AFRICA
Its Peoples and Their Culture History

AFRICA

Its Peoples and Their Culture History

GEORGE PETER MURDOCK
Professor of Anthropology, Yale University

McGRAW-HILL BOOK COMPANY
1959   New York   Toronto   London

On the title page, the upper photograph, of the two Keyu warriors overlooking the Rift Valley in Kenya, is used by courtesy of the British Information Service; the lower photograph, of a girl musician of the Kung Bushmen, by courtesy of the Peabody Museum of Archaeology and Ethnology, Harvard University

To Americans of African descent

PREFACE

This book does not present a distillation of long and intimate familiarity with the African continent. The author has had field experience only among indigenous peoples in North America and Oceania, and his first-hand knowledge of Africa has been limited to three brief visits—a week in Egypt in 1921, four days in Cape Town in 1945, and a fortnight in Kenya and Tanganyika in 1957. His interest in the area stems primarily from the accident of having undertaken, about eight years ago, to offer a graduate course in African ethnology. Exposure to the descriptive literature raised problems of unusual challenge and engendered a mounting enthusiasm. In contrast to regions which man has occupied for only a few thousand years, Africa offers the fascination of a continent inhabited, in all probability, from the very dawn of culture history, a continent in which diverse races have interacted in complex ways for millennia and in which survivals of extremely archaic cultural adjustments still emerge here and there only slightly masked by subsequent developments.

The book does reflect the difficulties encountered by the author in acquiring a comprehensive understanding of the peoples and cultures of Africa. He early discovered the virtual absence of reliable guides to a preliminary orientation. With rare exceptions, general works are incomplete in geographic scope, naïve in theoretical perspective, and inaccurate in factual detail; historical reconstructions reflect racial biases, outmoded concepts of the mechanics of diffusion, and undisciplined imagination; classifications of cultures and of languages are often impressionistic and technically defective; and regional summaries and analyses are fewer and less satisfactory than for most comparable ethnographic areas. From these strictures the author must hasten to except three generalizing anthropologists whose work has proved so extraordinarily helpful that he must single them out for a special accolade: Hermann Baumann, who, in *Völkerkunde von Afrika*, with R. Thurnwald and D. Westermann as coauthors, has made an invaluable scholarly contribution in sifting and organizing the descriptive data on the peoples of Negro Africa; Daryll Forde, whose monumental editorial enterprise, the *Ethnographic Survey of Africa*, has assembled and summarized masses of material, often from scattered, inaccessible, and unpublished sources, on a large number of

vii

African societies; and Joseph H. Greenberg, who has brought order out of chaos in African linguistic classification.

Disillusioned early about the value and dependability of most of the generalizing literature, the author decided to rely almost exclusively on the descriptive literature. Here Africa's disadvantage disappears. No other continent, with the possible exception of North America, can compare with it in either the volume or the quality of ethnographic coverage. Few peoples of consequence remain completely undescribed, and the wealth of information on many is unsurpassed elsewhere in the world. Most English-speaking readers will already be aware of the numerous penetrating analyses of indigenous social systems produced in recent decades by British Africanists—e.g., Evans-Pritchard on the Nuer, Fortes on the Tallensi, Schapera on the Tswana, and Monica Wilson on the Nyakyusa —and of comparable contributions by younger anthropologists from Great Britain, South Africa, and the United States. Commitment to the descriptive literature has brought the incidental reward of discovering many equally competent ethnographers who have written in other languages, among whom at least Grottanelli, Hulstaert, Maquet, and Paulme deserve special mention.

Having chosen to emphasize the ethnographic literature, the author made the further decision to embrace the entire continent in his survey. To exclude Egypt, Ethiopia, and North Africa, as has commonly been done, could only have the effect of obscuring the influences which have impinged on Negro Africa from the north and northeast and of injecting an element of unnecessary guesswork into their interpretation. To exclude Madagascar, moreover, would eliminate a prime source of information concerning the cultural impact on Africa of contacts with India and Malaysia by way of the ancient monsoon trade route across the Indian Ocean.

The assimilation of the complete corpus of ethnography for the entire continent of Africa constitutes a formidable task. Only through some process of selection could its realization be expected within a reasonable period of time. The decision was therefore reached to cover only a limited range of subject matter. This volume consequently makes no pretense of synthesizing available information on such important fields as religion, art, law, socialization, and technology. It deals only with food-producing activities, the division of labor by sex, housing and settlement patterns, kinship and marriage, the forms of social and political organization, and a few miscellanea such as cannibalism and genital mutilations.

A second limitation relates to time. No consideration is given to early man or to the long sequence of Paleolithic cultures revealed by prehistoric archeology. Nor is any attention paid to the modern period of intense social and political change on which most contemporary scholars have concentrated their efforts. The time span encompassed thus begins with the first achievement of a Neolithic agricultural civilization about 7,000 years ago and ends with the conclusion of European colonial penetration around the beginning of the present century. In general, the book aims to present a culture-historical base line to aid in the understanding of more recent events and ongoing trends.

In addition to attempting to reconstruct the major cultural developments and movements of peoples in Africa over the past 7,000 years, the book seeks to order existing ethnographic knowledge by summarizing the cultural data surveyed for each of the distinctive areas or provinces into which the peoples of the continent are divided. It combines these objectives by first presenting a few chapters of orientation on the topics of geography, race, language, economy, society, government, and history, which include distributional information and a consideration of theoretical problems, and following these by chapters on each of the cultural provinces of the continent, arranged in an order which may appear arbitrary but which is designed to introduce, in approximately their sequential chronological order, the major developments in African culture history since the end of Paleolithic times.

Besides summarizing the pertinent historical and cultural data, each regional chapter includes certain materials primarily of a reference nature. Tribes are classified into groups of essentially identical language and culture, arranged numerically in alphabetical order, with reasonably complete synonymies to facilitate identification through an index of tribal names included at the end of the book. Approximate population figures are given wherever available from ethnographic sources; census reports have not been separately consulted for this purpose. To each chapter is appended a selected bibliography. These include fewer than half the sources actually consulted by the author, listing only the works which he has found genuinely useful for the guidance of readers with similar interests who may wish to verify his interpretations or pursue particular subjects further. To conserve space, references are given in an abbreviated form, though sufficiently detailed to allow them to be readily located in library catalogues, and periodicals and symposia that are frequently cited are indicated by initials to which a key is provided following Chapter 55.

The author acknowledges especial personal indebtedness to the following persons: Harold D. Gunn, for making available his invaluable collection of unpublished manuscript material on the Plateau Nigerians; Alan H. Jacobs, for a personal introduction to the Arusha, Chaga, Iraqw, Kikuyu, Masai, and Meru tribes of Kenya and Tanganyika; Peter J. Wilson, for valued assistance in the analysis of political systems; David W.

Ames, Robert G. Armstrong, J. H. M. Beattie, A. Richard Diebold, John L. Fischer, Robert F. Gray, Philip H. Gulliver, Jean La Fontaine, Simon Ottenberg, Harold K. Schneider, Edward H. Winter, and others, for supplying unpublished ethnographic information; and Carmen S. Murdock, for her supportive interest and infallible editorial judgment.

George Peter Murdock

CONTENTS

Preface vii

List of Maps xiii

Part One: Orientation

1. Geography 1
2. Race 7
3. Language 12
4. Economy 17
5. Society 24
6. Government 33
7. History 40

Part Two: African Hunters

8. Pygmies 48
9. Bushmen and Their Kin 52
10. East African Hunters 59

Part Three: Sudanic Agricultural Civilization

11. Nuclear Mande 64
12. Voltaic Peoples 77
13. Plateau Nigerians 89

Part Four: North African Agricultural Civilization

14. Ancient Egyptians 101
15. Berbers 111
16. Saharan Negroes and the Caravan Trade 124
17. Negroes of the Sudan Fringe 133
18. Punic and Greco-Roman North Africa 148

Part Five: Synthesis in the Nile Corridor

19. Nubians 158
20. Nuba 164
21. Prenilotes 170
22. Central Ethiopians 181
23. Sidamo Peoples 187

Part Six: Southward Expansion of the Cushites

24. Southern Cushites 193
25. Megalithic Cushites 196
26. Ancient Azanians 204

Part Seven: Cultural Impact of Indonesia

27. Malagasy 212
28. Central Sudanic Peoples 222
29. Eastern Nigritic Peoples 230
30. Cameroon Highlanders 238
31. Southern Nigerians 242
32. Twi 252
33. Kru and Peripheral Mande 259
34. Senegambians 265

Part Eight: Expansion of the Bantu

35. Northwestern Bantu 271
36. Equatorial Bantu 278
37. Mongo and Luba 284
38. Central Bantu 290
39. Northeast Coastal Bantu 306

Part Nine: East African Pastoralism

40. Beja 314
41. Afar and Somali 318
42. Galla 323
43. Nilotes 328

Part Ten: Spread of Pastoralism to the Bantu

44. Kenya Highland Bantu 342
45. Interlacustrine Bantu 347
46. Tanganyika Bantu 357
47. Middle Zambesi Bantu 364
48. Southwestern Bantu 369
49. Shona and Thonga 374
50. Nguni 380
51. Sotho 386

Part Eleven: North and West African Pastoralism

52. Bedouin Arabs 392
53. Tuareg 405
54. Baggara 410
55. Fulani 413

Key to Bibliographical Abbreviations 422

Index of Tribal Names 425

LIST OF MAPS

1. Relief of Africa 2
2. Drainage Systems of Africa 3
3. Mean Annual Rainfall in Africa 4
4. Vegetation Zones of Africa 5
5. Distribution of Races in Africa 11
6. African Languages about A.D. 1500 15
7. Distribution of Types of Subsistence Economy 18
8. Distribution of Cattle and of Milking 20
9. Distribution of Rules of Descent 28
10. Culture Provinces of the Western Sudan 71
11. Areas of Berber Speech 112
12. Trans-Saharan Caravan Routes 128
13. Culture Provinces of the Yam Belt 223
14. Culture Provinces of Bantu Africa 272
15. East African Pastoralists 315
16. Major Concentrations of Fulani 414
17. Tribal Map of Africa . . . . . . [pocket inside back cover]

PART ONE
ORIENTATION

———◦•◦———

I

———◦•◦———

Geography

Among the continents, Africa stands second to Eurasia in size. It has an area of about 11,700,000 square miles, which is nearly 40 per cent greater than that of the Soviet Union and more than three times that of the United States including Alaska. It lies astride the equator, with about 80 per cent of its surface within the tropics. With approximately 240 million inhabitants, it ranks third in population, behind Eurasia and North America and appreciably ahead of South America, but it has more distinct peoples and cultures than any other continent.

Geologically, Africa consists largely of a single rigid block of rock of marine origin laid down perhaps 200 million years ago and later uplifted. This still lies on the surface in many places but is elsewhere covered by sedimentary rocks deposited subsequently on the floors of invading gulfs or shallow inland basins. The processes which raised this massive block thousands of feet above sea level produced remarkably little folding. Consequently, except for the relatively recent Atlas ranges in Morocco, Africa has no mountain chains comparable to the Alps, Andes, Himalayas, and Rockies of other continents. As shown in Map 1, it consists of a series of plateaus, generally higher in the south and east than in the north and west, falling sharply to an extraordinarily narrow coastal plain. On even the highest plateaus, with average altitudes of more than 7,000 feet, the surface is level or undulating rather than broken by ridges.

The chief exception to topographic monotony is presented by the great extinct volcanoes and spectacular rift valleys of East Africa. Among the

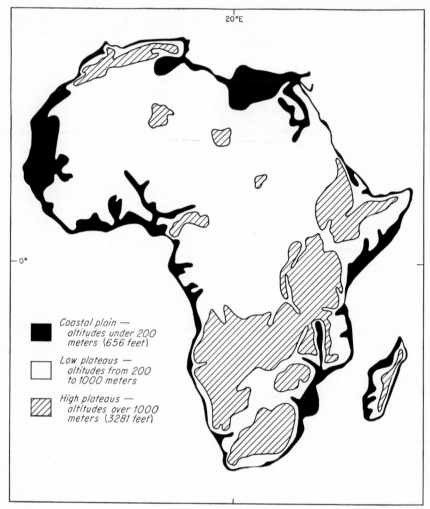

20°E

0°

Coastal plain —
altitudes under 200
meters (656 feet)

Low plateaus —
altitudes from 200
to 1000 meters

High plateaus —
altitudes over 1000
meters (3281 feet)

Map 1. Relief of Africa

former, Mounts Elgon, Kenya, and Ruwenzori average about 17,000 feet
in elevation, and majestic Kilimanjaro lifts its glacier-tipped cone 19,400
feet above sea level. The rift valleys, like the volcanoes, resulted from a
series of stupendous north-south fractures which occurred during the
uplifting of the continent and produced giant trenches often thousands of
feet in depth. Their lake-studded courses can readily be followed on
Map 2. The principal rift valley starts at the mouth of the Zambesi River
and runs northward via Lake Nyasa and the great interior drainage
basin of Tanganyika and western Kenya and thence northeastward across
Ethiopia to the coast, after which it forms the floors of the Red Sea, the

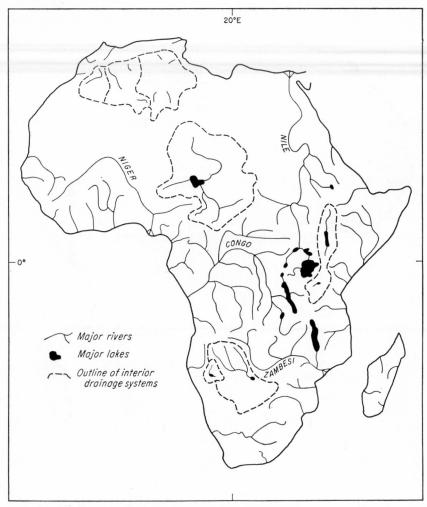

Map 2. Drainage Systems of Africa

Gulf of Aqaba, and the Dead Sea, and terminates in Syria. A second rift valley, later in origin, is marked by a chain of lakes to the west of the first—Lakes Tanganyika, Kivu, Edward, and Albert—of which the first has a bottom several thousand feet below sea level.

The geological history of Africa accounts for some of the peculiarities of its drainage system (see Map 2). Its great rivers, like the Congo, Niger, Nile, and Zambesi, are navigable for great distances on the interior plateaus but invariably plunge over impassable rapids or cataracts as they approach the coastal plain. The most spectacular of these, Victoria Falls on the Zambesi, has a drop of 343 feet, or more than twice that of Niagara. Riv-

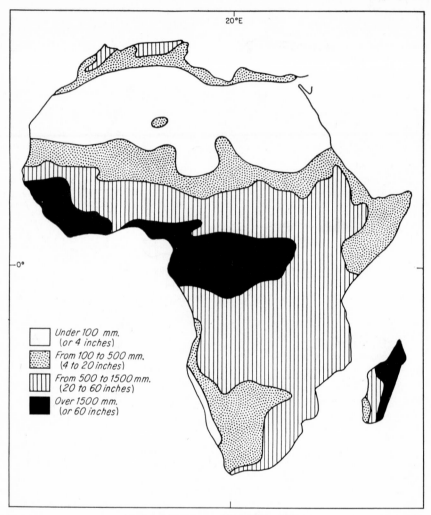

Map 3. Mean Annual Rainfall in Africa

Legend:
- Under 100 mm. (or 4 inches)
- From 100 to 500 mm. (4 to 20 inches)
- From 500 to 1500 mm. (20 to 60 inches)
- Over 1500 mm. (or 60 inches)

ers enter the ocean, not through navigable estuaries, but through deltas, often obstructed by shifting sand bars. Because of uplift, other harbors are extraordinarily few, except along the western Mediterranean coast. The irregular elevation of the continental mass also isolated a series of interior drainage basins which filled with shallow, brackish lakes, most of which have long since found outlets or, in arid regions, have dwindled to salt marshes. Curiously enough, the largest survivor, Lake Chad, contains fresh rather than brackish water, presumably through underground seepage into other basins.

Despite the tropical location, altitude moderates the temperature, which

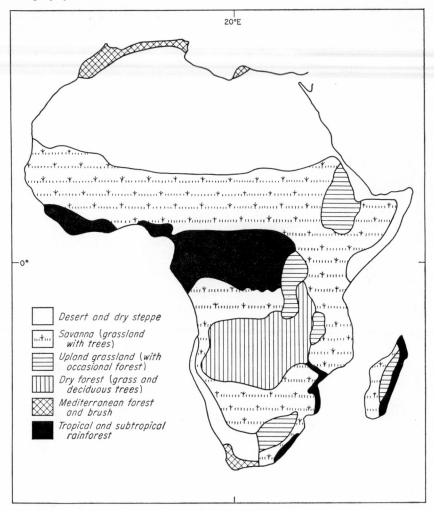

20°E

0°

Desert and dry steppe

Savanna (grassland with trees)

Upland grassland (with occasional forest)

Dry forest (grass and deciduous trees)

Mediterranean forest and brush

Tropical and subtropical rainforest

Map 4. Vegetation Zones of Africa

on the plateaus of East Africa averages 20 degrees Fahrenheit lower than on the adjacent seacoast. Frosts occur only in the extreme north and south of the continent and on the higher mountains and consequently do not exert a limiting influence on either agriculture or the natural vegetation. The chief controlling factor is drought, for in Africa rainfall is vastly more critical than temperature. Not only do various parts of the continent show wide differences in mean annual precipitation (see Map 3), but these are accentuated by uneven seasonal distribution and by large variations from year to year. The intertropical weather front, which regulates the climate over much of the interior, fluctuates widely because of the lack of mountain barriers, so that regions which receive plenty of rain in one year may suffer severe drought the next. Because of this extreme irregularity, the productivity of agriculture and the consequent density of population, as well as the nature of the vegetation cover, reflect not the annual means of precipitation but rather the minima of recurrent bad years.

Africa has three areas of desert—the Sahara in the north, the margins of the Horn in the east, and the coast and some hinterland in the southwest. Despite their substantial geographic extent, these arid regions belie the popular conception of desert as barren rock and sand dunes bereft of vegetation, for such features characterize less than 8 per cent of the area of the continent. Most of the desert surface supports scattered scrub and even, especially on the margins, grass, which provides excellent pasturage. Moreover, the Sahara in particular is dotted with oases which support intensive irrigated agriculture.

Popular opinion also greatly exaggerates the extent of tropical rainforest, or "jungle," in Africa. Actually this covers only restricted coastal strips in Madagascar, Mozambique, and the Guinea coast and a larger area in the northern Belgian Congo and adjacent Cameroon and French Equatorial Africa, and even here it is less dense than in comparable regions in Southeast Asia or South America. Small areas of temperate-zone woodland and brush occur at the northern and southern extremes of the continent. More extensive than tropical rainforest is the so-called "dry forest" of Northern Rhodesia and adjacent Angola, Belgian Congo, and Tanganyika. This consists of a relatively open stand of flat-topped deciduous trees, which shed their leaves during the hot dry season, with a fairly substantial grass cover underneath and between them.

By far the preponderant type of vegetation cover in Africa (see Map 4) is savanna, or grassland with scattered trees. Among the latter, baobab and species of *Acacia* tend to prevail where rainfall is sufficient, with thorny shrubs in more arid sections. At unusually high elevations savanna is replaced by upland grasslands, e.g., the High Veld of Transvaal, or by forests, where mountain slopes are steep. When one adds desert steppe and dry forest to savanna and mountain grasslands, the proportion of the surface of Africa which can support herbivorous animals is really extraordinary. Herein lies, of course, the geographical reason for both the fabled wealth of the continent in wild game and the exceptional role that pastoral activities play in the economies of the indigenous peoples.

A comparable richness in mineral resources suggests the probable economic position of Africa in the world of the future. They lie, however, outside the scope of this book, since only one of them, namely, iron, was important in the native economy prior to the present century. Iron has been smelted and made into tools and weapons by most of the inhabitants of the continent for at least the past thousand years, and the author greatly regrets not having included metallurgical technology among the subjects of his survey.

Selected Bibliography

Bernard, A. *Afrique septentrionale et occidentale.* 2 vols. Paris, 1937–1939.
Fitzgerald, W. *Africa.* 7th edit. London, 1950.
Klute, F., L. Wittschell, and A. Kaufmann. *Afrika in Natur, Kultur und Wirtschaft.* Wildpark-Potsdam, 1930.
Stamp, L. D. *Africa.* New York, 1953.

2

Race

Africa was probably the cradle of mankind. For several decades hardly a year has passed without some exciting new evidence of early man or of manlike apes in East or South Africa to strengthen this conclusion. These findings, however, lie beyond the time horizon of the present volume, which begins with the end of the Paleolithic period. From that time to the present, Africa has been inhabited by representatives of only five races: the Bushmanoid, Caucasoid, Mongoloid, Negroid, and Pygmoid.

Racial factors in themselves, of course, do not assist in explaining the development or distribution of cultures in Africa, since scientists have long since disproved popular assumptions of inherent racial differences in the capacity to create and maintain culture. We also recognize that the anthropometric and somatological criteria by which the five races have been distinguished are themselves becoming increasingly suspect as physical anthropology comes to lay its main emphasis upon genetic factors. Unfortunately, the distribution of O, A, B, and AB blood groups is rather similar in all five African races, and other genetically precise data are not yet available in sufficient quantity to render much assistance. Though we consequently neither regard race as relevant to culture nor consider traditional typologies as particularly respectable from the scientific point of view, we nevertheless insist that the older anthropometric and somatological criteria still serve a useful function as an aid in historical reconstruction. They show enough uniformity over limited areas, enough stability over time, and enough persistence in mixtures, to provide the archeologist and the ethnologist with a highly welcome additional tool for tracing important culture-historical movements in the past. We thus offer no apologies for the fivefold division presented herewith.

The Bushmanoid peoples, however insignificant numerically, clearly constitute a distinct race. The Xam, or Southern Bushmen, selected as the type because they are probably the least mixed, reveal the following physical characteristics: short stature, averaging no more than 4 feet 10 inches for adult males; exceedingly wrinkled skin of a light yellowish-brown color; very scanty facial and body hair; short, black hair on the head, clustering in very tight "peppercorn" spirals; medium to narrow head, with a cephalic index of 76; low forehead; flat, triangular face; high cheekbones; extremely broad nose, with a nasal index of 115; brown eyes reduced to narrow slits by a prominent but un-Mongoloid eye fold; thin but slightly protruding lips; pointed chin; slender body and limbs; and, in women, marked steatopygia (prominent buttocks) and the so-called "Hottentot apron" (elongation of the labia minora). Among more northern Bushmen the stature increases to about 5 feet 2 inches, and the prevailing skin color becomes reddish brown. The average Hottentot, with cattle and a milk diet, attains 5 feet 3 inches in stature and has a narrower head (cephalic index 73) and nose (nasal index 100).

The Pygmoid peoples, though perhaps ultimately somewhat more closely akin to the Negroid than to any other stock, display enough specialized features to warrant classification as a distinct race rather than as a subrace. The Mbuti of the Ituri Forest region, the group least affected by Negro contacts, exhibit the following physical traits: short stature, averaging about 4 feet 9 inches in adult males; light yellowish-brown skin densely covered with downy body hair (lanugo), which is blond to reddish in infants but dark brown in adults; black, kinky head hair; high, bulging forehead; large head of medium breadth, with a cephalic index of 76.5; broad, flat nose, with a nasal index of about 100; protruding brown eyes; oval face; lips of medium thickness, but not everted; slender legs and body, with protruding abdomen; and an average body weight for males of only 88 pounds. Other Pygmy groups are usually darker in color because of Negroid admixture but range in stature from as short as 4 feet 6 inches to as tall as 5 feet 1 inch.

The Negroid race, being familiar to most readers, requires a less detailed description. The Mande peoples of the western Sudan, who may be selected as a fairly representative group, are tall in stature, averaging 5 feet 8 inches for adult males, and dark brown in skin color. Other characteristics are a narrow head (cephalic index 74); black, kinky hair; bulging forehead; broad nose (nasal index 95); prognathous face; thick, everted lips; and scanty facial and body hair. On the Guinea coast the stature is usually somewhat shorter, and the skin color frequently approaches true black. The Bantu tend to be somewhat lighter, shorter, and less prognathous than other Negroes, and in the central Sudan a round, or brachycephalic, head form occasionally appears. The Nilotes of the eastern Sudan are sufficiently divergent to warrant their classification as a distinct subrace. The Dinka, a typical Nilotic tribe, exhibit the following characteristics: very tall stature, averaging 5 feet 10 inches for adult males; long limbs; extreme slenderness; dark-brown skin; narrow head (cephalic index 73); black, kinky hair; broad nose (nasal index 92); and medium to thick everted lips.

The Caucasoids of Africa belong to the Mediterranean subrace but tend to be much taller and somewhat more dolichocephalic (narrow-headed) than their kinsmen of southern Europe and the Near East. The Berbers of North Africa and the Cushites of Ethiopia and the Horn diverge in some respects. The former reveal certain affinities with the Nordic subrace of northwestern Europe, notably a definite, though relatively low, incidence of blondness in hair and eye color. The Cushites have long since incorporated a not insubstantial infusion of Negroid blood. This reveals itself in different ways in different tribes. Thus the lowland Somali are much darker than the peoples of highland Ethiopia but have hair that is wavy or occasionally straight and only rarely kinky, whereas this typically Negroid form prevails in 60 to 70 per cent of the plateau population. The Galla, a typical Cushitic people, exhibit the following traits: tall stature, averaging 5 feet 8 inches in adult males; medium-brown skin; curly to kinky hair on the head, with an appreciable amount also on the face and body; a head of medium breadth (cephalic index 77); narrow nose (nasal index 69); dark-brown eyes; medium to thick but not everted lips; prominent nose; and strong chin. The Kabyle of Algeria, a representative Berber people, may be characterized as follows: medium stature, averaging 5 feet 5 inches in males; light-brown skin; straight or wavy hair, which is usually black or dark brown, but occasionally red; abundant facial and body hair; head of medium breadth (cephalic index 77); moderately narrow nose (nasal index 74); dark- to light-brown eyes, with occasional lighter shades; medium to thin lips; and prominent nose.

Mongoloid peoples survive today only on the island of Madagascar, where they are usually heavily admixed with Negroids. The interior peoples of Borneo, their nearest kinsmen in Indonesia, have approximately the following characteristics: short stature, averaging 5 feet 2 inches for adult males; yellowish-brown skin; straight black hair, which is scanty on the face and body; head of medium breadth (cephalic index 77); broad and rather flat nose (nasal index 80); dark eyes; lips of medium thickness; and a high incidence of Mongolian spots and the epicanthic fold. The Merina of central Madagascar, in whom the Mongoloid element

Table I: Descriptive Characteristics of African Races

Race and people	Stature	Skin color	Head form	Nose form	Hair form	Lips	Special features
Pygmoid							
Mbuti	Very short	Light yellowish brown	Narrow to medium	Broad	Kinky	Medium but not everted	Protruding eyes Downy body hair Delicate frame
Bushmanoid							
Xam	Short	Light yellowish brown	Narrow to medium	Very broad	Peppercorn	Thin, slightly everted	Wrinkled face High cheekbones Steatopygia
Negroid							
Mande	Tall	Dark brown	Narrow	Broad	Kinky	Thick, everted	Prognathism
Dinka	Very tall	Dark brown	Narrow	Broad	Kinky	Medium, everted	Very slender Long limbs
Caucasoid							
Kabyle	Medium	Light brown	Medium	Narrow to medium	Straight or wavy	Medium to thin	Some hair and eye blondism
Galla	Tall	Medium brown	Medium	Narrow	Curly to kinky	Medium to thick	Prominent nose
Mongoloid							
Merina	Short	Yellowish brown	Medium to broad	Broad	Straight	Medium	Mongolian spots Epicanthic fold

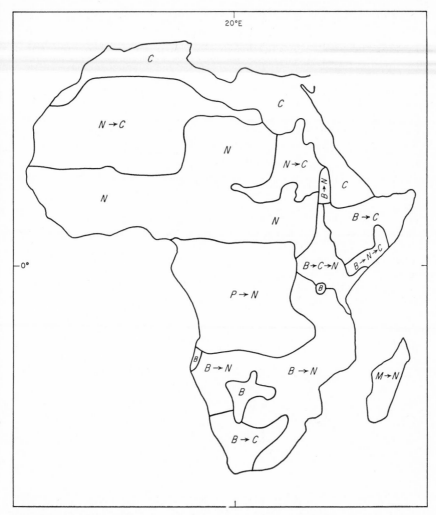

Map 5. Distribution of Races in Africa (*B*—Bushmanoid, *C*—Caucasoid, *M*—Mongoloid, *N*—Negroid, *P*—Pygmoid, → Displaced by)

is strongest today, resemble the Borneo Dayak in most respects, although the head is somewhat broader (cephalic index 81).

For purposes of ready comparison, the distinctive descriptive characteristics of the five African races are summarized in Table 1.

At the close of the Paleolithic period the Mongoloids had not yet made their appearance in Africa, and the other four races divided the continent in not notably unequal proportions. Subsequent historical movements, to be described in detail in later chapters, have practically eliminated the Pygmoids, the Bushmanoids, and even the latecoming Mongoloids.

Although the Caucasoids have made modest advances in certain areas, most of the territorial gains have accrued to the Negroid race. Map 5 shows the racial distribution in Africa at the end of the Paleolithic period and today. Regions whose ethnic occupation has remained unaltered are indicated by the initial of the race. Where one race has replaced or largely absorbed another, arrows show the order of succession. Thus B→C→N, for example, indicates that the area in question was originally occupied by Bushmanoids, who have since been replaced by Caucasoids, and these in turn by Negroids.

Selected Bibliography

Clark, W. E. LeG. *Fossil Evidence for the Evolution of Man.* Chicago, 1956.
Coon, C. S. *The Races of Europe.* New York, 1939.
Gates, R. R. *Human Ancestry from a Genetical Point of View.* Cambridge, 1948.
Gusinde, M. Pygmies and Pygmoids. *AQ,* 3:3–61. 1955.
Haddon, A. C. *The Races of Man and Their Distribution.* New York, 1925.
Martin, R. *Lehrbuch der Anthropologie.* 2d edit. 3 vols. Jena, 1928.
Schapera, I. *The Khoisan Peoples of South Africa.* London, 1930.
Seligman, C. G. *Races of Africa.* New York, 1930.

3

———•◦•———

Language

In the absence of written records, linguistic relationships provide by far the most dependable evidence of historical connections. If two peoples speak related languages, however much they may differ in race or in culture and however remote their geographical location, either both have descended from a single ancestral society or the ancestors of one have at some time had such intimate contact with a group thus related to the other that they abandoned their own language and adopted that of their neighbors. Even great paucity or a complete lack of other evidence cannot invalidate this conclusion. Thus the fact that the Malagasy speak a Malayo-Polynesian language proves beyond doubt the former existence of some direct contact between the inhabitants of Madagascar and of Indonesia, though this might never have been guessed from other clues.

This volume draws heavily upon the results of linguistic research.

Inferences from this source have frequently given the first intimation of some major historical movement, whether of migration or of cultural diffusion. Moreover, these have never proved false, for a careful search has invariably turned up corroborative data from written records, archeology, botany, physical anthropology, social structural analysis, ethnographic distributions, or more commonly several of these sources.

Although generations of linguists have analyzed the languages of Africa and have added immensely to the sum of our knowledge, various defects of method have delayed until recently the formulation of a comprehensive and dependable classification of all African languages comparable to that achieved in 1891 by J. W. Powell for native North America. Far too much stress, for example, has been laid on single traits like sex gender. Even more serious has been the reliance placed upon inferences from other aspects of culture, especially the presence or absence of a pastoral mode of life. Innumerable linguists have seemed to regard the herding and milking of cattle as a linguistic trait, and an overriding one at that. Repeatedly, for example, they have classed the Fulani, the Hottentot, and the southeastern Nilotes erroneously as "Hamitic" in language because of their dependence upon cattle, and have placed the Hausa, who are really Hamitic, in some other linguistic group because they are not pastoral. They have resorted to inadmissible processes of language formation such as the emergence of mixed intermediate languages implied in such terms as "Semi-Bantu" and "Nilo-Hamite." Finally, they have clung too tenaciously to traditional groupings, treating Bantu as an independent linguistic stock long after evidence was available to show that it is merely an enormously expanded division of one branch of a single subfamily of a very much larger stock.

Fortunately we need no longer depend upon this earlier work, for Greenberg (1949–1954) has now given us a complete and thoroughly satisfactory classification of the languages of Africa, superseding for our purposes everything that preceded it. Our own research has confirmed Greenberg on every point where he differs from his predecessors, and our classification of stocks and families is derived entirely from his. It deviates only on minor and inessential points, which should be noted.

First of all, we have renamed several of the stocks. Khoisan is preferred to "Click" since we accept Greenberg's own objections to classification in terms of a single linguistic trait. We propose Kanuric in place of "Central Saharan" since we prefer terms with ethnic connotations, like Algonkian and Arawakan, to geographical names. Similar considerations pertain in the cases of Greenberg's "Afroasiatic" and "Niger-Congo" stocks. Instead of the former we use Hamitic. The more generally accepted term "Hamito-Semitic" incorrectly implies that Semitic is paired with a coordinate Hamitic division, whereas it actually has four parallel subfamilies—Berber, Chadic, Cushitic, and Egyptian. Moreover, the name Hamitic is now available, having been replaced by Cushitic for the southeastern subfamily of the stock. For the awkward "Niger-Congo" we prefer the archaic name Nigritic, which seems especially fitting since its speakers comprise, and are largely confined to, the more typical representatives of the Negro race.

Two of Greenberg's stocks—Nyangiya and Temainian—are omitted from our list. Both are based on very short word lists, and their independence therefore awaits confirmation.* On Map 6 they appear in the areas of Eastern Sudanic and Kordofanian, respectively. All other changes are minor and obvious. A complete classification of the linguistic stocks and subfamilies of Africa, as used throughout this volume, is presented in the following list.

1. Furian [the Fur of Greenberg]
2. Hamitic [the Afroasiatic of Greenberg, the Hamito-Semitic of others]
   a. Berber
   b. Chadic [the Chad of Greenberg]
   c. Cushitic
        Branches: Central, Eastern, Northern, Southern, Western
   d. Egyptian [the Ancient Egyptian of Greenberg]
   e. Semitic
3. Kanuric [the Central Saharan of Greenberg]
4. Khoisan [the Click of Greenberg]
   a. Bushman
        Branches: Central, Northern, Southern
   b. Kindiga [the Hatsa of Greenberg]
   c. Sandawe
5. Koman
6. Kordofanian
   a. Katla
   b. Koalib
   c. Tagali
   d. Talodi
   e. Tumtum
7. Maban
8. Malayo-Polynesian [the Austronesian of some]
9. Nigritic [the Niger-Congo of Greenberg]
   a. Atlantic [the West Atlantic of Greenberg]

* Greenberg, in a personal communication while this book was in press, reports that new information definitely indicates the affiliation of both Nyangiya and Temainian with Sudanic. He likewise suggests a distant relationship between the Furian, Kanuric, Maban, Sudanic, and probably also the Koman and Songhaic stocks. On a still more tentative basis he considers a connection between Kordofanian and Nigritic to be probable.

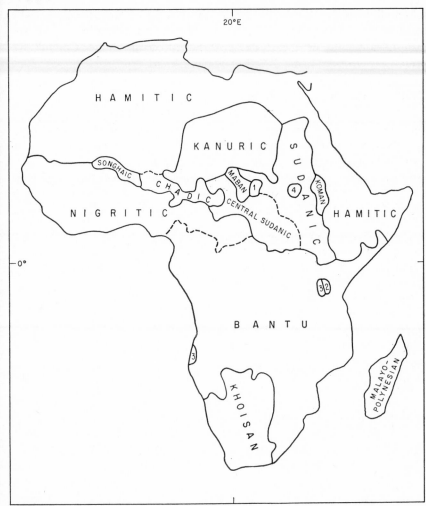

Map 6. African Languages about A.D. 1500 (1–Furian, 2–Hamitic, 3–Khoisan, 4–Kordo-fanian)

    b. Bantoid [the Central branch of Greenberg, the Semi-Bantu of others]
       Branches: about six in number, of which one, herewith called Macro-
       Bantu, has seven divisions: Bantu, Batu, Galim-Mambila, Jarawa-Mbula,
       Ndoro, Tiv [the Munshi of Greenberg], and Zuande [the Bitare of
       Greenberg]
    c. Eastern Nigritic [the Adamawa-Eastern branch of Greenberg]
    d. Ijaw [the Ijo of Greenberg]
    e. Kwa
       Branches: Edo, Ibo, Kru, Nupe, Twi, Yoruba
    f. Mande [the Mandingo of Greenberg]

   g. Voltaic [the Gur of Greenberg]
       Branches: Gur [the Mossi-Grunshi of Greenberg], Senufo
10. Songhaic [the Songhai of Greenberg]
11. Sudanic [the Macro-Sudanic of Greenberg]
   a. Bertan
   b. Central Sudanic
   c. Eastern Sudanic
       Branches: Barea, Beir [the Beir-Didinga of Greenberg], Dagu, Ingassana [the Tabi of Greenberg], Merarit, Nilotic [the Southern branch of Greenberg], Nubian
   d. Kunaman

Map 6 shows the location and geographic extent of these eleven stocks about A.D. 1500 and of three lesser groupings—Bantu, Central Sudanic, and Chadic—mapped separately because of their special historical significance. Several factors have prompted the selection of 1500 rather than the present as the basic date for the map. For one thing, this eliminates the necessity for indicating an extraneous linguistic stock, the Indo-European, in such regions as Algeria and South Africa. More important, it makes possible considerable simplification in areas where recent intrusive populations have shattered and dispersed the indigenous inhabitants and thereby produced complex distributions that are difficult to map clearly on a small scale. The principal deviations from a more recent situation are the following:

1. In South Africa the distribution of Khoisan remains unaffected by European settlement and by the late encroachments of the Tswana.
2. In the northern part of the eastern Sudan Arabic does not appear, leaving the linguistic situation approximately as it must have existed prior to the invasions of the Baggara, or Cattle Arabs.
3. In the southern part of the eastern Sudan the situation is reconstructed to show the Central Sudanic peoples before they were shattered by the Azande spearhead of the Eastern Nigritic migration from the west, the Nilotic penetration from the northeast, and the Arab slave raids of the nineteenth century.
4. On the middle Niger the Tuareg had not yet migrated south of the great bend of that river.
5. In Northern Nigeria the boundary between the Chadic and Nigritic languages is readjusted to discount the displacements that resulted from Fulani penetration.
6. In East Africa the Bantu are assigned areas which they apparently occupied prior to the last southward advance of the Masai and the expansion of the Somali and Galla toward the southwest.

The map likewise omits a few enclaves of intrusive tribes. It has the definite advantage, however, of delimiting quite clearly the major linguistic divisions of Africa. For specific tribal locations and more recent distributions the reader may consult the tribal map in the pocket at the back of the book.

Selected Bibliography

Greenberg, J. H. Studies in African Linguistic Classification. *SWJA*, 5:79–100, 190–198, 309–317; 6:47–63, 143–160, 223–237, 388–398; 10:405–415. 1949–1954. [Also published in book form, New Haven, 1955].

4

Economy

A survey of the entire range of indigenous economic life in Africa lies outside the scope of the present volume, which attempts to cover intensively only the subsistence economy, i.e., the major types of food acquisition. These are hunting and gathering, fishing, animal husbandry, agriculture, and their various combinations. Map 7 shows the distribution of these types of subsistence activity over the continent.

Hunting and gathering, by which man gained his livelihood throughout the Paleolithic period, survive today as the mainstay of existence only among a few remnant peoples, who will be considered in Chapters 8 to 10, notably the Pygmies of the Congo Basin, the Bushmen of arid southern Africa, the Kindiga of northern Tanganyika, and the Dorobo of western Kenya. As a subsidiary activity, of course, hunting still retains some importance over most of Africa, as is understandable in view of the plentitude of game animals for which the continent is famed. Gathering, too, provides a welcome addition to the diet in some regions, e.g., in the western Sudan, where locust beans, kola nuts, and shea fruits are extensively used.

Most African peoples practice fishing as a subsidiary economic pursuit wherever geographical conditions permit. One interesting exception, however, deserves special note. The Cushites of northeastern Africa impose a taboo on the eating of fish which compares in rigor to that of the Semites against pork. Fishing attains the status of the dominant subsistence activity in a few scattered regions. In no instance, however, does

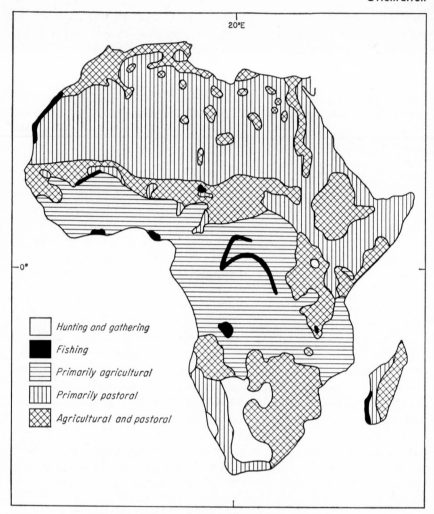

Map. 7. Distribution of Types of Subsistence Economy

this represent a survival from a preagricultural economy but occurs
only as a reflection of environmental influences. Coastal Mauritania,
inhabited by the Imragen, and the lagoons of the Ivory Coast exemplify
one type of favorable situation—a maritime location with an immediate
hinterland unsuited to agriculture. A second conducive situation is presented by the Congo and Niger Rivers and some of their principal tributaries. Here numerous tribes combine fishing with a profitable boat trade
and exchange dried or salted fish for the agricultural produce of their
neighbors. An occasional insular people, notably the Buduma of the

small islets in Lake Chad, has arrived at a comparable economic adjustment.

Animal husbandry as a subsistence activity—eliminating those domesticated species which contribute but slightly to the food supply—revolves in Africa around pigs, goats, sheep, cattle, and camels. All were introduced to the continent from Asia by way of Egypt, and all except the camel, which first appeared in Greco-Roman times, arrived along with agriculture in the early Neolithic period. The pig, once extremely important throughout North Africa, has nearly become extinct through the notion of its uncleanness, which first arose in Pharaonic Egypt and was reinforced by the much later invasion of Bedouin Arabs and Islamic culture. Except for places where it has recently been reintroduced by Europeans, the pig has survived into modern times in only a few small peripheral areas—among the Nuba and Prenilotes of the middle Nile, the Guanche of the Canary Islands, and the Senegambian tribes of Portuguese Guinea. The goat, except for the dog the most widespread of African domesticated animals, has penetrated even the tropical forest in many places. African sheep have fat tails and hair rather than wool, the familiar woolly sheep representing a relatively late introduction. The camel is confined to arid regions, though by no means exclusively to Arabs.

African cattle represent varieties of and crosses between two species— Mediterranean cattle (*Bos taurus*) and the Indian humped zebu (*B. indicus*)—each of which entered the continent twice in different forms. Long-horned Mediterranean cattle, presumably descended from the wild *B. primigenius*, appeared in Egypt at the beginning of the Neolithic period; short-horned Mediterranean cattle, probably derived from the wild *B. brachyceros*, arrived during the third millennium B.C. Both spread early throughout North Africa and the Sudan, where derivative and hybrid breeds survive, except where Arabs or Fulani have introduced the zebu within the past ten centuries. The zebu reached Egypt about 1600 B.C. and East Africa in another form during the first millennium after Christ. Most, but by no means all, East and South African cattle have a strong zebu ingredient. Cattle have penetrated the tropical-forest zone to only a very limited extent, and they are excluded from many sections by the presence of the tsetse fly.

Cows, goats, and, where they occur, camels are milked throughout North, East, and South Africa, and over most of this area butter is made —at least for cosmetic purposes if not for food. The inhabitants of the western Sudan, of the Guinea coast, and of northern Angola, however, do not milk their animals, except on the very fringe of the Sahara and in a few other places under recent Fulani influence. It would thus appear that the Negroes originally borrowed animal husbandry from the North African Caucasoids without its associated dairy complex and that the

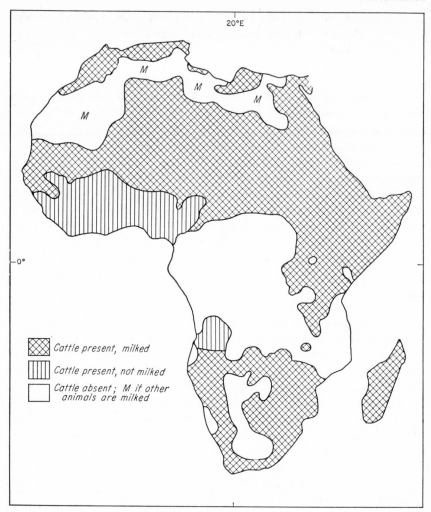

Map 8. Distribution of Cattle and of Milking

latter diffused southward only at a later date and over a smaller area.
Map 8 shows the distribution of cattle and of milking.

Animal husbandry plays varying roles in the economies of different
parts of Africa. It may make a negligible contribution to subsistence, as
in the tropical-forest zone. It may provide a significant, though subsidiary,
supplement to the products of tillage, as in many agricultural areas. It
may combine with cultivation in a balanced economy with approximately
equal dependence upon both activities, as in many societies that are commonly regarded as "pastoral," e.g., among the majority of the Berbers,
Galla, Nilotes, and Cattle Bantu. Or it may be in large measure detached

from agriculture, becoming the basis of an independent nomadic mode of pastoral life in which subsistence depends primarily upon milk and other animal products.

Independent pastoralism of this last type has existed from the dawn of recorded history among the Beja peoples between the Nile Valley and the Red Sea, deriving presumably from the neighboring Bedouin Arabs to the east. Elsewhere in Africa, however, it did not develop until a surprisingly late date, probably nowhere much earlier than A.D. 1000. It has nevertheless spread very widely during the past thousand years and is the prevailing pattern of life today among the Afar and Somali of the Eastern Horn, most North African Arabs, the Tuareg of the Sahara, the Fulani of the western and central Sudan, and the Herero and Hottentot of southwestern Africa. Pastoralism may center on sheep and goats, on camels, or on cattle. Primary dependence upon small livestock characterizes the Arab nomads in the hinterland of the Mediterranean coast in North Africa. The camel assumes first place among the Beja, the Afar and Somali, and the Arab and Berber tribes of the Sahara. Cattle play the dominant role among the Galla, the Baggara Arabs of the eastern Sudan, the Fulani, the Hottentot, and all Negro pastoralists.

Agriculture is practiced throughout the continent except among the surviving hunters and a few of the most exclusive fishing and independent pastoral peoples. Africans grow approximately nine-tenths of all the cultivated plant varieties known to man and have assembled them from every originating center in the world, though borrowings from China and highland America have been relatively few. Since the various plants first appeared in Africa at widely different places and times and have commonly been controlled by climatic and other geographical factors in their spread, the analysis of their distribution yields clues of the utmost importance in unraveling the paths of past migrations of peoples and diffusions of culture. The historical reconstructions in this volume consequently depend heavily upon this type of evidence.

Botanists can frequently identify the approximate place of origin of an indigenous cultigen by locating the native habitat of the wild form from which it was ennobled. Cultivated cotton (*Gossypium herbaceum*), for instance, can be traced to the Sahara-Sudan borderland because of the occurrence there of the wild *G. anomalum*, its presumptive ancestor. Botanists can also demonstrate the alien provenience of particular plants on the basis of genetic analysis. All African bananas (*Musa paradisiaca* and *M. sapientum*) are hybrids of two wild forms, *M. acuminata* and *M. balbisiana*, natives respectively of Malaya and India, and can have come originally only from Southeast Asia since neither wild form occurs anywhere in Africa. Cultivated plants have an immense advantage over domesticated animals as aids in historical reconstruction. One imported bull can alter appreciably the breed of a herd, but indigenous and introduced plants either retain their separate identities or, if they cross, readily yield evidence of their origins to genetic research.

Introduced plants rarely replace completely the species previously cultivated. The latter nearly always survive in some subsidiary status, as revealed in the full lists of cultivated plants compiled by conscientious ethnographers. In Africa, ethnographies written in the French and German languages are much the most useful from this point of view. Over wide regions of Africa today plants introduced in recent centuries from the New World, notably maize and manioc, have attained a dominant role as the staple crops, but analysis of ethnographic lists of subsidiary cultigens invariably reveals those which provided the basis of subsistence prior to A.D. 1500.

Each of the major complexes of food plants which have played a role in African culture history will receive full consideration in the regional chapter dealing with its introduction. At this point only a brief orientation is needed. Two of the complexes originated on the continent itself, one in West Africa and one in Ethiopia, considered, respectively, in Chapters 11 and 22. Two derive from Southwest Asia by way of Egypt and are treated in Chapters 14 and 18. They are differentiated on the basis of dates of introduction, i.e., prior or subsequent to the close of the Pharaonic, or Dynastic, period marked by the conquest of Egypt by Alexander the Great in 332 B.C. Two complexes, discussed in Chapter 26, derive from Southeast Asia by way of East Africa and are differentiated on the basis of whether their component plants were first domesticated in India or farther to the east. The last complex to reach Africa is the American (see Chapter 29), whose elements were introduced to the coasts of West and East Africa by Europeans during the course of the slave trade. A partial list of plants from these various sources, classified according to type of cultigen, is presented in Table 2.

It may also prove helpful to single out for brief mention all the plants which have attained the status of an outstanding staple in at least several of the societies of the continent. These are, roughly in order of their importance:

Sorghum and pearl millet, in a very large number of societies in Negro Africa and adjacent regions

Maize, in many societies in the tropical-forest zone and southern Africa and occasional ones in East Africa and the Sudan

Wheat and barley, in many parts of North Africa

Manioc, in many societies in the Belgian Congo, French Equatorial Africa, and adjacent regions

Yams and taro, on the Guinea coast and in a number of societies in the southern Sudan, Cameroon, and the Congo Basin

Bananas, in many societies in Uganda and the tropical-forest zone

Rice, in Madagascar, an occasional society in East Africa, and all of coastal
West Africa from Senegal to the Ivory Coast
Eleusine, in a considerable number of societies in East Africa
Date palm, in the oases of the Sahara Desert
Fonio, in a number of societies in the western Sudan
Ensete, in southwestern Ethiopia
Fig and olive, in a few societies along the Mediterranean littoral
Legumes, sweet potatoes, and teff, in an occasional isolated society

Table 2: Classification of African Cultivated Plants by Type and Origin

Type	Place of origin				
	West Africa	Ethiopia	Southwest Asia	Southeast Asia	America
Cereal grains	Fonio Pearl millet Sorghum	Eleusine Teff	Barley Wheat	Rice	Maize
Legumes	Cow pea	...	Broad bean Chick pea Lentil Pea	Gram bean Hyacinth bean Pigeon pea Sword bean	Haricot bean Lima bean
Tubers and root crops	Coleus Earth pea Geocarpa bean Guinea yam	Ensete	Beet Chufa Onion Radish	Taro Yam	Malanga Manioc Peanut Sweet potato
Leaf and stalk vegetables	Okra	Cress	Cabbage Lettuce	Jew's mallow	
Vine and ground fruits	Fluted pumpkin Gourd Watermelon	...	Grape Melon	Cucumber Eggplant	Pineapple Pumpkin Squash Tomato
Tree fruits	Akee Tamarind	...	Date palm Fig Pomegranate	Banana Coconut palm Mango	Avocado Papaya
Condiments and indulgents	Kola Roselle	Coffee Fenu-greek Kat	Coriander Garlic Opium poppy	Ginger Hemp (hash-ish) Sugarcane	Cacao Red pepper Tobacco
Textile plants	Ambary Cotton	...	Flax		
Oil plants	Oil palm Sesame	Castor Remtil	Olive Rape		

Among economic plants and cash crops grown for export the most important are cacao, coffee, cotton, flax, kola, the oil palm, peanuts, and sesame.

Selected Bibliography

[For sources on African agriculture see the bibliographies appended to Chapters 11, 14, 18, 22, 26, and 29.]

Bisschop, J. H. R. Parent Stock and Derived Types of African Cattle. *SAJS*, 33:852–870. 1936.

Dyson, R. H. Archeology and the Domestication of Animals in the Old World. *AA*, 55:661–673. 1953.

Phillips, R. W. Cattle. *Scientific American*, 198(6):51–59. 1958.

Simmonds, N. W., and K. Shepherd. The Taxonomy and Origins of the Cultivated Bananas. *Journal of the Linnean Society, Botany*, 55:302–312. 1955.

Simoons, F. The Non-milking Area of Africa. *Anthropos*, 49:58–66. 1954.

5

Society

Anthropologists have devoted special attention to the field of social organization for nearly a century and have made more striking scientific progress here than in any other branch of their subject. As a consequence, they have developed a somewhat complex technical vocabulary which it is necessary to employ in any discussion of African society. Since the concepts employed by specialists, though seldom difficult to grasp, are not always familiar to the general reader, and the terms are not always fully standardized, each subject considered below will be introduced by a set of definitions.

In some parts of the world, though rarely in Africa, marriages may be concluded relatively informally, involving only the consent of the parties and their kinsmen, a minimum of ceremonial, and no property transfer or other material consideration, except perhaps for gift giving or an exchange of presents. Most African societies, however, require some material consideration to legitimize and stabilize a marriage, to recompense the bride's parents for the loss of their daughter, and to serve as a guaranty that the husband will fulfill his obligations. Such a consideration may be tendered in goods, in services, or in kind. If paid in goods, e.g., in livestock or in currency, it is technically called a *bride-price*. If rendered in services, e.g., in agricultural labor for the wife's parents either before or after marriage, it is called *bride-service*. A payment in kind involves giving a woman of one's own group, e.g., a sister or a daughter, to a kinsman of the bride in exchange for her—a transaction known as an *exchange marriage*.

Payment of a bride-price strongly predominates in Africa as a whole and in the great majority of its individual culture provinces. Exchange marriage prevails in a number of societies on the Nigerian plateau, in a smaller cluster in western Ethiopia, and in sporadic instances elsewhere. Bride-service has a higher incidence. It often occurs as a supplement to, or a substitute for, a bride-price, and stands alone, as one might expect, chiefly among peoples who are poor in livestock or other valuable possessions, e.g., the Bushmen and the eastern Central Bantu.

Marriage can assume any one of three basic forms. *Monogamy* unites one man with one woman only, but a society cannot be characterized as monogamous unless plural marriages are either forbidden or disapproved, since the normal sex ratio assures a preponderance of monogamous unions in any society except under highly exceptional, and usually temporary, circumstances. *Polyandry* unites one woman with two or more husbands; *polygyny*, one man with two or more wives. The more familiar term "polygamy," which embraces both forms of plural marriage, will not be used in this book. Polygyny may be either *sororal* or *nonsororal* depending upon the presence or absence of a preference for marrying sisters rather than co-wives who are unrelated to each other. Polygyny often results from preferential rules governing the remarriage of widows, e.g., the so-called "inheritance" of widows by a brother, nephew, or son of the deceased husband. Actually these rules represent, not a form of property transmission, but a social security device assuring the support and maintenance of women in their old age. The rule prescribing secondary marriage with a brother of the deceased husband is known as the *levirate*, or if only the husband's younger brother is eligible, as the *junior levirate*. A parallel rule, called the *sororate*, gives a widower a preferential right to marry a sister of his deceased wife.

Polyandry is virtually nonexistent in Africa, and monogamy, except for intrusive Europeans and missionized natives, is confined almost exclusively to the Berbers of North Africa, the Monophysitic Christians of Ethiopia, and the remnant hunting peoples. Polygyny preponderates to an overwhelming extent, prevailing in 88 per cent of a representative sample of 154 societies drawn from the continent at large (Murdock, 1957). Africans have discovered means of making the institution work to the satisfaction of both sexes. No woman lacks a male provider. No polygynous wife has trouble finding a helper or baby sitter in time of need. Since the first wife normally enjoys for her lifetime a position of superior authority and prestige, every woman knows in advance of her marriage what her future status will be and has no fear of being superseded. Since men almost universally establish each of their wives in a separate dwelling and endow them individually with land and livestock, sources of friction are reduced to a minimum. Custom normally requires the husband to treat each wife with equal consideration, to eat and sleep with each in regular rotation, so that no married woman suffers public humiliation through any overt manifestation of favoritism. In consequence of these cultural adjustments, missionaries seeking to institute monogamy in African societies frequently encounter their strongest opposition from the women.

A household may consist either of an independent polygynous or monogamous family or of an *extended family*. In the latter type of organization two or more families of different generations are united by consanguineal kinship ties and common residence under a single head. The precise composition differs with the prevailing rule of residence (see below), but one common type, the patrilocal extended family, comprises a patriarchal head, his wife or wives, his unmarried children, his married sons with their wives and children, and not infrequently also his younger brothers or other collateral relatives with their wives and offspring. The distribution of the various types of family and household organization in Africa defies easy summarization and must therefore await consideration in the regional chapters.

Besides families and households, all societies possess kin groups of some kind whose members are bound together by ties of consanguineal kinship, or blood relationship, but not necessarily by common residence. Affiliation with such groups is accomplished by a rule of descent, of which there are two main types. *Bilateral descent*, which affiliates individuals with their close kinsmen on the basis of relationships traced equally through males and through females, need not concern us here since it prevails in only an insignificant handful of African societies. In contrast to most of the peoples of Europe and the New World, and many of those in Asia and Oceania, those of Africa adhere almost unanimously to one of the two alternative modes of *unilinear descent*, i.e., the *patrilineal* rule, which affiliates individuals with kin groups exclusively on the basis of relationships through males, or the *matrilineal* rule, in which it is only relationships through females that count. A not inconsiderable number even practice *double descent*, which affiliates individuals with some kin groups through the patrilineal rule and with others through the matrilineal rule, thus differing fundamentally from bilateral descent, which affiliates people with the same group regardless of the sex of the parent or other kinsman through whom they are related.

Bilateral descent doubtless once prevailed among the Bushmanoid hunters of South and East Africa since it still survives today among the less acculturated of their survivors. The Caucasoid peoples of northern Africa seem to have been characterized by patrilineal descent from time immemorial, since both matrilineal and bilateral descent occur among them very rarely and only in situations suggesting derivative developments. On the other hand, the Negroes, though preponderantly patrilineal today, may very probably once have been largely matrilineal. In nearly every subfamily of the major linguistic stocks in Negro Africa, e.g., the Nigritic, Sudanic, and Kordofanian, there are at least some tribes who adhere to the matrilineal rule even today, and techniques developed elsewhere by the author (Murdock, 1949) for ascertaining earlier forms of social organization demonstrate rather conclusively that in at least these linguistic stocks matrilineal descent prevailed generally in the not very distant past. Map 9 shows the distribution of the various patterns of descent in Africa today.

Both rules of unilinear descent produce kin groups of parallel type. These are called *lineages*, especially when relatively small and characterized by unmistakable corporate functions; *sibs*, especially when the members are numerous and geographically dispersed so that they cannot maintain a genuine corporate identity; *phratries*, when they are still larger and comprise a number of sibs; and *moieties*, when an entire society comprises only two very large groups, so that every individual must necessarily belong to either one or the other. To indicate succinctly whether the organizing rule of descent is patrilineal or matrilineal, these kin groups are commonly called patrilineages, matrisibs, etc. Some societies exhibit a tendency to constitute as separate groups the descendants of ancestors at each ascending generation, producing a hierarchy of lineages within lineages in what is called a *segmentary lineage system*. The Arab peoples provide particularly striking examples. In such systems it has been found helpful to employ a standard terminology for segments of increasing size and generation depth: minimal lineage, minor lineage, major lineage, maximal lineage, subsib, sib, subphratry, and phratry, or as many such terms as the number of recognized levels in the particular society requires.

Kin groups may or may not regulate marriage, and the same is true of local groups, social classes, age-grades, etc. Any social group which does not regulate marriage, i.e., which prescribes neither that its members marry amongst themselves nor that they marry outsiders, is called *agamous*. A group which does regulate marriage is called *endogamous* if in-marriage is favored, *exogamous* if out-marriage is strongly preferential. In general, kin groups tend to be exogamous, especially at the lineage level. Phratries, however, are often agamous or even endogamous.

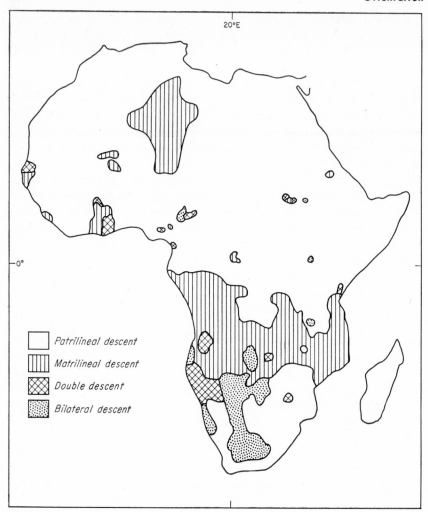

20°E

-0°

Patrilineal descent

Matrilineal descent

Double descent

Bilateral descent

Map 9. Distribution of Rules of Descent

and sibs occasionally so. Endogamy at the lowest lineage level is confined almost exclusively to the Arabs of North Africa and to indigenous peoples who have been subject to strong Islamic indoctrination.

Kinship systems, i.e., the classification of relatives into categories with reference to the kinship terms applied to them, reveal unmistakable correlations with particular configurations of kin groups. The complexities of kinship lie for the most part beyond the scope of the present volume, which will report on only one phase of the subject, namely, typology in the terminological classification of first cousins. Before presenting this, it will help to make one important distinction. A *cross-cousin* is the child of a father's sister or of a mother's brother; a *parallel cousin* is the child of a father's brother or of a mother's sister. In other words, cousins of the former type are the children of a brother and sister, whereas those of the latter type are the offspring of two brothers or of two sisters. The distinction has implications for subjects other than kinship. Cross-cousins, for example, are commonly permitted or even expected to marry, whereas unions between parallel cousins are usually forbidden as incestuous, except in the Islamic world.

First cousins can be designated in the six basically different ways discussed below.

Eskimo pattern. Cross- and parallel cousins are called by the same terms but are terminologically distinguished from siblings. The English term "cousin" illustrates this pattern, which is most typically associated with bilateral descent, independent nuclear families, and kin groups of the type known as personal kindreds.

Hawaiian pattern. Cross- and parallel cousins are both called by the same terms as brothers and sisters. This pattern occurs most commonly in bilateral societies with extended families or corporate kin groups but can also result from an incompletely assimilated shift from one rule of descent to another.

Descriptive pattern. Cousins of every category are terminologically distinguished not only from siblings but also from each other, and are called by compound terms which identify precisely their relationship to Ego, e.g., "father's brother's son" or "maternal uncle's daughter." In Africa this pattern occurs commonly in the Islamic area and on the Guinea coast and occasionally elsewhere, and seems to be correlated with patrilineal descent, a segmentary lineage organization, and the absence or weak development of exogamy.

Iroquois pattern. Cross-cousins are terminologically equated with each other and differentiated from both siblings and parallel cousins. This pattern normally coexists with a matrilineal or patrilineal rule of descent, under which cross-cousins cannot be members of Ego's kin group whereas parallel cousins either necessarily are or may be.

Omaha pattern. Cross-cousins are terminologically differentiated alike from siblings, parallel cousins, and each other, the children of a mother's brother being equated with kinsmen of a higher generation, e.g., being called "uncle" or "mother," whereas a father's sister's children are equated with kinsmen of a lower generation. This pattern occurs almost exclusively in patrilineal societies with strongly functional lineages and reflects a feeling that membership in one's mother's patrilineage, to which of course one's mother, maternal uncle, and the latter's children all belong, is more important than a difference in generation.

Crow pattern. This type is similar to the Omaha pattern. It reflects the lineage principle in the same way except that it occurs in matrilineal societies. Here it is the father's sisters' children who are classed with a higher generation, e.g., as "father" and "aunt," and the mother's brothers' children with a lower generation. When found in a patrilineal society, the Crow pattern provides an infallible indication of former matrilineal descent.

Like kin groups, local groups—or *communities*—represent a universal form of social organization. Under nomadic or seminomadic conditions the prevailing type of local group, comprising a number of families which wander and camp together, is called a *band*. With sedentary life the families which compose a local community may live in a *village*, or aggregate of clustered households; in a *neighborhood*, or aggregate of dispersed households; or in a settlement pattern of some intermediate or more complex form. Many societies recognize local groups intermediate in size between the household and the community. These are most widely known as *wards*, but in the African literature are more commonly called "quarters." Wards may adjoin one another closely or be separated by an intervening space, which, if great enough, may even convert them into dispersed hamlets.

The inhabitants of a local community, or of a ward within it, may be associated on the basis of common religious beliefs or ethnic ties or social status or economic specialization, or as a by-product of individual enterprise and self-interest; in such circumstances their integration rests on propinquity and interdependence alone and any kinship bonds among them are purely incidental. Members of bilateral societies of European origin tend to assume that this kind of community structure is universal. In unilinear societies, however, and perhaps especially in patrilineal cultures, this assumption commonly proves false, and the rule of descent often provides the primary bond of association in local groups as well as in kin groups, at least in the ward and the village, though admittedly only rarely in large urban centers. In Africa, particularly, no adequate conception of community life can be achieved without due recognition of the integrating role of unilinear kinship ties.

Very widely in Africa the village, or at least the ward, is itself a genuine kin group, united by unilinear descent. It cannot, of course, be a sib or a lineage according to the definitions given above, since such groups are normally exogamous. If husband and wife always and necessarily belong to different lineages or sibs, it is obvious that no local group, whether a household, a ward, or a village, can be composed entirely of members of a single unilinear consanguineal kin group. How, then, can we call any local group a kin group? The answer lies in the fact that only the core of a local group is affiliated through unilinear descent, their spouses being attached to the group through affinal rather than consanguineal ties. A local kin group is thus a compromise kin group, or, technically, a *clan* (Murdock, 1949).

A clan invariably owes its origin to a compromise between a rule of descent and a consistent rule of *residence*. Whenever a man and a woman marry, since unions between members of the same family are universally prohibited as incestuous, one or the other or both must change residence if they are to establish a common household. The alternative possibilities are few, and each has a scientific name. In the first possible solution to this problem, known as *neolocal* residence, both spouses leave their parental homes and establish a new household whose location is not determined primarily by the kinship ties of either. Though normal in many European societies, neolocal residence is all but unknown in Africa. In an alternative solution, known as *duolocal* residence, neither spouse leaves his natal home; instead of founding a common household they maintain separate establishments, each with his own kinsmen. This occurs nowhere in Africa as a permanent arrangement, although a few Twi tribes in Ghana practice duolocal residence for the first few years of married life.

With these insignificant exceptions, all African peoples adhere to a rule of *unilocal* residence, in which one spouse continues to reside with or near his or her kinsmen and is joined there by the other. Unilocal residence may assume any of three variant forms. In the first of these, called *matrilocal* residence, it is the wife who remains at home and the husband who leaves his relatives to reside with her. This rule, though common in matrilineal societies elsewhere in the world, occurs with extraordinary infrequency in Africa, being confined to a minority of the Central Bantu and not more than two or three scattered tribes elsewhere. In the second variant, called *patrilocal* residence, the wife leaves home and joins her husband, either in the household of his parents or in a new one in the vicinity. This rule has by far the widest distribution of all on the African continent.

Ranking second in incidence, far behind patrilocal residence but several times as common as all other rules put together, is a third unilocal variant, known as *avunculocal* residence. Under this rule it is again the woman who leaves home, but the couple set up housekeeping with or near, not the parents of the husband, but his maternal uncle. The man has also, of course, left his parental home, but in most cases he has done so long before marriage, in adolescence or even in boyhood. The term "virilocal," which has recently been gaining currency, is to be abjured as ambiguous since it needlessly confuses patrilocal with avunculocal and even with neolocal residence.

Clans can develop only in the presence of consistent rules of descent and residence. The conjunction of patrilineal descent and patrilocal residence produces a *patriclan*, a compromise kin group with the male members of a patrilineage as its core, to which are added their wives from other lineages who have joined them in patrilocal residence, and from which are subtracted their adult sisters who have left to reside in the clans of their husbands. The combination of matrilineal descent and matrilocal residence similarly gives rise to *matriclans* around a core of matrilineally related females plus their in-marrying husbands and minus their out-marrying brothers. When combined with avunculocal residence, matrilineal descent yields *avuncuclans*, in which the core consists of the males rather than the females of a matrilineage, and the fringe, as in the case of a patriclan, comprises the in-marrying wives of the adult men. Clans cannot arise or exist under other combinations, e.g., of matrilineal descent and patrilocal residence, and any clan organization dissolves as soon as social change produces any serious inconsistency between the rules of residence and descent.

Like other kin groups, clans vary in size. One which is coextensive with an entire village, neighborhood, or band is called a *clan-community*. One which is confined to a ward or comparable segment of a community is called a *clan-barrio*. On a still more reduced level, extended families can be regarded as minimal clans since they possess an identical structural composition. Whatever their scale, clans and lineages in the same society always share a common core, consisting of the members of one sex in the prevailing line of descent, and always differ in the relationship of the other sex to them, i.e., as spouses in the one case and siblings in the other. Where both types of group coexist in the same society, they typically reveal very different functions. In general it is the lineage which regulates marriage and inheritance, acts as a unit in life-crisis situations, and is associated with totemism and ancestor worship, whereas the clan functions primarily in the economic, recreational, political, and military spheres of life. These differences are unfortunately often obscured in the descriptive literature through the indiscriminate use of the term "clan" for both the sib or maximal lineage and the compromise kin group, to which the name is here restricted.

Selected Bibliography

Baumann, H. Vaterrecht und Mutterrecht in Afrika. *ZE*, 58:62–161. 1926.
Murdock, G. P. *Social Structure*. New York, 1949.
———. World Ethnographic Sample. *AA*, 59:664–689. 1957.

6

Government

In the survey of African ethnography conducted for the present volume, political systems received appreciably less attention than social organization. They were examined less from the point of view of function, or even of structure, than from that of form, which it was hoped might shed light on historical movements and the diffusion of culture in the past. This hope has been realized only in small part. A comprehensive survey of African political organization is still urgently needed, although Fortes and Evans-Pritchard (1940) have made a promising beginning. The present writer can do little more than offer a tentative classification and characterization of the major types of indigenous structures and propose a few suggestions for future research.

The first and simplest, as well as the most widespread, type of political system is one which may be called a *primitive democracy*. Leadership and a measure of prestige, but not authority, are vested typically in a headman and a council of elders or family heads with perhaps a few other semispecialized functionaries to direct hunting or conduct particular rituals. The headman, though often hereditary, is merely *primus inter pares*. Neither he nor any other leader has the power or the right to compel compliance. He can only advise or persuade. Decisions are reached through discussion and informal consensus, and sanctions are applied exclusively through the operation of informal mechanisms of social control. With rare exceptions political integration does not transcend the bounds of an autonomous local community, and nothing remotely approximating the structure of a state is detectable. Political relations tend to be indistinguishable from kinship relations. Under unilinear descent the structure of the clan is the structure of government. If a community comprises several clan-barrios, a very modest hierarchical order may emerge, with the senior or founding clan providing the headman and the others relating themselves to it in some real or fictive junior kinship capacity, e.g., as younger brothers, sisters' sons, or affines.

A second distinguishable type, particularly characteristic of the Bedouin Arabs and the Tuareg, may be named the *gentile aristocracy*. The political structure still rests primarily on a kinship foundation, specifically a segmentary lineage system. Coercive power, however, makes its appearance, based on superiority of weapons, mobility through the camel or the horse, lineage *esprit de corps*, and the fortunes of war. Through such ad-

33

vantages one powerful kin group or a confederation of such conquers weaker groups or defenseless alien peoples and reduces them to tributary status, serfdom, or slavery, exploiting them remorselessly. Extremely sharp class distinctions develop as a consequence. Stratification is not ordinarily achieved, however, through the subordination of individuals to individuals but of groups to groups, with the dominant kin group forming a ruling aristocracy at the apex of the hierarchy. Political hegemony tends, nevertheless, to be transitory since no adequate devices for achieving administrative stability have been achieved. Except for Islamic religious and judicial functionaries, leadership rests exclusively in the heads (sheikhs) of the hierarchical lineage segments, who ordinarily lead the same mode of life as their followers and must continually validate their authority through valor, generosity, sagacity, or piety. Since rivalries are rampant, strong fissive tendencies prevail. Power alignments are readily shattered, with a constant reshuffling of lineage segments. Even when dominant gentile aristocracies acknowledge the theoretical sovereignty of neighboring states or of colonial governments, they commonly remain essentially autonomous and undergo little significant structural change.

A highly distinctive type of political system, confined today to the less strongly Arabized parts of North Africa but formerly much more widespread, is the *Berber republic*. Its characteristic structure, unveiled by the researches of Montagne (1930), will receive detailed consideration in Chapter 15, and the briefest of summaries must suffice at this point. Except for emergency war leaders there are no chiefs or other authoritative functionaries. Government at the local level is conducted exclusively by a democratic assembly of all adult males, headed by an elected president who serves for a single year and functions only as the chairman or presiding officer at assembly meetings. At the district level authority is vested in a council or senate, with a similar elective presiding officer, which is composed of a representative of each lineage of the district. Since these tend to be the older and wealthier men, the body has an oligarchical rather than a democratic character. It is, however, in no sense aristocratic, for the independent Berbers are notably egalitarian and have developed no significant class or caste distinctions. Above the district level political integration is achieved solely through traditional alliances between groups of districts. Although its lineage substructure is still clearly apparent, this system has evolved some specifically political features of rather exceptional interest.

A fourth and genuinely unique political system, the *Gada republic*, has a fairly extensive distribution in East Africa. Especially characteristic of the Galla and neighboring Eastern Cushitic tribes of southern Ethiopia, it has spread to a series of adjacent Bantu and Nilotic peoples, though often in an attenuated form. It rests, not on kinship, but on a structure of formal age-grades. An *age-grade* may be defined as an organized social group in a hierarchical system of such groups stratified according to either the actual or the socially defined ages of their members. An *age-set* comprises the individuals who occupy a particular grade at a particular time. They become constituted as a group through initiation into the lowest grade of the system. After a specific period of time—eight years among the Galla—they are promoted collectively to the next higher grade, being succeeded by another set and themselves replacing the set ahead of them, which advances into the next grade. After a set has filled successively all the grades of the system—five in number among the Galla—its surviving members pass out of the system entirely. Specific communal and political functions are associated with each grade. The set or sets occupying a junior grade or grades serve as warriors. The senior set serve as respected elders and advisers but exercise no political authority, which is invariably reserved for the members of the set occupying the grade behind them, i.e., the second from the top in the hierarchy.

The Gada republic is a genuine state, integrating not a single community but entire tribes. Even among peripheral peoples like the Masai, among whom the formal political structure has become greatly simplified, the entire society constitutes a peace-group unified by a tribe-wide age-grade organization. Where the system is highly developed, political authority is vested in the holders of a diverse series of offices, including a tribal chief, a speaker of the tribal assembly, headmen of local communities, judges, legal advisers, and religious functionaries, all chosen from the age-set occupying the semifinal age-grade, all holding office only for the duration of their occupancy of that grade, and all retiring together at the termination of this period to become honored but politically powerless elders. Officeholders are elected on the basis of merit and past accomplishment, but eligible candidates for the highest positions are restricted to the sons of previous incumbents. Like the Berber system, from which it differs in so many other respects, the Gada political structure does not rest on kinship, aristocratic status, or despotic power. Since, moreover, neither system is truly democratic, though in both instances authority derives more from popular choice than from hereditary right, it seems appropriate to characterize both of them as republican.

A fifth type of political system may be called the *Oriental despotism*, after Wittfogel (1957), who has delineated its characteristic features and associated institutions with acumen and painstaking thoroughness. Pharaonic Egypt, with its agrarian economy based on irrigation, its absolutistic monarchy, its hierarchical administrative bureaucracy, its massive monuments and public works created by *corvée* labor, the conspicuous consumption of its rulers, and the complete domination of the state over property, religion, and other potential sources of autonomous power, represents the veritable prototype of the Oriental despotism. Under the same category clearly fall the political systems established in maritime North Africa by Rome, Byzantium, the Ottoman Turks, and the Arabs, as well as the derivative states known historically from Nubia and highland Ethiopia.

What concerns us more is the *African despotism,* a parallel form of political structure found widely in Negro Africa and extending to Madagascar and to the Cushitic-speaking Sidamo peoples of southwestern Ethiopia. Its striking resemblances to the Oriental despotisms analyzed by Wittfogel raise two extremely important questions. The first is historical. Do the despotic states of Africa represent an independent but parallel development, like those of Mexico and Peru in the New World, or did the peoples of the Sudan borrow the fundamental pattern of organization at some early date from Pharaonic Egypt, adapt it to their own needs, and transmit it to the rest of Negro Africa? The writer feels unable to give a categoric answer to this question and recommends it as a significant research problem for some historically oriented anthropologist. He can, however, record his own very tentative conclusions. These are, first, that African despotisms all derive from a single common source; second, that the balance of evidence favors an origin in the western Sudan rather than on the lower Nile; third, that significant increments to the basic pattern were in fact borrowed from Egypt at some subsequent period or periods.

The second important question is sociological or comparative. Is the African despotism merely a subtype of the Oriental despotism, or does it represent a separate major type of political system like the maritime state, the feudal state, the modern industrial democracy, and—we might add from the previous discussion—the primitive democracy, the gentile aristocracy, and the archaic republic? Again the writer cannot give a definite answer, and can only recommend the problem as one well worth independent investigation and record his own impressions. On the whole, the African despotism, even when all accretions reasonably attributable to diffusion from Pharaonic Egypt are stripped away, strikes him as much too similar to the Oriental despotism to warrant its establishment as a distinct major type of political system. On the other hand, he finds it impossible to ascribe the system to an economic basis in irrigated agriculture—the hydraulic foundation on which Wittfogel believes all except marginal and derivative Oriental despotisms rest. Irrigation is, to be sure, by no means unknown in Negro Africa, but the regions of greatest political complexity are almost invariably characterized by shifting swidden, or slash-and-burn, agriculture. What, then, provides the economic basis for the African despotic state? To the scholar who may wish to pursue the subject, the writer can offer only one suggestion: Is it, perhaps, the exploitation of slave labor, which Wittfogel finds surprisingly minimized in his Oriental despotisms but which is enormously developed in many of the most typical African states?

Specialists steeped in the African literature commonly discern wide differences among the complex political systems of different areas. To the present writer, coming to the subject after a survey of another continent, such differences appear superficial in comparison with the extraordinary resemblances in fundamental features and even in external forms. As contrasted with the diversity of complex political structures in aboriginal North America, exemplified by those of the Aztec, the Creek, the Iroquois, and the Natchez, the states of Negro Africa appear essentially as similar as the peas in a single pod. However geographically remote and however dissimilar the other aspects of culture, political forms seem everywhere to conform to a single fundamental pattern. Nor does the size of a state seem to make any essential difference. Even a petty paramount chief who has subjugated a few neighboring communities and destroyed the preexisting primitive democracy seems invariably to institute, in so far as he can on a small scale, the forms prevailing in larger states in the vicinity or even at some distance. It is almost as though all of Africa south of the Sahara were permeated, as it were, by a mental blueprint of a despotic political structure, transmitted from generation to generation as a part of traditional verbal culture, and always available to be transmuted into reality whenever some individual arises with the imagination, enterprise, strength, and luck to establish, with the aid of his kinsmen, an authoritarian regime over people residing beyond the limits of his local community.

Some of the widespread similarities in basic pattern and in details of form which have led the author to his conclusion of the essential uniformity and single origin of despotic states in Negro Africa may now be listed.

Monarchical absolutism. Each king or independent paramount chief enjoys absolute power, at least in theory.

Eminent domain. All land, livestock, and wild game in the state belong in theory to the monarch, providing a basis for his right to derive an income from them.

Divine kingship. Either the ruler himself is divine or he has unique personal access to the dominant divine powers.

Ritual isolation. The king is isolated from physical contact with all except a few attendants and intimates. Often he eats in private or must be fed by others, or his feet may not touch the ground, or he is concealed by curtains because his glance is considered dangerous.

Insignia of office. Royal status is symbolized by the possession of distinctive regalia, among which stools, drums, and animal tails are especially common.

Capital towns. The ruler resides in a capital town along with his attendants and ministers. Typically each new monarch founds a new capital or at least establishes a new royal residence.

Royal courts. The monarch maintains an elaborate court with pages, guards, entertainers, personal attendants, treasurers, and a variety of chamberlains with specialized functions.

Protocol. Behavior at court follows detailed rules of protocol, of which abject prostration in the presence of the monarch is a nearly universal ingredient.

Harems. The ruler is invariably surrounded by a large number of wives and concubines.

Queens. At most royal courts a Queen-Mother, a Queen-Consort, and a Queen-Sister, or at least two of the three, enjoy extraordinary prestige, even sometimes technically outranking the king himself. Queens are commonly endowed with independent estates and often exercise restricted political authority.

Territorial bureaucracy. For administrative purposes each state is divided into a territorial hierarchy of provinces, districts, and local communities with bureaucratic officials at each level responsible for maintaining order, collecting and transmitting taxes, and levying troops and *corvée* labor. Even where bureaucratic posts are hereditary rather than appointive, their occupants are firmly subordinated to the central authority.

Ministers. Resident at the capital as assistants to the ruler in the exercise of centralized authority are always a number of ministers of state, the most important of whom form a supreme advisory council. They are distinguished by specialized functions, e.g., a vizier or prime minister, a military commander in chief, a chief justice, a royal executioner, a custodian of the royal tombs, a supervisor of royal princes and princesses.

Duality of ministerial roles. Almost universally, the ministers combine their specialized functions at the capital with offices as provincial governors in the territorial organization.

Titles. Characteristic of African states is a great proliferation of titles. Although a few or many may be hereditary, there are always a large number bestowable by the monarch in return for loyal services, and competition for these is often keen.

Security provisions. To prevent palace revolutions a king's brothers, as the most likely usurpers, may be killed, blinded, incarcerated, or banished from the capital. To prevent revolts in the provinces, positions as governors are commonly filled, not by members of the royal lineage, but by persons of categories ineligible to succeed to the throne, e.g., commoners, elevated slaves, eunuchs, or, where succession is patrilineal, sisters' sons.

Electoral succession. Although the ruler often designates an heir presumptive, and may even invest him with ministerial authority, succession to the throne is almost never automatic. The decision usually rests in the hands of a committee of ministers with constitutional electoral powers, who are free to follow or ignore the late king's wishes. Not infrequently the succession shifts regularly from one to another branch of the royal lineage.

Anarchic interregnums. Since there is always a plurality of candidates with strong supporters, and considerable political maneuvering may be necessary before the electors can agree upon a successor, a period of several days or even weeks usually intervenes between the death of one king and the selection of the next. During this interregnum laws are relaxed and social disorder prevails, often accentuated by a resort to arms by the partisans of rival claimants.

Human sacrifice. In many Negro states the funeral of a king is accompanied by human sacrifices, sometimes on an extravagant scale.

Naturally not all the above features occur in every despotic state south of the Sahara, but the great majority usually do, and the degree of association among them is far too strong to be attributable to chance.

Selected Bibliography

Fortes, M., and E. E. Evans-Pritchard, eds. *African Political Systems*. London, 1940.

Irstam, T. The King of Ganda. *PEMS*, n.s., 8:1–203. 1944.

Montagne, R. *Les Berbères et le Makhzen dans le sud du Maroc*. Paris, 1930.

Onneken, D. A. *Die Königskultur Kaffas und der verwandten Königreiche*. Frankfurt am Main, 1956.

Schapera, I. *Government and Politics in Tribal Societies*. London, 1956.

Wittfogel, K. A. *Oriental Despotism*. New Haven, 1957.

7

History

The fact that this volume has a primarily historical objective makes it necessary to face squarely the issue of the validity of historical anthropology and of its various methods and techniques. This is the more imperative since a substantial number of outstanding anthropologists, especially in Great Britain, exhibit a profound distrust of the historical approach and consistently refrain from using it even in an auxiliary capacity. This prejudice, for it cannot be characterized otherwise, stems directly from Radcliffe-Brown (1923 and 1950), who throughout his career habitually referred contemptuously to the work of historical anthropologists as "pseudo history" or "conjectural history." This canard cannot be allowed to stand unchallenged.

The writer agrees with the great majority of his American colleagues that history and science are equally legitimate objectives in anthropological work and that neither approach is inherently more likely than the other to produce valid results. To be sure, only some of the historical research in anthropology can be characterized as sound; much is admittedly bad, and some, though laudable in scope and method, is unfortunately simply wrong. But scientific research in anthropology can be similarly categorized as sound, bad, and wrong, and in approximately the same proportions.

Work in the African field, whether historical or scientific, which the author considers definitely bad he simply ignores in this book, whatever the reputation of the persons responsible. He also abjures the methods which he considers fundamentally unsound, but these must be specified. One is the use of similarities in tribal or place names as a basis for drawing historical inferences. Such resemblances have absolutely no evidential value of themselves, and conclusions drawn from them cannot be accepted unless solidly buttressed by other and more dependable evidence. A second unsound method consists of postulating migration or diffusion from general similarities in complex social phenomena, e.g., from the occurrence of totemism, or mother-right, or potlatches and feasts of merit in geographically remote areas in the absence of any probability of a historical connection on other and more substantial grounds.

Equally unsound, but unfortunately extremely prevalent among both ethnologists and archeologists, is the technique which the writer dubs "trait chasing." This consists in drawing conclusions as to historical connections from specific and detailed cultural resemblances occurring in different regions, e.g., the presence of a similar type of adze blade in Polynesia and South China or of a double spiral motif in both the Caucasus and northwestern Argentina. Even the compilation of a number of supportive similarities between the same two regions has no evidential value if the probability of contact or migration cannot be established on other grounds. Linguists have estimated that, for any two unrelated languages selected at random from anywhere in the world, as much as 6 per cent of their total vocabularies may reveal such similarities in both form and meaning that competent specialists would unhesitatingly accept them as cognates if the languages were known to be related. Similarly, in ethnology, if one starts with a single resemblance between any two remote and unrelated cultures, a search for others can easily reveal scores or even hundreds.

More difficult to assess are those cases, in both scientific and historical anthropology, where wrong conclusions have been reached despite essential soundness in method. The great evolutionists like Morgan and Tylor provide, of course, the classic illustration. In scientific anthropology, or "comparative sociology," Radcliffe-Brown must be placed unequivocally in this category, for his interpretations of particular ethnographic phenomena have proved erroneous in every instance where they have been brought into question, e.g., by Deacon, Junod, Kroeber, and Lawrence. His strictures against historical anthropology can therefore probably be interpreted as a typical Freudian reaction formation against an equally just (or unjust) characterization of his own work as "pseudo science" or "conjectural sociology." This does not detract from the value of his contribution in stimulating others, for Morgan, whose interpretations were at least as erroneous, still enjoys a solid reputation as the grandfather of kinship studies.

A strictly parallel case in historical anthropology is the *Kulturkreislehre* of the German-Austrian "culture-historical" school. Despite a genuinely admirable methodology, e.g., in the criteria of form and quantity, this group reached erroneous conclusions in their postulation of a small series of culture complexes which allegedly spread as units over enormous areas of the world's surface. The culture history of the present volume has nothing in common with the approach of this group. A criticism, however, is not in order since the leading exponents of the theory publicly renounced it at a world anthropological congress in 1956, in what was perhaps the most laudable demonstration of scientific integrity in the history of our subject. In tribute we can at least cite Ankermann (1905), who investigated the culture history of Africa from this point of view, even though we cannot follow him.

Thoroughly sound work in historical and in scientific anthropology, leading to essentially dependable conclusions, is well exemplified on the one hand by Spier's North American researches and on the other by the recent British social anthropologists whose reports on African societies have proved indispensable in the compilation of this book. Greater sophistication in psychology and sociology may doubtless ultimately revise some of Spier's specific conclusions, and in occasional instances a greater awareness of history and process can demonstrate errors in the interpretations advanced by British Africanists; but incidental mistakes of this kind are thoroughly excusable and in no way detract from the essential merit of the work. On the whole, the present writer agrees heartily with Eggan (1950 and 1954) that the most productive procedure in both scientific and historical anthropology is one which combines the best in the two approaches and constantly tests conclusions in either by evidence from the other.

The techniques of historical reconstruction employed in this volume are those discovered to be reliable by a very simple empirical test, namely, whether their use leads invariably to conclusions consistent with those derived from other independent and dependable methods. Several sources of evidence fall unmistakably into this category. First, of course, is the direct testimony of contemporary written records. These are invaluable for North African history, but unfortunately rarely yield information of any considerable time depth elsewhere on the continent. The second is the equally direct testimony of materials excavated in archeological sites, from which, however, we must emphatically except the inferences that archeologists have drawn from these findings, unless their interpretations are buttressed by independent evidence. A third and equally dependable source is linguistic relationships, which have already been discussed in Chapter 3. A fourth is the evidence from botany and from the distribution of cultivated plants, as presented and analyzed in Chapter 4. A fifth is the methodology for inferring earlier forms of social organization in a particular society from internal structural inconsistencies reflecting the conservatism of certain features, as presented elsewhere by the author (Murdock, 1949). A sixth is ethnographic distributional analysis as applied by the more cautious American historical anthropologists, which is characterized particularly by its restriction to areas of continuous distribution of cultural forms and by its refusal to jump geographic gaps without exceedingly compelling reasons. This technique may be combined with a conservative utilization of the age-area hypothesis, although the author refrains from doing this except where the conclusions receive confirmation from at least one of the other five basic techniques.

As intimated above, these six independent methods of reconstructing the past support one another. The author has not encountered a single instance in Africa where suggestive leads from two or more of these sources have indicated inconsistent conclusions. One typical example of their mutual confirmation must suffice. The author was first led to suspect that the Barea and Kunama tribes of Eritrea might have come from the Nile Valley 300 miles to the west by Greenberg's demonstration that their languages belong to the Sudanic stock. Subsequent analysis of their cultivated plants revealed that these, unlike the crops of their present immediate neighbors, belong mainly to the Sudanic complex like those of Nubia. Their matrilineal social organization, contrasting sharply with the patrilineate of their neighbors, proved thoroughly consistent, according to the author's methods of social structural analysis, with what ethnographic distributions and age-area analysis indicated as probable in the Nile Valley before the Moslem conquest of the kingdom of Alwa in A.D. 1504. The author subsequently discovered a clinching confirmation of the validity of these various techniques in the chronicle of an Arab traveler who visited Alwa in 872 and referred to the "Barya" and "Cunama" as tribes then living on the borders of that kingdom.

The discussion thus far has ignored one source of historical information of which the African literature contains a vast quantity, namely, the oral historical traditions of the African peoples themselves. No dependence whatsoever is placed upon evidence of this type in the present volume, since repeated comparisons of local traditions regarding places or directions of origin with inferences from the six techniques of proven reliability have indicated, for time depths of over a century, an agreement of not greater than 20 or 25 per cent, or approximately what one could expect on the basis of chance alone. The author is consequently forced to conclude that indigenous oral traditions are completely undependable much beyond the personal recollections of living informants, unless they happen to be of the very unusual type, characteristic of Polynesia, where automatic self-correction results from their use for validating social status or land claims. It is ironical that British social anthropologists, as in the volumes of the *Ethnographic Survey of Africa*, invariably give serious consideration to native historical traditions, the one type of historical information that is virtually valueless, and completely ignore the evidence from every genuinely reliable source except written records.

The details of the culture history of Africa must, of course, await development in the regional chapters that follow. Since, however, the rationale of the particular sequence followed may not be immediately apparent, and since readers interested only in certain regions may require a summary orientation as a background, it seems desirable to insert at this point an extremely condensed synopsis of the major historical movements on the continent as a whole over the past 7,000 years.

5000 TO 4000 B.C.

Independent development of agriculture on the upper Niger River and its spread throughout the western Sudan.

Introduction of Neolithic agriculture and domesticated animals into Egypt from adjacent Southwest Asia.

4000 TO 3000 B.C.

Spread of Neolithic agriculture and animal husbandry westward along the Mediterranean coast of North Africa to the Atlantic.

Diffusion of Sudanic agriculture eastward across the Sudan to Ethiopia and Nubia.

Replacement of the indigenous Bushmanoid hunters by Negroes on the middle Nile and in western Ethiopia.

Conjunction of the two agricultural civilizations at the border of Egypt and Nubia, resulting in the borrowing by the Nubian Negroes of the Neolithic domesticated animals without the associated milking complex.

3000 TO 2000 B.C.

Development of a complex civilization in Dynastic Egypt.

Introduction of domesticated animals into highland Ethiopia and the improvement of certain Sudanic plants and development of new crops in this minor center of origination.

Spread of the Neolithic animals, without milking, westward across the Sudan to the Atlantic.

Initiation by the Berbers of trade across the Sahara Desert with the Sudan Negroes, resulting in the adoption of Southwest Asian agriculture and domestic animals by the indigenous Negro population of the Sahara.

2000 TO 1000 B.C.

Development of states on the Egyptian model in Nubia and Ethiopia.

Mercantile and technological advance and the rise of despotic states of African type along the northern border of the western Sudan.

Southward expansion of Cushites from southern Ethiopia to the Azanian coast of East Africa, occupying mountainous regions suitable to terraced agriculture but leaving the indigenous Bushmanoid hunters in possession of the inhospitable steppe country.

1000 TO 1 B.C.

Colonization of the North African coast by Phoenicians and Greeks.

Rise of Carthage to hegemony in North Africa based on maritime trade in the western Mediterranean and on the trans-Saharan caravan trade, terminating in annihilation by Rome in 146 B.C.

Decline of Pharaonic Egypt, marked by successive conquests by the Nubians (742 B.C.), the Macedonians (332 B.C.), and the Romans (32 B.C.).

Rise of Napatan power and Meroitic civilization in Nubia.

Invasion of Eritrea by Semites from Yemen, founding the kingdom of Axum and initiating the penetration of Ethiopia.

Introduction, through the maritime trade across the northern Indian Ocean, of Sudanic agriculture to western India and of Indian crops to East Africa.

Increasing prominence of Indonesians from Borneo in the monsoon trade across the Indian Ocean, resulting in their settlement on the East African coast and the introduction there of important Malaysian food plants.

Beginning of the westward spread of these crops across Africa north of the tropical forest to the Guinea coast.

A.D. 1 TO 500

Incorporation of coastal North Africa in the Roman Empire as the principal "granary" of the latter.

Rise of the empire of Ghana in the western Sudan.

Spread of the Malaysian food plants throughout the Guinea coast, laying there the foundation for a dense agricultural population and the rise of despotic states.

Penetration of Cameroon and the Congo Basin by Bantu tillers from Nigeria using Malaysian crops, resulting in their occupation of the territory of the Pygmy hunters and the reduction of the latter to a dependent symbiotic status.

Displacement of the Indonesians by Sabaean and Axumite Semites in the maritime trade with the East, resulting in the migration of the Indonesian settlers in East Africa to Madagascar as the ancestors of the modern Malagasy.

A.D. 500 TO 1000

Shift in political hegemony in coastal North Africa from Rome to Byzantium.

Political conquest of coastal North Africa after 639 by the Moslem Arabs and the conversion of the population to Islam, followed by the rise of independent Moorish states in Morocco, Algeria, and Tunisia.

Belated acquisition of the milking complex by Negroes of the Sudanic linguistic stock and by the Eastern Cushites of southern Ethiopia.

Emergence of the Bantu from the tropical forest into East Africa, adopting Ethiopian food plants from the Cushites and by means of them penetrating the Bushmanoid territory to the south and displacing its indigenous hunting population.

Founding of Zimbabwe and neighboring settlements for the mining of gold and its export to India, first by Cushites and subsequently by Moslem Arabs.

Penetration of Tanganyika and coastal Kenya and Somalia by the Bantu, displacing or absorbing the Bushmanoid hunters except in a few enclaves.

Displacement of the Sabaean Semites by Moslem Arabs in the maritime trade with the East and establishment by the latter of a series of trading posts along the East African coast.

Establishment of Arab settlements in northern Madagascar, initiating a heavy importation of Negro slaves and thereby modifying the racial composition of the Malagasy.

Mass migration of Bedouin Arabs into North Africa, destroying the agricultural productivity of the land and the previous urbane civilization over wide areas.

Displacement of Berbers from Tripolitania and Morocco into the west central Sahara and Mauritania, resulting in the reduction of the indigenous agricultural Negroes to serfdom and the adoption by their conquerors of a predatory nomadic mode of life.

Formation in Senegal of a hybrid race, the Fulani, characterized by a Nigritic language but a pastoral economy, and the beginning of their gradual penetration eastward throughout the western Sudan.

Displacement of Ghana by Mali as the dominant state in West Africa.

Conquest of the Christian state of Dongola in Nubia by the Moslem Arabs.

Completion of the Christianization and Semitization of central Ethiopia.

Development of independent nomadism among the Galla and Somali of southeastern Ethiopia, resulting in their spread south and east into the Horn, the wresting of the steppe country from the surviving Bushmanoid hunters, and the subjugation of the Bantu tillers in the valleys of the Shebelle and Juba Rivers.

Parallel development of independent nomadism among the Sudanic-speaking Nilotes, resulting in their expansion to the southeast and their absorption of the surviving Bushmanoid hunters and Cushitic tillers.

Penetration of Uganda, Ruanda-Urundi, and northwestern Tanganyika by the pastoral Nilotic Hima, leading to their establishment of political domination over the Pygmy and Bantu inhabitants but to their adoption of the Bantu language.

Conquest of North Africa by the Turks and its incorporation into the Ottoman Empire.

Establishment of the Moslem Fung state of Sennar on the middle Nile, overthrowing Christian Alwa and unleashing a migration of Cattle Arabs into the eastern Sudan.

Shift of political hegemony in the western Sudan from Mali to the Songhai state, itself overthrown by Moroccan conquest after a century of splendor.

Initiation of the trans-Atlantic slave trade by Europeans, resulting in the transplantation of Negroes to the New World and in the establishment of important American food plants on the coasts of Africa and their rapid spread into the interior.

Southwestward expansion of the Somali at the expense of the Galla, precipitating a return migration of the latter into southern and central Ethiopia.

Southward spread of milking from the Interlacustrine Bantu to the middle Zambesi and thence to the Southeastern and Southwestern Bantu and the Hottentot, resulting in a strong accentuation of pastoralism in southern Africa.

European settlement in South Africa, eventuating in the virtual annihilation of the Khoisan-speaking hunters and herders and in the subjugation of the Bantu-speaking tillers.

Eastward infiltration of the Fulani into the central Sudan, followed by political conquest and the displacement of indigenous Negro tribes.

European colonial expansion and the political partition of Africa.

Selected Bibliography

Ankermann, B. Kulturkreise und Kulturschichten in Afrika. *ZE*, 37:54–90. 1905.

Baumann, H., R. Thurnwald, and D. Westermann. *Völkerkunde von Afrika*. Essen, 1940.

Eggan, F. *Social Organization of the Western Pueblos*. Chicago, 1950.

———. The Method of Controlled Comparisons. *AA*, 56:743–763. 1954.

Murdock, G. P. *Social Structure*. New York, 1949.

Radcliffe-Brown, A. R. Methods of Ethnology and Social Anthropology. *SAJS*, 20:124–147. 1923.

———. Introduction. *ASKM*, pp. 1–85. 1950.

PART TWO
AFRICAN HUNTERS

———•••———

8

———•••———

Pygmies

Under the name Sangoan archeologists group a series of closely related prehistoric cultures found in central Africa west of the great lakes and extending from the Middle Paleolithic period to about the beginning of the Christian era. Their bearers were hunting and gathering peoples who centered in the equatorial rainforest (see Map 4) but extended south thereof to about 16°S, beyond which cultures of the Stillbay type occur. Their descendants are the Pygmies—also called Negrillos, Twa (Batwa), and Twides—of whom about 170,000 survive in the same region today. As noted in Chapter 2, they belong to the Pygmoid race, which resembles the Negroid in certain respects but differs in more.

No longer do the Pygmies roam the forest undisturbed, for about 2,000 years ago their territory was penetrated from the north by a series of agricultural Negro peoples—a few Central Sudanic tribes from the northeast, more speakers of Eastern Nigritic languages from across the northern border, but especially a horde of Bantu peoples from Nigeria and the Cameroon highlands in the northwest. At first the newcomers were doubtless welcome since they could offer agricultural produce and superior tools in exchange for game, forest products, and ivory. Indeed, wherever Pygmies survive today they are characterized by a symbiotic relationship with the neighboring Negroes involving precisely this kind of economic interdependence. Ultimately, of course, the invaders, with their more advanced economy, multiplied in number and achieved complete dominance. Almost nowhere today do Pygmies occupy independent tracts of land. Rather, they are attached in small bands to particular Negro chiefs or headmen in a relationship which, though reciprocal, is clearly dependent. In many parts of their former territory, moreover, they have disappeared through absorption, and in others they have become strongly acculturated.

Although archeologically Sangoan cultures extend westward into the tropical-forest zone along the Guinea coast, no Pygmoid peoples survive in this region today. The Gagu of the Ivory Coast, once considered a possible remnant, are now recognized as true Negroes despite their relatively short stature. A few markedly acculturated Pygmy groups are found in the savanna country along the Kwango, Kasai, and other southern tributaries of the Congo River, and a few pockets still exist in the dry-forest zone farther south. One lone outpost is found, for example, in the Nyaneka country in the southwest (ca. 15°S, 13°E), and in the southeast, in Northern Rhodesia and the adjacent Belgian Congo, a few thousands have escaped complete assimilation by adopting a fishing economy in the swamps near Lake Mweru (ca. 8°S, 29°E), Lake Bangweulu (ca. 11°S, 30°E), and the Kafue River (ca. 15°39'S, 27°E).

The great majority of the Pygmies still live in their ancient heartland, in or on the edge of the zone of tropical rainforest. Among them four principal groups can be distinguished.

1. Binga (Babenga, Babinga, Yadinga), embracing the Beku, Bongo (Babonga), Jelli (Badiele, Baguielli, Bayele, Bodjili, Boyaeli), Koa (Akoa, Bakoa), Kola (Bakola), Kuya (Bakouya), Rimba (Barimba), and Yaga (Bayaga, Bayaka). This group extends along the Atlantic coast and its immediate hinterland from 5°N to 5°S, and inland north of the equator to about 19°E. They number about 27,000 and are only slightly mixed and acculturated.

2. Central Twa. This group, for whom no special tribal names are reported, live among the great Mongo nation of Bantu in the central Belgian Congo between 1°N and 4°S and between 18° and 23°E. They number around 100,000 and are considerably Mongoized in physique and culture, though they still depend largely upon hunting, fishing, and gathering for subsistence.

3. Gesera (Bagesera), with the Zigaba (Bazigaba). These tribes live in Ruanda and Urundi (ca. 1–3°S, 29–30°E) and number about 9,000. About 2,500 still follow their old mode of life in the mountains, but the remainder have adopted a sedentary life on the plains near Lake Kivu, with pottery making as a specialty.

4. Mbuti (Bambuti, Wambuti), with the Aka (Akka) and Efe (Eve). These tribes, with a total population of about 32,000, inhabit the Ituri Forest (ca. 0–4°N, 26–31°E) and reveal the least Negro influence in physique and culture.

Presumably the Pygmies once spoke languages of their own, but no record of their former speech survives today. Every group, without exception, speaks the dialect of the Negro tribe to which it is attached, whether Bantu, Eastern Nigritic, or Central Sudanic.

Subsistence is derived principally from hunting and gathering. The men hunt small animals and also deer, wild boar, and even the hippopotamus and the elephant, whereas the women collect wild fruits and roots, insects and larvae, lizards, and often shellfish. Fishing, which also assumes considerable importance in many groups, is done mainly by women among both the Binga and the Mbuti. The Pygmies keep no domestic animals except the dog, which they use in hunting, and they practice no agriculture except under Negro influence.

All unacculturated Pygmies live in nomadic bands, which number from twenty to as many as a hundred individuals, and wander over recognized hunting territories owned collectively by the group. At each camp site the women erect their huts in a circle around an open space. The typical dwelling is hemispherical in shape and consists of a framework of flexible poles set in the ground in a circle or ellipse, bent together and fastened at the top, and covered with leaves. Often this is reduced to a mere windbreak covered with leaves or bark, but among the Binga the hut is sometimes elaborated by extending one end to form a low entrance tunnel.

Marriage is usually monogamous, but polygyny is not forbidden and occurs to a limited extent. In such cases each co-wife has a separate hut. A man obtains a wife by making substantial gifts to her relatives. These sometimes amount to a genuine bride-price. In one Binga case, for instance, they included a new bow, two hundred arrows, two vessels of arrow poison, a knife, a spear, two new barkcloths, a string of beads, and two iron bracelets. Exchange of sisters is the preferred mode of marriage among the Mbuti and may well have been the original Pygmy practice. Each nuclear family constitutes an independent household. Related

Group of Congo Pygmies. (Courtesy of the American Museum of Natural History.)

families commonly erect their huts side by side, but true extended families are lacking. Local exogamy is universal, and marriage is usually forbidden between first cousins and all closer kinsmen. A widow normally marries a brother or other close relative of her deceased husband.

Residence is patrilocal and descent patrilineal. A wife always joins the band of her husband, to which their children also belong, and marriage is not permitted with any known relative in the male line. Nearly all authorities report exogamous totemic patrisibs, but their evidence strongly suggests that it is only the localized lineage or patriclan which is exogamous. Since nearly all the Negro tribes amongst whom the Pygmies live are characterized by patrilineal descent and patrilocal clan-communities, this feature of social organization may well have been borrowed from them, and it is possible, if not probable, that the Pygmies were originally bilateral in descent, even though patrilocal residence and local exogamy may have prevailed.

The Pygmies do not practice slavery and have no stratification into social classes. The band is basically egalitarian and democratic, with an older and experienced man as its informal leader. In consultation with the other men he decides when and where to hunt and move camp. There is no higher political integration except for the usual dependence of each band on the chief or headman of the associated Negro group. Formal age-grades are lacking, as is circumcision except under Negro influence. Though the Pygmies are in general peaceful, interband feuds and even warfare sometimes occur. Unlike their Negro neighbors, however, the Pygmies do not indulge in cannibalism.

Selected Bibliography

Bruel, G. Les Babinga. *RES*, 1:111–125. 1910.

Czekanowski, J. *Forschungen im Nil-Kongo-Zwischengebiet*, vol. 2. Leipzig, 1924. [Mbuti].

Douet, L. Les Babingas ou Yadingas. *Ethnographie*, n.s., 2:15–32. 1914.

Gusinde, M. Pygmies and Pygmoids. *AQ*, 3:3–61. 1955.

Immenroth, W. Kultur und Umwelt der Kleinwüchsigen in Afrika. *SV*, 6:1–380. 1933.

Regnault, M. Les Babenga. *Anthropologie*, 22:261–288. 1911.

Schebesta, P. *Bambuti*. Leipzig, 1932.

———. *Among Congo Pygmies*. London, 1933. [Translation of the above].

———. Die Bambuti-Pygmäen vom Ituri. *MIRCB*, 1:1–438; 2:1–551; 4:1–253. 1938–1950.

Schumacher, P. Die Kivu-Pygmäen. *MIRCB*, 5:1–404. 1950. [Gesera].

Seiwert, J. Die Bagielli. *Anthropos*, 21:127–147. 1926. [Binga].

Trilles, H. *Les Pygmées de la forêt équatoriale*. Paris, 1932. [Binga].

9

Bushmen and Their Kin

From the beginning of the Upper Paleolithic period until relatively recent times the Sangoan cultures of the prehistoric Pygmies of the tropical rainforest were bounded on the south and east by a different complex of hunting and gathering cultures known collectively as Stillbay. These blanketed all of South Africa as well as East Africa between the great lakes and the Indian Ocean as far north as Ethiopia and the Horn. The boundary between them coincided roughly with that now prevailing between regions having an annual rainfall of more than 40 inches and those having less than this amount. Stillbay cultures are characteristically associated with skeletal remains of the Bushmanoid rather than the Pygmoid racial type. Numerous peoples of this physical type have survived into modern times in South Africa, and their cultures form the subject of this chapter. Remnants of hunting peoples in East Africa are fewer, their cultures more modified, and their Bushmanoid racial characteristics less certain. Their treatment will therefore be reserved for the next chapter.

For millennia the South African hunters occupied the region now embraced by the Union of South Africa, South-West Africa, Bechuanaland, Basutoland, Swaziland, Southern Rhodesia, and portions of southern Angola and Northern Rhodesia. A few centuries before the arrival of Vasco da Gama, however, two waves of intrusive agricultural Bantu penetrated the area deeply from the north—the Southwestern Bantu along the west coast and the Southeastern Bantu along the east coast. After 1720 one group of the latter, the Tswana, advanced westward and occupied the region now known as Bechuanaland. In the meantime Europeans, who had established their first settlement at Table Bay in 1652, had begun a progressive expansion toward the northeast, which ultimately gained for them large tracts of desirable land in Orange Free State and the Transvaal. In consequence, the indigenous inhabitants who still maintain even a semblance of their ancient way of life are now confined to a few relatively inhospitable areas in South-West Africa, the Kalahari Desert, and the Okavango Swamp region.

The aboriginal population falls into three distinct groups: the Bushmen, the Hottentot, and the Bergdama. The Hottentot differ culturally from the other two groups in that they had obtained cattle from the Southwestern Bantu and had adopted a pastoral mode of life. Physically, however, they closely resemble the Bushmen, varying only to about the degree one would expect in a people with a superior diet and a more secure livelihood. Compared with the Bushman physical type described in Chapter 2, the Hottentot tends to be 4 or 5 inches taller and to have a slightly narrower head and nose, but in other respects he reveals all the typical Bushmanoid stigmata. The Bergdama, most of whom are herdsmen or servants to the pastoral Hottentot or Bantu Herero, are, on the contrary, Negroid rather than Bushmanoid in physique. The Koroca of coastal Angola, long regarded as a detached group of Bushmen, have been reported by Lang and Tastevin (1937) to resemble the Bergdama in both language and physical type. In culture, however, both these groups affiliate closely with the Bushmen. Unfortunately, the physical anthropological evidence is insufficient to solve the problem of Negroid hunters in this part of Africa. They might be assumed to be Bushmen strongly admixed with Bantu blood were it not for specific statements that they differ markedly in appearance from the Bantu. Possibly they are akin to some of the hunting tribes of East Africa (see Chapter 10), who are reported to be Bushmanoid in culture and sometimes in language but often Negroid in racial characteristics.

The surviving representatives of the indigenous population number rather more than 100,000 today: about 55,000 Bushmen, most of whom are serfs of the Tswana; 30,000 Bergdama, many with a strong Hottentot or Herero admixture; and perhaps 35,000 Hottentot, many of them mixed with European blood. In addition, the Hottentot, and to a lesser extent the Bushmen, constitute an important ingredient in the large detribalized and mixed-blood population of the present Union of South Africa known as the Cape Coloured. The indigenous tribes can be grouped and classified as follows (the peculiar symbols represent the various clicks or implosive consonants).

1. Bergdama (Haukoin, Mountain Damara). They number about 30,000.
2. Cape Hottentot, comprising the Attaqua, Chainoqua, Chariguriqua (Little Grigriqua), Goringhaiqua, Grigriqua, Hancumqua, Hessequa, Kochoqua, Kora (Gorachouqua), and Outeniqua, together with the Damaqua, Gonaqua, and Inqua who are known collectively as the Eastern Hottentot. This group is now extinct.
3. Heikum (Hei//om). This tribe is to a considerable extent mixed with, and acculturated to, the Ambo and Herero tribes of the Southwestern Bantu.
4. Hiechware. These people are largely serfs or dependents of the Bantu Tswana.
5. Hukwe (Kwengo, Makwengo), with the kindred Galikwe (Dennassena, Madennassena). These tribes have long been subject in varying degrees to neighboring Bantu peoples—the Mbukushu, Subia, Tawana, and especially the Lozi.
6. Korana (!kora). These people, who number perhaps 10,000 today, split off from the Kora tribe of the Cape Hottentot in the late seventeenth century, withdrawing inland to escape the Dutch.
7. Koroca (Bakoroka, Coroca, Mucoroca). This isolated group in coastal Angola, numbering about 15,000, comprise the Luheka (Valuheke) on the seacoast, the

Zorotua (Vasorontu) on the edge of the desert, and the Kwise (Bacuisso, Moquisse, Vakuise) in the mountain foothills.

8. Kung (!kung), including the Agau, Auen (≠aukwe, //kau//en), Kungau (≠kungau), Nogau, and Ogowe (!ogowe), together with detached remnants in southern Angola known collectively as Okung (!o !ku). A number of bands of this group, which has a total population of perhaps 4,000, still follow an unaffected, primitive way of life.

9. Nama (Naman, Namaqua). These people, who still number about 25,000, are the only Hottentot group whose aboriginal culture survived long enough to be studied by anthropologists.

10. Namib, embracing the Ganin (≠ganin), Geinin (/geinin), Koma (/koma), and Obanen (//obanen). This group occupies the desert coast of South-West Africa, separated from other Bushmen by the Nama Hottentot.

11. Naron (//aikwe), including the Amkwe (≠amkwe), Ginkwe (!ginkwe), Gokwe (≠gokwe), Tsaukwe, and Tsonokwe.

12. Nusan (/nu//en), including the Auni (/auni), Ngke (//ng!ke), and the detached Sarwa (Masarwa) of the Kalahari Desert. They are largely subject today to the Bantu tribes of the Tswana nation.

13. Ohekwe (Tete), with the related Dukwe (≠dukwe), Hura, and Kabakwe (≠kabakwe). These people are largely subject to the Tswana.

14. Tannekwe (/tannekwe), including the Bugakwe and Garikwe (≠garikwe). These people are marsh dwellers, subject to the Tawana and other Tswana tribes.

15. Xam (Cape Bushmen, /xam), including remnants of unnamed tribes farther east in Basutoland and the Transvaal. This group is extinct or nearly so.

All the above peoples speak languages of the Bushman subfamily of the Khoisan linguistic stock, whose geographical distribution is shown in Map 6. The Bushman subfamily has three branches: (1) Southern, embracing the Nusan and Xam; (2) Northern, including the Heikum and Kung; and (3) Central, spoken by all the other Bushman tribes and also by the peoples of Hottentot culture and those of the Bergdama physical type.

The Khoisan languages have long been noted for their peculiar implosive consonants called clicks. Clicks also occur in the speech of several of the intrusive Bantu tribes of the region—the Koba of northern Bechuanaland, the Sotho of Basutoland, and the Nguni peoples of Natal and adjacent areas. Their presence in these alien languages is best explained on the hypothesis that the invading Bantu married Bushman women, and that these, in learning the speech of their husbands, substituted their own implosive consonants for some of the normal consonants of the latter, transmitted this pronunciation to their children, and thus initiated a phonetic innovation which their children perpetuated. It would follow from this, of course, that the territories now occupied by Bantu click speakers were previously inhabited by Bushmen—an inference which has substantial archeological support.

Since the Hottentot differ from the other tribes of the group in their pastoral mode of life, the description of their culture will be postponed until after we have considered the Bushmen and the Bergdama. The latter peoples subsist almost exclusively by hunting and gathering. Fishing also assumes considerable importance among the Tannekwe and coastal Koroca and is of subsidiary significance in a few other groups, notably the Bergdama, Hiechware, and Xam. Agriculture is totally unknown except for a little millet cultivation by the Tannekwe under Bantu influence. Animal husbandry is almost equally undeveloped. The Bushman tribes and the Koroca have no domesticated animals except the dog, and some groups, e.g., the Naron, lack even the dog. The Bergdama keep goats, but the sources disagree as to whether this feature of their culture is truly aboriginal. The division of labor by sex follows everywhere a single pattern, with men doing the hunting and fishing, women the gathering.

A nomadic life in migratory bands characterizes the entire area. Settlements are shifting camps, except among the Hukwe and Tannekwe, who occupy semipermanent villages during the rainy season though they wander at other times of the year. Use is frequently made of natural caves and rock shelters or, in the case of the coastal Koroca, of artificial caves dug in sand dunes. More often, however, these nomads build simple windbreaks, consisting of a semicircle of saplings set in the ground, tied together and fastened at the top, and covered with grass or occasionally reed mats. The Bergdama and many Bushman tribes often extend the framework of the windbreak to a complete circle, thus producing a hemispherical or dome-shaped hut reminiscent of Pygmy dwellings. The huts of a temporary camp are typically pitched in a circle—at least among the Bergdama and Northern Bushmen.

Nowhere does marriage involve payment of a bride-price. The groom merely brings his future parents-in-law a few gifts, most typically of game to demonstrate his prowess as a hunter. He then takes up his residence with them, rendering postmarital bride-service. Shortly after the birth of his first child he normally removes with his family to his own paternal band, but in some Bushman tribes, notably the Xam, he may elect to remain in permanent matrilocal residence. Marriage is predominantly monogamous. Polygyny, to be sure, is everywhere permitted, but it is nowhere common, except possibly among the Bergdama, and in some tribes, e.g., the Koroca and Kung, it is exceedingly rare. When it occurs, the sororal form is usually preferred. Local exogamy appears to be universal except among the Hiechware. Marriage between first cousins is usually permitted, though not preferred, but the Bergdama and Heikum are reported to bar unions with a parallel cousin. The levirate and sororate, in the senior as well as the junior form, are reported for a number of tribes and nowhere denied.

A household consists typically of a single nuclear family. In cases of polygyny each wife usually has a hut of her own, though co-wives some-

Bushman Woman Drilling Hole in an Ostrich
Eggshell Bead. (Courtesy of South African
Government Information Office, New York.)

times occupy one shelter among
the Namib and the Naron. The
sources contain no suggestion of
any form of extended family organization. Descent is bilateral,
but the combination of local exogamy with patrilocal residence
gives the local band a structure resembling that of a patriclan. Kinship terms for cousins conform to
either the Eskimo or the Hawaiian
pattern. Recent data on the Kung
reveal an interesting subordination
of kinship terminology to naming
patterns; every individual is named
after some relative and is referred
to by a kinship term indicative, not
of his own, but of his namesake's
relationship to Ego. The same
tribe divides all relatives, according to the kinship terms applied
to them, into two categories—
those with whom one may and
must joke and those with whom
joking behavior is strictly taboo.

Each band has its own defined
territory, which is communally
owned and used. Private property is recognized only in movables, and
these are inconsequential. Inheritance is basically patrilineal and by primogeniture, but among the Bergdama, at least, a woman's possessions descend
to her eldest daughter. Slavery is absent, and class distinctions are unknown. Bergdama, however, often hire themselves out as herdsmen to
the Nama and Herero for a share in the increase of the herd, and most
of the surviving Bushmen have been subjected and reduced to the status
of serfs by the dominant Bantu tribes. Primitive democracy prevails,
with minimal political integration. Each band is autonomous under a
headman with nominal authority, who is normally succeeded by a son.
Warfare is confined to petty raids and blood feuds among neighboring
bands.

Most authorities differentiate the Hottentot sharply from the Bushmen, and many classify them as "Hamites" and derive them by migration
from the pastoral peoples of the Eastern Horn. This is sheer nonsense,

reflecting only the unfortunate tendency of the earlier Africanists to regard cattle as a linguistic trait. The Hottentot are indisputably closely akin to the Bushmen in physical characteristics, and their language is not Hamitic but is specifically affiliated with the Central branch of the Bushman subfamily of the Khoisan stock. They are, to be sure, pastoral, keeping large herds of long-horned cattle and fat-tailed sheep and a fair number of goats, and the milk of these animals constitutes a staple element in their diet. All other aspects of their culture, however, show such striking affinities with that of the Bushmen that we are left with no reasonable alternative except to regard them as a Bushman group who adopted cattle from the Southwestern Bantu and made modest readjustments in their culture in adaptation to the new and more stable mode of life.

A brief review of Hottentot culture reveals clearly its dependence upon a Bushman substratum. The division of labor by sex is identical, except that men have added herding to their hunting and fishing activities, women milking to their food-gathering duties. The pattern of life in nomadic bands remains unchanged, and the dwellings of a camp are still pitched in a circle. Even the huts themselves are hemispherical, as among the Bushmen, though the Hottentot, having pack oxen for transport purposes, do not have to depend upon improvised materials at each camp site but use permanent and well-made poles and rush mats, which are dismountable and portable.

Like the Bushmen, but unlike their Bantu neighbors and alleged Hamitic kinsmen, the Hottentot pay no bride-price but do postmarital matrilocal bride-service, shifting to patrilocal residence after the birth of the first child. Polygyny is rare rather than common and preferential. Extended families are lacking; local exogamy prevails, as do the levirate and sororate; and cross-cousin marriage is permitted but not preferred.

With the more stable mode of life, patrilocal bands have crystallized into definite patriclans, with the resulting recognition of patrilineal descent and the adaptive development of cousin terminology of the Iroquois type. Inheritance is still patrilineal and by primogeniture. Slavery and hereditary aristocracy remain unknown, although the possession of cattle has given rise to incipient status distinctions in terms of wealth. The incidence of warfare has increased, with the result that groups of neighboring bands have become loosely federated into subtribes for offensive and defensive purposes, the senior headman serving as titular chief and the other leaders forming a sort of council. All in all, Hottentot culture is still recognizably Bushman in all its basic patterns, and its deviations are about the minimum to be expected in a hunting people adapting to a more stable pastoral economy.

Selected Bibliography

Barrow, J. *An Account of Travels into the Interior of South Africa.* 2 vols. London, 1801–1804. [Xam].

Bleek, D. F. Bushman Terms of Relationship. *BS*, 2:57–70. 1924.

———. *The Naron.* Cambridge, 1928.

———. Bushmen of Central Angola. *BS*, 3:105–125. 1929. [Kung].

Correia, J. A. Une étude de l'ethnographie d'Angola. *Anthropos*, 10:321–331. 1925. [Koroca].

Dornan, S. S. Notes on the Bushmen of Basutoland. *Transactions of the South African Philosophical Society*, 18:437–450. 1909.

———. The Tati Bushmen. *JRAI*, 47:37–112. 1917. [Nusan].

———. *Pygmies and Bushmen of the Kalahari.* London, 1925. [Hiechware].

Fourie, L. The Bushmen of South-West Africa. *NTSWA*, pp. 79–105. 1928. [Heikum].

Fritsch, G. T. *Die Eingeborenen Süd-Afrika's.* Breslau, 1872. [Xam].

Hoernlé, A. W. The Social Organization of the Nama Hottentots. *AA*, 27:1–24. 1925.

Kaufman, H. Die ≠Auin. *MDS*, 23:135–160. 1910. [Kung].

Lang, A., and C. Tastevin. Le tribu des Va-Nyaneka. *Mission Rohan-Chabot*, 1:1–213. Corbeil, 1937. [Koroca].

Lebzelter, V. *Eingeborenenkulturen in Südwest- und Südafrika.* Leipzig, 1934.

Marshall, L. The Kinship Terminology of the !Kung Bushmen. *Africa*, 27:1–25. 1957.

Passarge, S. Das Okawangosumpfland und seine Bewohner. *ZE*, 37:649–716. 1905. [Tannekwe].

———. *Die Buschmänner der Kalahari.* Berlin, 1907. [Naron and Ohekwe].

Schapera, I. *The Khoisan Peoples of South Africa.* London, 1930.

———. *The Early Cape Hottentots.* Cape Town, 1933.

Schmidt, M. Die Nama, Bergdama und Namib-Buschleute. *ER*, 2:269–397. 1930.

Schultze, L. *Aus Namaland und Kalahari.* Jena, 1907. [Nama].

Seiner, F. Die Buschmänner des Okawango- und Sambesigebietes. *Globus*, 97:341–345, 357–360. 1910. [Tannekwe].

———. Ergebnisse einer Bereisung der Omaheke. *MDS*, 26:225–316. 1913. [Kung].

Stow, G. W. *The Native Races of South Africa.* London, 1905.

Trenk, P. Die Buschleute der Namib. *MDS*, 23:166–170. 1910.

Vedder, H. *Die Bergdama.* Hamburg, 1923.

———. The Berg Damara. *NTSWA*, pp. 37–78. 1928.

Werner, H. Anthropologische, ethnologische und ethnographische Beobachtungen über die Heikum- und Kungbuschleute. *ZE*, 38:241–268. 1906.

Wilhelm, J. H. Die !Kung-Buschleute. *JMV*, 12:91–189. 1953.

———. Die Hukwe. *JMV*, 13:8–44. 1954.

Zastrow, B. von, and H. Vedder. Die Buschmänner. *ER*, 2:399–435. 1930. [Kung].

10

East African Hunters

No true Bushmen have ever been encountered by Europeans in that portion of East Africa which extends from the border of the Transvaal northeastward to southern Ethiopia and the Gulf of Aden between the Indian Ocean and the great lakes. Yet archeological evidence demonstrates unmistakably the former presence of Bushmanoid hunters and gatherers with cultures of the Stillbay complex throughout this area, and indeed as far north as Singa on the Blue Nile, within about 300 miles of Khartoum. They appear early in the Upper Paleolithic period and endure until the beginning of the Iron Age, shortly before A.D. 1000, except in southern Ethiopia, western Kenya, and adjacent northern Tanganyika, where alone in the region a genuine Neolithic period is attested. Confirmatory evidence of their presence is provided by prehistoric rock paintings found widely in Kenya, Somaliland, and Tanganyika which strikingly resemble those which Bushmen were still making in historical times in South Africa.

In the northern part of the former range of the Stillbay cultures there still live a number of scattered hunting peoples who almost certainly represent the lingering remnants of the Paleolithic inhabitants of East Africa. They may be enumerated and identified as follows.

1. Boni (Bon, Waboni, Walangulo). A small tribe, numbering not many more than a thousand, these people inhabit a portion of the coast of southern Somalia between the lower Tana and Juba Rivers. They speak the Cushitic language of their dominant Galla neighbors, by whom they are despised as unclean. Until recently they lived exclusively by hunting, fishing, and gathering, shooting elephant, rhinoceros, hippopotamus, antelope, and smaller game with the bow and poisoned arrows.

2. Dorobo (Andorobo, Asa, Okiek, Wandorobbo). These people, numbering about 1,400, live in small dispersed groups in mountainous sections of the Nandi and Masai country in Kenya, here and there extending southward into Tanganyika. They speak the Eastern Sudanic dialects of their neighbors, to whom they are commonly attached in a partly servile and partly symbiotic relationship. Until very recently their economy was based exclusively on hunting and gathering, the former done with poisoned arrows.

3. Kindiga (Hadzapi, Hatsa, Kangeju, Tindega, Wakindiga, Watindega). These people still lead an independent life of hunting and gathering near Lake Eyasi in northern Tanganyika. They number about 600 and speak a Khoisan language.

4. Manjo, with the Bacha, Fuga, Idenic, Koigi, Kwayegu (Kouayegou), Molosa, Watta (Wayto), and Yidi. These groups, numbering several thousand, survive as endogamous pariah castes of hunters among the various Cushitic tribes of southern

59

Ethiopia, living in a partly dependent and partly symbiotic relationship with their dominant neighbors, whose languages they speak.

5. Midgan, with the Ribi (Waribi). These people, probably numbering several thousand, constitute a despised and endogamous caste of hunters who live dispersed among the various Somali tribes and a few pastoral Galla. They speak languages differing from, but apparently akin to, the Cushitic tongues of their superiors.

6. Sandawe (Wassandaui). This independent tribe in northern Tanganyika, numbering about 25,000, has now adopted intensive agriculture and animal husbandry from its Bantu neighbors; when first observed, however, one section was still living by hunting and gathering. These people speak a language of the Khoisan stock which is only remotely related to that of the Kindiga.

7. Sanye (Sania, Wasanye, Wassania). A small scattered hunting tribe, numbering only a few hundred, these people live southwest of the Tana River in Kenya. They are subject to the Bararetta Galla, whose language they now speak and from whom they have recently adopted the rudiments of animal husbandry.

8. Teuso. These people, who number about 1,200, live scattered among the Nilotic Jie, Karamojong, and Turkana. Basically nomadic hunters and gatherers, they have turned recently to agriculture and animal husbandry. A report by the Gullivers (1953) that they speak a completely independent language awaits confirmation by linguists.

All these peoples appear to be basically Negroid in physique, although the occurrence of subsidiary Bushmanoid characteristics has been specifically alleged for the Boni, Dorobo, Kindiga, and Teuso, as well as for occasional agricultural tribes in western Ethiopia as far north as the Koma. It is possibly significant, for example, that adult males among the Kindiga attain an average stature of only 5 feet 3 inches and that women show some tendency toward steatopygia, a distinctive Bushmanoid trait. The Teuso are also short in stature and noticeably light-skinned. The Midgan, though they appear not to differ appreciably in physique from the Somali, are definitely regarded by the latter as the descendants of the aboriginal inhabitants of the country. The absence of more marked Bushmanoid racial stigmata among the surviving East African hunters may be due simply to mixture with the intrusive Negroid peoples, Bantu or Nilotic, or alternatively it may point to the existence in East Africa of an old Negroid population with a Bushmanlike culture, possibly akin to the Bergdama of South-West Africa.

The linguistic evidence is more conclusive. The Kindiga and Sandawe of northern Tanganyika both speak languages of the Khoisan stock. These fall, however, into subfamilies that are separate alike from each other and from the Bushman subfamily of South Africa. Clicks are nevertheless characteristic of all three divisions.

Cultural traits other than hunting and gathering in nomadic bands confirm the affiliation of the East African hunters with the Bushmen. Thus dome-shaped huts with a framework of branches thatched with leaves or grass are characteristic of the Boni, Dorobo, Kindiga, Sanye, and, until

very recently, the Sandawe. Marriage involves only gifts of game
or honey among the Boni and
some Dorobo, though elsewhere at
least a modest bride-price seems
customary. Monogamy or very
limited polygyny, occasionally sororal, prevails among the Dorobo,
Kindiga, Sandawe, and Teuso.
Only the Sanye practice general
polygyny. Local exogamy is the
rule among the Boni, Dorobo,
Sandawe, Sanye, and apparently
the Teuso. Residence is patrilocal
in all reported cases, but among
the Sandawe is alternatively matrilocal until the birth of the first
child. Descent is still bilateral
among the Kindiga, but the
Dorobo, Sandawe, and Sanye have
adopted exogamous patrisibs from
their Negro or Cushitic neighbors.
Slavery and class distinctions are
reported for none of these peoples

Dorobo Physical Type with Markedly Un-
Negroid Hair and Features. (Courtesy of British Information Services.)

and specifically denied for most.
And in none of them does political integration transcend the level of the
local community.

A review of the evidence presented in this and the two preceding
chapters shows that the entire southern and eastern half of the African
continent was inhabited by hunting and gathering peoples from Paleolithic times until quite recently and that actual remnants of that ancient
population and their cultures have survived into the historical period in
almost every section of this vast area. In sharp contrast to this, not a
single hunting and gathering society has been observed in modern times
in all the rest of Africa. Archeology, of course, has revealed traces of
Paleolithic food gatherers everywhere on the continent. Throughout
North and West Africa they have been succeeded by Neolithic food
producers whose cultures have endured for millennia and have long
since obliterated all traces of their simpler predecessors. In East and South
Africa, however, Neolithic occupation appears appreciably later and, as
previously noted, is confined to a surprisingly restricted area. Elsewhere
in this region the Paleolithic period is succeeded directly, without any
transitional Mesolithic or Neolithic phase, by Iron Age cultures, brought

in by intrusive peoples well after the time of Christ. Not until the Iron Age, moreover, does archeology reveal the presence of Negroes anywhere in the southern and eastern half of the continent, although today, of course, they constitute the overwhelming bulk of its population.

The cultures of the preagricultural peoples of East Africa and the equatorial rainforest resemble one another so closely in fundamental respects that they can be regarded as constituting a single ancient culture area. The hunting, fishing, and gathering subsistence activities differ little more than might be anticipated from the varying resources provided by diverse geographical environments. Technological achievements seem remarkably uniform, as witnessed by the universality of the bow and poisoned arrows and the dome-shaped shelter of bent poles thatched with leaves or grass. Social organization reveals such widespread common features as a uniform division of labor by sex, marriage by gifts or at most a very moderate bride-price, patrilocal residence, infrequent and usually preferential sororal polygyny, minimal bilateral extension of incest taboos, the sororate and levirate, independent nuclear-family households, exogamous bands, bilateral descent (except under strong influence from patrilineal Negroes), absence of slavery and of differentiated social classes, and lack of any political integration transcending the local level.

Probably no other region of comparable size in the entire world for which ethnographic as well as archeological evidence exists reveals so high a degree of cultural uniformity. By comparison the Bantu, who occupy roughly the same territory today and who, moreover, constituted, about 2,000 years ago, a single group with a uniform language and culture, now exhibit the widest diversity in technology, in types of economy, in marriage forms and practices, and in social and political organization. The singular cultural uniformity among the African hunters must have an explanation. Among possible reasons the author proposes the influence of local exogamy.

Other regions in the world which reveal cultural homogeneity over wide areas, like aboriginal Australia and the central and southern Northwest Coast of North America, are characterized by local exogamy, whereas local endogamy preponderates in such culturally heterogeneous ethnographic regions as Melanesia and central California. In the presence of a rule of local exogamy, whether derived from localized clans or from an exogamous band or village structure, every marriage unites individuals from two different communities having at least slightly variant cultures, and children grow up exposed to the cultures of both parents with a choice among alternatives. This makes it possible for diffusion to operate through the socialization process, a much more perfect mechanism for transmission than is cultural borrowing through contact on the adult level. Under such conditions diffusion, mediated through every marriage, can proceed automatically and inevitably from group to group until checked by some major geographic barrier, of which there are remarkably few in Africa, or by some cultural boundary beyond which local endogamy is in vogue. The process of cultural leveling through diffusion can thus gain ascendancy over the processes of cultural differentiation and thereby produce a high degree of cultural uniformity over wide areas.

Selected Bibliography

Bagshawe, F. J. The Peoples of the Happy Valley. *JAS*, 24:25–33, 117–130, 219–227, 328–347. 1925–1926. [Kindiga and Sandawe].

Barrett, W. E. H. Notes on the Wa-sania. *JRAI*, 41:29–39. 1911. [Sanye].

Bleek, D. F. The Hadzapi or Watindega. *Africa*, 4:273–285. 1930. [Kindiga].

Cerulli, E. *Peoples of South-West Ethiopia and Its Borderland*. London, 1956. [Manjo].

Clark, J. D. *The Prehistoric Cultures of the Horn of Africa*. Cambridge, 1954.

Cole, S. *The Prehistory of East Africa*. London, 1954.

Cooper, B. The Kindiga. *TNR*, 27:8–15. 1949.

Dempwolff, O. *Die Sandawe*. Hamburg, 1916.

Gulliver, P., and P. H. Gulliver. *The Central Nilo-Hamites*. London, 1953. [Teuso].

Huntingford, G. W. B. Modern Hunters. *JRAI*, 59:333–378. 1929. [Dorobo].

——. The Social Organization of the Dorobo. *AS*, 1:183–200. 1942.

——. The Social Institutions of the Dorobo. *Anthropos*, 46:1–48. 1951.

——. *The Southern Nilo-Hamites*. London, 1953. [Dorobo, Kindiga, and Sandawe].

——. The Political Organization of the Dorobo. *Anthropos*, 49:123–148. 1954.

——. *The Galla of Ethiopia*. London, 1955. [Manjo].

Kimmenade, M. van de. Les Sandawe. *Anthropos*, 31:395–416. 1936.

Kohl-Larsen, L. *Auf den Spuren des Vormenschen*. 2 vols. Stuttgart, 1943. [Kindiga and Sandawe].

Le Roy, A. Au Zanguebar anglais. *MC*, 22:582–586, 593–594. 1890. [Boni].

Lewis, I. M. *Peoples of the Horn of Africa*. London, 1955. [Midgan].

Mylius, N. Ehe und Kind im abflusslosen Gebiet Ostafrikas. *AV*, 3:44–135; 4:38–153. 1948–1949. [Kindiga and Sandawe].

Reche, O. *Zur Ethnographie des abflusslosen Gebietes Deutsch-Ostafrikas*. Hamburg, 1914. [Kindiga].

Wayland, E. J. Preliminary Studies of the Tribes of Karamoja. *JRAI*, 61:212–218. 1931. [Teuso].

Werther, C. W. *Die mittleren Hochländer des nördlichen Deutsch-Ost-Afrika*. Berlin, 1898. [Sandawe].

PART THREE
SUDANIC AGRICULTURAL CIVILIZATION

———◆•◆———

II

———◆•◆———

Nuclear Mande

Until about 5000 B.C. the entire continent of Africa still lingered in the Stone Age—either the Upper Paleolithic period or the Mesolithic period, which in North and East Africa and in parts of West Africa provided a transition to the Neolithic. None of its inhabitants practiced any agriculture whatsoever or possessed any domestic animal, save perhaps the dog. Then Neolithic civilization, marked by a shift from food gathering to food production through the raising of cultivated plants and domesticated animals, made its appearance independently in two widely separated parts of the continent—Egypt and the western Sudan.

Ancient Egypt acquired agriculture and domestic animals from adjacent Southwest Asia. Here sedentary village life with tillage and the herding of goats had developed in the hills of east central Iraq by about 6500 B.C. These achievements spread throughout the Fertile Crescent and, with increments, reached Lower Egypt around 4500 B.C., as we know from radiocarbon dating. After more than a millennium of further elaboration they became the basis of the resplendent civilization of Pharaonic Egypt.

It has hitherto escaped attention, however, that agriculture was independently developed at about the same time by the Negroes of West Africa. This was, moreover, a genuine invention, not a borrowing from another people. Furthermore, the assemblage of cultivated plants ennobled from wild forms in Negro Africa ranks as one of the four major agricultural complexes evolved in the entire course of human history.

64

Interestingly enough, the innovators have belonged to four distinct races. Along with the Caucasoids who developed the Southwest Asian complex, the Mongoloids who achieved the Southeast Asian complex, and the American Indians who elaborated the Middle American complex, we must now align the West African Negroes as one of mankind's leading creative benefactors.

Several factors account for the failure to recognize this contribution of the Negro. Botanists, though long aware of the African origin of many important cultivated plants, have had no means of determining their antiquity, and prehistoric archeology has been unable to supply the needed information because of the paucity of research in precisely the most crucial areas. Moreover Vavilov, the botanist who has contributed more than any other to our knowledge of the origins of cultivated plants and who personally investigated at first hand every other major and minor center of independent domestication in the world, never happened to visit Negro Africa. He thus fell into the error of ascribing its cultigens to regions where he found them, particularly to the lesser Ethiopian and Indian centers. The mistake was especially difficult to correct in the case of India; many of the more important crops of Negro Africa had spread there before the dawn of the Christian era, so that Europeans, who first encountered them in India, not unnaturally assumed them to be local cultigens. Finally, we cannot ignore the vulgar assumption, widespread among Asiatics as well as Europeans, that the Negro is an inferior race incapable of making any substantial contribution to civilization, with its corollary that all complex manifestations of culture in Africa south of the Sahara must have emanated from some other and "higher" race like the Caucasoid "Hamites."

Identification of the Negro's contribution requires solutions to three distinct but interrelated problems: (1) a determination of which of the world's cultivated plants were first brought under cultivation in Negro Africa; (2) a delimitation of the precise location of the originating center or centers; (3) an estimation of the approximate date at which the transition from hunting and gathering to agriculture first occurred south of the Sahara.

To solve the first problem, we began by excluding all crops which botanists agree were first brought under cultivation elsewhere than on the African continent, i.e., in the major centers of Southwest Asia, Southeast Asia, and Middle America and in the minor centers of China, India, the Mediterranean (southern Europe), and lowland America. A few doubtful instances, especially where botanists are in dispute about the African or Indian origin of a plant, were resolved by examining distributions. In most cases these crops were assigned to India because their cultivation in Africa was found to center in eastern sections of the continent where archeology demonstrates that the introduction of agriculture has been comparatively recent.

The next step consisted in segregating the indigenous cultigens of North Africa and Ethiopia from those of Negro Africa. This proved relatively easy. The opinions of leading botanists were found to coincide well with the distributional evidence. North African crops have spread south of the Sahara to a surprisingly limited extent—in almost no instance beyond the northern, or Islamic, fringe of the Sudan. Ethiopian cultigens, on the other hand, have often diffused far south into Bantu Africa, but in no case have they spread westward any considerable distance into the regions occupied far earlier by Negroid peoples. The list of plants remaining after these eliminations was considered to comprise those whose original domestication is to be credited to the Negro.

The second problem was to delimit the most probable center of origin within the area clearly occupied by Negro agricultural societies prior to the time of Christ. This is the great region bounded on the east by the Nilotic pastoralists, on the north by the edge of the Sahara Desert, on the west by the Atlantic Ocean, and on the south by the Gulf of Guinea and the northern border of the Bantu-speaking peoples. The Bantu were excluded because other evidence demonstrates that, with the probable exception of a few tribes along the present boundary between Nigeria and Cameroon, they did not occupy any of their present territory until less than 2,000 years ago, a date much too late to ascribe to them the origin of African agriculture. Lists of crops were compiled, mainly from ethnographic sources, on most of the tribes of this area, numbering well over 250.

When distributions were plotted for all the plants in these lists, a few, notably the Guinea yam and the oil palm, were found to center on the Guinea coast, all the rest in the Sudan. Within the latter area, moreover, they centered in the western rather than in the central or eastern Sudan. The more important crops, to be sure, extend from the shores of the Atlantic to Ethiopia and the coast of the Indian Ocean, but all those of more limited distribution were found to be confined to the region between Senegal and Northern Nigeria, with the greatest concentration near the headwaters of the Niger River. This location receives modest support from archeologists, on the basis of admittedly fragmentary evidence from the very few relevant excavations reported to date, and from botanists who have identified the ranges of wild species from which the domesticated forms have presumably been ennobled.

The strongest confirmation, however, comes from linguistic distributions. We should expect the particular people who first advanced from a hunting and gathering economy to an agricultural one to have multiplied in number and to have expanded geographically at the expense of their more backward neighbors, with the result that the group of languages which they spoke should have spread over an unusually wide expanse of territory. This condition does not prevail in either the central or the eastern Sudan, where we find numerous linguistic groupings occupying areas of relatively modest size, e.g., Songhaic, Chadic, Kanuric, Maban, Furian, and the several divisions of Sudanic. Our criteria are fully satisfied, however, in the western Sudan by the far-flung Nigritic stock and particularly by its Mande subfamily, which centers on the upper Niger River. Not only do the speakers of Mande exhibit Negro agriculture in its fullest and most developed form, but their distribution demonstrates that they have spread in all directions at the expense of their immediate neighbors—westward into the original habitat of the Atlantic subfamily, southwestward among the Kru group of the Kwa subfamily, eastward into numerous pockets among the tribes of the Voltaic subfamily, and even northward into some of the Saharan oases.

We therefore conclude that the invention of agriculture in Negro Africa is most probably to be credited to the Mande peoples around the headwaters of the Niger in the extreme western part of the Sudan, less than 1,000 miles from the shores of the Atlantic Ocean. It is probably no accident that the earliest and most complex civilizations in this part of Africa of which we possess actual historical records, as we shall shortly see, were exhibited by Mande-speaking peoples.

Determination of the precise date of the invention of agriculture on the upper Niger must await archeological research using radiocarbon and other chronological techniques. In the absence of any evidence of this type to date, we can only arrive at a rough approximation by inference from other sources of information. One clue comes from ethnographic distributions. Agriculture must have been fully established in the Sudan before this region was exposed to the diffusion of Southwest Asian crops from Egypt, which could not have been many centuries after 4500 B.C., or else borrowing of cultivated plants from this source would surely have been more extensive than it has been in actual fact. Fewer than ten Negro tribes in the entire Sudan, for example, have adopted either barley or wheat, the staples of ancient Egypt, and in no single instance does either occupy a place in the economy comparable in importance to that of indigenous Sudanic cereals.

More decisive is the indirect evidence, to be presented in Chapter 19, that Sudanic agriculture had spread to the Nubian border of ancient Egypt by at least the end of the fourth millennium B.C. and by suggestions that it had reached Ethiopia by approximately the same date. These countries lie at the end of routes of diffusion of more than 3,000 miles, and over most of this distance the progress of agriculture involved the conversion of one reluctant hunting tribe after another, belonging to a number of different linguistic stocks, to an entirely novel mode of life. Comparative evidence indicates that this process is vastly slower and more difficult than the diffusion of new crops from one agricultural people to another. The time required for such a transcontinental transmission is more likely to be measurable in millennia than in centuries.

Moreover, no new agricultural complex has ever sprung into being full-grown. Other regions invariably reveal a long period of cautious initial trial and error, followed by more confident attempts to improve old plants and experiment with new ones. Investigators of the origins of agriculture in the Fertile Crescent (e.g., Braidwood, 1958) allow at least a thousand years for the development of the full Southwest Asian complex from its first tentative beginnings, and a comparable period should presumably be accorded to the western Sudan. On the basis of these various inferences the writer inclines to the conclusion that agriculture was probably invented independently on the upper Niger before it had diffused from Asia to the lower Nile, though doubtless later than its earliest development in the Near East.

Since the cultivated plants indigenous to Negro Africa were for the most part first developed in the Sudan rather than on the Guinea coast, we shall designate them collectively as the Sudanic complex. They can now be identified and listed by categories.

CEREAL GRAINS *

Fonio, acha grass, or hungry rice (*Digitaria exilis*). Continuously distributed from Senegal to northern Cameroon, often as a staple, this grain has not diffused to other regions of Africa or the world.

Pearl millet, or bulrush millet (*Pennisetum spicatum* or *P. typhoideum*). A staple throughout most of Negro Africa, this cereal has also spread to India and elsewhere. In view of its economic importance in Africa it will be hereinafter designated simply as millet, and the introduced and much less widely distributed common millet (*Panicum miliaceum*) will be called Asiatic millet.

Sorghum (*Sorghum vulgare*, formerly *Andropogon sorghum*). Of its numerous varieties three are especially important in its West African center of origin: dry-season corn (var. *cernuum*), feterita (var. *caudatum*), and Guinea corn (var. *guineense*). Others have been developed in the regions to which it has spread, notably Ethiopia, India, China, and North America.

LEGUMES

Cow pea (*Vigna unguiculata* or *V. sinensis*). Widespread in Negro Africa, whence it spread at an early date to India.

* A fourth indigenous Sudanic cereal, African rice (*Oryza glaberrima*), was brought to the author's attention while this book was in press. See B. F. Johnston, *The Staple Food Economies of Western Tropical Africa* (Stanford, 1958), pp. 26, 63, 94, and references cited therein.

TUBERS AND ROOT CROPS

Coleus, or Kafir potato (*Coleus dazo* and *C. dysentericus*). Common in the southern Sudan and adjacent areas, whence it was early carried to India.

Earth pea, or Bambara groundnut (*Voandzeia subterranea*, formerly *Glycine subterranea*). This plant, whose habit of growth resembles that of the American peanut, is widely distributed in Africa.

Geocarpa bean, or geocarpa groundnut (*Kerstingiella geocarpa*). This plant, which is somewhat similar to the peanut and earth pea, is confined to the western Sudan.

Guinea yam (*Dioscorea cayenensis* and *D. rotundata*). A native of the Guinea coast, this root crop extends into the adjacent southern Sudan.

Rizga (*Plectanthus floribundus*). This cultigen is confined mainly to Northern Nigeria and immediately adjacent regions.

Yam bean (*Sphenostylis stenocarpa*). This plant, which is grown for its seeds as well as for its tuber (reported to taste like a potato), has a modest distribution in west and central Africa.

LEAF AND STALK VEGETABLES

Okra, or gumbo (*Hibiscus esculentus*). Widespread in Africa and today also in the New World.

VINE AND GROUND FRUITS

Fluted pumpkin (*Telfairia occidentalis*). Confined mainly to West Africa.

Gourd, bottle gourd, or calabash (*Lagenaria vulgaris*). This plant was culti-vated in pre-Columbian times in both the Old and the New World, and its present distribution is practically universal. Most authorities agree that the Old World gourds were first domesticated in the western Sudan, whence they spread to Egypt during the second millennium B.C. and also at a very early date to India.

Watermelon (*Citrullus vulgaris*). It is used in Africa not only for its fruit but also for the oil extracted from its seeds. It spread from the Sudan to Egypt in the second millennium B.C. and has today a nearly universal dis-tribution.

Yergan, or egusi (*Cucumeropsis edulis* and *C. mannii*). This squashlike ground fruit is confined mainly to West Africa.

TREE FRUITS

Akee, or akee apple (*Blighia sapida*). This fruit tree, native to West Africa, was carried to the New World during the slave trade.

Tamarind (*Tamarindus indica*). Probably Sudanic in origin, this tree spread both to Egypt and to India at an early date.

CONDIMENTS AND INDULGENTS

Kola (*Cola acuminata* and *C. nitida*). This tree, sometimes cultivated but more often protected in its wild state, is a native of the western Sudan, where its nuts, the source of a major ingredient in modern "cola" drinks, have long been gathered as a favorite indulgent.

Roselle, or red sorrel (*Hibiscus sabdariffa*). Widespread in Africa, whence it has spread to India and the New World.

TEXTILE PLANTS

Ambary, or hemp-leafed hibiscus (*Hibiscus cannabinus*). Widespread in the Sudan and sporadic in East Africa.

Cotton (*Gossypium herbaceum*). Originally ennobled in the western Sudan from the indigenous wild *G. anomalum*, this textile plant was transmitted very early to India but did not reach Egypt until the sixth century B.C.

OIL PLANTS

Oil palm (*Elaeis guineensis*). Widespread in tropical West Africa.

Sesame, benniseed, or gingelly (*Sesamum indicum*). Widespread in Africa, this plant spread to India at a very early date, and thence to Mesopotamia, but it was not adopted in Egypt until the Greco-Roman period.

Shea tree, or shea-butter tree (*Butyrospermum parkii*). The nuts of this tree, which grows semiwild and is only occasionally fully cultivated, provide an important source of fat in the zone north of the habitat of the oil palm.

The foregoing list excludes food plants of minor significance, such as those whose leaves are used like spinach, as well as all medicinal herbs. Inspection reveals that, like the other three major complexes of the world, the Sudanic cultigens include representatives of all the principal categories of cultivated plants. Among them are some of genuinely outstanding importance, notably sesame, probably the world's foremost oil plant; cotton, the greatest of all textile crops; and sorghum, which ranks with American maize, Southeast Asian rice, and Southwest Asian wheat as one of the world's four leading cereal grains. In the realm of domesticated animals Negro Africa has not made a comparable contribution, the guinea fowl (*Numida meleagris*) constituting its sole original domesticate.

With the exception of the Guinea yam and the oil palm, whose center of distribution lies in the adjacent tropical forest, all the crops of the Sudanic complex extend practically throughout the western Sudan. They are cultivated with approximately equal intensity in the three culture provinces delineated in Map 10. On the basis of evidence from linguistic distributions and cultural complexity, however, we assume that they diffused at an early date to the Voltaic and Plateau Nigerian provinces from a center of origin among the Mande-speaking peoples.

The latter fall into two main divisions—the Nuclear Mande, or Mande-tan, and the Peripheral Mande, or Mande-fu. The Peripheral Mande (see Chapter 33) represent an early expansion southwestward into the tropical-forest region among peoples of other subfamilies of the Nigritic linguistic

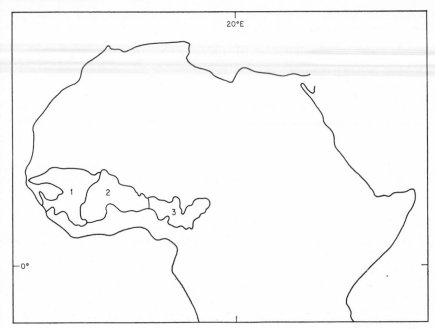

Map 10. Culture Provinces of the Western Sudan (1—Nuclear Mande, 2—Voltaic peoples, 3—Plateau Nigerians)

stock, where they have remained culturally stagnant or have perhaps even retrogressed. Though it was doubtless the possession of agriculture that facilitated this spread, the actual origin of cultivation must be ascribed to the much more progressive Nuclear Mande, with whom we are concerned in the present chapter. Nor shall we deal here with a number of Mande tribes that are now found scattered in enclaves throughout the Voltaic province, where some have penetrated in a commercial capacity and others presumably settled during the periods of political expansion under the empires of Ghana and Mali.

The major ethnic groupings within the limited confines of the Nuclear Mande province can be identified as follows.

1. Bambara (Banmana), including the Somono, a caste of fishermen on the Niger River. They number about a million and are mainly pagan, though the Somono are Moslems.
2. Bozo. This Moslem tribe, numbering about 30,000, lives largely by fishing and boat trade on the Niger and Bani Rivers but also engages in agriculture on the flood plains between them.
3. Dialonke (Dyalonka, Jallonke). This tribe, displaced from Fouta Djalon by the Fulani in the eighteenth century, numbers about 75,000 and is incompletely Islamized.
4. Kagoro (Bagane). This scattered group of pagans, numbering about 25,000, is a mixture of Bambara, Fulani, and Soninke elements.

5. Kasonke (Kasson, Khasonke). This group, of mixed Malinke and Fulani origin, numbers about 70,000, mainly pagans.
6. Konyanke (Konianke), with the kindred Mau (Diamande, Gyomande, Mahu, Old Diula), who are politically dominant over the Gyo tribe of Dan among whom they live. They number about 65,000 and are pagan.
7. Koranko (Kuranko), with the detached Lele in Kissi territory. They number about 125,000 and are pagan.
8. Malinke (Manding, Mandingo, Wangara), with the kindred Bambugu, Mikifore, Sankaran (Gangaran), Sidyanka, Toronka, Tubakay (Diakhambe), and Wasulunka (Ouassoulou, Wassulu). They number about a million, most of whom are still pagan.
9. Nono. With their fellow urbanized inhabitants of the town of Djenne, especially the Songhaic-speaking Djennenke, they number about 10,000 and are mainly Moslems.
10. Soninke (Sarakole, Seraculeh), with the Diawara, the dispersed Marka, and the Aser (Adjer), a small remnant group still inhabiting the desert oases of Tichit and Walata. They are considerably mixed with Bambara, Berber, Fulani, and Malinke elements. They number about 360,000, and almost all are Moslems.
11. Susu (Soso, Soussou). They number about 300,000, most of whom are Moslems.
12. Yalunka. A detached branch of the Dialonke, of which their name is simply an Anglicized version, they live in Sierra Leone. They number about 30,000, and about half are Moslems.

The Nuclear Mande, like their dispersed kinsmen, are typical representatives of the Negroid race (see Chapter 2) and speak related dialects of the Mande subfamily of the Nigritic linguistic stock. As the presumptive inventors of Sudanic agriculture, they early assumed cultural leadership in West Africa. Somewhat later, trade with the Berbers of Morocco across the Sahara Desert stimulated the development of handicraft manufactures, the growth of mercantile towns, and eventually the evolution of complex political institutions. In these advances the Soninke assumed the lead by virtue of their geographical position on the edge of the Sahara. When the Arabs first arrived on the fringes of the western Sudan, they found the Soninke organized in a powerful state known as Ghana, with its capital near modern Walata. It spanned most of the country from the Atlantic to the Niger, extended northward into Mauritania, and prospered greatly through a flourishing trade with Morocco. The Arabs were informed that it had had twenty-two kings prior to the Hegira, which would carry its founding back to perhaps the fourth century.

Our direct historical information concerning Ghana comes chiefly from El Bekri, an Arab who visited the country about A.D. 1067. He reports that the capital consisted of two towns about 6 miles apart—one occupied by Moslems and the other the fortified residence of the king and his court. The ruler was assisted by a number of ministers and claimed all gold found in the kingdom—the principal export commodity at the time. When a king died, there were human sacrifices at his funeral, and he was succeeded by a sister's son. From these scanty data it appears clear that the political system was a typical African despotism.

In 1076 the capital was captured, sacked, and occupied for a time by the Almoravid Berbers from Morocco. The Soninke fled to the southern province of Soso and established a state there. This flourished for a while, and even reconquered Ghana in 1205, but the state never fully regained the splendor of the past.

In the meantime, during the eleventh century, the Malinke had founded a small state on the Niger River, later known as Mali. It expanded rapidly in the thirteenth century, defeated Soso in 1235, and in 1240 occupied the remnants of Ghana. Mali reached its apogee about 1325 with the conquest of Timbuktu and Gao. It then dominated all West Africa from the edge of the tropical rainforest in the south to Senegal in the northwest and Air in the northeast, and maintained diplomatic relations on a plane of equality with the Sultan of Morocco and the King of Portugal. Gradually, however, Mali went into a decline, losing Timbuktu in 1433 to the Tuareg, and Djenne in 1473 to the Songhai.

With the Songhai empire engaged in other directions, Mali retained a tenuous hold for a time on the homeland of the Malinke. About 1670, however, the subject Bambara threw off the yoke and established the independent states of Segou and Kaarta, which soon absorbed the last remnants of the kingdom of Mali. The Bambara occupied Djenne from 1670 to 1810, and for a brief period Timbuktu as well. After 1810, however, the Fulani of Masina rose to dominance and, between 1854 and 1861, finally destroyed the Bambara states. In 1893, with the arrival of the French in Djenne, a new political era was initiated.

The civilization of the western Sudan, as of Egypt, lies deep in the past. Contemporary ethnography, which we shall now summarize for the province, can give little conception of the complexity of culture and the richness of life under the ancient empires of either region. This must await the spade of the archeologist, which has thus far lifted perhaps an ounce of earth on the Niger for every ton carefully sifted on the Nile.

The Nuclear Mande subsist primarily by agriculture, which they occasionally conduct with the aid of irrigation but mainly by shifting hoe cultivation. As might be expected of the presumptive originators of the Sudanic complex, they still raise practically all its component crops and, in addition, have borrowed onions from Egypt, rice from the Arabs, bananas and yams from Southeast Asia, and a substantial number of plants from the New World: haricot and lima beans, maize, manioc, peanuts, peppers, squash, sweet potatoes, tobacco, and tomatoes. The leading crop is millet, followed closely by rice, sorghum, and maize, but rice achieves first place among the Koranko and Susu. Cotton and fonio are likewise important.

Animal husbandry holds a significant, though subsidiary, place in the economy. When the Negroes of the Sudan came into contact with the Neolithic peoples of North Africa, they readily borrowed the domestic animals of the latter, though rejecting most of their cultivated plants. They did not, however, adopt milking, which even today occurs in West Africa only where introduced in recent times by the Fulani. All the Nuclear Mande peoples keep cattle, but these serve primarily for prestige, bride-price payments, and occasional sacrifices, since their meat is rarely used and they are milked only in tribes having Fulani herdsmen, like the Bambara and Soninke, and in others that have experienced strong Fulani influence, notably the Kasonke and Yalunka. Other domestic animals include goats, sheep, dogs (often eaten), chickens, guinea fowl, bees, and occasionally horses, donkeys, and ducks. Hunting is less productive than fishing, which constitutes the principal subsistence activity of the Bozo and is common elsewhere along the rivers. Most tribes gather considerable quantities of wild seeds, of baobab and other fruits, and of kola, palm, and shea nuts.

Trade assumes substantial proportions everywhere, and regular markets are apparently universal. Commerce with the northeast is largely monopolized by the Nono and with the Atlantic coast by the Susu, whereas the Diula and Marka, mercantile branches of the Soninke, conduct most of the trade that flows east, north, and south. The Nono of Djenne, who may serve as an example, export local agricultural products, shea butter, cloth and other native manufactures, and transshipped imports; they import dried fish and fish oil from the Bozo, milk and butter from the Fulani of Masina, salt and livestock from the north, and gold, kola nuts, and slaves from the south. In the division of labor by sex, the men hunt, fish, tend livestock, conduct foreign trade, clear land, and do most of the agricultural work; the women gather, care for poultry, milk (wherever this is done), cultivate garden crops, and participate in market trading.

All the tribes of the province inhabit compact permanent villages or towns, which are sometimes fortified by an encircling palisade among the Malinke and Susu. The prevailing house type is a round hut with cylindrical walls of mud or sun-dried brick and a conical roof of thatch; these dwellings are typically grouped in compounds around a courtyard and surrounded by a fence. A very different kind of structure, of North African origin, occurs in the northeast—among the Bozo, the Nono, the eastern Bambara and Soninke, and a few Malinke. This is a rectangular house with a flat terrace roof of beaten earth, an interior courtyard, and an external wall of sun-dried brick surmounted by crenelated parapets.

Towns with this type of dwelling are normally divided into separate wards, or quarters.

Marriage regularly involves a bride-price, paid in livestock, slaves, or cowries, and often bride-service as well. Sister exchange can occur as an alternative among the Bambara, Bozo, and Malinke. The Moslem Bozo and Soninke permit unions between parallel cousins, and preferential cross-cousin marriage is reported for the Koranko (with MoBrDa only), Susu, and some groups of Bambara and Malinke. All the Nuclear Mande practice general polygyny, but only in the nonsororal form. The first wife enjoys a superior status, but co-wives are individually established in separate quarters and the husband usually rotates among them. Levirate unions are preferential, but usually only with the widow of an elder brother, and the sororate is optional. A son may inherit his father's widow, if she is not his own mother, among the Bambara, Malinke, and Nono, but not among the Koranko. Patrilocal extended families exist as the norm in every society of the province. Each has a patriarchal head, who administers the group's collective property and who is succeeded when he dies by his next younger brother.

Descent, inheritance, and succession follow the patrilineal principle. Agamous patrisibs with associated totemic taboos occur in most, if not all, societies. They are composed of lineages, which are exogamous except among Islamized tribes and are usually localized as clan-barrios in distinct quarters of a town or village. Cousin terminology of the Iroquois type is specifically reported for the Bambara, Malinke, and Susu and may well be general. Apart from El Bekri's report of matrilineal succession in ancient Ghana, the only suggestion of possible former matrilineal descent in the area is a pair of allegations, made independently for the Bambara and Malinke, that a maternal uncle has an obligation to provide his sister's son with a wife. Even these are more plausibly to be interpreted as oblique references to preferential marriage with a mother's brother's daughter.

Age-grades for both sexes, functioning in communal labor, are reported for the Bambara and Malinke alone, but puberty initiation ceremonies marked by circumcision and clitoridectomy are widespread. Secret societies are attested only among the Koranko, Malinke, and Susu, but even these tribes lack the famed Poro and Bundu societies of the adjacent coastal peoples.

Local government rests on a special supernatural relationship between the land of a community and the lineage which first settled it. The chief of the latter, called Master of the Land among most tribes but appropriately Master of the Water among the riverain Bozo, controls the land of the village, at least in theory, though it is usually parceled out in collective usufruct among the various extended families. He likewise exercises priestly functions, sacrificing to the ancestral spirits, and with the aid of a council of family heads he handles local administrative and judicial matters.

Villages are aggregated into districts with similar priest-chiefs. The Koranko, Nono, Susu, and Yalunka have petty states with paramount chiefs. The Bambara, Malinke, and Soninke, though they retain no trace of the great monarchical states under which they were formerly organized, differ from the other tribes of the province in possessing a differentiated class of hereditary nobility. Until recently, however, slavery was universal and debt slavery widespread. Slaves born into a household usually enjoyed a preferred status as compared with those acquired by purchase or through capture in war, and after three or four generations they became assimilated to freemen. Long exposure to Arab influence presumably accounts for the widespread prevalence of despised endogamous castes, including smiths, leatherworkers, sometimes other artisans and fishermen, and usually the so-called *griots*, who are musicians, bards, and genealogists.

Selected Bibliography

Anderson, E. *Plants, Men, and Life*. Boston, 1952.
Anonymous. Coutume Soussou. *PCEHS*, ser. A, 10:575–610. 1939.
Aubert, A. Coutume Bambara. *PCEHS*, ser. A, 9:1–126. 1939.
Aubert, M. Laws and Customs of the Susus. *SLS*, 20:67–87. 1936.
Bazin, H. Les Bambara et leur langue. *Anthropos*, 1:681–694. 1906.
Boyer, G. Les Diawara. *MIFAN*, 29:1–122. 1953. [Soninke].
Braidwood, R. J. Near Eastern Prehistory. *Science*, 127:1419–1430. 1958.
Burkill, I. H. Habits of Man and the Origins of the Cultivated Plants of the Old World. *Proceedings of the Linnean Society of London*, 164:12–42. 1953.
Candolle, A. de. *Origin of Cultivated Plants*. 2d edit. London, 1904.
Chevalier, A. La région des sources du Niger. *Géographie*, 19:337–352. 1909. [Koranko].
Clozel, F. J., and R. Villamur. *Les coutumes indigènes de la Côte d'Ivoire*. Paris, 1902. [Malinke].
Coutouly, F. de. Coutume Marka-Sarakollé. *PCEHS*, ser. A, 9:203–246. 1939. [Soninke].
Dalziel, J. M. *The Useful Plants of West Tropical Africa*. London, 1937.
Daniel, F. Étude sur les Soninkés ou Sarakolés. *Anthropos*, 5:27–49. 1910.
Delafosse, M. *Haut-Sénégal-Niger*. 3 vols. Paris, 1912.
Haswell, M. R. Economics of Agriculture in a Savannah Village. *CRS*, 8:1–142. 1953. [Malinke].
Henry, J. *Les Bambara*. Münster, 1910.
Holderer, P. Note sur la coutume Mandingue du Ouli. *PCEHS*, ser. A, 8:323–348. 1939. [Malinke].
Irvine, F. R. The Indigenous Food Plants of West African Peoples. *Journal of the New York Botanical Garden*, 49:224–236, 254–267. 1948.
———. *A Textbook of West African Agriculture*. 2d edit. London, 1953.
Kamara, K., and D. B. Drummond. Marriage Customs amongst the Kurankos. *SLS*, 16:57–66. 1930.

Labouret, H. Les Manding et leur langue. *BCEHS*, 17:1–270. 1934. [Malinke].

Lavergne de Tressan, M. de. Inventaire linguistique de l'Afrique Occidentale Française et du Togo. *MIFAN*, 30:1–241. 1953.

Malzy, P. Les Bozos du Niger et leurs modes de pêche. *BIFAN*, 8:100–132. 1946.

Mauny, R. La préhistoire. *Afrique Occidentale Française*, ed. E. Guernier, 1:23–32. Paris, 1949.

——. Notes historiques autour des principales plantes cultivées d'Afrique occidentale. *BIFAN*, 15:684–730. 1953.

——. The Question of Ghana. *Africa*, 24:200–213. 1954.

McCulloch, M. *The Peoples of Sierra Leone Protectorate.* London, 1950. [Koranko, Susu, and Yalunka].

Monteil, C. *Les Khassonké.* Paris, 1915.

——. *Les Bambara de Ségou et du Kaarta.* Paris, 1924.

——. *Djénné.* Paris, 1932. [Nono].

Nicole. Die Diakite-Sarrakolesen. *REVAO*, pp. 93–138. 1903. [Soninke].

Ortoli, J. Coutume Bambara. *PCEHS*, ser. A, 9:127–159. 1939.

——. Coutume Bozo. *PCEHS*, ser. A, 9:161–202. 1939.

Paques, H. *Les Bambara.* Paris, 1954.

Reinhardt, L. *Kulturgeschichte der Nutzpflanzen.* 2 vols. München, 1911.

Saint-Père, L. J. B. *Les Sarakollé du Guinimakha.* Paris, 1925. [Soninke].

Sauer, C. O. *Agricultural Origins and Dispersals.* New York, 1952.

Schiemann, E. Entstehung der Kulturpflanzen. *Handbuch der Vererbungswissenschaft*, 3:1–377. Berlin, 1932.

Sidibé, M. Coutumier du cercle de Kita. *BCEHS*, 17:1–270. 1934. [Malinke].

Snowden, J. D. *The Cultivated Races of Sorghum.* London, 1936.

Thomas, N. W. *Anthropological Report on Sierra Leone*, vol. 1. London, 1916. [Koranko, Susu, and Yalunka].

Tothill, J. D., ed. *Agriculture in the Sudan.* London, 1948.

Urvoy, Y. *Petit atlas ethno-démographique du Soudan.* Paris, 1942.

Westermann, D. *Geschichte Afrikas.* Köln, 1952.

12

Voltaic Peoples

East of the Nuclear Mande and south of the Niger River, largely in the interior watershed of the Volta River, live a block of Negro peoples who, for the most part, belong to the Voltaic subfamily of the Nigritic linguistic stock. They share with the Nuclear Mande so many features, not only of subsistence economy, but also of other basic aspects of culture, that, despite an almost complete lack of direct evidence, we can safely assume that they borrowed the fundamental elements of Sudanic agricultural civilization from their western neighbors at a very early date. They have had, however, only a small part in the political history of the western Sudan as compared with the peoples to the west, north, and east of them. To be sure, the large Gurma and Mossi tribes in the north of the province have had strong states for at least the past 800 years and have frequently warred with their powerful neighbors on the Niger. They have not, however, either created great empires by conquest or suffered subjection to alien states. On the contrary, they seem to have served as buffers, protecting their weaker southern neighbors from exposure to the political upheavals that have racked the Nuclear Mande, the Songhai, and the Hausa. Even the impact of Islam has been slight and sporadic. For these reasons their culture probably reflects fairly closely what that of the Mande must have been like prior to their embarkation on a career of empire building and to the advent of the Berbers and Arabs from the north.

The Voltaic peoples attain today a total population of approximately 6 million, or appreciably more than the Nuclear Mande. Unlike the latter, however, they do not consist of a few great and relatively homogeneous nations but rather, probably because of their relative isolation, form a large number of culturally distinct tribes. In the classification that follows, even extensive combination has been unable to reduce the number of separate ethnic groups below forty-eight. These are divided into clusters on the basis of linguistic affiliations. Unless otherwise noted, each tribe is to be understood as pagan in religion and as belonging to the appropriate branch of the Voltaic subfamily of the Nigritic stock.

SENUFO CLUSTER

1. Guin (Gouin, Gwin, Mbouin), with the kindred Turuka (Kpin, Pain, Pin, Tourouka, Turka). They number about 55,000, and their linguistic affiliation is still uncertain.
2. Karaboro, with the Tyefo. They number about 35,000, and the linguistic affiliation of the Tyefo is uncertain.
3. Komono, with the kindred Falafala, Pala, and Sikolo. They number less than 10,000.
4. Minianka, with the Nanerge, Pomporo, Sankan, Syenere (Sendere), and Tagba. They number about 200,000, of whom roughly 20,000 are Moslems.
5. Nafana (Nafame, Nafarha), with the Pantera. They number about 15,000.
6. Senufo (Sene, Siena). They number about 540,000, of whom a very few are Islamized.
7. Wara (Guala, Ouara), with the Natioro (Samino, Sanmu). The linguistic affiliations of these small tribes, with a total population of about 6,000, are still uncertain.

HABE CLUSTER

8. Bobo, embracing the Bua (Black Bobo, Boua, Bwa), Kian (Kyan, Tian, White Bobo), Nienige (Niniga), Tara (Red Bobo), and Sankura (Zara). They number about 250,000 and have been very slightly influenced by Islam.
9. Deforo. They number about 10,000.
10. Dogon (Dagom, Habe, Hambbe, Kado, Makbe, Tombo, Toro). They number about 225,000.

LOBI CLUSTER

11. Dian (Dya), with the Puguli. They number about 11,000.
12. Dorosie (Dokhosie, Dorhosye), with the Gan and Padorho. They number about 10,000.
13. Kulango (Kolano, Koulango, Kulambo, Ngoulango, Parkhalla), with the Loron (Lorho, Loro), Nabe (Nembai), and Tese (Tegue). They number about 30,000.
14. Lobi, with the kindred Tegessie (Loron-Lobi, Touna, Tuna). They number about 110,000.
15. Tusyan, with the Semu (Same) and Vigye. They number about 25,000.

GRUSI CLUSTER

16. Builsa (Boura, Bulea, Bulo, Buluk, Bura, Kanjaga). They number about 55,000.
17. Dagari (Dagaba, Dagati), with the Zanga. They number about 140,000.
18. Degha (Dga, Diammou, Dyamu, Mo). They number about 8,000.
19. Grunshi (Gorise, Gourounsi, Gruinse, Grussi, Gurunsi), embracing the Awuna (Aculo, Adjolo, Atyulo, Frafra, Kassonfra, Yulu), Fera (Fra), Isala (Debe, Galebagba, Hisala, Isalen, Pasala, Sissala, Tamboboda), Kasena (Kasom, Kassonboura, Kassuna), and Nagwa. They number about 110,000.
20. Lilse (Lyela), with the Fulse (Akurumba, Foulse, Kouroumba, Kurumba), and Nioniosse (Nyonyose). These three tribes, with a total population of about 60,000, are quite distinct, probably even linguistically, though often confused.
21. Nunuma (Nanoumba, Nibulu, Nounouma), with the kindred Menkiera. They number about 35,000 and are frequently classed as Grunshi.
22. Vagala (Site, Vagele), with the detached Tampolense (Tamprussi). These small remnant tribes number about 2,000.

MOLE CLUSTER

23. Birifor (Birifon), with the Lober. They number about 85,000.
24. Dagomba (Dagbamba, Dagboma), with the kindred Nanumba (Nanune). They number about 175,000, and Islam is making some inroads among them.
25. Gurensi (Gorensi), embracing the Kusasi (Kousansi, Kusae, Kusale, Kusan, Kussi), Namnam (Nabdam, Nabte), Nankanse (Gurensi proper, Nankana), and Tallensi (Talene, Talni). They number about 170,000.
26. Mamprusi (Mampelle, Mampulugu). They number about 50,000.
27. Mossi (Mole, Moshi), with the Yarse, a mercantile people of Mande origin. They number about 1,750,000, of whom fewer than 100,000, mainly Yarse, are Moslems.
28. Naudeba (Loso, Losso, Naoudemba). They number about 50,000.
29. Wala (Oule, Wile, Wule). They number about 55,000.

GURMA CLUSTER

30. Basari (Bassari, Bedjelib, Ntchan, Tobote), with the Chamba (Akasele, Kaselem, Tschamba). They number about 80,000.
31. Gurma (Gourmantche). They number about 180,000.
32. Konkomba (Bekpokpak, Komba, Konko, Kpankpam, Lekpokpam, Pangpana), with the Bekwom (Bikwombe) and Ngaga. They number about 50,000.
33. Moba (Bmoba, Moab, Moare, Mwan). They number about 50,000.

TEM CLUSTER

34. Kabre (Bekaburum, Cabrai, Kabure, Kaure, Kobore), with the kindred Difale, Dompago, Logba, Manganapo, Namba (Lamba), and Tamberma. They number about 205,000.
35. Tem (Chaucho, Kotokoli, Temba, Timu, Tsautsho). They number about 45,000.

BARGU CLUSTER

36. Bargu (Barba, Bariba, Borgawa, Burgu). They number about 150,000, of whom perhaps 10,000 are Moslems.
37. Kilinga (Kilir, Kyilina, Sugu, Tsylina, Yom), with the Tamba (Taneka) and Yowa (Pilapila). They number about 50,000.
38. Somba (Sombaru, Some), embracing the Berba, Betammaribe (Betammadibe), Betiabe, Bulba (Boulba, Boulea), Dye (Die), Natimba (Natemba, Natyab), Nautuba, Niende (Nyende), Soruba (Besorube), and Woaba (Ouabou, Waba, Yoabu). They number about 150,000.

INTRUSIVE PEOPLES

39. Busa (Boussa, Busawa), with the Boko. They number about 30,000, including a very few Moslems, and belong to the Mande subfamily of the Nigritic linguistic stock.
40. Busansi (Bisa, Bisano, Bisapele, Bousanou, Bouzantchi, Busanga, Bussansi). They number about 130,000 and belong to the Mande subfamily of the Nigritic linguistic stock.
41. Chakossi (Anufo, Chokosi, Dyakosi, Mangu, Tschokossi, Tyoko). Descended from Akan mercenaries who served the Dagomba and Konkomba rulers several centuries ago, they belong to the Twi branch of the Kwa subfamily of the Nigritic linguistic stock. They number about 10,000 and are partially Islamized.
42. Dafi (Dafing, Southern Marka). They are a specialized branch of the Marka subgroup of the Soninke and belong to the Mande subfamily of the Nigritic linguistic stock. They number about 90,000 and are Moslems.
43. Diula (Dioula, Dyoura, Gyula). They are a widely scattered mercantile group, probably of Soninke origin, and belong to the Mande subfamily of the Nigritic linguistic stock. They are Moslems and number about 160,000, of whom one group has established a state near Kong and mixed there with the Falafala, a subject tribe of the Senufo cluster.
44. Gan (Ben, Ganne, Ganra, Gben, Ngan), with the kindred Mangoro and the dominant Anno. They number about 5,000. The Gan and Mangoro belong to the Mande subfamily of the Nigritic linguistic stock, and the Anno to the Kwa subfamily.
45. Ligbi (Ligoue, Nigbi, Nigwe), with the kindred Huela (Vuela) and Numu (Noumou). They belong to the Mande subfamily of the Nigritic linguistic stock and number perhaps 12,000, of whom about half are Moslems.

46. Samo (San, Somno), with the kindred but isolated Samoro (Samogho). They belong to the Mande subfamily of the Nigritic linguistic stock, number about 135,000, and are partially Islamized.
47. Sia (Bobofign, Sya, Tusia). They belong to the Mande subfamily of the Nigritic linguistic stock, number about 75,000, are considerably mixed with Bobo, and are Moslems.
48. Tienga (Kengawa, Kienga, Kyenga, Tyenga), with the Shanga (Tshanga). They belong to the Mande subfamily of the Nigritic linguistic stock, number about 20,000, and are partially Islamized.

Among the enclaves of intrusive Mande peoples, the Busa, Busansi, and Tienga in the east presumably date from the period of expansion of the great Malinke empire of Mali. The Dafi, Diula, Ligbi, Samo, and Sia, however, seem first to have penetrated the region in a mercantile capacity. With them should also be included the Yarse subgroup among the Mossi, though these people no longer retain their ancestral language.

The Voltaic peoples cultivate practically the entire roster of Sudanic plants, with millet, sorghum, and occasionally fonio as the staples. They have also borrowed extensively from other complexes: melons and onions from Southwest Asia; bananas, cucumbers, eggplant, rice, taro, and yams from Southeast Asia; haricot and lima beans, maize, manioc, papayas, peanuts, peppers, squash, sweet potatoes, tobacco, and tomatoes from the New World. Among these introduced crops, maize assumes first place among the Nafana, rice among the Wara, and yams among the Dagomba, Degha, Diula, Gan, Kilinga, and Kulango; and all three are also widely grown elsewhere. The Bobo, Dogon, and Kabre practice some irrigation, but the prevailing agricultural technique is shifting hoe cultivation with crop rotation and fallowing. The Dogon, Gurensi, Kabre, Mamprusi, and Nunuma use animal manure, and often human manure as well, to fertilize their fields.

Hunting, fishing, and gathering, especially of shea nuts, all occur in the area, but rarely do they provide more than a modest supplement to the diet. Animal husbandry assumes considerably more importance. All tribes keep at least a few cattle, mainly of a humpless short-horned breed. Generally, however, they use them exclusively for sacrifices, for marriage payments, and for their hides and manure, almost never for their milk. Some milking, indeed, is reported for the Basari, Bobo, Dagari, Gurensi, Kilinga, Minianka, Moba, Mossi, and Tem, but in every case, except that of the Gurensi, the sources specifically attest that this practice is confined almost entirely to intrusive Fulani herdsmen. Nearly all the Voltaic peoples possess numerous goats, sheep, dogs (commonly eaten), chickens, guinea fowl, and bees, and many keep a few donkeys and horses. Pigs. cats, ducks, and pigeons appear only sporadically and in small numbers.

Trade is highly developed, and regular markets are practically universal. Commerce is conducted largely by groups of Mande origin, notably the Diula in the southwest, the Dafi in the northwest, and the Yarse in the northeast. Cowrie shells serve everywhere as a medium of exchange. The basis of trade among the Diula consists in the exchange of livestock imported from the north for kola nuts and slaves obtained in the south, but they also deal in Senufo cloth, shea butter, and gold mined by the Kulango. Women do most of the market trading, but the men handle other than local commerce. Hunting is done by men, gathering by women, and fishing by both sexes. The men tend the livestock, clear land, and perform the bulk of the agricultural work. The women, however, everywhere render considerable assistance in the fields, and among the Bargu, Dogon, Gurma, and Mossi their contribution rises to equal participation.

The prevailing pattern of settlement is a neighborhood of dispersed family homesteads, but compact villages occur among most Mande and Senufo groups and among scattering other tribes, notably the Dagomba, Dogon, Gurma, Kilinga, Mamprusi, some Somba, and the Isala subtribe of the Grunshi. Round huts with cylindrical walls of mud or sun-dried brick and conical thatched roofs, grouped in circular walled compounds, must once have prevailed throughout the area and still constitute the predominant type of habitation. From the north, however, has penetrated a distinct house type, presumably favored by its adaptability to defense. This is a rectangular structure with a flat roof of beaten earth, an interior courtyard, and an exterior wall of mud or sun-dried brick commonly surmounted by a crenelated parapet, and it prevails today among the Birifor, Bobo, Busansi, Dagari, Dian, Diula, Dogon, Dorosie, Grunshi, Komono, Minianka, Nunuma, Samo, Sia, Vagala, and Wala. The Degha, Gan, Nafana, and some Ligbi have adopted the rectangular frame houses with thatched gable roofs which characterize the coastal tribes to the south.

Few tribes impose restrictions on premarital sex relations. Marriages are usually arranged by the heads of two extended families, often while the girl is still an infant. The most typical procedure is that followed by the Birifor, Dagari, Grunshi, Gurensi, and Wala, and with slight modifications also by the Basari, Bobo, Builsa, Dagomba, Dian, Komono, Mamprusi, Senufo, Tem, and Wara. Here formal negotiations are conducted by a special go-between, who must always be a patrilineal kinsman of the youth and at the same time a close relative of the girl, preferably the son of one of her female lineage mates, and who thereafter mediates between the two kin groups in all matters arising out of the union. These tribes usually require three kinds of material consideration: (1) agricultural bride-service between the betrothal and the wedding and commonly even thereafter; (2) a substantial and standardized bride-price in livestock, cowries, or both; and (3) special placation gifts donated by the groom's lineage at some time after the bride has come to live with them and whose acceptance by the bride's kinsmen makes the union a fully legitimate one and consolidates all the reciprocal obligations entailed by it.

Variant modes of marriage prevail in other parts of the area. The Chakossi, Dafi, Diula, Gan, Guin, Moba, Mossi, and Nunuma, for example, require a bride-price but apparently neither bride-service nor placation gifts. The Dogon, Dorosie, Kabre, Konkomba, Kulango, Lobi, Naudeba, and Somba omit the bride-price but demand premarital bride-service. Among the Deforo, Gurma, Lilse, Samo, and Vagala a marriage involves gifts but no other form of material consideration. Although collusive abduction appears rather widely as an alternative to other modes, marriage by exchange is reported only for the Mossi and Senufo, and it is said to be rare even in these tribes.

Polygyny is permitted everywhere and has a high incidence except among the Dogon and Naudeba. The sororal form is attested as either preferential or common in thirteen tribes and as forbidden only among the Dagomba, Diula, Dogon, Konkomba, Mossi, Wala, and the Tallensi subtribe of the Gurensi. The first wife enjoys a superior status, but the co-wives each have separate quarters and the husband distributes his time equally among them in rotation. The levirate and sororate are nearly universal, the former being denied only for the Mamprusi. Among the Dagari, Grunshi, Nunuma, Somba, and Wala, married women commonly have recognized lovers, who make gifts to the husband and do field work for him in return for the wife's favors. The group that occupies a household is typically a patrilocal extended family, ranging in size from a small unit of married brothers or a father and one married son to a large aggregate embracing the families of various collateral patrilineal relatives. Only in the extreme north, among the Dogon, Lilse, Minianka, and Mossi, are extended forms of the family consistently absent.

The tribes of the Grusi and Mole clusters reveal a distinctive pattern of social organization, characterized by patrilocal residence, patrilineal descent, exogamous totemic patrisibs, segmentary lineages, patrilineal inheritance and succession, local exogamy, kinship terminology of the Hawaiian type, and the prohibition of marriage between first cousins of any kind. A settlement is occupied by a localized major lineage, thus constituting a patrilocal clan-community, within which the component minor lineages are commonly localized in distinct quarters as clan-barrios and the minimal lineages, of course, as patrilocal extended families. The tribes of the Bargu, Gurma, Habe, and Tem clusters appear, on the basis of incomplete evidence, to possess social systems of essentially similar character. The Dogon, however, have cousin terminology of the Iroquois rather than the Hawaiian pattern, and only the quarters of a village have the structure of patriclans.

The tribes of the Lobi and Senufo clusters, together with the Birifor of the Mole cluster, exhibit a markedly divergent pattern, one that sheds considerable light on the probable evolution of social organization in the province as a whole. The Dorosie, Kulango, and Lobi are characterized by matrilineal rather than patrilineal descent, by agamous matrisibs and exogamous matrilineages, by matrilineal inheritance, by preferential cross-cousin marriage, and by kinship terminology of the Crow type. Though residence is prevailingly patrilocal today, avunculocal residence appears as a patterned alternative, and with sufficient frequency to suggest that it may once have been the norm. These tribes presumably represent the first step in a transition from an avunculocal form of the matrilineate to the patrilocal and patrilineal structures now dominant in the region as a whole, namely, the shift from avunculocal to patrilocal residence as the norm.

The second step, the development of patrilineal descent on the basis of patrilocalization, is represented by the neighboring Birifor. These people have evolved exogamous patrisibs and patrilineages without losing their earlier matrilineal sibs and lineages, and are thus characterized by double descent. They retain both the preference for cross-cousin marriage and the original Crow type of cousin terminology. Inheritance, however, has changed in adaptation to the new conditions. Movable property, notably livestock and money, still descends to a man's matrilineal heir—his next younger brother or, if he has none, the eldest son of his eldest sister. On the other hand, property which is attached to a particular locality, e.g., a man's dwelling, land, and private shrines, has yielded to the pressure of patrilocal residence and is now transmitted to a patrilineal heir, the eldest son.

The third step, the final disappearance of matrilineal kin groups under the unfavorable influence of patrilocal residence, is exemplified by the Dian, who are strictly patrilineal in descent but retain the older Crow terminology, an unfailing diagnostic of previous matrilineal descent, as well as the preference for cross-cousin marriage and the intermediate rule of mixed inheritance. The Senufo tribes fall somewhere in this series of transitions, for they all follow either a matrilineal or a mixed rule of inheritance and exhibit at least remnants of avunculocal residence, but their exact position cannot be identified in the absence of precise data on either kinship terminology or kin-group structure.

The fourth step involves an adaptive change in kinship terminology and the correlative banning of cross-cousin marriage. Since Crow terms for cross-cousins are functionally inconsistent with patrilineal descent, they tend to disappear and to be replaced by the sibling terminology already in use for parallel cousins, thus yielding the Hawaiian pattern, which we have already found prevalent in the Grusi and Mole clusters. The incest taboos previously preventing marriage with a sibling or parallel cousin are extended at the same time to the cross-cousins, who now fall into the same social category. All that remains of the former matrilineate is a series of survivals. Thus the patrilineal Dagari and Vagala still cling to certain forms of matrilineal inheritance, and the Builsa, Dagomba, Grunshi, Gurensi, and Mamprusi continue to prohibit marriage with any known relative in the female line despite the complete disappearance of all corporate matrilineal kin groups.

Conceivably the Dogon represent the fifth and final step in this evolutionary sequence—that in which even the lingering survivals of the former matrilineate have been discarded and kinship terms have been altered to the Iroquois pattern, which is better adapted to the patrilineate. The social structure of the Dogon conforms to the so-called Dakota type, which is statistically the most common among patrilineal peoples throughout the world.

Age-sets, functioning mainly to assist fellow members in the performance of bride-service obligations, occur in a few societies, notably the Dogon, Kabre, and Lobi. Circumcision is reported only for the Bobo, Chakossi, Dagomba, Deforo, Diula, Dogon, Gurma, Minianka, Mossi, Samo, Somba, Tienga, and Wala. Clitoridectomy, on the other hand, is widely practiced, being cited as absent only for the Dagomba, Deforo, Gan, Kabre, Mamprusi, and Nafana. Neither cannibalism nor headhunting is found in the area, though the latter may once have prevailed among the Dagari and Mamprusi. Slavery is universal, but otherwise the Voltaic peoples are relatively egalitarian. Differentiation of a hereditary noble class appears only among the Bargu, Dagomba, Gurma, Mamprusi, Mossi, and Wala. Endogamous despised castes of smiths and leatherworkers are confined to a few peripheral tribes, notably the Bobo, Dogon, Minianka, Mossi, and Senufo, and thus are clearly not indigenous to the area.

Political organization derives largely from a religious conception—the deification of the earth. Each local community has a ritual headman charged with responsibility for maintaining good relations with the earth and thus assuring the welfare of his people. He is regularly the head of the lineage that traditionally first occupied the land, and on his death he is succeeded by the eldest surviving male of the lineage. He propitiates the earth with sacrifices at planting and harvest time and must ritually validate any conversion of untilled land to agricultural use. The spilling of blood upon the earth is believed to be especially abhorrent to the deity. A killing in war or a murder defiles the earth and must be expiated by extraordinary sacrifices. To prevent such contamination and its possible awful consequences, the headman has the ritual authority to put a stop to feuding or warfare and to mediate in disputes which threaten to provoke them. This complex of beliefs and practices obviously exerts a powerful influence toward peace and social order.

In some tribes a local chief has usurped secular authority within the

A Ritual Headman of the Tallensi. (Courtesy of Meyer Fortes.)

community, but rarely has he disturbed the ritual powers of his predecessor. Relatively few of the Voltaic peoples have evolved any form of political integration transcending the local level. Petty paramount chiefships over small districts have developed among the Dagari, Deforo, Lilse, Moba, and Senufo, and larger ones among the Basari, Busa, Chakossi, Dafi, Kilinga, and Tem. True monarchical states exist only among the Bargu, Dagomba, Gurma, Mamprusi, Mossi, and Wala. The organization of the larger of the two Mossi states may be briefly described as fairly representative of them all.

At the head of this typical African despotism stands the Mogho-Naba, or king, who maintains an elaborate court at a capital town, where he is served by numerous eunuchs, bodyguards, page boys (selected for their good looks), and various specialized officials. His many wives live in special villages, scattered throughout the kingdom, where all the male inhabitants are eunuchs. He administers the country through five provincial governors and numerous appointive district chiefs, commonly eunuchs, who collect regular taxes and special imposts from the local headmen. The governors, whose offices are hereditary from father to eldest son, also hold particular posts at court. One is the prime minister and the chief over all eunuchs. The others are, respectively, the commander of the cavalry, the keeper of the royal tombs, the commander of the infantry, and the commandant of the palace and chief over its page boys. The death of a ruler is followed by an interregnum, marked by anarchy and widespread pillage, until his successor is installed. The latter is selected from among the sons of the deceased king by an electoral college composed of the second, third, and fourth ministers and the commander in chief of the army. Sons of kings, forbidden to live at the capital, maintain small courts in provincial villages. The daughters of kings enjoy an exceptionally high status; they dominate their husbands and commonly lead profligate lives.

Selected Bibliography

Arnaud, R. Notes sur les montagnards Habé. *RETP*, 2:241–318. 1921. [Dogon].
Asmis, G. Die Stammesrechte des Bezirkes Sansane-Mangu. *ZVR*, 27:71–128. 1912. [Chakossi, Konkomba, and Moba].
Castinel, J. Le mariage et la mort dans la région du Yanga. *BIFAN*, 7:148–155. 1945. [Gurma].
Charles, L. Les Lobi. *RES*, 2:202–220. 1911.
Chéron, G. Les Minianka. *RES*, 4:165–186. 1913.
Cremer, J. *Les Bobo*. 2 vols. Paris, 1924–1927.
Delafosse, M. Le peuple Siéna ou Sénoufo. *REES*, 1:17–32, 79–92, 151–159, 242–275, 448–457, 483–486; 2:1–21. 1908–1909.
Desplagnes, L. *Le plateau central nigérien*. Paris, 1907. [Dogon].
Dim Delobsom, A. A. L'empire du Mogho-Naba. *ESEJ*, 9:1–308. 1933. [Mossi].

Ferréol. Essais d'histoire et d'ethnographie sur quelques peuplades de la subdivision de Banfora. *BCEHS,* 7:100–127. 1924. [Komono].

Fisch, R. Die Dagbamba. *BA,* 3:132–164. 1913. [Dagomba].

Fortes, M. Kinship, Incest and Exogamy among the Tallensi. *Custom is King,* ed. L. H. D. Buxton, pp. 237–256. London, 1936. [Gurensi].

———. The Political System of the Tallensi. *APS,* pp. 239–271. 1940.

———. *The Dynamics of Clanship among the Tallensi.* London, 1945.

———. *The Web of Kinship among the Tallensi.* London, 1949.

Fortes, M., and S. L. Fortes. Food in the Domestic Economy of the Tallensi. *Africa,* 9:237–276. 1936. [Gurensi].

Froelich, J. C. Généralités sur les Kabrè. *BIFAN,* 11:77–105. 1949.

———. Les Konkomba. *BIFAN,* 11:409–437. 1949.

———. Notes sur les Naoudeba. *BIFAN,* 12:102–121. 1950.

Guébhard, P. Notes contributives à l'étude de la religion, des moeurs, et des coutumes des Bobo. *RES,* 2:125–145. 1911.

Haumant, J. C. *Les Lobi et leur coutume.* Paris, 1929.

Klose, H. *Togo unter deutscher Flagge.* Berlin, 1899. [Basari].

Labouret, H. Les tribus du Rameau Lobi. *TMIE,* 15:1–510. 1931. [Birifor, Dian, Dorosie, and Lobi].

Lavergne de Tressan, M. de. Inventaire linguistique de l'Afrique Occidentale Française et du Togo. *MIFAN,* 30:1–241. 1953.

Mangin, E. Les Mossi. *Anthropos,* 9:98–124, 477–493, 705–736; 10–11:187–217, 323–331. 1914–1916.

Manoukian, M. *Tribes of the Northern Territories of the Gold Coast.* London, 1952.

Menjaud, H. Documents ethnographiques sur le Gourma. *JSA,* 2:35–47. 1932.

Mercier, P. The Social Role of Circumcision among the Besorube. *AA,* 53:326–337. 1951. [Somba].

———. L'habitat et l'occupation de la terre chez les "Somba." *BIFAN,* 15:798–817. 1953.

Paulme, D. *Organisation sociale des Dogon.* Paris, 1940.

Puig, F. *Étude sur les coutumes des Cabrais.* Toulouse, 1934. [Kabre].

Rattray, R. S. *The Tribes of the Ashanti Hinterland.* 2 vols. Oxford, 1932. [Birifor, Dagari, Grunshi, Gurensi, and Mamprusi].

Roure, M. Notes sur les coutumes et traditions des Tankamba. *PCEHS,* ser. A, 10:557–572. 1939. [Somba].

Sidibé, M. Famille, vie sociale et vie religeuse chez les Birifor et les Oulé. *BIFAN,* 1:697–742. 1939.

Tauxier, L. *Le noir du Soudan.* Paris, 1912. [Bobo, Builsa, Dafi, Diula, Grunshi, Gurensi, and Mossi].

———. *Le noir du Yatenga.* Paris, 1917. [Lilse, Mossi, and Samo].

———. *Le noir de Bondoukou.* Paris, 1921. [Degha, Diula, Gan, and Kulango].

———. Les Dorhosié et Dorhosié-Fingg. *JSA,* 1:61–110. 1931.

———. Les Gouin et les Tourouka. *JSA,* 3:77–128. 1933.

———. Deux petites populations peu connues de l'Afrique Occidentale Française. *JSA,* 9:159–195. 1939. [Wara].

Vendeix, M. J. Nouvel essai de monographie du pays Senoufo. *BCEHS,* 17:578–652. 1935.

Worsley, P. M. The Kinship System of the Tallensi. *JRAI,* 86:37–75. 1956. [Gurensi].

13

Plateau Nigerians

The techniques and products of agriculture, after their elaboration by the Nuclear Mande, gradually spread eastward across 3,000 miles of the Sudan to Nubia and Ethiopia. They were not carried by a single migrating people but were transmitted by diffusion to successive peoples of different linguistic stocks—a slow and laborious process since each in turn had painfully to learn the complex new techniques of food production and to substitute these for the old familiar modes of food acquisition through hunting and gathering. The transition may thus easily have required a thousand years for its completion, a period probably roughly coinciding with the fourth millennium B.C. During the third millennium there occurred a second major process of diffusion in the reverse direction, carrying the Neolithic domesticated animals obtained through contact with the ancient Egyptians westward to the headwaters of the Niger. Only the animals themselves, however, were adopted at this time, not the associated milking complex, which diffused very much later and over a much more restricted territory.

The eastward diffusion of agriculture and the westward diffusion of animal husbandry probably followed practically the same path, though in opposite directions. Linguistic and distributional evidence allows us to reconstruct this route with a high degree of probability. Between the upper Niger and Northern Nigeria the carriers were clearly the Voltaic peoples. Between Lake Chad and the Nile they were as certainly the peoples speaking the Central and Eastern Sudanic languages, for the Maban, Furian, and Kordofanian speakers occupy areas much too small to have played a major mediating role. In Northern Nigeria and the adjacent section of Cameroon, however, two alternative routes are possible—a southern one through the mountainous plateau region and a northern route through the country now occupied by the great Hausa and Kanuri nations.

The geographical disadvantages of the southern route, coupled with the vastly more complex civilizational attainments of the peoples of the north, make it highly probable that the mediators in both the eastward and the westward diffusion were the Hausa and Kanuri rather than the Plateau Nigerians. To be sure, the cultural superiority of the former rests in large measure on two subsequent historical developments—the growth of the important caravan trade across the Sahara Desert with the peoples of

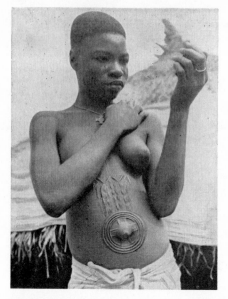

Tiv Girl with Characteristic Navel Scarification. (Courtesy of British Information Services.)

North Africa and the spread of the Arabs and of Islam to the fringe of the Sudan during the past thousand years. These developments render it preferable to defer consideration of Hausa and Kanuri civilization until Chapter 17.

In the present chapter, consequently, we shall confine our attention to the inhabitants of the central plateau region of Nigeria and adjacent Cameroon, which lies east and southeast of the Voltaic province. Even though the Plateau Nigerians presumably played no direct role in mediating the diffusion of either Sudanic agriculture or Neolithic animal husbandry, they certainly acquired both at an early date, for no traces of earlier forms of subsistence economy survive today. With rare exceptions, however, they did not assume the associated elements of a more complex civilization. They remain, so to speak, a cultural cul-de-sac characterized by a series of interesting archaic traits ranging from widespread complete nudity to certain utterly unique marriage practices.

The historical role of the Plateau Nigerians has not, however, been entirely negligible. Their southern tribes, at about the time of Christ, mediated the diffusion of Malaysian food plants from the east to the Guinea coast, effecting here a complete transformation of the local economy. From their midst, soon thereafter, came the Bantu, who penetrated the equatorial rainforest and ultimately most of the southern third of the African continent. One plateau tribe, the Jukun, evolved a complex state, that of Kororofa, which made extensive conquests in Northern Nigeria in the seventeenth century. In general, however, the Plateau Nigerians have been politically weak and defenseless. During the nineteenth century, in particular, they suffered heavily from incursions by the Fulani (see Chapter 55), who infiltrated large tracts of territory suitable to grazing, drove the indigenes into mountain enclaves or reduced them to subjection, and even here and there wrought some acceptance of Islam.

The Plateau Nigerians are typically Negroid in physical characteristics. Linguistically, however, they fall into several distinct groups. The largest of these comprises members of the Bantoid subfamily of the Nigritic stock. In the east and west live a few tribes of the Eastern and Kwa subfamilies of the Nigritic stock, and in the northeast are a considerable number of Negro peoples speaking languages of the Chadic subfamily of the Hamitic stock. The latter differ notably from their linguistic kinsmen of the great Hausa nation to the northwest. Although for the sake of convenience the peoples of the province are classified below according to language, it should be emphasized that in this region cultural and linguistic differences reveal an extremely low degree of correlation.

BANTOID PEOPLES

1. Afusare (Fizere, Hill Jarawa), with the Anaguta (Naguta). They number about 30,000.
2. Basa (Bassa), with the kindred Basakomo (Bassa-Komo) and Kaduna (Bassa-Kaduna). They number about 50,000.
3. Batu (Boko), with the Akonto. They number fewer than 2,000.
4. Birom (Berom, Burum, Kibbo, Kibyen), with the Aten (Ganawuri, Jal, Ngell) and Pyem (Fem, Paiema, Pem). They number about 70,000.
5. Borrom (Boghorom, Burmawa, Burrum), with the Basherawa. They number about 30,000.
6. Butawa (Mbotuwa, Mbutawa), with the Kudawa and Ningawa. They number about 15,000, of whom half are Moslems.
7. Chawai (Atsam), with the Irigwe (Aregwa, Irrigwe, Rigwe). They number about 25,000.
8. Dakakari (Dakarawa), embracing the Bangawa, Fakawa, Kelawa, and Liliwa subtribes. They number about 65,000.
9. Galim, with the Ndoren and Suga. This small remnant group was separated from the kindred Mambila by the Fulani invasion.
10. Gure (Guri), with the Dungi (Dwingi) and Kahugu. They number about 6,000.
11. Jarawa (Jar), with the Badawa, Bamberawa (Bambaro), Bankalawa, and Barawa (Mbarawa). This group numbers about 100,000 and is Islamized to a slight extent.
12. Jerawa, with the Amap (Amo), Buji (Bujawa), Chara (Fachara, Pakara, Teria), Chokobo, Gusuwa (Gussum, Ibau), Janji (Jenji), Piti (Pitti), Rebinawa (Narabuna), Ribam, Rukuba, Sangawa, and Taurawa. They number about 50,000.
13. Jibu (Dschubu, Jubu). They number about 5,000.
14. Jukun (Jukon, Kororofawa), with the Bashar, Kona, and other remnant groups in the north. They number about 30,000.
15. Kadara (Adara), with the Ajure (Kajuru) and Kuturmi (Ada). They number about 25,000.
16. Kamberi (Kambali, Kambari), with the kindred Achifawa (Atshefa) and Dukawa. They number about 85,000.
17. Kamuku, with the Baushi, Ngwoi, Pongo (Arringeu), and Uru. They number about 25,000.
18. Katab, with the Ataka, Ikulu (Ikolu), Jaba (Ham), Kachicheri, Kagoma, Kagoro (Agolik), Kaje (Baju, Kache, Kajji), Kamantan, Kaninkon (Tum), Lungu (Adong), and Morwa (Asolio, Moroa). They number about 115,000.

19. Kentu (Kyato, Kyeto), with the Nyidu (Nidu, Nyivu). They number about 5,000, of whom a considerable proportion are Moslems.
20. Kurama, with the Binawa, Kaibi, Kiballo, Kinuku, Kitimi, Kono, Rishuwa, Rumaiya, Ruruma, and Srubu. They number about 25,000.
21. Mada, with the Aike, Ayu (Ayob), Egon (Eggon, Hill Mada), Lindiri, Ninzam (Sanga), Numana (Numuna), and Nungu (Lungu). Some of these people, who number in all about 100,000, may possibly speak languages of the Kwa subfamily.
22. Mama, with the Kaleri. They number about 15,000.
23. Mambila (Torbi), with the Abo (Abong), Daga, Guroji, Kamkam, Magu, and Wawa (Baba, Warwar). They number about 25,000.
24. Mbula (Bula, Bulla), with the kindred Bari (Bare). They number about 15,000.
25. Ndoro. This tribe numbers about 5,000.
26. Reshe (Bareshe, Gungawa). This tribe numbers about 15,000.
27. Tigon (Tigum, Tugong, Tugun, Tukum), embracing the Ashaku (Atsuku), Mbembe (Dumbo), Mfumte (Kaka, Kaka-Banjo), Misaje (Metcho), and Nama. They number about 15,000.
28. Tiv (Mitshi, Munshi), with the Iyon, Ugbe, and Utange. They number about 800,000.
29. Yergum (Yergam), with the Dollong, Sayirr, and Tarok (Talok). They number about 35,000.
30. Yeskwa (Jesko, Yankpa, Yasgua, Yesko). They number about 15,000.
31. Zuande (Bitare, Yukutare). This tribe numbers about 1,000.
32. Zumper (Djompra, Djumperi, Kutev, Mbarike, Zomper). They number about 15,000.

CHADIC PEOPLES

33. Angas (Angassawa), with the Ankwe, Bwol, Chip, Dimuk, Goram (Gworam), Gurka (Gerkawa), Jorto, Kwolla, Miriam (Merniang), Montol (Montoil), Pai, Ron (Baram, Baron), Seiyawa (Sayawa, Seawa), Sura, and Tal. They number slightly more than 200,000.
34. Bachama (Bashama), with the Demsa (Bata, Batta). They number about 15,000.
35. Bata (Batta), embracing the Bolki, Bulai, Gudo, Kofo, Malabu, Muleng, Njei (Jenge, Kobochi, Nyei, Nzangi, Zani), and Zumu (Jimo). This partially Islamized group numbers about 30,000.
36. Bura (Burra), with the Pabir (Babur, Barburr). This group numbers about 100,000. A few Pabir are Moslems.
37. Dera (Kanakuru). This slightly Islamized tribe numbers about 10,000.
38. Gerawa, with the Denawa, Galembawa, Gerumawa (Germawa), Gezawa, and Kirifawa. This group, numbering about 50,000, is slightly Islamized.
39. Gisiga (Gisohiga, Guissiga), with the Balda, Gauar, Mofu (Muffo), Musgoi (Musugeu), and Muturua (Moutou). A population figure of 15,000, reported in 1935, probably refers to the Gisiga tribe alone.
40. Gude (Cheke), with the Bana, Daba, Djimi, Gidder (Gidar, Guider), Hina, Holma, Kola, and the so-called "Fali" of Jilbu and Mubi. They number about 60,000.
41. Gwandara, with the Gade and the detached Nimbia. This group, numbering about 10,000, is not merely Chadic but specifically Hausa in language.
42. Hona, with the kindred Gabin. They number about 10,000.
43. Kapsiki, with the Baza, Hiji (Higi, Hill Margi), and Nkafa. They number about 25,000.
44. Margi (Marghi), with the kindred Chibak (Chibbuk, Cibak, Kibaku), Kilba,

Sukur (Sugur), and the so-called "Fali" of Wuba. This group numbers about 75,000 and is partially Islamized.
45. Matakam (Wula), with the Bulabai, Diele (Zele), Hide, Mabass, Mineo (Minew), Ndare, and Vusei. They number about 80,000.
46. Podokwo (Podogo), with the Mada, Molkwa, Mora, Muktale, Mukulehe, Sawa, Tala, Udjila, and Urzal. They number about 15,000.
47. Tangale, with the Billiri, Cham, Chongee, Chongwom, Dadiya, Kamu (Kamo), Lofa, Pero (Fero), Tula, Ture, and Waja. They number about 100,000.
48. Tuburi (Toubouri, Tubori, Tupuri). This tribe numbers about 65,000.
49. Wakura, embracing the Chikide, Gelebda, Gbuwhe, Hidkala, Kuvoko, Tur, Vemgo, Vizik, and Woga. They number about 60,000.
50. Warjawa (Warji), with the Afawa (Faawa, Paawa), Ajawa, Diryawa, Lipkawa, Miyawa, and Sirawa. They number about 40,000, of whom 10 per cent are Moslems.
51. Wurkum (Urku, Wuruku), including the Bandawa, Kulu, Pia (Piyawa), and Walo. This group, numbering about 45,000, is of heterogeneous linguistic composition. Though most of its members are Chadic, the Kulu are Bantoid.

EASTERN NIGRITIC PEOPLES

52. Chamba (Camba, Dschamba, Tsamba), including the Donga, Lekon (Laego, Leco), Mumbake, and Wom. They number about 20,000, of whom some 15 per cent are Moslems.
53. Daka (Dakha, Dekka), embracing the Dirrim, Gandole, Lamja, Taram, and Tsugu. They number about 5,000.
54. Jen, with the kindred Munga. They number about 1,000.
55. Kam. This tribe numbers about 5,000.
56. Longuda (Nunguda). This tribe numbers about 15,000.
57. Mumuye, with the kindred Gengle, Gola (Gomla, Gori), Kugama, Kumba, Teme, Waka, Yendang (Yandan), Yofo, and Zinna (Zin). They number about 70,000.
58. Vere (Werre), embracing the Bai, Boi, Koma, Lima, Marki, Sablo, Togi (Tuki), Vomni, and Zango. They number about 15,000.
59. Yungur (Binna, Yunguru), with the Banga, Betta, Handa, Kwotba, Lala, Libo, Mboi (Mboyi), Pella, Pirra, Roba, Subktu, Tambo, and Yang. They number about 25,000.

KWA PEOPLES

60. Gbari (Goale, Gwali, Gwari). They number about 180,000 and are linguistically akin to the Nupe. The majority are Moslems.
61. Koro (Korro), embracing the Ache (Koro Ache), Huntu (Koro Funtu, Koron Huntu), Iya (Koron Iya), Zani (Koron Zani), and Zuba. This group, numbering about 20,000, is slightly Islamized, and most of its members speak dialects of Gbari.

The Plateau Nigerians are sedentary tillers, practicing shifting hoe cultivation with fallowing and crop rotation. They grow practically all the plants of the Sudanic complex and have added onions from Southwest Asia, eleusine from Ethiopia, bananas, rice, taro, and yams from Southeast Asia, and maize, manioc, peanuts, peppers, pumpkins, sweet potatoes, tobacco, and tomatoes from America. The three Sudanic cereals—

sorghum, millet, and fonio—constitute the staples almost everywhere. They receive their principal support from the introduced grains and from tubers and root crops, both native and borrowed.

Most tribes, except in the extreme south, keep a few cattle, mainly of a dwarf humpless breed. They value these, amongst other reasons, for their manure, which they commonly use as fertilizer, but they almost never milk them except under direct Fulani influence. Goats, sheep, dogs (often eaten), and chickens are practically universal, and most groups keep a few horses for riding. Apiculture occurs sporadically. Hunting, fishing, and gathering, though widely practiced, rarely contribute substantially to the diet. Trade is not highly developed, but regular markets are reported for a number of groups. The men hunt, tend livestock, and do all or most of the fishing, except among the Kadara and Kamberi. Both sexes, however, share in agricultural labor, with their relative participation shifting slightly from tribe to tribe.

Compact villages, often protected by walls or hedges, constitute the prevailing settlement pattern, but clusters of smaller, discrete hamlets are common in the northeast, and neighborhoods of dispersed homesteads predominate among the Birom, Tiv, Yergum, and some Angas groups. The riverain Reshe live in quadrangular pile dwellings, but all other peoples occupy round huts with conical thatched roofs and cylindrical walls of mud or of wattle and daub, typically grouped in enclosed family compounds. This house type, however, is often modified in particular localities. Among the Katab, for example, the ground plan is oval rather than round, and the roof is asymmetrical with its peak in the rear. Angas, Borrom, Mada, Mama, and Yeskwa dwellings have two concentric walls, the inner cylinder serving as a granary and the space between it and the outer wall as living quarters. The Gisiga construct houses in pairs with an enclosed hall connecting them.

Political authority at the local level is usually vested in a hereditary headman assisted by a council of elders. The sources give no hint of a special ritual relationship between the headman and the land such as prevails among the Voltaic peoples and in vestigial form among the Nuclear Mande. About a third of the peoples of the area lack completely any political integration above the local level. Another third are organized under petty paramount chiefs over subtribes or small districts. The remaining third are subject, directly or indirectly, to Fulani emirs.

In the entire province only the Jukun ever developed a genuinely complex state. After a period of expansion in the seventeenth century, the state declined and was finally conquered by the Fulani early in the nineteenth century. At its head stood a typical divine king, the representative of and mediator with the gods. His person was sacred; his feet could not touch the ground, and he spoke to others only from behind a screen. Theoretically he enjoyed absolute power and could appropriate any property or woman he desired. If, however, he failed in his primary function of controlling the forces of nature—as was evidenced if he coughed, or sneezed, or became ill, or fell from his horse—he was put to death, and in no event was he permitted to reign for more than seven years. He ruled with the aid of a council composed of titled members of the royal family, who also served as provincial governors and collected tribute, but who could not be removed from office. In addition to household officials like a chief steward, a chief chamberlain, a chief groom, and a supervisor of the royal harem, the monarch was served by a prime minister, a chief priest, a military commander in chief, and a special minister, known as the Abun Achuwo, whose duty it was to kill the king and choose his successor. Two female figures held positions of special status and respect—the Queen-Mother, a widow of the previous monarch, and the Queen-Sister, a sister of the former king who had authority over all the women at the court.

Slavery is universal, and debt slavery common. In addition to war captives, the northern tribes frequently enslave criminals and suspected witches. Differentiated ruling classes are reported only for the Angas, Bata, Dera, Gude, Jukun, Ndoro, and Tigon. In a few Chadic groups, i.e., the Bachama, Bata, Gude, Margi, and Matakam, smiths form an endogamous but not a despised caste. Age-grades assume social importance only among the Kadara. Circumcision occurs regularly among the Angas, Birom, Butawa, Chamba, Chawai, Gerawa, Gude, Gure, Gwandara, Jarawa, Jerawa, Jibu, Kadara, Katab, Kurama, Mada, Mambila, Ndoro, Reshe, Tiv, Vere, Warjawa, and Zumper, and sporadically in several other tribes; but clitoridectomy is attested only for the Mada, Yeskwa, and some Basa and Gwandara. Nearly all groups formerly practiced headhunting, which the sources specifically deny only for the Borrom, Bura, Dera, and Hona. Cannibalism prevailed among the Jarawa, Jerawa, Longuda, Mama, Mambila, Ndoro, Tangale, Tigon, Warjawa, Yergum, and Zumper and in some subtribes of the Angas, Birom, Mada, and Mumuye.

Marriage involves a prolonged period of agricultural bride-service, coupled with gifts or a modest bride-price, in three-fourths of the tribes of the area. The requirement of service is omitted only in groups which have adopted marriage by exchange or a truly substantial bride-price. Monogamy—a rare phenomenon among African Negroes—prevails among the Daka and Jibu, but all other tribes permit polygyny and usually practice it extensively, though only in the nonsororal form. The first wife enjoys a special status, but the co-wives each have a separate hut and the husband rotates among them. The household is typically an extended family occupying a compound, but among the Bura, Kapsiki, Podokwo, and Yergum extended families either do not occur or exist only as non-residential units. Except among the Jen, Jibu, Ndoro, and Zuande, who prefer marriage with a cross-cousin, incest taboos prevent unions with any first cousin. The levirate is preferential, especially with the widow of an elder brother, but the sororate is rare and usually expressly forbidden.

One unique feature especially characterizes the marriage customs of most Plateau Nigerians, being reported from the Kamberi in the west to the Margi in the east and apparently absent only among the Chadic tribes of the extreme east and among the Macro-Bantu tribes in the south. This is the extraordinary latitude allowed to a married woman in eloping with a new husband. The situation among the Katab and their neighbors, being particularly well described, may serve as an example, but it is closely paralleled in many other groups. A woman marries her first husband in return for a small bride-price paid to her father. Thereafter she is free, with the consent of her parents, to elope with a man from some other village. The latter is obligated only to make the customary marriage payments to her father, but not to recompense her first husband—except, in a few tribes, when she has not yet borne him a child. She may repeat this procedure a number of times, but in no case does it terminate the previous unions. Whenever a woman visits the village of a former husband, she resumes her marital relations with him for the time being. The entire social structure reflects these arrangements. No person of either sex can take a spouse, either primary or secondary, from among the members or residents of his own local community. Other communities, or sometimes particular segments thereof, are divided into two groups. From one of these a primary spouse can be taken, but never a secondary spouse. The other includes localities into which an original marriage is strictly forbidden but whose residents are freely available for secondary elopements.

Social organization on the Nigerian plateau presents a complex checkerboard of contrasting patterns. Fortunately the ethnographic sources contain reasonably satisfactory information on this subject for all groups save the Afusare, Angas, Butawa, Dakakari, Gerawa, Gisiga, Gwandara, Jarawa, Kamberi, Koro, Mama, Reshe, Tuburi, Wakura, Yergum, Yeskwa, and Zumper. Data on the other forty-four tribes enable us to reconstruct with a high degree of assurance not only the system which originally prevailed in the province but also the various steps by which it has been modified to produce the forms occurring today.

The Daka, Gure, Kam, and Ndoro still retain the essential features of the presumptive original structure, namely, matrilineal descent, inheritance, and succession, premarital bride-service with nominal gifts or a very small bride-price, avunculocal residence and avuncuclans, and cousin terminology of the Crow type. The sole reported deviation from this pattern is the Hawaiian cousin terms of the Gure, due perhaps to the influence of the Kahugu subtribe, who have made the transition to patrilineal descent.

Modification of this system, involving a shift to patrilocal residence, occurred as a result of two innovations in the mode of marriage—either an increase in the bride-price to a substantial amount or the adoption of preferential marriage by the exchange of sisters. Since these had somewhat different effects, we shall consider them separately.

Sister exchange may well have been developed as a device to stabilize marital unions, since a woman's relatives would naturally be less likely to sanction her elopement if they were to lose thereby the woman for whom she had been exchanged. At any rate, almost the only tribes which do not permit unrestricted elopement are those which have adopted sister exchange—the Basa, Batu, Kentu, Mambila, Tiv, Wurkum, and Zumper in the south and an occasional subtribe or local group elsewhere. All these tribes permit a man who has no sister or other close female relative available for exchange to obtain a wife in the older fashion by paying a nominal bride-price. This, however, gives the husband only a right of cohabitation, not a claim to the children, who are affiliated with the kin group from which their mother came. The sons of such unions normally go to live with their maternal uncles and bring their wives there when they marry, i.e., in avunculocal residence. Since matrilineal descent has yielded precedence to the patrilineal rule, cousin terms of the Crow type have proved nonfunctional and have been abandoned in favor of Hawaiian terminology, as is specifically attested for the Kentu and Tiv.

The tribes following the alternative course of increasing the bride-price have in some instances failed to make the complete transition to patrilocal residence. Thus the Jibu, Jukun, and Vere still adhere to avunculocal residence in 50 per cent or more of all marriages. Their extended families consequently exhibit a mixed composition, lacking a central core of either matrilineally or patrilineally related males. This has destroyed the local basis for matrilineal descent without providing one for the development of patrilineal affiliation, with the result that all three tribes are today strictly bilateral. Cousin terminology has shifted to the Hawaiian pattern among the Jibu and Jukun, although the Vere have terms of the Iroquois type, doubtless a survival from their earlier unilinear phase.

All the other tribes have adopted patrilineal descent. The Chamba, Dera, and Longuda, however, have done so without abandoning their earlier matrilineal kin groups, and are thus characterized by double descent. Understandably enough, the Chamba and Longuda retain their old Crow cousin terms, since these have not lost their supportive matrilineal

framework. All other groups have completed the transition to the patrilineate. The Bata, Chawai, Hona, Jerawa, Katab, Margi, Mumuye, Tangale, and Yungur, in doing so, have made the expected shift to the
Hawaiian kinship pattern. Six tribes have even achieved new types of
cousin terminology inherently adapted to patrilineal descent—the Bura
and Kurama with an Iroquois pattern and the Birom, Gbari, Kadara, and
Matakam with Omaha terminology.

This reconstruction can by no means be discounted as speculative since
the bilateral and patrilineal societies of the area, practically without exception, still display within their own social structures a variety of elements that point specifically to matrilineal antecedents. Several of these
deserve special notice. Significant traces of matrilineal inheritance survive
among the Bachama, Jibu, Jukun, Kentu, Mambila, Mbula, Tigon, Vere,
Yergum, and Yungur. Avunculocal residence still prevails, at least as a
patterned alternative, among the Bachama, Bata, Chawai, Gwandara,
Hona, Jibu, Jukun, Kadara, Katab, Kentu, Kurama, Mambila, Margi,
Mbula, Mumuye, Tigon, Tiv, Vere, Wurkum, Yergum, Yeskwa, and
Yungur. Submerged traces of matrilineal affiliation, including matrilineal exogamy, the matrilineal descent of totems, and the ascription of
responsibility for blood vengeance and witchcraft exclusively to rela-
tives in the female line, are specifically attested for the Bachama, Batu,
Butawa, Chawai, Jen, Jibu, Kapsiki, Katab, Mambila, Mbula, Vere,
Wurkum, and Yungur. It can scarcely be doubted, therefore, that the
Plateau Nigerians were formerly characterized by social systems of a
matrilineal and avunculocal type.

Linguistic relationships in this province hold a special importance for
the understanding of African culture history. The Bantoid subfamily of
the Nigritic stock breaks down into a number of distinct divisions. One
of these, including such tribes as the Anyang, Boki, Ekoi, Ibibio, and Yako,
is located in adjacent Southern Nigeria, where it extends to the Guinea
coast. Of those confined to the present area, one embraces the Batu,
Galim, Jarawa, Mambila, Mbula, Ndoro, Tiv, and Zuande tribes. This
may be termed the Macro-Bantu division, since all the far-flung Bantu
languages, which extend from the borders of the Plateau Nigerian province eastward to Kenya and southward to Natal, resolve themselves
upon analysis, as Greenberg has shown, into a single branch of this division and are strictly coordinate, for instance, with Galim-Mambila or
with Tiv. Far from being a linguistic stock in its own right, Bantu is
merely one branch of one of several divisions of one of seven major subfamilies of the Nigritic stock.

Since genetic relationships in language invariably reflect historical contacts and movements, the established facts in the present case force us
inescapably to a historical conclusion of the utmost significance, namely,

that the Bantu peoples originated in the area now under discussion, and specifically in its southern part, where most of the tribes with the most closely cognate languages still reside. Moreover, the degree of linguistic differentiation indicates that they originated not much more than 2,000 years ago, since which time the Bantu peoples have undergone an extraordinary explosive expansion. It will be the task of Chapters 35 to 39 and 44 to 51 to explain, date, and trace this remarkable spread. For the present it must suffice merely to call attention to the fact and to draw from it one very important deduction.

If the Bantu originated on the Nigerian plateau, they must have started their dispersion with the type of culture and social organization then characteristic of this area. Since they have subsequently faced vast differences in geographic environments and cultural contacts, which have inevitably wrought substantial changes, whereas conditions have apparently remained far more static in the comparative isolation of the Nigerian plateau, it is probable that the related peoples who have stayed behind have preserved a number of the characteristics of original Bantu culture. It is a reasonable working hypothesis, for example, that the Bantu began their widespread dispersal with an avunculocal and matrilineal social system such as we have reconstructed for their nearest kinsmen.

Selected Bibliography

Abraham, R. C. *The Tiv People*. Lagos, 1933.

Ames, C. G. *Gazetteer of the Plateau Province*. Jos, 1934.

Best, O. H. Burmawa of Kanam. Unpublished ms. [Borrom].

Bohannan, L., and P. Bohannan. *The Tiv of Central Nigeria*. London, 1953.

Bohannan, P. Tiv Farm and Settlement. *CRS*, 15:1–87. 1954.

Clifford, M. Notes on the Bassa-Komo Tribe. *Man*, 44:107–116. 1944. [Basa].

Downes, R. M. *The Tiv Tribe*. Kaduna, 1933.

East, R., ed. *Akiga's Story*. London, 1939. [Tiv].

Eustace, R. B. B. Report on the Hill Pagans of the Dikwa Division. Unpublished ms. [Wakura].

Fegan, E. S. Some Notes on the Bachama Tribe. *JAS*, 29:269–279, 376–400. 1930.

Fitzpatrick, J. F. J. Some Notes on the Kwolla District and Its Tribes. *JAS*, 10:16–52, 213–221. 1910. [Angas and Yergum].

Gunn, H. D. *Peoples of the Plateau Area of Northern Nigeria*. London, 1953. [Afusare, Birom, Chawai, and Jerawa].

———. *Pagan Peoples of the Central Area of Northern Nigeria*. London, 1956. [Butawa, Gure, Kadara, Katab, Kurama, and Warjawa].

Hall, J. S. Religion, Myth and Magic in Tangale. Unpublished ms.

Harris, P. G. Notes on Yauri. *JRAI*, 60:283–334. 1930. [Reshe].

———. Notes on the Dakarkari Peoples. *JRAI*, 68:113–152. 1938.

Helser, A. D. *In Sunny Nigeria*. New York, 1926. [Bura].

Hinderling, P. Versuch einer Analyse der sozialen Struktur der Matakam. *Africa*, 25:405–426. 1955.

Lamouroux, R. La région du Toubouri. *Anthropologie*, 24:679–692. 1913.

Lembezat, B. Kirdi. *MIFCC*, 3:1–95. 1950.
——. *Mukulehe*. Paris, 1952. [Podokwo].
MacBride, D. F. H. Yungur District. Unpublished ms.
Macdonald-Smith, S. Report on the Koro Tribe. Unpublished ms.
Mathews, A. B. Mumuye District. Unpublished ms.
Meek, C. K. *The Northern Tribes of Nigeria*. 2 vols. London, 1925.
——. The Katab and Their Neighbors. *JAS*, 27:104–126, 269–280, 364–379; 28:43–54.
    1928–1929.
——. *A Sudanese Kingdom*. London, 1931. [Jukun].
——. *Tribal Studies in Northern Nigeria*. 2 vols. London, 1931. [Invaluable brief
    accounts of many tribes].
——. The Kulū in Northern Nigeria. *Africa*, 7:257–269. 1934. [Wurkum].
Monckton, G. C. Anthropological Notes on the Gerkawa Tribe. Unpublished ms.
    [Angas].
Percival, D. H. The Mambila Area. Unpublished ms.
Rowling, C. W. Marghi District Assessment. Unpublished ms.
Shaw, J. H. The Mubi Area of Adamawa Province. Unpublished ms. [Gude].
Smith, M. G. Secondary Marriage in Northern Nigeria. *Africa*, 23:298–323. 1953.
    [Kadara and Katab].
——. The Social Structure of the Northern Kadara. Unpublished ms.
——. Social Organisation and Economy of the Kagoro. Unpublished ms. [Katab].
Temple, O. *Notes on the Tribes, Provinces, Emirates and States of the Northern
    Provinces of Nigeria*, ed. C. L. Temple. 2d edit. Lagos, 1922.
Tremearne, A. J. N. Notes on the Kagoro and Other Nigerian Head-Hunters. *JRAI*,
    42:136–199. 1912. [Katab].
——. *The Tailed Head-Hunters of Nigeria*. London, 1912. [Katab].
Varvill, M. H. Report of Yeskwa District. Unpublished ms.
Wilson-Haffenden, J. R. Anthropological Notes on the Yeskwa Tribe. Unpublished
    ms.
Woodhouse, C. A. Some Account of the Inhabitants of the Waja District. *JAS*,
    23:110–121, 194–207. 1924. [Tangale].

PART FOUR
NORTH AFRICAN AGRICULTURAL CIVILIZATION

14

Ancient Egyptians

Around 5000 B.C., when the Negroes of the upper Niger were apparently making their first experiments with the cultivation of plants, the inhabitants of the lower Nile were taking a parallel step. Sebilian, a Mesolithic hunting and gathering culture, was being replaced by Neolithic cultures, variously called Merimdean, Fayum, Tasian, and Bedarian, borne by people indistinguishable in physical type from the later Dynastic Egyptians. From adjacent Southwest Asia, where agriculture and animal domestication had already been practiced for perhaps 2,000 years, they borrowed the means and techniques of food production and freed themselves from their earlier dependence upon food gathering. Radiocarbon dating shows that they had made this advance by 4500 B.C.

From the Egyptian Neolithic culture developed the so-called Predynastic cultures—Amration, Gerzean, and Semainian—and then, around 3000 B.C., the civilization of Dynastic Egypt, marked by a further revolutionary advance to life in cities, differentiated manufactures, extensive trade, and the emergence of complex political institutions. A peak was reached during the Old Kingdom (ca. 2900–2550 B.C.) under the III and IV dynasties. After a recession, during which occurred the transition from the Copper to the Bronze Age, civilization again flowered in the Middle Kingdom (ca. 2160–1780 B.C.) under the XI and XII dynasties. The third and greatest climax came in the New Kingdom or Empire (ca. 1580–1100 B.C.) under the XVIII to XX dynasties. Gradual deterioration followed, broken temporarily by the Saite Revival under the XXVI dynasty (ca.

663–525 B.C.). In 332 B.C. Egypt fell to Alexander the Great, bringing to a close the Pharaonic period of Egyptian history and inaugurating the Greco-Roman period.

Egypt—being, in geographical terms, essentially an elongated river oasis through a desert—could contribute little out of her own plant and animal resources to the Neolithic revolution. She derived her domesticated species largely from parts of the Fertile Crescent lying to the northeast. We shall nevertheless designate them collectively as the Egyptian complex since, from the point of view of the rest of Africa, Egypt was the funnel for nearly all contributions from Southwest Asia, whatever their specific point of origin, and the center from which they spread westward and southward to other parts of the continent. In enumerating below the elements of the Egyptian complex, we shall indicate for each the probable region of origin and time of adoption and shall exclude all elements introduced after the close of the Pharaonic period, since their spread has been due to other historical forces and can therefore give no measure of the influence of Egyptian civilization upon other African peoples.

CEREAL GRAINS

Barley (*Hordeum vulgare* and *H. distichum*). Of Middle Eastern origin, appearing in Egypt from the very beginning of the Neolithic period.

Wheat (*Triticum vulgare*), including emmer (*T. dicoccum*) and spelt (*T. spelta*). This Middle Eastern grain likewise dates from the earliest Neolithic period in Egypt.

LEGUMES AND FORAGE CROPS

Alfalfa, or lucerne (*Medicago sativa*). Middle Eastern in origin.

Broad bean (*Vicia faba* or *Faba vulgaris*). Of either Mediterranean or Middle Eastern origin, this legume appears in Egypt by at least 2000 B.C.

Chick pea (*Cicer arietinum*). This Middle Eastern crop appears in Egypt relatively late in the Pharaonic period.

Chickling vetch (*Lathyrus sativus*). This Middle Eastern plant is late and may actually not have reached Egypt until the Greco-Roman period.

Clover (*Trifolium alexandrinum*). An indigenous Egyptian cultigen but relatively late.

Lentil (*Lens esculenta* or *Ervum lens*). This Middle Eastern plant reached Egypt no later than 2000 B.C.

Lupine (*Lupinus termis*). An indigenous Egyptian cultigen.

Pea, or garden pea (*Pisum sativum*). An early introduction from the Mediterranean or the Middle East.

Vetch (*Vicia sativa*). Introduced from the Middle East.

TUBERS AND ROOT CROPS

Beet (*Beta vulgaris*). This Mediterranean plant is recorded in Egypt early in the second millennium B.C.

Chufa, or earth almond (*Cyperus esculenta*). An indigenous Egyptian cultigen.
Onion (*Allium cepa*). This Middle Eastern plant appears in Egypt before 3000 B.C.
Parsnip (*Pastinaca sativa*). Mediterranean in origin, and perhaps late.
Radish (*Raphanus sativus*). This Middle Eastern root crop, which was both eaten and used as a source of oil, appears in Egypt by at least 2900 B.C.

LEAF AND STALK VEGETABLES

Artichoke (*Cynara scolymus*). A Mediterranean plant, possibly introduced into Egypt in Greco-Roman rather than Pharaonic times.
Asparagus (*Asparagus officinalis*). Mediterranean in origin, this plant reached Egypt by at least the first half of the third millennium B.C.
Cabbage (*Brassica oleracea*). This Mediterranean plant was not introduced into Egypt until the sixth century B.C. The cabbage differs from other cultivated species of the genus *Brassica* in the number of its chromosomes, having nine whereas black mustard has eight, the turnip ten, and rape eighteen.
Celery (*Apium graveolens*). This Mediterranean plant first appears in Egypt late in the second millennium B.C.
Endive (*Cichorium endivia*). This Mediterranean plant is the "bitter herbs" of ancient Palestine.
Lettuce (*Lactuca sativa*). This Middle Eastern plant, apparently first cultivated for the oil in its seeds, dates in Egypt from at least the early third millennium B.C.

VINE AND GROUND FRUITS

Grape, or vine (*Vitis vinifera*). This Middle Eastern plant dates from the earliest Dynastic period in Egypt.
Melon, or cantaloupe (*Cucumis melo*). This plant was introduced from the Middle East by at least 2000 B.C.

TREE FRUITS

Almond (*Amygdalus communis*). Introduced from the Middle East about 1500 B.C.
Apple (*Malus pumila* or *Pyrus malus*). Middle Eastern in origin and introduced about 1500 B.C.
Date palm (*Phoenix dactylifera*). An early introduction from southern Arabia.
Fig (*Ficus carica*). This Middle Eastern plant reached Egypt about 2000 B.C.
Mimusops (*Mimusops schimperi*). Indigenous to Egypt, this tree was cultivated from the third millennium B.C.
Mulberry (*Morus nigra*). Middle Eastern in origin and introduced relatively late.
Pomegranate (*Punica granatum*). This Middle Eastern plant is first attested in Egypt about 1500 B.C.

CONDIMENTS AND INDULGENTS

Anise (*Pimpinella anisum*). Mediterranean in origin.
Black caraway (*Nigella sativa*). Of Mediterranean origin.

Caraway (*Carum carui*). Mediterranean in origin.

Chive (*Allium schoenoprasum*). Introduced into Egypt from the Middle East.

Coriander (*Coriandrum sativum*). This Middle Eastern plant was introduced into Egypt about 1000 B.C.

Cumin (*Cuminum cyminum*). Probably Mediterranean in origin.

Dill (*Anethum graveolens*). Of Mediterranean origin.

Fennel (*Foeniculum vulgare*). Mediterranean in origin.

Garlic (*Allium sativum*). This Middle Eastern plant reached Egypt by at least the beginning of the third millennium B.C.

Leek (*Allium porrum*). Middle Eastern in origin and very early in Egypt.

Opium poppy (*Papaver somniferum*). Middle Eastern in origin and probably very early since it also appears among the Neolithic lake dwellers of Switzerland.

OIL AND DYE PLANTS

Flax (*Linum usitatissimum*). Probably an indigenous Egyptian cultigen. It is first attested in the V dynasty, when it was used primarily for linseed oil. After the XII dynasty it was also used for its fibers.

Henna (*Lawsonia inermis* or *L. alba*). Introduced from India during the second millennium B.C.

Olive (*Olea europea*). Mediterranean in origin, its fruit was used from very early times as a major source of oil.

Rape (*Brassica napus*). A Mediterranean plant, probably first used for its oil.

Saffron (*Crocus sativa*). This dye plant was introduced from the Middle East in late Pharaonic times.

DOMESTIC ANIMALS

Cat (*Felis domestica*). Probably indigenous in Egypt, where it appears first to have been domesticated around 2000 B.C.

Cattle (*Bos taurus* and *B. indicus*). Long-horned cattle date from earliest Neolithic times in Egypt, and short-horned cattle are nearly as early. The humped zebu breed was introduced in the sixteenth century B.C.

Chicken, or barnyard fowl (*Gallus domesticus*). Originally domesticated in Southeast Asia, the chicken was introduced into Egypt about 1450 B.C. and independently into East Africa about a thousand years later.

Goat (*Caprus hircus*). Dates from at least the Predynastic period in Egypt.

Goose (*Anser* sp.). Occurs very early in Egypt.

Honeybee (*Apis mellifera*).

Horse (*Equus caballus*). Introduced into Egypt from Central Asia just before the middle of the second millennium B.C.

Mallard duck (*Anas boschas*). Occurs very early in Egypt.

Pig (*Sus scrofa*). Dates from the earliest Neolithic period in Egypt.

Pigeon, or dove (*Columba* sp.).

Sheep (*Ovis aries*). The hairy, flat-tailed sheep dates from the earliest Neolithic in Egypt. Woolly sheep were introduced from the Middle East about 2000 B.C.

The camel, despite is popular association with the pyramids, did not reach Egypt until the Roman period. On the other hand the donkey or ass (*Equus asinus*), though probably first domesticated in Ethiopia, was adopted by the Egyptians early in the third millennium B.C. To complete the roster of plants cultivated in Pharaonic Egypt there should be added several which do not appear in the above list because they originated in Ethiopia or the Sudan or because they were independently introduced from India into Negro Africa.

Castor (*Ricinus communis*). Borrowed at an early date from Ethiopia.

Cotton (*Gossypium herbaceum*). This Sudanic cultigen reached Egypt in the sixth century B.C.

Cress (*Lepidium sativum*). Ethiopian in origin, this plant probably reached Egypt in Pharaonic times, though it is not actually attested until the second century B.C.

Gourd (*Lagenaria vulgaris*). This Sudanic plant spread to Egypt during the second millennium B.C.

Gram or mung bean (*Phaseolus aureus* and *P. mungo*). A fairly early introduction from India.

Safflower (*Carthamus tinctorius*). This plant, used both as a dye and for oil, was introduced into Egypt from Ethiopia about 1500 B.C.

Tamarind (*Tamarindus indica*). Introduced at an early period from the Sudan.

Watermelon (*Citrullus vulgaris*). This Sudanic plant spread to Egypt in the second millennium B.C.

Egyptian agriculture depended upon the waters of the Nile and the fertilizing silt deposited by its annual inundations. Retaining basins conserved water, and mechanical appliances like water wheels and the shadoof lifted it into irrigation ditches which carried it to the fields. The dependable and carefully regulated water supply, the automatic annual renewal of the soil's fertility, and the use of plows drawn by oxen resulted in extremely intensive cultivation and high productivity. Cereal grains, particularly wheat, made the chief contribution to subsistence, followed in importance by the date palm, flax, and an array of legumes and forage crops. These last permitted animal husbandry, despite the desert environment, to play a significant auxiliary role in the economy. Cattle, sheep, and goats, the principal domesticated species, provided meat, hides, wool, and milk, from which butter and cheese were prepared. Oxen were used for draft, donkeys as beasts of burden, and horses eventually to some extent as riding animals. The pig had a curious history in Egypt. From a position of extreme importance at the beginning of the Neolithic period it gradually declined in significance, and records from the Dynastic period reveal the development of an increasing prejudice against it as an unclean animal.

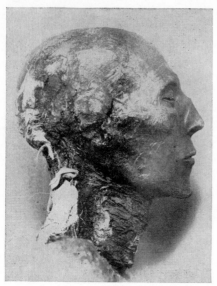

Mummified Head of Pharaoh Seti I of the XIX Dynasty. (Courtesy of the Peabody Museum of Archaeology and Ethnology, Harvard University.)

With the establishment of agriculture and animal husbandry, hunting and gathering became insignificant as a source of food, although fishing retained some minor importance. Handicraft specialization and trade, however, expanded enormously. Markets were general, and caravan routes radiated out in all directions. In the division of labor by sex the men did the herding, milking, and most of the agricultural labor.

There is no need to recapitulate here the more spectacular aspects of ancient Egyptian civilization—the monumental art and architecture, the extraordinarily expert craftsmanship, the complex hierarchy of gods with animal attributes, the familiar but much overrated attempt to institute monotheism, and the morose preoccupation with death exemplified by mummification and the cult of Osiris. These matters are widely known, and fully reported in numerous scholarly and popular works, for the Egyptians were a literate nation, and their hieroglyphic inscriptions and papyri have left us a record of their life and thought infinitely richer than that of any other African people of the past.

We must, however, examine those aspects of culture which this volume attempts to cover for other parts of Africa, so that we may be able later to assess the influence of ancient Egyptian civilization elsewhere in the continent. This impact is to be sought first of all, of course, in the cultures of the peoples who bordered Pharaonic Egypt. These were four in number: the Berbers, who inhabited the Mediterranean coast and adjacent desert oases immediately to the west; the Beja, who occupied the arid region lying between the Nile Valley and the Red Sea to the southeast; the Nubians, who dwelt along the Nile to the south beyond Wadi Halfa; and, across a stretch of uninhabitable desert to the southwest, the Teda of Fezzan and Tibesti. The last two were Negro peoples with completely alien languages. The Berbers and Beja, however, were Caucasoid, like the Egyptians, and the three peoples spoke languages of different subfamilies of the same Hamitic stock, namely Berber, Cushitic, and Egyptian. Traces of borrowing from Pharaonic civilization discovered in the cultures of these neighboring groups may then be pursued into other areas as far as the evidence leads.

The ancient Egyptians laid no stress on premarital chastity. Marriages were arranged by parents, sometimes in childhood. Unions between full brothers and sisters were preferred in the royal family and also occurred among the nobility, but their frequency is difficult to determine because of the custom of applying the term "sister" to a wife or sweetheart, even though she was not actually related. Since uncles also commonly married their nieces in the upper classes, it is probable that even the lower classes did not extend incest taboos to first cousins. Marriages between non-kin seem to have involved some kind of a property transaction, presumably a modest bride-price. Monogamy strongly predominated. Polyandry did not occur, and polygyny was rare, although harems of concubines were common in the higher official circles. A newly married couple established an independent household, apparently in neolocal residence. Descent seems clearly to have been bilateral, even though a number of authorities have inferred matrilineal descent from the fact that funerary inscriptions more often cite the mother's name than the father's. Inherited family surnames were definitely lacking, and the sources yield no intimation of extended families, lineages, sibs, or clans.

The Egyptians lived in compact villages, towns, and cities, in which the buildings were aligned on streets. They built stately palaces and temples of stone masonry, but the bulk of the population inhabited rectangular dwellings with walls of sun-dried brick and flat roofs. These commonly had two stories, sometimes more, and faced on a courtyard, of which walls often formed one or more sides. Settlements extended thickly along the banks and on the delta of the Nile River over the lower 600 miles of its course. The population of ancient Egypt has been variously estimated at between 2 and 7 million people.

The country, during most of its long history, was politically organized in a single, unified bureaucratic state under a despotic king or pharaoh. The ruler, occasionally a woman, was regarded as a god and the son of a god, and in recognition of his divinity all persons prostrated themselves in his presence. In theory he possessed absolute power, but actually, of course, his kinsmen, his officials, the army, and the priesthood exerted a substantial check over its exercise. Among the insignia of his high office he carried a scepter or mace, wore an animal tail around his waist, and bore on his head the uraeus or double crown of Upper and Lower Egypt. A ruler was succeeded ideally by his eldest son, but civil wars between rival claimants and even usurpations by powerful commoners occurred with considerable frequency.

The pharaoh resided in a capital city, where he maintained an elaborate court and indulged himself in conspicuous consumption, constructing huge monuments, endowing temples, and distributing largesse among those who rendered him loyal service. He surrounded himself with personal attendants, including bodyguards, fanbearers, butlers, scribes, a "bearer of the royal stool," an "overseer of the royal wardrobe," a "stable master of the great stable," an "overseer of the palace," a "superintendent of the royal chamberlains," and a "great steward of the Lord of the Two Lands," who was charged with the administration of the king's personal landed estates. Although the pharaoh maintained harems of concubines in various cities, he had but one legitimate Queen-Consort, commonly his own sister or half sister but sometimes a foreign princess or even a commoner. She kept a separate household and was endowed with independent landed estates administered by her own stewards. On the death of the king she preserved her independent status as the Queen-Mother of the new ruler.

At the head of the administrative hierarchy stood a vizier, or prime minister, who also served as chief justice of the kingdom and as governor of the capital city. During the New Empire, to which our data primarily pertain, there were commonly separate viziers for Upper and Lower Egypt, both reporting daily to the pharaoh. The heir apparent, or crown prince, enjoyed high status and not infrequently occupied important posts such as that of commander in chief of the army or that of a viceroy or a provincial governor. A "first king's herald of His Majesty" was charged with the communication of royal decrees and with arranging interviews with the monarch. An "overseer of the granaries of Upper and Lower Egypt" and an "overseer of the treasury of silver and gold" exercised extremely important fiscal functions. Other prominent officials included a chief "overseer of cattle," the "dispatch writer of the pharaoh," the "chief taxing master of the entire land," and two "overseers of river mouths" responsible for the supervision, respectively, of external and internal trade. The principal ministers bore the honorific title of "fanbearer on the right of the king" and formed a privy council which advised the monarch on appointments and other administrative matters.

From earliest times Egypt was administratively organized into a varying number of provinces, or nomes, each consisting of a sizable town and its environing territory and each headed by a governor, or nomarch, directly responsible to the vizier. A nome comprised a number of lesser districts with administrative heads, which in turn consisted of a number of villages with local headmen. At each level the responsible official combined judicial, military, and commonly also ecclesiastical functions with the bureaucratic ones of collecting and transmitting taxes and raising *corvées* for public works. Reforms under the New Empire created three great administrative regions—the delta and two divisions of Upper Egypt—comprising about forty fiscal districts each, and established "Kenbet courts" in each town to collect imposts and handle other administrative matters as well as to dispense justice. At each level of this bureaucratic hierarchy controllers, or overseers, reported through their superiors to the vizier and maintained granaries and treasuries, which served not merely as storehouses but also as repositories for land, tax, and court records.

The invaluable Wilbour Papyrus indicates that arable and pasture land under the New Empire was divided into plots averaging perhaps 10 acres but ranging from less than a single acre to more than 50. Many formed portions of the royal domains, but the great majority were owned by temples and shrines, endowed with land, herds, and slaves by previous pharaohs or occasionally by wealthy and pious laymen. No evidence suggests the reservation of special estates for the support of administrative officials, but private property in land certainly existed, although it constituted only a small fraction of the total. With few exceptions holdings were comparatively small, and they represented practically every class in society. The frequency of ownership by women suggests hereditary transmission; that by common soldiers and mercenaries suggests either payment or reward for services. The repeated distinction between "holders of land" and "cultivators" or "herdsmen" would seem to indicate widespread tenancy and a near absence of small independent farmers.

Viceroys administered conquered provinces. A ring of fortresses protected the boundaries of the empire and facilitated the collection of duties on imported and exported commodities. The army consisted largely of conscripts and of foreign mercenaries, although charioteers seem to have constituted an elite corps drawn from the upper classes. The pharaoh himself assumed over-all command of the armed forces, assisted by a supreme general and by lieutenant generals for both Upper and Lower Egypt. The infantry was divided into divisions of 5,000 men, brigades of 250, and companies of 50, each with an officer in charge. A prince of royal blood commanded the chariotry, which was organized into squadrons.

Far from being independent, the administrative, military, and ecclesiastical hierarchies formed together a unified monolithic structure. The pharaoh appointed all priests, and he bestowed all military promotions in person. Priests served on the "Kenbet courts," provincial administrators functioned as chief priests, and local headmen commonly combined the role of prophet with their other activities.

Egyptian society exhibited a complex stratification into social classes: royalty but no hereditary aristocracy; a bureaucratic nobility comprising priests and military officers as well as administrative officials; a diversified bourgeoisie including scribes, teachers, merchants, and petty bureaucrats; an equally diversified class of specialized artisans; an agricultural peasantry reduced practically to the status of serfs; and a class of hereditary slaves composed of war captives and their descendants. Individual freedom was as lacking as in modern totalitarian states. The little man faced the constant threat of arbitrary exactions and of forced labor, and extant papyri contain detailed references to administrative oppression. The "splendour that was Egypt" had a broad basis in human misery.

Selected Bibliography

Baumgartel, E. J. *The Cultures of Prehistoric Egypt*. London, 1947.

Budge, E. A. W. *Dwellers on the Nile*. London, 1926.

Burkill, I. H. Habits of Man and the Origins of the Cultivated Plants of the Old World. *Proceedings of the Linnean Society of London*, 164:12–42. 1953.

Bury, J. B., S. A. Cook, and F. E. Adcock, eds. *The Cambridge Ancient History*, vols. 1–3. New York, 1923–1925.

Caminos, R. A. *Late Egyptian Miscellanies*. Oxford, 1954.

Childe, V. G. *New Light on the Most Ancient East*. 4th edit. London, 1952.

Cline, W. Notes on Cultural Innovations in Dynastic Egypt. *SWJA*, 4:1–30. 1948.

Dyson, R. H. Archeology and the Domestication of Animals in the Old World. *AA*, 55:661–673. 1953.

Erman, A. *Aegypten und aegyptisches Leben im Altertum*, ed. H. Ranke. Tübingen, 1923.

Gardiner, A. H. *The Wilbour Papyrus*. 4 vols. Oxford, 1941–1952.

———. *Ancient Egyptian Onomastica*. 2 vols. London, 1947.

Hartmann, F. *L'agriculture dans l'ancienne Egypte*. Paris, 1923.

Kees, H. *Aegypten*. München, 1923.

Keimer, L. *Die Gartenpflanzen im alten Aegypten*. Hamburg, 1924.

Montet, P. *La vie quotidienne en Egypte au temps des Ramsès*. Paris, 1946.

Murray, M. A. *The Splendour That Was Egypt*. New York, 1949.

Paton, D. *Animals of Ancient Egypt*. Princeton, 1926.

Reinhardt, L. *Kulturgeschichte der Nutzpflanzen*. 2 vols. München, 1911.

Schiemann, E. Entstehung der Kulturpflanzen. *Handbuch der Vererbungswissenschaft*, 3:1–377. Berlin, 1932.

Vavilov, N. I. The Origin, Variation, Immunity and Breeding of Cultivated Plants, transl. K. S. Chester. *Chronica Botanica*, 13:1–364. 1949–1950.

Wilkinson, J. G. *The Manners and Customs of the Ancient Egyptians*, ed. S. Birch. 3 vols. New York, 1923–1925.

Wittfogel, K. A. *Oriental Despotism*. New Haven, 1957.

15

Berbers

Since late Paleolithic times the Mediterranean littoral of North Africa has been inhabited by people of Caucasoid race. Sometime after 4000 B.C., following a transitional Mesolithic period called Capsian, they acquired cultivated plants and domesticated animals from Egypt and entered a Neolithic phase. In the second millennium B.C. they received metals from the same source. When the Phoenicians and Greeks, and later the Romans, colonized the North African coast, they found the region occupied by a people of comparatively homogeneous culture known collectively as the Berbers. These had occupied a few marginal oases but in general had penetrated only slightly into the Sahara Desert. In the west, however, they extended somewhat farther south and had even settled the Canary Islands.

In physical type the Berbers resemble the Mediterranean subrace of southern Europe, although they appreciably exceed the latter in average stature and show a somewhat higher incidence of blondness in beard, hair, and eyes. Their languages, which are so closely related as to be almost mutually intelligible, constitute the distinct Berber subfamily of the Hamitic linguistic stock.

Though they had withstood earlier foreign invasions with considerable success, the Berbers were shattered by the Arab conquests of the seventh century and particularly by the mass Bedouin immigrations beginning in the eleventh century. Some fled or were driven into the desert, where they in turn displaced or subjugated the indigenous Negroes. Others submitted, becoming Arabized in language and to some extent racially mixed. All, without exception, embraced Islam. Nearly thirteen centuries of acculturation have brought about such a degree of fusion and assimilation that North Africa today must be classed as an integral part of the great Middle Eastern culture area. Berber speech survives, as shown in Map 11, only in mountain fastnesses and other relatively protected pockets in the original homeland and in areas of dispersion in the desert.

Although some groups who have adopted the Arabic language are still basically Berber in culture and some Berber speakers are strongly Arabized, it is nevertheless generally true that the tribes who have retained their original language have also preserved more of their ancient customs. We shall therefore adopt a strictly linguistic classification in segregating the Berbers from the Arabs in North Africa. The peoples who still speak Berber, at least in part, fall into the following twenty-nine groups.

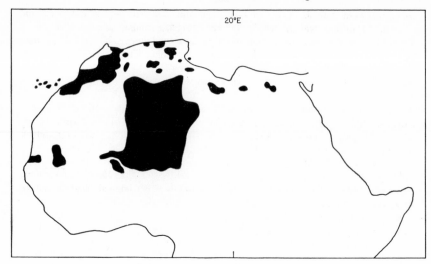

Map 11. Areas of Berber Speech

1. Atta (Ait Atta), with the Yahia (Ait Yahia). These tribes are akin to the Beraber and, like the latter, are transhumant pastoralists. Many, however, have established themselves in the plains as "protectors" of the sedentary Drawa, and some engage in the desert caravan trade. They number about 50,000.
2. Beraber, including the Idrassen, Ndhir (Ait Ndhir, Beni Mtir), Seri (Ait Seri), Serruchen (Ait Seghrouchen), Sokhman (Ait Chokhman), Yafelman (Ait Iafelman), Yussi (Ait Youssi), Zaer, Zayan (Isaian), Zemmur, and other tribes of the Middle Atlas Mountains. Though they have permanent agricultural settlements, most of them also practice extensive transhumance. Their population was reported in 1921 as about 450,000.
3. Drawa, including the Dades (Ait Dades), Mesgita (Mezguita), Seddrat (Ait Seddrat), and Zerri (Ait Zerri, Uled Jerri) tribes as well as the Arabized and detribalized residents of the districts of Fezwata, Ktawa, Mhammid, Ternata, and Tinzulin. All are sedentary date cultivators living in walled towns along the Dra River and its tributaries in southern Morocco. They number at least 150,000.
4. Duaish (Idaouich). This tribe of semisedentary millet cultivators and sheepherders in the French Sudan is culturally indistinguishable from the Arabic-speaking Zenaga tribe except that about 4,000 of its members still speak a Berber language.
5. Figig (Figuig), embracing the 10,000 inhabitants of ten fortified, date-growing oasis towns on the upper Zusfana River in the Algerian Sahara.
6. Filala, including the inhabitants of the river oases of Ferkla, Gheris, Tafilalet, and Todga in southeastern Morocco. They number more than 100,000, occupy several hundred walled towns, and raise dates and other crops.
7. Gadames (Ghadames, Rhadames), including the approximately 5,000 inhabitants of the oasis and important caravan center of Gadames in western Libya.
8. Guanche. The aboriginal inhabitants of the Canary Islands.
9. Jalo (Gialo), including the sedentary Modshafra, Suaya, and Wadshili (Uadschili) tribes of the oases of Jalo in eastern Libya. They number about 10,000, but only the Wadshili of Augila still retain their Berber speech.
10. Jerba (Djerba, Gerba), including the 40,000 inhabitants of the island of Jerba

in southeastern Tunisia. They are sedentary cultivators of cereals and fruits and, like the Mzab and Nefusa, belong to the schismatic Ibadite sect of Islam.

11. Jofra (Djofra, Giofra), embracing the sedentary inhabitants of the Libyan oases of Forgha, Jofra (with Sokna and Wadan), and Zella. They number about 6,000 and are linguistically akin to the Jalo and Siwa.

12. Kabyle, including nearly a million sedentary cultivators in a compact section of coastal Algeria.

13. Matmata. A small remnant tribe in the Tabaga Mountains of southern Tunisia.

14. Menasser (Beni Menasser), including the remnant tribe of this name in the Cherchel region of coastal Algeria and the even smaller (and unmapped) islands of Berber speech in the Dahra, Mascara, Ouarsenis, and Teniet regions.

15. Mzab (Beni Mzab, Mozabites), including the sedentary inhabitants of Berrian, Guardaia, Guerara, and other date-growing oases of the Ued Mzab region of the Algerian Sahara. They belong to the heretical and puritanical Ibadite sect of Moslems and number about 30,000.

16. Nefusa (Nafusa, Nefousa) including the Berbers of the Ibadite sect and some intrusive Arab tribes who occupy the Nefousa Mountains of Tripolitania. They number about 45,000 and subsist mainly by agriculture.

17. Rif (Riffians), including the Metalsa (Mtalsa) and Znassen (Beni Iznacen) tribes and numerous subtribes of the Ghomara (Ghomera), Riffian, and Senhaja (Sanhadja) nations occupying the mountainous Rif region of northern Morocco. They number about 700,000 and subsist by cereal agriculture.

18. Shawia (Chaouia), embracing the inhabitants of the Aures Mountains in eastern Algeria. They are sedentary cereal cultivators and numbered 126,000 in 1926.

19. Shluh (Chleuch), including the Aghbar (Achbar), Fruga (Frouga), Gedmiwa, Glawa (Glaoua), Gontafa (Gentafa, Goundafa, Gundaffa), Haha, Hawara (Haouara), Jerrar (Ait Djerrar), Ksima, Mamud (Ida ou Mamoud), Massat (Ait Massat), Menaba (El Menaba, Mnebba), Mentaga (Imentagen), Mesgina (Imssegin), Mtuga (Imtuggen, Mtioua, Mtougga), Ntifa (Entifa), Seksawa (Iseksawan, Seksioua), Semlal (Ida ou Semlal), Semmeg (Ait Ssimig), Shtuka (Chtouka), Tanan (Ida ou Tanan), Unein (Ounein), Uzgita (Ousgita), Zal (Ida u Sal), Ziki (Ida u Siki), and numerous other tribes of the Grand Atlas, the Anti-Atlas, the intervening valley of the Sous River, and the adjacent coast of Morocco. They number over a million and are sedentary cereal cultivators.

20. Siwa, including the sedentary inhabitants of the oasis of Siwa in western Egypt. They grow dates and olives, and number about 4,000.

21. Tasumsa, with the Hadj (Ida-u-el-Hadj), Hassan (Idab-el-Hassan), and Tendega. These seminomadic Mauritanian tribes form part of the Arabic-speaking Trarza nation, from whom they differ chiefly in the fact that some 13,000 of their 29,000 members still preserve their original Berber speech.

22. Tekna (Tekena), including the Aglu (Ahel Aglou), Akhsas (El Achsass), Azuafidi (Azouafit), Bamrane (Ait Ba Amran), Bella (Ait Bella), Brahim (Ait Brahim), Iaggut (Ait Djagut, Djeggut, Iggout, Jagut, Yakout), Izargien (Asergiin, Izerguiin), Jemel (Aid Djemel, Ait Yemel), Lhassen (Ait Lahsen), Mejjat (Ait Medjat, Mojat), Musawali (Ait Moussa ou Ali), Sahel (Ahel Sahel, Ait Sahel), Usa (Ait Jussa, Ait Oussa), and numerous other tribes of extreme southwestern Morocco, Spanish Ifni, and northern Rio de Oro. They number about 200,000 and are linguistically akin to the Shluh, from whom they differ chiefly in being more nomadic.

23. Tuareg (Touareg), including the Ahaggaren (Hoggar Tuareg, Ihaggaren, Kel Ahaggar), Antessar (Kel Antessar), Asben (Air Tuareg, Kel Air), Aulliminden

(Awellimiden, Oulliminden), Azjer (Adjeur, Ajjer, Kel Azdjer), Ifora, Ihajenen (Gat Tuareg, Ghat, Rhat), and other tribes of the central Sahara north of the Niger River. They number about 200,000, of whom more than half are Bella or Negro serfs.

24. Tuat (Touat), including the sedentary inhabitants of the oases of Gurara, Kerzaz, Tidikelt, and Tuat in the Algerian Sahara, together with the Khebbache (Ait Khebbache) and other neighboring seminomadic tribes. They are primarily date cultivators and number about 50,000.

25. Udalan (Oudalen, Wadalen), with the Igwadaren, Irreganaten, Logomaten, and other Tuareg tribes that have penetrated in recent centuries into the region south of the Niger River. They number about 100,000, largely Negro serfs.

26. Uregu (Ait Oureggou), with the Feqqus (Ahl Feqqous) and Tinerst (Ait Tinerst). These small tribes are sedentary tillers on the middle Moulouya River in eastern Morocco.

27. Warain (Ait Warain, Beni Ouarain). This seminomadic tribe, numbering about 100,000, inhabits the eastern part of the Middle Atlas Mountains in Morocco.

28. Wargla (Ouargla), embracing the inhabitants of the oasis of Wargla in the Algerian Sahara. They are sedentary cultivators and formerly played an important part in the trans-Saharan caravan trade.

29. Zekara (Zkara), with the neighboring Bekhti (Uled Bekhti), Chebel (Beni Chebel), Yala (Beni Yaala), and Zeggu (Beni Bou Zeggou) of eastern Morocco and the Snus (Beni Snous) across the border in Algeria. They are semisedentary and number about 50,000.

To comprehend original Berber culture, we must find some way of peeling off, so to speak, its Arab veneer. This feat is facilitated by the fact that we possess early accounts of the now extinct Guanche of the Canary Islands, who were never subjected to Arab influence. Until conquered by the Spaniards in the late fifteenth century, they had been almost completely isolated from the mainland by their lack of boats for several millennia and thus preserved into recent historical times a genuine Neolithic culture, unaffected by any of the innovations in the arts that have occurred since the discovery of metalworking. Though its descriptions leave much to be desired, Guanche culture provides us with a solid base line of unusual historical depth.

Cereal agriculture formed the basis of subsistence, with barley as the staple and possibly also wheat. The sources also mention figs and beans but no other crops. The Guanche kept goats, sheep, pigs, and dogs, ate the flesh of them all, and used the milk of the first two to make butter and cheese. They did very little hunting or fowling but gathered wild plants to some extent and augmented their diet substantially with fish, which they caught by means of hook and line, nets, harpoons, and poison. Men did the hunting and fishing, but both sexes participated in agricultural work.

A bride was fattened up for her wedding, and the groom paid a brideprice in livestock. Wealthy men on the island of Tenerife practiced polygyny, and Lanzarote women are reported to have been polyandrous, cohabiting for a month with each husband in rotation, but these constituted exceptions to the prevailing rule of absolute monogamy. Marriage was permitted between first cousins, and in the ruling family of Tenerife even between brother and sister.

The Guanche inhabited compact villages of rectangular stone houses with flat roofs. These were aggregated into districts—one or several to an island—under paramount chiefs. Beside the chief stood a high priest, who also acted as judge. A council of nobles, belonging to a hereditary class distinct from commoners, assisted the ruler. Since succession to the chiefship on certain islands followed the female line and since a man's sisters' sons regularly inherited his movable property, most authorities have concluded that the Guanche were matrilineal in descent.

The Berber-speaking peoples now inhabiting sections of the Sahara and adjacent Sudan, whence they were driven or carried by the Arab invaders, have undergone so profound a cultural readjustment to the altered conditions of life that their ethnographic descriptions can be utilized only with extreme caution for purposes of reconstruction. In the case of the Tuareg and Udalan, the adaptation to a desert environment has involved so many genuine innovations, as well as borrowings from both the indigenous Negroes and the Bedouin Arabs, that we shall treat them separately in Chapter 53. In the more rugged mountain regions of their original habitat, however, the Berbers have been able, in greater or lesser measure, to resist Arab political and cultural penetration and to cling conservatively to many of their ancient ways. In attempting to isolate indigenous Berber culture we have therefore depended primarily upon descriptions of the mountain tribes, which are particularly satisfactory for the Beraber, Kabyle, Rif, and Shluh, and have used other sources principally for supplementation.

Since the separation of the Neolithic Guanche, the mainland Berbers have acquired the plow, improved techniques of irrigation, and a vast array of new cultivated plants. These include practically all those known to the ancient Egyptians and those introduced into North Africa in Greco-Roman times (see Chapter 18) as well as a fair number of Sudanic and American origin. Barley and wheat, however, remain the staples, supplemented to some extent by other grains, especially maize, millet, and sorghum. Arboriculture generally ranks second in importance to cereal agriculture and frequently surpasses it. Thus figs and olives are the staples of the Nefusa and some Kabyle, and the date palm among most oasis dwellers.

The mainland Berbers have likewise acquired a number of domestic animals unknown to the Guanche: cattle, horses, donkeys, mules, camels, chickens, and bees, as well as a few cats, pigeons, and rabbits. Only rarely, however, do any of these rival sheep and goats in importance, the chief exception being the place of cattle among the Rif. The importance of the pig in both ancient Egypt and the Canary Islands suggests that this animal, whose flesh constitutes an abomination in the eyes of all good Moslems, may also have played a prominent role in the economy of the Berbers prior to the introduction of Islam. A few isolated facts lend support to this inference. Thus the heterodox Zekara still eat pork, and a few pigs are kept even today by the Zaer tribe of Beraber and, surreptitiously, by the Rif.

The native Berber economy rests on a fine balance between animal husbandry and agriculture. Every tribe, without exception, depends heavily upon domestic animals for burden and usually draft, for meat, for hides and wool, and for milk and dairy products; nor is there a single undisplaced tribe that does not rely upon agriculture for a substantial portion of its subsistence. Even those that practice extensive transhumance, like the Beraber, have permanent settlements where the majority of the population lives throughout the year while a minority accompanies the flocks to the mountains in summer, to the plains in winter, or both. In contrast to most other areas of pastoralism in the world, it is the sedentary population that controls the land. Districts grant seasonal grazing rights to one another through reciprocal agreements. Unlike the Bedouin Arabs, the Berbers did not divorce pastoralism from agriculture. Historical accounts, to be sure, frequently mention Berber nomads, but they were only seminomads, attached to permanent agricultural settlements and resorting only seasonally to transhumant pastoralism. Until a thousand years ago, when a few of them learned differently from the Arabs, they never adopted an independent pastoral mode of life.

Hunting and gathering rarely add significantly to the food supply. Fishing, on the other hand, assumes importance wherever geographical conditions permit, as among the Drawa, Jerba, Rif, Shluh, and Zekara. The Berbers engage extensively in commerce and maintain regular markets nearly everywhere. It was they, indeed, who first initiated the trans-Saharan caravan trade, probably as early as the third millennium B.C.

In the division of labor by sex the men do the hunting, fishing, and herding, whereas gathering, shellfishing, and milking, if we may judge by fragmentary information, are assigned to women. Men alone engage in agricultural work in the oases and other regions of strong Arab influence, but women assist them to a substantial extent in all the less acculturated Berber tribes.

Marriage regularly involves a bride-price, paid sometimes in livestock, sometimes in money. The fact that in a number of tribes, including the Shawia, Shluh, and Zekara, the bride's father does not retain the marriage payment but turns it over to his daughter as a dowry suggests that this may once have been the general Berber practice. A similar inference can perhaps be drawn from the custom of fattening up a bride for her wedding, which is reported for tribes as remote from one another as the Guanche, Jerba, and Tuat. The marriage of first cousins is permitted or even favored. This might be attributed to Arab influence were it not for the fact that it is reported even for the isolated Guanche and for the additional fact that the Rif, who allow other cousin marriages, forbid a man to marry his father's brother's daughter, though such a union is regularly preferred by the Arabs.

Particularly striking, in view of the general acceptance of Islam, is the strong preference for monogamy among nearly all Berber peoples, including even the oasis dwellers and the Tuareg. Polygyny is reported only for the Jerba, the Kabyle, the Rif, and a few scattered Beraber and Warain tribes. In most of these cases, moreover, it is confined to a few wealthy men or results, as among the Rif, from the operation of preferential levirate. So firmly held is the monogamous ideal that it has even been adopted by some of the intrusive Arabs.

Nuclear families are reported to be independent social groups only among the Mzab. Elsewhere they are aggregated into patrilocal extended families, each with a patriarchal head. An extended family consists ordinarily only of the head, his wife and unmarried children, and his married sons with their families. It usually breaks up with the death of the father, but occasionally brothers continue to live together even thereafter. The group may occupy a single house, as among the Nefusa and Shluh; a compound, as among the Kabyle; or a cluster of adjacent dwellings, as among the Beraber and Rif.

If matrilineal descent once prevailed among the Berbers, as the Guanche data suggest, it must have disappeared long ago, for no traces survive among the mainland tribes. The Tuareg, to be sure, have recently evolved a peculiar type of matrilineal system under a very special set of circumstances, to be described in Chapter 53, but all other tribes observe the patrilineal rule today. Their forms of social organization, indeed, reveal a striking uniformity. The fundamental unit is a small patrisib or major lineage, usually called a "bone" (*ighs*), which is typically localized as a clan in a hamlet or small village, or in a ward, or quarter, of a larger settlement. The sib is always composed of a number of minimal patrilineages, each the core of an extended family and sometimes, but not invariably, also of intermediate minor lineages. Sibs are never exogamous and are often preferentially endogamous, but in some tribes, e.g., the Rif and Shluh, exogamy prevails within the component lineages. The indigenous system appears not to be a truly segmentary one, for when a segment removes to another community the kinship tie is soon forgotten, and no distinctions are recognized between senior and junior lines. Cousin terms of the Omaha type are reported for the Semlal tribe of Shluh, and of the descriptive type for the Siwa.

Groups larger than the sib, e.g., the community, the district, and the tribe, are political rather than genealogical units. Although a fictional kinship tie may be invoked to cement them, this is not typical and probably reflects Arab influence. Beyond the sib, the bonds that unite society are primarily territorial.

The Berbers in general recognize private property in movables and in cultivated land but only collective rights in grazing grounds and forest. Inheritance, like descent, is patrilineal. Sons divide equally the estate of the father. Daughters are usually excluded, even though it is necessary to use some fiction to circumvent the Koranic law, which prescribes that they shall receive half shares. Distinctions in wealth are widely reported, and poor men often tend the herds or work on the lands of the rich for a share of the product.

Except for differences in wealth, often only moderate, the Berbers are remarkably egalitarian. Although a distinct noble class, as reported for the Guanche, doubtless also existed in the petty Berber states of pre-Arab times, no distinction between nobles and commoners is recognized today in the tribes that still occupy essentially their original habitat. Serfdom is absent in the same regions, and even slavery is undeveloped, rare, or lacking entirely. Only occasionally, too, do we hear of despised and endogamous outcaste groups, e.g., smiths, musicians, and town criers among the Rif. The minimal development of social stratification among the less acculturated Berbers contrasts sharply with the situation in those groups who have been politically subjugated by the Arabs and among those who have themselves subjugated indigenous Negro peoples. Here we find everywhere the typical Arab caste structure, with segregated classes of nobles, subject commoners, agricultural serfs, despised groups of artisans, and domestic slaves. The line is absolutely clear-cut. Among oasis dwellers, for example, those, like the Mzab and Siwa, who have not displaced Negroes are relatively egalitarian, whereas the rest, e.g., the Drawa, Filala, and Wargla, reveal the full range of caste stratification. The contrast can even appear within a single group, e.g., between the Shluh of the Grand Atlas and Anti-Atlas Mountains and those of the intervening valley of the Sous River, which alone had an earlier Negro population.

Chronic warfare has constituted a dominating condition of Berber social life from time immemorial. Raids, blood feuds, and even more severe forms of conflict are a constant factor, both as a threat and as a reality. They occur between districts, between communities of the same district, and even between lineages, wards, or factions of the same community.

They even characterize groups that have achieved some measure of political integration. Modern colonial powers find the unruly Berber tribesmen no less difficult to pacify than did the Carthaginians, the Romans, and the Turks in earlier epochs.

The conditions of perpetual warfare determine the patterns of settlement. Neighborhoods of dispersed family homesteads are impossible because indefensible. They occur only among the Jerba, who are uniquely protected from external aggression by their insular location. Tents and other flimsy shelters must be eschewed except when absolutely necessary, as in temporary camps during seasons of nomadism, and then they must be protected by temporary barricades and a constant watch. Consequently all Berbers except the Jerba and Tuareg live in compact and fortified settlements. In the oases and other densely populated locations the people congregate in towns or large villages protected by a high encircling wall, often equipped with towers and battlements. At the highest or most defensible point within the settlement, moreover, there is frequently a strong fortress or citadel, which commonly also serves as a communal granary. In areas of sparser population the units of settlement are hamlets, each protected by the high walls of its external houses and often, too, by an almost impenetrable surrounding hedge of thorny shrubs. In such cases the group of hamlets which forms a community usually also possesses a fortified granary at some central location, where each family stores its valuables and surplus food in special locked chambers. When danger threatens, the people drive their flocks into the central courtyard of the granary and man its battlemented walls against attack. In regions where the people have been subjugated by some powerful state with an Arab or Arabized Berber ruler, e.g., the Sultan of Morocco, the military and administrative officials build forts at strategic locations and strong castles as residences in order to defend themselves not so much from enemies as from their oppressed subjects.

Several house types are distinguishable. The more nomadic tribes, e.g., the Beraber, Shawia, Tasumsa, Tekna, Warain, and Zekara, have adopted tents from the Arabs but ordinarily use them only during the periods of transhumance. The Jerba, Nefusa, and lowland Shluh, some groups of Rif, Uregu, Warain, and Zekara, and all the oasis tribes occupy rectangular houses with flat terraced roofs, interior courtyards, and thick external walls of stone or sun-dried brick. The Beraber, Shawia, mountain Shluh, and northern Warain likewise have rectangular houses with flat roofs and stone walls, but the interior courtyard is lacking. The Kabyle, some Uregu, and the Ghomara and Sanhaja tribes of the Rif live in rectangular houses with gable roofs covered with thatch, shingles (common among the Rif), or tiles (common among the Kabyle). Flimsier shelters of the last type, with dismountable wooden frames, are used by some groups in their pastoral camps and were doubtless generally so used before the adoption of the Arab tent.

Native Berber political organization reveals a striking degree of homogeneity when allowance is made for the wide range in the size of settlements, from small hamlets to oasis towns with several thousand inhabitants. Three levels of integration can be distinguished, namely, the community, the district, and the tribe. The community is a political aggregation of clans, i.e., of localized lineages or sibs. It may consist of a cluster of small hamlets or, where settlements are larger, of a single sizable village; in the large oasis towns it is recognizable in the ward, or quarter. The district constitutes an aggregation of communities, i.e., a union of several hamlet clusters or villages or, in the oases, a town. The tribe represents an aggregation of districts, characterized by a common territory, name, and culture. The community is always, and the district usually, a firm political unit. The tribe, however, except under conditions of alien conquest and subjugation, reveals little political cohesion. It functions as a unit only under extreme emergencies. An impromptu tribal council may, for example, be assembled to meet the threat of a foreign invasion. Normal regulative functions, however, are observable only within the community and the district.

Government at the community level is notably democratic. All authority is vested in an assembly (*jemaa*) composed of all adult males, which usually meets weekly in the mosque or under a tree in the open. The assembly commonly appoints certain executive agents, e.g., a presiding officer, a secretary, and a custodian of mosque funds, but it reserves to itself all important decisions, which are reached by unanimous consent after general discussion. The heads of lineages and extended families usually exert a major influence and are often assigned special seats, but younger men may always attend and express their opinions. In some instances, especially in the oasis towns, the local assembly has become rudimentary or has disappeared entirely.

The district is governed by a council, usually also called a *jemaa*, composed normally of representatives of each of the sibs or major lineages of the component communities. Since these groups tend to appoint their older, wealthier, and more influential men, the district council has a somewhat oligarchical character in contrast to the democratic local assembly. Each year the council elects one of its members as president (*moqaddem*), usually selecting him from the various communities in rotation. He presides at council meetings, executes the decisions of the council with the help of appointed assistants or policemen, and may, if influential, be called upon to arbitrate private disputes, but his authority is severely limited and he is jealously watched lest he usurp autocratic

powers. The council reserves for itself all legislative, administrative, judicial, and fiscal functions.

Among the Drawa, Filala, and Mzab, whose original assemblies have de-
generated, the council of the district, i.e., of the town, has become subdivided into two bodies, a senate and an assembly. Among the Todga
group of Filala the former body deals with external and the latter with
internal affairs. Among the Mzab, the senate is composed of the clergy and
of literate men, the assembly of ordinary male citizens; the former
legislates regulations in accordance with the dogmas of the Ibadite sect,
whereas the latter executes these and exercises all temporal functions.
In the Drawa town of Nesrat the senate is controlled by a few wealthy
families and leaves to the assembly, whose members it appoints, only
minor police functions.

When a district becomes involved in a war, the council appoints a
military leader (*amghar*) with absolute authority for the duration of the
emergency. A strong and successful military leader, even though closely
watched by the council, occasionally succeeds in usurping personal power
and in subordinating or suppressing the democratic institutions of his
people. Usually such usurpation is temporary and ceases with his death,
but in favorable circumstances it may be extended and perpetuated in the
form of an authoritarian state, of which Berber history shows numerous
examples. This has happened within the past century in the Glawa, Gontafa, and Mtuga tribes of the Shluh, where *amghar* first established
authoritarian power over their respective tribes and then, by allying
themselves with the Sultan of Morocco, embarked on careers of conquest
by which they acquired very large semi-independent domains. In the
process they have completely shattered the local democratic institutions
and substituted the rule of force.

Though comparable developments have occurred from time to time
throughout the nearly 3,000 years for which we have some record of
Berber history, they seem, on the whole, to have been localized and exceptional. In general, the Berbers have achieved a measure of political
integration transcending that of the district in a very different manner.
For our understanding of the peculiar mechanism by which this has been
accomplished we are heavily indebted to the acute field observations and
comparative research of Montagne.

In nearly every Berber society each district, and sometimes also each
community, is divided into two opposing and rivalrous factions called
sof. Membership is hereditary and apparently determined by lineage membership. In the oasis of Gadames each faction occupies a separate walled
section of the town, which members of the other may not enter. They
meet only on neutral ground, e.g., the mosque or the market, and their

encounters are commonly marked by bloody fights. In the oasis of Siwa their residential areas are separated by a street rather than a wall, and each of several hamlets lying outside the main town is affiliated with one or the other. Again, fighting and feuding have occurred constantly between them. Similar divisions are reported for the Drawa, Kabyle, Mzab, and other tribes. Their existence frequently makes it necessary for elective or appointive officials to be selected alternately from each, or for a principal and his assistant to be chosen from opposite factions.

Among the tribes which have not been displaced from their original habitat political units are allied with one another in dual divisions of a higher level, called *lef*. Though best described for the Shluh, these groups are also well attested for the Kabyle and Rif and are reported in lesser detail for the Beraber and Warain. Since they function in a strictly comparable manner in all these societies, the situation among the Shluh will serve sufficiently as an illustration.

The *lef* of the Shluh are composed of districts which, when mapped, reveal a checkerboard pattern. Each district is bounded by some which belong to its own *lef* and by some belonging to the opposite one. The districts comprising a *lef* are bound to one another through treaties which provide for mutual assistance in defensive war, for reciprocal grazing rights during transhumance, and for peaceful trade with one another. The bonds of alliance are cemented by traditional forms of hospitality and by great annual feasts to which the members invite one another.

Warfare is confined almost exclusively to districts of opposite *lef*. When a Shluh district is attacked, messengers fire recognized gunshot signals at each border of an allied district, and shortly the forces of the *lef* allies pour in from every quarter and the aggressors are overwhelmed. Since *lef* are primarily defensive rather than offensive alliances, they operate strongly to preserve peace in a region where warfare is endemic. The Rif illustrate the mode of operation where several districts are involved in an act of aggression. An *ad hoc* council of all the districts of the victimized *lef* is called and assesses a heavy fine against each aggressor district. If this is not paid, the forces of the entire *lef* assemble and attack the aggressor districts one at a time. As each district is defeated, the fine is collected and divided among the victors, and the vanquished are compelled to join in the attack on the next district, sharing in the division of its fine. Understandably enough, submission usually occurs well in advance of the conquest of the last offending district.

Substantial traces of the *lef* system still survive even among many Arabized Berbers, including the Jebala of Morocco and practically all the peoples of Tunisia. It seems to have prevailed for millennia as the major adjustment for the preservation of peace in a war-ridden land. Though distinctive, it is by no means unique in human culture. The Creek confederacy of the American Southeast, for example, was based on a comparable moietylike division into rivalrous Red and White towns. And the alert reader may already have noted the striking resemblance between the Berber *lef* and the balance-of-power alignment of modern European states. Perhaps some may even derive a shred of comfort from the fact that the Berber balance of power, though it by no means prevented war, nevertheless survived as a peace-enforcing mechanism for thousands of years. The Berbers seem, indeed, to have found it clearly preferable to total despotic power under an authoritarian state.

Selected Bibliography

Abès, M. Les Izayan d'Oulmès. *AB*, 1:265–278. 1916. [Beraber].

———. Les Aith Ndhir. *AB*, 2:149–194, 337–416. 1917. [Beraber].

Adam, A. La maison et le village dans quelques tribus de l'Anti-Atlas. *Hesperis*, 37:289–362. 1950. [Shluh].

Alimen, H. *Préhistoire d'Afrique*. Paris, 1955.

Bates, O. *The Eastern Libyans*. London, 1914.

Beaurpère. Note provisoire sur les vallées du Todga, de l'Imider et du Saghro oriental. *VTM*, 9:203–266. 1931. [Filala].

Belgrave, C. D. *Siwa, the Oasis of Jupiter Ammon*. London, 1923.

Bernard, A. *Afrique septentrionale et occidentale*. 2 vols. Paris, 1937–1939.

Berque, J. *Les Seksawa*. Paris, 1954. [Shluh].

Bertholon, L. Exploration anthropologique de l'île de Gerba. *Anthropologie*, 8:318–326, 399–425, 559–583. 1897. [Jerba].

Célérier, J. La transhumance dans le Moyen-Atlas. *Hesperis*, 7:53–68. 1927. [Beraber].

Chapelle, F. de la. Une cité de l'Oued Dra' sous le protectorat des nomades. *Hesperis*, 9:29–42. 1929. [Drawa].

Chavanne, J. *Die Sahara*. Wien, 1879.

Cline, W. Notes on the People of Siwah and El Garah. *GSA*, 4:1–64. 1936.

Cook, A. C. The Aborigines of the Canary Islands. *AA*, 2:451–493. 1900. [Guanche].

Coon, C. S. Tribes of the Rif. *HAS*, 9:1–417. 1931.

Despois, J. *Le Djebel Nefousa*. Paris, 1935.

Destaing, E. *Etude sur le dialecte berbère des Beni-Snous*. 2 vols. Paris, 1914. [Zekara].

———. *Etude sur le dialecte berbère des Aït Seghrouchen*. Paris, 1920. [Beraber].

Dubié, P. L'îlot berbérophone du Mauritanie. *BIFAN*, 2:316–325. 1940. [Tasumsa].

Espinosa, A. de. *The Guanches of Teneriffe*, ed. C. Markham. London, 1907.

Gaudry, M. *La femme chaouia de l'Aurès*. Paris, 1929. [Shawia].

Goichon, A. M. *La vie féminine au Mzab*. Paris, 1927.

Hanoteau, A., and A. Letourneux. *La Kabylie et les coutumes kabyles*. 2d edit., 2 vols. Paris, 1893.

Hooton, E. A. The Ancient Inhabitants of the Canary Islands. *HAS*, 7:1–401. 1925. [Guanche].

Joly, F. Les Ait Khebbache de Taouz. *Travaux de l'Institut de Recherches Sahariennes*, 6:129–159. Alger, 1951. [Tuat].

Justinard. Les Aït Ba Amran. *VTM*, 8:1–144. 1908. [Tekna].

Marcy, G. Les Ait Jellidasen. *Hesperis*, 9:79–142. 1929. [Warain].

Marty, P. L'orf des Bani M'tir. *Revue des Études Islamiques*, 2:481–511. 1928. [Beraber].

Maunier, R. *Mélanges de sociologie nord-africaine.* Paris, 1930. [Kabyle].

Mercier, L. Notice économique sur le Tafilalet. *RCD,* 15:210–221. 1905. [Filala].

Mercier, M. *La civilisation urbaine au Mzab.* Alger, 1922.

Meunié, D. J. Les oasis des Lektoua et des Mehamid. *Hesperis,* 34:397–420. 1947. [Drawa].

Michaux-Bellaire, E. Rabat et sa région. *VTM,* 5:1–372. 1921. [Beraber].

Montagne, R. Le régime juridique des tribus du sud marocain. *Hesperis,* 4:313–331. 1924. [Shluh].

———. Massat. *Hesperis,* 4:357–403. 1924. [Shluh].

———. L'Aghbar et les hautes vallées du Grand-Atlas. *Hesperis,* 6:1–32. 1927. [Shluh].

———. *Les Berbères et le Makhzen dans le sud du Maroc.* Paris, 1930. [Shluh].

Mouliéras, A. *Le Maroc inconnu,* vol. 1. Paris, 1895. [Rif].

———. *Une tribu zénète anti-musulmane au Maroc.* Paris, 1905. [Zekara].

Murdock, G. P. Political Moieties. *The State of the Social Sciences,* ed. L. D. White, pp. 133–147. Chicago, 1956.

Niéger, J. Le Touat. *RCD,* 14:170–177, 184–203. 1904.

Piquet, V. *Le peuple marocain.* Paris, 1925.

Querleux. Les Zemmour. *AB,* 1(2):12–61. 1915. [Beraber].

Rohlfs, G. *Kufra.* Leipzig, 1881. [Jofra].

Spillmann, G. Districts et tribus de la haute vallée du Dra'. *VTM,* 9:1–201. 1931. [Atta and Drawa].

Steindorf, G. *Durch die libysche Wüste zur Amonsoase.* Bielefeld and Leipzig, 1904. [Siwa].

Stuhlmann, F. *Ein kulturgeschichtlicher Ausflug in den Aures.* Hamburg, 1912. [Shawia].

Suter, K. Timimum. *MGGW,* 94:31–54. 1952. [Tuat].

Ubach, E., and E. Rackow. *Sitte und Recht in Nordafrika.* Stuttgart, 1923. [Shluh].

Wulsin, F. R. The Prehistoric Archaeology of Northwest Africa. *PPM,* 19(1):1–173. 1941.

Wysner, M. G. *The Kabyle People.* New York, 1945.

16

Saharan Negroes and the Caravan Trade

The Sahara Desert covers slightly more than one-fourth of Africa's land surface—an area greater than that of the continental United States. The region receives an average rainfall of less than 1 inch per year, and nowhere more than 5 inches. Several thousand square miles are completely uninhabited, consisting of scattered areas of *erg,* or shifting sand dunes; of *hammada,* or exposed bedrock; or of flat stretches of gravel and windblown sand, called *reg*. Contrary to common opinion, however, a considerably larger part of the Sahara's surface is capable of supporting human life through animal husbandry and oasis agriculture and has actually been occupied by a sparse population from time immemorial. When one adds to this the barren reaches traversed by important caravan routes operated or controlled by the inhabitants, the area actually utilized by man constitutes so large a proportion of the total territory that we have rarely found it necessary to indicate unoccupied country in mapping tribal boundaries.

Racially, the Sahara affiliates with the Sudan. It had an indigenous Negroid population at the time of the Arab invasions, and the archeological discovery of a tall Negroid skeleton 250 miles north of Timbuktu indicates that the inhabitants had not undergone ethnic change since Paleolithic times. Economically and culturally, however, the Sahara affiliates with North Africa rather than the Sudan—a connection as clear in antiquity as it has been since the advent of Islam.

This tie almost certainly dates back to the original adoption of agriculture. Environmental factors and the lack of advanced irrigation techniques prevented early Sudanic agriculture from spreading northward into the Sahara, either through migration or through diffusion. But when the Berbers acquired the Egyptian complex, along with its associated domestic animals and methods of irrigation and fertilization, the situation changed. The Saharan Negroes could use what their northern neighbors had to offer, and borrowing became inevitable when the Berbers discovered the advantages to be derived from trade with the civilizations of the Sudan, advantages which could be achieved only by crossing the Sahara. In view of the manifest superiority of their own habitat, the Berbers lacked any incentive to colonize the Sahara, but they did need the cooperation of its inhabitants in exploring trade routes and probably also in the actual conduct of commerce itself. Through such intimate contacts the Negroes of the desert came to abandon their old life of hunting and gathering and to adopt the food plants, livestock, and associated techniques of their Caucasoid neighbors to the north, which have distinguished them ever since from their racial kinsmen to the south.

Under the conditions of extreme aridity prevailing in the Sahara, human occupation depends primarily upon the availability of water. One source is provided by rivers, which arise in regions of greater rainfall and then traverse portions of the desert. The Dra and Sis, for example, carry water from the Atlas Mountains into the arid country of southern Morocco. A second but important source is the infrequent rains. They produce a lush temporary growth of grass and weeds highly nutritious to grazing animals, and their runoff in otherwise dry streambeds leaves enough subsoil moisture to nourish a quick crop. Thirdly there are scattered natural springs which bring subterranean waters to the surface, where they can be distributed by canals to irrigated fields. Finally there is the permanent lens of underground water which can be tapped in various ways. It can be brought to the surface with buckets in artificial wells dug at suitable places along caravan trails to quench the thirst of man and beast, or, where more plentiful, can be raised by shadoof or well sweeps and conveyed to irrigated fields. A particularly ingenious device is the *foggara,* an underground tunnel constructed at a slight slope from a natural source of subsurface water, which is then conducted by gravity, sometimes for miles, to the place of use without loss through evaporation. Another is the sunken garden—a pit sometimes as much as 40 feet in depth, at the bottom of which crops are grown on prepared soil at an elevation so low that their roots can reach ground water without irrigation.

Through these means the scattered oases of the Sahara support an amazingly rich and varied agriculture. The crops include most of those of the Egyptian and Greco-Roman complexes as well as numerous introductions from the Sudan and America. All those enumerated below are specifically reported in ethnographic sources for true oases, i.e., excluding those watered by permanent streams.

Grains: Asiatic millet, barley, maize, millet, rice, rye, sorghum, wheat.
Legumes and forage crops: alfalfa, broad beans, chick peas, hyacinth beans, lentils, peas, vetch.
Root crops: beets, carrots, chufa, onions, radishes, turnips.
Leaf and stalk vegetables: cabbage, celery, okra, purslane, rape.
Vine and ground fruits: cucumbers, eggplant, gourds, grapes, melons, pumpkins, squash, tomatoes, watermelons.
Fruits and nuts: almonds, apples, apricots, dates, figs, jujubes, olives, oranges, peaches, pears, plums, pomegranates, quinces.
Condiments and indulgents: black caraway, coriander, cumin, garlic, peppers, tobacco.
Textile plants: ambary, cotton, flax, hemp.
Dye plants: henna, indigo, saffron.

Animal husbandry, which is of subsidiary importance to the tillers of the oases, becomes the primary basis of subsistence to an approximately equal number of pastoral nomads. These people live in part directly on the meat and milk of their herds, in part indirectly on the "protection," i.e., tribute, which they exact from caravan merchants and the sedentary population. Cattle and horses are few in number, the principal animals being sheep, goats, donkeys, and camels. The camel, more properly called the one-humped dromedary and more poetically "the ship of the desert," dates only from the Roman period. First mentioned historically in 46 B.C., it did not become established in substantial numbers until the fourth century.

Despite a widespread belief that the Sahara is undergoing progressive desiccation, there is no actual evidence that its water resources have diminished appreciably during the past 7,000 years. The impression stems basically from the fact that wells and water holes along the caravan trails have grown fewer through disuse and lack of maintenance with each technological advance permitting a longer journey without water —the shifts first from human porters to donkeys, then from donkeys to camels, and finally from camels to automotive vehicles. It has also, of course, been accentuated by cases of actual abandonment due exclusively to political factors.

The Sahara assumes importance less for its sparse human population and their ingenious adaptations to an unfavorable environment than for its crucial role in history as an artery of trade and cultural diffusion between the Mediterranean region and Negro Africa. Old caravan trails crisscross it in every direction, following routes where dependable sources of water succeed one another at the shortest maximal intervals. Along these routes the native inhabitants have traded with one another, and with the Sudan and the Mediterranean littoral, from time immemorial, and have brought the products of the heart of Africa to the ancient seats of civilization, and vice versa. This traffic doubtless dates from early in the Neolithic period, for along stretches where some of the principal trails pass over rocky *hammada* the bedrock has been polished smooth by the bare feet of countless thousands of human porters before animal transport came into general use.

Map 12 shows the principal caravan routes. Four of them occupy positions of especial historical importance. The first of these, proceeding from west to east, is the Taodeni Trail, linking Morocco—via Abuam, Terhaza, Taodeni, and Arawan—with Walata and the middle Niger region at Timbuktu. The second, the Gadames Trail, connects modern Tunisia and ancient Carthage with the Hausa country of Nigeria via Gabes, Gadames, Gat, Assiu, and Agades. The third, or Bilma Trail, links Libya in the north with the native states of Bornu and Kanem on Lake Chad by way of Sokna, Murzuk, and Bilma. The fourth, the Selima Trail, connects ancient and modern Egypt with Darfur and Wadai in the central Sudan via the oases of Kharga, Selima, and Bir-Natrun. Alternative or combined routes, of course, might also be chosen; two of the most popular in the early Middle Ages led from Egypt to Gao and Timbuktu—the one passing through Siwa and other northern oases and thence southwest through Murzuk, Gat, and Tamanrasset, the other running southwest through Kufra and thence via either Tekro and Nguimi or Bilma and Agades. Of considerable consequence, too, are the routes leading

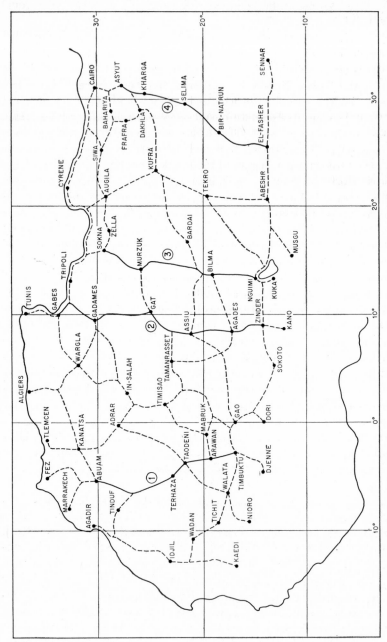

Map 12. Trans-Saharan Caravan Routes (1—Taodeni Trail, 2—Gadames Trail, 3—Bilma Trail, 4—Selima Trail)

south from Algeria either through Wargla and In-Salah or through Kanatsa and Adrar.

To the trade along these routes the oasis dwellers have contributed their own products—dates, livestock, hides, dried and salted meat, milk products, saltpeter, and especially salt, which has always been in high demand in the Sudan. Important salt mines are located near Tekro and In-Salah, but the greatest producer is Taodeni. The fact that salt caravans from Taodeni to Timbuktu have been observed, even in the present century, with as many as 25,000 camels each gives some conception of the magnitude of the Saharan traffic. The products shipped southward from the Mediterranean region throughout the historical period have consisted chiefly of grain to the Sahara and of arms, glass, other manufactured goods, and luxury items to both the Sahara and the Sudan. The Sudan has supplied the Sahara with grain, dried fish, kola nuts, and cotton goods, and the Mediterranean region with a constant flow of ivory, gold, ebony, ostrich feathers, and slaves. A substantial proportion of the gold and ivory held by the peoples of Europe and the Near East prior to the Discoveries Period seems to have been derived ultimately from Negro Africa through the trans-Saharan trade. The contribution of Africa to economic history can scarcely be overestimated.

West of Nubia, where culture history has followed a very different course, the Sahara falls ethnically into three divisions. In the east, from Tibesti south to the borders of Bornu, Bagirmi, and Wadai, the Negroes still substantially hold their own. In Greek and Roman times, when they were known as the Garamantes, they extended considerably farther north, occupying all of Fezzan, where Negroid physical traits are still prominent. The Arabs expelled them from the oasis of Kufra as recently as 1813. The modern descendants of the Garamantes, like the inhabitants of Bornu to the southwest, speak languages of the independent Kanuric stock (see Map 6) and fall into the following tribal groups.

1. Berti. These people, who are linguistically akin to the Zaghawa, inhabit the Tagabo Hills in Darfur.
2. Bideyat (Anna, Awe, Baele, Bedeyat, Terawia), with the kindred Gaida (Gaeda) and Murdia (Mourdia) of Ennedi and the Unia of Unianga. Numbering about 18,000, they are partly pagans and partly indifferent Moslems. Their language is closely related to but not mutually intelligible with Zaghawa.
3. Bulgeda (Boulgheda), including the Bultoa (Bolto), Dalea (Dalia), Irie (Iria), Jagada (Diagada), and Sangada (Koroa, Sagada) of Borku.
4. Daza (Dasa, Dazagarda), including the Dogorda (Gorane), Dongosa (Doza, Dozza), Famalla (Haualla, Medela), Kokorda, Nakaza (Akaza, Anakatza, Nakatsa), Wandala (Ouendallah), and other subtribes of northern Kanem. With the Bulgeda they number about 20,000, all Moslems.
5. Kawar. The natives of Kawar are partly Teda, partly Kanembu and Kanuri, with Kanuri as the prevailing language. They number about 6,000.

6. Kreda (Karra), including the kindred Kacherda, each division having numerous subtribes. They number about 20,000 and speak a language akin to Daza.
7. Teda (Tebu, Tibbu, Toubou, Tubu). This tribe, comprising about 10,000 in Tibesti and another 2,000 in Fezzan, was converted to Islam in the late eighteenth century.
8. Zaghawa (Soghaua, Zegaoua, Zorhaua). This tribe, resident in northern Darfur, is still only partially Islamized.

Of these Saharan tribes, the Berti and Kawar are sedentary and primarily agricultural, the Bideyat, Bulgeda, Kreda, and Zaghawa largely pastoral, and the Daza and Teda almost equally composed of nomadic herders and of sedentary or semisedentary tillers. They grow most of the Saharan crops previously enumerated, with the date palm usually the staple. All tribes keep numerous camels, sheep, goats, and donkeys, and all except the Kawar and Teda have cattle as well. They do very little hunting and fishing but gather quantities of wild-palm nuts in season, and the caravan trade looms very large in their economy. The men herd and milk the larger animals, engage in trade, and hunt, whereas the women gather, fish, and tend and milk the smaller livestock. Both sexes share the labor of cultivation where this is not performed by slaves.

The sedentary tribes live, at least seasonally, in permanent compact villages, whereas the nomads wander in migratory bands. Three house types are reported. The nomads occupy rectangular or elliptical tents with dismountable wooden frames, vertical walls, and either flat or pitched roofs covered with palm-leaf mats or, occasionally, with skins. The Kawar and most of the sedentary Daza have rectangular dwellings with mud walls and gabled roofs thatched with palm leaves, but the sedentary Teda, a few of the Daza, and probably the Berti live in round huts with cylindrical walls of dry stones or mud and conical thatched roofs.

Each local community, which is structurally often a patriclan, has a hereditary headman. He is in some instances essentially autonomous and in others subordinate to a petty paramount chief. The Kawar and Teda each have a tribal "sultan," selected in rotation from two or more noble lineages, but he possesses only nominal authority. The Bideyat and Zaghawa acknowledge the suzerainty, respectively, of the Wadai and Darfur states. All tribes possess slaves and have despised and endogamous castes of smiths, and the Daza, Kawar, and Teda distinguish certain noble sibs from ordinary commoners. Warfare, though frequent, is confined in the main to raiding and blood feuds.

Marriage involves a substantial bride-price in livestock and is universally forbidden with any first cousin. Polygyny, though everywhere permitted, is only moderately common among the Daza, Kreda, and Teda. Patrilocal residence prevails, but it is preceded by an initial period of matrilocal residence among the Bideyat, Daza, and Teda. The evidence on social organization, though scanty, strongly suggests the prevalence of agamous patrisibs divided into exogamous lineages, and at least the Teda have cousin terminology of the Iroquois pattern. Inheritance and succession follow the patrilineal rule. Primogeniture prevails among the Zaghawa, but the other tribes conform approximately to Islamic law, according to which a portion of a man's estate is reserved for his widow and the remainder divided equally among his children with full shares to sons and half shares to daughters.

The central portion of the Sahara, to the west of the Kanuric-speaking Negroes, is dominated today by the Tuareg (see Chapter 53), a nation of camel nomads who speak a Berber language and are unquestionably Caucasoid. Among them and outnumbering them, however, lives a depressed caste of Negroes who are usually known by the Songhai name of Bella, though locally called Haratin. Various facts belie the common assumption that the Bella are descendants of Negro slaves imported from the Sudan. The Tuareg do possess such slaves, whom they employ as house servants, but they call them Iklan and distinguish them sharply from the Bella, who are agricultural serfs owned by or attached to particular Tuareg families or lineages whom they support by their labor either directly or through annual tribute in agricultural products. This status suggests subjugation and exploitation rather than slave descent.

The Bella subsist by sedentary agriculture, and even today have not adopted the Tuareg tent but live either in hemispherical shelters of poles covered with grass mats or in rectangular huts with flat roofs and walls of sun-dried brick or stones laid in mud. The Tuareg, on the other hand, follow an exclusively pastoral mode of life—a relatively recent development in North Africa—and refrain contemptuously from any kind of agricultural labor. This intimation that they are latecomers to the Sahara is confirmed by historical evidence, cited by Urvoy (1936), that they originally inhabited Tripolitania, whence they were forced into the desert by the pressure of Arab expansion between the eleventh and sixteenth centuries. Records from classical antiquity, moreover, show that oases as far north as Gadames in Tunisia and Gurara, Tuggurt, and Wargla in Algeria were then inhabited by Negroes. The Berber seizure of Wargla, indeed, can be specifically documented as occurring in the ninth century.

If Negroid peoples still occupied the central Sahara until medieval times, as now seems indisputable, to what linguistic group did they belong? Urvoy (1936) tells us explicitly that the present Tuareg country of Air was originally inhabited by Hausa-speaking Negroes, who retreated thence into Gobir under pressure from the invading Berbers. Moreover, for the oasis of Gadames, located at approximately the point where the present boundaries of Libya, Tunisia, and Algeria meet, all the earliest European explorers—e.g., Richardson (1848), Duveyrier (1864), and

Chavanne (1879)—report Hausa as the prevailing language of the Negro population, although they do not make absolutely clear whether they are referring to the Bella or to slaves imported from Nigeria. The Hausa nation of today enjoy a reputation throughout the Sudan for their mercantile propensities, which is precisely what one might expect in a people habituated for millennia to the trans-Saharan caravan trade. The conclusion that the ancestors of the Bella spoke Hausa would also solve a problem of linguistic distribution. It would bring the Chadic subfamily of Hamitic, to which Hausa belongs, into geographical contiguity with the Berber subfamily, whereas today the speakers of Chadic are separated by the entire breadth and half the length of the Sahara Desert from any other representatives of the Hamitic linguistic stock except latecoming Arab and Tuareg groups.

The western third of the Sahara, extending from the Tuareg country to the Atlantic Ocean, is largely occupied today by a series of Arab and Arabized Berber tribes. In practically every instance we possess definite historical evidence of their derivation from the north, usually from Morocco, as a part of or in consequence of the westward expansion of the Arabs. We know, for example, that the Zenaga tribe had established themselves in the Hodh region of the French Sudan by the ninth century. With the exception of an uninhabitable section in the center, the western Sahara was originally inhabited exclusively by Negroes. They still survive there as the Haratin, a subject group of agricultural serfs whose status almost exactly replicates that of the Bella among the Tuareg and who are equally distinct from imported Sudanese slaves and their descendants.

In the north, we know that the oases of the Dra and Sis Rivers in southeastern Morocco originally had an indigenous Negroid population. The earliest historical sources likewise report the presence of Negroes as well as Berbers in present Shluh territory along the Atlantic coast and in the valley of the Sous River, but they had apparently disappeared from this region by A.D. 1100. We lack any evidence indicative of their possible linguistic affiliations.

On the fringe of the Sudan farther south, however, the present Haratin are probably descended from Negroes of the Mande subfamily of the Nigritic stock. It was these people, and not some unidentified Caucasoid group as is sometimes alleged, who formed the core of the great empire of Ghana, which flourished for centuries prior to A.D. 1000 in the general vicinity of modern Walata. Ghana maintained extensive trade relations with North Africa, and it was probably in this connection that a number of Mande peoples (variously called Dafi, Diula, Marka, etc.) now scattered throughout the western Sudan, where they play an economic role comparable to that of the Hausa in the central Sudan, acquired their exceptional mercantile interest and skill. The fact that the Aser, a small remnant group of Mande speech, still survive in the desert oases of Tichit and Walata provides confirmation of this inference.

Selected Bibliography

Bouillié, R. *Les coutumes familiales au Kanem.* Paris, 1937. [Daza].
Bovill, E. W. *Caravans of the Old Sahara.* London, 1933.
Carbou, H. *La région du Tchad et du Ouadaï,* vol. 1. Paris, 1912.
Chavanne, J. *Die Sahara.* Wien, 1879.
Cline, W. The Teda of Tibesti, Borku, and Kawar. *GSA,* 12:1–52. 1950.
Dalloni, M. Mission au Tibesti. *Mémoires de l'Academie des Sciences de l'Institut de France,* 62:405–449. 1936. [Teda].
Duveyrier, H. *Les Touareg du nord.* Paris, 1864.
Fuchs, P. Ueber die Tubbu von Tibesti. *AV,* 11:43–66. 1956. [Teda].
Gamory-Dubourdeau, P. M. Notes sur les coutumes des Toubou du nord. *BCEHS,* 9:131–152. 1926. [Teda].
Gautier, E. F. *Sahara, the Great Desert.* New York, 1935.
Le Coeur, C. Dictionnaire ethnographique Téda. *MIFAN,* 9:1–213. 1950.
MacMichael, H. A. *The Tribes of Northern and Central Kordofan.* Cambridge, 1912.
Meigs, P. Outlook for Arid North Africa. *Focus,* 5(4):1–6. 1954.
Nachtigal, G. Die Tibbu. *ZGE,* 5:216–242, 289–316. 1870. [Teda].
———. *Sahara und Sudan.* 2 vols. Berlin, 1879–1881.
Prall. Le secteur nord du cercle de Gouré. *BIFAN,* 7:1–46. 1945. [Teda].
Richardson, J. *Travels in the Great Desert of the Sahara,* vol. 1. London, 1848.
Schiffers, H. *Die Sahara und die Syrtenländer.* Stuttgart, 1950.
Urvoy, Y. Histoire des populations du Soudan central. *PCEHS,* ser. A, 5:1–350. 1936.
Westermann, D. *Geschichte Afrikas.* Köln, 1952.

17

Negroes of the Sudan Fringe

The early agricultural civilization which arose around the headwaters of the Niger River and gradually diffused eastward across the entire breadth of the Sudan to the Nile Valley also spread northward to the edge of the Sahara as far as geographical conditions permitted. As we have seen, however, it did not penetrate the desert, where the Negro inhabitants continued to live a nomadic life of hunting and gathering until their Caucasoid neighbors to the north had received from Southwest Asia the Neolithic crops and techniques that could be adapted to oasis conditions. It was not, of course, until much later that the Berbers occupied portions of the Sahara. But they, and presumably the Egyptians even earlier, did establish trade relations across the desert with the Sudan, thus stimulating the adoption of agriculture by the Saharan Negroes.

As this trade developed, its impact was naturally felt first and strongest by the Negro peoples inhabiting the northern fringe of the Sudan. It was they who enjoyed the resulting economic prosperity, who benefited by the new products of Mediterranean origin, and who were in a position to enrich their cultures by borrowing adaptive elements from those with whom they traded. In consequence, they must then have achieved the cultural leadership in the Sudan which they seem to have held ever since. During the historical period most of them have accepted Islam and much of its associated culture, so that they must be regarded today as constituting the African frontier of the Moslem world and of the great Middle Eastern culture area. Elements of Arabic origin now obtrude so prominently, indeed, that it is no easy problem to isolate the features of culture borrowed during earlier periods.

The most intensive impact must naturally always have been felt in the immediate vicinity of the Sudanic termini of the four major trans-Saharan caravan routes. At precisely these points, from the dawn of recorded history to modern times, there have existed strong native states with relatively complex cultures and comparatively elaborate political systems, whose antecedents doubtless go far back into the prehistoric past. The spheres of influence of these states enable us to divide the Sudan fringe into a number of distinct provinces. At the termini of the easternmost trail, the Selima, leading from Egypt, lie the states and provinces of Darfur and Wadai. Farther west, the Bilma Trail links Libya with the states and provinces of Bagirmi and Bornu. The Gadames Trail from ancient Carthage and modern Tunisia terminates at the major cities of the Hausa states and province. From Morocco the Taodeni Trail leads to the middle and upper Niger. The states of the latter, notably Ghana and its successors, have already been described, together with the cultures of their surviving populations, in Chapter 11. The alternative terminus on the middle Niger, with Timbuktu as the principal mercantile center, is occupied by the Songhai nation and province. The several provinces in order from east to west, with the peoples who compose them, are briefly characterized below.

DARFUR PROVINCE

Exclusive of Arabic and other intrusive peoples described elsewhere, all the constituent groups of this province speak languages of the Dagu branch of the Eastern Sudanic subfamily, with the single exception of the Fur, who constitute the sole members of the independent Furian stock.

The province has a total population of about 750,000, but no reliable breakdown by tribes is available. Although Darfur was doubtless the first province to experience contact with ancient Egypt, via either the Selima Trail or the Nile Valley, its actual historical record does not begin until the fourteenth or fifteenth century.

1. Dagu (Dadio, Dago, Daju, Tagu), with the kindred Bego (Baygo, Beigo).
2. Fur (For, Forawa), embracing the Dalinga, Forenga, Kamminga, Karakarit, Kungara, and Temurka. They are the dominant people of the province politically and probably also numerically.
3. Kimr (Ermbeli, Guemra, Guimr). They are the inhabitants of Dar Kimr.
4. Sila (Sula). They are a branch of the Dagu, from whom they split off several centuries ago to settle in Dar Sila. An offshoot of the Sila, the Shatt (Dagu), later migrated to Kordofan and settled in the western Nuba Hills, where about 2,000 still survive.
5. Tama, with the kindred Erenga (Djebel, Iringa) and Sungor (Soungor). They are a branch of the Sila who settled Dar Tama, whence they displaced the Kimr.

WADAI PROVINCE

Except for two groups, the Merarit and Mubi, all the indigenous tribes of this province speak languages of the independent Maban stock. They have a total population of nearly a million. The historical record begins at the same late date as does that for Darfur.

6. Maba (Wadaians), embracing the Bandula (Banadoula, Madala), Fala (Bakka), Ganyanga, Kashmere (Kachmere), Kadjanga (Abu Derreg), Karanga (Malanga), Kelinguen (Kelingane), Kodvi (Kudu), Madaba, Marfa, Matlambe, and Moyo. They number nearly 300,000 and dominate Wadai politically.
7. Masalit (Massalat).
8. Merarit (Mararet), with the kindred Ali, Chale, Kubu (Koubou), and Oro. These tribes constitute the distinct Merarit branch of the Eastern subfamily of the Sudanic linguistic stock.
9. Mimi (Mima, Moutoutou).
10. Mubi (Moubi), with the kindred Karbo (Korbo, Kourbo). These people speak languages of the Chadic subfamily of the Hamitic stock and are doubtless intrusive from the west.
11. Runga (Rounga). They are the inhabitants of Dar Rounga.

BAGIRMI PROVINCE

Since the beginning of dependable history in the early sixteenth century, political hegemony in this province has rested with peoples of the Central Sudanic linguistic subfamily, but they are probably intrusive into the area from the south. The Bua group of Eastern Nigritic speech presumably represents an even later arrival from the southwest. The original inhabitants appear to have belonged to the Chadic subfamily of the Hamitic linguistic stock, which is still numerically strong. Cultural and demographic data are nearly as scanty as for Wadai, but a total population of 150,000 was reported in 1925. Islam has not as yet penetrated the entire province.

12. Bagirmi, with the Busso. The Central Sudanic Bagirmi, who dominate the province politically, were reported to number 31,000 in 1925.
13. Bua, with the Koke (Khoke), Nielim (Njillem, Nyelem), and Tunia (Tounia). This Eastern Nigritic group, reported in 1925 to number about 7,000, is still mainly pagan.
14. Fanyan (Fagnia, Fanian, Nuba). This tribe, reported to number 1,200 in 1925, is only partially Islamized. The linguistic affiliation of this group, though not specifically reported, is probably Chadic.
15. Gaberi (Gabri, Ngabre), with the Chiri (Chere, Shere, Tshire), Dormo, Lele, and Nangire (Nancere). This Chadic group is pagan in religion.
16. Kenga (Kenya, Khenga), with the Babalia, Diongor, Masmadje, and Saba. This Central Sudanic group, numbering about 3,000 in 1925, is still pagan.
17. Kun (Kuang, Kung). The linguistic affiliation of this pagan group is not reported but is presumably Chadic.
18. Lisi, embracing the Bulala (Boulala, Maga), Kuka (Kouka), Midogo (Medogo, Mudogo), and Semen (Abu Semen). These peoples, who are also found in Kanem, are Central Sudanic in speech, indifferent Moslems in religion, and considerably mixed with Caucasoid elements.
19. Musgu (Mousgou, Musgum, Musuk). This Chadic tribe, numbering about 35,000, is only slightly Islamized.
20. Sokoro (Bedanga), with the Barein (Barain) and Yalna. This Chadic group, still pagan in religion, was reported to number about 13,000 in 1925.
21. Somrai, with the Deressia, Kabalai, Mesme, Miltu (Miltou), Modgel, Ndam, Sarwa (Sarua), and Tumak (Toummak, Tummok). This Chadic group is still pagan.

BORNU PROVINCE

The indigenous population of this province, as of Bagirmi, appears to have been Chadic in language but not specifically Hausa. They have long been politically dominated, however, by peoples of the Kanuric linguistic stock akin to the Saharan Negroes who control the Bilma Trail and who very probably penetrated the region from the north with the aid of superior sociocultural techniques acquired from the North African Berbers in the caravan trade. They enter history in the eighth century with the establishment of the Sef dynasty, which held power, first in Kanem and later in Bornu, until 1846—perhaps the longest dynastic reign on record anywhere in the world.

22. Auyokawa, with the Shirawa and Teshenawa. This Chadic people, now largely acculturated to the Hausa, number about 50,000. They were Islamized in the seventeenth century.
23. Bede (Bedde). This Chadic group, numbering about 50,000, is still largely pagan.
24. Beriberi, with the Dogara (Dagra). This Kanuric people, numbering about 110,000, are strongly acculturated to the Hausa, whose language some of them have adopted.
25. Bolewa (Bole, Borlawa, Fika). This Chadic group, with a semi-independent kingdom, has a population of about 35,000.

26. Buduma (Boudouma, Jedina, Yedina), with the Kuri (Kouri). These Chadic people, who number about 20,000, inhabit about seventy islands in Lake Chad, where they subsist primarily by fishing and animal husbandry with only aux- iliary agriculture.

27. Kanembu (Hamedj), embracing the Bade, Baribu, Chiroa (Tschiroa), Dalatoa, Danoa (Danawa, Haddad), Diabu, Galabu, Gudjiru, Kaburi, Kadjidi, Kankena, Kanka (Konku), Maguemi, Ngejim (Ngischem), and Sugurti (Tsugurti). This Kanuric nation, numbering about 75,000, was Islamized in the late eleventh cen- tury.

28. Kanuri (Beriberi, Kanoury), with the Magumi (Magomi). This Kanuric nation, numbering nearly a million, has been politically dominant since 1380, when the ruling dynasty moved from Kanem to Bornu.

29. Karekare (Kerekere), with the kindred Ngamo (Gamawa). This Chadic group, still largely pagan, numbers about 55,000.

30. Kotoko (Logone, Makari), with the kindred Ngala. These Chadic people prob- ably number in excess of 100,000.

31. Koyam (Kai, Kojam). This Kanuric tribe numbers about 15,000.

32. Mandara (Ndara, Wandala), with the Gamergu and Maya. This Chadic group numbers about 80,000, mainly Moslems.

33. Manga (Mangawa). This Kanuric nation numbers about 100,000.

34. Mober (Mobber). This Chadic tribe has a population of about 25,000.

35. Ngizim (Ngezzim). This Chadic tribe, numbering about 25,000 is only partially Islamized.

36. Tera (Kemaltu, Terawa), with the kindred Hina (Hinna) and Jera (Jara, Jerra). This Chadic group, numbering about 40,000, is incompletely Islamized.

HAUSA PROVINCE

All the peoples of this province speak languages of the Hausa branch of the Chadic subfamily of the Hamitic stock. As indicated in Chapter 16, at least some of them appear to have come from the north, where they once occupied the central portion of the Sahara, whence they were driven by the Berbers under Arab pressure. That Chadic peoples have long inhabited the Sudan, however, is indicated by the presence of other branches of the subfamily, not only in the Bornu and Bagirmi provinces, but also in the Nigerian plateau area. Though never politically unified until their conquest by the Fulani in the nineteenth century, the Hausa peoples, probably as a result of long experience in the trans-Saharan caravan trade, have achieved a degree of cultural unity comparable to that of the great nations of Europe in modern times and are perhaps the only nation of Negro Africa where this can definitely be said to have happened prior to European colonial occupation. They are likewise liter- ate. Long ago they adopted the Arabic alphabet for writing their own language and have since produced an extensive literature, especially of a historical character. The famous Kano Chronicle, for example, gives us unusual historical depth for this part of the Sudan, although the events recorded before the fourteenth century deal mainly with wars among the various Hausa states.

37. Adarawa (Aderaoua), with the Azna (Anna, Arna, Asna, Azena), Gubei, and Tulumi (Touloumey). They number about 250,000 and are incompletely Islamized.
38. Hausa (Haoussa), embracing the indigenous inhabitants of the former states of Daura (the Daurawa), Gobir, Kano (the Kanawa), Katsena (the Katsenawa), Kebbi (the Kebbawa), Zamfara, and Zaria (the Zazzagawa). With their pagan kinsmen, the Maguzawa, they number about 5 million.
39. Kurfei (Kourfey, Soudie). They number about 40,000 and are largely pagan.
40. Maguzawa (Pagan Hausa). These people are pagan in religion but otherwise indistinguishable from the Hausa proper. Since they are geographically interspersed with the latter, the mapping of their territory is arbitrary.
41. Mauri (Maouri). This pagan tribe numbers about 75,000.
42. Tazarawa, with the Tegamawa and substantial remnants of the Hausa of Daura and Gobir now residing in French territory. They number about 600,000, of whom approximately a third are still pagan.

SONGHAI PROVINCE

West of the Hausa, along the Niger River where its great bend touches the edge of the Sahara Desert, reside the peoples who constitute the sole representatives of the independent Songhaic linguistic stock. They appear to have come from the western part of the Hausa country, whence they ascended the Niger to their present location. They enter history about A.D. 700.

43. Dendi. These people, who number about 40,000, occupied their present territory by conquest from the Mande-speaking Tienga about 150 years ago.
44. Songhai (Songhoi, Sonhray). This nation, numbering about 330,000, has usually exercised political domination in the province.
45. Zerma (Djerma, Dyerma, Zaberma). These people number about 250,000.

Since actual recorded history begins earlier in the western than in the eastern provinces of the Sudan fringe, we may present our historical summary in reverse geographical order. When the Songhai first appeared in history, they were ruled by a dynasty of pagan Lemta Berbers who had been driven from Tripolitania in the first Arab conquest. From their capital at Kukia on the Niger below Gao they gradually extended their sway up the river and, in 1009, removed their administrative center to Gao. The conversion of the people to Islam began at about this time. In 1325 the Malinke of Mali captured Timbuktu and Gao and dominated the middle Niger until 1433, when they lost Timbuktu to the Tuareg. In 1465 a Songhai prince of Gao, named Sonni Ali, drove the Tuareg from Timbuktu and, in 1473, occupied Djenne. After his death one of his principal lieutenants, a Soninke named Askia, overthrew Sonni Ali's son and founded a new dynasty in 1493. Askia tried unsuccessfully to reduce the Mossi state, but he wrested large territories from Mali and, in 1512, launched a series of attacks against the Hausa states, conquering Gobir, Zamfara, Katsena, Zaria, and Kano in rapid succession. In 1515 he turned against the Tuareg, occupied Agades, expelled the bulk of the local population, and established there a Songhai colony, of which remnants survive to the present day. Under Askia the Songhai enjoyed enormous prosperity, a university was established at Timbuktu, and the fame of the kingdom was spread throughout the Moslem world by a pilgrimage which the ruler made to Mecca with a large force of retainers and a huge gift in gold for charitable foundations in the holy city.

The wealth of the Songhai state aroused the cupidity of the Sultan of Morocco, Ahmed el Mansur, who seized the rich salt mines of Terhaza in the Sahara in 1585 and, in 1591, dispatched an army equipped with firearms which took Gao by surprise. Within a year his forces had also occupied and sacked Timbuktu and Djenne. The Moroccans withdrew their military forces in 1618 and left the administration in the hands of a pasha. After 1660 the pashas of Timbuktu achieved independence, but the Moroccan regime of pillage and extortion had so disrupted the economy of the region that the trans-Saharan trade shifted to more easterly routes and prosperity vanished. After 1780 the Tuareg achieved political dominance on the middle Niger and held it, except for a brief period of Bambara rule around 1800, until the French occupation in 1893.

The Hausa peoples received their first knowledge of Islam from the west in the fourteenth century, when the Malinke kingdom of Mali, then at its apogee, dispatched merchants and emissaries to their country. The conversion of King Yaji of Kano (1349–1385) initiated the penetration of this new religion, which has proceeded at fluctuating rates ever since and is today nearly complete. After their conquest by King Askia of Songhai, the Hausa gradually recovered their independence. With the Moroccan conquest of Gao and Timbuktu in 1591 they entered on a period of great economic prosperity. Under the disturbed conditions prevailing on the middle Niger the bulk of the trans-Saharan caravan trade, which had heretofore followed the Taodeni Trail to Timbuktu, shifted to the Gadames Trail, whose termini, Kano and Katsena, now became the great mercantile metropoles of the Sudan. A new threat soon appeared from the south with the rising power of the Jukun state of Kororofa, which repeatedly invaded the Hausa country and exacted tribute from Kano and some of its neighbors throughout most of the seventeenth century. The pastoral Fulani, who had begun to infiltrate the region in the fifteenth century, had become a significant element in the population by the eighteenth century, but the story of the holy war waged by Osman dan Fodio and of his conquest of the Hausa states (1804–1809) must be reserved until Chapter 55.

Islam penetrated the Bornu province in the latter part of the eleventh century. During the early thirteenth century, political and military expansion carried the borders of the state of Kanem to Fezzan in the north, Wadai in the east, and the Niger River in the west. In 1380, however, the Bulala tribe of Lisi from Bagirmi occupied Kanem, and the ruler fled to the west of Lake Chad, where he founded the state of Bornu, the center of political power in the province ever since. King Idris Alowa (1571–1603) of Bornu, obtaining firearms from the Turks of Tunisia, embarked on an ambitious career of conquest. He subjugated the Asben Tuareg of Air, the Hausa state of Kano, and the Kotoko, Mandara, Margi, Musgu, and Ngizim tribes to the south and, in the seventeenth century, also reduced Bagirmi to tributary status. During the latter part of the eighteenth century the Fulani began to infiltrate the country, but an attempt by the followers of Osman dan Fodio to conquer Bornu was repulsed in 1809. Kanem, however, suffered invasions by the Bagirmi and the Soliman Arabs, and Bornu, weakened by these struggles, was conquered by Wadai in 1846, bringing to a close the long reign of the Sef dynasty. In 1894, Rabeh, an Arabized Negro slave raider and adventurer from Sennar on the Nile, after a career of depredation and conquest in the central Sudan, reduced Bornu and established there the capital of a completely exploitative state. He was defeated and slain by the French in 1898, and shortly thereafter his country was parceled among the British, French, and Germans.

Although Islam was introduced into the Bagirmi province around 1600, its spread there has been relatively limited. Throughout much of their history, the dominant Bagirmi have fought and frequently subjugated the Lisi, Kotoko, Mandara, Sokoro, and Somrai. Wedged in, however, between the stronger states of Bornu on the west and Wadai on the east, the Bagirmi have usually been tributary to one or the other and at best have been able only to harass them by an occasional attack without the prospect of conquest. Tribes of Baggara, or Cattle Arabs, began to infiltrate the province from the east during the seventeenth century, and the Fulani from the west somewhat later. In the early nineteenth century the Soliman Arabs from Tripolitania ravaged Bagirmi, which survived only with help from Wadai. Rabeh conquered the province in 1892 and, from his subsequent capital in Bornu, subjected it to nearly a decade of systematic plunder.

The Arabic-speaking Tungur arrived in Darfur in the fourteenth or fifteenth century and later spread to Wadai. Because of their language the Tungur have usually been assumed to be Arabs, but they do not regard themselves as such, and the assumption is further contradicted by indications that they did not accept Islam until the seventeenth century, the period of the conversion of the other peoples of Darfur and Wadai. The fact that they still use the sign of the cross suggests that they may formerly have been Christians, and there are other intimations that they were originally Arabized Berbers or Nubians who reached the Sudan from, or by way of, the Christian kingdom of Dongola in

Nubia. They intermarried with the Dagu, who had previously been politically dominant in Darfur, and succeeded them in power. Soon afterward they extended their sway to Wadai. Race mixture and acculturation continued, and after 1600 dynasties of native origin replaced them in both states. Since then the Fur have been the dominant group in Darfur and the Maba in Wadai. The two states, traditional rivals, have waged war intermittently throughout their history. Darfur, the stronger until the seventeenth century, also had political ambitions in the east and even conquered Kordofan and temporarily reduced the Fung kingdom of Sennar. Wadai dominated Bagirmi and frequently warred with Bornu. Both yielded considerable territory to the Baggara, or Cattle Arabs, in the expansion of the latter into the central Sudan, and Darfur succumbed to the Egyptians in 1875 and to the Mahdists in 1883 before the establishment of British rule.

The basic economy differs remarkably little throughout the Sudan fringe. With the sole exception of the Buduma of Lake Chad, all peoples depend for subsistence primarily upon hoe cultivation. The influence of North Africa reveals itself in the fairly widespread practice of irrigation, the occasional appearance of the Egyptian shadoof, the use of animal manure as fertilizer, and the cultivation of a few of the crops of the Egyptian complex, notably garlic, melons, onions, and occasionally even wheat and the date palm. Nevertheless, the Sudanic complex unquestionably takes precedence. Sorghum and millet are everywhere the staples, and the sources attest every other crop of this complex except coleus, the Guinea yam, the oil palm, and yergan. Ambary, fonio, and rizga, however, are confined to the two westernmost provinces. Borrowings from all other sources, omitting very exceptional occurrences, include rice and yams from Southeast Asia, cucumbers and mangoes from India, and maize, manioc, peanuts, peppers, pumpkins, sweet potatoes, tobacco, and tomatoes from the New World.

Animal husbandry regularly provides an important supplement to agriculture. All tribes possess cattle, sheep, goats, dogs, and chickens in substantial numbers, and many of them also keep horses, donkeys, pigeons, bees, and, at caravan centers, camels. In sharp contrast to most of their southern neighbors, the fringe peoples milk their cows and goats and make butter—an indubitable reflection of North African influence. Hunting is negligible everywhere, but fishing assumes considerable importance except in the Hausa province. The tribes around Lake Chad gather wild rice and waterlily roots, and the Hausa peoples collect substantial quantities of locust beans, shea nuts, and wild baobab and tamarind fruits.

Regular markets, both local and regional, are universal, with cowrie shells and strips of cotton cloth serving as the most widespread media of exchange. Specialized handicraft manufactures are highly developed, and the caravan trade, of course, plays a dominating role in the economy. In Bornu, to select but a single example, caravans bring cotton fabrics, leather goods, and kola nuts from the Hausa country and salt, natron, and Mediterranean manufactured articles from the north, returning with dried fish, ivory, ostrich feathers, and slaves. In the division of labor by sex the men hunt, do most of the fishing, clear the land for agriculture, herd the larger animals, and conduct the caravan commerce, whereas women engage in petty trade and do most of the milking. Agricultural field work and the care of smaller animals, once shared nearly equally by the two sexes, tend to become increasingly masculine concerns where Islam has become firmly established.

The prevailing pattern of rural settlement is a compact village of round huts with conical thatched roofs and cylindrical walls of mats or mud, grouped in rectangular compounds fenced with sorghum stalks or earth walls. Many groups in the Hausa and Bornu provinces, however, live in neighborhoods of dispersed family homesteads, and in the Buduma and Kanembu tribes the dwellings more commonly assume a beehive shape

Kanuri Horsemen of Bornu. (Courtesy of British Information Services.)

without distinct walls. The larger towns and cities in all provinces, however, diverge from this characteristically Sudanic pattern toward one more typical of North Africa. Usually divided into wards, or quarters, they are frequently fortified with turreted walls of brick or stone laid in mud and often contain rectangular houses with flat roofs of beaten earth, battlemented walls of sun-dried bricks, and interior courtyards. The urban Musgu build dwellings of a unique and architecturally striking type. These are very tall and of beehive shape and are constructed of mud with a waterproof coating of clay and dung and with ribbed projections to prevent erosion from rain.

Marriage universally involves a bride-price in livestock or money, and the Karekare, Tera, and some Tazarawa also require premarital bride-service. In all reported cases the preferred union is with a cross-cousin, and wherever Islam is strong, marriage with a parallel cousin is almost equally favored. Polygyny prevails everywhere in the nonsororal form and has a high incidence except among the Fur. The first wife enjoys a privileged status, but each co-wife has her own hut and the husband circulates from one to another in regular rotation. The Ngizim practice cicisbeism; a man may pay another man half of the normal bride-price for the privilege of sleeping with the latter's wife. Moslem tribes ordinarily forbid levirate and sororate unions, but pagans commonly permit them, especially in the junior form.

The Fur, who constitute the only exception to the otherwise universal rule of patrilocal residence, are organized in matrilocal extended families, each with a common men's mess. Elsewhere the residential unit varies between an independent polygynous household and a patrilocal extended family. Except for the Dagu, who follow the matrilineal rule of inheritance, property is always transmitted in the male line, usually in accordance with the Koranic provision that sons participate equally while daughters receive half shares.

With the possible exception of the Fur, descent is invariably patrilineal. Pagan tribes like the Maguzawa are often organized in exogamous but noncorporate patrisibs with totemic food taboos, but Moslem groups have only agamous patrilineages. Kinship terminology of the Iroquois type is reported for the Buduma, Songhai, and Tera; of the Hawaiian type for the Bolewa, Hausa, Karekare, Maguzawa, and Ngizim. Clitoridectomy is not customary, but all tribes save the Musgu apparently practice circumcision. The Bolewa and Tera formerly took the heads of slain enemies as trophies, but cannibalism is completely unknown in the area.

All except the most marginal groups reveal a complex social stratification. The major classes are (1) a privileged nobility, often headed by a royal lineage; (2) free commoners, frequently divided into wealthy merchants, artisans, and peasant farmers; and (3) slaves, including debt

slaves. In addition, endogamous depressed castes of smiths, leatherworkers, hunters, and *griots* are commonly differentiated in the westernmost
provinces.

The cultures of the Sudan fringe, as described up to this point, represent a mixture of elements derived from a variety of sources (see Table
3). We may now face the moot problem of the culture-historical affilia-

Table 3: Affiliations of the Cultures of the Sudan Fringe

Segment of culture	*Historical affiliation*
Language	Negro African except for the very old connection of Chadic with Hamitic
Religion	Preponderantly recent Southwest Asian, i.e., Islamic
Agriculture	Overwhelmingly Sudanic with modest Egyptian and American increments
Animal husbandry	Exclusively Southwest Asian, ranging from Neolithic through Greco-Roman times
Commerce and industry	Predominantly North African, especially Berber and Carthaginian
House type and settlement pattern	Basically indigenous Sudanic but with strong North African increments
Marriage, family, and kinship	Fundamentally Sudanic with important Arab-Islamic modifications
Social stratification	Primarily North African Arabic, overlying an indigenous foundation

tions of the political institutions of the area, already alluded to in Chapter 6. All the major societies of the Sudan fringe, together with those
previously encountered among the Nuclear Mande, Voltaic, and Plateau
Nigerian peoples, as well as others to be examined in future chapters,
are characterized by monarchical bureaucratic states which conform to
a strikingly uniform pattern. Because of certain basic resemblances to
Oriental despotisms in other parts of the world, we have designated this
pattern as the African despotism. The question arises whether this type
of political system represents an indigenous development in the Sudan
or has been derived from North Africa, and, if the latter, from what
specific source.

We can quickly eliminate a series of North African societies as the
primary source: (1) the Berbers and Carthaginians because their republican institutions diverge from the despotic ones of the Sudan in almost
every conceivable respect; (2) the Arabs both because their advent in
North Africa is much too late to have provided a model for the Sudan
states and because their characteristic political organization in North Africa, described in Chapter 52, also differs sharply from the Sudanic
pattern; and (3) Roman, Byzantine, and Turkish North Africa because
their political systems, though also despotic, were themselves derivative

and particularly because their capitals lay in faraway Europe and their colonial administrations in Africa could not have provided a sufficiently complete model of centralized bureaucratic organization for successful copying. This leaves ancient Egypt as the only possible North African source from which the Sudanic peoples could have derived their governmental institutions.

Secondary influences from some of the above sources cannot, of course, be excluded and in certain instances, indeed, are readily demonstrable. Arab-Islamic features, for example, obtrude themselves in nearly all the more recent Sudan states. Moreover, the extensive employment of eunuchs as palace officials and favorites, specifically reported for the Bagirmi, Hausa, Kanuri, Maba, and Mandara, finds no historical prototype in ancient Egypt and can only have been derived from Byzantium through the mediation of the Arabs or Turks.

Excluding such minor accretions, we are left with only two fundamental alternatives—indigenous local development or borrowing from Pharaonic Egypt. Independent evolution of complex absolutistic states in the Sudan certainly cannot be excluded as a possibility since this has occurred in many other parts of the world, e.g., in Babylonia, China, India, Mexico, and Peru, where conditions comparable to those in the prehistoric Sudan have been present, notably intensive agriculture, specialized handicraft industries, urban concentrations of population, and extensive foreign commerce. Moreover, as Steward (1949) has shown, striking parallels occur in all such cases of independent evolution. The issue would appear to rest basically on a question of probabilities. Do the political systems of the Sudan bear only a general resemblance to those of ancient Egypt, as in the cases of the Aztecs, Chinese, and Incas, which would be consistent with independent evolution, or are the likenesses so specific and detailed that cultural borrowing seems the more probable explanation?

As in Egypt and many other early agrarian societies, the Sudanic state is ruled by a theoretically absolute monarch, who administers his domains through a complex bureaucratic hierarchy which maintains order and collects and transmits taxes and tribute of various kinds. The territorial officials receive their support from a share or percentage of the revenues they collect. Though occasionally hereditary, these positions are much more commonly appointive, being filled either by relatives or by favorites of the king. The latter resides in a capital city, where he is surrounded by a harem, a council of ministers with administrative and advisory functions, and a court of personal attendants with specialized duties, such as a palace chamberlain, chief steward, treasurer, commander of the royal bodyguard, harem supervisor, royal spokesman or herald, inspector-general, and royal executioner. Court life is suffused with elaborate protocol, and etiquette demands extreme obeisance toward those of superior status.

The ecclesiastical and military organizations integrate closely with the administrative. The ruler normally serves as the chief mediator with the supernatural; he himself is frequently, though not universally, considered a divine figure and hedged in with ritual taboos; and he commonly has a chief priest as one of his principal ministers. Provincial governors bear military as well as administrative obligations, and the council of ministers typically includes such figures as the commander in chief of the army and the captain of cavalry.

Official positions at all levels are associated with a graded series of honorific titles, some but not all of which are confined to the aristocracy. Since they are rarely strictly hereditary, competition and intrigue to obtain them are rife. At the apex of the structure stands a privy council of higher ministers, who in the Sudan usually combine offices in the territorial organization with specialized functions at the capital. They commonly include, in addition to ecclesiastical and military functionaries, a prime minister or vizier, a chief justice, a supervisor of public works, a chief of police, and an heir designate. Succession, however, is rarely automatic, as by primogeniture, although it is regularly confined to sons of former kings. In many states, a small group of leading ministers who are not themselves eligible for the succession serve as an electoral college with power to select the new ruler without reference to the wishes of his predecessor.

This generalized description of the Sudanic state accords closely with what we know of the political organization of Pharaonic Egypt. Since, however, it reveals no notable inconsistencies with the structure of Oriental despotisms in other parts of the world, it cannot be taken as proof of Egyptian derivation. Even the use of elevated slaves as ministers and territorial officials, attested for the Bagirmi, Hausa, Kanuri, Lisi, and Maba, has precedents elsewhere. However, the Sudanic and Pharaonic states share a few highly specific features that are absent or rare in historically independent absolutistic and bureaucratic systems. Particularly striking among these is the high prestige accorded to certain female statuses of royal rank.

The Pharaonic Egyptians recognized two such statuses, each associated with independent landed estates: the Queen-Consort, or status wife of the king, and the Queen-Mother, the widow of the previous monarch, the mother of the reigning one, or commonly both at the same time. The Queen-Consort occurs, as might perhaps be expected, in practically every Sudanic state, while a prestigeful Queen-Mother, a much less universal status, is specifically attested for the Bagirmi, Bolewa, Kanuri, Maba, and Mandara. In addition, a number of Sudanic states, notably those of the

Bagirmi, Fur, and Kanuri, recognize a third great royal female figure, a Queen-Sister, who is usually the eldest sister of the monarch with authority over all the women of the palace or court. Among the ancient Egyptians, who practiced dynastic incest, the Queen-Consort was commonly also the king's sister. If the Negroes of the Sudan borrowed their political institutions from Egypt, it is quite understandable that, with the prevailing strong taboos against primary incest, they might have separated the dual status of the Pharaonic queen into its constituent functional elements of Queen-Consort and Queen-Sister.

As already indicated in Chapter 6, the writer feels incapable of rendering a final decision between the two alternatives, although he suspects a combination of original independent parallelism with subsequent cultural borrowing.

Selected Bibliography

Anonymous. Coutume Azna. *PCEHS*, ser. A, 10:303–316. 1939. [Adarawa].

———. Coutume Dendi. *PCEHS*, ser. A, 10:317–335. 1939.

———. Coutume Maouri. *PCEHS*, ser. A, 10:337–357. 1939.

———. Coutumes Haoussa et Peul. *PCEHS*, ser. A, 10:261–301. 1939. [Tazarawa].

Ardant du Picq. Les Dyerma. *BCEHS*, 14:461–704. 1931. [Zerma].

Arkell, A. J. The History of Darfur. *SNR*, 32:37–70, 207–238; 33:129–155, 244–275. 1951–1952.

Barth, H. *Travels and Discoveries in North and Central Africa,* vol. 2. London, 1857. [Kanuri].

Beaton, A. C. The Fur. *SNR*, 29:1–39. 1948.

Bouillié, R. *Les coutumes familiales au Kanem.* Paris, 1937. [Buduma and Kanembu].

Bovill, E. W. *Caravans of the Old Sahara.* London, 1933.

Bruel, G. *L'Afrique Equatoriale Française.* Paris, 1918.

Carbou, H. *La région du Tchad et du Ouadaï.* 2 vols. Paris, 1912.

Coutouly, F. de. Les populations du cercle de Dori. *BCEHS*, 6:269–301, 471–496, 637–671. 1923. [Songhai].

Davies, R. The Masalit Sultanate. *SNR*, 7(2):49–62. 1924.

Denham, D., and H. Clapperton. *Narrative of Travels and Discoveries in Northern and Central Africa.* London, 1826. [Kanuri].

Devallée. Le Baghirmi. *BSRC*, 7:3–76. 1925.

Duchamp. Coutume Sonraï. *PCEHS*, ser. A, 9:303–337. 1939. [Songhai].

Ellison, R. R. Marriage and Child-birth among the Kanuri. *Africa*, 9:524–535. 1936.

Felkin, R. W. Notes on the For Tribe. *PRSE*, 13:205–265. 1885. [Fur].

Forde, D., and R. Scott. *The Native Economies of Nigeria.* London, 1946. [Hausa].

Greenberg, J. H. The Influence of Islam on a Sudanese Religion. *Monographs of the American Ethnological Society*, 10:1–73. New York, 1946. [Maguzawa].

———. Islam and Clan Organization among the Hausa. *SWJA*, 3:193–211. 1947.

Hagen, G. von. Einige Notizen über die Musgu. *BA*, 2:117–122. 1912.

Hillelson, S. Notes on the Dago. *SNR*, 8:59–73. 1925. [Dagu].

Krusius, P. Die Maguzawa. *AFA*, 42:288–315. 1915.

Macintosh, E. H. A Note on the Dago Tribe. *SNR*, 14:171–178. 1931. [Dagu].

Macleod, O. *Chiefs and Cities of Central Africa.* London, 1912. [Buduma].

MacMichael, H. A. *A History of the Arabs in the Sudan,* vol. 1. Cambridge, 1922.

Meek, C. K. *The Northern Tribes of Nigeria.* 2 vols. London, 1925.
————. *Tribal Studies in Northern Nigeria.* 2 vols. London, 1931. [Karekare and Ngizim].
Miner, H. *The Primitive City of Timbuctoo.* Princeton, 1953. [Songhai].
Nachtigal, G. *Sahara und Sudan.* 2 vols. Berlin, 1879–1881. [Bagirmi, Buduma, Kanuri, and Kotoko].
Robin, J. Description de la province de Dosso. *BIFAN*, 9:56–98. 1947. [Zerma].
Rouch, J. *Les Songhay.* Paris, 1954.
Schultze, A. *The Sultanate of Bornu*, ed. P. A. Benton. London, 1913. [Kanuri].
Smith, M. F. *Baba of Karo.* New York, 1955. [Hausa].
Smith, M. G. The Economy of Hausa Communities of Zaria. *CRS*, 16:1–264. 1955.
Steward, J. H. Cultural Causality and Law, *AA*, 51:1–27. 1949.
Talbot, P. A. The Buduma of Lake Chad. *JRAI*, 41:245–259. 1911.
Temple, O. *Notes on the Tribes, Provinces, Emirates and States of the Northern Provinces of Nigeria*, ed. C. L. Temple. 2d edit. Lagos, 1922.
Tremearne, A. J. N. *Hausa Superstitions and Customs.* London, 1913.
Trenga, G. Le Bura-Mabang du Ouadai. *TMIE*, 49:1–300. 1947. [Maba].
Urvoy, Y. Histoire de l'empire du Bornou. *MIFAN*, 7:1–166. 1949.
Vieillard. G. Coutumier du cercle de Zinder. *PCEHS*, ser. A, 10:95–179. 1939. [Tazarawa].
Westermann, D. *Geschichte Afrikas.* Köln, 1952.
Wittfogel, K. A. *Oriental Despotism.* New Haven, 1957.
Wood, W. M. Tera Notebooks. Unpublished ms.

18

Punic and Greco–Roman North Africa

If the trans-Saharan caravan trade stimulated economic and political development among the Negroes on the southern fringe of the desert, it similarly brought progress and prosperity to the Berbers along its northern borders. The great Phoenician mercantile city of Tyre, which had extended its trading relationships to the western Mediterranean during the eleventh century B.C. and had begun to establish a series of colonies and trading posts in Sicily, Sardinia, and southern Spain, was induced to do likewise in North Africa in order to tap the flourishing trade with the Sudan. The most famous of her African colonies was Carthage, founded near the site of modern Tunis in 814 B.C., according to Punic tradition.

From relatively modest beginnings, Carthage gradually rose to power and prosperity, and in the sixth century B.C., when the mother city was conquered by the Persians, she assumed political hegemony over all the Phoenician settlements in the western Mediterranean. She extended her control of North Africa from Tripolitania in the east to the Atlantic coast of Morocco in the west, establishing trading posts at strategic points. She dominated most of this region, however, through allied or conquered and tributary Berber tribes, and her own area of intensive settlement was mainly confined to the northern part of modern Tunisia and an adjacent strip on the Algerian coast. Here the Carthaginians replaced Berber with their own Semitic language and attained a population, according to Strabo, of about 700,000, which must certainly have included a high proportion of Punicized Berbers.

A sea-borne merchant people like the parent Phoenicians, the Carthaginians ranged far beyond the Straits of Gibraltar to trade with the Britons and with the Berbers of western Morocco. Sometime before 400 B.C. Hanno, a Carthaginian admiral, embarked with a fleet of sixty vessels on a famous voyage of exploration down the Atlantic coast of Africa. He certainly reached the Gulf of Guinea and, from his report of gorillas, probably the shores of modern Gabon, but he did not circumnavigate the continent as some have claimed. The discovery, two centuries ago, of a cache of Carthaginian coins of the fourth century B.C. in the Azores—a third of the way across the Atlantic from Portugal—raises the question whether some stray Punic navigator may not even have discovered the New World.

In Sicily, Carthage contended for supremacy with Syracuse and other Greek colonies from the fifth to the third centuries B.C., with varying military success. When, however, she succeeded in expanding her territory in 275 to the Strait of Messina opposite continental Italy, she presented a serious threat to the rising power of Rome. This precipitated the three Punic Wars (265–146 B.C.), which terminated in her utter destruction.

The Carthaginian economy rested on intensive agriculture, with irrigation and the plow. Although the subject Berbers grew wheat and barley as their staple crops, supplemented by legumes, flax, and sesame, the Carthaginians themselves seem to have concentrated on arboriculture, growing orchards of almonds, figs, grapes, olives, pears, pomegranates, and walnuts. They made noteworthy advances in scientific agriculture, as even the hostile Romans recognized when they translated into Latin the thirty-two treatises of Mago on the subject. Animal husbandry yielded wool, hides, meat, milk, butter, and cheese. The Carthaginians kept cattle, sheep, goats, horses, donkeys, poultry, and bees. They bred mules, and tamed wild African elephants for use in warfare as early as the third century B.C. They did little hunting or gathering, but fishing was economically important.

Above all else, however, the Carthaginians were a mercantile people. They built their power and wealth on the basis of the trans-Saharan trade with Negro Africa and extended it after the fall of Tyre by inheriting the latter's monopoly of all commerce beyond the Straits of Gibraltar. They imported dates and hides from the Sahara; ivory, ostrich feathers, gold, and slaves from the Sudan; grain and copper from Sardinia; silver from Spain; and quantities of tin from Britain to fill the widespread demand in the Mediterranean for its use in the manufacture of bronze. In exchange, they gave their own products—grain, wine, olive oil, beeswax, timber for naval construction, linen cloth, rugs, pottery, glassware, metal tools and weapons, and ornaments of precious stones. Carthage conducted this immense and far-flung trade mainly by barter, for she had no coinage of her own until the fourth century B.C. The state bent every effort to protect and expand its commercial monopolies with its fleet and its armies.

As might be expected in so mercantile a society, social stratification was highly developed. In addition to a plutocratic aristocracy, there were differentiated classes of intelligentsia, petty bourgeoisie, artisans, proletarians, and slaves. Land was held in large estates, obtained by conquest, owned by the wealthy, and worked by slave labor. Next to nothing is specifically reported concerning the domestic institutions of Carthage, but the sources contain some intimations that the great merchant families were in reality corporate patrilineages.

The urban population lived in cities and towns of considerable size. The city of Carthage itself was built on a T-shaped peninsula with two landlocked harbors, one for merchant ships and the other for naval vessels. Its defenses included strong city walls and a citadel. Narrow streets radiated out from a forum or central plaza. Houses were rectangular in shape, up to six stories in height, and constructed of sun-dried brick.

Carthage originally had a monarchical form of government modeled on that of Tyre. Around 450 B.C., however, there occurred a revolution in which the kingship was abolished and a republic established. At the head of the state stood two chief magistrates, or presidents, called *shofet*, elected annually for a term of one year. They exercised judicial functions, but their executive authority was limited to convening and presiding over the two houses of a bicameral legislature, in which all political power was vested. A senate of 300 exercised executive as well as legislative authority. This body, or usually an executive committee composed of thirty of its more influential members, decided on matters of war and peace, sent and received embassies, levied troops, imposed taxes, and determined over-all military strategy. The senators were chosen exclusively from the aristocratic merchant families or lineages, inferentially as their formal representatives. The lower house was a popular assembly, which every free male Carthaginian was privileged to attend and where he could express his opinions with complete freedom. The assembly elected the presidents by popular vote and probably appointed a treasurer and finance minister. Its legislative and executive powers, however, were limited to issues brought before it at the instigation of the senate. This was done whenever the upper house failed to achieve essential unanimity or wished an expression of public opinion. The assembly also appointed military and naval commanders in time of war, investing them with powers for the duration of the emergency.

An obscure feature of the Carthaginian constitution was the pentarchies, or boards of five. We know that they were self-perpetuating, and they seem to have been recruited from members of the senate. Some authorities believe that they were identical with the executive committee of the latter. In any event, they were clearly controlled by the mercantile oligarchy, and considerable venality marked their appointment. They chose, commonly from their own ranks, the higher judiciary—a corps of 104 judges of senatorial rank, who allegedly had the authority to demand from all major officials an accounting of their behavior while in office and who became the dominant power in the state during the last half century before its downfall.

Aristotle, our fullest and most objective authority on the Carthaginian political system, stresses the nonhereditary character of all positions, the complete freedom of speech in the assembly, the frequency with which a single individual held several governmental posts at the same time, and the dual desiderata of merit and wealth for election to office, the latter being necessary because officials received no salaries but dangerous because tending to induce corruption. He also comments on the long duration of the system without either a revolution or the emergence of a dictator (it endured for about two centuries after he wrote). He weighs carefully the relative incidence of aristocratic, oligarchic, and democratic elements and finds the system a combination of all three, although curiously, according to modern standards, he considers election by voting rather than by lot to be a definitely undemocratic feature.

The constitution of Carthage has attracted the interest, and aroused the speculations, of political scientists ever since Aristotle's time. They have commonly compared it, unconvincingly, with those of ancient Greece, early Rome, and later European democracies. The mystery of its marked divergence from all these systems and of its complete lack of parallels among Semitic peoples elsewhere disappears, however, in the light of the ethnographical researches of Montagne (1930). We can now understand it as an obvious borrowing from the political institutions of the Berbers.

The Carthaginian constitution had the Berber combination of a democratic popular assembly and an oligarchic council or senate, with essentially the same composition and functions. It had the same dual chief magistrates, chosen in the same way for terms of the same length and with the same distinctive lack of executive power, from which we may reasonably conclude, despite the absence of direct evidence, that one Carthaginian *shofet* served as presiding officer in the senate and the other over the assembly. In both systems, moreover, generals were chosen for the duration of a war—a factor which frequently gave Hannibal an advantage over the Roman generals, who were appointed for specific terms and were thus likely to be relieved of command at a critical point in a campaign. The only feature of the Carthaginian system for which no obvious Berber parallel exists is the pentarchies, and even these may conceivably bear some relation to the artificial groupings called "fifths" (*khom*) that are widely reported in the Berber literature.

When the author first encountered ethnographic descriptions of Berber forms of government, he immediately suspected a Carthaginian derivation. As he covered more of the literature, however, it became apparent that the similarities were clearest in the most remote Berber tribes, whose ancestors could never have had contact with Punic culture, and it gradually dawned upon him that the borrowing must have taken place in the opposite direction. It then became obvious what happened in the revolution of 450 B.C. Having overthrown their traditional monarchy, the Carthaginians had no political model to copy save that of the neighboring Berbers. The imitation of the latter must have been rendered even more inevitable by the presence in the Punic body politic of numerous Berbers in various stages of acculturation, many of them thoroughly habituated to the traditional institutions of their own people. It is one of the fascinations of anthropology that field work and comparative research conducted in the twentieth century can shed direct light on important historical events of the fifth century B.C.

Greco-Roman influence in North Africa began in the seventh century B.C., when Greeks, mainly from Crete, established a series of colonies on the coast of Cyrenaica. Like Carthage, these prospered greatly from the trans-Saharan caravan trade. The city of Cyrene, for example, had 100,000 inhabitants in A.D. 115, when its large population of Jews revolted. Enormous numbers were massacred, and the rest dispersed throughout the Maghreb or western Mediterranean coast of Africa, where many survive today.

Egypt, after its conquest by Alexander the Great and the installation of Ptolemy I as pharaoh in 323 B.C., embarked upon its Hellenistic period. The Ptolemies, so to speak, merely stepped into the shoes of the earlier native rulers and retained the traditional administrative organization almost intact, so that they became, in effect, just one more in the long series of Egyptian dynasties. However, they surrounded themselves with Greek officials and advisers, adopted Greek as the court language, encouraged Greek immigration, and promoted trade and cultural interchange with the Greek world. Under their rule Egypt thus acquired a strong Hellenic veneer.

After the destruction of Carthage in 146 B.C., Rome organized the former possessions of the latter as the province of Africa with its capital at Utica, an ally in the last Punic War. The subsequent conquests of Cyrenaica in 96 B.C., of Egypt in 30 B.C., and of Morocco in A.D. 40, and their incorporation in the empire as additional provinces, gave Rome administrative control over the entire North African coast. She proceeded to develop these territories for her own economic advantage, extending irrigation by the construction of great hydraulic works, instituting ambitious systems of soil conservation, and building long aqueducts to bring water to the major cities settled by her colonists, retired veterans, and loyal Berber allies.

In consequence, North Africa became the granary of the empire, supplying approximately two-thirds of all the grain consumed in Rome itself. In part this was purchased, in part obtained through land taxes payable in kind. One lasting result of this development, as well as of Ptolemaic and later Byzantine and Arab enterprise, was the introduction into North Africa of a series of new cultivated plants unknown to earlier Pharaonic Egypt. The most important of these, which we shall designate collectively as the Greco-Roman complex, are listed below.

CEREAL GRAINS

Asiatic millet (*Panicum miliaceum*). This Middle Eastern grain occurs sporadically in North Africa.

Italian millet (*Setaria italica*). This Middle Eastern grain is infrequently reported in North Africa.

Oats (*Avena sativa*). Though this grain originated in the Middle East during the Bronze Age, it still occurs only sporadically in North Africa.

Rye (*Secale cereale*). This grain also was cultivated in the Middle East in the Bronze Age but is grown only sporadically in North Africa.

LEGUMES

French lentil (*Vicia ervilia* or *Ervum ervilia*). This Middle Eastern plant was introduced into North Africa by the Arabs in the eighth century.

ROOT CROPS

Carrot (*Daucus carota*). This Middle Eastern plant was apparently first introduced to North Africa in the Greco-Roman period.

Salsify (*Tragopogon porrifolium*). This Mediterranean plant appears to have been taken to Africa by the Romans.

Turnip (*Brassica rapa*). This Middle Eastern plant was apparently introduced into North Africa during the Greco-Roman period.

LEAF AND STALK VEGETABLES

Chervil (*Anthriscus cerefolium* or *Scandix cerefolium*). This Mediterranean plant appears to have been introduced into Africa in the first century.

Purslane (*Portulaca oleracea*). This Mediterranean plant was introduced into Africa during the Greco-Roman period.

Spinach (*Spinacia oleracea*). This Middle Eastern plant seems to have entered North Africa with the Arabs.

TREE FRUITS AND NUTS

Apricot (*Prunus armeniaca*). Introduced into Africa from the Middle East about the time of Christ.

Carob (*Ceratonia siliqua*). Introduced from the Mediterranean or the Middle East about the beginning of the Christian era.

Cherry (*Prunus avium* and *P. cerasus*). Introduced into Egypt from the Middle East during the Hellenistic period.

Citron (*Citrus medica*). A native of India, the citron was introduced into Egypt during the Hellenistic period.

English walnut (*Juglans regia*). Introduced into Egypt from the Middle East early in the Hellenistic period or perhaps even in late Pharaonic times.

Filbert, or hazelnut (*Corylus avellana*). Brought from the Middle East to Egypt at about the same time as the English walnut.

Jujube (*Zizyphus vulgaris* or *Z. jujuba*). A native of China, the jujube was introduced into North Africa in the Greco-Roman period.

Lemon (*Citrus limon*). An Indian cultigen introduced into Egypt during the Hellenistic period.

Lime (*Citrus aurantifolia*). Introduced from India with the lemon.

Medlar (*Mespilus germanica*). Introduced from the Middle East during the Greco-Roman period.

Orange (*Citrus aurantium*). Entered North Africa with the Arabs.

Peach (*Prunus persica*, formerly *Amygdalus persica*). A very old Chinese cultigen, the peach was introduced into Egypt during the Hellenistic period.

Pear (*Pyrus communis*). This Middle Eastern plant reached Egypt early in the Hellenistic period and was grown in Punic Carthage.

Pistachio (*Pistacia vera*). Although the Egyptians obtained pistachio nuts by trade from Babylonia from a relatively early period, they apparently did not introduce the tree itself until the first century.

Plum (*Prunus domestica*). Probably introduced into Egypt from the Middle East during the Hellenistic period.

Quince (*Cydonia oblonga*). This Middle Eastern plant probably reached Egypt in the Hellenistic period.

CONDIMENTS

Marjoram (*Origanum majorana*). This Mediterranean plant probably reached Egypt during the Hellenistic period.

Peppermint (*Mentha piperita*). This Mediterranean plant was possibly, though not probably, cultivated in Egypt as early as the Pharaonic period.

Rosemary (*Rosmarinus officinalis*). Highly dubious evidence suggests that this Mediterranean plant may have been cultivated in Egypt as early as the Pharaonic period.

Shallot (*Allium ascalonicum*). This Middle Eastern plant was introduced into Africa early in the Christian era.

OIL AND DYE PLANTS

Black mustard (*Brassica nigra*). Middle Eastern in origin.

Indigo (*Indigofera tinctoria*). Of Indian origin.

Madder (*Rubia tinctorum*). This Mediterranean plant was probably introduced into Africa during the Roman period.

Rocket (*Eruca sativa*). This oil plant is of Middle Eastern or Mediterranean origin.

Turmeric (*Curcuma longa*). This dye plant is ultimately of Southeast Asian origin.

White mustard (*Sinapis alba*). This oil plant is of Mediterranean origin.

Rome experienced relatively little difficulty in defending her conquests in Egypt. The change of rulers meant little to the people on the local level, especially since the old administration into nomes remained in force until A.D. 307. Military forces, being needed chiefly for border protection against Beja and Nubian incursions, were in time substantially reduced. The Garamantes, or Saharan Negroes, gave more trouble. Rome found it necessary to occupy Fezzan in 19 B.C. and remained there until the fifth century. Punitive expeditions, such as one into Tibesti in A.D. 100, kept the remoter Teda at bay. Much harder to cope with was the Berber spirit of independence, the more so since Rome controlled only the coastal fringe of Berber territory. The "barbarians" farther inland made repeated raids into the administered territory. In defense, the Romans erected walls along the border in places lacking natural protection, with watchtowers beyond them and supportive forts, camps, and military roads behind them, and induced veterans and trustworthy natives to settle on the frontier by giving them free land in return for the obligation of military service in support of the regular occupying forces.

The trans-Saharan caravan trade continued to flourish, with a new element added in the importation of wild animals for public spectacles at Rome. Curiously enough, however, we have no record from Greco-Roman times of Europeans actually visiting the Sudan as traders, explorers, or tourists. Italian settlers brought Latin to Africa, where it became established as the official language. Punic, however, did not completely disappear until the fifth century, and even the early Christian bishops in Africa had to learn it for their missionary endeavors. Acculturation proceeded apace, especially in former Carthaginian territory, and the province of Africa even produced such eminent Romans as Apuleius, Augustine, and Tertullian.

We shall not describe the culture and social institutions of Greco-Roman North Africa, for they actually belong more properly to European history, and their effects, moreover, were relatively transitory. Despite economic prosperity, unrest developed and steadily intensified. Through political confiscations land fell increasingly into the hands of the state, of officials, and of private absentee landlords. The peasants, forced progressively into the status of unfree serfs, sought refuge in Christianity and suffered martyrdom, then formed schismatic sects against the official church and suffered persecution. Harsh exactions resulting from the farming out of taxes provoked the Berbers to repeated revolts. In A.D. 429 the Vandals under Genseric, summoned to quell tribal rebellions, took advantage of the opportunity to seize for themselves all the Roman colonies from Morocco to Cyrenaica. They were in turn conquered by Byzantium in 533. In 639, shortly after the death of Mohammed, the Arabs of the Abbassid, or Baghdad, caliphate occupied Egypt, and by the end of the century had seized all the former Roman possessions in North Africa, initiating the conversion of the entire Christian population to Islam. This story, however, must be continued in Chapter 52.

Selected Bibliography

Aristotle. *Politics.* [The reader is warned to consult one of the older scholarly editions rather than more recent ones, tailored for philosophers, which omit the sections on the Carthaginian constitution as "mainly of antiquarian interest"].

Baradez, J. *Fossatum Africae.* Paris, 1949.

Bevan, E. *A History of Egypt under the Ptolemaic Dynasty.* London, 1927.

Burkill, I. H. Habits of Man and the Origins of the Cultivated Plants of the Old World. *Proceedings of the Linnean Society of London,* 164:12–42. 1953.

Bury, J. B., S. A. Cook, F. E. Adcock, and M. P. Charlesworth, eds. *The Cambridge Ancient History,* vols. 4, 6–7. New York, 1926–1930.

Cagnat, R. L. V. *Carthage, Timgad, Tébessa et les villes antiques de l'Afrique du Nord.* 3d edit. Paris, 1927.

Candolle, A. de. *Origin of Cultivated Plants.* 2d edit. London, 1904.

Diehl, C. *L'Afrique byzantine.* Paris, 1896.

Gsell, S. *Histoire ancienne de l'Afrique du Nord.* 8 vols. Paris, 1913–1928.

Hubac, P. *Carthage.* Paris, 1946.

Johnson, A. C. *Egypt and the Roman Empire.* Ann Arbor, 1951.

Julien, C. A. *Histoire de l'Afrique du Nord.* Paris, 1931.

Montagne, R. *Les Berbères et le Makhzen dans le sud du Maroc.* Paris, 1930.

Reinhardt, L. *Kulturgeschichte der Nutzpflanzen.* 2 vols. München, 1911.

Rostovtzeff, M. *The Social and Economic History of the Roman Empire*. 2d edit. Oxford, 1942.

Schiemann, E. Entstehung der Kulturpflanzen. *Handbuch der Vererbungswissenschaft*, 3:1–377. 1932.

Schnebel, M. *Die Landwirtschaft im hellenistischen Aegypten*. München, 1925.

Vavilov, N. I. The Origin, Variation, Immunity and Breeding of Cultivated Plants, transl. K. S. Chester. *Chronica Botanica*, 13:1–364. 1949–1950.

Warmington, B. H. *The North African Provinces from Diocletian to the Vandal Conquest*. Cambridge, 1954.

Wheeler, R. E. M. *Rome beyond the Imperial Frontiers*. London, 1954.

PART FIVE
SYNTHESIS IN THE NILE CORRIDOR

———————•••••———————

19

———————•••••———————

Nubians

The Nile Valley south of ancient and modern Egypt, from the second cataract near Wadi Halfa to the junction of the Blue and White Niles at Khartoum, is known as Nubia. Archeology reveals that the southern part of this area was occupied as early as the Mesolithic period by a Negroid people who lacked domesticated animals and plants and subsisted partly by hunting and gathering but mainly by spearing fish and river hippopotamus. We also know that they lived in huts of wattle and daub, made stone implements of the Capsian type, manufactured pottery, and removed the lower incisor teeth. Since the knocking out of incisor teeth is confined today in Africa almost exclusively to speakers of the Sudanic languages and occurs in practically all the tribes of this linguistic stock who have not adopted circumcision as an alternative initiatory rite, we can reasonably assume that the Mesolithic inhabitants were the ancestors of the modern Nubians and, like the latter, spoke languages belonging to the Nubian branch of the Eastern subfamily of the Sudanic stock. The Nubian language is spoken today as far north as the first cataract at Aswan, but the original population of southern Egypt between the first and second cataracts appears to have been Caucasoid rather than Negroid and to have been akin to the Predynastic inhabitants of the rest of Egypt.

Shortly after 3900 B.C., as shown by radiocarbon dating, an early phase of Neolithic culture makes its appearance in southern Nubia in the vicinity of Khartoum. The people were still Negroid in physique, and the advent of shell fishhooks and barbed harpoon heads indicates that they still subsisted largely by fishing, albeit with improved techniques. Stone axes and adzes with ground edges suggest advances in boat building. Among the numerous remains of hunted animals, moreover, there appear for the first time a few bones of domesticated species—dogs, sheep, and goats. This demonstrates incipient contact with the Neolithic culture which had been established in northern Egypt for at least 500 years, a conclusion confirmed by other concrete resemblances to the Predynastic cultures of Egypt.

These early Neolithic Nubians had apparently not yet learned to till the soil. To be sure, they manufactured pestles of sandstone, but they seem to have used these for pulverizing red ocher rather than for grinding grain. The acceptance of agriculture cannot, however, have been long delayed. When it arrived, it must have been introduced first from the west, for even today the basic crops of Nubia are those of western Sudanic origin. These are, however, supplemented by a number of plants of the Egyptian complex. In subsistence economy, as in other aspects of culture, Nubia appears to have been the scene of an early synthesis of the two oldest agricultural civilizations of the African continent.

According to the archeological evidence, from about 3100 to 2250 B.C., a period roughly contemporaneous with the first six dynasties of Pharaonic Egypt, there were intermittent contacts with and borrowings from Egypt, including the introduction of copper tools and the quarrying of stone for Egyptian monuments. Nubia had clearly achieved a full-fledged agricultural civilization by this time, and probably considerably earlier.

Shortly after 2250 B.C. a new Caucasoid population, the so-called C group, appears for a time in northern Nubia. Its association with a notable increase in the remains of domesticated cattle, sheep, and goats suggests an influx of pastoral Beja from the east. The newcomers presumably introduced the use of milk and the manufacture of butter, since the Beja, like the Bedouin Arabs across the Red Sea to the east, have been characterized from time immemorial by their primary dependence upon dairy products for subsistence. The Nubians had already, of course, borrowed animal husbandry from Egypt and had transmitted it to their Negro neighbors. The fact that the Negroes of the Sudan as far west as the Atlantic possess cattle and sheep but do not milk them, as we have seen, strongly suggests that the diffusion of these animals through Nubia occurred during the late fourth or early third millennium B.C., at a time when the Nubians had not yet adopted milking from the Beja.

Between 1970 and 1520 B.C. Dynastic Egypt gradually extended its political sway up the Nile from the second to beyond the fourth cataract, establishing forts and garrisons, and maintained this control with few interruptions until about 1050 B.C. During this period Nubia became thoroughly acculturated, accepting even the Egyptian religion and conception of divine kingship. Economic prosperity seems to have prevailed. Nubia exported to its northern neighbor great quantities of gold as well as ivory, ebony, gums and perfumes, ostrich feathers, precious stones, slaves, and the skins of wild animals.

After 1050 B.C. Egypt underwent a serious decline, and Nubia became independent. A strong state was established at Napata on the Egyptian model, e.g., with brother-sister marriages in the royal family. In 750 B.C. the Napatan king, Kashta, invaded Upper Egypt, and in 742 his successor, Piankhi, completed the conquest of Egypt, founding the XXV, or Napatan, dynasty. Though expelled from Egypt in 663 B.C., this dynasty continued to rule Nubia, first from Napata and after 550 from Meroe. Egyptian civilization persisted in Nubia but gradually deteriorated. Around 200 B.C. hieroglyphic writing was replaced by a cursive script, still undeciphered, in the local language. It may well have been from Meroe that iron, the divine kingship, and other elements of Egyptian culture were introduced into Negro Africa. Finally, about A.D. 350, the Meroitic state was overthrown by the Semitic kingdom of Axum.

After an anarchic period marked by Beja incursions, Christianity was introduced into Nubia in A.D. 543, and shortly thereafter two petty states fused to form the strong kingdom of Dongola with its institutions modeled on those of Byzantium. In 580 the state of Alwa, located farther south, with its capital near modern Khartoum, also accepted Christianity. The Arab conquest of Egypt in 639 isolated Dongola from Mediterranean Christendom, but, by paying tribute, this Christian state was able to escape absorption by Moslem Egypt. It was even strong enough to withstand the Hilalian invasion of Bedouin Arabs which overran most of North Africa after 1045. It was nevertheless subject to attrition, through conversions to Islam and the infiltration of Arabs, until in 1315 the last Christian king was succeeded by a Moslem. In the north the people quickly accepted Islam, and the mixed population between the first and fourth cataracts, constituting the Barabra nation of today, has become strongly Arabized, though still retaining the Nubian language.

Above the fourth cataract the Bedouin invaders swamped the indigenous Nubians, and the present mixed Gaaliin population is Arabized in language as well as in culture. Farther south, the Christian kingdom of Alwa resisted Arab penetration until 1504, when it succumbed to the Moslem Fung state of Sennar. This removed the last barrier to Bedouin expansion in this part of Africa, and the Baggara, or Cattle Arabs, poured south and west into the eastern and central Sudan (see Chapter 54). Groups of Nubians, resisting absorption, sought refuge in the hills of Kordofan and Darfur, where remnants survive to the present day.

The Nubians of today, i.e., the peoples who still speak languages of the Nubian branch of the Eastern subfamily of the Sudanic stock, are listed and identified below.

1. Anag (Nuba). These people live scattered in the hills of northern Kordofan around 15°N, 30°E. They are strongly Arabized, and the majority now speak Arabic rather than Nubian.
2. Barabra (Berberi, Nile Nubians), embracing the Kenuzi (Beni Kanz, Kenozi, Kenous, Kunuzi, Nubi) between the first and second cataracts, the Sukkot and Mahas between the second and third cataracts, and the Danagla between the third and fourth cataracts. They constitute the only undisplaced survivors of the pre-Islamic Nubians and probably number at least 200,000.
3. Birked (Birguid, Kajjara). This group now live in Darfur (ca. 13°N, 26°E), whence they fled after the downfall of the kingdom of Dongola.
4. Dilling, with the detached Gulfan, the Kadero (Kadaru), and other subtribes. They live in the Nuba Hills of Kordofan, where they have been penetrated to some extent by nomadic Arabs. They number about 20,000 and are still largely pagan.
5. Midobi (Meidob, Mydob). These displaced people occupy the mountains of Jebel Midob in Darfur and are Moslems.
6. Nyima (Nyamang), including the detached Afitti (Sidra). These people live west of the Dilling in the Nuba Hills, are pagan, and number about 37,000.

Although Negroid in origin, all the Nubians reveal a strong Caucasoid admixture. The Barabra, indeed, represent a hybrid race in which the Caucasoid component probably predominates. Their ancestral Negro element has been diluted by substantial ancient Egyptian and modern Arab increments, by a lesser Beja one, and by a considerable European and Asiatic infusion from the Bosnian, Hungarian, Circassian, Kurdish, and Turkish troops stationed for centuries on the Nubian outpost of the Ottoman Empire; the Negro element has been reinforced, however, by Negro slaves introduced from the eastern Sudan, especially during the nineteenth century. The modern Barabra are characterized by the following traits: moderately tall stature (5 feet 6 or 7 inches in adult males), slender body, medium- to dark-bronze skin, head of medium breadth (cephalic index 77), oval face, short but straight nose of moderate width (nasal index 80), scanty facial hair, thick lips, and black hair, which is curly rather than kinky.

Agriculture remains the basis of the economy except among the Birked and Midobi of Darfur, who have come to emphasize pastoral activities. Sudanic crops predominate, as previously noted, with sorghum and millet as the staples, along with watermelons, gourds, okra, sesame, and cotton. They are augmented by crops from the Egyptian complex, especially barley and the date palm but also peas, lentils, figs, carob, and some wheat and grapes. This is to be expected, of course, from the historical record of Pharaonic penetration, but it is noteworthy that these crops have scarcely spread beyond the Barabra. Even these people rarely use the plow, although they employ the Egyptian shadoof and ox-driven water wheel in irrigating their fields. A few plants of American origin, notably maize, peanuts, peppers, and squash, have found a minor place in the economy of the Dilling and Nyima. None of these increments, however, can disguise the basic Sudanic pattern of Nubian agriculture. The Egyptian impact upon animal husbandry has been vastly greater. All groups keep cattle, sheep, goats, donkeys, and dogs; use milk; and make butter. Horses and chickens are likewise common, and the Barabra and Midobi keep camels. The pig, prominent in Christian and pre-Christian times, survives today only among the Nyima and some Dilling. The Nubians depend to only a limited extent upon hunting, fishing, and gathering, but the caravan trade has been important throughout recorded history. In general, the men hunt, fish, herd the larger animals, and do the milking, whereas the women gather, tend pigs and chickens, and share equally in agricultural labor. Among the Barabra, however, only men work in the fields, and among the Midobi and Barabra women participate in the herding and milking of livestock.

Marriage involves a bride-price generally in livestock but occasionally in money. Residence is patrilocal, although at least the Barabra, Dilling, and Nyima require an initial period of matrilocal residence with bride-service. Polygyny is permitted, but only in the nonsororal form. Each nuclear or polygynous family occupies an independent household. Marriage is permitted or even favored with a cross-cousin, except among the Nyima, but only the Barabra allow unions with a parallel cousin. A preference for local endogamy appears to be universal.

Descent is everywhere patrilineal today, with cousin terminology of the descriptive pattern. The Barabra have adopted the agamous segmentary lineage organization of the Arabs, but the other tribes possess exogamous patrisibs, and these are further aggregated into exogamous patriphratries among the Dilling and Nyima. True clans are reported only for the Dilling, where each sib tends to be localized in a hamlet. Despite the indubitably patrilineal character of the social organization today, a number of indications suggest that matrilineal descent may formerly have prevailed. In addition to the common requirement of initial matrilocal residence, avunculocal residence crops up occasionally among the Dilling. Inheritance is strictly matrilineal—by a sister's son—among the Midobi, and the same rule applies to movable property among some of the Dilling. Finally, succession to political positions is definitely matrilineal among the Anag and Midobi, and to priestly offices among the Nyima, and this rule is also definitely attested for the Nubians of Christian and pre-Christian Dongola, whom most authorities consider to have been matrilineal even in descent.

The seminomadic Midobi live in dome-shaped shelters of branches covered with grass, but most Nubian tribes occupy permanent hamlets or small villages of round huts with cylindrical walls and conical thatched roofs. The walls are of dry masonry among some Barabra, of stones set in mud among the Anag, of wood and wattle among the Nyima, and of mud among the Dilling. In the last two tribes the huts are grouped in rings with connecting walls to form family compounds. The prevailing house type among the Barabra, however, is a rectangular dwelling of North African derivation with mud or brick walls, a flat roof, and an interior courtyard. In the Kenuzi subtribe the roof is often arched or vaulted rather than flat, a common characteristic of ancient Egyptian houses in the same general region.

Circumcision is universal, and the Barabra subject girls to clitoridectomy, excision of the labia minora, and infibulation. All tribes kept slaves until recently, but social stratification is not otherwise complex. The Nyima acknowledge no authority beyond that of a priest who renders ritual services to the several hamlets of a "hill community." Many Dilling subtribes, however, recognize "kings" over a number of such communities; they are elective within a royal sib, possess special insignia (e.g., a skullcap and a sacred drum among the Kadero), and exercise minor ritual functions. The Birked and Midobi also have royal families and petty kings, two such in the latter tribe. These survivals, however, give few clues to the complex political structures which must have prevailed in Napatan, Meroitic, and Christian times, but for these periods we unfortunately possess only exceedingly fragmentary direct historical evidence.

Selected Bibliography

Arkell, A. J. *Early Khartoum*. London, 1949.
———. *Shaheinab*. London, 1953.
———. *A History of the Sudan*. London, 1955.
Budge, E. A. W. *The Egyptian Sudan*. 2 vols. London, 1907.
Burckhardt, J. L. *Travels in Nubia*. 2d edit. London, 1922. [Barabra].
Dunham, D. The Kingdom of Kush at Napata and Meroe. *SNR*, 28: 1–10. 1947.
Herzog, R. *Die Nubier*. Berlin, 1957. [Barabra].
Kauczor, P. D. The Afitti Nuba of Gebel Dair. *SNR*, 6:1–34. 1923. [Nyima].
Lampen, E. A Short Account of Meidob. *SNR*, 11:55–67. 1928. [Midobi].
MacMichael, H. A. *The Tribes of Northern and Central Kordofan*. Cambridge, 1912. [Anag].
———. Nubian Elements in Darfur. *SNR*, 1:33–53. 1918. [Midobi].
———. Darfur Linguistics. *SNR*, 3:197–216. 1920. [Birked].
Nadel, S. F. The Hill Tribes of Kadero. *SNR*, 25:37–79. 1942. [Dilling].
———. *The Nuba*. London, 1947. [Dilling and Nyima].
Rafalowitsch. Ethnographische Bemerkungen über die Bewohner des niederen Nubiens. *Archiv für Wissenschaftliche Kunde von Russland*, ed. A. Erman, 13:100–140. 1854. [Barabra].
Stevenson, R. C. The Nyamang of the Nuba Mountains. *SNR*, 23:75–98. 1940. [Nyima].

20

Nuba

South of Nubia and west of the White Nile lies the region called Kordofan, the homeland of a distinctive Negro people known as the Nuba. The similarity in names should not mislead us into confusing them with the Nubians, even though the Nubian Dilling and Nyima tribes now live near them in the Nuba Hills and are commonly regarded as Nuba. The inhabitants of the Nuba Hills have no archeological record and only a very brief history. Protected by their mountain environment, they have remained relatively untouched by the movements of peoples and cultures in the Nile Valley and between the latter and the central Sudan. They thus constitute a sort of cultural eddy or backwash and probably retain many cultural characteristics of the Nile Negroes before the latter felt the impact of Pharaonic civilization.

The Baggara, or Cattle Arabs, who inundated the eastern Sudan after the downfall of the Christian kingdom of Alwa in A.D. 1504, displaced and partially absorbed the Nuba who lived in the plains country, forming tribes of mixed racial composition, like the Bederia and Messiria. They penetrated the Nuba Hills, however, to only a limited extent, so that nearly a quarter million Nuba still maintain a foothold in these mountain fastnesses. Racially the Nuba are indisputably Negroid, with but inconsequential admixture, and are distinguished by very dark skin color, heads of medium breadth (cephalic index 76), kinky hair, and tall stature, averaging about 5 feet 8 inches for adult males. The men go completely naked; the women wear a tuft of leaves in front and behind.

Unlike the Sudanic-speaking Nubians, the Nuba speak languages of a completely independent stock, the Kordofanian. This is divided into five subfamilies: the Katla in the northwest, the Koalib in the center, the Tagali in the northeast, the Talodi in the south, and the Tumtum in the southwest. To these we have added the Temainian group in the west central part of the Nuba Hills, originally classed by Greenberg (1950) as an independent linguistic stock. Since information received from Greenberg while this book was in press indicates that this group actually affiliates with the Eastern subfamily of the Sudanic stock, its members should probably be treated as Nubians rather than as Nuba. Inasmuch as the Nuba tribes, though very numerous, do not differ widely from one another in culture, the classification below follows the linguistic divisions.

1. Katla, with the kindred Gulud and the distantly related Tima.
2. Koalib (Kawalib), embracing the Abol, Delami, Gabri, Heiban, Kalkadda, Kattei, Kinderma (Kanderma), Koalib proper, Laro (Alleira), Lebu, Lukha, Moro, Mummu, Ndorno, Ngadhado, Nukr (Nyukur), Nyaro, Otoro, Shwai, Tendik, and Tira.
3. Tagali (Tageli, Tekele), embracing the Kajaja, Moreb (Morib), Rashad, Tagali proper, Tagoi, Tumeli, Tumuk (Tumak), Turjak, and Wadelka.
4. Talodi (Tasoni, Tata), embracing the Acheron, Buram, Dakoka, central and southern Eliri, Lofofa, Lumun (Luman), Mesakin, Tacho, Talodi proper, and Torona.
5. Tumtum, embracing the Demik, northern Eliri, Fama, Kadodo, Kadugli, Kamdang, Kanga, Karondi, Keiga, Korongo (Krongo), Miri, Murta, Tabanya, Teis, Tullishi (Tuleshi), Tumtum proper, and Turug.
6. Temein (Temain), with the kindred Keiga-Girru and Teis-um-Danab.

The Nuba economy rests primarily upon agriculture, with terraced fields, hoe cultivation, and some irrigation, crop rotation, fallowing, and use of animal manure as fertilizer. The Sudanic complex predominates, with millet and sorghum as the staples, supplemented by sesame, okra, watermelons, gourds, and cotton. From the Egyptian complex the Nuba have received only onions, and they have borrowed none of the Greco-Roman crops. From India, however, they have adopted cucumbers and from America peanuts, peppers, and especially maize, which now rivals the Sudanic cereals in importance. They possess numerous cattle, originally of a dwarf variety now being replaced by the Arab long-horned breed. They milk cows, as well as goats, and make butter. They also keep sheep, chickens, and a few donkeys, horses, and guinea fowl. Especially interesting, however, is the prominence of pigs. This animal, as we have seen, held a very important place in early Egypt but came to be considered unclean and fell into disrepute sometime after the Middle Kingdom. Subsequently the Arabs, with their even more extreme taboo against pork, practically obliterated the pig throughout North Africa and later in Nubia as well. The Nuba, who are still mainly pagan, thus stand almost alone in their continuation of Neolithic pig culture into the modern era.

Other economic activities, like hunting, gathering, and trade, are inconsequential, and the sources do not even mention fishing. In the division of labor by sex the Nuba assign land clearance and the herding and milking of cattle and goats to men, gathering and the tending of pigs and chickens to women. Both sexes participate almost equally in agricultural labor, although the men do more work on the distant fields, women on those closer to the home.

Marriage regularly involves a bride-price in livestock, usually substantial in amount but relatively small in the southern tribes of the Talodi group and among the neighboring Korongo and Nyaro. In most cases it is supplemented by premarital bride-service in the form of several days of agricultural labor each year for the prospective father-in-law, and in many tribes it is partially offset by a dowry of much smaller amount. The Nuba forbid marriage with any first cousin but everywhere exhibit a strong preference for local endogamy outside the limits set by incest taboos and kin-group exogamy. Monogamy is the rule. To be sure, polygyny, exclusively in the nonsororal form, is always permitted, but in actual fact it occurs rather rarely except in the tribes of the Koalib group, where it is extremely frequent. The levirate is common or preferential except among the Koalib proper, but only the tribes of the Talodi and Tumtum groups allow sororate unions. The normal residential unit consists of an independent nuclear family. In cases of polygyny, each co-wife occupies a hut of her own, or even a separate compound, as among the Korongo, Otoro, and Talodi. The Koalib proper have patrilocal extended families, each occupying a homestead under the leadership of the eldest male member. Elsewhere, although related families often reside close together, they do not actually coalesce as larger household units.

Residence is normally matrilocal until after the birth of the first child and patrilocal thereafter. The northern tribes of the Koalib and Tumtum groups, however, follow the patrilocal rule from the outset, whereas in the Talodi group and the southern tribes of the Tumtum group avunculocal residence occurs at least as frequently as patrilocality and perhaps more often. Kinship terminology of the Iroquois type appears among the Mesakin of the Talodi group, but all other tribes have either Hawaiian or descriptive terms for cousins. Unilinear sibs are universal. They are exogamous except where large, when exogamy is often confined to their component subsibs or lineages. They are commonly associated with special food taboos, ritual numbers and directions, magical functions, and a joint responsibility for blood vengeance. Magical functions usually differ from sib to sib, each being dependent upon others for their proper performance. This creates a symbiotic relationship among sibs which contributes substantially to social integration. Clans are absent except in the Koalib group, where sibs tend to be localized in hamlets or wards.

Though all the Nuba have unilinear kin groups, the rule of descent varies. The Talodi group and the southern tribes of the Tumtum group follow exclusively the matrilineal rule, the northern and central tribes of the Koalib group are as exclusively patrilineal, and the southern tribes of the Koalib group and the northern tribes of the Tumtum group are characterized by double descent. Whichever unilinear principle predominates, its rule of exogamy is extended to the group of the parent with whom Ego is not affiliated, as well as to that of the other parent and himself.

Analysis of the distributional evidence enables us to reconstruct the development of social organization in this area with a high degree of assurance and yields valuable insights which are unattainable by those anthropologists who confine themselves arbitrarily to purely synchronic methods of structural and functional interpretation.

Geographical contiguity provides us with our first clue. We note that the Nuba tribes with patrilineal descent are precisely those who have been most exposed to Arab contact and who are located in closest proximity to the strongly patrilineal Dilling tribe of Nubians.

Linguistic relationships offer a second line of analytical attack. Peoples whose languages are genetically related have normally participated in a single cultural community at some time in the past, whereas those with unrelated languages are likely to have had different culture histories, even though they may happen to occupy contiguous territories at a given time. On the basis of language we have already been able to separate the Sudanic-speaking Dilling and Nyima from the Kordofanian-speaking Nuba proper, with whom they are commonly confused, and to relate them historically rather to the Nubians. The next step consists in grouping the Nuba tribes by the subfamilies of the Kordofanian stock to which their languages belong. When this is done we discover that data on social organization are lacking for the small Katla and Tagali subfamilies but available for at least three tribes each of the Koalib, Talodi, and Tumtum divisions. This enables us to note that matrilineal sibs occur in every tribe of the Talodi and Tumtum subfamilies and in at least one important tribe (the Nyaro) of the Koalib division, significantly the one farthest removed geographically from the patrilineal Dilling. This strongly suggests that all the Nuba were originally matrilineal and that a shift to patrilineal descent has occurred at a relatively recent time in the presence of Nubian neighbors who have provided a model for cultural borrowing.

Comparative studies provide a third and supporting type of evidence. They have demonstrated that double descent, attested for the Nyaro tribe of the Koalib group and the Tullishi tribe of the Tumtum group, reflects, wherever else it occurs in the world, the temporal priority of matrilineal over patrilineal descent in the particular group. The emergence of patrilineal descent in a previously matrilineal society is a commonplace, whereas matrilineal descent can ordinarily appear in a formerly patrilineal society only after an intervening period of bilateral descent. When assessed with this developmental hypothesis in mind, the distributional evidence lends striking confirmation.

Among the southernmost and least disturbed Nuba tribes, who are all characterized by bride-service, a very small bride-price, rare polygyny, initial matrilocal residence, and a high incidence (50 to 70 per cent) of avunculocal residence, the Mesakin tribe of the Talodi group, who are the most protected of all by their interior location, have Iroquois cousin

terminology. It is thus reasonable to reconstruct the original social structure of the Nuba as belonging to the Avuncu-Iroquois type of Murdock
(1949, p. 244). Its most characteristic features would have been matrilineal descent, initially matrilocal but permanently avunculocal residence,
bride-service rather than bride-price, monogamy, and Iroquois cousin
terminology.

The next phase of development is exemplified by the Talodi proper and
by the Korongo tribe of the Tumtum group, both near neighbors of the
Mesakin. It may well have been initiated by the introduction of cattle,
which, since they were owned and tended by men, strengthened the
influence and economic position of the male sex. Cattle provided a
wherewithal for paying a bride-price and thus resulted in a decreasing
emphasis on bride-service. Their possession favored patrilineal inheritance
and patrilocal residence and made polygyny much more readily achievable. Thus the Talodi and Korongo are characterized by a modest bride-
price, limited polygyny, mixed rules of inheritance, and a moderate
incidence of patrilocal residence, although they still adhere strictly to
matrilineal descent. The Iroquois pattern of designating cousins, losing
its original support in kin-group localization, yielded to the practice, either
of extending sibling terms to cousins, as among the Lofofa, or of applying descriptive terminology.

The Tullishi tribe of the Tumtum group, northwest of the foregoing
and in contact with the patrilineal Nyima tribe of Nubians, illustrate the
next step. Here the bride-price has already become substantial, and
patrilocal residence has completely replaced the avunculocal practice.
Moreover, the new pattern of localization has given rise to definite patrilineages, although they are still agamous and subordinate to the older
matrisibs. This development is carried forward by the Nyaro, the
southernmost tribe of the Koalib group who live to the east of the matrilineal core. Here the incipient and agamous patrilineages have evolved
into full-fledged exogamous patrisibs, which have taken over the association with food taboos and the responsibility for various rituals, leaving
blood vengeance and certain funerary obligations in the hands of the
still flourishing matrisibs.

The culmination of the entire process is reflected in the other tribes of
the Koalib group, notably the Heiban, Koalib proper, Moro, Otoro, and
Tira. Here the bride-price has become really substantial. Residence has
become exclusively patrilocal; only the Tira, significantly the southernmost of the five, have retained the initial matrilocal period. Polygyny
has become general; in many of the tribes more than 50 per cent of all
married men possess plural wives. Finally, patrilineal descent has become
absolute; the original matrilineal kin groups have completely disappeared.
The postulated transition in social organization has run its full course.

The Nuba live in small sedentary hamlets, several of which are commonly united to form a hill community. Dwellings are round, with cylindrical mud walls and conical thatched roofs. Untilled land belongs collectively to the hill community, but individuals (with rare exceptions only men) acquire private property in plots which they bring under cultivation, and they can transmit their rights to this land through sale or inheritance. Livestock constitute the principal form of wealth, and status distinctions between rich and poor are of considerable consequence. A mild form of domestic slavery also prevails, but war captives are usually ultimately adopted into the family. Among the Tullishi, the hill community is ruled by a hereditary headman whose person is sacred and taboo. In general, however, the office of chief is weakly developed, and political power is vested in influential rainmakers or in wealthy men, who can exercise only informal sanctions. With few exceptions, all of them recent, political integration does not transcend the level of the hill community save for the temporary influence of individual "big men" and for the unity achieved, especially in the Koalib group, through the symbiotic interdependence of sibs based on their specialization in magic. Intergroup warfare occurs frequently but is usually confined to blood feuds and to raids for slaves and cattle.

Age-grades are common, though not universal. Initiation by circumcision or other genital mutilations does not occur, but the Otoro have adopted from the Sudanic-speaking peoples the custom of knocking out the incisor teeth of both sexes at puberty. The same tribe has by far the most complex age-grade system in the area. Boys and young men between the ages of eleven and twenty-six are organized into five grades, and at an important ceremony every third year each age-set is promoted to the next higher grade. A set acts as a unit in cooperative labor, and members of the two junior grades have special clubhouses. Unmarried girls are organized into three grades and live in a special dormitory which they use as a club.

Selected Bibliography

Bell, G. W. Nuba Agricultural Methods and Beliefs. *SNR*, 21:237–249. 1938. [Talodi and Tumtum].
Greenberg, J. H. Studies in African Linguistic Classification. *SWJA*, 6:388–398. 1950.
MacDiarmid, P. A., and D. N. MacDiarmid. Languages of the Nuba Mountains. *SNR*, 14:149–162. 1931.
Murdock, G. P. *Social Structure*. New York, 1949.
Nadel, S. F. *The Nuba*. London, 1947.
———. Dual Descent in the Nuba Hills. *ASKM*, pp. 333–359. 1950. [Koalib and Tumtum].
Seligman, C. G., and B. Z. Seligman. *Pagan Tribes of the Nilotic Sudan*. London, 1932. [Koalib, Talodi, and Tumtum].

21

Prenilotes

The basin of the White and Blue Nile Rivers south of Khartoum, together with the adjacent slopes of the Ethiopian plateau to the east and probably also the section of the western highlands now known as Wallega, seems to have been occupied at the end of the Paleolithic period by the northernmost extension of the East African hunters. The evidence for this rests mainly on the discovery of a Bushmanoid skull with associated Paleolithic artifacts at Singa (ca. 13°N) on the Blue Nile and on the occurrence of individuals with marked Bushmanoid features among the present-day Koman peoples of western Ethiopia.

At some later time, probably during the fourth millennium B.C., a wave of Negroid peoples entered the region from the west and practically obliterated the indigenous hunters. Since they spoke languages of the Sudanic stock, in some instances specifically of the Nilotic subdivision thereof, we shall adopt the suggestion of Grottanelli (1948) that they be called the Prenilotes. It was almost certainly these Negro invaders who first introduced Sudanic agriculture into this part of Africa and transmitted it to both the Nubians in the north and the Caucasoid Cushites of highland Ethiopia to the east.

Pharaonic Egypt never extended its political control over the Prenilotes, though elements of its culture must have penetrated to them via the Nubians of Napata and Meroe. Christianity, shortly after its spread to Dongola, was accepted in A.D. 580 by the Prenilotes of Alwa, a state with its capital near modern Khartoum. It was Christian Alwa, as we have already noted, which held up the expansion of the Bedouin Arabs into the eastern Sudan until it succumbed to Moslem conquerors in 1504.

An Arab traveler who visited Alwa in A.D. 872 mentions incidentally in his chronicle the names of two tribes, the "Barya" and "Cunama," as then resident on the borders of the kingdom. Thereafter they disappear from history until rediscovered in the nineteenth century several hundred miles to the east in the highlands of Eritrea. It is to be presumed that they fled there to escape the shattering impact of the Arab advance. That the Barea and Kunama of Eritrea are in fact emigrants from the Nile Valley is clearly demonstrated by the contrasts they present to the Cushitic and Semitic peoples who completely surround them today. They are still partially Negroid rather than fully Caucasoid in physique, Sudanic rather than Hamitic in language, matrilineal rather than patrilineal in social organization, and pagan rather than Moslem in religion, and their agriculture is basically Sudanic rather than Egyptian or Ethiopian. Since they are culturally more conservative, and somewhat better described, than most of the groups that still survive in the original homeland, they contribute substantially to our knowledge of earlier Prenilotic culture.

The Moslem conquerors of Alwa were the Fung, an Arab people with considerable Negro admixture. They founded a strong state at Sennar, dominating the region between the White and Blue Niles, and established subject or tributary states among a number of adjacent Prenilotic tribes. After 1580 the Fung state underwent considerable expansion, waging intermittent warfare with Darfur to the west and extending its political control eastward to the Red Sea. Its political institutions conformed to the Arabic pattern. A sultan headed the state, appointed governors over districts for the collection of taxes and tribute, and was assisted by a council of state composed of a vizier, a chamberlain with the grim duty of killing the ruler's brothers on his accession, and other officials. Fung prospered commercially, since Sennar stood at the crossroads of trade routes leading in all directions. Ivory, gold, horses, sesame, coffee, gum, hides, ebony, and ostrich feathers flowed in from Ethiopia and the south; slaves, iron, and gold dust from the west; dates, cloth, iron implements, mirrors, and beads from the north.

By 1780 a decline had set in, and in 1821 the territory was conquered and annexed by the Turkish government of Egypt. After 1850 came successive incursions from the north by Arab slave traders and fanatic Mahdists, which decimated many of the native tribes. Others, in the east, had been expelled from the highlands and subjected to slave raids by the Galla since the sixteenth century. In 1899, when British administration was established in the Anglo-Egyptian Sudan, the remnants of the Prenilotes, except for the resistant Shilluk tribe and the encapsulated Barea and Kunama, were largely restricted to the hill country between the White Nile and the edge of the Ethiopian plateau.

Physically the Prenilotes are Negroid and in general resemble the Nuba, with whom they were formerly contiguous. An unmistakable Caucasoid admixture, however, appears among the Shilluk and especially the Barea and Kunama. Several groups along the Ethiopian border speak languages of the independent Koman stock, conceivably a heritage from the ancient hunting population, but the great majority belong to various divisions of the Sudanic linguistic stock. The total population of the surviving Prenilotes scarcely exceeds 250,000, distributed among the following ethnic groups.

1. Anuak (Jambo, Yambo). They number about 40,000 and belong to the Nilotic branch of the Eastern subfamily of the Sudanic stock.

2. Barea (Baria, Barya). They number about 10,000 and constitute the sole members of the Barea branch of the Eastern subfamily of the Sudanic linguistic stock.

3. Berta (Barta, Beni Shangul, Gamila, Scioghile, Shangalla), embracing the Agaro, Dashi, Fazoglo, Jebelawin, Kosho, Rikabiyyah, Sillok, Watawit, and other subtribes. They number about 10,000, many of whom are strongly Arabized, and constitute the distinct Bertan subfamily of the Sudanic linguistic stock.

4. Gule (Hameg, Hamej), with the Kadallu (Kadalo). They belong to the Koman linguistic stock and probably number fewer than 10,000. The Gule formed the basic population of the former Fung kingdom of Sennar.

5. Gumuz (Djumus, Gimz, Gumus, Gumzawi, Guniz, Gunza), with the Dach, Gubba, Naga (Nagaya), and Shinasha (Bworo). They belong to the Koman linguistic stock and probably number not more than 10,000.

6. Ingassana (Engassana, Ingessana, Mamidza, Metabi, Tabi). They number about 12,000 and form the distinct Ingassana branch of the Eastern subfamily of the Sudanic linguistic stock.

7. Koma (Coma, Khoma, Komo), with the kindred Buldiit, Gwama, Kigelle, Roro, San, and Uduk (Ganza, Kebeirka, Korara). They number about 8,000 and belong to the Koman linguistic stock.

8. Kunama (Bazen, Cunama). They number about 20,000 and constitute the sole members of the Kunaman subfamily of the Sudanic linguistic stock.

9. Mao (Amam, Anfillo, Mau, Mayo), with the Busasi. They number about 10,000 and originally spoke a Koman language, though many have now adopted the Western Cushitic speech of the Busasi, a conquering group of Kafa origin.

10. Masongo (Magengo, Magianghir, Magiano, Masango, Mashongo, Ojang, Tama, Yjang), with the Bula (Buna) and Olam (Nyilam). They number about 6,000 and belong to the Beir branch of the Eastern subfamily of the Sudanic linguistic stock.

11. Meban (Gura, Maban), with the kindred Burun, Jumjum, and Ulu. They belong to the Nilotic branch of the Eastern subfamily of the Sudanic linguistic stock and probably number in excess of 10,000.

12. Shilluk. They number about 110,000 and belong to the Nilotic branch of the Eastern subfamily of the Sudanic linguistic stock.

The Prenilotes depend for subsistence primarily upon agriculture. In addition to sorghum, the universal staple, they grow such other crops of the Sudanic complex as cotton, cow peas, gourds, millet, okra, sesame, and watermelons. The Egyptian complex has contributed only broad beans, melons, and—in sporadic instances—barley, cabbage, and radishes. The tribes that border Ethiopia have commonly borrowed castor, eleusine, remtil, safflower, and teff from this originating source. Plants from remoter regions attested for two or more societies include gram and sword beans and cucumbers from India, sugarcane and yams from Malaysia, and maize, manioc, peanuts, peppers, pumpkins, and tobacco from America.

Fishing plays a prominent role in the economy of the Prenilotes, and occasionally hunting as well. Animal husbandry everywhere provides an important auxiliary source of livelihood. Cattle are kept, and milked, in all except a few areas infested with the tsetse fly. Goats, sheep, and dogs are universal; donkeys, cats, and chickens nearly so; and all groups except the Anuak, Shilluk, and the two Eritrean tribes are reported to keep pigs. Though the Shilluk have usually been classed with the pastoral Nilotes, they differ markedly from the latter in their completely sedentary mode of life, in their abstention from drinking the fresh blood of their animals, and in the relative unimportance of cattle, whose per capita incidence is scarcely a quarter of that among the neighboring Nuer. Men alone do the hunting, herding, and milking, but both sexes participate in the labor of cultivation.

Circumcision and clitoridectomy have invaded part of the area under Arab, Beja, or Galla influence, notably among the Barea, Ingassana, Kunama, Mao, and some Berta and Gumuz. Elsewhere, as among the Anuak, the southern Berta, the Koma, and the Meban, the old Sudanic practice of extracting the lower incisor teeth in both sexes still prevails. Cannibalism and headhunting are completely unknown.

Marriage involves the payment of a substantial bride-price in livestock or other valuables among the Anuak, Barea, Kunama, and Shilluk. The Berta, Ingassana, and Meban, however, require at best only a very nominal marriage payment, the consideration consisting mainly in several years of premarital and postmarital bride-service. The Gumuz, Koma, Mao, and some Berta groups follow a third procedure, that of exchanging a sister or other female relative for a wife. Marriage is usually forbidden with any first cousin. Only the Barea, Meban, and Shilluk are reported to practice general polygyny, which is preferably sororal among the Shilluk. In most other tribes monogamy strongly predominates, plural marriages being uncommon and confined mainly to men of wealth. The normal residential unit is an independent nuclear or polygynous family, occupying a compound within which each married woman has her own hut.

Patrilocal residence is the norm, but it is commonly preceded by about a year of initial matrilocal residence among the Barea, Ingassana, Kunama, Shilluk, and the Burun and Ulu subgroups of the Meban. Avunculocal residence, however, occurs as a patterned alternative very frequently among the Berta and Ingassana and moderately often among the Anuak and Shilluk. This, coupled with the fact that the Uduk subtribe of the Koma follow the matrilineal rule in regard to both inheritance and succession, suggests the possibility of former matrilineal descent, as among the Nubians and the Nuba. One source (Hilke and Plester, 1955), indeed, maintains that "mother-right" still survives among the Berta and Gumuz. Even more conclusive confirmation comes from the Barea and Kunama, who have been isolated in Eritrea from all recent intrusive influences along the Nile and remain matrilineal in both inheritance and descent to the present day. The Ingassana are now bilateral and are characterized by cousin terminology of the Hawaiian type. All other tribes today exhibit a patrilineal structure of noncorporate patrisibs and exogamous patrilineages, each of the latter tending to be localized in a hamlet. The Shilluk have cousin terms of the descriptive type and a segmentary lineage organization; their sibs, in contrast to those of most other tribes, are exogamous.

All the Prenilotes are sedentary. The local community consists either of a single compact village or of a cluster of hamlets. The prevailing house type is a round hut with cylindrical walls of wattle and daub and a conical roof thatched with grass, but among the Barea and Kunama the roof extends to the ground, giving a beehive effect. Among the Anuak, Shilluk, and apparently at least some of the other tribes, each local community has one dominant lineage that provides the headman and other lineages that have attached themselves to it, often through an original matrilocal or avunculocal marriage, and whose members are regarded as "sisters' sons" of the ruling lineage. The headman commonly has a ritual relationship to the soil. Among the Shilluk he is elected by the local council of hamlet heads from among the men of the senior minor lineage within the dominant major lineage. The cluster of hamlets which forms a Shilluk community is also united by a common age-grade organization of Nilotic type with military functions, but formal age groupings are not reported elsewhere in the area.

Formerly, perhaps, political integration did not transcend the local level. Democratic atomism still prevails among the Barea and Kunama, who lack paramount chiefs and are ruled by local assemblies of adult males in which the old men exert strong influence. Whatever the original situation, it certainly underwent change at some early period, and a distinctive type of political organization made its appearance. This probably either evolved or was perpetuated under the Christian kingdom of Alwa, for it did not prevail in the Fung state of Sennar, though it is recorded for a number of peoples who were tributary to the latter. We shall first summarize the scanty data on the Berta, Gule, and Meban and then present the much richer descriptive material on the Anuak and Shilluk.

The dependent states established under Fung domination among the Gule of Sennar, the Berta of Fazoglo and Kele, and the Meban of Ulu were all characterized by institutionalized regicide. The king was killed when it was felt he had outlived his usefulness. At Fazoglo the decision as to whether the ruler should be slain or spared rested in the hands of a council of high officials, and if their decision was unfavorable the execution was carried out by a near relative of the king, most commonly his father's brother's son, who thereupon succeeded to the throne. At Kele, too, there had to be preliminary consent by a family council, and the killer had to be a relative descended from a common grandparent. At Ulu the decision was reached by a council of the ruling family, which usually chose a half brother of the king, but sometimes a first cousin, to slay the monarch, usually by ambushing him at night, and to succeed to his office. The kings of Ulu were understandably nervous, surrounding themselves with a bodyguard of armed slaves and, for safety, sleeping each night in a different place.

Among the Anuak one source of the kingship and of regicide is observable in the status of the local headman. Each village or cluster of hamlets normally has a headman, called Father of the Land, who has a special ritual relationship to the soil, and whose office is characterized by the possession of symbolic insignia, e.g., strings of beads, heirloom spears, and village drums. The office enjoys extraordinary respect and deference, but this is maintained only by continual generosity and feast giving. As soon as a headman becomes impoverished or otherwise suffers loss of standing, others begin to conspire for the position. Anyone who is the son of a former headman is eligible to succeed, but sons and half brothers by the same mother never attempt a usurpation, leaving the competition mainly to the headman's paternal cousins and half brothers by the same father. The one who mobilizes the strongest popular support overthrows the incumbent, sometimes killing him but more commonly permitting him to retire to the village of his mother's patrilineage. Because of their insecurity, headmen rarely sleep at night but wander about the village eavesdropping for plots against them.

Somewhere in the southeastern part of the Anuak country, the position of one local headman seems to have acquired exceptional prestige and such wide renown that its occupant was accorded the title of "king." Competition for this office became especially strong, and regicide so common that the number of eligible candidates became legion. The brothers of the "king" and the sons of former rulers customarily took refuge in the villages of their mothers' patrilineages, there plotting with their maternal relatives to attack the royal village, seize the insignia of office, and thereby acquire the coveted title for themselves. After some time a resolution was reached whereby the king, to escape regicide, voluntarily yielded the symbols of office at the first sign of an approaching army and was allowed to retire unmolested to the settlement of his mother's lineage. Here he continued to hold the royal title and to receive the homage due his high status. Ultimately any son of a former king was permitted to visit the royal court and be ceremonially invested with the emblems. In consequence, every member of the royal line became a "king," and each new village to supply a ruler with a wife might anticipate the honor of having kings of its own. With this incentive the system spread outward from its point of origin until today it is shared by nearly half the Anuak nation, and its expansion continues unchecked. Wherever it has spread the "kings," i.e., former kings, tend to become established as a noble class and ultimately to usurp the political authority of the earlier headmen, whose functions become reduced to such ritual activities as magically inducing rain, soil fertility, and abundance of fish.

The whole system is based on prestige alone. There is no central government, no administration. The king exercises no political authority or judicial functions outside his own village. There is not even any joint military enterprise or any restraint upon intervillage warfare. Nor is there actually a capital, for the king ordinarily moves from village to village, each feeling honored to support him for a while. The Anuak seem to have succeeded better than any political cartoonist on a European anti-royalist newspaper in producing an effective caricature of the kingship.

The political organization of the Shilluk, being especially adequately described, provides the capstone, as it were, for our understanding of the area as a whole. The communities of the Shilluk country, numbering about a hundred, are politically integrated into a single tribal state under a prestigeful divine king called *reth*. He resides in the capital town of Fashoda, where he maintains a court and is served by a large body of retainers and a harem of wives. Some authorities report that it was formerly common for a Shilluk king to marry his sisters or half sisters. His office is symbolized by a royal stool. The man who sits upon it must be the son of a former king and a direct patrilineal descendant of Nyikang, the culture hero of the people and the traditional founder of the kingdom through conquest. It is, indeed, not the king who rules but the spirit of Nyikang who rules through him, and it is upon the power and beneficent influence of Nyikang that the entire state and society are believed to depend. The ruler must serve the interests of Nyikang, e.g., by maintaining and replenishing the latter's herds of sacred cattle. It is his responsibility to bring the divine power of Nyikang to bear for societal objectives, which he does by making sacrifices for rain and for victory in war. As high priest of the country, the king must maintain himself in a state of ritual purity and perfect health. If he weakens physically or if his people suffer misfortune, this suggests his loss of divine power and the danger that Nyikang may desert his people. Regicide offers a solution, but before considering this we must examine the class structure, electoral system, and administrative organization of Shilluk society.

Six distinct social classes can be distinguished. The first, or royal, class is composed of the king himself, his children, and the surviving offspring of former rulers. The females are forbidden to marry—except possibly the king himself—or to bear children, which, of course, renders impossible any matrilineal succession to the throne. The males are all eligible to succeed to the kingship, and to thwart untoward ambitions all are banished from the capital and compelled to live in the settlements of their mothers' lineages. The second class consists of all other members of the royal sib, i.e., of those who are not themselves the children of a king and are thus ineligible to succeed to the throne. They number about 7 per cent of the total population and are treated with deference by the lower classes, but they lack any political authority unless they happen to be lineage heads in the communities where they reside. Third comes a small class of "degraded royalty," comprising the patrilineal descendants of royalty who were in former times, for various reasons, declared ineligible to succeed to the kingship. They form a single sib and enjoy a status which is definitely noble except that, unlike commoners, their women may not marry men of the royal sib. The fourth class, that of commoners, includes the mass of the population, specifically the patrilineal descendants of the followers of Nyikang in his conquest of the country. Next comes a class of retainers (*bang reth*), who are organized into a single artificial exogamous sib and are even more numerous than the royal sib. They are composed of war captives kept by the king as personal servants, of convicted murderers and their brothers, of aliens and poor commoners who have attached themselves to the king in return for cattle to marry with, and of the patrilineal descendants of all such persons. They are the personal attendants and clients of the king and owe primary allegiance to him. Since they are ineligible to hold land or to intermarry with royalty, they have a status slightly lower than that of commoners. The sixth class is that of privately owned slaves, comprising war captives, victims purchased from the Arabs, children bought from poor parents during a famine, and the descendants of all such people.

Returning to the kingship, we may note the electoral procedure. The death of a ruler is followed by an anarchic interregnum while his successor is being selected from among the men of the royal class. The decision is vested in a sort of electoral college, consisting of the chief of one community on the northern frontier, of another on the southern frontier, of nine others traditionally descended from those among whom Nyikang originally divided his conquered territory, of three heads of ineligible royal lineages, and of the especially influential chiefs of the two provinces, northern and southern, into which the country is divided. The electors naturally favor different candidates—the provincial chiefs, in particular, being motivated by extreme rivalry. Compromises are therefore inevitable and are characteristically achieved by one faction agreeing to support another's candidate in return for a promise of reciprocal support at the next election. Hence the succession rarely passes from father to son but shifts from one branch to another of the royal lineage.

Once the electoral college has reached its decision, the king-elect proceeds to raise an army in the southern province. Meanwhile the priests of Nyikang remove his effigy from its shrine in the north and parade it through the northern province, collecting a second army. The two forces meet in mock combat on the provincial border, and that of the king-elect suffers defeat. The priests escort both the divine effigy and the royal captive to the capital, placing first the former, then the latter, on the royal stool. As the king-elect takes his seat he is seized with trembling. The spirit of Nyikang has passed from the effigy through the stool and taken possession of the body of the new ruler. This is symbolized by a second mock battle in which the king's force emerges triumphant.

Neither the provinces nor the districts represented by the electors are administrative units. The chiefs of the hundred communities are responsible directly rather than indirectly to the king. Even they are not appointive. The king, to be sure, must confirm them in office, but they are elected by local procedure. From these facts Evans-Pritchard (1948) infers that the Shilluk king has no administrative authority or judicial power, that his influence rests solely upon his divinity and his ritual functions, and that the political structure is consequently not that of a true state. It is possible, of course, that men like Hofmayr, Howell, and Westermann, who accomplished the basic field research, erred in stressing the absolute power and "theoretical omnipotence" of the Shilluk king, but it is also conceivable that Evans-Pritchard was swayed by his own earlier discovery of a stateless government among the Anuak. Perhaps, too, the original power of the Shilluk monarchy has been obscured by the long period of Turkish, Egyptian, Mahdist, and British domination. The fact that the Shilluk alone, among all the tribes of their culture area, have escaped being shattered by these outside forces would seem to argue for at least some measure of political solidarity.

Complete internal peace certainly did not prevail, for local chiefs often raided one another for cattle. It is nevertheless clear that when such depredations became excessive the king intervened. He possessed, in his large body of retainers, a major instrument of force. With their help and the assistance of warriors levied from the injured neighbors, he descended on the recalcitrant local chief, burned his homestead, and expropriated his cattle. According to the canons of political science, the existence of an agency of force under central control and its use for the application of punitive sanctions are the prime criteria of a true state.

If their monarch could not muster a sufficient force to overawe, and if necessary defeat, a wayward local chief, it must certainly have appeared to the Shilluk that he had lost the divine power of Nyikang and thus deserved to be removed from the scene. This brings us back to the topic of regicide. All the earlier sources report that if a reigning king manifested a loss of power—e.g., by growing ill or senile, by failing to satisfy his wives sexually, or by allowing the state to undergo some major misfortune such as a famine, an epidemic, or defeat in war—it became necessary to kill him in order to preserve the society. The Shilluk themselves say, and unquestionably believe, that in such circumstances the ruler may be ambushed and strangled or walled up in a house and left to die. Though admitting that "Shilluk kings generally met a violent death," Evans-Pritchard doubts that regicide ever actually occurred through assassination. What happened, he believes, is that a prince would take advantage of rising popular discontent and marshal his supporters in an armed rebellion; if this succeeded, the king lost his life.

If the ruler did not fear assassination, why did he rid his capital of every eligible successor? Why did he surround himself with a loyal body of retainers beholden to no one else? Why did he take such extraordinary precautions against ambush as to sleep only in the daytime and remain awake all night with his harem around him to raise an alarm? We may also wonder why an ambitious prince and his supporters should have preferred an open military attack upon the king's substantial body of loyal retainers when their ends might be achieved more safely and surely through conspiracy and private assassination.

As happens so frequently, evidence from ethnographic distributions contributes to the solution of this problem. We know definitely that in four neighboring Fung dependencies regicide not only occurred but was planned and approved by a council of relatives, accomplished by surprise, and executed by a collateral patrilineal kinsman who became the next king. Among the Anuak, too, an overthrown headman was killed by a paternal half brother or cousin who succeeded to his position. Of Ulu, the Fung kingdom closest to the Shilluk, finally, we are told that the king took special precautions against being ambushed at night. With the reports of actual field workers supported by the areal pattern and confirmed by the behavior of the kings themselves, the expressed beliefs of the Shilluk can probably be accepted as not without foundation.

If we look back from the Shilluk to ancient Egypt, it is difficult to convince ourselves that the influence of the latter has been confined to the importation of domestic animals and a few cultivated plants. Since diffusion is always selective, the absence of specific resemblances in such aspects of culture as settlement pattern, house type, marriage, and kinship structure is not conclusive. That some social as well as economic institutions may have spread far up the Nile is suggested by certain similarities between the political systems of ancient Egypt and the Shilluk. Among these we may list the very explicit divinity of the king, his ritual isolation, a stool as his symbol of office, the prevalence of brother-sister marriages in the ruling dynasty, and the traditional and symbolic division of the kingdom into a northern and southern half. The number and specificity of these parallels cast doubt on the assumption that they are due to chance alone. If they have actually been acquired by diffusion from ancient Egypt, the intervening Nubians, about whose aboriginal culture we know so little, must have shared at least these, and doubtless other, social institutions with the African colossus of the north.

Selected Bibliography

Bacon, C. R. K. The Anuak. *SNR*, 5:113–129. 1922.

Conti Rossini, C. Popoli dell'Etiopia occidentale. *Rendiconti della Reale Accademia dei Lincei*, 28:251–285, 319–325. Roma, 1919. [Gumuz].

Corfield, F. D. The Koma. *SNR*, 25:123–265. 1938.

Crawford, O. G. S. *The Fung Kingdom of Sennar*. Gloucester, 1951.

Evans-Pritchard, E. E. A Preliminary Account of the Ingassana Tribe. *SNR*, 10:69–83. 1927.

———. Ethnological Observations on Dar Fung. *SNR*, 15:1–61. 1932. [Berta and Meban].

———. The Political System of the Anuak. *MSA*, 4:1–164. 1940.

———. Further Observations on the Political System of the Anuak. *SNR*, 28:62–97. 1947.

———. The Divine Kingship of the Shilluk. Cambridge, 1948.

Grottanelli, V. L. *I Mao*. Roma, 1940.

———. I Pre-Niloti. *AL*, 12:282–326. 1948.

Haberland, E. Ueber einen unbekannten Gunza-Stamm in Wallega. *RSE*, 12:139–148. 1953. [Gumuz].

Hilke, H., and D. Plester. Forschungsreise in das Land der Präniloten. *ZE*, 80:178–186. 1955. [Berta and Gumuz].

Hofmayr, W. *Die Schilluk*. Wien, 1925.

Howell, P. P. The Shilluk Settlement. *SNR*, 24:47–67. 1941.

———. Observations on the Shilluk. *Africa*, 22:97–119; 23:94–109. 1952–1953.

Munzinger, W. *Ostafrikanische Studien*. Schaffhausen, 1864. [Barea and Kunama].

Paul, A. Some Aspects of the Fung Sultanate. *SNR*, 35(2):17–31. 1954.

Pumphrey, M. E. C. The Shilluk Tribe. *SNR*, 24:1–45. 1941.

Seligman, C. G., and B. Z. Seligman. *Pagan Tribes of the Nilotic Sudan*. London, 1932. [Ingassana, Meban, and Shilluk].

Tucci, G. I Baria e i Cunama. *Revista di Etnografia*, 4:49–75. Napoli, 1950.

Westermann, D. *The Shilluk People*. Berlin, 1912.

22

Central Ethiopians

The Paleolithic hunting and gathering inhabitants of the Ethiopian plateau belonged to two distinct races. Bushmanoid peoples with cultures of the Stillbay complex have left indubitable traces in the southwest, whereas Caucasoids apparently occupied the northeast, but much archeological work remains to be done before the distribution and geographical movements of the two can be more accurately determined. It is clear, however, that the Caucasoid element came ultimately to prevail over the entire area. These people undoubtedly spoke languages of the Cushitic subfamily of the Hamitic stock, for these constitute the linguistic substratum over all the plateau today.

At some time prior to 3000 B.C. the Negroid ancestors of the Prenilotes penetrated the plateau from the west, bringing with them agriculture of the Sudanic type. They displaced or absorbed the indigenous Bushmanoid inhabitants in the western part of the highlands and must also have made certain inroads among the Caucasoid Cushites farther east, for all the peoples of Ethiopia today reveal at least a slight admixture of Negro blood. On the whole, however, the Cushites stood their ground, apparently by adopting agriculture and a sedentary mode of life from the culturally more advanced Negroes.

From this point on, the Cushitic peoples of the highlands begin to differentiate into three very distinct divisions, which must be treated separately. In the southeast, isolated from the rest of the plateau by the great rift valley, developed a cluster of peoples speaking languages of the Eastern branch of the Cushitic subfamily. We shall deal with them and their modern descendants in Chapters 25, 43, and 44. In the southwest evolved a second cluster, the Sidamo peoples, speaking languages of the Western branch of the Cushitic subfamily. They will provide the subject of consideration in the following chapter.

The third cluster of highland Cushites, the Agau peoples, spoke languages of the Central branch of the Cushitic subfamily. They once occupied most of the central and northern part of the Ethiopian plateau but have been displaced or absorbed over most of this region within the historical period by intrusive Semitic peoples coming from southern Arabia. It is with the Central Ethiopians, both Agau and Semites, that this chapter is primarily concerned.

Only a few scattered remnants of the Agau, numbering in all probably not more than 100,000, survive today, and they have apparently become nearly completely acculturated to the dominant Semites. Moreover, they are almost completely unstudied, so that we possess no reliable information on which to reconstruct their cultural past. This is unfortunate since the Ethiopians known to the Pharaonic Egyptians must have been the ancestors of the Agau, and any cultural influences on highland Ethiopia emanating from ancient Egypt must have been mediated by them, and are certainly not recoverable from the latecoming Semites.

The lack of information is doubly regrettable since all indications point to the Agau as one of the culturally most creative peoples on the entire continent. Not content with adopting Sudanic agriculture from the Prenilotes, they improved the crops which they borrowed and produced important new varieties, notably the durra variety of sorghum. They also experimented with wild plants in the search for new cultigens, as a result of which central highland Ethiopia ranks with China and India as one of the world's important minor centers of origination of cultivated plants. Their principal contributions, which we may term collectively the Ethiopian complex, are listed below.

CEREAL GRAINS

Eleusine, or finger millet, or ragi (*Eleusine coracana*). This cultigen spread early to India, as well as widely in East and South Africa.
Teff (*Eragrostis abyssinica*). This cereal has spread to a very limited extent into the eastern Sudan.

ROOT CROPS

Ensete, or the Abyssinian banana (*Ensete edulis*, formerly *Musa ensete*). This plant, used for its edible roots rather than its fruit, was first domesticated in southwestern Ethiopia, where it is still the staple crop.

LEAF AND STALK VEGETABLES

Cress, or garden cress (*Lepidum sativum*). This plant is also used for the oil expressed from its seeds.

CONDIMENTS AND INDULGENTS

Coffee (*Coffea arabica*).
Fenugreek (*Trigonella foenumgraecum*).
Kat, or Arab tea (*Catha edulis*).
Vegetable mustard (*Brassica carinata*).

OIL AND DYE PLANTS

Castor (*Ricinus communis*). This oil plant spread to Egypt early in the Dynastic period.
Remtil, or nug (*Guizotia abyssinica*). An important oil plant.

Safflower (*Carthamus tinctorius*). This plant, used both as a dye and for oil, spread to Egypt about 1500 B.C.

The Agau obtained cattle, sheep, and goats from ancient Egypt, presumably via the Nubians and Prenilotes and probably around the beginning of the third millennium B.C., but it is unlikely that they acquired the milking complex at that time. They themselves apparently domesticated the donkey, or ass, and later learned to cross it with the horse to produce mules. They maintained intermittent contacts with Pharaonic Egypt, which during periods of expansion, notably under the XVIII dynasty of the New Empire, even conquered and temporarily incorporated portions of their territory. This must certainly have stimulated cultural borrowing, possibly of political forms as on the middle Nile. Some of the crops of the Egyptian complex, which hold a prominent place in the economy of Ethiopia today, may also have diffused to the highlands at this time. In view of the fact, however, that they spread to intervening Nubia to such a very limited extent, it seems more reasonable to assume that they were mainly introduced from Arabia by the Semites at a somewhat later date.

During the first millennium B.C. a highly complex agricultural civilization flourished among the Sabaean Semites of southern Arabia, whose prosperity appears to have been founded in part on the development of a profitable sea-borne trade with India. Around 700 B.C., during a period of expansion, a wave of Sabaeans crossed the Red Sea from Yemen and seized from the Agau a portion of their territory in the northeastern section of modern Ethiopia and adjacent Eritrea. Later they established a powerful state with its capital at Axum, where archeological research has revealed a complex civilization of southern Arabian type. This seems to have had its economic basis, not only in trade, but in the cultivation of wheat, barley, and other Southwest Asian crops, which, as previously suggested, the Sabaeans presumably brought with them from Arabia. It was doubtless also the latter who first introduced the milking complex to Ethiopia.

The Axumites accepted Christianity early in the fourth century and thereafter maintained close commercial and diplomatic relations not only with the Christian states of Alwa and Dongola in Nubia but also with the nations of the eastern Mediterranean. Such was their strength that they twice invaded and conquered Yemen, once in the fourth and once in the sixth century, on both occasions holding that country for a period and gaining control over its rich trade with India. With the rise and spread of Islam in the seventh century, the Ethiopian Semites were isolated from their Mediterranean co-religionists by Moslem encirclement, and Axum disappears from history.

During the Axumite period a second and smaller band of Semitic immigrants invaded southeastern Ethiopia, leaving as their modern descendants the Gurage and Harari peoples. Jews formed a third Semitic increment. During the Diaspora many of them fled to Ethiopia, settled among the Agau, and converted some of the latter to Judaism. The most famous of their descendants are the Falasha, or "Black Jews," who today constitute a section of the Cushitic-speaking Kemant tribe.

After the fall of Axum its place in northern Ethiopia was taken by other dynasties, sometimes Semitic, sometimes Agau. During the twelfth and thirteenth centuries Islam, which had been established on the coasts of southern Eritrea and adjacent Somaliland, penetrated into the southeastern and eastern highlands. It was checked temporarily after 1270 by the strong Solomonid dynasty, which extended its political control from the Tigrinya to the Amhara country. The bulk of the Agau population was now converted to Christianity and became so strongly acculturated to their Semitic conquerors that today only a few dwindling islands of Central Cushitic speech survive in the midst of the dominant Amhara and Tigrinya nations.

In the early sixteenth century the Moslem Somali repeatedly invaded the territory of the Christian Semites, who ultimately defeated them with Portuguese help in 1543. Weakened by their exhausting wars with the adherents of Islam, the Ethiopians were unable to withstand a new threat from the south. The pastoral Galla began to infiltrate the southern plateau before 1550, and by 1600 had occupied a substantial portion of central Ethiopia as well, displacing speakers of Western Cushitic as well as of Semitic languages. They quickly exchanged their nomadic habits for a sedentary agricultural life and became acculturated to the Amhara in other important respects, though many of them still cling to their pagan religion and their indigenous social institutions. The Ethiopian Semites and the Galla have long since become politically reconciled and have played approximately equal roles in the recent history of the country.

The Central Ethiopians are preponderantly Caucasoid, though containing a subordinate Negroid strain. They all speak languages of the Hamitic stock, either Semitic or Central Cushitic. They subscribe in the main to the Coptic, or Monophysitic, branch of Christianity, though they include a small pagan and a larger Moslem minority. They fall into seven distinguishable ethnic groups, as follows:

1. Amhara. The dominant group in modern Ethiopia, they probably number at least 3 million. They are Semitic in speech, and most are Christian.
2. Awiya (Agaumeder, Awawar), with the kindred Damot. This Agau remnant, speaking a Central Cushitic tongue, is mainly Christian.
3. Gurage (Gouraghe). This Semitic-speaking group numbers about 350,000, of whom approximately a third are Christian, a third Moslem, and a third pagan.

4. Harari. This Moslem group, speaking a Semitic language, numbers about 35,000 in and around the city of Harar.
5. Kamir (Chamir, Hamir, Khamir), with the related Khamta (Hamta). This Agau remnant, Central Cushitic in language, is mainly Christian.
6. Kemant (Camant, Chemant, Kamant, Qemant), with the Falasha (Black Jews, Kayla) and Quara (Kwara). These Central Cushitic speakers are pagan except for 20,000 Falasha, who are Jewish in religion. Together with the other Agau remnants, the Awiya and Kamir, they probably number about 100,000.
7. Tigrinya. These Semitic people are mainly Christians, though they include a few Moslems. They number about 1,150,000, of whom 430,000 (the Akkele-Guzai, Hamasien, and Serae tribes) live in Eritrea.

The Central Ethiopians subsist primarily by agriculture, in which they employ an ox-drawn plow and occasionally irrigation. In addition to the cultigens of local origin, they grow cotton, cow peas, gourds, millet, sesame, and sorghum from the Sudanic complex; barley, black caraway, broad beans, chick peas, flax, garlic, grapes, lentils, peas, rape, vetch, and wheat from the Egyptian complex; small quantities of oats, peaches, and purslane from the Greco-Roman complex; bananas and sugarcane from Southeast Asia; and maize, peanuts, peppers, and tobacco from the New World. Their economy rests largely on the cultivation of cereal grains, with barley, eleusine, sorghum, teff, and wheat as the staples. Oil plants, particularly castor, flax, and remtil, occupy an unusually prominent position. As compared with North Africa, Ethiopian agriculture differs most strikingly in the near absence of vegetables and fruit trees.

Animal husbandry, though always subsidiary to tillage, assumes great importance. Cattle, sheep, goats, horses, donkeys, dogs, cats, chickens, and bees are universal, and, in addition, the Tigrinya keep a few camels. Pigs, however, are unreported. All groups milk their cows, ewes, and goats and make butter, which they use, however, chiefly as a cosmetic. They do practically no hunting, fishing, or gathering, but they engage extensively in trade and maintain a system of regular markets. In the division of labor by sex, the men do most of the herding, the women most of the milking (except among the Tigrinya), and both sexes participate in agricultural work, with the larger share falling to the men.

Most groups live in compact permanent villages, but neighborhoods of dispersed homesteads are reported for the Gurage. Cities are rare, the largest being Addis Ababa with a population of approximately 150,000. The prevailing type of dwelling is a round hut with cylindrical walls of wattle and daub and a conical thatched roof, but wealthy town dwellers among the Amhara, Harari, and Tigrinya occupy flat-roofed rectangular houses with interior courtyards and stone walls plastered with mud.

The Agau peoples and the Amhara apparently require no material consideration in connection with a marriage, though gifts are given. A dowry, however, is customary among the Tigrinya and a bride-price among the

Gurage. All groups, even those who adhere to Islam, forbid unions with a first cousin. Polygyny prevails among pagans and Moslems, but Christians cleave officially to monogamy, though informally tolerating concubinage. The Falasha and Tigrinya proscribe the levirate, which in other groups is always permissible and often preferential. Residence regularly follows the patrilocal principle, but extended forms of the family do not occur. Descent, though apparently bilateral among the Amhara, is definitely patrilineal among the Gurage and Tigrinya. The Semitic peoples employ cousin terminology of the descriptive pattern.

The Central Ethiopians differentiate a landed aristocracy from commoners and until recently had a class of hereditary slaves. Smiths and hunters commonly form segregated and endogamous castes. Inheritance invariably follows the patrilineal principle, with males alone participating and with sons taking precedence over brothers. The Amhara adhere to primogeniture, but among the Tigrinya all sons share alike. Boys are subjected to circumcision and girls to clitoridectomy, and sometimes also to infibulation, in infancy. Both the Agau and the Semites have been habituated to monarchical forms of government from time immemorial. The present Ethiopian state is headed by an emperor (*Negus*), who is advised by a council of ministers and rules his country through provincial governors (*ras*) and an administrative hierarchy filled mainly by nobles. Since the end of the nineteenth century, except during an interim of Italian rule, the state has exercised effective sovereignty over the peoples of southeastern and southwestern as well as of central and northern Ethiopia.

Selected Bibliography

Azais, P., and R. Chambard. Notes sur quelques coutumes observées au Guragé. *RETP*, 8:39–44. 1927.
Cecchi, A. *Da Zeila alle fronteire del Caffa*. 2 vols. Roma, 1885. [Amhara and Gurage].
Conti Rossini, C. *La langue des Kemant en Abyssinie*. Wien, 1912.
Flad, J. M. A. *A Short Description of the Falashas and Kamants*. Chrishona, 1860.
Hildebrandt, J. M. Gesammelte Notizen über Landwirthschaft und Viehzucht in Abyssinien. *ZE*, 6:318–340. 1874.
Leslau, W. Ethiopic Documents: Gurage. *Viking Fund Publications in Anthropology*, 14:1–176. New York, 1950.
——. Falasha Anthology. *Yale Judaica Series*, 6:1–222. New Haven, 1951.
——. Coutumes et croyances des Falachas. *TMIE*, 61:1–98. 1957.
Munzinger, W. *Ostafrikanische Studien*. Schaffhausen, 1864. [Tigrinya].
Nadel, S. F. Land Tenure on the Eritrean Plateau. *Africa*, 16:1–22, 99–109. 1946. [Tigrinya].
Parkyns, M. *Life in Abyssinia*. 2 vols. London, 1853. [Tigrinya].
Paulitschke, P. *Beiträge zur Ethnographie und Anthropologie der Somâl, Galla und Harari*. 2d edit. Leipzig, 1888.

Perham, M. *The Government of Ethiopia*. London, 1948.
Rey, C. F. *Unconquered Abyssinia*. London, 1923. [Amhara].
Sanford, C. *Ethiopia under Haile Selassie*. London, 1946.
Sauer, C. O. *Agricultural Origins and Dispersals*. New York, 1952.
Schiemann, E. Entstehung der Kulturpflanzen. *Handbuch der Vererbungswissenschaft*, 3:1–377. Berlin, 1932.
Snowden, J. D. *The Cultivated Races of Sorghum*. London, 1936.
Stern, H. A. *Wanderings among the Falashas in Abyssinia*. London, 1862.
Stiehler, W. Studien zur Landwirtschafts- und Siedlungsgeographie Aethiopiens. *Erdkunde*, 2:257–282. 1948.
Trimingham, J. S. *Islam in Ethiopia*. Oxford, 1952.
Vavilov, N. I. The Origin, Variation, Immunity and Breeding of Cultivated Plants, transl. K. S. Chester. *Chronica Botanica*, 13:1–364. 1949–1950.

23

Sidamo Peoples

Along the southwestern margin of the Ethiopian plateau dwell a group of culturally very distinctive peoples known collectively as the Sidamo. Though racially very much mixed, they retain no traces of the Bushmanoid hunting population that originally inhabited their country. Authorities agree that they contain strong ingredients of both Caucasoid and Negroid blood but disagree about which predominates. The Caucasoid element is certainly Cushitic, for all the peoples of the area speak languages of the Western branch of the Cushitic subfamily of the Hamitic stock, with the single exception of the Gibe, who have adopted the Galla language through conquest within the historical period. The Negroid element, reflected in such characteristics as kinky hair and a chocolate-brown skin color, presumably derives from the Prenilotes who brought Sudanic agriculture to highland Ethiopia about 5,000 years ago. We lack sufficient evidence, however, to determine how the mixture occurred, whether through early Negro infiltration among Caucasoids after the latter had expelled the Bushmanoids or through later Caucasoid expansion into territory where Negroes had previously displaced the indigenous hunters.

East of the Sidamo peoples live the Darasa, Kambata, Konso, and Reshiat tribes, who exhibit a similar mixed racial composition and who are consequently often classed with them. They differ substantially, however, in many aspects of culture and speak languages of the Eastern rather than the Western branch of the Cushitic subfamily, affiliating in both respects more closely with the Galla. We shall therefore segregate them for special treatment in Chapter 25.

The total population of the Sidamo tribes approaches 1,500,000. They are divisible into the following seven major groups:

1. Bako, with the Amar (Amarcocche, Ammur, Hamarkoke, Hummurcocche), Ari (Are, Arro, Shangama), Bachada (Baciada, Bagata, Bashada), Bana (Banna, Bunno), Biya (Bio, Biye), Boda, Borali (Burle), Dime (Dima), Gayi, Kerre (Cherre, Karo, Kere, Koure, Kure), Oida, Sido, Tdamoo, Tsamai (Cule, Duma, Dume, Koule, Kule, Samai, Tsamako), and Ubamer. It is possible that a few of these tribes speak Eastern Sudanic rather than Western Cushitic languages. They are pagans and probably number at least 30,000.
2. Gibe, embracing the Enarya, Garo (Bosha), Gera, Gomma, Guma, and Limmu. Conquered by Galla invaders in the sixteenth century, they are now Moslems and have adopted the Eastern Cushitic language of their rulers.
3. Gimira (Gemirra, Ghimirra), with the kindred Benesho (Benischo, Bennecho, Bienescio, Bimenso), Kaba (Caba, Kabo), Nao (Naa, Naho, Naji, Nayo), Shako (Chako, Mocha, Saco, Sciacco, Shekke), and She (Dissu, Dizu, Schewe, Sewo, Shewo). They number about 20,000 and are pagans.
4. Janjero (Yamma, Yangaro, Yem). They are pagans in religion.
5. Kafa (Goffa, Gonga, Kafficho). The population of this primarily pagan nation was estimated at half a million in 1905.
6. Maji (Maciu, Madsche, Magi, Mancho, Masi, Mazi). This group, a detached branch of the Gimira, numbers about 6,000 and is pagan.
7. Ometo (Omati, Ometi), embracing the Alga, Baditu (Amara, Amarro, Badditu, Coira, Hamarro, Koira, Kuera, Kwera), Basketo (Baskatta), Bodi (Bodu), Borodda, Chara (Ciara, Tsara, Zara), Doko (Doco, Dokko, Sidi, Sido), Dollo, Dorse (Dorze), Gamo (Zagitse), Gofa, Haruro (Aruro, Gagembe, Gatzamba, Kachama, Katsamma, Tzademba), Konta (Conta, Gobo, Kobo, Kuontab, Uaratta, Waratta), Kucha (Cuccia, Cuiscia, Koisha), Kullo (Cullo, Dauro, Dawaro, Omati, Wammate), Malo, Uba (Ubba), Walamo (Ualamo, Uollamo, Walaitsa, Wallamo, Wollamo), Zala (Sala, Tsala, Zalla), and Zaysse (Seysse, Zaisse). They number several hundred thousand, and most are pagan.

Recorded history among the Sidamo peoples does not extend back beyond about A.D. 1400, when the Kafa kingdom was founded. The Gibe were conquered by Galla invaders shortly before 1550, and the Gimira were subjugated by the Kafa in the eighteenth century. In wars of territorial aggrandizement between 1886 and 1900, Menelik II conquered the Gibe, Janjero, and Kafa and incorporated them in the Ethiopian state, which today exercises suzerainty over the entire area.

The Sidamo peoples cultivate the soil with exceptional intensity. Many of them practice irrigation on terraced fields fertilized with animal manure, and about half of them have adopted the ox-drawn plow. They raise all the crops of the Ethiopian complex, but unlike the Central Ethiopians depend, except for the Gibe, primarily on root crops rather than on cereals. The staple is ensete, an original local cultigen, to which have been added the Sudanic coleus, the American sweet potato, and the Malaysian taro and yams. Grains, which come next in importance, include barley, eleusine, maize, millet, sorghum, teff, and wheat. Auxiliary crops include cotton, cow peas, gourds, and sesame from the Sudanic complex; black caraway, cabbage, chick peas, coriander, flax, garlic, lentils, opium poppies, peas, and vetch from the Egyptian complex; lemons and limes from the Greco-Roman complex; ginger from India; bananas and sugar-cane from Malaysia; and haricot beans, pumpkins, tobacco, and tomatoes from America.

The peoples of the area keep cattle, sheep, goats, donkeys, dogs, chickens, and bees, and they utilize milk and butter. The Gibe and Kafa also catch and tame wild civet cats, keeping them for the extraction of a glandular secretion which is used for perfume and which constitutes an important export item. On the whole, however, animal husbandry plays a role distinctly subordinate to agriculture. Little hunting and gathering are done, and no fishing, except by a few Bako, for the Sidamo peoples in general observe the widespread Cushitic taboo against eating fish. Men tend the livestock, but women ordinarily milk them. Men do the plowing, but hoe cultivation usually devolves upon the women.

In contrast to the village pattern of settlement among the Central Ethiopians, most Sidamo tribes live in neighborhoods of dispersed homesteads, each surrounded by its own plot of cultivated land. Some groups of Bako and Ometo occupy compact and sometimes palisaded villages, but they constitute a distinct minority. Dwellings are typically round, with cylindrical walls of wattle and daub and conical thatched roofs supported by a central wooden column, and are usually clustered in compounds.

Marriage requires payment of a bride-price and is forbidden with any first cousin. Most tribes practice general polygyny, establishing each wife in a separate hut within the compound, but the Janjero limit plural wives to men of noble rank. Patrilocal residence prevails generally but does not usually give rise to extended forms of the family. Descent, inheritance, and succession universally follow the patrilineal rule. Sibs and lineages, though usually exogamous, are only rarely localized as clans.

Most, if not all, Sidamo tribes have hereditary slaves and despised endogamous castes of smiths, hunters, and leatherworkers. In addition, the Gibe, Janjero, and Kafa observe a sharp differentiation into three social classes—royalty, nobles, and commoners. The Gibe and Kafa practice clitoridectomy, but the Janjero do not. In addition to circumcision, which is nearly universal in the area, Janjero males have their nipples and one testicle excised. Cannibalism does not occur, but a number of tribes take the genitals of slain enemies as trophies.

Monarchical forms of political organization prevail throughout the Sidamo area and exhibit a single characteristic pattern, which is particularly elaborate among the Gibe, Janjero, and Kafa. The Kafa system, described below, may be taken as generally applicable to the other tribes as well, subject to a reduction in scale for the Bako, Maji, and Ometo and to the loss of the ruler's religious sanctity in the five Gibe states, in consequence of the Galla conquest.

At the head of the Kafa state stands a divine king (*tato*), in whom the spirit of the sky god is incarnate. His eyes are compared to the sun, and so dangerous is their power that the populace hides when he leaves his palace, and only his wives, attendants, and high officials may look upon him or speak to him. His life is hedged in with taboos; he cannot, for example, touch food himself and must therefore be fed. He lives in a fortified palace in the capital town of Bonga, where he is surrounded by a harem of wives, a bodyguard of eunuchs, and personal officials with specialized functions, e.g., four chamberlains and a private treasurer and commissary. His insignia of office include a golden armband, various other ornaments of gold and silver, a conical hat or crown, a drum, an umbrella, and two thrones, one a bed and the other a chair. He is both the chief judge of the kingdom and its high priest, conducting sacrifices to the sky god on a sacred hill.

In addition to conquered and tributary states, the realm is divided into 134 administrative districts with salaried heads, and these are grouped into twelve provinces. Although the provincial governors are appointive in most of the states of the area, in Kafa they are hereditary within particular patrisibs, though they must be invested in office by the king. The territorial officials judge disputes; raise troops in case of war; levy taxes in cattle, slaves, cloth, and ivory, but not in agricultural products; and conscript *corvées* to build and maintain roads and to labor on the royal estates. The entire administrative hierarchy is responsible, not to the king, but to the Katama, a vizier or prime minister, who is also the commander in chief of the army and the immediate administrator of the capital town.

Supreme authority in the state, however, is vested, not in the Katama or in the king, but in a privy council (*mikirecho*) of seven ministers, without whose concurrence no major decision can be made. Except for the Katama, its members are all provincial governors, and most of them have other specialized functions. Thus one is the king's speaker, master of ceremonies at court, and foreign minister; another is minister of public works and commandant of the palace guard; a third is the supervisor of the king's slaves and of labor on the royal domains. The minister of trade and markets, however, does not belong to the council; he holds office by appointment from the king and is responsible to him alone.

Although in some of the Sidamo states, e.g., Janjero, the relatives of the king fill appointive offices in the administrative hierarchy, they play a relatively unimportant role in the political life of the Kafa. An important exception is the Gabirecho or Queen-Mother, who exercises supreme supervision over the royal court, the members of the royal family, and the palace stores. When the occupant, who is in the first instance the mother of the ruler, dies, she is succeeded in her important office by the Queen-Consort, or chief wife of the king.

When the monarch falls ill, the fact is concealed; and when his death approaches, all his male kinsmen are put in chains until his successor is chosen. The heir is always a son of the deceased ruler, but the selection is made, during an interregnum of eight days, by the privy council acting as an electoral college. The corpse of the dead king is wrapped in many cloths (a reflex of mummification?), and human sacrifices mark his funeral. The council not only appoints the king but may depose him, although this has actually happened only once in history—by poisoning. The only other specific evidence of regicide in the Sidamo area is a report that Janjero kings who are wounded in battle are put to death.

The Kafa conduct war for slaves, cattle, and other plunder as well as for territorial aggrandizement. All males except the members of four privileged sibs are liable to military service. The king retains one-tenth of all war captives and half of all other booty, the remainder being divided among the captors. The country is thoroughly organized for war. In addition to a system of highways connecting the major towns and markets, with bridges over rivers and resthouses at intervals, the state maintains a special system of military roads. Even more rapid communication, for mobilizing an army or other emergencies, is achieved through a special signaling system using slit gongs. Finally, the entire state of Kafa, and those of the Gibe and Janjero as well, is completely surrounded, except where impregnable geographical barriers exist, by a single or double palisade, a deep ditch, and an outside strip of cleared land, with fortified gates at moderate intervals manned constantly by armed guards. With the exception of the Great Wall of China, and possibly a few sections of imperial Rome's frontier defenses, no other known people has lavished such effort in military protection.

If certain resemblances between the Sidamo political systems and those of the Prenilotes suggest to the reader a historical connection between them, and the possible derivation of both from Dynastic Egypt, he should bear in mind an alternative route of diffusion, namely via central Ethiopia, where all traces of conceivable Pharaonic influence on governmental forms have long since been obliterated by millennia of Sabaean, Byzantine, Islamic, and recent European contacts.

Selected Bibliography

Bieber, F. K. *Kaffa.* 2 vols. Münster, 1920–1923.

Borelli, J. *Ethiopie méridionale.* Paris, 1890. [Ometo].

Bryan, M. A. A Linguistic No-man's Land. *Africa,* 15:188–205. 1945.

Cecchi, A. *Da Zeila alle fronteire del Caffa.* 2 vols. Roma, 1885. [Gibe].

Cerulli, Enrico. *Etiopia occidentale.* 2 vols. Roma, 1932–1933. [Gibe and Janjero].

Cerulli, Ernesta. *The Peoples of South-west Ethiopia and Its Borderland.* London, 1956. [Gimira, Maji, and Ometo].

Chiomio, G. I Magi. *RSE,* 1:271–304. 1950.

Huntingford, G. W. B. *The Galla of Ethiopia; the Kingdoms of Kafa and Janjero.* London, 1955.

Montandon, G. Le Ghimirra. *Géographie,* 25:1–20. 1912.

———. *Au pays des Ghimirra.* Neuchâtel, 1913.

Onneken, D. A. *Die Königskultur Kaffas und der verwandten Königreiche.* Frankfurt am Main, 1956.

Pauli, E. Die Splitterstämme nördlich des Rudolfsees. *AL,* 14:61–189. 1950. [Bako, Gimira, and Ometo].

Ricci, M. Notizie etnografiche sugli Amar. *RSE,* 11:49–95. 1952. [Bako].

Stiehler, W. Studien zur Landwirtschafts- und Siedlungsgeographie Aethiopiens. *Erdkunde,* 2:257–282. 1948.

PART SIX
SOUTHWARD EXPANSION OF THE CUSHITES

24

Southern Cushites

Throughout the Upper Paleolithic and Mesolithic periods, as noted in Chapters 9 and 10, a population of Bushmanoid hunters and gatherers occupied all of East Africa from western Ethiopia and the Eastern Horn south to the Cape of Good Hope. They possessed cultures of the type known to archeologists as Stillbay and, in the main at least, spoke languages of the Khoisan stock. Though Negroid peoples inhabit nearly all of this region today, not a single trace of this race appears archeologically anywhere in the area until well after the time of Christ, and this noteworthy absence is abundantly confirmed by other forms of evidence.

The Bushmanoid hunters did not, however, enjoy exclusive possession of this vast territory throughout the period in question. Archeology attests the presence of a second race in a small part of the area. Rather surprisingly, these people were not Negroid but Caucasoid, and they came from the north, not from the west. Even if there were no other evidence, this fact would suggest that they were Cushites, akin to the inhabitants of the Ethiopian plateau.

The first trace of a Caucasoid occupation dates from the Upper Paleolithic period and is confined to an extremely restricted region—the lake-studded rift valley which extends from Lake Rudolf on the border of Ethiopia southward across Kenya into adjacent Tanganyika in the vicinity of Lakes Natron, Manyara, and Eyasi. The newcomers brought with them a new culture, known as Kenya Capsian from its clear affinity with the Capsian cultures of prehistoric North Africa, which were likewise borne by peoples of Caucasoid race. They subsisted exclusively by hunting and gathering, like their Bushmanoid predecessors and neighbors, but their implements consisted mainly of stone blades as contrasted with the flakes characteristic of the Stillbay cultures. They possessed the bow and arrow and in time came to use microliths and make pottery. At some time around 3000 B.C. the descendants of these immigrants developed derivatives of Kenya Capsian known as the Stone Bowl cultures, e.g., Hyrax Hill and Gumban, which were characterized by pestles and bowls of stone.

At some time before 1000 B.C., new waves of Caucasoid peoples began to fan out from southern Ethiopia, occupying a very much wider expanse of territory and bringing with them a full Neolithic culture with agriculture and domestic animals. We shall deal with them in the next chapter, presenting evidence linking them culturally and linguistically with the present inhabitants of southern Ethiopia.

There remains for consideration here, however, a small but interesting cluster of tribes in northern Tanganyika speaking languages of the Southern branch of the Cushitic subfamily. It is tempting to regard them as the living descendants of the prehistoric Kenya Capsian and Stone Bowl peoples, even though they are in large degree racially mixed with and culturally assimilated to their present Negro neighbors. Two kinds of evidence lend a measure of support to this hypothesis. In the first place, three of the four surviving groups of Southern Cushites live in, or immediately adjacent to, the rift valley in northern Tanganyika, i.e., at precisely the probable southern limit of the narrow former range of Kenya Capsian, in a region, moreover, which is a geographical cul-de-sac for other remnant peoples, like the Khoisan-speaking Kindiga. In the second place, no speakers of Southern Cushitic languages survive in Ethiopia or anywhere else—a fact that suggests a long period of isolation and linguistic differentiation. Moreover, such evidence as we possess indicates that the Neolithic Cushitic immigrants spoke Eastern or Western rather than Southern Cushitic languages.

More than 400 miles now separate the tribes of this cluster from other speakers of Cushitic languages. The component groups may be identified as follows.

1. Burungi (Mbulunge), with the kindred Alawa (Uassi, Wasi). They number about 20,000.
2. Goroa (Fiome, Gurumo). They number about 18,000.
3. Iraqw (Erokh, Iraku, Mbulu). They number approximately 100,000.
4. Mbugu (Wambugu). A remnant group, numbering about 10,000, located considerably to the east of the other three and now largely assimilated to the Pare tribe of Bantu.

All the modern Southern Cushites practice cereal agriculture, with sorghum, millet, maize, and eleusine as the staple crops. They also raise beans, peanuts, and a few sweet potatoes. Animal husbandry generally ranks almost on a par with agriculture and surpasses it among the Mbugu. Numerous cattle, sheep, goats, and donkeys are kept. Milk is drunk, and apparently blood as well, and animal manure is used to fertilize the fields. Men tend and milk the livestock and do most, but not all, of the agricultural work.

All groups live in neighborhoods of dispersed homesteads rather than in compact villages. The typical dwelling is of the type called *tembe* in Tanganyika. Long and rectangular in shape, it has a nearly flat roof covered with earth and in some tribes, notably the Goroa, is semisubterranean. The Iraqw, however, in their area of original settlement, build round houses with walls of wattle and daub, conical roofs thatched with reeds, and a second story for sleeping quarters. This particular area, which the writer is fortunate to have visited, makes an indelible impression upon the European because of its sharp contrast to the settlement patterns of most African tribes. One sees no brush, no fallow or unoccupied land. The rolling countryside presents a vista of alternating cultivated fields, neat strips of green pasture, homesteads, and well-tended plots of woodland—the whole strongly reminiscent of prosperous peasant sections in certain parts of Europe.

The Southern Cushites keep no slaves and recognize no class distinctions. They practice both circumcision and clitoridectomy but apparently lack an organization into age-grades. They are governed by councils of elders with a presiding head but have no political integration transcending the level of the local community.

Marriage involves a substantial bride-price in livestock. Limited polygyny prevails, with the first wife enjoying a superior status. Levirate unions are permitted with a younger brother of the deceased husband, but any children born are ascribed to the latter rather than to the new spouse. A homestead comprises a single nuclear or polygynous family, never an extended family. Descent, inheritance, and succession follow the patrilineal principle, and residence is patrilocal. There are numerous patrisibs, which reveal some tendency toward localization as clan-communities. The Iraqw also possess unnamed matrilineages of little importance and follow the Crow pattern of designating cousins. Since these matrilineal features occur among the adjacent Bantu tribes, they are more reasonably attributable to intermarriage and cultural borrowing than to survival from an earlier matrilineal social system.

Selected Bibliography

Baumann, O. *Durch Massailand zur Nilquelle*. Berlin, 1894. [Burungi and Goroa].
Cole, S. *The Prehistory of East Africa*. London, 1954.
Huntingford, G. W. B. *The Southern Nilo-Hamites*. London, 1953.
Leakey, L. S. B. *The Stone Age Cultures of Kenya Colony*. Cambridge, 1931.
Mylius, N. Ehe und Kind im abflusslosen Gebiet Ostafrikas. *AV*, 3:44–135; 4:38–153.
    1948–1949.
Reche, O. *Zur Ethnographie des abflusslosen Gebietes Deutsch-Ostafrikas*. Hamburg,
    1914. [Burungi and Goroa].
Storch. Sitten, Gebräuche und Rechtspflege bei den Bewohnern Usambaras und
    Pares. *MDS*, 8:310–331. 1895. [Mbugu].
Winter, E. H. Some Aspects of Political Organization and Land Tenure among the
    Iraqw. Unpublished ms.

25

Megalithic Cushites

In East Africa, archeologists have unearthed evidences of true Neolithic cultures only in western Kenya, adjacent northern Tanganyika, and central Uganda. Elsewhere the Iron Age appears to have followed Paleolithic cultures without any intervening transition. The discoveries in Uganda may engage our attention first, since we have the least information on this area.

Wayland (1934) and Lanning (1953) have reported a considerable number of extremely impressive prehistoric earthworks in the vicinity of the equator in central Uganda. They include artificial reservoirs, one of which exceeds 300 feet in length; earth dams for impounding water for irrigation; deep shafts of unknown purpose; and extensive systems of trenches, averaging as much as 15 feet in width and 11 feet in depth, which seem clearly to have served as fortifications, since they are sometimes concentric. With them are associated pit dwellings and middens containing the bones of cattle and game animals.

The construction of the earthworks must have required a mass organization of labor. The fortifications remind us forcefully of the massive defense systems of the Sidamo states, the more so since the Sidamo peoples also practice irrigated agriculture. Moreover, nowhere in East Africa are Negro peoples, either Bantu or Nilotic, known to have built structures even remotely comparable to these. Cole (1954) therefore seems justified in attributing the remains to "a Hamitic tribe that arrived from the north and apparently established an empire in Uganda." These people can only have been Western Cushites of the Sidamo group, not only for the reasons advanced above but also because of the remarkable detailed resemblances between the political system of the modern Ganda (see Chapter 45) and the Kafa state of southwestern Ethiopia (see Chapter 23). We can, therefore, safely postulate a prehistoric expansion of the Western Cushites into central Uganda, though unfortunately we as yet lack any information on its approximate date.

Much richer information on the East African Neolithic culture comes from western Kenya. Here unmistakable evidences of agriculture and domesticated animals begin to appear in the late habitation sites of the Caucasoid bearers of the Stone Bowl cultures. The Njoro River Cave, for example, has yielded stone pestles, grindstones, and gourd fragments as evidences of agriculture, as well as stone bowls, obsidian blades, and pottery akin to those in remains of earlier date. It also contained beads of agate, chalcedony, and amazon stone allegedly resembling those found in prehistoric Egypt and Nubia. The remains of cattle and sheep appear in Gumban sites of about the same age. Archeologists have estimated the date of these deposits as about 850 B.C., but indirect evidence suggests that this estimate may be too late by several centuries.

A new group of immigrants must have brought these innovations, for Neolithic remains are no longer confined to the narrow rift valley but begin to appear throughout the mountainous region of western Kenya and adjacent Tanganyika, an area bounded by Mounts Kenya and Kilimanjaro in the east, Mount Elgon and Lake Victoria in the west, and Lakes Eyasi and Manyara in the south. Prominent among these remains are stone-walled habitation enclosures, pit dwellings, menhirs, stone-faced cultivation terraces, irrigation ditches, and graded roads with a predominantly north-south orientation. They give evidence of a relatively dense population practicing an intensive form of agriculture coupled with animal husbandry. In the main, however, the sites are confined to elevated locations with substantial precipitation. The semiarid intervening country continued to be occupied, apparently, only by Bushmanoid hunters and gatherers with cultures of the Stillbay complex.

The Neolithic Caucasoids have left no obvious descendants in this region today, unless possibly the Southern Cushites derive from them rather than from the earlier Capsian immigrants as we have assumed. With this possible exception, no people either of Caucasoid race or of Cushitic language survives anywhere in the area, which is populated exclusively by Negroids of either Bantu or Nilotic speech. Who were the Neolithic Caucasoids, and what has become of them?

They can only have been Cushites, expanding southward from the Ethiopian plateau, as did the Western Cushites into central Uganda. Although we shall shortly attempt to identify them, this identification can only be tentative, and it therefore seems advisable to give the vanished people a name of their own. We shall call them the Megalithic Cushites because of the prominence of stonework in their archeological remains. In addition to the stone walls and terraces already alluded to, we may note the characteristic large stone phalli which turn up in even the most remote regions to which these people once spread (see Chapter 26). In certain sections of southern Ethiopia, moreover, whole fields of stone phalli averaging around 12 feet in height provide one of our clues to their place of origin.

It seems in the highest degree improbable that a people as widely distributed as the Megalithic Cushites, and possessed of so complex a culture, should have vanished without a trace. The Bantu, coming from the tropical forest several centuries after the time of Christ, must certainly have had at first a much simpler technology; and the Nilotes, arriving somewhat later from the northwest, were more concerned with herding than with cultivation. Why should the Megalithic Cushites have proved equally vulnerable in the face of both groups of immigrant Negroes? The answer may well lie in their dispersed distribution in restricted mountain locations where there was sufficient rainfall to conduct their irrigated agriculture. The newcomers, particularly the pastoral Nilotes, might have infiltrated the less favored intervening tracts of land, first isolating the Cushites in scattered enclaves, then gradually engulfing them through intermarriage, and ultimately producing a mixed population that had lost the Cushitic language and acquired a strong Negroid physical ingredient.

Various lines of evidence indicate that this is precisely what happened. It is certainly no accident that the Bantu of highland Kenya are commonly styled the "Hamitized Bantu" and that the Nilotes of the same general area are usually called "Nilo-Hamites" in contradistinction to their kinsmen in northern Uganda and the adjacent Sudan, where the Megalithic Cushites never penetrated. The peculiarities that distinguish the so-called "Nilo-Hamitic" languages from the closely related "Nilotic" languages of the Eastern Sudanic subfamily are almost exactly what one might expect to find in a population that once spoke Cushitic and gradually shifted through intermarriage to a Sudanic tongue.

Cultural evidence proves equally instructive. Intensive agriculture with terraced fields, irrigation, and the use of animal manure as fertilizer survives today in precisely those well-watered mountain areas where the Megalithic Cushites must once have been concentrated, e.g., among the Nilotic Hill Suk, Keyu, Kipsigi, and Nandi tribes northeast of Lake Victoria and among the Bantu Chaga, Meru, Pare, and Teita of the Mount Kilimanjaro region. The crops which the Bantu and Nilotes cultivate in the area consist largely of those that were developed, like eleusine, or improved, like durra, in highland Ethiopia.

A whole series of other culture traits distinctive of the Cushites occur also among the Bantu and Nilotes, but only among tribes inhabiting country formerly occupied by the Megalithic Cushites. The author has demonstrated this by plotting actual distributions for the following traits:

1. Age-grades of the peculiar cycling type characteristic of the Galla and other Eastern Cushites, or forms clearly related thereto.
2. The distinctive Cushitic taboo on the eating of fish.
3. The practice of drinking blood drawn from the necks of living animals by means of a miniature arrow.
4. The presence of despised and endogamous castes of smiths.
5. Circumcision for both sexes as contrasted with its absence, its restriction to one sex, or, in the case of the Nilotes, with the extraction of the lower median incisor teeth as an initiatory rite.

The distributions of these traits reveal a remarkable degree of correspondence, not only with one another but also with the area of former Megalithic Cushite occupation. They occur in practically every Bantu and Nilotic people now residing south of the Ethiopian highlands, east of Lake Victoria, and north of 6°S, but in practically no tribe of either linguistic group living west or south of these limits. Altogether, the evidence seems conclusive that the Megalithic Cushites, far from vanishing without a trace, have transmitted a considerable part of their former culture to their Negroid successors and have doubtless also contributed substantially to their genetic composition.

The same cultural evidence sheds light on the probable origin of the Megalithic Cushites. Among the various Cushitic peoples residing in southern Ethiopia, we can probably eliminate the Sidamo group as ancestral since they lack cycling age-grades and do not drink fresh blood. The Somali likewise have no age-grades, and, moreover, are geographically too remote. The Galla, though they share many of the elements in question, do not build megaliths or practice intensive irrigated agriculture on terraced fields. This leaves one small group of Cushitic tribes, located between the Galla and Sidamo, that we shall designate as the Konso cluster, since the Konso are the best described among them. They exhibit in well-developed form all the traits that we have enumerated, as well as others that we have not mentioned. Among these is the stall feeding of animals, a rare practice confined, as far as we know, to the Konso, the Chaga of Mount Kilimanjaro, and the Kara of the island of Ukara near the eastern shore of Lake Victoria.

If the Megalithic Cushites do in fact represent an early southward expansion of peoples belonging to the Konso cluster, the surviving culture of the latter should shed light on the civilization of the former. Since, moreover, the Konso and their neighbors are characterized by a very strong infusion of Negroid blood on a Caucasoid base, the absence of more obvious Caucasoid physical traits in their further mixture with Bantu and Nilotes becomes entirely understandable. The surviving tribes of the Konso cluster, who probably number several hundred thousand people though they have never been enumerated, are listed and identified below.

1. Darasa (Darassa), with the neighboring Gudji, Jamjam, and Sidamo. They are pagans.
2. Kambata (Cambate), with the kindred Alaba (Allaba), Hadya (Adea, Gudela, Gudilla, Hadea, Hadiya, Kontomba, Wutella), and Tambaro (Sambaro, Tembaro, Tzambaro). The Kambata are Christians, the rest mainly Moslem. All have been strongly influenced by both the Sidamo peoples and the Amhara.
3. Konso (Conso), with the Burji (Alada, Cirra, Tchirra), Busso, Gamole, Gardula, Gauwada, Gidole (Ghidole), Gowaze, and Majolo. They are pagans.
4. Reshiat (Lareschiat, Rachiat, Rissiat, Russia), also known as the Dathanaic (Darsonich, Dathanik), Geleba (Gallab, Galuba, Gelab, Gelubba, Gheleba, Goliba, Gullop), and Marille (Marle, Marmale, Merelle, Morille). With them are included the neighboring Arbore (Harbora). They are pagan and in many cases seminomadic.

The tribes of the Konso cluster practice an exceptionally intensive agriculture, with irrigation and the terracing of mountain slopes with stone retaining walls. The staple crop is durra, a variety of sorghum, among the Konso and Reshiat, ensete among the Darasa and Kambata. Cotton is cultivated extensively, and varying quantities of maize, teff, barley, oats, taro, sweet potatoes, beans, peas, cabbage, ginger, coffee, and tobacco are also grown. The Reshiat, like many of the Galla, have become primarily pastoral but continue to practice at least some terraced cultivation. Elsewhere animal husbandry holds a distinctly subsidiary position in relation to agriculture, and the Konso go so far as to keep their animals in stalls, feeding them by hand rather than grazing them, in order to conserve the manure for their fields. Cattle, sheep, goats, and donkeys are kept in considerable numbers, as well as a few horses in the north and camels in the extreme south. Both the milk and the fresh blood of the animals are consumed. Hunting is insignificant, and fish are specifically tabooed as food. Trade is well developed, and all groups except the Reshiat have regular markets. Men do the herding and hunting and women the milking and market trading, but both sexes participate in agricultural labor.

Some of the tribes of the cluster live in neighborhoods of dispersed family compounds, but the Konso and the sedentary Reshiat occupy compact villages, which the Konso surround with massive wooden palisades. The prevailing house type is a round structure with cylindrical walls of planks or wattle and daub and with conical thatched roofs, which in some instances extend to the ground. The western Konso, however, occupy pit dwellings with rounded stone walls and flat terraced roofs. One writer has called the Konso a "living megalithic culture." In addition to the stone retaining walls of their irrigated fields and the stone construction of some of their houses, they erect stone menhirs over the graves of prominent men and on the plazas of their villages, and outside each men's house there are stone back rests for its members. The Burji erect stone tumuli, and the sources contain unspecific references to stone phalli.

The Konso demand no consideration in contracting a marriage, but the other tribes require a bride-price. General polygyny prevails, each wife having her separate hut within the compound. Residence tends to be patrilocal but without producing an extended-family organization. The Konso constitute a partial exception in this respect, for the eldest son, who will inherit the home, continues to reside in his father's compound after marriage, and only younger sons build or purchase another dwelling. Descent is patrilineal, with exogamous but nonlocalized sibs. Both circumcision and clitoridectomy (or a more drastic operation) are practiced, the former normally occurring relatively late in life.

Slavery is presumably rare, being specifically reported only for the Burji, but pariah castes of smiths, tanners, and potters are general. With this exception, the peoples of the Konso cluster reveal a markedly egalitarian social system. They differ sharply from their Sidamo neighbors in this respect and likewise in the absence of a monarchical political structure, except where this has been borrowed from the west, as in the Kambata group. Integration at the tribal level is achieved, instead, by an elaborate age-grade organization, the so-called Gada system.

The original Eastern Cushitic system, still preserved by the Reshiat as well as by most Galla tribes, comprises five cycling grades with promotion to the next higher grade occurring every eighth year, with a concentration of political functions in the fourth grade, and with sons entering the first grade as their fathers graduate from the fifth, i.e., forty years later. Since membership in a grade bears no necessary relation to actual age and since the average generation difference is less than forty years, such a system tends to be vitiated by "senectation," i.e., by sons reaching a relatively advanced age before their father's graduation qualifies them to enter the first grade. Some tribes, notably the Darasa and Konso, have apparently sought to compensate for this by instituting changes in the system. The Darasa have seven cycling grades with promotion occurring every tenth year, but a son joins the first grade when his father enters the third, i.e., only twenty years later. The Konso system is worth summarizing in detail both because of its intrinsic interest and because it is unusually fully described.

To comprehend the Konso system one must distinguish between age-classes, age-grades, and age-sets. Age-classes correspond to actual age, and they exist for both sexes. A new class is established every thirteen years, at which time it is constituted of all persons of the appropriate sex who have reached nine years of age since the formation of the previous class. A boy at this time is assigned to a particular men's house, of which there are several in each village, and goes to live there. One who reaches puberty before his class is formed removes to a men's house anyhow, but does not become a member until the establishment of his class. A person remains a member of his age-class for life, and classes of males act as military units in warfare. A man must take his first wife from the female class corresponding to his own, and if she dies or is divorced he must take a substitute wife from the same class. Secondary wives, however, may be taken from junior age-classes.

An age-set consists of the men of a particular generation who enter the same age-grade together and advance together through successive grades. Thus membership in an age-set, as in an age-class, is for life.

An age-grade is a level in a hierarchical series of four, named respectively (1) Fareita, (2) Chela, (3) Gada, and (4) Orshada, through which age-sets advance periodically. Membership in a grade endures, not for life, but for a period of eighteen years. Once every eighteen years, at a spectacular tribe-wide ceremony, every age-set moves into the next higher grade. The previous occupants of the fourth, or Orshada, grade, of course, move out of the system entirely at this time, and the first, or Fareita, grade is filled by the sons of the men who are passing from the Chela into the Gada grade. A man thus enters any grade exactly thirty-six years after his father did.

Men of the first grade occupy themselves largely with community labor, e.g., in the construction or repair of palisades, plazas, public buildings, paths, and irrigation ditches. They are not permitted to marry, but sexual intercourse is not denied them, for they have the privilege of sleeping with the older married women. The husbands of the latter cannot object, for since a male is believed to be sterile until he has been initiated into the second age-grade, the paternity of children is not involved.

After eighteen years in the first grade a man enters the second, or Chela, grade. He marries and establishes a household at this time. This is compulsory, and his actual physical age does not matter. Whether he is a man of thirty-five or a boy of nine, he can neither marry before this time nor defer his first marriage until later. His period of eighteen years in the second grade he devotes primarily to founding a family and rearing children. Under this system, of course, marriages occur in clusters eighteen years apart, with none except secondary unions occurring during the intervals between.

The age-set which occupies the third, or Gada, grade fills most of the responsible political, ecclesiastical, and judicial offices in Konso society and runs the government over a span of eighteen years. Officials fall into two categories: Bogalla and Heiyu. The former are hereditary, with succession from father to eldest son in alternating grades, whereas the latter are elective, being chosen from rich and poor alike on the basis of personal qualifications. The Heiyu serve mainly as judges, magistrates, and legal advisers, and the Bogalla hold administrative and priestly positions. The highest Bogalla, called Abba Jila, acts as chief and high priest of the entire Konso tribe, assisted by his "opposite number" in the second grade, who will succeed to his office. A Miskatta Bogalla serves as headman in each village, and three special Bogalla, called "kings" though they exercise no political functions, live hermit lives in isolation on mountain peaks. Other lesser Bogalla have sacrificial functions.

On entering the fourth, or Orshada, grade, men relinquish the offices they have held and serve henceforth only in an advisory capacity to their successors. Formerly they were circumcised at this time and thereafter withdrew from all active sexual life. If an individual had held a particularly high office in the Gada grade, there are intimations that he now became a transvestite and assumed thenceforth the social role of an old woman.

Selected Bibliography

Borelli, J. *Ethiopie méridionale.* Paris, 1890. [Kambata].

Cerulli, E. *Peoples of South-west Ethiopia and Its Borderland.* London, 1956.

Cole, S. *The Prehistory of East Africa.* London, 1954.

Höhnel, L. von. Ostäquatorial-Afrika. *PME,* 21(99):1–44. 1890. [Reshiat].

Jensen, A. E. *Im Lande des Gada.* Stuttgart, 1936. [Darasa and Konso].

———. Elementi della cultura dei Conso. *RSE,* 2:217–259. 1942.

———. Das Gada-system der Konso und die Altersklassen-systeme der Niloten. *Ethnos,* 19:1–23. 1954.

Lanning, E. C. Ancient Earthworks in Western Uganda. *UJ,* 17:51–62. 1953.

Leakey, M. D., and L. S. B. Leakey. *Excavations at the Njoro River Cave.* Oxford, 1950.

Nalder, L. F., ed. *A Tribal Survey of Mongalla Province.* London, 1937. [Reshiat].

Nowack, E. *Land und Volk der Konso.* Bonn, 1954.

Pauli, E. Die Splitterstämme nördlich des Rudolfsees. *AL,* 14:61–189. 1950. [Reshiat].

Prins, A. H. J. *East African Age-Class Systems.* Groningen, 1953.

Ricci, M. Notizie etnografiche sugli Arbore. *RSE,* 9:5–40. 1950. [Reshiat].

Stiehler, W. Studien zur Landwirtschafts- und Siedlungsgeographie Aethiopiens. *Erdkunde,* 2:257–282. 1948.

Wayland, E. J. Some Ancient Earthworks in Northern Buddu. *UJ.* 2:21–32. 1934.

26

Ancient Azanians

The coast of Kenya and of adjacent Somalia and Tanganyika, from Kisimayu in the north to Kilwa in the south and including the off-lying islands of Pemba and Zanzibar, was known to Mediterranean antiquity as Azania. This region has been a major center of mercantile activity for well over 2,000 years. The predominant population today consists of the people known as Swahili (see Chapter 39), a mixture of Bantu Negroes with Islamic Arabs. Neither element in this amalgam, however, arrived in the area until shortly before A.D. 1000. Prior to that time most of the coast and hinterland of East Africa was occupied only by hunting and gathering tribes of Bushmanoid race and Stillbay cultures. Such simple people could scarcely have embarked on a career of foreign trade, nor could they have produced goods of sufficient value and in sufficient quantity to have attracted merchant mariners from distant lands to their shores. The problem then is to discover who these ancient Azanians were, with whom they traded, on what their mercantile activity was based, and what influence it exerted on the culture history of Africa.

Ancient Egyptian chronicles report trading expeditions as early as the XI and XII dynasties beyond the Red Sea to the land of Punt, most reasonably identified as the coast of modern French Somaliland, but it was probably the Sabaeans of southern Arabia who first made the long passage around the Eastern Horn and reached the Azanian coast. This may have occurred as early as the first half of the first millennium B.C., and cannot have occurred very much later, since Roman and Ptolemaic coins of the third century B.C. have been excavated at Bui Kavo. Greek geographers of the second century B.C. speak of the great wealth of the Sabaeans derived from their trade with India, and we may assume also with East Africa. This is the first actual historical mention of the Sabaean Lane, as the great trade route from Azania to India via southern Arabia has been termed, although it had doubtless been established several centuries earlier. Not until about A.D. 47, however, did Europeans, in the person of a certain Hippalus, learn that this route could be sailed readily in both directions by utilization of the alternating monsoon winds; thus the Romans gained access to the Indian trade previously monopolized by others.

About A.D. 60 an anonymous Greek merchant mariner made a voyage around the Eastern Horn and down the African coast at least as far as Dar es Salaam and perhaps even farther. What is more, he described the coast and ports of Azania in a famous book entitled *Periplus of the Ery-thraean Sea*. This work, which in modern English would be entitled "Sailing Directions for the Indian Ocean," has doubtless survived because of its utility to seamen for many centuries thereafter. The author explicitly records the existence of a flourishing trade not only with southern Arabia but also with India, and he tells us of resident Yemenite merchants who were married to local women and understood the native language. In addition to a list of Azanian imports and exports, he gives fragments of information about the inhabitants. They had plank boats and dugout canoes with which they fished, caught sea turtles, and indulged their "piratical habits." They lacked any complex form of political organization, but each town had its own independent chief. Of their physical characteristics he reports only that they were "very great in stature."

Although all commentators assume that the Azanians were Negroes, it is significant that the author remarks only on their stature. He seems, therefore, to assume that they were Caucasians, for, to a Greek of his day, Negroes would have been strange beings whose characteristics would certainly have been noted. In this assumption, of course, he was right, since, as noted above, the archeological evidence demonstrates indisputably the complete absence of Negroes in this part of Africa for centuries to come. The Cushitic peoples, however, are noted for their tall stature. The inhabitants can therefore have been no other than Megalithic Cushites who had descended the few miles from the Kenya highlands to the coast and there turned to maritime pursuits. This is attested by the numerous megalithic remains, including stone phalli, which still dot the Azanian coast.

The Yemenite Arabs dominated the trade with Azania until about A.D. 575, except for portions of the fourth and sixth centuries when the Ethiopian kingdom of Axum conquered Yemen and assumed control of the rich commerce with India. From 575 to 879 the Persians played the chief role in the trade with the East, which they extended to China. During this period Chinese merchants participated for the first time in the African trade, as evidenced by the discovery, at Mogadisho and Kilwa, of Chinese coins dating from the eighth century on. From 879 until the establishment of the Portuguese on Zanzibar in 1503 the trade with Azania was again dominated by the Arabs, who in this period were Moslems, as they had been since the seventh century, but this is the story for another chapter.

The great bulk of the East African trade seems always to have been with India via the Sabaean Lane rather than with Egypt and the Mediterranean by way of the Red Sea. Not only were distances appreciably shorter in the former instance, but the monsoon winds of the Indian

Ocean were far more favorable for sailing vessels. The author of the *Periplus* reports that in his day the principal exports from Azania were ivory, rhinoceros horn, tortoise shell, and coconut oil, which were exchanged for metal implements and glass. Not long after A.D. 500 the sources begin to add gold and slaves as major exports and iron and beads as imports. Records from the Far East attest the importation of Negro slaves into Java and China as early as the ninth century.

One major effect of the Azanian commerce with southern Arabia and India upon the culture history of Africa appears to have been the introduction of ironworking to East Africa. Although the writer has made no effort to cover this subject in his ethnographic survey, he is impressed by the close correlation in time between the appearance of iron among the imports to Azania and the estimates of archeologists as to the first appearance of this metal in the interior. Iron Age sites in highland Kenya typically reveal other evidences of trade with the coast, e.g., beads, cowrie shells, and pipe bowls for the smoking of hashish. The analysis of iron technology in Negro Africa in the light of its apparent dual introduction via Azania and from Meroitic Nubia suggests itself as an interesting historical problem.

By far the most significant impact of ancient Azania upon world history, without question, was that wrought by the interchange of cultivated plants with India by way of the Sabaean Lane. Merchant vessels traveling with the monsoons in either direction loaded up at the port of origin with supplies there available and disposed of any surpluses at their destination, with the result that the coasts of Azania and western India early came to share the same roster of food plants. Although present evidence indicates that this probably happened around the middle of the first millennium B.C., further archeological work in Africa and historical research in India might conceivably press the date of the exchange still further back in time.

The cultivated plants of Indian origin which reached East Africa by way of the Sabaean Lane, most of which were also carried to North Africa at about the same time, may be designated as the Indian complex. Its constituent elements are enumerated below.

LEGUMES

Gram bean, or mung bean (*Phaseolus aureus* and *P. mungo*).

Hyacinth bean, or lablab bean (*Dolichos lablab*). Some botanists consider this plant an African cultigen, but its distribution on the continent makes an Indian origin more probable.

Pigeon pea (*Cajanus cajan* or *C. indica*). Again botanists are in dispute concerning an African or an Indian origin, and again distributional evidence favors the latter.

Sword bean, or jack bean (*Canavalia ensiformis*).

LEAF AND STALK VEGETABLES

Jew's mallow (*Corchorus olitorius*).

VINE AND GROUND FRUITS

Cucumber (*Cucumis sativa*).
Eggplant, or garden egg (*Solanum melongena*).

TREE FRUITS

Balsam pear (*Momordica charantia*).
Mango (*Mangifera indica*).

CONDIMENTS AND INDULGENTS

Ginger (*Zingiber officinale*). This plant is possibly Malaysian rather than Indian in origin.
Hemp (*Cannabinus sativa*). This plant, a native of Inner Asia, was early introduced from India to East Africa, not for its fibers but for smoking as hashish.

None of the above plants has achieved any particular importance in Africa. The contrary is true, however, of the cultigens that traveled in the opposite direction, of which the following are the most important:

Castor	Cow pea	Gourd	Sesame
Cotton	Eleusine	Pearl millet	Sorghum

The seventeen major crops of India, whose distribution Janaki Ammal (1956) has mapped for that subcontinent, include five of African origin, namely, castor, cotton, pearl millet, sesame, and sorghum. All five, significantly, reveal similar distributions in western India, in the very region to which the monsoon winds would carry vessels coming from East Africa, whereas all twelve non-African crops are concentrated in quite different areas. We cannot escape the conclusion that western India owes its agricultural civilization very largely to importations from Negro Africa.

The crops of the Indian complex by no means exhaust the list of cultivated plants which reached Azania via the Sabaean Lane. A considerable number, including several of very great importance, had their origin farther to the east, in Southeast Asia or Indonesia. We shall designate these collectively as the Malaysian complex, whose component elements are listed below.

CEREAL GRAINS

Rice (*Oryza sativa*). The dry, or swidden, cultivation of rice reached Africa via the Sabaean Lane but became established at that time only on the island of Madagascar. Wet, or paddy, cultivation was accepted, on the continent of Africa as well as on Madagascar, at a much later date, mediated in both cases by the Moslem Arabs.

TUBERS AND ROOT CROPS

Polynesian arrowroot (*Tacca pinnatifida*). This plant became established only on Madagascar.

Taro, or coco yam (*Colocasia antiquorum*, formerly *Arum colocasia*). This plant is widely cultivated in equatorial Africa.

Yam (*Dioscorea alata, D. bulbifera*, and *D. esculenta*). This plant is very widely distributed in tropical Africa.

TREE FRUITS AND NUTS

Banana (*Musa paradisiaca* and *M. sapientum*). This plant is widely cultivated in equatorial Africa.

Breadfruit (*Artocarpus incisa*). This plant became established only on Madagascar, the Comoro Islands, and Zanzibar.

Coconut palm (*Cocos nucifera*). This tree has a modest distribution in the tropical coastal regions of Africa.

CONDIMENTS AND INDULGENTS

Areca palm (*Areca catechu*). The nut is chewed with betel.

Betel (*Piper betle*). This plant became established, along with the areca palm, only on Madagascar and the Comoro Islands.

Sugarcane (*Saccharum officinarum*). This plant is widely cultivated in tropical Africa.

The introduction of Malaysian plants into East Africa raises the question of whether they might not have been brought by some Indonesian people. Evidence of several independent kinds—linguistic, ethnographic, and historical—yields an affirmative answer to this question.

The inhabitants of Madagascar, as has long been known, speak a language of the Malayo-Polynesian stock, and this indicates that they must have come from Indonesia, where cognate tongues are spoken. Most authorities agree, moreover, that they did not sail directly across the Indian Ocean but followed a coastwise course by way of India, southern Arabia, and East Africa. They usually date the arrival of the ancestors of the Malagasy somewhere between the second and the fourth centuries and derive them from either Sumatra or Java, where great Hinduistic civilizations were then coming into being. Attempts to relate their departure to conditions in these islands at the time have proved vain, however, for conclusive evidence has recently been adduced indicating that they came from neither island but rather from Borneo, which Hinduistic civilization had not reached. The disproof of these assumptions paves the way for advancing the probable date of the departure from Indonesia by several centuries.

The new evidence is linguistic in nature. Dahl (1951) has shown grounds for assuming an especially close relationship between Malagasy and the Maanyan language of south central Borneo, and Dyen (1953) has corroborated this conclusion by the application of recent lexicostatistical methods. These indicate that Malagasy has been separated from Maanyan for about 1,900 years, whereas from 3,000 to 3,800 years must be allowed for its separation from other Indonesian languages, such as Malay, Toba Batak, and even the adjacent Ngaju Dayak, and almost as much time for the separation of any of these three from Maanyan. If accurate, these calculations indicate the early first century as the approximate time of the departure from Indonesia—even earlier, of course, if the emigrants maintained close contacts with their homeland.

Scholars have sought for ethnographical evidences, other than culti-vated plants, indicating that Malaysian peoples reached the east coast of continental Africa, and have discovered a fair number. These include the flat-bar zither, which occurs only in Indonesia, Madagascar, and East Africa and nowhere in India, Arabia, Egypt, or other parts of Africa; a coconut grater of specifically Malayo-Polynesian design; a special type of eel pot; a peculiar method of catching sea turtles which utilizes the suck-ing propensities of lampreys; and perhaps even the predilection for fish-ing itself, which is notoriously anathema to most Cushites beyond the bounds of Azania. Especially convincing, perhaps, is the occurrence in coastal East Africa of two types of boats, both of which experts ascribe to borrowing from an Indonesian source. One of them is the *mtepe*, a vessel of Malaysian design constructed of planks lashed together with cordage of sennit (coconut) fibers, decorated with round oculi on the bow and near the stern, and propelled by rectangular mat sails. The sec-ond is the *dau*, a dugout canoe with double outriggers connected with the boom by indirect attachments, which is demonstrably of Indonesian origin and which occurs in Africa only in Zanzibar, the Bajun Islands, the Mozambique coast, the Comoro Islands, and Madagascar.

In view of the striking coincidence in dates between the linguistic estimate for the separation of Malagasy and the visit of the author of the *Periplus of the Erythraean Sea*, let us reexamine this historical document for possible evidences of Indonesian influences on coastal East Africa in the middle of the first century. We find two such: (1) specific men-tion of the coconut, a Malaysian plant, and of trade in coconut oil, and (2) references to two types of watercraft, namely, "sewed boats" and "canoes hollowed from single logs." These strongly suggest, respec-tively, the *mtepe*, with its planks "sewed" with sennit fibers, and the *dau*, which is hollowed from a single log. In the latter case, to be sure, the *Periplus* does not mention outriggers, but these are later specifically attested by Ibn al-Mujawir.

We thus have abundant grounds for assuming that the Maanyan or some closely kindred Malayan people were already frequenting the Azanian coast in the first century. Definite historical reports of Indonesians in East Africa become increasingly numerous and explicit until the twelfth century, after which they cease entirely. One of these, by the Arab geographer Edrisi, states: "The people of the isles of Zabag [Indonesia] come to the country of the Zenjs [the inhabitants of Azania] in large and in small ships. They trade with them and export the Zenj merchandise, for they understand each other's language." This suggests actual colonies of Malayo-Polynesian speakers in the port towns of Azania, as would indeed be expected under the prevailing conditions of steady and lucrative trade. Presumably, too, they intermarried with the local population, as had the earlier Yemenite Arab traders according to the *Periplus*. Since by this time the Bantu had become a significant element in the population, the result would be a hybrid race—part Malay, part Caucasian, and part Negro—like the contemporary Malagasy.

The ancient Azanians, stimulated by the trade with the East, must have explored their hinterland for exportable products in high demand. It is tempting to assume that in this way they discovered the rich gold resources of Southern Rhodesia and the adjacent Transvaal and established settlements there to exploit them, such as Zimbabwe with its famed megalithic ruins and Mapungubwe with its wealth of gold artifacts. Such an assumption would have seemed fantastic a few years ago, when scholars ascribed these sites and the activities they reveal to late Bantu tribes under Arab direction. Recently, however, independent samples of carbon from Zimbabwe have, upon analysis, yielded unexpectedly early dates, around the beginning of the seventh century. These force a complete reconsideration of the problem.

The period now indicated considerably antedates that of Arab expansion on the adjacent coast and falls at the very beginning of the Bantu penetration into East Africa. Analysis of skeletal remains reveals Bantu physical types at Zimbabwe in Rhodesia but only Bushmanoid types (Fauché, 1937) at Mapungubwe in the Transvaal. Since the latter site contains evidence of sorghum, cow peas, and watermelons, it cannot be ascribed to the preagricultural Bushmen or to the not yet present Bantu but only to some other people who cultivated Sudanic crops. Could these have been the Cushites of Azania?

The stone platforms, terraces, monoliths, and enormous structures of dry-stone masonry at Zimbabwe suggest a specific connection with the Megalithic Cushites, an interpretation bolstered by the wealth of stone phallic representations reminiscent of those on the Azanian coast and in southern Ethiopia. The presence of beads of apparent Indian and Malay origin in the earliest deposits and of Chinese porcelains at a later period—

from the eleventh century on—indicates that the exploiters of the local gold deposits were deeply involved in the trade with the East. Gold working in the Zimbabwe region continued, of course, under Arab and other auspices until the Portuguese period, or long after the Azanians disappear from history. Mining experts have estimated the total yield of the prehistoric workings of the region at anywhere from 15 to 75 million pounds sterling, which would account in considerable measure for the fabulous wealth of medieval Indian rulers. Though the riddle of Zimbabwe cannot yet be considered solved, it now appears more reasonable than formerly to ascribe a prominent role in its development to the Cushites of Azania.

Selected Bibliography

Anderson, E. *Plants, Men, and Life.* Boston, 1952.

Burkill, I. H. Habits of Man and the Origins of the Cultivated Plants of the Old World. *Proceedings of the Linnean Society of London,* 164:12–42. 1953.

Candolle, A. de. *Origin of Cultivated Plants.* 2d edit. London, 1904.

Cole, S. *The Prehistory of East Africa.* London, 1954.

Dahl, O. C. Malgache et maanjan. *Avhandlinger utgitt av Egede-Instituttet,* 3:1–408. Oslo, 1951.

Dale, I. R. The Indian Origins of Some African Cultivated Plants and African Cattle. *UJ,* 19:68–72. 1955.

Dyen, I. Book Review [of Dahl, 1951]. *Language,* 29:577–590. 1953.

Fouché, L. *Mapungubwe.* Cambridge, 1937.

Grandidier, A., and G. Grandidier. *Ethnographie de Madagascar.* 4 vols. Paris, 1908–1928.

Grottanelli, V. L. *Pescatori dell'Oceano Indiano.* Roma, 1955.

Hornell, J. Indonesian Influence on East African Culture. *JRAI,* 64:305–332. 1934.

———. The Sea-going *Mtepe* and *Dáu* of the Lamu Archipelago. *TNR,* 11:1–10. 1941.

Huntingford, G. W. B. Azania. *Anthropos,* 35–36:209–220. 1940–1941.

Ingrams, W. H. *Zanzibar.* London, 1931.

Janaki Ammal, E. K. Introduction to the Subsistence Economy of India. *Man's Role in Changing the Face of the Earth,* ed. W. L. Thomas, pp. 324–335. Chicago, 1956.

Matheson, J. K., and E. W. Bovill, eds. *East African Agriculture.* London, 1950.

Sauer, C. O. *Agricultural Origins and Dispersals.* New York, 1952.

Schiemann, E. Entstehung der Kulturpflanzen. *Handbuch der Vererbungswissenschaft,* 3:1–377. Berlin, 1932.

Schoff, E. H., ed. *The Periplus of the Erythraean Sea.* London, 1912.

Simmons, N. W., and K. Shepherd. The Taxonomy and Origins of the Cultivated Bananas. *Journal of the Linnean Society, Botany,* 55:302–312. 1955.

Summers, R. The Dating of the Zimbabwe Ruins. *Antiquity,* 29:107–111. 1955.

Vavilov, N. I. The Origin, Variation, Immunity and Breeding of Cultivated Plants, transl. K. S. Chester. *Chronica Botanica,* 13:1–364. 1949–1950.

Wainwright, G. The Founders of the Zimbabwe Civilization. *Man,* 49:62–68. 1949.

Wieschhoff, H. A. The Zimbabwe-Monomotapa Culture. *GSA,* 8:1–115. 1941.

PART SEVEN
CULTURAL IMPACT OF INDONESIA

27

Malagasy

Madagascar, the fourth largest island in the world, is about 1,000 miles in length and some 300 miles in width and has a total land surface of nearly 230,000 square miles and a population of more than 4 million. Despite its size and topographical diversity, its inhabitants reveal a considerable degree of homogeneity in language and culture. In ethnic composition, on the other hand, they represent a highly complex mixture of physical types—Negroid, Mongoloid, and Caucasoid. The Negroid element predominates, especially in the coastal regions, whereas the Mongoloid element is strongest on the interior plateau. The Caucasoid element, much the least significant, is most noticeable in precisely the regions where there is definite historical evidence of Arab or European settlement. Malagasy culture, however, is basically Malaysian (Mongolian) with a strong Arabic (Caucasian) overlay and a relatively weak Bantu (Negro) component. The language belongs to the Malayo-Polynesian stock but has a modest increment of loan words from both Arabic and Bantu.

Recorded history gives little help in explaining or reconciling the above facts and may therefore be summarized very briefly. Dependable records do not begin until about A.D. 900, i.e., at about the time when the Arabs replaced the Persians as the dominant maritime power in the Indian Ocean and began the establishment of a series of strong mercantile colonies along the East African coast, first at Mogadisho and Brava but ultimately extending to Sofala. These Arabs were orthodox Sunnites, and as a consequence of their expansion various heterodox Arabs from Oman,

Yemen, and Azania sought refuge in eastern Madagascar, eventually establishing themselves in the Antaimoro country in the southeast and introducing certain Arabian and Islamic cultural elements to the population already established on the island. The expanding Sunnites soon followed them to Madagascar for purposes of trade and established colonies, especially in the northwest. In contrast to their predecessors they were illiterate, and the culture they brought with them was basically that of the mixed Swahili type which developed in former Azania after the advent of the Bantu. They imported large numbers of Negro slaves to perform their own agricultural labor and for sale to the Malagasy. The arrival of the Portuguese in 1500 put an end to Arab domination. As Portuguese power waned, the British and French competed for control, with the latter achieving political occupation in 1896.

These historical facts probably account sufficiently for the Arabian and Islamic elements in modern Malagasy culture and in part for the Negroid and Caucasoid elements in the population of the island, the one introduced through slaves and the other through traders and colonists. They leave unexplained, however, most of the problems raised by the complex ethnic, linguistic, and cultural composition of the Malagasy. Theories attempting to answer these problems are legion. They have, however, been built largely out of conjecture and inference, and they conflict with one another on practically every point. Their authors, moreover, with the notable exception of Linton, have lacked either experience in other areas or competence in general ethnology. Instead of discussing the theories, consequently, we shall first list a series of facts which seem indisputable, indicating the prevalent theories which each renders untenable, and then formulate a historical reconstruction that is consistent with all the facts and accounts for them with the highest degree of probability.

First, no archeological site on the island has revealed either skeletal remains of any racial type other than the three already mentioned or evidence of any culture notably different from, and possibly antecedent to, that of the present Malagasy. We therefore reject the almost universally accepted theory of an earlier Pygmoid occupation, whether of Oceanic Negritos or of African Twides, and see no reason for assuming that the island was other than completely uninhabited when the first Malagasy arrived on its shores.

Second, competent physical anthropological studies of the Malagasy, when compared with similar studies of both African and Oceanic Negroids, have demonstrated an incidence of blood types and somatic traits consistent with the derivation of the Negroid element in Madagascar from a Bantu source but inconsistent with the Papuo-Melanesian origin postulated by Grandidier and others.

Third, archeology on the adjacent continent has established conclusively that the Bantu did not reach East Africa until after the middle of the first millennium after Christ and that there were no other Negroes on the coast or its immediate hinterland prior to that time. This renders untenable the assumption of several leading theorists that a Bantu migration preceded that of the Malagasy to the island. The present Negroid element must therefore have entered the island after it had been populated by other elements or else, in part, contemporaneously with the latter.

Fourth, the Malagasy language not only belongs to the Malayo-Polynesian linguistic stock but is especially closely related to the Maanyan language of south central Borneo, as was pointed out in the preceding chapter. We must consequently reject the common assumption that the Mongoloid element in Madagascar is derived primarily from Sumatra or Java, together with the alternative conjecture of a Polynesian origin.

Fifth, the fact that the dialects of Malagasy are similar, all of them being reported as mutually intelligible, suggests immigration by a relatively unified linguistic and cultural group. This contradicts the various theories of the peopling of the island by diverse Indonesian elements arriving at different times and places from different points of origin, for in that case Madagascar should still preserve some measure of linguistic diversity.

Sixth, none of the remote islands of the Indian Ocean, such as Mauritius or Reunion, was inhabited at the time of their discovery by Europeans, nor has any of them revealed a trace of any earlier occupation, either permanent or transient. Coupled with the indisputable evidence of Indonesians on the Azanian coast, this fact argues strongly against the various theories which would bring one or more of the elements in the population of Madagascar to that island by direct voyages from Indonesia or the Pacific islands, and supports the alternative hypothesis of a coastwise passage via India, South Arabia, and East Africa.

With the underbrush of untenable theories cleared away, the landmarks of attested fact stand out in sufficient clarity and number to enable one to map the actual topography of events with only a minimum of inference. The story, as reconstructed, may be summarized as follows.

At some time prior to the beginning of the Christian era the coastal Maanyan of southeastern Borneo, close kinsmen of the people bearing this name who still survive in the adjacent interior of that island, had developed skills in navigating their outrigger canoes in trading with the inhabitants of nearby islands. Their territory lay along a trade route no less famous than the Sabaean Lane—one connecting Malaya, Sumatra, and Java with the southeast coast of China through the Philippine Islands and Formosa. The first ambitious overseas ventures of the coastal Maanyan doubtless occurred along this route. That it was being plied at the time, and had already been connected with the Sabaean Lane, is indicated by information received from Professor H. Otley Beyer of Manila, in a personal communication, that coins of Alexander the Great have been unearthed in the Philippine Islands in sites along the route.

With experience gained in this eastern maritime trade the coastal Maanyan ventured ever farther to the west—to the Nicobar Islands and Ceylon, to the Laccadives and the west coast of India, to southern Arabia, and ultimately to Azania, where we have already found evidences of them in the first century. Such dauntless mariners would certainly not have hesitated to venture farther south along the East African coast in the quest for profit, and in doing so they would inevitably have discovered the Comoro Islands and Madagascar, at that time completely uninhabited.

If they found products of commercial value in Madagascar, some would doubtless have settled there to exploit them. They would have found the virgin forests of the island ideal for the swidden (slash-and-burn) cultivation of the dry rice and the root and tree crops which they were wont to grow for subsistence on their home island. It is significant that the cultivation of wet, or paddy, rice, already established at that time in Java, Sumatra, and Malaya, had not yet been introduced to Borneo, where most inhabitants subsist by swidden cultivation even today.

In Azania the Maanyan probably functioned mainly as merchants and mariners. Those who settled there, temporarily or permanently, probably constituted an urban group, leaving agriculture to the local Cushites. The latter, who may be assumed to have perpetuated the crops (including perhaps ensete, or the Abyssinian banana) and the irrigation techniques of their forefathers, would have found the Malaysian banana and root crops highly acceptable but may well have rejected rice because they were not accustomed to swidden cultivation. This would account for the failure of this crop to become established on the East African coast even though it doubtless became the staple on Madagascar from earliest settlement.

Through intermarriage with the local Cushites the Indonesians may have incorporated a certain amount of Caucasian blood and even a trickle of Negro blood, derived ultimately from the Cushitic population of southern Ethiopia. With the arrival of the Bantu in East Africa this trickle must have increased to a steady stream. The spread of the Bantu will receive full consideration later. For present purposes it is sufficient to note the slave-trading record of the Arabs, the testimony of Zimbabwe, and the evidence of race mixture in the present-day Swahili, and to draw the conclusion that in Azania the Arabs, Cushites, and Indonesians alike acquired numbers of Bantu slaves, mixed with them, and produced hybrid offspring.

One gains an impression from the historical record that the India-Africa trade was open to the ships and merchants of all nations during the Yemenite and Persian periods but that after the Moslem Arabs achieved dominance—especially after their establishment, beginning in the early tenth century, of a series of fortified trading posts from Mogadisho to Sofala—they strove for a mercantile monopoly and sought to discourage their rivals of other nationalities. This was clearly the situation when the Portuguese arrived and shattered the monopoly by armed force. We may assume that the Indonesians and Chinese were among the unwelcome visitors who were thus gradually squeezed out. At any rate, as previously noted, all historical mention of Indonesians on the Azanian coast ceases completely by the end of the twelfth century.

Traditions and genealogies of the Merina tribe of the Madagascar plateau ascribe their ruling caste, the Andriana, to a migration occurring around the beginning of the second millennium, and practically all authorities infer from this that the lighter-skinned and more Mongoloid inhabitants of the interior of the island owe their origin to a separate and late movement from Indonesia. The traditions conceivably have a basis in the evacuation of the Malayan Azanians to Madagascar, but the assumption of a special migration has none. On the contrary, by this time the Indonesians of Africa had probably already been permanently cut off from their homeland, or at least would be before long.

The Indonesian and Bantu components in the Malagasy race and culture can now be simply accounted for. The original culture was exclusively Indonesian, and all immigrants prior to the middle of the first millennium were overwhelmingly Mongoloid. Later voluntary immigrants from Azania were at first predominantly Indonesian in culture but with considerable absorbed elements of Negro, Arab, and Cushitic blood, varying probably with the place and date of their departure, and later increasingly Negroid in physique with a culture of the emerging mixed Swahili type. During this period and after the final exodus from Azania the involuntary immigrants, or slaves, an element probably appreciably larger than either of the others, consisted exclusively of Negroes. As in the tropical New World, their effect upon the ethnic composition of the population was large but their contribution to the total culture was relatively small—and for identical reasons. The variable distribution of physical types by regions in Madagascar doubtless reflects specific historical influences which can no longer be reconstructed, although Linton's hypothesis of natural selection on the basis of the differential susceptibility of the two races to malaria may offer a partial explanation.

The numerous Malagasy tribes can be conveniently reduced to eleven major groups, as follows:

1. Antaisaka (Taisaka, Tesaki), with the neighboring Antaimoro (Antimorona, Taimoro, Tenuro), Antambahoaka (Tambahuaca), Antifasy (Antifasina, Taifasy, Tefasi), and Sahafatra (Antimanambondro). They number about 420,000 and reveal a noticeable infusion of early Arabic physical and cultural traits.
2. Antandroy (Tandruy), with the neighboring Antanosy (Tanosy, Tanusi). They number about 390,000.
3. Bara, with the kindred Barobe, Imamono, Sautsauta, Timonjy, and Vinda. Their population totals about 180,000.
4. Betsileo, embracing the Arindrano, Ilalangina, Isandra, and Manadriana. They number about 500,000.
5. Betsimisaraka, with the Betanimena. They number about 630,000.
6. Mahafaly (Mahafali). They have a population of about 80,000.
7. Merina (Antimerina, Hova, Imerina, Ovah). These plateau people, markedly Malayan in physical type, have exerted political hegemony over their neighbors since about 1600. Their present population is about a million.
8. Sakalava, embracing the Antankarana, Antiboina, Antifiherena, Antimailaka, Antimaraka, Antimena, Antimilanja (Antambongo), and Vezu (Veso). Though probably the most Negroid of all in physique, they are the only group in Madagascar that still preserves the Indonesian outrigger canoe. They number about 300,000.
9. Sihanaka (Antisihanaka). They have a population of about 85,000.
10. Tanala (Antanala), embracing the Ikongo and Menabe and including the neighboring Bezanozano (Antaiva, Antankay, Tankay). They number about 200,000.
11. Tsimihety. Their population totals about 300,000.

The Malagasy peoples fall into four subareas, differentiated mainly in basic economy: the interior Plateau, the East Coast, the Escarpment between them, and the Plains of the west coast, which also includes the extreme north and south of the island. The tribes of the Plateau (Betsileo and Merina) depend primarily on irrigated rice cultivation, with auxiliary animal husbandry. The East Coast peoples (Antaisaka and Betsimisaraka) subsist by the swidden cultivation of dry rice, supplemented by fishing and animal husbandry. The Escarpment tribes (Sihanaka, Tanala, and Tsimihety) fall into an intermediate position, characterized in many instances by an incipient transition from dry- to wet-rice cultivation. The Plains peoples (Antandroy, Bara, Mahafaly, and Sakalava) are pastoral cattle herders, who also depend heavily on fishing near the coast and to a considerably lesser extent upon agriculture.

Among the major food complexes, the Malaysian easily ranks first. All its component plants are cultivated in Madagascar. Among them, rice is the staple everywhere except in the Plains; taro and bananas are both widely cultivated; and Polynesian arrowroot is important in the Plains. Nearly all the crops of the Indian complex are likewise cultivated, but they are relatively insignificant. Of the Sudanic complex, sorghum assumes first place among the Mahafaly, earth peas are widely cultivated, and smaller quantities of gourds, watermelons, sesame, and cotton are also grown. Among plants of American origin, sweet potatoes assume first place among the Antandroy and Sakalava; manioc and maize are important everywhere; and considerable amounts of peanuts, haricot and lima beans, pumpkins, and tobacco are also raised. Many additional crops have been introduced by Europeans within the past century.

The Malagasy keep relatively small numbers of goats, fat-tailed sheep, pigs (introduced by the Portuguese), dogs, cats, chickens, and other animals of more recent introduction. Cattle, however, are exceedingly numerous. Milk, which is used everywhere, constitutes a major item in the diet of the pastoral tribes. Elsewhere, however, cattle are kept primarily as economic capital and for prestige. Their manure is utilized for fertilizer, but beef is rarely eaten except on sacrificial occasions. Fishing assumes considerable importance among many tribes, but hunting and gathering are inconsequential. In the division of labor by sex, the men ordinarily hunt, prepare land for cultivation, and herd and milk cattle, whereas both sexes engage in fishing and agriculture. In the Plains, however, the men do most of the fishing and the women most of the cultivation.

All groups occupy compact villages, commonly fortified with palisades. One house type prevails throughout the island—a rectangular structure with a thatched gable roof and walls of wood, bamboo, reeds,

Merina Dancers. (Courtesy of the Peabody Museum of Archaeology and Ethnology, Harvard University.)

or mats. On the East Coast, dwellings are commonly elevated on piles. Boys are everywhere circumcised in infancy or childhood, but clitoridectomy is not reported. Warfare is endemic. It is usually waged on a petty scale for booty in cattle and slaves, but among the Merina and some other tribes it has served as an instrument of state building. Headhunting and cannibalism are not practiced.

All Malagasy condone sexual freedom in the unmarried, and a period of trial cohabitation is often customary before a marital union is considered definitive. A bride-price of some kind appears to be universal, though its amount is frequently nominal. General polygyny prevails—sometimes, but never preferentially, in the sororal form. The first wife enjoys a favored status except among the Antandroy. A man always establishes his wives in separate dwellings and distributes his time equally among them. Residence is regularly patrilocal. Among the Tanala married sons attach themselves to their paternal households, forming patrilocal extended families. Among the Antaisaka and Bara this is true only of the eldest son, who will ultimately succeed as the household head; younger sons set up independent establishments. Extended families are also reported for several other tribes, but in most cases the reference seems to be to groups socially united by ancestor worship rather than to common residential units, which are normally independent nuclear or polygynous families.

Sons and daughters share equally in inheritance except among the Antandroy, where sons alone inherit, and among the Bara and Tanala, where daughters are restricted to movable property. All Malagasy tribes are patrilineally organized into sibs and lineages, which are typically localized either as clan-communities or as clan-barrios. Sib exogamy, however, prevails only among the Antaisaka, Bara, and Betsileo. Elsewhere sibs, and usually lineages as well, are agamous or even show a tendency to endogamy, as among the Merina, the Sihanaka, and the Menabe subtribe of the Tanala. Curiously enough, taboos against sex relations and marriage are usually extended farther in the female than in the male line, though corporate matrilineal kin groups do not occur. Matrilineal exogamy is specifically attested for the Bara, Merina, and Tanala, and it may possibly be inferred for the southwestern Plains tribes from the fact that they forbid marriage with a mother's sister's daughter, though permitting, or even preferring, a union with any other type of first cousin. Kinship terminology of the Hawaiian type is attested for the Antaisaka and Merina. The Tanala, however, employ Iroquois terms for cross-cousins of opposite sex.

The Malagasy do not treat smiths or other artisan groups as pariah castes, but they recognize a sharp division into three endogamous classes: (1) hereditary nobles, often with royalty as a special subclass;

(2) free commoners; and (3) slaves, who are recruited through capture in war or through enslavement for debt or crime and whose status is transmitted to their children. The Bara and the Plateau tribes also distinguish a subclass of royal slaves, who possess some of the privileges of commoners. Political organization everywhere transcends the level of the local community with its headman and council of lineage heads. Even the peripheral tribes possess despotic paramount chiefs, and the more central groups all have well-developed states with monarchical institutions. Political integration reaches its apex in the conquest state of the Merina, with its royal capital and elaborate court, its privy council of specialized officials, and its territorial administrative organization. According to Grandidier, the ruler, being regarded as divine, is exempted from the usual incest taboos and may marry a sister or other close relative. Reminiscent of many continental African despotisms is the high rank held at court by the king's mother and his chief wife.

The social organization of the Malagasy, like their economy, clearly reflects the Indonesian antecedents of their culture. In particular, the generational character of their kinship terminology contrasts sharply with all Arabic, Bantu, and Cushitic systems. The whole social structure, indeed, corresponds almost exactly to what one would expect in a Bornean bilateral society that was subjected to patrilocal influences through Arab and Cushitic contacts and that had to adapt to the increasing importance of cattle. Matrilineal exogamy, which constitutes the sole discrepancy, possibly reflects the mass impact of Bantu slaves, most of whom probably came from societies with matrilineal descent.

Specific features of Arabic derivation in Malagasy culture are numerous, but most of them fall into categories that lie beyond the scope of our survey, such as magic, divination, and value systems. Wet-rice cultivation seems also to have been introduced by the Arabs at a relatively late period, since this has been its origin wherever else it occurs in Africa.

Influences from the African continent obtrude most prominently in the realms of animal husbandry and government. Cattle may derive, of course, from either a Bantu or a Cushitic origin, but the latter seems more probable from the presence of such diagnostic traits as the keeping of livestock in pens to conserve their manure but especially from the fact that the Northeast Coastal Bantu themselves obtained cattle from the Cushites. Dynastic incest reminds us, naturally, of ancient Egypt, but it is probably safer in this case to invoke cultural parallelism. The despotic monarchical government of the Merina, however, with its territorial administrative organization, its specialized ministers, and especially the prominence of a Queen-Mother and a Queen-Consort, unmistakably reflects a widespread pattern in Africa, perhaps derived ultimately from Pharaonic Egypt. Possible immediate sources in East Africa include the kingdoms of southwestern Ethiopia and Uganda, and, as we have seen, the form of the latter is perhaps traceable to that of the former. If the political institutions of the Merina are basically African, then this people must have entered Madagascar from Azania, as we have inferred from other evidence, not by a special late migration from Indonesia.

Selected Bibliography

Aujus, L. Notes sur l'histoire des Betsimisaraka. *BAM*, ser. 1, 4:104–115. 1906.

Cotte, V. *Regardons vivre un tribu malgache.* Paris, 1946. [Betsimisaraka].

Decary, R. *L'Androy.* 2 vols. Paris, 1930–1933. [Antandroy].

———. *Moeurs et coutumes des Malgaches.* Paris, 1951.

Deschamps, H. J. *Les Antaisaka.* Tananarive, 1936.

Drury, R. *Madagascar,* ed. P. Oliver. London, 1890. [Mahafaly].

Dubois, H. M. Monographie des Betsileo. *TMIE,* 34:1–1510. 1938.

Faublée, J. L'alimentation chez les Bara. *JSA,* 12:157–201. 1942.

———. *Ethnographie de Madagascar.* Paris, 1946.

———. *La cohésion des sociétés Bara.* Paris, 1953.

Fenard, G. *Les indigènes fonctionnaires à Madagascar. ESEJ,* 31:1–278. 1939. [Merina].

Ferrand, G. *Les Musulmans à Madagascar et aux Iles Comores.* 3 vols. Paris, 1891–1902. [Antaisaka].

Grandidier, A., and G. Grandidier. *Ethnographie de Madagascar.* 4 vols. Paris, 1908–1928.

Kurze, G. Das Volk der Süd-Sakalava. *MGGJ,* 5:115–128; 7:106–120. 1886–1889.

Launois, P. L'état malgache et ses transformations. *ESEJ,* 14:1–131. 1932. [Merina].

Le Barbier, C. Notes sur le pays des Bara-Imamono. *BAM,* n.s., 3:63–142. 1916–1917.

———. Contribution à l'étude des Bara-Imamono. *Anthropologie,* 31:69–93, 319–328, 495–517. 1921.

Linton, R. Culture Areas of Madagascar. *AA,* 30:363–390. 1928.

———. The Tanala. *FMAS,* 21:1–334. 1933.

Mattei, L. Les Tsimihety. *BAM,* n.s., 21:131–196. 1938.

Michel, L. *Moeurs et coutumes des Bara.* Tananarive, 1957.

Rajohnson, H. Etude sur les Antanosy et les Antandroy. *BAM,* ser. 1, 6:177–196. 1908.

Schnakenberg, H. *Beitrag zur Ethnographie Madagaskars.* Strassburg, 1888.

Sibree, J. *The Great African Island.* London, 1880. [Merina].

28

---·•·---

Central Sudanic Peoples

The ancestors of the Malagasy, as we have seen, introduced a series of Malaysian cultivated plants on the Azanian coast during the centuries immediately preceding or following the time of Christ. Of these, three in particular, namely, bananas, taro, and yams, came subsequently to play an extremely important role in the economic and cultural development of the African continent. They constituted, for example, the staple crops along most of the West African coast when the first Europeans arrived. The possibility of independent ennoblement from related wild forms on the Guinea coast and in Southeast Asia can be ruled out on botanical grounds. There are, to be sure, wild yams in West Africa, and some of them have been improved to produce the Guinea yam, but the latter belongs to different subspecies from the Malaysian yams. In the case of taro, no wild forms are known in Africa. The banana, as we have seen (Chapter 4), cannot have originated anywhere in Africa since both the cultivated species are complex hybrids of wild forms which occur only in India and Malaya. We can thus assume, as a firm induction from known facts, that the Malaysian food plants of West Africa came from Southeast Asia.

They cannot have arrived by sea around the Cape of Good Hope, for the Azanians, the Maanyan-Malagasy, and the later Arabs apparently never sailed farther south than Mozambique, and no shred of evidence exists that any navigator of any nation anticipated Vasco da Gama in rounding the Cape in either direction. Transportation by way of the as yet undiscovered New World lies, of course, completely beyond the bounds of possibility for this period. The diffusion of the Malaysian crops to the Guinea coast must consequently have taken place overland across the African continent from east to west.

Here, however, we run squarely up against the clear archeological evidence that most of East Africa from the Cape to the Horn and the entire Congo Basin were occupied exclusively by hunting and gathering peoples, Bushmanoid and Pygmoid, until a period very much later than the diffusion must have occurred. Societies without agriculture cannot transmit cultivated plants. We are compelled, therefore, to look for an uninterrupted corridor of agricultural peoples running, at around the time of Christ, across the Bushmanoid territory and north of the Pygmy country

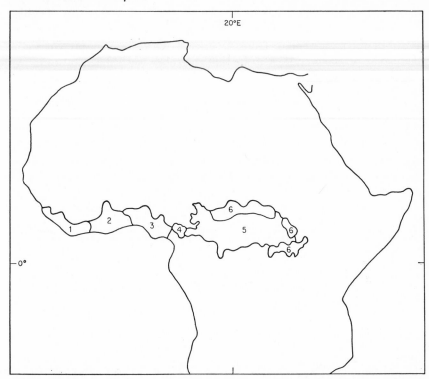

Map 13. Culture Provinces of the Yam Belt (1—Kru and Peripheral Mande, 2—Twi, 3—Southern Nigerians, 4—Cameroon Highlanders, 5—Eastern Nigritic Peoples, 6—Central Sudanic Peoples)

to the Guinea coast—a corridor, moreover, throughout whose length geographical conditions are favorable to the cultivation of bananas, taro, and yams.

In this and the ensuing chapters we shall explore this corridor, stopping occasionally on the way to describe the cultures of the indigenous peoples. Map 13 outlines the cultural provinces of the Yam Belt, as we shall term this corridor because of the special prominence of the yam in this region. To be sure, bananas and taro invariably accompanied the yam, and commonly sugarcane as well. Here we must pause to explode a bombshell, for several sorts of evidence suggest that the sweet potato reached Azania as part of the Malaysian complex and accompanied the latter in its transcontinental diffusion.

The author is aware, of course, that the sweet potato is botanically a New World plant. He also admits that in many parts of West Africa its distribution coincides so closely with the spread of other American root crops, notably malanga and manioc, as to indicate its probable introduction from the west along with the latter. He is, moreover, familiar with the controversial literature regarding the time and mode of the spread of the sweet potato from America to Oceania. The present status of this last problem appears to be that the tuber was carried by man—we do not yet know when or by whom—from South America to the Pacific islands prior to Magellan's voyage and that it there diffused throughout most of Polynesia and Melanesia as far west as New Guinea, where it has long been established as the staple crop in the mountainous interior. Most authorities have assumed, however, that it did not reach Indonesia and the Philippines, where it is an extremely important crop today, until the beginning of the colonial period.

If the sweet potato actually arrived in Azania from the east along with bananas, sugarcane, taro, and yams, its trans-Pacific spread must have taken place very much earlier than even the most uninhibited theorists have as yet dared to assume. It need not, of course, have become established more than locally in Indonesia until long after it reached Africa, for the sea-faring Maanyan of Borneo, who ventured as far as Azania and Madagascar, could certainly have made the short voyage to New Guinea and have picked up the plant there, provided it had already been locally adopted at the time.

The writer cannot bring himself to accept the early transmission of the sweet potato to Azania as more than a hypothesis worthy of special investigation. He feels, however, that the reader should be informed of the evidence which ultimately evoked in his mind the startling possibility. First, throughout the corridor which we shall shortly explore, the sweet potato is associated as nearly invariably with bananas, taro, and yams as are these plants with one another. Second, in many tribes of East Africa the sweet potato occurs without manioc, the most widely distributed of American tubers—even in regions, like southwestern Ethiopia, where the inhabitants subsist primarily through the cultivation of root crops and might be expected to accept a new one with avidity.

Finally, in certain societies which segregate their crops into groups with differential ritual associations, sweet potatoes receive the same ceremonial treatment as plants which have unquestionably been introduced via the Sabaean Lane and are differentiated in this respect from other American crops. Thus Gutmann (1913) divides the crops of the Chaga of Mount Kilimanjaro into three groups: (1) those cultivated by women with extremely elaborate rituals; (2) those grown by men with modest ceremonial associations; and (3) those raised indifferently by either sex and completely devoid of attendant rituals. He believes these reflect three successive levels of historical introduction. Sweet potatoes fall into the first and oldest group, along with taro, yams, and beans (of unidentified but presumably Indian species). The only other American crop of any consequence cultivated by the Chaga is maize, and this falls into the third group, that without ritual incrustations and thus presumably the most recent. What we need is a reasonable explanation of facts like these which does not resort to the unsatisfactory assumption of "historical accident."

The Megalithic Cushites, of course, carried the Malaysian complex on the first leg of its westward journey, providing the necessary corridor through otherwise Bushmanoid territory. That the complex spread throughout the area of Megalithic Cushite occupation is demonstrated by the fact that even the remote Sidamo peoples cultivate bananas, sugarcane, taro, yams—and sweet potatoes. The Cushites must also have carried the complex to Uganda, where we have already encountered archæological evidence of a pre-Bantu civilization of Sidamo origin, since the Interlacustrine Bantu, who inhabit the country today, still grow the same five crops, with bananas as the ranking staple in most groups and yams occupying a prominent position in many.

This brings the entire Malaysian complex to the border of the Central Sudanic province, the particular subject of the present chapter. The speakers of the Central Sudanic languages, who occupy a position at almost the exact geographical center of the African continent, have played the role of mediators in a long series of important diffusion processes. It was certainly they who transmitted the Sudanic complex in the fourth millennium B.C. from the peoples of the Lake Chad region to the Eastern Sudanic inhabitants of the Nile Valley. It was again they who, in the third millennium B.C., mediated the westward diffusion of the Neolithic animals from Southwest Asia and the Nile Valley. Much later, as we shall presently see, they had an important part in the transmission of pastoral practices to the Interlacustrine Bantu. In passing on the Malaysian food plants, therefore, they were playing no unaccustomed role.

We have already encountered three tribes of Central Sudanic speech —the Bagirmi, Kenga, and Lisi—on the Sahara-Sudan fringe just east of Lake Chad. The remaining members of this linguistic subfamily form a fringe, as Map 13 reveals, around the northern, eastern, and southeastern borders of the Eastern Nigritic province. This suggests that they have been pressed back by the inhabitants of this province and extruded from a portion of their former territory. The last phase of this process, indeed, is a matter of historical record, occurring through the eastward expansion of the Azande during the late eighteenth and the nineteenth centuries.

All the tribes of the Central Sudanic province are fully Negroid in physical characteristics, and all speak languages of the Central subfamily of the Sudanic stock. Certain regional differences in culture and history, however, make it advisable to divide them below into separate northern, eastern, and southeastern clusters.

SARA CLUSTER

The tribes of the northern, or Sara, cluster constitute one of the least adequately described groups of comparable size on the entire continent of Africa. We lack population data and good ethnic maps, and even tribal groupings and linguistic affiliations are by no means always certain. Consequently the following classification doubtless contains serious errors and omissions.

1. Gula (Goula, Gulla), with the Gele, Kudia (Koudia), Kulfa (Koulfa, Kulfe), Mali, and Mufa (Moufa).
2. Kara, with the Binga, Homr (Mogum), Mamun, and Yulu (Youlou).
3. Kreish (Gbaya, Kapala, Krech, Krejy, Kreki), with the Aja, Feroge (Farogga), Mere, Naka, Woro, and Yomamgba. They are largely Moslem today.
4. Nduka (Ndouka, Tane), with the Akunga (Akounga), Awaka (Aouaka), Leto (Aretou, Luto, Routou, Ruton), and Udio (Oudio). They are partially Islamized.
5. Ngama, with the Dakpa (Dagba), Day (Daya), Gulai (Goulay), Madjinngay, and Vale.
6. Sara, with the Barma, Dindje (Dendje, Djinge), Joko (Djioko), Kaba (Kabba), Kumra, Mbai (Bai), Ndara, Ndemi, Tele, and Tie.

MADI CLUSTER

The tribes of the eastern, or Madi, cluster are reasonably well described. Those in the extreme east reveal considerable acculturation to the pastoral Nilotes, and those in the northeast have suffered heavily from Arab slave raids.

7. Bongo (Dor). The population of this tribe, estimated at 100,000 around 1870, has been reduced to about 5,000 today.
8. Lendu (Alendu, Balendu, Walendu), with the Mabendi. They number about 155,000 and are often miscalled Bale, Drugu, or Lega (Balega, Malegga, Walegga).
9. Logo, with the Avukaya, Do (Dongo, Ndo), and Kaliko (Keliko). They number about 75,000.
10. Lugbara (Laccara, Logbwari, Louagouare, Lubare, Lugbari, Lugori, Lugwaret), with the Avare and Okefu. They number about 250,000.
11. Madi, with the kindred Luluba. They number about 70,000.
12. Mittu, with the Baka (Abaka), Beli (Behli), Biti (Bite, Bitu), Gberi (Gehri), Kodo (Moru-Kodo), Lori, Nyamusa, Sofi, Wadi (Moru-Wadi), and Wira. They number about 35,000.
13. Moru (Miza, Moru-Misi), with the Agi (Moru-Agi, Ogi, Ojiga, Uggi), Andri (Moru-Endri, Ondri), Kediru (Kederu, Moru-Kediru), and Lakamadi. They number about 20,000.

MANGBETU CLUSTER

The tribes of the southeastern, or Mangbetu, cluster inhabit former Pygmy territory, into which they began to infiltrate perhaps a thousand years ago. They entered into symbiotic relationships with the autochthones of the Mbuti group, who still survive in appreciable numbers nearly everywhere. Subsequently Eastern Nigritic and Bantu peoples began to penetrate the area, from the northwest and southwest respectively. Although both seem to have enjoyed some initial success, the Mangbetu tribe ultimately seized the initiative and during the eighteenth century conquered and subjected most of the other peoples, Central Sudanic as well as Bantu and Eastern Nigritic. Not until 1873 did the Mangbetu finally succumb to the more numerous and more aggressive Azande, the spearhead of the last Eastern Nigritic advance. Along with its Central Sudanic members, the Mangbetu cluster includes three strongly acculturated tribes of Nigritic speech—the Bangba, Mayogo, and Ngbele.

14. Badjo (Madjo). This tribe is a late offshoot of the Mangbetu.
15. Bangba (Abangba, Amiangbwa, Bomba, Mangba), with the Bote (Bogoro, Mayanga). This is a medley of peoples, partly Bantu but mainly Eastern Nigritic in speech, who have been shattered by Mangbetu and Azande expansion.
16. Lese (Balesa, Balesse, Balissi, Walese), with the kindred Mvuba (Bahuku, Bambuba, Bamouba, Mbuba, Wakuko, Wambuba). They number about 20,000.
17. Makere, with the kindred Malele and Niapu. They number about 20,000.
18. Mamvu (Momfou, Momvu, Mumvu), with the kindred Mangutu (Mangbutu, Momboutou). They number about 35,000.
19. Mangbetu (Mambecto, Mombattou, Monbuttu, Mongbutu), with the Babelu (Babeyru).
20. Mayogo (Bayugu, Maigo, Mayugu). They are an Eastern Nigritic tribe formerly subject to the Mangbetu.
21. Mbae (Bamanga, Bambanga, Mambanga, Manga, Mbanga, Umanga, Wamanga). They are a detached tribe living in Bantu territory to the south.
22. Medje, with the Mabisanga (Abisinga).
23. Ngbele (Bangbele, Mambere, Mangbele). Originally a Bantu people, they have become largely acculturated to their Mangbetu conquerors.
24. Popoi (Bagunda, Bapopoie, Mopoi). They number about 10,000.
25. Rumbi (Barumbi, Lombi, Walumbi, Warumbi). This detached tribe, living in Bantu territory, numbers about 8,500.

All the Central Sudanic peoples subsist primarily by shifting hoe cultivation, supplemented by considerable hunting, fishing, and gathering. For millennia they have participated fully in the Sudanic complex, growing ambary, cow peas, earth peas, gourds, okra, roselle, sesame, watermelons, and in the south the oil palm, in addition to sorghum and millet, the long-standing staples. Diffusion by way of the Yam Belt brought them eleusine from Ethiopia and gram, hyacinth, and sword beans from the Indian complex, as well as sweet potatoes and all the principal Malaysian crops. Taro, yams, and sweet potatoes occur nearly everywhere, but bananas do not extend as far north as the Sara cluster. This plant, however, constitutes the outstanding staple in the Mangbetu cluster and, together with the yam, certainly made possible the penetration of the Pygmy-held tropical-forest region which the tribes of this cluster now occupy. At a later period the Central Sudanic peoples acquired a number of additional crops from the New World: cucurbits, lima beans, maize, manioc, peanuts, peppers, and tobacco.

The inhabitants of this province have long kept cattle, sheep, goats, dogs, and chickens, and the tribes of the Sara cluster also possess small horses. Those of the Mangbetu cluster, however, lost cattle and sheep when they entered the tropical forest and, perhaps as a consequence, adopted cannibalism from their Nigritic neighbors. With this exception, all the Central Sudanic tribes milk their animals and make butter. Trade has developed to only an extremely limited extent in this province. In general, the men hunt, fish, tend livestock, and clear land for agriculture, and the women gather and participate equally in the task of cultivation. In the Mangbetu cluster, however, women do most of the field work and some of the fishing. Also, in this group, interestingly enough, in contrast to most Eastern Sudanic peoples, it is the men alone who do the milking. The separation of women and cattle, long looked upon erroneously as a Cushitic trait, may thus actually have originated among the Central Sudanic peoples and have been borrowed from them by the Interlacustrine and other cattle-raising Bantu.

Marriage entails a substantial bride-price in livestock or iron implements, and in the Madi cluster often a period of bride-service as well. Unions between first cousins are forbidden, at least by the Bongo, Logo, and Mangbetu tribes. Polygyny prevails everywhere, and a man establishes his wives in separate dwellings and divides his time equally among them. The household unit usually, and perhaps always, assumes the form of a polygynous rather than an extended family. Residence is invariably patrilocal, although the Madi, Mittu, and Moru normally require an initial period of matrilocal residence. Descent, inheritance, and succession follow the patrilineal rule. All tribes are organized in exogamous and often totemic patrisibs, each localized as a clan-community. The Gula, Lendu, and all members of the Mangbetu cluster practice circumcision, but the Sara, some Mamvu, and most tribes of the Madi cluster dispense with all forms of genital mutilation and extract the lower (in the case of the Sara, the upper) median incisor teeth as an initiatory rite. Formal age-grades are reported only for the Moru and the Kaliko subtribe of the Logo.

The Lese, Mamvu, Mbae, Popoi, and Rumbi occupy compact villages with dwellings aligned on either side of a single street, but elsewhere the settlement pattern consists of dispersed family homesteads or of isolated small hamlets. The prevailing house type is a round hut with a conical thatched roof and cylindrical walls of wood, mats, or wattle and daub. In the south, however, the rectangular dwelling with thatched gable roof characteristic of the adjacent Equatorial Bantu has replaced the older house form among the Badyo, Makere, Mangbetu, Mbae, Medje, Rumbi, and some Lese, Mayogo, Ngbele, and Popoi; and the Lendu have adopted the beehive structures of the nearby Interlacustrine Bantu.

Political organization rarely transcends the level of an autonomous local community with a headman and a council of elders. The Logo are reported to have paramount chiefs, though their authority is slight, and some of their neighbors acknowledge the religious influence, though not the secular power, of special rainmakers over small groups of settlements. The Mangbetu alone developed conquest states and a hereditary ruling class. Slavery prevails in the Mangbetu and Sara clusters, but the tribes of the Madi cluster neither take nor keep slaves.

Unfamiliar with warfare, except in the form of petty raiding, and defenseless because of their dispersed settlement pattern, the peoples of the Madi and Sara clusters have been unable to offer serious resistance to better-organized groups impinging upon them from all directions. Consequently they have retired before the Azande expanding from the west, the Nilotes advancing from the north, and the Baggara, or Cattle Arabs, coming from the east. During the nineteenth century, moreover, they suffered severe depopulation from systematic slave raiding, conducted first as a government monopoly by the Turkish administration of Egypt and then through concessions to rapacious Arab entrepreneurs. The establishment of colonial rule by the British and French saved a number of tribes from complete extinction.

Selected Bibliography

Baxter, P. T. W., and A. Butt. *The Azande and Related Peoples.* London, 1953.
Bernard, G. Notes sur les Badjo. *RC*, 3:311–332, 385–400. 1912.
Bruel, G. *L'Afrique Équatoriale Française.* Paris, 1918.
Costermans, B. J. Mosaïque Bangba. *MIRCB*, 28(3):1–175. 1953.
Czekanowski, J. *Forschungen im Nil-Kongo-Zwischengebiet*, vol. 2. Leipzig, 1924.
Delafosse, M. *Essai sur le peuple et la langue Sara.* Paris, 1897.
Delhaise, C. Les Bapopoïe. *BSRBG*, 36:86–113, 149–202. 1912.
Evans-Pritchard, E. E. The Bongo. *SNR*, 12:1–61. 1929.
Felkin, W. Notes on the Madi or Moru Tribe. *PRSE*, 12:303–353. 1883. [Moru].
Gutmann, B. Feldbausitten und Wachstumsbräuche der Wadschagga. *ZE*, 45:475–511. 1913.
Hutereau, A. Notes sur la vie familiale et juridique de quelques populations du Congo Belge. *AMCB*, ser. 3, 1(2):61–84. 1909. [Mangbetu and Medje].
Maenhaut, M. Les Walendu. *BJIDC*, 7:1–7, 25–37, 65–77, 97–116. 1939.
Maes, J. Les Warumbi. *Anthropos*, 4:607–629. 1909.
McConnell, R. E. Notes on the Lugwari Tribe. *JRAI*, 55:439–467. 1925. [Lugbara].
Middleton, J. Notes on the Political Organization of the Madi. *AS*, 14:29–36. 1955.
Nalder, L. F., ed. *A Tribal Survey of Mongalla Province.* London, 1937. [Madi and Moru].

Schebesta, P. *Vollblutneger und Halbzwerge*. Leipzig, 1934. [Mamvu].
———. *My Pygmy and Negro Hosts*. London, 1936. [Translation of the above].
Schweinfurth, G. Das Volk der Monbuttu. *ZE*, 5:1–27. 1873. [Mangbetu].
———. *The Heart of Africa*. 2 vols. New York, 1874. [Bongo and Mangbetu].
Seligman, C. G., and B. Z. Seligman. *Pagan Tribes of the Nilotic Sudan*. London, 1932. [Bongo, Mittu, and Moru].
Stuhlmann, F. *Mit Emin Pascha ins Herz von Afrika*. Berlin, 1894. [Lendu].
Van den Eynde, P. Notes sur les Walendu ou Bale. *Congo*, 4(2):520–530. 1923.
Van Geluwe, H. Les Bira et les peuplades limitrophes. *AMRCH*, 2:1–161. 1956. [Rumbi].
———. *Mamvu-Mangutu et Balese-Mvuba*. London, 1957.
Van Mol, P. Het huwelijk bij de Mambutu's. *Congo*, 13(2):204–224. 1932.
Van Overbergh, C. Les Mangbetu. *CME*, 4:1–594. 1909.

29

————•◦•————

Eastern Nigritic Peoples

South and west of the Central Sudanic tribes lies a broad band of Negro peoples speaking languages of the Eastern subfamily of the Nigritic stock. Bordered by the Bantu on the south, they extend westward to the Plateau Nigerian province, to which, in fact, we have already assigned some of their linguistic kinsmen (see Chapter 13). Paucity of ethnographic information makes it difficult to fix with certainty the border line between the tribes with Plateau Nigerian cultures and those affiliating more closely with the Eastern Nigritic province proper. Unquestionably there exists a zone of transition. In general, we have assigned groups to the Plateau Nigerian province where the sources specifically attest traits characteristic of that culture, such as traces of matrilineal descent and the patterned elopement of married women; tribes not so characterized are treated in the present chapter.

The southern half of the Eastern Nigritic province falls within the zone of tropical rainforest, whereas the northern half lies in savanna territory (see Map 4), a fact of the utmost importance in understanding the cultures of the region and in reconstructing their history. It is also imperative to distinguish a small cluster of tribes in Adamawa, in the extreme northwest, from the main body, which lies astride the boundary of savanna and rainforest. This is done in the following tribal classification.

ADAMAWA CLUSTER

The tribes of this cluster have in all probability occupied roughly their present territory since the earliest development of agriculture in the western Sudan. Their recorded history, however, does not begin until a century and a half ago, when a Fulani chieftain, Modibo Adama, with assistance from Osman dan Fodio, embarked in 1809 on a career of conquest in the Adamawa region. He first shattered the western tribes, seizing much of their land and separating the Fali and Kotopo from their eastern kinsmen. He then moved south against the Mbum and Wute, conquering both, expropriating large tracts for his pastoral followers, and isolating the Kepere from the main body of Mbum. Peace came only with the establishment of German rule around 1900.

1. Dama, with the Kali and Mono.
2. Dari, with the Lame.
3. Duru (Dui, Durru). They number about 14,000.
4. Fali (Falli), including the Bori, Kangu (Kangou), Peske, and Tingelin (Tinguelin). They number about 20,000.
5. Kepere (Byrre, Kper, Pere, Ripere). They are a branch of the Mbum, from whom they were separated by the invading Fulani.
6. Kotopo (Kotofo), with the Kutin (Koutinn).
7. Laka (Lakka, Tolakka), with the Dek.
8. Masa (Bana, Banana, Massa), with the Budugum, Gisei, Kim, Kossob, Marba, and Mussoi (Musei). They number at least 50,000.
9. Mbere (Mberre), with the kindred Kare (Kaya, Tali).
10. Mbum (Bum).
11. Mundang (Moundan), with the Kiziere, Mangbei, and Yasing (Imbara, Jassing, Zazing). They number about 25,000.
12. Namshi (Namchi, Namdji), with the kindred Doado, Kolbila, Pape, Sari, Sewe, and Woko (Boko, Voko). They number about 20,000.

EQUATORIAL CLUSTER

More than half of the area occupied by the tribes of this cluster lies in the zone of tropical rainforest originally inhabited by Pygmy hunters and gatherers, remnants of whom still survive throughout most of the region. Occupation by the Eastern Nigritic peoples must, therefore, have occurred relatively recently, probably within the last 2,000 years. The section of savanna country which they also occupy forms a narrow strip between the rainforest to the south and the territory inhabited by the Central Sudanic tribes of the Sara cluster on the north. This suggests that an eastward expansion by the Eastern Nigritic peoples along a former border between the Pygmies and the Central Sudanic peoples displaced these groups respectively to the right and left. Projection backward of the eastern movement historically attested for the Azande in recent centuries would lead to the same conclusion.

13. Abarambo (Barambo), with the Amadi (Amago, Aogo, Madi, Madyo), Duga, and Pambia (Apambia). They number about 50,000.
14. Azande (Asandeh, Niam-Niam, Sande, Zande), with the Bandya (Abandia). They number about 750,000.
15. Babukur (Abuguru, Buguru), with the Huma. This was one of the groups subjugated by the Azande.
16. Banda, with the Dakpwa, Langbwasse, and numerous other subtribes.
17. Bangandu (Bangangtu, Bumbe). This group, numbering fewer than 2,000, is a detached offshoot of the Baya living in Bantu country.
18. Banza (Mbanza). This tribe is a detached branch of the Banda.
19. Banziri (Gbanziri), with the Buraka (Bouraka). A fishing tribe on the Ubangi River.
20. Baya (Baja, Gbaya), with the detached Bogoto. They number in excess of 200,000.
21. Bofi (Boffi). This tribe is considerably mixed with the Bantu Pande.
22. Bondjo (Bandjo, Bongio, Bonjo, Mbondjo), with the Mondjembo.
23. Bwaka (Bouaka, Gbwaka, Mbaka, Ngbwaka). They numbered 180,000 in 1940.
24. Gobu, with the Togbo. They are a detached branch of the Banda.
25. Idio (Adio, Makaraka). They are a detached offshoot of the Azande.
26. Ikasa, with the Ikenga. These tribes are detached offshoots of the Baya in Bantu territory.
27. Kare (Akale, Akari, Bakare). Originally a Bantu tribe, they have become strongly acculturated to the Azande.
28. Mandja (Mangia). They were reported in 1904 to number 24,000.
29. Mundu (Mondu, Mountou). They number about 10,000 and are subject to the Azande.
30. Ndogo (Ndouggo), with the Bai (Bare, Bari), Biri (Birri, Viri), Bviri (Gamba, Gumba, Mbegumba, Mvegumba), Golo, Sere (Abire, Basiri, Chere, Serre, Shaire, Sheri, Siri), and Tagbo. This group, numbering about 30,000, has been shattered and decimated by Azande incursions and Arab slave raids.
31. Ngbandi (Angbandi, Gbandi, Mogwandi, Mongbwandi, Wangandi).
32. Nzakara (Nsakkara, Sakara).
33. Wute (Babute, Bafute, Bute, Mfute). This tribe, numbering about 40,000, belongs to the Bantoid rather than the Eastern subfamily of the Nigritic stock.
34. Yakoma, with the Dendi and Sango. This fishing group on the Ubangi River number about 25,000.
35. Yangere (Jangere, Ngere, Yangeli). This tribe, numbering about 3,000, is a detached offshoot of the Banda.

The incidence and distribution of cultivated plants among the Eastern Nigritic peoples illuminate their culture history with exceptional clarity. They must have acquired Sudanic agriculture at a very early period, for the tribes of the Adamawa cluster still grow sorghum and millet as their staples and cultivate varying amounts of coleus, cotton, cow peas, earth peas, fonio, okra, oil palms (in the south only), roselle, sesame, watermelons, and yergan. In the Equatorial cluster, however, sorghum retains its status as a staple or co-staple only among the Banda, Mandja, Ndogo, and Wute tribes. Other Sudanic crops disappear entirely (like fonio), decline markedly in importance, or occur only sporadically, especially as one moves southward.

This happened, presumably, in consequence of the introduction of the Malaysian complex from the Central Sudanic peoples. Yams and taro appear even in the Adamawa cluster, and both crops, along with bananas, increase in importance toward the south in almost exact proportion to the decreasing significance of the Sudanic cultigens. In addition, there are other contemporary introductions from the east, notably sugarcane, Ethiopian eleusine (the Abarambo and Azande staple), and from the Indian complex, cucumbers, gram beans, hemp, Jew's mallow, and pigeon peas. Very few of these, however, extend as far as the Adamawa cluster. The inference appears inescapable that the adoption of the Malaysian crops enabled the Eastern Nigritic peoples to penetrate the rainforest habitat of the Pygmies, which had previously been impossible owing to the unsuitability of the Sudanic cultigens to this environment. This expansion once begun, its momentum seemingly carried it eastward at the expense of the Central Sudanic peoples.

Although bananas, taro, and yams appear in all the tribes of the Equatorial cluster, and in most of them clearly outrank the Sudanic cereals, they no longer retain their former position. This they have yielded to cultigens of New World origin which have been introduced within the last four centuries. Maize, manioc, or both together rank as the staples today in the great majority of tribes; cucurbits, peanuts, and sweet potatoes follow not far behind; and numerous crops of lesser importance likewise appear—lima beans, papayas, peppers, pineapples, and tobacco. These have spread to the Adamawa cluster as well but have not attained a comparable position there. Since these American plants seem to have reached the Eastern Nigritic peoples by way of the Congo River and its Ubangi tributary, they acquired them in advance of their Central Sudanic neighbors, and this may have been the critical factor that enabled them to dominate the latter.

In earlier chapters we have frequently encountered crops of American origin playing a subordinate role to those of some

Azande Boy Spinning Cotton. (Courtesy of the American Museum of Natural History.)

other complex—Sudanic, Egyptian, Ethiopian, or Malaysian. Here for the first time we find them occupying the leading position, and it therefore seems appropriate to inject a discussion of them at this point.

All the cultivated plants of New World origin now found in Africa have arrived during the course of the last four and a half centuries, for, with the possible exception of the sweet potato, no convincing evidence has yet been adduced to suggest the introduction of any American cultigen into Africa prior to the discovery of the New World. Even before Columbus had completed his voyages of discovery and exploration, the Portuguese and Spaniards began sending to Africa for Negroes to assist them in exploiting the agricultural and other resources of the two American continents, and the slave trade, thus initiated, continued well into the nineteenth century.

The ships engaged in this human commerce were naturally provisioned on either side of the Atlantic by the foods there available, and any stores remaining were traded or even purposely planted on the opposite shore. Since the environmental conditions in tropical Africa and tropical America are nearly identical, the products from each continent became readily established on the other. Native African plants are common today in Brazil and the West Indies, and American plants early gained a foothold on the coasts of Africa. The tropical-forest cultigens from the New World quickly marched inland from their ports of entry in Africa and established themselves firmly over wide regions of the interior which resembled their native American habitat; thus by the time Europeans got around to exploring the interior of the continent they frequently found the New World plants already occupying a dominant position and the earlier varieties so submerged that identification was possible only by careful scrutiny of ethnographic crop lists and distributional evidence.

It is noteworthy that the American species that have become established in Africa do not include the sunflower (*Helianthus annuus*) or any other species confined to the arid regions of the New World; nor do they include the potato (*Solanum tuberosum*) or any other species confined to the high Andes. All, without exception, had been established in lowland South America or the West Indies prior to their transplantation. The potato, to be sure, has reached Africa today, but it apparently was nowhere introduced before the twentieth century. The component elements of the American complex, as introduced into Africa, are enumerated below.

CEREAL GRAINS

Maize, or Indian corn (*Zea mays*)

LEGUMES

Haricot bean, or kidney bean (*Phaseolus vulgaris*)
Lima bean (*Phaseolus lunatus*)

TUBERS AND ROOT CROPS

Arrowroot (*Maranta arundinacea*)
Malanga, or yautia (*Xanthosoma sagittifolium*)
Manioc, or cassava (*Manihot utilissima*)
Peanut (*Arachis hypogaea*)
Sweet potato (*Ipomoea batatas*, formerly *Convulvulus batatas*)

VINE AND GROUND FRUITS

Pineapple (*Ananas comosus* or *Ananassa sativa*)
Pumpkin (*Cucurbita pepo*)
Squash (*Cucurbita maxima* and *C. moschata*)
Tomato (*Lycopersicum esculentum*)

TREE FRUITS

Avocado, or alligator pear (*Persea gratissima*)
Guava (*Psidium guajava*)
Papaya, or pawpaw (*Carica papaya*)

CONDIMENTS AND INDULGENTS

Cacao (*Theobroma cacao*)
Red pepper, or chili pepper (*Capsicum annuum*)
Tobacco (*Nicotiana rustica* and *N. tabacum*)

DOMESTIC ANIMALS

Guinea pig (*Cavia* sp.)
Muscovy duck (*Cairina moschata*)
Turkey (*Meleagris gallopavo*)

Although agriculture provides the primary basis of subsistence among most Eastern Nigritic tribes, it is surpassed by fishing and river trading among the Banziri, Yakoma, and some Bondjo and Ngbandi. The Adamawa peoples possess goats, sheep, dogs, chickens, and occasionally horses and bees. Except in the south, they also keep cattle and milk them, thus representing the limit of the early westward diffusion of the milking complex. In the Equatorial cluster, however, animal husbandry dwindles to insignificance. Cattle and horses disappear entirely, sheep occur only sporadically, and some tribes even lack goats. Nowhere does either hunting or gathering add substantially to the food supply, and trade is confined mainly to the larger rivers. The men normally hunt, fish, tend and milk livestock, where these occur, and clear new land for tillage, leaving the tasks of gathering and agriculture to the women. In Adamawa, however, the women often participate in fishing and the men to a limited extent in cultivation.

Most tribes live in neighborhoods of dispersed homesteads or in clusters of isolated hamlets, but the Banziri, Baya, Bondjo, Bwaka, Mbum, Mundang, Ngbandi, Wute, Yakoma, and a few other peoples occupy compact villages. These usually consist of either a single row of dwellings along a riverbank or a double row facing a street. Round huts of Sudanic type, with conical thatched roofs and cylindrical walls of mud or wattle and daub, strongly preponderate, but a few tribes in the extreme south, i.e., the Bangandu, Bondjo, Bwaka, Ikasa, and Yangere, have adopted the Bantu rectangular house with mat or plank walls and a thatched gable roof.

The Adamawa and Equatorial tribes differ little in social organization. All require a substantial bride-price, usually paid in iron implements, but the Fali require premarital bride-service as well, and the Banda formerly preferred the exchange of sisters. Unions with a first cousin are forbidden, and most groups insist upon local exogamy. General polygyny prevails, with a separate dwelling for each wife and a special status for the first. The Banda prefer the sororal form, but the Baya and Wute forbid it. Residence follows the patrilocal rule, although the Ngbandi and Wute allow a man to reside with his maternal uncle in special circumstances. Extended forms of the family are reported only for the Laka, Masa, and Wute. Descent, inheritance, and succession adhere strictly to the patrilineal principle. Sibs are usually, and lineages invariably, exogamous. Except among the Azande, Fali, and Laka, patrilineal kin groups tend to be localized as clan-communities. The Azande have cousin terminology of the descriptive type, but the Banda and Ngbandi appear to conform to the Omaha pattern.

Each village has a headman, and most tribes acknowledge no higher political authority. The Azande, Mbum, and Wute, however, are ruled by paramount chiefs over subtribes or districts. Among the Wute, each of these maintains a court with specialized officials, a council of noble kinsmen, and a prestigeful Queen-Mother. Mbum chiefs possess the attributes of divine kings. They eat only in secret and are killed if they fail in their primary responsibility of maintaining the welfare of their people, e.g., if they permit a severe drought to occur. Among the Azande a ruling sib, the Avungara, has established a series of personal states based on military conquest and apparently modeled on those of the Central Sudanic Mangbetu. All groups keep slaves, whose status is usually hereditary but is not so among the Azande and Banda. Although the Adamawa tribes rarely practice either circumcision or cannibalism, the Equatorial peoples —with occasional exceptions, as among the Banziri and Ndogo—have adopted both customs.

Selected Bibliography

Anderson, E. *Plants, Men and Life.* Boston, 1952.

Baxter, P. T. W., and A. Butt. *The Azande.* London, 1953.

Bruel, G. *L'Afrique Équatoriale Française.* Paris, 1918.

Brussaux, E. Notes sur les Moundans. *BSAP*, ser. 5, 8:273–295. 1907.

Cabot, J. Kim. *BIEC*, n.s., 5:41–67. 1953. [Masa].

Caldwell, M. G., and H. Sheldon. The Culture of the Baya Tribe. *Scientific Monthly*, 30:321–325. 1930.

Calonne-Beaufaict, A. de. *Azande.* Bruxelles, 1921.

Candolle, A. de. *Origin of Cultivated Plants.* 2d edit. London, 1904.

Carlier, E. Notice sur les Bondjos. *BSG*, ser. 7, 20:241–248. 1899.

Clozel, F. J. *Les Bayas.* Paris, 1896.

———. The Banziris. *Popular Science Monthly*, 49:673–677. 1896.

Crabbeck, G. Les Gbwaka. *BJIDC*, 11:85–108. 1943. [Bwaka].

Czekanowski, J. *Forschungen im Nil-Kongo-Zwischengebiet*, vol. 2. Leipzig, 1924. [Abarambo and Azande].

Daigre. Plantes alimentaires du pays Banda. *BSRC*, 8:123–134. 1927.

———. Les Bandas. *Anthropos*, 26:647–695; 27:153–181. 1931–1932.

Darré, E. Coutumes de la tribu Bondjo. *BSRC*, 3:53–73. 1923.

Evans-Pritchard, E. E. The Mberidi (Shilluk Group) and Mbegumba (Basiri Group) of the Bahr-el-Ghazal. *SNR*, 14:15–48. 1931. [Ndogo].

———. *Witchcraft, Oracles and Magic among the Azande.* Oxford, 1937.

Froelich, J. C. Le commandement et l'organisation sociale chez les Fali. *EC*, 53–54:20–50. 1956.

Gaud, F. Les Mandja. *CME*, 8:1–574. 1911.

Gillier. Les Banda. *RCD*, 23:346–355, 386–396. 1913.

Girard, H. Yakomas et Bougous. *Anthropologie*, 12:51–91. 1901.

Hagen, G. von. Die Bana. *BA*, 2:77–116. 1912. [Masa].

Harttmann, H. Ethnographische Studie über die Baja. *ZE*, 59:1–61. 1927.

Hutereau, A. Notes sur la vie familiale et juridique de quelques populations du Congo Belge. *AMCB*, ser. 3, 1(1):13–39. 1909. [Azande].

Lagae, C. R. Les Azande ou Niam-Niam. *BC*, 18:1–224. 1926.

Larken, P. M. An Account of the Zande. *SNR*, 9:1–55; 10:85–134. 1926–1927.

Lembezat, B. Kirdi. *MIFCC*, 3:1–95. 1950. [Masa].

Leynaud, E. Parenté et alliance chez les Bandas. *BIEC*, n.s., 7–8:109–159. 1954.

Lotar, L. Polygamie et mariage Zande. *Congo*, 6(1):574–581. 1925.

Malzy, P. Les Fali du Tinguelin. *EC*, 51:3–27. 1956.

Martin, R. Note sur les Mundang. *BIEC*, 2:99–105. 1947.

Nalder, L. F., ed. *A Tribal Survey of Mongalla Province.* London, 1937. [Idio].

Nys, F. *Chez les Abarambos.* Anvers, 1896.

Poupon, A. Étude ethnographique des Baya. *Anthropologie*, 26:87–144. 1915.

Poutrin. Notes ethnographiques sur les populations M'Baka. *Anthropologie*, 21:35–54. 1910. [Bwaka].

Reinhardt, L. *Kulturgeschichte der Nutzpflanzen.* 2 vols. München, 1911.

Santandrea, S. Il gruppo Ndogo del Bahr-el-Ghazal. *AL*, 2:175–353. 1938.

Sauer, C. O. *Agricultural Origins and Dispersals.* New York, 1952.

Schiemann, E. Entstehung der Kulturpflanzen. *Handbuch der Vererbungswissenschaft*, 3:1–377. Berlin, 1932.

Schweinfurth, G. *The Heart of Africa.* 2 vols. New York, 1874. [Azande].

Seligman, C. G., and B. Z. Seligman. *Pagan Tribes of the Nilotic Sudan*. London, 1932. [Azande].

Sieber, J. *Die Wute*. Berlin, 1925.

Tanghe, B. *De Ngbandi naar het leven geschetst*. Brussel, 1928.

Tessmann, G. Die Mbaka-Limba, Mbum und Lakka. *ZE*, 60:305–352. 1929.

——. *Die Baja*. 2 vols. Stuttgart, 1934–1937.

Thorbecke, F. Anthropogeographie des Ost-Mbamlandes. *AHKI*, 36:1–94. 1916. [Wute].

Vavilov, N. I. The Origin, Variation, Immunity and Breeding of Cultivated Plants, transl. K. S. Chester. *Chronica Botanica*, 13:1–364. 1949–1950.

Vergiat, A. M. *Moeurs et coutumes des Manjas*. Paris, 1937.

30

Cameroon Highlanders

The grassy uplands of central Cameroon, which connect the Eastern Nigritic and Southern Nigerian provinces, apparently lay on the very margin of original Negro territory, for a few Pygmy remnants still survive among the Tikar tribe in the east. The inhabitants doubtless acquired Sudanic agriculture at an early period, for they raise coleus, earth peas, gourds, millet, oil palms, okra, roselle, watermelons, and yergan, and sorghum ranks as one of the staple crops everywhere except in the extreme south.

They nevertheless fall clearly into the Yam Belt, since all groups cultivate substantial amounts of bananas, yams, and especially taro, which is a staple or co-staple in most tribes. They have added Jew's mallow, pigeon peas, and sword beans from the Indian complex, and in some instances have also adopted Ethiopian eleusine. The Cameroon Highlanders may well have mediated the transmission of the Malaysian crops from the Eastern Nigritic peoples to the inhabitants of coastal Nigeria. On the other hand, the route may have lain slightly farther to the north among the adjacent Plateau Nigerians, for the southern tribes of the latter also adopted bananas, taro, and yams and still cultivate them, with the last two ranking as major crops. But whatever the route may have been, it completed the transcontinental diffusion of the Malaysian complex from the Indian Ocean to the shores of the Atlantic.

The Cameroon Highlanders belong to the Bantoid subfamily of the Nigritic linguistic stock. More than that, they all speak languages of the

Bantu subdivision of the Macro-Bantu branch of that subfamily. Together with the adjacent lower country to the southwest along the Nigerian border, upland Cameroon appears to have constituted the original
homeland of the Bantu and the region to which they were confined until
the advent of the Malaysian food plants. These gave them, like their
Eastern Nigritic neighbors, the wherewithal to penetrate for the first time
the tropical rainforest to the south previously inhabited exclusively by
Pygmoid hunters and gatherers. The resulting enormous expansion of the
Bantu peoples, which we shall consider beginning with Chapter 35, represents one of the most important indirect effects of the cultural impact
of Indonesia on the peoples of Africa.

The Cameroon Highland Bantu, who are located on Map 13, fall into a
very large number of distinct tribes, of which only the best known are
mentioned in the following classification.

1. Bamileke, embracing the Babadjou (Babudschu), Bafang, Bafoussam, Bagam
   (Eyap), Baham, Bamendjou (Bamendzo), Bandjoun (Bandschu), Bangangte, Ban-
   gou (Bangu), Bangwa, Bapi (Bapei), Batongtu, Chang, and numerous other tribes
   and chiefdoms. They number in excess of 450,000.
2. Fia (Bafia), with the Balom, Bape, Djanti (Njanti), Lemande (Omand), Mehele,
   Yambasa, and Yambeta (Njabeta). They number about 50,000.
3. Fungom, with the Bum (Bafumbum). They number about 50,000.
4. Fut (Bafut, Fu), with the Babanki, Bafreng, Bamenda, and Bandeng. They number about 35,000.
5. Kom (Bahom, Bamekom, Bekom, Bikom, Hom, Nkom). They number about
   30,000.
6. Li (Bali, Balu, Bani). They number about 23,000.
7. Mum (Bamoum, Bamum, Banun, Mom). They number about 75,000 and have
   been largely Moslem for more than half a century.
8. Ndob (Mburukem, Ndop), embracing the Baba, Babessi (Bamessi), Babungo
   (Bamungo), Bamessing (Nsei), and other subtribes. They number about 45,000.
9. Nen (Banen, Banend, Banyin, Penin, Penyin), embracing the Ndiki (Indiki),
   Nyokon, and other subtribes. They number about 32,000.
10. Nsaw (Bansaw, Banso, Nso). They number about 60,000.
11. Nsungli (Dzungle, Ndzungli, Njungene, Zungle), embracing the Mbaw, Mbem,
    Tang, War (Mbat, Wa, Wot), and Wiya (Ndu, Ndum, Wimbu). They number
    about 40,000.
12. Tikar (Mbam, Ndomme). They number about 10,000 and have long been domi-
    nated by intrusive Fulani. The Fungom, Fut, Kom, Ndob, Nsaw, and Nsungli
    are sometimes classed as Tikar in a broader sense.
13. Widekum, embracing the Befang, Esimbi (Age), Menka, Meta (Menemo),
    Mogamaw, Ngemba (Bapindji), Ngie, and Ngwo (Ngunu). They number nearly
    100,000.
14. Wum (Aghem). They number about 10,000.

The Cameroon Highlanders subsist primarily by agriculture. Long after
their adoption of the Malaysian complex they, like their Eastern Nigritic
neighbors, acquired a series of American food plants. Maize, in particular,
ranks widely as a staple or co-staple today. Manioc, peanuts, and sweet

potatoes are likewise important, and lesser American crops include cucur-bits, haricot and lima beans, malanga, peppers, and pineapples. All in all, the American, Malaysian, and Sudanic complexes play approximately equal roles in the contemporary agriculture of the province.

Most groups possess goats, sheep, pigs (apparently recent), dogs, and chickens. The Bamileke, Li, Mum, and Tikar also keep a very few cattle but do not milk them. Hunting and fishing augment the food supply to a variable, though rarely significant, extent. The majority of tribes do a considerable amount of trading and maintain regular markets. Men hunt, clear land, and do most of the trading. Except among the Tikar and some Nsungli, they leave tillage largely to the women, who also engage in fishing, sometimes exclusively.

The Bamileke, Fia, Li, and Widekum reside in neighborhoods of dispersed family homesteads, but all other groups occupy compact villages. Among the Mum and Tikar these consist of a double row of compounds along either side of a single street. The prevailing house type is a square dwelling with a pyramidal thatched roof and walls of wattle and daub, but the Tikar and Widekum build cone-cylinder huts of Sudanic type, and the transitional Fia and Nen construct rectangular houses with gable roofs like those of the adjacent Equatorial Bantu.

Nsaw Village. (Courtesy of United Nations.)

Each village has a hereditary headman, who is usually advised by a council of lineage heads. The Fia, Nen, and Widekum lack political institutions of greater complexity, but all other groups are organized into states under paramount chiefs. Though for the most part small, these attain substantial size among the Kom, Li, Mum, Nsaw, and some Bamileke. Whether large or small, they exhibit the usual characteristics of African despotisms: divine kings; territorial administrative organizations; and capitals with elaborate courts, specialized officials, and prestigeful queen-mothers. Though slavery is universal, hereditary aristocracies ordinarily appear only in conjunction with complex states. Circumcision is widespread, but clitoridectomy is not reported, and cannibalism is apparently confined to the marginal Fia and Tikar tribes.

Marriage normally entails the payment of a substantial bride-price, but the Nsaw and Tikar require only token gifts, the Fia more often resort to abduction, and the Nen and occasionally the Bamileke and Nsungli practice sister exchange. Unions between cross-cousins are forbidden, at least among the Bamileke, Kom, Nsaw, and Tikar. Polygyny prevails everywhere, and co-wives always occupy separate huts. The household unit tends to be an independent polygynous family among the southern tribes, an extended family in the north.

Except among the Kom and Wum, residence follows the patrilocal rule, and descent, inheritance, and succession the patrilineal principle. Exogamous patrilineages are generally localized as clan-barrios but occasionally as clan-communities, e.g., among the Fia, Nen, and Widekum. In contrast to all other tribes, residence is avunculocal among the Kom and often so among the Wum, and both groups adhere to the matrilineal rule in regard to inheritance and descent. These facts, coupled with a few seeming survivals in other tribes, support the hypothesis, advanced in Chapter 13, that the Bantu were originally matrilineal and avunculocal. Most of the Cameroon Highlanders, however, seem to have completed the transition to the patrilineate before they began to expand into the tropical rainforest.

The Mum share with the Vai (see Chapter 33) the distinction of being the only Negro tribes to have invented a system of writing. When first observed, in 1907, they were using 348 signs, largely ideographic or pictographic. King Njoya, knowing of both the German writing and the Arabic script employed by Hausa traders and feeling a need for communicating secretly with his local officials, called a meeting of his council and proposed the creation of a form of writing. Since the language consisted largely of monosyllabic roots, the original signs were readily converted, by 1909, into a syllabary, and after further evolution were developed into a true alphabet.

Selected Bibliography

Ankermann, B. Bericht über eine ethnographische Forschungsreise ins Grasland von Kamerun. *ZE*, 42:288–310. 1910. [Li, Mum, and Nsaw].
Delafosse, M. Naissance et évolution d'un système d'écriture de création contemporaine. *RETP*, 3:11–36. 1922. [Mum].
Dugast, I. Inventaire ethnique du Sud Cameroun. *MIFCC*, 1:1–159. 1949.
———. Monographie de la tribu des Ndiki. *TMIE*, 58:1–824. 1955. [Nen].
Edgerton, F. C. C. *African Majesty*. New York, 1939. [Bamileke].
Hutter, F. Politische und soziale Verhältnisse bei den Graslandstämmen Nordkameruns. *Globus*, 76:284–289, 303–309. 1899. [Li].
———. *Wanderungen und Forschungen im Nord-Hinterland von Kamerun*. Braunschweig, 1902.
———. Bamum. *Globus*, 91:1–6, 26–32, 44–47. 1907.
Kaberry, P. M. *Women of the Grassfields*. London, 1952.
Malcolm, L. W. G. The Social-Political Organisation of the E-yap Tribe. *Anthropos,* 21:233–243. 1926. [Bamileke].
McCulloch, M., M. Littlewood, and I. Dugast. *Peoples of the Central Cameroons*. London, 1954.
Rein-Wuhrmann, A. *Mein Bamumvolk im Grasland von Kamerun*. Stuttgart, 1925.
Schmidt, A. Feld-Forschungen über das Leben der Frau im Grasland von Kamerun. *AV*, 4:165–185. 1949. [Ndob].
Sieber, D., and J. Sieber. Das Leben des Kindes im Nsungli-Stamm. *Africa*, 11:208–220. 1938.
Tessmann, G. Die Völker und Sprachen Kameruns. *PM*, 68:113–120, 184–190. 1932.
———. *Die Bafia und die Kultur der Mittelkamerunbantu*. Stuttgart, 1934.
Thorbecke, F. Anthropogeographie des Ost-Mbamlandes. *AHKI*, 36:1–94. 1916. [Tikar].
Thorbecke, F., and M. P. Thorbecke. Die Kultur der Tikar. *AHKI*, 41:13–178. 1919.

31

———•◆•———

Southern Nigerians

The tropical forest which blankets the Congo Basin also extends along the Guinea coast of West Africa. Archeological research reveals essentially the same distribution for the prehistoric hunting and gathering cultures known collectively as Sangoan. Since these are associated in the Congo with peoples of the Pygmoid race, many authorities have assumed that Pygmies once inhabited the Guinea coast as well. No remnants, however, are found there today. Negroid peoples speaking languages of the Nigritic stock occupy the coastal zone as exclusively as they do the interior. No dependable evidence of an older Pygmoid population has yet been adduced, despite traditions—always unreliable—of an earlier "little people" and unverified reports of localized groups with short stature. Until archeology definitely establishes the contrary, therefore, it is safer to assume that the bearers of Sangoan cultures on the Guinea coast were Negroes rather than Pygmies.

The present chapter deals with the inhabitants of Southern Nigeria. These Negro peoples for the most part speak languages of the Kwa subfamily of the Nigritic stock, but the Bantoid subfamily prevails in the extreme east, and the Ijaw tribe constitutes the only representative of the Ijaw subfamily. Analysis of the culture of the area will be facilitated by a classification of the component societies into five clusters.

BANTOID CLUSTER

All the tribes of this cluster speak languages of the Bantoid subfamily of the Nigritic stock. It is probable that they descended from the Nigerian plateau to the adjacent coast upon acquisition of the Malaysian food plants from the east.

1. Anyang (Anjang, Bascho), with the kindred Banyang (Banjangi, Konguan, Manyang). They number about 50,000.
2. Boki (Nki), with the Bete, Uge, and Yakori (Yakoro). They were reported in 1921 to have a population of 92,000.
3. Ekoi, embracing the Akaju (Ahaju), Atam, Ejagham (Ekoi proper), Keaka, Manta, Nde (Ndei), Obang, Olulumaw, and other subtribes. Their population was reported as 90,000 in 1921.
4. Ibibio (Agbisherea), with the Anang, Andoni, Efik, Eket, Enyong, Ibeno, and detached Abuan. They number slightly more than a million.
5. Mbembe, with the Adun (Arun), Igbo, Oshopong (Eshupum), and other small groups. They were reported in 1921 to number about 38,000.
6. Ododop (Erorup), with the Korop (Korawp) and Okoiyang. They number about 5,000.
7. Orri, embracing the Effium, Okpoto-Mteze, and Ukelle. They number about 75,000.
8. Yako, with the Abayong (Abaiyonga), Abine (Abani), Agoi, Akunakuna (Agwa-aguna), Asiga (Essiga), Ekumuru (Ikumunu), Ekuri, Enna, and Uyanga. They number about 40,000.

IDOMA CLUSTER

The tribes of this cluster all speak languages of the Kwa subfamily of the Nigritic stock, but whether they are affiliated primarily with the Nupe or the Yoruba branch of this subfamily is not always clear.

9. Afo (Afao, Afu). They number about 8,000.
10. Arago (Alago). They number about 15,000.
11. Egede, with the Akweya, Yachi (Iyace), and detached Etulo. They number about 85,000.

12. Gili (Koro of Lafia, Migili). They number about 7,000.
13. Idoma, with the Agala, Agatu, Igumale, Okpoto (Akpoto), Okwaga, and Oturkpo. They number about 250,000.
14. Igala (Atagara, Igara, Igula), with the Ibaji. They number about 200,000.
15. Iyala (Ingkum, Yala), with the Nkum (Nkim). They number about 30,000.

NUPE CLUSTER

The tribes of this cluster speak languages of the Nupe branch of the Kwa subfamily of the Nigritic stock. Islam has been widely accepted.

16. Igbira (Egbiri, Kotokori), with the Igu (Egu), Okene (Okeni), and Panda (Hima, Kwotto, Wushishi). They number about 250,000.
17. Nge (Basange, Bassange). These people, numbering about 20,000, are an offshoot of the Nupe who fled to escape Fulani conquest.
18. Nupe, embracing the Batache, Beni (Bini), Benu, Chakpang (Cakpang), Dibo (Ganagana, Zitako), Ebagi, Ebe (Abewa), Gbedye, Gwagba, Kakanda (Akanda, Hyapa), Kede (Kyedye), Kupa (Gupa), Kusopa, and Zam. They number about 360,000 and were conquered by the Fulani around 1820.

CENTRAL CLUSTER

The tribes of this cluster are linguistically somewhat diverse, though all speak Nigritic languages.

19. Edo (Bini), with the Ishan (Esa, Isa). They number about 400,000 and belong to the Edo branch of the Kwa subfamily of the Nigritic stock.
20. Ibo, embracing the Ada (Edda), Ika, Onitsha, and other subtribes. They number nearly 4 million, and constitute the Ibo branch of the Kwa linguistic subfamily.
21. Ijaw (Ijo), with the Brass and Kalabari. They constitute the sole members of the Ijaw subfamily of the Nigritic linguistic stock. In 1921 they had a reported population of about 175,000.
22. Isoko, with the Erakwa and Urhobo (Sobo). They belong to the Edo branch of the Kwa linguistic subfamily and number about 435,000.
23. Itsekiri (Awerri, Jakri, Jekri, Oere, Ouere, Owerri, Warri). They belong to the Yoruba branch of the Kwa linguistic subfamily. They number about 33,000 and subsist primarily by fishing.
24. Kukuruku, embracing the Akoko, Etsako, Ineme, and Ivbiosakon subtribes. They number slightly under 200,000 and belong to the Edo branch of the Kwa linguistic subfamily.

YORUBA CLUSTER

The tribes of this cluster all speak closely related languages belonging to the Yoruba branch of the Kwa subfamily of the Nigritic stock. Most of them have been notably urban for centuries.

25. Ana (Atakpame, Ife), with the Dume and Kpedji. This group, numbering about 15,000, split off from the Ife in the sixteenth century and migrated west into Togo and Dahomey.
26. Bunu (Kabba), embracing the Aworo (Akanda), Bunu, Ijumu (with the Ibbedde and Adda), Owe (Kabba), and Yagba. They number about 100,000.

27. Egba, with the Awori (Dje, Holli), Badagri, Dassa, Egabo, Itsha (Tsha), Ketu, Manigri, Nago (Anago, Nagot), and Tshabe (Tschebe). They number about 550,000.
28. Ekiti, with the Akoko, Ondo, and Owo-Ifon. They number about 370,000.
29. Ife, with the Ilesha (Ijesha) and Illa. They number about 170,000.
30. Ijebu, including the kindred inhabitants of Lagos and the adjacent coast. They number about 550,000.
31. Yoruba proper, embracing the Ibadan, Igbolo, Igbona (Igbomina), Ilorin, and Oyo. They number about 1,600,000. Islam is fairly widespread among the Ilorin, who were conquered by the Fulani in 1831.

Sudanic agriculture doubtless penetrated Southern Nigeria from the north at an early period. Since, however, its crops are not in general well suited to tropical-forest conditions, it probably replaced the earlier primary dependence upon hunting, fishing, and gathering only in favorable locations, especially along the northern fringe of the area. This is suggested by the surprisingly minor role which plants of the Sudanic complex play in the present economies. Sorghum and millet, for example, appear as staples only among the Nupe, and in many tribes are grown only sparingly or not at all. Akee, ambary, cotton, earth peas, fluted pumpkins, gourds, okra, sesame, and yergan are cultivated fairly widely but not in great quantities. Guinea yams and especially the oil palm, however, are important, and these were presumably brought under cultivation originally on the coast rather than in the interior. Even though agriculture probably held only a subordinate place in the coastal economies for a long time, its antiquity cannot be denied. Otherwise we could scarcely account for the fact that the cultivation of certain Sudanic crops, notably millet, is often heavily incrusted with ritual.

The arrival of the Malaysian complex by overland transmission from the east, which probably occurred around the beginning of the Christian era, must have wrought an explosive transformation in the economy. Population catapulted with the introduction of a new and abundant food supply, until today it is appreciably denser in this region than in any other part of the African continent. Yams proved particularly well adapted to local conditions and are today the outstanding staple in the majority of the tribes of the province. Taro, known locally as the coco yam, is likewise important everywhere, and in several tribes it rises to the status of a co-staple. Bananas constitute the chief crop of the Anyang but have achieved only a subsidiary position farther west.

The introduction of American cultivated plants from Brazil and the West Indies after 1500, mediated by the European slave traders, gave a new fillip to the economy. Being native to a similar environment in the New World, they readily became established on the Guinea coast. They soon outstripped the crops of the Sudanic complex and today are second only to those of the Malaysian complex. Peppers, pineapples, pumpkins, squash, sweet potatoes, tobacco, and tomatoes occur fairly widely, and maize, manioc, and peanuts rank among the mainstays of the present economy. Among the Ijebu and Itsekiri, indeed, manioc has even supplanted yams as the principal crop.

Nearly all tribes keep a few cattle, but do not milk them. Goats, sheep, dogs, and chickens are general, and there are occasional reports of horses, pigs, cats, ducks, and guinea fowl. Hunting and gathering are less productive today than formerly, but fishing adds an important increment to the food supply in most tribes and provides the primary basis of subsistence for the Itsekiri. Trade and handicraft industries are highly developed, and regular markets are practically universal. Men hunt, clear land for agriculture, and do most of the fishing, whereas women engage in market trading. Both sexes participate in cultivation, but men do more of the work among the western tribes, women among those in the east.

The Egede, most Ibo, and some Idoma live in neighborhoods of dispersed family homesteads, but most tribes occupy compact villages and towns. These are typically divided into wards, or quarters, which sometimes, as among the Ibibio and Nupe, are physically separated as distinct hamlets. Anyang, Edo, and Ekoi villages often consist of a double row of habitations along a single village street. In the more populous tribes, settlements sometimes attain the size of true cities. Ibadan in the Yoruba country, for example, has a population of 400,000 and is the largest exclusively Negro city in all Africa. Cone-cylinder huts of the familiar Sudanic type prevail among the Boki and the tribes of the Idoma and Nupe clusters, which border the Plateau Nigerians, but elsewhere we encounter a new and distinctive house type—a rectangular dwelling with walls of mats or wattle and daub and a gable roof thatched with palm leaves. These houses are grouped in compounds around a central courtyard, usually rectangular in shape. Where huts are round, on the other hand, compounds tend to be circular.

All Southern Nigerians require a consideration in marriage. This consists primarily of bride-service and gifts among the Ekoi and Igbira and of a woman given in exchange among the Afo and some Idoma and Ibo, but it assumes the form of a substantial bride-price in all other groups. The Ijaw and Kukuruku, to be sure, permit marriages with but a minimal consideration as an alternative, but in such cases the children belong not to the father but to the mother's family. The Ekoi, Ibibio, and Ibo systematically fatten a girl for her wedding, sometimes for periods exceeding a year. The Ekoi and Nupe allow cousins to marry, and the Yako and eastern Ibo prefer unions with a father's sister's daughter, but most groups regard any cousin marriage as incestuous. Polygyny is favored by all the peoples of the region. The sororal form is permitted among the Idoma and Igala but forbidden in most other tribes. The first wife enjoys a

Onitsha Ibo Girl with Characteristic Leg Bangles. (Courtesy of British Information Services.)

preferred status, but each co-wife normally has a separate hut or apartment. Residence is regularly patrilocal, but the Yako require an initial matrilocal period, and the Kukuruku follow the avunculocal rule in certain instances. With only inconsequential exceptions the patrilocal extended family everywhere constitutes a strongly functional unit, though it may be composed of distinct polygynous households.

Descent, inheritance, and succession usually follow the patrilineal principle. Patrilineages are apparently universal, but among the Arago, Egede, Idoma, Itsekiri, and Nupe they are not exogamous. On the other hand, exogamy extends not only to lineages but also to sibs in the Yoruba cluster and among the Anyang, Edo, and Yako. Kin groups are nearly always localized as clans—usually in wards or barrios but occasionally in whole settlements, e.g., among the Anyang and Arago. Kinship terminology follows a number of different patterns: descriptive among the Ibibio, Hawaiian in the Edo and Yoruba groups, Iroquois among the Yako, and Omaha among the Ibo and Igbira. The social systems of a few eastern tribes give internal evidence of possible former matrilineal descent. Among the Yako, for example, there are exogamous matrilineal as well as patrilineal sibs and lineages, and the rule of inheritance is matrilineal for movables though patrilineal for land. The adjacent Afikpo Ibo and some Ekoi also reveal double descent and mixed norms of inheritance, and the neighboring Mbembe, for whom matrilineal inheritance is reported, may well fall into the same category. Among the Kukuruku, descent depends upon the mode of marriage, being patrilineal when a bride-price has been paid for the mother but otherwise usually matrilineal.

Most Southern Nigerian tribes practice circumcision. Clitoridectomy is nearly as prevalent but is specifically denied for the Afo, Idoma, Ijaw, and Itsekiri tribes. Age-grades occur very widely but are not quite universal. Among the eastern Ibo, who may serve as an example, young men are organized into age-sets every third year in each village, where they engage in communal labor. Approximately every ninth year the three oldest sets, including men from thirty-five to forty-five years of age, are reconstituted as an age-grade, with police functions and the responsibility for executing the decisions of the village elders. After a period in this grade they are promoted to the first of three grades of "elders," who exercise political authority not only in the village but also in the district.

States of considerable magnitude occur among the Edo, Igala, Igbira, Ijaw, Itsekiri, Nupe, and all tribes of the Yoruba cluster, but elsewhere political integration does not transcend the level of the local community with a headman and a council of elders or of a small district with an age-grade organization or a petty paramount chief. Among the tribes of the Idoma and Nupe clusters succession to chiefly positions commonly alternates among two or more royal lines. Slavery is universal, but differentiated royal and noble classes appear only in conjunction with a complex political organization. Elsewhere status depends upon seniority and especially on the acquisition of titles. These are commonly organized in elaborate hierarchical systems, in which titles of different grades are achievable in a defined order through feasts and large payments to the holders of higher titles. Human sacrifice is reported for the Arago, Bunu, Edo, Ibo,

Fine Examples of Ife Yoruba Sculpture. (Courtesy of the American Museum of Natural History.)

Igala, Ijaw, and Yoruba; cannibalism for the Boki, Ekoi, Ibo, and some Igbira and Ijaw; headhunting for the Boki, Egede, Ekiti, Ekoi, Ibo, Idoma, Igala, Igbira, Ijaw, Kukuruku, Nge, Orri, and some Iyala and Nupe.

The larger states are headed by absolute monarchs, who maintain elaborate courts in capital towns and rule their countries through administrative hierarchies of provincial governors and district chiefs. The heads of the Ife, Igala, and Igbira states are divine kings, whose persons are sacred, who are hedged in by a multitude of taboos, and who exercise sacerdotal as well as secular functions. Rulers are served by palace officials, who are often eunuchs, and by titled ministers, who commonly form a council of state. A Queen-Mother often maintains a separate court and retinue, and in the Igbira state of Panda a Queen-Sister holds an exalted position and the ranking Queen-Consort exercises authority over all the women of the palace. The Edo state of Benin, which was founded in the twelfth century and which conquered and subjugated most of the neighboring peoples in the fifteenth and sixteenth centuries, may be described in some detail as representative of the more complex political institutions of the region.

The Edo king maintains a court and a large harem at the capital city of Benin. Here he concerns himself primarily with state rituals, cult activities, and judicial cases. A Queen-Mother and a Queen-Consort hold positions of great influence and prestige, as does the heir apparent, the ruler's eldest son. A hierarchical administrative organization assures the support of the state apparatus by levying *corvée* labor and collecting tribute semiannually in palm oil, livestock, and agricultural produce.

These sources of revenue are augmented by court fines, trade monopolies, fees received from prospective titleholders, and the booty obtained in war. Routine decisions are made by a supreme council of seven ranking ministers, including the heir apparent and the hereditary governors of the six major provinces. The latter also have specialized functions, e.g., as chief priest, commander in chief of the army, and keeper of the royal shrines. For decisions of greater moment they are joined by eighteen town chiefs and twenty-nine palace chiefs to form a grand council. All but one official in each of the latter categories hold their offices by appointment —as territorial administrators in the one case and as functionaries of the royal household in the other. Below them stand the holders of titles of numerous subsidiary orders, each of whom has obtained his original appointment and each promotion by the payment of generous fees.

Selected Bibliography

Ajisafe, A. K. *The Laws and Customs of the Yoruba People.* London, 1924. [Egba].
Ardener, E. W. The Kinship Terminology of a Group of Southern Ibo. *Africa,* 24:85–99. 1954.
Armstrong, R. G. The Igala; the Idoma-speaking Peoples. *Peoples of the Niger-Benue Confluence,* ed. D. Forde, pp. 77–155. London, 1955.
Asmis, G. Die Stammesrechte des Bezirks Atakpame. *ZVR,* 25:67–130. 1911. [Ana].
Audric, M. F. Coutumes Nago et Djèdj. *PCEHS,* ser. A, 10:475–530. 1939. [Egba].
Bascom, W. R. The Principle of Seniority in the Social Structure of the Yoruba. *AA,* 44:37–46. 1942. [Ife].
Basden, C. T. *Niger Ibos.* London, 1938.
Bradbury, R. E. *The Benin Kingdom and the Edo-speaking Peoples.* London, 1957.
Brown, P. The Igbira. *Peoples of the Niger-Benue Confluence,* ed. D. Forde, pp. 53–74. London, 1955.
Butcher, H. L. M. Some Aspects of the *Otu* System of the Isa Sub-Tribes of the Edo People. *Africa,* 8:149–162. 1935.
Byström, K. Notes on the Ekparabong Clan. *Orientalia Suecana,* 3:3–26. Uppsala, 1954. [Ekoi].
Clifford, M. A Nigerian Chiefdom. *JRAI,* 66:393–436. [Igala].
Forde, C. D. Land and Labour in a Cross River Village. *GJ,* 90:24–51. 1937. [Yako].
———. Fission and Accretion in the Patrilineal Clans of a Semi-Bantu Community. *JRAI,* 68:311–338. 1938. [Yako].
———. Government in Umor. *Africa,* 12:129–162. 1939. [Yako].
———. Kinship in Umor. *AA,* 41:523–553. 1939. [Yako].
———. Marriage and the Family among the Yakö. *MSA,* 5:1–121. 1941.
———. Ward Organization among the Yakö. *Africa,* 20:267–289. 1950.
———. Double Descent among the Yakö. *ASKM,* pp. 285–332. 1950.
———. *Yoruba-speaking Peoples of South-Western Nigeria.* London, 1950.
———. The Nupe. *Peoples of the Niger-Benue Confluence,* ed. D. Forde, pp. 17–52. London, 1955.
Forde, C. D., and G. I. Jones. *The Ibo and Ibibio-speaking Peoples.* London, 1950.
Granville, R. K., and F. N. Granville. Notes on the Jekris, Sobos and Ijos. *JRAI,* 28:104–126. 1898. [Edo, Ijaw, and Itsekiri].
Green, M. M. *Ibo Village Affairs.* London, 1947.

Lloyd, P. C. The Yoruba Lineage. *Africa*, 25:235–251. 1955.

———. *The Itsekiri*. London, 1957.

Mansfeld, A. *Urwald-Dokumente*. Berlin, 1908. [Anyang, Boki, and Ekoi].

Meek, C. K. *Law and Authority in a Nigerian Tribe*. London, 1934. [Ibo].

Nadel, S. F. The Kede. *APS*, pp. 165–195. 1940. [Nupe].

———. *A Black Byzantium*. London, 1942. [Nupe].

Odgers, C. N. F. The Migili Tribe. Unpublished ms. [Gili].

Ottenberg, S. Stability and Change in the Afikpo Family and Lineage Systems. Unpublished ms. [Ibo].

Partridge, C. *Cross River Natives*. London, 1905. [Mbembe].

Roth, H. L. *Great Benin*. Halifax, 1903. [Edo].

Ruel, M. J. The Family Structure of Banyang Society. *Proceedings of the Third Annual Conference of the West African Institute of Social and Economic Research*, pp. 66–70. 1956. [Anyang].

Schuster, F. Die soziale Verhältnisse des Banjange-Stammes. *Anthropos*, 9:948–955. 1914. [Anyang].

Schwab, W. B. Kinship and Lineage among the Yoruba. *Africa*, 25:352–374. 1955.

Seton, R. S. The Igala Tribe. *JAS*, 29:42–52, 149–163. 1929–1930.

Simmons, D. C. The Influence of Various Christian Sects upon an Indigenous African Society. Unpublished ms. [Ibibio].

Staschewski, F. Die Banjangi. *BA, Beihefte*, 8:1–66. 1917. [Anyang].

Talbot, D. A. *Woman's Mysteries of a Primitive People*. London, 1915. [Ibibio].

Talbot, P. A. *In the Shadow of the Bush*. London, 1912. [Ekoi].

———. *Life in Southern Nigeria*. London, 1923. [Ibibio].

———. *The Peoples of Southern Nigeria*. 4 vols. London, 1926.

———. *Tribes of the Niger Delta*. London, 1932. [Ijaw].

Tepowa, A. A Short History of Brass and Its People. *JAS*, 7:32–88. 1908. [Ijaw].

Thomas, N. W. *Anthropological Report on the Edo-speaking Peoples*. 2 vols. London, 1910.

———. *Anthropological Report on the Ibo-speaking Peoples*. 6 vols. London, 1913–1914.

Tschudi, J. Aus dem sozialen Leben der Afo. *BA*, 29:147–171. 1956.

Ward, E. Marriage among the Yoruba. *Catholic University of America Anthropological Series*, 4:1–55. Washington, 1937. [Ekiti].

Welch, T. W. The Isoko Tribe. *Africa*, 7:160–173. 1934.

Wilson-Haffenden, J. R. Ethnological Notes on the Kwottos. *JAS*, 26:368–379; 27:24–46, 142–154, 281–286, 380–393. 1927–1928. [Igbira].

———. *The Red Men of Nigeria*. London, 1930. [Igbira].

32

Twi

If the reader compares Maps 4 and 13, he will observe that the zone of tropical rainforest along the Guinea coast is interrupted for a stretch at the western border of the Southern Nigerian province. The break marks the beginning of another province, which extends westward across southern Dahomey, Togo, and Ghana to the eastern Ivory Coast. It is inhabited by kindred Negro peoples speaking languages of the Twi branch of the Kwa subfamily of the Nigritic stock. The newly independent state of Ghana, which occupies the heart of the province, has adopted the name of the old Mande empire discussed in Chapter 11, but no relationship whatsoever exists between the two. Despite attempts to invent a connection through a misreading of legendary evidence, the inhabitants of the ancient and modern states of Ghana belong to separate branches of the Negro stock which differ markedly both in culture and in language.

Because of the geographical difference noted above, the original Sudanic agricultural complex may have become somewhat more firmly established in the Twi province than in the Southern Nigerian province. Akee, ambary, cotton, cow peas, earth peas, fluted pumpkins, gourds, Guinea yams, millet, oil palms, okra, roselle, sesame, sorghum, and yergan are all grown today in at least certain sections of the province. But only on the northern fringe, particularly in the hill region of central Togo, do they retain a significant position in the agricultural economy. Elsewhere they have been in very large measure replaced by Malaysian plants, especially yams and taro, which have wrought a revolution comparable to that already noted for the Southern Nigerians.

Culturally and linguistically the Twi peoples fall into four major clusters, under which their component tribes are classified below.

EWE CLUSTER

Several populous nations, who exhibit a considerable degree of cultural homogeneity, inhabit the eastern part of the province, mainly in coastal Dahomey and Togo.

1. Adangme (Adampa), embracing the Ada, Kpone, Krobo, Ningo, Osuduku, Prampram, and Shai. Together with the adjacent Ga, they probably number at least 200,000.
2. Ewe (Eibe, Ephe, Krepe), embracing the Anglo, Glidyi, Ho, and numerous other subtribes. They number about 700,000.

3. Fon (Dahomeans, Fonnu), with the Adja, Agonglin, Aizo (Aizangbe, Whydah), Djedj, Hwelanu, Mahi (Maxi), and Watyi (Wachi). Together with the Gun, they number nearly a million.
4. Ga (Gan), with the Awutu (Afutu, Ofutu), Gomwa (Domwa), and Gwan (Akripon).
5. Gun (Egun, Goun, Popo), with the Tofinu and Wemenu.
6. Popo, embracing the Ge (Anecho, Gen, Mina), Hula (Pla), and Peda. They number about 70,000.

CENTRAL TOGO CLUSTER

In the highlands of Central Togo reside a number of so-called "splinter tribes" that appear to have been driven into the region by the expansion of more vigorous neighboring peoples like the Ashanti, Dagomba, Fon, and Yoruba. In many respects their cultures are transitional toward those of the Voltaic peoples who adjoin them on the north.

7. Adele (Adeli, Bedere), with the Delo and Lolo. They number about 5,000.
8. Akposo (Kposo), embracing the Litime, Otadi, and Sodo. They number about 30,000.
9. Atyuti (Atjuti, Atyode), with the Anyana (Agnagan) and Chambuli (Bassen, Tchumbuli). They number a few thousand.
10. Avatime (Afatime, Kedemane, Siya), with the Logba, Nyangbo (Nyankpo), and Tafi (Trugbo). They number a few thousand.
11. Basila (Akpenu, Baseda, Windjinwindjin), with the detached Bazanche (Podo). They number a few thousand.
12. Buem (Balemi, Boem, Bwenum, Lafana, Lefana), with the Ahlo (Achlo, Bogon, Ogo), Akpafu (Lolobi, Matuka, Siwu), Boro, Likpe (Bakpele), and Santrokofi. They number at least 10,000.
13. Kebu (Akabu, Akebu, Ekbebe, Kabu). They number about 15,000.
14. Krachi (Kratyi), with the Basa (Ayesegn), Cangborong (Nchumbulung, Nchumuru, Tchangbore, Tchimboro), Chimboro (Agnamkpase), Kunya (Ahenklo, Nkogna, Nkunya), and Nawuri (Nawuli, Nawura, Nkatshina). They are akin to the Guang of the Akan cluster and probably number at least 20,000.
15. Tribu (Ntribu). This intrusive tribe, numbering a few thousand, belongs to the Tem branch of the Voltaic linguistic subfamily.

AKAN CLUSTER

About two-thirds of the entire Twi province is occupied by peoples of the Akan linguistic subdivision, who likewise exhibit marked cultural uniformity.

16. Akyem, with the Akwamu, Akwapim, and Kwahu (Akwahu). They number about 65,000.
17. Anyi (Agni), embracing the Arichin, Asaye (Sadqi), Betye (Bettie), Binye (Ano, Bini), Bonda (Bonai, Bonna, Bouanda), Brisa (Aowin, Brossa, Brussa), Buresya, Dadye (Asikaso, Asuamara, Diabe), Kumwe, Moro (Morunu), Ndenye (Indenie), Sanwi (Brofi, Samvign), Sefwi, and Sika. They number about 100,000.
18. Ashanti (Asante), with the Ahanta, Asen-Twifo, and Wasa. They number over 700,000.

19. Attie (Akye), embracing the Bodde, Kuroba (Krobu), and Nedde. They number about 55,000.
20. Baule (Baoule), with the Agbegnyau, Ayahu, Bomofwe, Ndamefwe, Ngannufwe, and Wure. They number about 400,000.
21. Brong (Abron). They number in excess of 75,000.
22. Fanti (Fante). They number at least 200,000, and some estimates run much higher.
23. Guang (Bandja, Gbandja, Gibya, Gonya, Gwan, Gwanya, Ngbanye). They number about 50,000 and have been Islamized to some extent.

LAGOON CLUSTER

Along the lagoons which line the southern shores of the Ivory Coast, and in the hinterland immediately behind them, reside a number of small groups that depend for subsistence very largely upon fishing but otherwise affiliate culturally with the tribes of the Akan cluster.

24. Abe (Abbe, Abi, Aby). They number about 30,000.
25. Ajukru (Adioukrou, Agyukru, Burburi, Ogykru). They number about 27,000 including the Aizi, an intrusive Kru people.
26. Alagya (Aladia, Alladians, Aragya, Jackjack). They number about 5,000.
27. Ari (Abidji, Adidji). They number about 10,000.
28. Assini (Issinese, Issynois), embracing the Abure (Akapless, Asoko, Essouma, Esuma), Afema, Evalue (Sahue), and Nzima (Amanaya, Apollonians, Zema). They number about 12,000.
29. Avikam (Avekwom, Brignan, Brinya, Gbanda, Kwakwa). They number about 5,000.
30. Ebrie (Gyuman, Kyama, Tyaman), with the kindred Mbato (Agwa, Goua, Gwa, Gwabyo). They number about 16,000.
31. Mekyibo (Byetri, Ewoutire, Ewutile, Vetere, Vitre, Vyetre). They number about 4,000.

Hunting and gathering contribute little to the food supply, but the Ga, the Gun, and all the Lagoon tribes except the Abe and Ari depend heavily upon fishing. The remaining peoples of the province live primarily by agriculture, with shifting hoe cultivation and fallowing. For most of them yams are the staple crop, but bananas and taro are also widely cultivated, and assume first place among the Anyi and Assini. The Sudanic plants, as previously noted, retain a significant position only in the Central Togo cluster, and even here they rarely attain the status of staples. Hyacinth beans and pigeon peas have been adopted from the Indian complex, and rice, though only recently introduced, has come to occupy a prominent place in the economy of the Buem. Through the slave trade the Twi have acquired a number of American crops—notably maize, manioc, peanuts, peppers, squash, sweet potatoes, and tomatoes— and cacao ranks with the indigenous oil palm as a major modern commercial resource. Although introductions from the New World clearly overshadow the original Sudanic cultigens, they have not succeeded in supplanting the Malaysian food plants, except among the Adele and Krachi, where manioc and maize, respectively, have become leading crops.

The Twi peoples keep sheep, goats, dogs, chickens, and smaller numbers of pigs, cats, guinea fowl, ducks, and pigeons. Nearly all possess a few cattle, though they never milk them, and horses appear sporadically in the Central Togo and Ewe clusters. Regular markets, normally held every fourth day in all towns and most villages, facilitate the distribution of agricultural produce, the products of local handicraft industries, and articles traded between the north and south. In general, the men hunt, clear land, and do most of the fishing; women engage in petty trade; and both sexes participate in agricultural labor.

Except for the Anyi and some Adele and Guang, who live in neighborhoods of dispersed homesteads, the Twi peoples occupy compact villages and towns, commonly divided into quarters, or wards, and into family compounds. The latter are sometimes aligned on either side of a single village street, as among the Attie, Baule, and Ebrie, but more commonly along narrow paths radiating from a central market place. Dwellings conform in the main to the type prevalent throughout the Guinea coast—rectangular houses with thatched gable or shed roofs and walls of reeds or of wattle and daub, arranged around a quadrangular interior courtyard. In the Lagoon cluster they are sometimes elevated on piles. The Guang and most tribes of the Central Togo cluster differ from the rest of the area in building cone-cylinder huts of the Sudanic type. The Buem and some Akposo and Krachi, however, construct rectangular dwellings with mud walls and flat roofs like those of some adjacent Voltaic peoples.

Marriage normally entails the payment of a substantial bride-price in livestock, cowrie shells, or other valuables; and the Ajukru, Attie, Brong, and the tribes of the Ewe cluster require premarital bride-service as well. Nearly all groups prefer cross-cousin unions, and some of them even forego the bride-price in such cases. The Adangme, Popo, and some Ga differ from the overwhelming majority in permitting marriages between parallel cousins. General polygyny prevails throughout the area, but only the Fon allow it in the sororal form. The first wife enjoys a preferred status, but each co-wife has a hut or apartment of her own and the husband spends an equal period with each in rotation. A preference for local endogamy appears to be universal.

Kin-group organization reveals significant regional variations. The tribes of the Central Togo cluster adhere to the patrilocal rule of residence and to the patrilineal rule in descent, inheritance, and succession. The Akposo, Atyuti, and Kebu, at least, have totemic patrisibs, and lineages appear to be localized as clans. The tribes of the Ewe cluster exhibit structures of essentially the same type. All of them have localized patrilineages, which are exogamous except among the Adangme, Ga, and Popo, and with the same three exceptions lineages are aggregated in noncorporate patrisibs. The Ewe and Ga use cousin terminology of the Hawaiian type, and the

Fon follow the descriptive pattern. Despite the patrilocal and patrilineal character of the present social systems of the Ewe peoples, these yield faint intimations of possible former matrilineal descent. Thus in certain subtribes of the Ewe, e.g., the Anglo and Glidyi, the eldest sister's eldest son inherits a man's movable property although his land and social status descend to his eldest son. The Fon are noted for a bewildering array of alternative modes of marriage, and some of these, which do not involve a bride-price, result in the affiliation of the children with the mother's rather than the father's lineage.

In all societies of the Akan and Lagoon clusters matrilineal descent, inheritance, and succession become, not a hypothesis, but a present reality. The Ashanti, Fanti, and perhaps other tribes, however, also possess partially exogamous patrilineages and are thus characterized by double descent. Cousin terminology follows the descriptive pattern among the Fanti and Guang, the Crow pattern among the Akyem and, with complications, the Ashanti. Variable residence rules produce an extraordinary complexity in household composition. Only for the Ashanti do we possess descriptive data sufficiently accurate and detailed to make possible a satisfactory analysis.

Marriage among the Ashanti begins with duolocal residence. The young wife continues to live for several years with her own parents and does not remove to her husband's home until about the time when her older children begin to require a father's attention. When his first wife joins him, a man may still be living in his father's compound, which consequently assumes the structure of a patrilocal extended family. More commonly, however, he will already have shifted to the home of a maternal uncle and, if not, will usually do so within a few years. This change in residence produces an avunculocal extended family. Unless he is his uncle's heir, a man, as soon as he has means to afford it, builds a new home, where he establishes his mother and perhaps some of his younger siblings (but not his father), and removes there with his own family. When his mother dies, he succeeds her as head of the household and is gradually joined by his sisters' sons as his own sons leave him to live with their uncles. As an old man, consequently, he again finds himself a member of an avunculocal extended family, this time as its head and not as a dependent.

Slavery and debt slavery prevail throughout the area, and the Attie have a class of hereditary serfs, but endogamous castes are unknown and a special class of nobles occurs only in the societies with complex political institutions. Some of the societies of the Lagoon cluster, e.g., the Ajukru and Ebrie, possess age-grade systems of considerable complexity. The Twi peoples do not practice clitoridectomy, and only the Guang and the tribes of the Ewe cluster subject boys to circumcision. Human sacrifice is confined to the larger societies of the Akan and Ewe clusters, but cannibalism and headhunting are completely absent.

A headman and a council of elders, usually representing the local lineages, handle public affairs within the village. Districts of varying size are politically organized under petty paramount chiefs, who commonly exercise sacerdotal as well as secular functions, and the Assini, Fon, and most societies of the Akan cluster have evolved complex states with kings, hierarchical administrative organizations, and courts with titled ministers and specialized palace officials. The Fon kingdom of Dahomey, which conquered a series of petty coastal states in the early eighteenth century and thereafter prospered extraordinarily for a century and a half through a virtual monopoly of all external trade on the Slave Coast, merits a summary description.

The King of Dahomey was an absolute monarch, ruling the country through an administrative hierarchy of provincial governors, district chiefs, and local headmen, who were responsible for tax collections. At the capital town of Abomey he maintained an elaborate court, where all who approached his person had to prostrate themselves and throw dust on their heads. One of his sons, not necessarily the eldest, held the honored position of heir apparent, but to guard against insurrection, no other kinsman was allowed to hold any post of power or influence. The royal princes and princesses led idle and profligate lives. The leading ministers at court, all appointive officials and commoners, included the Minga, who was commander in chief of the army, prime minister, and chief executioner; the Meu, chief of protocol, collector of taxes, and guardian of the royal princes and princesses; the Yovoga, governor of the port of Whydah and a sort of foreign minister, charged with all dealings with Europeans; the Adjaho, supervisor of the palace and head of the secret police and espionage systems; the Soga, commander of cavalry and overseer of the king's slaves; the Tokpo, minister of the interior and supervisor of markets and agriculture; the Benazo, royal treasurer and chief commissary; and the Totonu, or chief eunuch, who had charge of the king's harem and personal attendants.

Each official had a deputy and a female counterpart called his "mother," who took precedence over him at court. The king, similarly, was technically outranked by a Queen-Mother. The power of the state and the steady flow of lucrative slaves were maintained by a large standing army, whose shock troops were the redoubtable Amazons, a corps of 2,500 female warriors. Once a year the royal lineage paid tribute to its ancestors in the Annual Custom, an extravagant ceremony culminating in the sacrifice of about a hundred war captives and slaves, but even this was dwarfed by the sanguinary Grand Custom which followed the death of a ruler.

Selected Bibliography

Asmis, G. Die Stammesrechte des Bezirks Atakpame. *ZVR*, 25:67–130. 1911. [Akposo].
——. Die Stammesrechte der Bezirke Misahöhe, Anecho und Lome-Land. *ZVR*, 26:1–133. 1911. [Buem, Ewe, Krachi, and Popo].
Audric, F. Coutumes Aïzo, Fon, Nago. *PCEHS*, ser. A, 10:455–473. 1939.
Beckett, W. H. Akokoaso. *MSA*, 10:1–95. 1944. [Akyem].
Bohannan, L. Dahomean Marriage. *Africa*, 19:273–287. 1949. [Fon].
Bouscayrol, R. Notes sur le peuple Ébrie. *BIFAN*, 11:382–408. 1949.
Burton, R. F. *A Mission to Gelele, King of Dahome*. 2 vols. London, 1864. [Fon].
Busia, K. A. *The Position of the Chief in the Modern Political System of Ashanti*. London, 1951.
Christensen, J. B. *Double Descent among the Fanti*. New Haven, 1954.
Clozel, F. J., and R. Villamur. *Les coutumes indigènes de la Côte d'Ivoire*. Paris, 1902. [Ajukru, Anyi, Avikam, Baule, and Brong].
Conradt, L. Das Hinterland der deutschen Kolonie Togo. *PM*, 42:11–20, 29–33. 1896. [Adele].
Crosson. L'ethnographie de la Côte d'Ivoire. *RCD*, 10:93–99, 111–118. 1900. [Attie].
Danquah, J. B. *Akan Laws and Customs*. London, 1928.
Delafosse, M. Les Agni. *Anthropologie*, 4:402–445. 1893. [Baule].
Ffoulkes, A. The Fanti Family System. *JAS*, 7:394–409. 1908.
——. Fanti Marriage Customs. *JAS*, 8:31–48. 1909.
Field, M. J. *Social Organization of the Ga People*. London, 1940.
——. *Akim Kotoku*. London, 1949. [Akyem].
Fortes, M. Time and Social Structure: An Ashanti Case Study. *SS*, pp. 54–84. 1949.
——. Kinship and Marriage among the Ashanti. *ASKM*, pp. 252–284. 1950.
Grivot, R. Le cercle de Lahou. *BIFAN*, 4:1–154. 1942. [Avikam].
Herskovits, M. J. *Dahomey*. 2 vols. New York, 1938. [Fon].
Hinderling, P. Notizen von den Togo-Restvölker. *Tribus: Jahrbuch des Linden-Museums*, pp. 361–378. Stuttgart, 1952–1953. [Buem].
Klose, H. *Togo unter deutscher Flagge*. Berlin, 1899. [Ewe].
Köbben, A. J. L'héritage chez les Agni. *Africa*, 24:359–363. 1954.
——. Le planteur noir. *Études Éburnéennes*, 5:7–190. 1956. [Anyi].
Labouret, H. Notes contributives à l'étude du peuple Baoulé. *RES*, 5:83–91, 181–194. 1914.
Lavergne de Tressan, M. de. Inventaire linguistique de l'Afrique Occidentale Française et du Togo. *MIFAN*, 2:1–241. 1953.
Le Herissé, A. *L'ancien royaume du Dahomey*. Paris, 1911. [Fon].
Loyer, G. Abstract of a Voyage to Issini on the Gold Coast. *New General Collection of Voyages and Travels*, ed. T. Astley, 2:417–445. London, 1745. [Assini].
Lystad, R. A. *The Ashanti*. New Brunswick, 1958.
Manoukian, M. *Akan and Ga-Adangme Peoples of the Gold Coast*. London, 1950.
——. *The Ewe-speaking People of Togoland and the Gold Coast*. London, 1952.
Mead, M. A Twi Relationship System. *JRAI*, 67:297–304. 1937. [Akyem].
Ménalque, M. *Coutumes civiles des Baoulés*. Paris, 1933.
Mouezy, R. *Assinie et le royaume de Krinjabo*. Paris, 1942.
Plehn, R. *Beiträge zur Völkerkunde des Togogebietes*. Halle, 1898. [Akposo and Buem].
Quénum, M. Au pays des Fons. *BCEHS*, 18:141–335. 1935.
Rattray, R. S. *Ashanti*. Oxford, 1923.

Rattray, R. S. *Ashanti Law and Constitution*. Oxford, 1929.
Reichenbach, J. C. Étude sur le royaume d'Assinie. *BGS*, ser. 7, 11:310–349. 1890.
Renaud and Akindélé. La collectivité chez les Goun. *PCEHS*, ser. A, 10:531–556. 1939.
Sarbah, J. M. *Fanti Customary Laws*. London, 1897.
Spieth, J. *Die Ewe-Stämme*. Berlin, 1906.
Tauxier, L. *Le noir de Bondoukou*. Paris, 1921. [Brong].
——. *Religion, moeurs et coutumes des Agnis*. Paris, 1932.
Vincenti, J. Coutumes Attié. *BCEHS*, 5:58–76. 1922.
Westermann, D. *Die Glidyi-Ewe in Togo*. Berlin, 1935.
Wolf, F. Beitrag zur Ethnographie der Fō-Neger in Togo. *Anthropos*, 7:81–94, 296–308. 1912. [Fon].

33

Kru and Peripheral Mande

West of the Twi, in the southwestern Ivory Coast and in Liberia and Sierra Leone, lies a detached area of tropical rainforest (see Map 4). Its inhabitants, who exhibit markedly less complex cultures than their neighbors, speak languages of three distinct subfamilies of the Nigritic stock but nevertheless reveal an appreciable measure of cultural homogeneity. A solid block of tribes in the southeast, both along the coast and in the hinterland, belong to the Kru branch of the Kwa linguistic subfamily. Northwest of them, in Sierra Leone and adjacent Liberia, live six scattered tribes of the Atlantic subfamily, akin to the Senegambians farther north. These two groups presumably represent the older inhabitants of the province. A third group, belonging to the Mande linguistic subfamily, has invaded the coastal region from the interior, interpenetrating and largely replacing the Atlantic tribes and, to a lesser extent, also pressing back the Kru peoples. Since they exhibit none of the cultural complexity of the Nuclear Mande, these Peripheral Mande, as we shall call them, probably left the Niger Basin prior to the rise of the great Malinke empire and civilization of Mali. We may reasonably assume that their original expansion into the region was stimulated by the development of Sudanic agriculture among the Mande peoples of the interior, enabling some of them to spread toward the coast and to displace the indigenous hunting, fishing, and gathering peoples in places suited to the cultivation of the Sudanic crops. Once isolated in the tropical-forest zone, they remained relatively unaffected by subsequent cultural advances in the western Sudan.

The present cultural homogeneity has presumably resulted from inter-tribal contacts and borrowing within the area. Since the original cultural differences among the three linguistic groups have become very much blurred, the following threefold classification of tribes must not be interpreted as a division into distinct cultural clusters.

KRU TRIBES

1. Bakwe (Kroumen), with the Abriwi (Abrignon, Abrinyo), Bakone, Bapo, Bokwe (Bokre, Irapwe, Iribue), Budukwa, Debue, Digbue, Dioro, Giti, Grippuo, Guagui (Gigeagi), Haulo, Hena, Hwine (Bodo, Houne, Hwanne), Inemu, Kapo (Irecapo, Kopo), Nedio, Nene, Nigabani, Nigbi, Nozo, Obli, Pia (Omelokue, Pie, Pya), Plawi (Blapo, Plapo), Prufa, Tabetuo, Tahu, Toagi, Toyo (Tuy), Tuopo, Ubi, Urepo (Orepue), Uroko (Aulopo), and Yabue. They number about 20,000.
2. Bassa (Basa, Basso, Gbasa), with the kindred De (Dewoi, Do), Givi (Kwia, Queah), Klepo, and Sikon (Gbe).
3. Bete, with the Bobwa (Banua, Ouaga, Waga), Kuya (Dakuya, Kouya), Kwadya (Kwa, Kwadre), Neyo (Neyaux, Niyo), Niabua (Nyabwa), Sokwele (Sokya), and other small related tribes. They number about 150,000.
4. Dida (Dyida, Kuka), with the Ega (Dye, Egwa), Ekopo (Kwaya, Zegbe), Godye, and Newole. They number about 80,000.
5. Grebo (Gweabo, Kre, Krebo, Trebo), with the Jabo (Dyabo) and Tewi (Tepo).
6. Kran (Bush Kru, Karan, Kra), with the Padebu (Bush Grebo) and Tie (Gien, Kien). They number about 15,000.
7. Kru (Crau, Krao, Krawi, Nana). Together with the closely related Bassa, Grebo, and Sapo, they probably number in the neighborhood of a million.
8. Sapo (Pahn, Sapahn).
9. Wobe (Ouobe). They number about 30,000.

ATLANTIC TRIBES

10. Bulom (Bolom, Bulem, Bullom). They number about 20,000 and are strongly acculturated to the Temne.
11. Gola. They number about 100,000 and are strongly acculturated to the Mende.
12. Kissi (Ghizi, Gissi, Kisi). They number about 200,000.
13. Limba. They number about 175,000.
14. Sherbro (Mampua), with the kindred Krim. They number about 200,000.
15. Temne (Timne). They number about 525,000.

MANDE TRIBES

16. Dan (Da), with the kindred Gio (Grio, Gyo, Nyo), Tura (Toura, Wen), and Yafuba (Diaboula, Diafoba, Yabouba, Yakuba). They number about 150,000.
17. Gagu (Gagou, Gban). They number about 15,000.
18. Gbande (Gbassi), with the kindred Belle (Bere), Gbundi (Kimbuzi), and Weima. They number about 30,000.
19. Guro (Gouro, Gwio, Kwendre, Kweni, Lo), with the kindred Mwa (Mono) and Nwan. They number about 115,000.
20. Kono (Kolo, Konnoh). They number about 80,000.
21. Kpelle (Gbese, Gerse, Kpese, Pessy). They number about 250,000.

22. Loko (Landro, Lokko). They number about 80,000.
23. Mende (Kossa, Mendi), embracing the Ko (Comende, Kolomende), Kpa (Gbamende), and Sewa. They number nearly a million.
24. Ngere (Guere, Guerze, Nguerze), embracing the Boo, Doo, Fleo (Grio), Ge (Gbe), Mano (Mah, Mana), Niadrubu, Niao, Zague, and Zahon. They number about 100,000.
25. Toma (Busy, Buzi, Loma). They number about 150,000.
26. Vai (Gallina, Vei). They number about 200,000.

All the tribes of the province are Negroid, and most are pagan, although a majority of the Vai and very small minorities in several other tribes have accepted Islam. The Vai share with the Mum of the Cameroon highlands the distinction of having invented independently their own system of writing. In 1848 an American officer discovered among them an original syllabary with 226 characters, which he estimated as perhaps two decades old at that time.

The peoples of the province subsist today primarily by agriculture, with shifting swidden cultivation and fallowing. Since they cultivate small quantities of cotton, fonio, okra, millet, sesame, sorghum, and yergan, we may assume that they acquired the Sudanic complex at an early date from the Nuclear Mande in the interior. From the relative unimportance of these crops, however, we must conclude that they were not well adapted to the tropical-forest environment and thus perhaps did not seriously modify the earlier primary dependence on hunting, fishing, and gathering. The transition to a truly sedentary agricultural mode of life presumably did not occur until their eastern neighbors, the Akan peoples of the Twi province, transmitted to them the Malaysian banana, taro, and yam at some relatively early period in the Christian era. All three plants still occupy very important places in the economy, each outranking any cultigen of Sudanic origin.

It is, however, none of these three but a fourth Malaysian crop, rice, which today holds the position of the outstanding staple of the area. This arrived, not from the east, but from the northwest, having been introduced into West Africa by the Arabs at a date not later than A.D. 1500, when historical documents first mention it on the Niger. On becoming established in the Senegambian province, rice gradually diffused southward to the Peripheral Mande and the Kru. Its spread still continues, for it did not reach the Guro until the beginning of the present century and has not yet been adopted by the Gagu, whose staples are bananas and taro. Nearly everywhere else in the province, however, it now constitutes the mainstay of the diet. Only American plants of still more recent introduction rival the Malaysian crops in importance, especially lima beans, maize, malanga, manioc, peanuts, and sweet potatoes. Of these, manioc has now achieved second place in the local roster of cultivated plants, next to rice, and maize the fifth position, behind bananas and yams.

Fishing provides a substantial supplement to the food supply, except among a few inland tribes. The inhabitants also do some hunting and considerable gathering, especially of kola and oil-palm nuts. Trade is not highly developed, and regular markets are reported only for the Dan, Gbande, Kissi, northern Kpelle, Kran, Toma, and the Mano subtribe of the Ngere. Nevertheless, a unique type of currency, consisting of bundles of T-shaped pieces of forged iron, finds acceptance over much of the region. All tribes keep at least a few cattle, of a long-horned humpless breed, but use them mainly for sacrifices and marriage payments and never milk them. Other domestic animals of general prevalence include goats, sheep, dogs (often eaten), chickens, Muscovy ducks, and guinea fowl, but not horses, donkeys, pigs, or bees. Men hunt, harvest palm and kola nuts, and clear the land, but women perform the bulk of other agricultural work. Both sexes fish, but usually by different techniques. Only men, for example, engage in deep-sea fishing.

House types reveal a basic cleavage along linguistic lines. Kru tribes tend to construct rectangular dwellings with thatched gable roofs and walls of split raffia midriffs or of wattle and daub, whereas Atlantic and Mande tribes reveal a general preference for round huts with conical thatched roofs and cylindrical walls of mud, wattle, or wood. Borrowings, however, have occurred in both directions. Thus some Gagu, Guro, Kpelle, Sherbro, and Vai build rectangular houses, and all Wobe, most Kran, and some Bakwe, Grebo, and Kru have adopted the cone-cylinder hut. In either case, the dwellings are usually grouped in family compounds, and these are aggregated in small compact villages clustered around a central plaza with a council house and surrounded by a protective wall or palisade. In the Ivory Coast, however, compounds, palisades, and council houses tend to be absent. The Mende, Temne, and adjacent tribes have as their prevailing settlement pattern a large central village with outlying satellite hamlets.

Marriage regularly involves a bride-price, which, among the Kissi, Kpelle, and Mende, is commonly coupled with premarital bride-service. The Mende and a few of their immediate neighbors favor marriage with a mother's brother's daughter, but most groups forbid unions with any first cousin. Polygyny is general, but occurs only in the nonsororal form. The first wife is the chief wife, but the co-wives each have a separate hut, and the husband distributes his time equally among them. Preferential levirate appears to be universal. The household unit consists of a patrilocal extended family in most of the area, but it is an independent polygynous family among the Gbande, Kpelle, Ngere, Toma, and all tribes of the Kru group.

Residence is regularly patrilocal. Descent, inheritance, and succession follow the male line exclusively, with only the Sherbro revealing their ancient linguistic and cultural connection with the Senegambian peoples to the north by their retention, until very recently, of the matrilineal rule in all three respects. Most groups are organized into agamous patri-sibs and exogamous patrilineages, with the latter localized as clans in particular sections of each village. Not infrequently the village itself, or a small district, also constitutes a clan in a more tenuous sense. Kinship terminology of the Omaha type is reported for the Vai, of the descriptive type for the Limba, of the Eskimo type for the Temne, and of the Hawaiian type for the Kissi, Mende, and Sherbro.

Political authority on the local level is normally vested in a headman and a council of elders. The Bete, Dan, and Gagu lack any more complex type of integration, but all other tribes are organized under petty paramount chiefs over small districts. In the interior, the headman or district chief commonly has a special ritual relationship to the land, as among the neighboring Nuclear Mande and Voltaic peoples. Even in other regions he is usually responsible for the administration of the land, which is typically distributed among lineages or extended families and parceled out by them to individuals in heritable usufruct. Nowhere, apparently, does title to land carry with it the right of sale, gift, or lease.

All groups practice slavery and debt slavery and normally make a distinction between slaves obtained by purchase or by capture in war and those born within the family. The latter enjoy a superior status and cannot be sold. Otherwise social stratification is minimal. Endogamous castes are lacking, as are differentiated hereditary aristocracies. Among the Mende, however, the descendants of the original settlers of a district enjoy special prestige and constitute a sort of gentry. All tribes except the Gagu and Guro practice circumcision, but clitoridectomy is reported only for the Dan, Kissi, Kran, Mende, Ngere, Toma, and Vai. These mutilations usually occur in connection with elaborate initiation ceremonies at puberty, which involve special instruction in a "bush school" and result in admission to a secret society. Two such societies—one for males, called Poro, and another for females, known either as Sande or Bundu—occur widely throughout the area, though they are not specifically reported for certain tribes of the Ivory Coast. The Poro society often exercises a controlling influence in political life. The Dan, Kran, Ngere, Wobe, and some Bete formerly indulged in cannibalism.

Selected Bibliography

Aubert, M. Kisi Customs. *SLS*, 20:88–95. 1936.
Becker-Donner, E. Ueber zwei Kruvölkerstämme. *WBKL*, 6:71–108. 1944. [Kran].
Chevalier, A. Les massifs montagneux du nord-ouest de la Côte d'Ivoire. *Géographie*, 20:207–224. 1908. [Dan].

Clozel, F. J., and R. Villamur. *Les coutumes indigènes de la Côte d'Ivoire.* Paris, 1902. [Bakwe].

Coutouly, F. de. Quelques coutumes des Kroumen du Bas-Cavally. *BCEHS,* 3:79–98. 1920. [Bakwe].

Crosby, K. H. Polygamy in Mende Country. *Africa,* 10:249–264. 1937.

Delafosse, M. Les Vaï. *Anthropologie,* 10:129–150, 294–314. 1899.

Dunglas, E. Coutumes et moeurs des Bété. *PCEHS,* ser. A, 10:361–451. 1939.

Ellis, G. W. *Negro Culture in West Africa.* New York, 1914. [Vai].

Gamory-Dubourdeau, P. M. Notes sur les coutumes des Tomas. *BCEHS,* 9:288–350. 1926.

Genevray, J. Eléments d'une monographie d'une division administrative libérienne. *MIFAN,* 21:1–135. 1952. [Bassa].

Germann, P. *Die Völkerstämme im Norden von Liberia.* Leipzig, 1933. [Gbande and Kissi].

Hall, H. U. *The Sherbro of Sierra Leone.* Philadelphia, 1938.

Hallouin, J. Géographie humaine de la subdivision de Daloa. *BIFAN,* 9:18–55. 1947. [Bete].

Köbben, A. J. Le planteur noir. *Études Éburnéennes,* 5:7–190. 1956. [Bete].

Langley, E. R. The Temne. *SLS,* 22:64–80. 1939.

Little, K. L. *The Mende of Sierra Leone.* London, 1951.

McCulloch, M. *The Peoples of Sierra Leone Protectorate.* London, 1950.

Néel, H. Note sur deux peuplades de la frontière libérienne. *Anthropologie,* 24:445–475. 1913. [Kissi and Toma].

Paulme, D. *Les gens du riz.* Paris, 1954. [Kissi].

Poiret, J. Village kissien. *BCEHS,* 16:667–678. 1933. [Kissi].

Ronnefeldt, F. Die Heiratssitten der Vai. *ZE,* 67:317–321. 1935.

Schwab, G. Tribes of the Liberian Hinterland, ed. G. W. Harley. *PPM,* 31:1–526. 1947. [Gbande, Grebo, Kpelle, Kran, Ngere, Sapo, and Toma].

Tauxier, L. *Nègres Gouro et Gagou.* Paris, 1924.

Thomas, N. W. *Anthropological Report on Sierra Leone,* vol. 1. London, 1916. [Limba, Loko, Mende, Sherbro, Temne, and Vai].

Vendeix, M. Ethnographie du cercle de Man. *RETP,* 5:149–169, 287–294. 1924. [Dan and Wobe].

Viard, L. *Les Guérés.* Paris, 1934. [Ngere].

Westermann, D. *Die Kpelle.* Göttingen, 1921.

Wilson, J. L. *Western Africa.* New York, 1856. [Kru].

34

Senegambians

Northwest of the Peripheral Mande, along a narrow strip of the Atlantic seaboard extending northward to the border of the Berber-speaking Tasumsa of Mauritania, live a group of peoples whom we shall denote collectively as the Senegambians since the majority reside in Senegal and Gambia. Some, however, inhabit Portuguese Guinea and French Guinea, where the westward expansion of the Nuclear Mande has confined them to an even more restricted coastal zone and has enveloped one remnant group, the Tenda, in an interior pocket. All are Negroes, and all speak languages of the Atlantic subfamily of the Nigritic stock. They are consequently linguistic cousins to the six Atlantic tribes whom we found, in the preceding chapter, similarly submerged by the expanding Peripheral Mande. Their principal tribal divisions are listed and identified below.

1. Baga (Bago), embracing the Binari, Fore (Mbulunich), Kalum, Koba, Mandenyi, Manduri, Sitemu, and Sobane. They number about 45,000, of whom a few have been converted to Islam.
2. Balante (Ballante), with the Kunante. They number about 170,000.
3. Banyun (Bagnoun, Bainuk, Banhun), with the kindred Kassanga and Kobiana. They number about 10,000.
4. Biafada (Biafar, Bifra, Byafada). They number about 10,000.
5. Bijogo (Bidyago, Bijago, Bijuga, Bisago, Bissago). They occupy the Bijagos Archipelago and number about 20,000.
6. Diola (Dyola, Yola), embracing the Bayot (Adayamat), Felup (Ayamat, Fulup, Huluf, Kabil, Karon), Filham (Filhol, Fogny, Fulun), Her, and Jiwat (Djiwat). They number about 150,000.
7. Landuma (Landoma, Landouman), with the detached Tiapi (Tyapi). They number about 20,000.
8. Nalu (Nalou). They number about 10,000.
9. Pepel (Papel), with the Bram (Bola, Burama), Mandyako, and Mankanya (Mancagne). They number about 135,000.
10. Serer (Kegueme, Sarer), embracing the Non (Nono) and Sin (Sinsin). They number about 300,000.
11. Tenda, embracing the Badiaranke (Badian, Badyaranke, Udyade), Bassari (Basari, Biyan), Boeni (Tenda Boeni), Koniagi (Awunlen, Coniagui), and Mayo (Tenda Mayo). They number about 25,000, of whom the Boeni alone are Moslems.
12. Wolof (Djoloff, Jaloff, Jolof, Ouolof, Yallof), with the Lebu. They number about 850,000 and are Moslems.

At one time the Senegambians extended farther north into coastal Mauritania. Around the eleventh century, however, the Berbers, pressed

265

from the north by the Arabs, pushed the Wolof southward to near the mouth of the Senegal River, and the latter in turn partially displaced the Serer. The Tukulor of the middle Senegal, who were then politically dominant in the region, accepted Islam at that time and proselytized the Wolof. Several centuries elapsed, however, before the conversion of the latter was complete, and Islam has never penetrated the rest of the area to any appreciable extent. About 1350 the Wolof conquered the Tukulor and ruled a kingdom of some magnitude until around 1520. Though the Wolof never succumbed to the Malinke, the latter advanced deeply into Serer and Diola country. The Senegambians suffered further losses of territory with the occupation of Fouta Djalon by the Fulani and the westward advance of the Susu at the expense of the Baga. Despite these reverses, they still number almost 2 million.

Geographical conditions being much more favorable than in the coastal areas previously described, Sudanic agriculture penetrated the Senegambian territory effectively at an early date. The inland Tenda still preserve the full roster of Sudanic plants, but the coastal tribes today cultivate only cotton, cow peas, earth peas, gourds, millet, oil palms, okra, roselle, sesame, and sorghum. We cannot attribute their loss of status to the Malaysian bananas, taro, and yams, for the last two never spread this far north. The crop to which the Sudanic complex has yielded precedence is rice, which we have previously found as the staple also among the Kru and Peripheral Mande.

Historical records attest the cultivation of rice in the western Sudan in the fifteenth century, but it doubtless arrived considerably earlier, not by overland diffusion from East Africa but through the mediation of the Arabs. The Senegambians grow both the swamp and upland varieties of this cereal, using as their basic agricultural implement the spade, or foot-plow, rather than the usual African hoe and digging stick. Maize and manioc from the New World provide a significant supplement to rice and the Sudanic crops, and lesser borrowings include melons, peppers, squash, sweet potatoes, and tomatoes. As in North Africa, but in contrast to most other Negro areas of the continent, tree crops assume a position of considerable importance, notably bananas and coconuts from the Malaysian complex, mangoes from the Indian, papayas from the American, and limes and oranges from the Greco-Roman.

All tribes keep cattle, sheep, and goats, but only the Balante, Pepel, Serer, Wolof, and the Bayot subtribe of the Diola milk their animals. Dogs and chickens appear to be universal, but horses, donkeys, ducks, and bees are kept only sporadically. Of particular interest is the prominent place held by pigs in the animal husbandry of at least the Balante, Banyun, Biafada, Bijogo, Diola, and Pepel groups. Unfortunately our sources do not reveal whether these animals represent a recent introduction by the Portuguese or a survival, as among the Nuba and Prenilotes, of the ancient pig culture of North Africa, now largely obliterated through Islamic influence.

Except among the Tenda, fishing assumes an importance second only to agriculture. It is accompanied by the extensive use of shellfish, whose antiquity is evidenced by innumerable kitchen middens along the coast. Hunting holds a much less significant place in the economy, but there is considerable gathering of wild fruits and roots, berries, and kola, shea, and palm nuts. Trade is well developed in the north, and regular markets appear among the Diola, Pepel, Serer, and Wolof. Men hunt, fish from boats, clear new land, and tend cattle, horses, and donkeys, whereas women fish along the shore and in inland streams, collect shellfish, tend pigs, goats, sheep, and poultry, and do such milking as is practiced. Both sexes engage in agricultural work, but male participation tends to predominate in the north, female in the southern tribes. Gathering is done largely by men among the Baga, Banyun, and Bijogo, by women among the Balante, Tenda, and Wolof.

The Senegambians live in extended-family compounds, each consisting of a cluster of huts arranged, usually in a circle, around an open space and often surrounded by a fence or, in the north, by a hedge, wall, or palisade. Among the Baga, Biafada, Bijogo, Tenda, and Wolof the compounds adjoin one another to form compact villages, but elsewhere they are semidispersed with intervening gardens or plantations. The dwellings conform in general to the widespread cone-cylinder pattern with mud walls and thatched roofs, but local variations are marked. Thus walls are sometimes constructed of mats, plaited bamboo, sun-dried bricks, or stone rather than mud, and rectangular or elongated structures with pyramidal or hipped roofs appear among the Baga and Diola, some Banyun, Pepel, and Landuma, and a few Wolof.

Petty paramount chiefs exercise political authority over the Baga, Bijogo, Landuma, Nalu, Pepel, and Tenda, but the Biafada, Balante, Banyun, Diola, and some Serer recognize no government beyond the level of the local headmen and councils of elders. Complex states exist only among the Wolof and certain Serer whose dynasties appear to be of Wolof origin. Succession is matrilineal—normally by the next younger brother or, in default of such, by the eldest son of the deceased's eldest sister. The sources specifically attest this rule for the Landuma, Serer, and Tenda, and even for several states of the strongly Islamized Wolof, but suggest that succession is patrilineal among the Baga, Banyun, and Diola.

Comprehension of the complex political structures of the extreme north requires some preliminary understanding of the prevailing social stratification. The other tribes of the area either possess only a few slaves or lack them altogether. They have no endogamous castes—except for *griots*, or bards, among the Tenda—and in other respects they reveal an essentially egalitarian organization. The Serer and Wolof, however, reflect Islamic influence in an extraordinary multiplication of stratified statuses. The monarchical Serer, for example, clearly distinguish the following levels: (1) royalty; (2) a landed aristocracy of Malinke origin; (3) a seminoble class embracing the sons of aristocratic fathers and common mothers; (4) a class of superior commoners descended from indigenous Serer of high status; (5) a hereditary military class, descended from former Malinke warriors by nonnoble wives, who constitute the standing army, pay no taxes, and enjoy special privileges, such as stealing from commoners; (6) free peasants; (7) a special class of crown servants, recruited from war captives and free volunteers, who owe allegiance solely to the king, live in special villages, and share some of the privileges of the warrior class; (8) debt slaves pawned by the heads of matrilineages who find themselves in financial straits; (9) hereditary house servants, who are descended from slaves but who, unlike the latter, may not be sold; (10) true slaves, acquired by purchase; and (11) members of several despised endogamous castes, notably smiths, leatherworkers, butchers, and *griots*.

Each state of the Wolof type is ruled by a powerful paramount chief whose person is taboo and who has certain of the attributes of a divine king. The following details pertain to the Serer of Sine and Saloum, whose political structure has been particularly fully described. The king maintains an elaborate court in a capital town and collects taxes in kind through an administrative organization of district chiefs and local headmen. He is served by crown servants, who sometimes even hold minor administrative posts. His mother—or, if she is dead, her sister—enjoys exceptional prestige, rules a number of villages in her own right, and exercises judicial authority over all adulterous women. The highest minister of state, always a commoner lest he aspire to the kingship, exercises judicial powers over all freemen, supervises the chiefs of the three important frontier provinces, appoints a new king when the office becomes vacant, and, though he himself is appointed by the king, has the power to depose him. A second minister commands the army, represents the slaves and hereditary servants of the kingdom, and judges offenses in these classes. Like the prime minister, however, he is subject to the appellate jurisdiction of the king, who reserves to himself all judicial cases involving nobles and royalty. The third minister similarly represents and judges all crown servants and in addition serves as palace minister, master of ceremonies, chief of police, and royal executioner. The ruler is permitted to marry only women of common origin, so that his sons are ineligible to succeed him. He selects an heir presumptive from among his close matrilineal kinsmen and endows him with a special fief, but when the king dies, the prime minister is free either to confirm his choice or to appoint another royal male to ascend the throne.

Circumcision is general, and most tribes also practice clitoridectomy. These are usually, though not universally, associated with initiation ceremonies at puberty, which typically involve a period of instruction in a sequestered "bush school," as among the Peripheral Mande tribes farther south. The Pepel take the heads of slain enemies as trophies, and the Tenda occasionally practice ceremonial cannibalism, but neither custom seems to prevail elsewhere.

All tribes save the Wolof tolerate premarital sex freedom for girls. Marriage involves a bride-price in livestock, commonly including pigs, and frequently premarital bride-service as well. Preferential cross-cousin marriage prevails in several tribes. Polygyny occurs to only a limited extent among the Bijogo and Tenda but appears to be general elsewhere. The Serer and Wolof permit it only in the nonsororal form. Each co-wife has a hut of her own, and the husband spends a fixed period with each in rotation. The household unit is invariably an extended family, but the precise form which it assumes can rarely be ascertained from the in-complete data usually presented on residence rules.

Matrilocality is specifically reported for the less acculturated Bijogo, where women own the houses, but elsewhere the sources usually mention only patrilocal residence. However, the data on inheritance and succession, which are definitely matrilineal among the Landuma, Serer, Tenda, and some Wolof, make it clear that avunculocal residence also occurs with some degree of frequency, and this is supported by reports of matrilineal descent for the same tribes and for the Bijogo. The Serer and Tenda definitely possess exogamous matrisibs, and the Wolof observe double descent, having agamous kin groups of both unilinear types. The Baga in the extreme south possess exogamous patrilineages, but for the central tribes our principal authority, who shows no comprehension of social structural principles, merely denies totemism and asserts patrilocal residence and patrilineal inheritance. Until these allegations are confirmed we must probably assume, with Arcin (1907), that "the matrilineate is general among these peoples" and that deviations from it are attributable to recent historical influences.

Selected Bibliography

Ames, D. W. The Economic Basis of Wolof Polygyny. *SWJA*, 11:391–403. 1955.

——. The Selection of Mates, Courtship and Marriage among the Wolof. *BIFSH*, 18:156–168. 1956.

Arcin, A. *La Guinée Française*. Paris, 1907.

Aujas, L. Les Sérères de Sénégal. *BCEHS*, 14:293–333. 1931.

Bérenger-Féraud, L. J. B. *Les peuplades de la Sénégambie*. Paris, 1879.

Bernatzik, H. A. *Aethiopien des Westens*. 2 vols. Wien, 1933. [Balante, Banyun, Bijogo, Diola, and Pepel].

Bourgeau, J. Notes sur la coutume des Sérères du Sine et du Saloum. *BCEHS*, 16:1–65. 1933.

Campistron, M. Coutume Ouolof du Cayor. *PCEHS*, ser. A, 8:117–146. 1939.

Corre, A. Les Sérères de Joal et du Portudal. *RE*, 2:1–20. 1883.

———. Les peuplades du Rio Nunez. *MSAP*, ser. 2, 3:42–73. 1888. [Landuma].

Cunha Taborde, A. de. Apontamentos etnográficos sobre as Felupes de Suzana. *BCGP*, 5:187–223. 1950. [Diola].

Delacour, A. Les Tenda. *RES*, 3:287–296, 307–381; 4:31–53, 105–120, 140–153. 1912–1913.

Dulphy, M. Coutume des Sérères None. *PCEHS*, ser. A, 8:213–236. 1939.

———. Coutume Sérère de la Petite-Côte. *PCEHS*, ser. A, 8:237–321. 1939.

Fayet, J. C. Coutume des Ouolof Musulmans. *PCEHS*, ser. A, 8:147–193. 1939.

———. Coutume des Sérères N'Doute. *PCEHS*, ser. A, 8:195–212. 1939.

Gamble, D. P. *The Wolof of Senegambia*. London, 1957.

Gomes Barbosa, O. C. Breve notícia dos caracteres étnicos dos indígenas da tribo Biafada. *BCGP*, 1:205–274. 1946.

Lafont, F. Le Gandoul et les Nominkas. *BCEHS*, 21:385–458. 1939. [Serer].

Leca, N. Les pêcheurs de Guet N'Dar. *BCEHS*, 17:275–382. 1934. [Wolof].

Leprince, M. Notes sur les Mancagnes ou Brames. *Anthropologie*, 16:57–65. 1905. [Pepel].

Lestrange, M. de. *Les Coniagui et les Bassari*. Paris, 1955 [Tenda].

Mendes Moreira, J. Breve ensaio etnográfico acerca dos Bijagós. *BCGP*, 1:69–115. 1946.

Méo. Études sur le Rio-Nunez. *BCEHS*, 2:281–317, 341–369. 1919. [Baga].

Nogueira, A. I. P. Monografia sobre a tribo Banhun. *BCGP*, 2:973–1008. 1947.

Paulme, D. Structures sociales en pays Baga. *BIFSH*, 18:98–118. 1956.

Santos Lima, A. J. Organizacão económica e social dos Bijagós. *Centro de Estudos da Guiné Portuguesa*, 2:1–154. Lisboa, 1947.

Techer, H. Coutumes des Tendas. *BCEHS*, 16:630–666. 1933.

PART EIGHT

EXPANSION OF THE BANTU

---•••---

35

---•••---

Northwestern Bantu

The Bantu peoples occupy today approximately one-third of the African continent (see Map 14). As has been repeatedly noted, however, practically all of this vast territory was, until after the time of Christ, preempted by other peoples—mainly hunters and gatherers of the Pygmoid race in the west and of the Bushmanoid race in the east and south. During the past 2,000 years the Bantu have revealed a capacity for explosive expansion paralleled, among all the other peoples of the world since the dawn of recorded history, only by the Arabs after Mohammed, the Chinese, and the European nations since the Discoveries Period. It now becomes our task to locate the place of origin of the Bantu and to date, trace, and account for their phenomenal dispersion.

Linguistic evidence clearly indicates the region from which they came. As Greenberg (1949) has demonstrated, the Bantu languages as a group, despite their wide distribution, constitute but one of seven branches of the Macro-Bantu subdivision of the Bantoid subfamily of the Nigritic stock. The other six branches of Macro-Bantu, each of which is strictly coordinate with Bantu as a whole, are confined to a very small area near the Cameroon-Nigerian border. On linguistic grounds it is impossible that the Bantu can have come from anywhere else.

The original homeland of the Bantu must have lain immediately adjacent to the territory of the speakers of the other Macro-Bantu languages, i.e., in the Cameroon highlands and a thin lowland strip connecting the

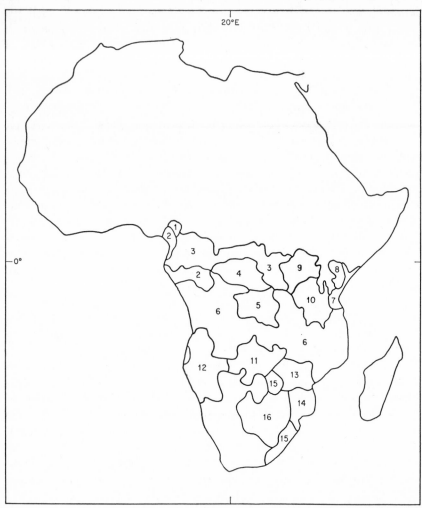

Map 14. Culture Provinces of Bantu Africa (1–Cameroon Highlanders, 2–Northwestern Bantu, 3–Equatorial Bantu, 4–Mongo, 5–Luba, 6–Central Bantu, 7–Northeast Coastal Bantu, 8–Kenya Highland Bantu, 9–Interlacustrine Bantu, 10–Tanganyika Bantu, 11–Middle Zambesi Bantu, 12–Southwestern Bantu, 13–Shona, 14–Thonga, 15–Nguni, 16–Sotho)

latter with the coast opposite the island of Fernando Po. It must have covered an extremely restricted area, for surviving remnants of Bongo hunters provide telltale evidence of former Pygmy occupation only a few miles to the south and east.

The Eastern Nigritic peoples (see Chapter 29) have already illustrated the means which first enabled the Negroes to penetrate the tropical forest. Sudanic agriculture developed in savanna country in more northerly latitudes, and its plants were adapted to these geographical conditions and not to the equatorial rainforest. The Malaysian banana, taro, and yam, on the other hand, had originated in a nearly identical environment in Southeast Asia and were thus ideally suited to the habitat of the Pygmies. Once the ancestral Bantu had borrowed these crops, their expansion to the south and east became inevitable.

This conclusion rests not on speculation but on a solid induction from the lists of food plants reported in ethnographic sources. The writer has compiled such lists, containing from eight to more than twenty cultigens each, for nine tribes of Northwestern Bantu, the subject of the present chapter. Bananas, taro, and yams appear in every one of the nine, and in nearly every instance as staples, whereas no crop of the Sudanic complex except the oil palm occurs in more than one list, even including four additional shorter ones. One can scarcely conceive of stronger proof that the Northwestern Bantu could not have entered their present habitat until they received the Malaysian food plants—unless, of course, they had reverted to a hunting and gathering economy, a sacrifice which tillers throughout history have invariably refused to make.

In the absence of direct historical and archeological radiocarbon evidence, we possess only two methods of arriving at an approximate date for the beginning of the Bantu penetration of the tropical forest. One comes from linguistics. The close genetic relationship among the various Bantu languages indicates the relative recency of their differentiation from a single ancestral speech community. Olmsted (1957) has applied modern glottochronological techniques to this problem, comparing ten maximally diverse Bantu languages with one another. Though his estimates of the time of separation vary with the particular pairs compared, and especially with differences in the purely technical treatment of doubtful cognates and use frequency, his results on the whole suggest an elapsed period of about three millennia. If one allows for a thousand years of linguistic differentiation in the Bantu homeland before the dispersion began, this estimate would accord perfectly with the conclusions from the alternative line of reasoning.

The second method depends upon inferences from known historical facts. We have already examined the evidence indicating that the Malaysian food plants were established on the Azanian coast of East Africa by A.D. 60, the approximate date of the visit by the author of the *Periplus of the Erythraean Sea* (see Chapter 26). They might have been introduced several centuries earlier, but not much more than that if we accept the archeological evidence dating the southern expansion of the Megalithic Cushites. Radiocarbon dating places Bantu at Zimbabwe in Southern Rhodesia in the seventh century. We thus have a time span of roughly 600 to 900 years within which the Malaysian crops diffused across the continent to the Cameroon-Nigerian border and the Bantu subsequently traversed the equatorial forest into East Africa. Since the Yam Belt was occupied by full-fledged agricultural peoples capable of borrowing new crops with ease, the westward diffusion presumably required considerably less time than the eastward migration, with its necessary successive adaptations to new geographical conditions. We cannot be far wrong, then, if we fix the first century as an estimated date for the beginning of the Bantu expansion.

One obvious route into the tropical forest ran southward along the Atlantic coast, and this seems to have been followed at an early period by emigrants from the lowland portion of the Bantu homeland. This chapter deals with the present inhabitants of this region. They need not, of course, be the direct descendants of the first emigrants, for the latter doubtless pressed forward into new territory, to be followed by later waves from the homeland. One such wave, indeed, originating apparently in the Cameroon highlands and spearheaded by the Fang nation, has pushed southward in fairly recent times into the hinterland of the Northwestern Bantu, confining the latter to a narrow coastal strip in the north, and has even reached the Atlantic in Gabon, on the equator, dividing its predecessors into a northern and a southern cluster. The component tribes of the two clusters are classified below.

NORTHERN CLUSTER

The peoples of this cluster, with the possible exception of the Bubi, are doubtless the latest to leave the original homeland and the most strongly influenced by recent historical developments there.

1. Bubi (Adija, Boobe, Ediye). These people, numbering about 10,000, inhabit the offshore island of Fernando Po. Presumably because of their isolation, they are linguistically somewhat divergent.
2. Duala (Diwala, Douala, Dwela), with the Bodiman, Limba (Lemba, Malimba), Mungo (Mongo), Oli (Buli, Ewodi, Eyarra, Wouri, Wuri), and Pongo. They number about 70,000.
3. Koko (Bagoko, Bakoko, Betjek, Edea, Mwele), with the Bassa (Basa), Bimbi (Babimbi), Bongkeng, Dibum, Mbang, and Ndogpenda. They number about 180,000.
4. Kossi (Bakosi, Kosi, Nkossi), with the Abo (Abaw, Bankon, Bo), Babong, Bafo (Bafaw), Bakaka, Bakem, Balong (Balon, Balung), Balondo, Baneka, Bareko, Elong, Manehas, Mbo, Miamilo, Musmenam, Ninong, and Sossi (Basosi, Sosi). They number about 60,000.
5. Kpe (Bakwedi, Bakwele, Bakwiri, Kpeli, Kweli, Kwiri, Wakweli), with the Isuwu (Bimbia, Mbia, Subu, Usuwu), Kole (Bakolle), Mboko (Bamboko, Bambuku, Boko, Womboko), and Wovea (Bobe, Bobea, Bota). They number about 50,000.
6. Kundu (Bakundu), with the Baji (Bao, Bavo, Bayi, Bolo, Bulu), Balue (Ballue, Barue), Efu, Issangili, Kogo (Bakogo), Kombe (Ekombe, Ewuni, Kumbe), Lundu

(Balongo, Balundu, Barondo, Murundu), Mbonge (Barombi), and Ngolo. They probably number about 50,000.
7. Ngumba (Mgoumba, Mvumba), with the Mabea (Bujeba, Ibea, Kaschua, Magbea). They number about 12,000.
8. Puku (Bapuku, Buku, Puko), with the Benga (Benge, Mabenga, Mbenga), Beundo, Kumbe (Kombe, Ngumbi), Noko (Banaha, Banoh, Banoko, Noho, Noo), Nyong, Tanga (Batanga), and Yasa. They number about 10,000.
9. Seke (Baseke, Basheke, Basiki, Museki, Segami, Sekiani, Shake, Sheekan, Sheke, Shekiani), with the Lengi (Balenge, Molingi). They number a few thousand.

SOUTHERN CLUSTER

In this cluster an unusually large number of Pygmies of the Bongo division live interspersed among the dominant Bantu in a symbiotic relationship with them. The ethnographic sources rarely give population data and are unfortunately deficient in many other respects.

10. Duma (Aduma, Badouma, Baduma, Douma, Maduma, Ndumu), with the Changi (Batchangui), Kanike (Bakanike), Mbete (Ambete, Bambete, Oumbete, Umbete), Ndumbo (Andumbo, Bandumbo, Mindoumbo), and Njawi (Bandjabi, Ndjavi, Njabi).
11. Lumbo (Balombo, Baloumbo, Balumbu, Lumba), with the Bwissi (Babouissi, Babwissi), Ngove, Rama (Barama, Bavarama, Varama), Shango (Asango, Ashango, Assongo, Machango, Masango, Massange), Shira (Echira, Eshira), Vungo (Bavoungo, Bavungo), and Yaka (Bayaka, Yakka).
12. Mpongwe (Bayugu, Empoongwe, Pongo, Pongoue), with the Galoa (Galloa, Galoi, Galua, Igulua, Ngaloi), Ininga (Anenga, Enenga), Jumba (Adjumba), Nkomi (Camma, Commi, Kama), and Orungu (Oroungou, Rungu).
13. Shogo (Ashogo, Ishogo, Issogo, Mitchogo), with the Kanda (Okanda, Okande), Pubi (Bapoubi, Pobi, Poubi, Pove, Powi), Puno (Apingi, Apinyi, Apono, Bapindji, Bapouno, Bapuno), and Simba (Asimba, Cimba). The Puno alone number about 40,000.
14. Teke (Bateke), with the Atyo, Fumu (Bamfono, Bamfumungu, Banfumu, Banfunuka, Mfumungu, Wamfumu), Lali (Balali), Ngangulu (Bangangoulou), Ntere, Nunu (Banunu), Shikuya (Achikouya), Tegue (Ategue, Bategue), Tende, and Tsaya (Mutsaya).

The Northwestern Bantu subsist primarily by agriculture, which they conduct by the swidden, or slash-and-burn, technique. We have already noted the utter insignificance of the Sudanic plants and the predominance of the Malaysian ones. Bananas constitute the staple crop in four of the fourteen societies of the province, taro in three, yams in two, and combinations of them in two others. Besides the Malaysian complex, only the American is represented other than sporadically—by beans, cucurbits, maize, malanga, manioc, peanuts, peppers, and sweet potatoes. Of these, maize, malanga, peanuts, and sweet potatoes have achieved modest importance in several societies, and manioc has attained the status of a staple or co-staple among the Mpongwe, Ngumba, and Teke.

In addition to agriculture, the Northwestern Bantu depend substantially upon fishing, hunting, animal husbandry, and gathering, in order of decreasing importance. Most groups keep at least a few goats, sheep, dogs, and chickens, as well as occasional cats and Muscovy ducks. Some of the tribes of the northern cluster also possess pigs and cattle, but the latter are not used for milk. Though regular markets are reported only for the Duala, intertribal trade assumes modest proportions everywhere. Most tribes recognize some conventional medium of exchange, commonly bars of iron. Men do all the hunting and most of the gathering. Although they also clear the land, women perform all other agricultural operations. Both sexes engage in fishing, but female participation consists chiefly in the catching of small fry with baskets and hand nets.

The Koko, the Teke, and the Mabea subtribe of the Ngumba live in neighborhoods of dispersed family homesteads, but the prevailing settlement pattern is a fairly compact village consisting of dwellings aligned on either side of a single street. Most villages have a "palaver house" at one end or else several such, one for each lineage, located at intervals along the middle of the street. Dwellings conform to one uniform type— a rectangular hut with a gable roof thatched with palm leaves and low walls of wood, bark, palm-leaf mats, or wattle and daub. Land is collectively owned, sometimes by the village but more commonly by its component lineages, and is parceled out to individuals in heritable usufruct without right of sale.

The Bubi, Duala, Koko, Kossi, and Puku have petty paramount chiefs. Elsewhere, however, each village enjoys complete political autonomy under a headman and a council of elders. Secret societies control the government in several tribes of the northern cluster, but age-grades are reported only for the Duala. Intervillage feuding and petty warfare are endemic, but only the Koko, Kundu, Shogo, and Teke practice cannibalism, presumably borrowed in most instances from the adjacent Equatorial Bantu. Although circumcision is nearly universal, being absent only among the Bubi, girls are not subjected to clitoridectomy. All the Northwestern Bantu keep slaves, recruited by purchase, by capture in war, or by enslavement for debt or crime. Only the Bubi, however, recognize a hereditary aristocracy, and status differences among freemen based on relative wealth are reported only for the Duala and Kpe.

Marriage invariably involves a substantial bride-price, but no other form of consideration. The Bubi and Koko favor unions with cross-cousins; the Kpe and Puku forbid them. All tribes practice extensive polygyny, which, for the Kpe at least, is always nonsororal. Each wife has a separate hut, and the husband visits each in regular rotation. The household normally comprises an independent polygynous family, extended families being highly exceptional. Among the Koko and Kpe a man has two status wives, the first supplied by his father and the second normally by his mother's brother. He divides his household between them into two sections, to which he assigns alternately the additional wives whom he obtains through his own efforts. Preferential secondary marriages of the levirate type appear to be universal, and, except for the Kpe, most tribes also practice the sororate.

The sources, though rarely satisfactory on social organization, demonstrate clearly that the area is basically matrilineal. They specifically attest matrilineal descent for all the tribes of the southern cluster, with the possible exception of the Duma. In the northern cluster, however, the influence of the adjacent Equatorial Bantu, Cameroon Highlanders, and Southern Nigerians has frequently wrought a transition to patrilineal descent. Even here, however, evidences of an earlier matrilineate still survive. The Bubi follow the matrilineal rule in regard to succession. The Kundu and Puku show traces of matrilineal inheritance. The Duala, though patrilineal today, still adhered to matrilineal descent when first studied by German ethnographers. The Kpe retain exogamous matrilineages to the present day, along with agamous patrilineal sibs and lineages, and are thus characterized by double descent. The same might well prove to be true of the patrilineal Koko, Kundu, and Puku, or of some of them, if we possessed more detailed information about their social systems. Cousin terminology is reported only for the Duala and Kpe, who follow the Iroquois pattern.

Residence in marriage is always virilocal from the first. Although it is certainly patrilocal in all patrilineal societies, it is at least sometimes avunculocal in the matrilineal tribes, and this rule may well predominate in those groups that are reported to have localized lineages and matrilineal inheritance, e.g., the Lumbo, Mpongwe, and Shogo. On the whole, the weight of the evidence strongly suggests the derivation of the social organization from the matrilineal and avunculocal system which we have already reconstructed for the ancestral Macro-Bantu peoples of the southern Nigerian plateau (see Chapter 13).

Selected Bibliography

Ardener, E. *Coastal Bantu of the Cameroons*. London, 1956. [Duala and Kpe].

Badier. Monographie de la tribu des Batékés. *BSRC*, 10:37–43. 1929.

Balandier, G. Les villages gabonais. *MIEC*, 5:1–86. 1952. [Shogo].

Bonnefond and J. Lombard. Notes sur les coutumes Lari. *BIEC*, n.s., 1(Supplement): 141–177. 1950. [Teke].

Buchner, M. *Kamerun*. Leipzig, 1887. [Duala].

Bufe, E. Die Bakundu. *AFA*, 40:228–239. 1913.

Conradt, L. Die Ngúmba. *Globus*, 81:333–337, 350–354, 369–372. 1902.

Deboudaud, J., and H. Chombart de Lauwe. Carte schématique des populations du Cameroun. *JSA*, 9:197–203. 1939.

Decazes, E. Chez les Batékés. *RE*, 4:160–168. 1885.

Dugast, I. Inventaire ethnique du Sud-Cameroun. *MIFCC*, 1:1–159. 1949.
Gil-Delgado, C. C. *Notas para un estudio antropologico y etnologico del Bubi de Fernando Poo*. Madrid, 1949.
Greenberg, J. H. Studies in African Linguistic Classification. *SWJA*, 5:309–317. 1949.
Guiral, L. Les Batékés. *RE*, 5:134–166. 1886.
Lenz, O. *Skizzen aus Westafrika*. Berlin, 1878. [Mpongwe].
Lessner, O. Die Baluë- oder Rumpiberge und ihre Bewohner. *Globus*, 86:273–278, 337–344, 392–397. 1904. [Kundu].
Le Testu, G. *Notes sur les coutumes Bapounou*. Caen, 1920. [Shogo].
Leuschner. Die Bakwiri. *REVAO*, pp. 14–26. 1903. [Kpe].
Maclatchy, A. L'organisation sociale des populations de la région de Mimongo. *BIEC*, 1:53–86. 1945. [Lumbo and Shogo].
Nicol, Y. *La tribu des Bakoko*. Paris, 1929.
Oertzen. Die Banaka und Bapuku. *REVAO*, pp. 27–56. 1903.
Olmsted, D. L. Three Tests of Glottochronological Theory. *AA*, 59:839–842. 1957.
Tessmann, G. *Die Bubi auf Fernando Poo*. Hagen, 1923.
Trézenem, E. Les Bateke Balali. *JSA*, 10:1–63. 1940.
Zenker, G. Die Mabea. *EN*, 3(3):1–24. 1904. [Ngumba].

36

———•••———

Equatorial Bantu

In a broad band across the tropical-forest zone of the Congo Basin, within 5°N and 5°S of the equator, live a block of Bantu peoples with remarkably homogeneous cultures, whom we shall call the Equatorial Bantu (see Map 14). They have wrested their present territory from the indigenous Pygmies, remnants of whom survive among the Bira, Budu, Dzem, Fang, Kalai, Kota, Sanga, and doubtless other tribes. That these remnants are notably fewer than among the Northwestern Bantu and the Mongo peoples, who adjoin the province on the west and the south, respectively, may well bear some relationship to the notorious addiction of the Equatorial Bantu to the practice of cannibalism.

The culture of these Bantu tribes shows striking resemblances to that of the Eastern Nigritic peoples to the north. This need not entirely reflect recent diffusion. If, as seems likely, the bulk of the Equatorial Bantu came from highland Cameroon and if the Eastern Nigritic peoples, as we have surmised (Chapter 29), originated in adjacent Adamawa, the ancestors of the two groups have been neighbors for thousands of years, thereby explaining at least some of the similarities between them. In both instances, of course, the penetration of the tropical forest followed, and was made possible by, the acquisition of the Malaysian food plants.

The Bantu occupation of the province must have occurred at a relatively early date—certainly prior to the expansion of the Mangbetu cluster of the Central Sudanic peoples, since, as we have seen (Chapter 28), the Mangbetu subjugated some of the Bantu tribes whom they found in possession of the country when they arrived. It was almost certainly the vanguard of the Equatorial Bantu who emerged from the tropical forest into Uganda, encountering there the Cushites, whom they were ultimately to absorb but not until they had borrowed from them the elements of East African agriculture.

The postulated derivation of the Equatorial Bantu from upland Cameroon rests in part on the near universality of patrilineal descent among them. The original Bantu appear to have been matrilineal and avunculocal, but the Cameroon Highlanders, as we have noted (Chapter 30), seem early to have achieved the transition to the patrilineate. On the other hand, certain features of Equatorial Bantu culture, particularly the prevailing house type and settlement pattern, point definitely to an origin on the Guinea coast. These suggest an intrusion of peoples from the coastal region akin to the Northwestern Bantu. Numerous authorities, indeed, have noted linguistic and other resemblances between the latter and tribes like the Dzem, Kaka, and Sanga who became separated from them by the late southward expansion of the Fang. Such groups presumably have made the shift from matrilineal to patrilineal descent since their arrival at their present location in consequence of pressures exerted by their neighbors.

The lack of notable cultural differences among the Equatorial Bantu makes it unnecessary to divide their numerous component tribes into clusters.

1. Amba (Awamba, Baamba, Bahamba, Bamba, Bwamba, Wawamba), embracing the Bulibuli, Bwezi (Babwizi), and Vonoma. They number about 60,000.
2. Babwa (Ababua, Baboa, Bobwa), with the Babeo (Bangelima, Mongelima), Bakango, Bangba, and Boyeu.
3. Bangi (Abango, Babangi, Bayanzi, Bobangi, Bubangi), with the Furu (Apfourou, Bafourou), Loi (Ballohi, Baloi, Balui), Ngiri (Bangili, Bangiri, Bonguili), and numerous lesser tribes. The Bangi proper number about 60,000, the Ngiri about 65,000.
4. Bati (Baati, Babati, Bobate, Mobati, Mombati), with the Benge (Amubenge, Bange, Mobanghi, Mubenge).
5. Binza (Babinja, Babinza, Mabinja, Vinza, Wavinza).
6. Bira (Babeyru, Babila, Babira, Baburu, Bagbira, Bavira, Wabira, Wavira), with the Pere (Babili, Bapere, Bapili, Peri). They number about 45,000. The Forest Bira and Plains Bira differ appreciably in culture.
7. Bomitaba, with the Bodongo, Boka (Bokaka), and Bonga.
8. Budja (Boudja, Mbudja), with the Bale (Mabale, Mbali, Mobali), Bango (Babangi, Bobango, Mobango), and Maginza.

9. Budu (Babudu, Banabuddu, Mabodo, Mabudu, Wabuddu).
10. Dzem (Diezem, Djem, Ndzem, Njiem, Nyem), with the Badjue, Guma (Gouma), Kwele (Bakuele, Bakwili), Ndsime (Medjimi, Mendsime), and Nzimu (Dsimu, Dzimou, Ndsimu, Zimu). They number about 30,000.
11. Fang (Fan, Fanwe, Mfang, Mpangwe, Pahouin, Pangwe), with the Bane (Bene), Bulu (Boulou), Eton (Etun, Toni), Mvae (Mwai, Mwei), Mvele (Mwelle), Ntum (Ntumu), Tsinga (Batchenge, Betsinga), Yaunde (Jaunde, Yadunde, Yaounde), and numerous lesser subtribes. They number in excess of 700,000.
12. Kaka, with the Bakum (Biakumbo, Bjakum), Besimbo, and Pol. They number about 50,000.
13. Kalai (Akalai, Akelle, Bakalai, Bakale, Bakelle, Bangomo, Bangone, Bembance, Ingouesse, Kele, Mboue), with the Bangwe, Basissiou (Mochebo), and Ongomo. Their population was estimated at 25,000 in 1906.
14. Kota (Bakota, Bandjambi, Ikota, Kuta, Okota), with the Chamai (Bouchamai), Hungwe (Mahoungoue, Ongwe), Kiba (Bokiba), Mbamba (Ambamba, Babamba, Bambamba, Obamba, Ombamba), Mbao (Bambao, Mbaon), Ndasa (Bandassa, Mindassa, Umdasa), Ndomo (Bandomo, Ndumu), Ngie (Banghie, Banguie), Pu (Bapou, Bapu), and Wumbu (Bahoumbou, Bavoumbou, Bawumbu, Vumbo, Wuumbu).
15. Kumu (Babumbu, Bakoumou, Bakumbu, Bakumu, Komo, Vuakumu, Wakumu). They number about 21,000.
16. Lengola (Balengora, Walengola).
17. Lika (Balika, Malika, Walika).
18. Lokele (Likile, Lukelle, Lukerou), with the Turumbu (Torumbu). They number about 30,000.
19. Maka, with the Bikay, Bikele, and So. They number about 55,000.
20. Mbesa (Bombesa, Mombesa), with the neighboring Ngombe (Gombe).
21. Mituku, with the Baleka and Balulu.
22. Ndaka (Bandaka, Wandaka), with the Bali (Babale, Babango, Mabali, Mbale, Mubali, Wabali, Yambuya).
23. Ndoko (Doko).
24. Ngala (Bamangala, Bangala, Mangala, Mongalla, Ngola, Wangala), with the Boloki (Baloki, Boluki), Lobala (Lubala), Ngombe (Gombe), and numerous other tribes. Their population was estimated at 110,000 in 1907.
25. Nyari (Babvanuma, Bandjali, Banyari).
26. Pande, with the Gundi (Bagunda, Goundi, Ngundi).
27. Poto (Bapoto, Foto, Mafoto, Upoto), with the Mondonga.
28. Rega (Balegga, Barega, Bulega, Kalega, Lega, Ouregga, Valega, Vuaregga, Walega, Warega), with the Bembe (Balembe, Vabembe, Wabembe).
29. Sanga (Bassanga, Bosanga, Masanga, Misanga), embracing the Besom (Binjombo, Dscherma, Jasua, Minjombo), Bidjuk, Bumali (Bomali, Boumaoali), Bomam (Bomome, Mpomama), Bombo (Bumbon, Bungbon), Esel (Essel, Lissel), Konambembe (Kunabembe), Lino, Mbimu, Ngwili (Bangili, Bounguili, Bungwili), and Pomo (Bongondjo). They number about 20,000.
30. Soko (Basoko, Bazoko).
31. Songola (Basongola, Goa, Usongora, Watchongoa), with the Enya (Baenya, Ouenya, Vouaghenia, Waenya, Wagenia, Wenja), Gengele (Bagengele), and Kwange (Bakwange).
32. Topoke (Eso, Geso, Tofoke, Tovoke).

The Sudanic complex plays but a minor role in the agricultural economy. Only the Amba, Babwa, and Plains Bira in the extreme northeast cultivate either sorghum or millet, and a compilation of twenty-five lists of food plants reveals the isolated occurrence of oil palms, okra, sesame, and yergan. On the other hand, the Malaysian complex, which made possible the Bantu occupation of the province, still holds a very strong position. Yams are mentioned in ten lists, taro in a like number. Bananas, included in all lists, attain the status of the prime staple in fourteen and of a co-staple in seven others. All other crops reported belong to the American complex, introduced very much later. Manioc is a staple or co-staple in nine societies and maize in four societies; sweet potatoes and peanuts are next in importance, with haricot beans, malanga, peppers, squash, and tobacco occurring only sporadically.

Fishing and boat trade rival agriculture, or even take precedence, in the economies of most tribes living along the larger rivers—the Bangi, Ngala, Poto, Soko, Songola, and some groups of the Babwa, Budja, Lengola, and Lokele. Hunting often assumes considerable subsidiary importance but tends to be reserved to the Pygmies where they are present. Gathering is so inconsequential that few sources even mention it. Most tribes engage to a considerable extent in intergroup trade and use various forms of iron or copper money. Markets, however, are specifically reported only for the Bira, Fang, Mbesa, Poto, and Rega.

The Plains Bira, who adjoin the pastoral Hima, stand alone in the area in keeping a few cattle, in milking cows and goats, and in making butter. Most tribes possess only goats, dogs, and chickens, though ten groups are reported to keep sheep as well. Human flesh replaces animal meat, for the sources specifically report the eating of slain and captive enemies in all the tribes of the province—except the Bomitaba, Kaka, Ndaka, Ndoko, and Poto—for whom we possess more than fragmentary information. Men hunt, but women commonly do some or most of the fishing, except in the societies that depend for their subsistence primarily upon this activity. Men clear the land, but leave all other agricultural work to the women.

The Equatorial Bantu reside in compact settlements consisting of two rows of rectangular houses along either side of a village street or, in riverain tribes, of a single row along the shore. The dwellings have walls of bark, leaves, bamboo, or planks and gable roofs thatched with leaves, and are sometimes grouped in quadrangular compounds. The Amba, Babwa, and Nyari, however, have adopted the Sudanic cone-cylinder hut from the adjacent Eastern Nigritic peoples, and the Plains Bira live in neighborhoods of dispersed homesteads of beehive dwellings like the Interlacustrine Bantu to the east. Except in the northeast, most villages have at least one men's house, located in the middle of the street or at one end, and in some cases there is one at each end.

Each settlement normally has a headman with limited authority and often, in addition, a council composed of the older men or of family or lineage heads. Only the Lengola, Mituku, Rega, Songola, Topoke, and northern Babwa recognize paramount chiefs over groups of settlements, and none has an elaborate political structure. The Equatorial Bantu observe no significant caste or class distinctions except for slavery, and the Amba, Bira, Fang, Kumu, and Rega do not even keep slaves. The sources contain only sporadic references to age-grades and secret societies. Circumcision, though not practiced by the Plains Bira, is otherwise nearly universal. Females, however, are not subjected to genital mutilations.

The Amba, Fang, and Ndaka often arrange marriages by exchanging sisters, and the Bomitaba and Poto occasionally do likewise, but a substantial bride-price constitutes the prevailing mode of obtaining a wife. Nearly all groups forbid unions with any first cousin and insist upon local exogamy. Polygyny, which is universal, can occur in the sororal as well as the nonsororal form among at least the Amba, Babwa, Poto, and Songola. Most groups, if not all, favor secondary marriages with a deceased wife's sister and the widow of a father or brother. The household unit tends to be an independent polygynous family in the east, a large extended family in the center and west.

Social organization is exceedingly uniform in the area, a single type characterizing nearly the entire province. Descent, inheritance, and succession follow the patrilineal principle, and residence is patrilocal from the first. Exogamous patrisibs are divided into lineages, without exhibiting a truly segmentary structure, and are localized as clan-communities or occasionally as clan-barrios. The men of a settlement thus form an integrated kin group as opposed to their wives, who are assembled from a number of other communities. The sources report cousin terminology of the Hawaiian type for the Poto, Songola, and Topoke, but the Amba follow the Omaha and the Rega the Iroquois pattern.

Only for the Ndoko does the evidence reveal any substantial deviation from the structural type described above. This tribe definitely adheres to the avunculocal rule of residence and to the matrilineal rule in descent, inheritance, and succession, thus conforming precisely to the ancestral Bantu pattern. Since avunculocal residence also occurs as an alternative in a few other tribes, e.g., the Amba and Babwa, we may reasonably assume that at least some of the immigrants into the province still adhered to the ancestral structure at the time of their arrival.

Selected Bibliography

Allys. Monographie de la tribu des Dzems. *BSRC*, 11:3–21. 1930.
Andersson, E. Contribution à l'ethnographie des Kuta. *SEU*, 6:1–364. 1953. [Kota].
Bertaut, M. *Le droit coutumier des Boulous*. Paris, 1935. [Fang].

Bertrand. Quelques notes sur la vie politique, le développement, la décadence des petites sociétés Bantou du bassin central du Congo. *RIS*, 1(1):74–91. 1920. [Lokele].

Bouccin. Les Babali. *Congo*, 16(2):685–712; 17(1):26–41. 1935–1936. [Ndaka].

Bruel, G. Les Pomo et les Boumali. *RES*, 1:3–32. 1910. [Sanga].

Czekanowski, J. *Forschungen im Nil-Kongo-Zwischengebiet*, vol. 2. Leipzig, 1924. [Amba, Babwa, Bira, Budu, Lika, Ndaka, and Nyari].

Darré, E. Note sur les Kaka. *BSRC*, 1:11–19. 1922.

——. Notes sur la tribu des Bomitaba. *RETP*, 3:304–325. 1924.

Delhaise, C. Les Warega. *CME*, 5:1–376. 1909.

——. Chez les Wasongola du sud. *BSRBG*, 33:34–58, 109–135, 159–214. 1909.

Dugast, I. Inventaire ethnique du Sud-Cameroun. *MIFCC*, 1:1–159. 1949.

Halkin, J. Les Ababua. *CME*, 7:1–616. 1911.

Heepe, M. *Jaunde-Texte*. Hamburg, 1919. [Fang].

Hermant, P. Les coutumes familiales des peuplades habitant l'État Independant du Congo. *BSRBG*, 30:149–173, 283–298, 406–438. 1906.

Hutereau, A. Notes sur la vie familiale et juridique de quelques populations du Congo Belge. *AMCB*, ser. 3, 1(1):1–104. 1909. [Babwa].

——. Les Mafoto. *BSRBG*, 34:138–152, 173–197. 1910. [Poto].

Ishmael, G. C. The Babinza. *Man*, 10:114–117. 1910.

Joset, P. E. *Les Babira de la plaine*. Anvers, 1936.

Koch, C. W. H. Die Stämme des Bezirks Molundu. *BA*, 3:257–312. 1913. [Dzem and Sanga].

Liétard, L. Les Waregas. *BSRBG*, 48:133–145. 1924.

Lindemann, M. Les Upotos. *BSRBG*, 30:16–34, 117–141. 1906. [Poto].

Maes, J. Quelques notes sur les Mongelima. *Anthropos*, 7:342–358. 1913. [Babwa].

Maes, J., and O. Boone. *Les peuplades du Congo Belge*. Bruxelles, 1935.

Moeller, A. Les grandes lignes des migrations des Bantous de la province orientale du Congo Belge. *MIRCB*, 6:1–578. 1936.

Salmon, J. Le droit matrimonial des Warega. *BJIDC*, 21:121–128, 229–248. 1953.

Schebesta, P. *Vollblutneger und Halbzwerge*. Leipzig, 1934. [Ndaka].

——. *My Pygmy and Negro Hosts*. London, 1936. [Translation of the above].

Smith, H. S. *Yakusu*. London, n.d. [Lokele].

Soupart, J. Les coutumes Budja. *BJIDC*, 6:269–274, 299–310. 1938.

Stuhlmann, F. *Mit Emin Pascha ins Herz von Afrika*. Berlin, 1894. [Bira].

Tessmann, G. *Die Pangwe*. Berlin, 1913. [Fang].

Torday, E. Der Tofoke. *MAGW*, 41:189–202. 1911.

Torday, E., and T. A. Joyce. Notes ethnographiques sur des populations habitant les bassins du Kasai et du Kwango oriental. *AMCB*, ser. 3, 2(2):1–359. 1922. [Topoke].

Trézenem, E. Notes ethnographiques sur les tribus Fan. *JSA*, 6:65–93. 1936.

Trilles, H. *Le totemisme chez les Fan*. Münster, 1912.

Van Geluwe, H. Les Bira et les peuplades limitrophes. *AMRCB*, 2:1–161. 1956. [Bira and Kumu].

Van Overbergh, C. Les Bangala. *CME*, 1:1–458. 1907.

Vedy. Les A-Babuas. *BSRBG*, 28:191–205, 265–294. 1904.

Verbeke, A. A. L. Étude sur la peuplade des Bombesa. *BSRBG*, 52:49–72. 1928.

Wayland, E. J. Notes on the Baamba. *JRAI*, 59:517–524. 1929.

Weeks, J. H. Anthropological Notes on the Bangala. *JRAI*, 39:87–136, 416–459; 40:360–427. 1909–1910.

——. *Among Congo Cannibals*. London, 1913. [Ngala].

Wijnant, D. Het Doko volk. *Congo,* 6(1):206–215; 6(2):410–426; 7(1):584–595. 1925–1926. [Ndoko].

Winter, E. H. Bwamba Economy. *East African Studies,* 5:1–44. Kampala, 1955. [Amba].

———. *Bwamba.* Cambridge, 1956. [Amba].

37

Mongo and Luba

In the very heart of the equatorial rainforest, almost surrounded by the curve of the Congo River, live a number of populous Bantu tribes belonging to the great Mongo nation. Amongst them reside a considerable body of Pygmies, intermarriage with whom in the past has produced an even larger population of mixed bloods, who are today indistinguishable in culture from the dominant Negroes. The Mongo peoples lie wedged between the matrilineal Central Bantu in the south and the patrilineal Equatorial Bantu in the north. Being unusually well described, they shed considerable illumination on the process whereby the transition from the one to the other form of social organization has occurred in this general region.

Southeast of the Mongo, in the adjacent savanna country, live a number of quite different peoples, mainly belonging to the Luba nation. In language, political institutions, and certain other aspects of culture they affiliate with the Central Bantu to the south. We have nevertheless chosen to treat them with the Mongo largely because, like the latter, they exhibit patrilineal forms of social organization. Moreover, the eastern and southeastern Mongo tribes manifest an unmistakable transition between them and the main body of the Mongo nation.

Since the two sets of tribes basically constitute distinct culture provinces (see Map 14), they are separated in the following classification.

MONGO PROVINCE

1. Bosaka (Saka), with the Ekota and Elinga. They number about 110,000.
2. Ekonda (Baseka), with the Batitu, Bokongo, Bolia, Ipanga, Iyembe, Mpama, Ntomba (Matumba, Ntumba, Tomba), and Sengele (Basengele, Mosengere). They number about 200,000.
3. Kela (Akela, Bakela, Ekele, Ikele), with the Balanga, Bambuli, and Boyela (Yela). They number about 150,000.

4. Kutshu (Akutshu, Bakutsu, Bankutshu), embracing the Bokala, Bolendu, Bolongo, Booli, Dengese (Bonkesse, Ndengese), and Yaelima. They number about 80,000.
5. Mbole (Bole, Imoma, Mboe). They number about 100,000.
6. Mongo (Balolo, Bamongo, Bomongo, Mbongo, Lolo). They number in excess of 200,000.
7. Ngandu (Bangandu, Bolo, Bongandu, Mongandu), with the Bambole, Lalia (Dzalia, Lolia), and Yasayama. They number about 250,000.
8. Ngombe (Bangombe, Bongombe, Gombe), with the Kutu (Bakoutou, Bakutu), Linga (Balinga, Baringa, Elinga, Waringa), and Ntomba.
9. Nkundo (Bankundu, Elanga, Gundo, Inkundo, Kundu), with the Bolemba (Bokote, Elonga, Lifumba, Wangata) and numerous other subtribes. They number about 200,000.
10. Songomeno (Basonge-Meno, Bassongo-Meno), with the Wankutshu (Ankutshu, Bankusu, Bankutsu, Bankutu, Nkutu).
11. Tetela (Batetela), also called Hamba (Bahamba) and Kusu (Bacusu, Bakoussou, Vuakussu, Wakusu), embracing the Okale, Olemba, Sungu, and other subtribes. Together with the Songomeno, they number about 300,000.

LUBA PROVINCE

12. Luba (Balouba, Balunga, Baluva, Bulaba, Louba, Turruba, Waluba), with the Bena Kalundwe and Bena Kanioka.
13. Lulua (Bena Lulua, Luluwa), with the Lange (Bachilangue, Bashilenge, Kaschilange, Tusilani, Tusselange).
14. Lunda (Alunda, Arunda, Balonda, Baloundou, Bamlunda, Kalunda, Lounda, Malhundo, Valunda).
15. Mbagani (Babagani, Babindi, Bindi, Tubindi), with the Kete (Baketa, Tukete).
16. Songe (Basonge, Bassongo, Bassonje, Wasonga), with the Zimba (Bazimba, Wazimba).
17. Yeke (Bayeke). This is not a tribe but a state established over Central Bantu indigenes by Nyamwezi conquerors from Tanganyika in the nineteenth century.

Except for a number of riverain fishing groups, the peoples of the area subsist primarily by swidden agriculture. Their principal crops, in order of importance, are manioc, bananas, yams, maize, peanuts, sweet potatoes, and taro. Here, as elsewhere in the tropical forest, the Bantu clearly began with the Malaysian complex and subsequently adopted the American food plants. The tribes of the Luba province, however, inject a novel element, for they also cultivate a number of Sudanic crops, including a modest amount of sorghum and millet and small quantities of ambary, earth peas, and sesame. The story of how these spread to the savanna country south of the rainforest must, however, be deferred until the next chapter.

All groups keep goats, dogs, and chickens, but sheep occur only in the Luba province and cattle not at all. Hunting and gathering have only negligible importance. Trade attains, in general, only a relatively modest development, although iron implements and bars or rings of copper are widely employed as currency. The men hunt, tend all livestock except fowls, and clear land for agriculture. The women participate in fishing and do most of the field labor. Cannibalism occurs only sporadically, being reported only for the Lulua, Songe, and some subtribes of the Nkundu, Songomeno, and Tetela.

Both the Mongo and Luba peoples live in villages or hamlets consisting of two rows of huts along a single street. In most tribes a cluster of several such settlements forms a community. Rectangular houses with thatched gable roofs predominate, but the Lunda, Songe, southern Tetela, and Yeke prefer dwellings of the cone-cylinder type. Socially both the settlement and its component hamlets are clans, i.e., localized sibs and lineages, respectively. Political authority is vested in a headman and a council of lineage or family heads within the local community, but over them nearly always stand district or subtribal chiefs with important ritual functions. Genuine states occur only among the Luba, Lulua, Lunda, and Yeke peoples of the Luba province. Except for the royal and official classes in these societies and wealth distinctions of considerable consequence among the Songe, Songomeno, and Tetela, class distinctions among freemen are minimal. All groups, however, keep slaves, whose status is hereditary except in the western tribes of the Mongo province, and the social position of the dependent Pygmies often approximates that of hereditary serfs.

Political integration attained such extraordinary magnitude in the Luba province and among the adjacent Central Bantu that it merits brief consideration. As an example of the states of this region we may select the great empire of Mwata Yamwo, founded among the Lunda by a Luba dynasty around 1625. It expanded through conquest after 1675 to within 300 miles of the Atlantic coast, dominating all the Central Bantu peoples of this vast territory until near the close of the nineteenth century. The ruler possessed the attributes of divinity, and no one might observe him eat or drink, on pain of death. He appointed provincial governors and lesser district chiefs, who supplied troops for his army and levied tribute in ivory, salt, copper, slaves, and produce. They resided at the capital town, where they exercised additional functions. The four highest among them formed an advisory council called the Kannapumba. Ranking even above them, however, was the Lukokesha, or Queen-Mother. Always the daughter of a former king, she remained unmarried, possessed independent tributary territories for her support, maintained her own court, and shared supreme authority with the monarch. When a king died, the Queen-Mother and the Kannapumba constituted an electoral college to choose his successor from among his own sons or those of former rulers.

Marriage regularly involves the payment of a substantial bride-price, with certain exceptions among the western tribes of the Mongo province. All groups observe strict rules of sib and hamlet or even village exogamy, and—except for the eastern Songe, who permit unions with a father's sister's daughter—all forbid marriage with any first cousin. General polygyny prevails, occurring in both the sororal and the nonsororal forms. Both the levirate and the sororate are customary, as well as secondary unions with a father's widow other than one's own mother. The household unit assumes the form of an independent polygynous family in the Luba province, of an extended family among the Mongo. Patrilineal descent, inheritance, and succession and patrilocal residence provide everywhere the underlying structural principles. From the point of view of static synchronic analysis, therefore, the social systems of the Mongo and Luba peoples appear nearly identical with those of the Equatorial Bantu.

A historical perspective, however, leads to a different conclusion. We note, first of all, that most peoples who speak languages of the Luba group live, not in the present area, but in the Central Bantu province, where they follow the avunculocal rule of residence and the matrilineal rule in regard to descent, inheritance, and succession. This arouses a suspicion that all the Luba peoples may once have had a similar social system, a suspicion confirmed by evidence that succession to the Luba kingship was formerly matrilineal. The southern kinsmen of the Lunda are also matrilineal, as are the subject peoples of the Yeke state. Moreover, in every tribe of the Mongo province, without exception, the sources report unmistakable survivals of the matrilineate. The social systems of the Ekonda, Mbole, Mongo, and Nkundu in the west, which are especially well described, provide structural evidence of a still more conclusive character.

When we subject the social organization of these four seemingly patrilocal and patrilineal peoples to close scrutiny, we observe several surprising facts. All of them, for example, have kinship systems of the classic Crow pattern, which elsewhere in the world is associated almost universally with matrilineal descent. We also discover that the four tribes permit a young man whose paternal kinsmen cannot provide him with a bride-price to remove to the village whence his mother came and to reside there in avunculocal residence with a maternal uncle. The latter, moreover, becomes obligated thereby to obtain a wife for him—an obligation taking precedence over that of the uncle toward his own sons. The nephew becomes permanently affiliated with his uncle's, i.e., his mother's, patrisib and lineage, and acquires rights of inheritance and succession there prior to those of his uncle's own sons. Some authorities even maintain that the natives interpret their own social systems as essentially matrilineal, rather than patrilineal as the structural anthropologist would characterize them.

The explanation of this ambiguity lies in a unique institution known as *nkita.* Whenever a female member of an extended family marries, her bride-price is employed to obtain a wife for one of its male members, usually one of her full brothers. She thereby becomes *nkolo* to her brother's wife, who is known as her *nkita.* The sons of the *nkita* acquire the right to inherit from and succeed their father only because the latter used his sister's bride-price to marry their mother, so that they are, in a certain sense, really his sister's sons. Patrilineal inheritance and succession are justified, so to speak, on a matrilineal principle.

The sons of the *nkolo,* on the other hand, acquire two definite rights against their maternal uncle, the husband of the *nkita,* by virtue of the fact that he has profited from the bride-price obtained for their mother. The first of these rights is that of receiving from their uncle the bride-price he obtains for his first daughter by the *nkita.* The second is the privilege of joining the uncle if their paternal kinsmen cannot provide them with a bride-price and, if this is exercised, of taking priority over that uncle's own sons in regard to inheritance and succession.

The whole system, however bizarre it may appear, reveals thorough-going functional integration. Even the Crow kinship terminology becomes entirely understandable. Brothers regularly take precedence over sons in matters of inheritance and succession. Thus a nephew who has exercised his *nkita* privilege by going to live with his mother's brother in avunculocal residence, though ranking ahead of that uncle's sons in precedence, ranks behind the uncle's younger brothers and cannot inherit or succeed until they have died. From the point of view of his cross-cousins, the uncle's sons, he becomes, as it were, the most junior among their paternal uncles, and it is quite natural that they should call him "father," as they do the latter, in characteristic Crow fashion. He in turn, of course, calls them "sons," the term applied to a brother's as well as one's own sons, regardless of their relative age.

This system illustrates the incomplete understanding that comes from even the most meticulous synchronic structural analysis. It can be fully comprehended only from the point of view of a theory of cultural dynamics which visualizes social systems as undergoing modification over time in adaptation to changing life conditions, and as doing so in moving equilibrium without necessary loss of functional integration at any point in the process. In the present instance, full enlightenment appears once we make a single very reasonable historical assumption, namely, that the Mongo peoples formerly had a matrilineal and avunculocal social system precisely like that which still survives among all their immediate neighbors to the southwest and south, as will be described in Chapter 38.

Let us imaginatively project ourselves backward to the time when the then matrilineal and avunculocal Mongo encountered the first influences favoring a transition to patrilocal residence, perhaps their original acquisition of iron or copper money. A prosperous father, wishing to keep his sons with him, would, after providing wives for his nephews, do the same for his sons, using for this purpose the bride-prices received for his nieces—ultimately those for his daughters, as fathers gradually acquired control over the latter. When in time most fathers had come to do this, the preexisting matrilineages and avuncuclans would have become converted by easy gradations into patrilineages and patriclans. Since, however, not all fathers could do so, as is still the case today, the old avunculocal rule and privileges were retained as a patterned alternative to cover such special cases. The original Crow kinship terminology, since it continued to be functional, underwent no change. The social structure prevailing today, since no other reasonable explanation is conceivable, can only have developed in this way. If the Mongo have undergone this transition from an original matrilineal and avunculocal system, other groups of now patrilineal and patrilocal Bantu may well have had a comparable history.

Selected Bibliography

Boelaert, E. De Nkundo-maatschappij. *KO*, 6:148–161. 1940.

———. Terminologie classificatoire des Nkundo. *Africa*, 21:218–223. 1951.

Brausch, G. La justice coutumière chez les Bakwa Luntu. *AS*, 1:235–242. 1942. [Lulua].

Brepoels, H. Het familienhoofd bij de Nkundo negers. *Congo*, 11(2):332–340. 1930.

Brown, H. D. The Nkumu of the Tumba. *Africa*, 14:431–447. 1944. [Ekonda].

Burton, W. F. P. The Country of the Baluba. *GJ*, 70:321–342. 1927.

Empain, A. Les Bakela de la Loto. *BSRBG*, 46:206–265. 1922.

Engels, A. *Les Wangata*. Bruxelles, 1912. [Nkundo].

Gilliard, L. Étude de la société indigène. *Congo*, 6(1):39–76. 1925. [Ekonda].

Grevisse, F. Les Bayeke. *BJIDC*, 5:1–16, 29–40, 65–74, 97–113, 165–175; 6:200–216, 238–241. 1937–1938.

Heusch, L. de. Valeur, monnaie et structuration sociale chez les Nkutshu. *RIS*, 28(1):73–97. 1955. [Songomeno and Tetela].

Hulstaert, G. Le mariage des Nkundó. *MIRCB*, 8:1–519. 1938.

———. Carte linguistique du Congo Belge. *MIRCB*, 19(5):1–67. 1950.

Kaptein, G. Familieleven en zeden bij de inboorlingen van den Evenaar. *Congo*, 3(1):531–549. 1922. [Mbole and Nkundo].

Laufant, R. Coutumes juridiques des Baluba. *BJIDC*, 3:51–57, 78–83. 1935.

Liétard, L. Étude sommaire sur la tribu des Lulua. *BSRBG*, 53:40–43. 1929.

Louillet, L. Le "lusalo" ou mariage monogamique par échange de sang. *Congo*, 7(2):209–217. 1926. [Luba].

Maes, J. *Notes sur les populations des bassins du Kasai, de la Lukenie, et du Lac Leopold II*. Bruxelles, 1924. [Ekonda and Kutshu].

———. Notes sur les populations Lalia et Yasayama. *Congo*, 15(1):172–179. 1934. [Ngandu].

Molin, S. Notes sur les Boyela. *Congo*, 14(1):388–401. 1933. [Kela].

Müller, E. W. Soziologische Terminologie und soziale Organisation der Ekonda. *ZE*, 81:188–202. 1956.

Philippe, R. Le mariage chez les Ntomb'e Njale. *Aequatoria*, 17:129–153. Coquilhat-ville, 1954. [Ekonda].

Pogge, P. *Im Reich des Muata Jamwo*. Berlin, 1880. [Lunda].

Ruskin, E. A., and L. Ruskin. *Dictionary of the Lomongo Language*. London, 1928.

Schebesta, P. *Vollblutneger und Halbzwerge*. Leipzig, 1934. [Nkundo].

———. *My Pygmy and Negro Hosts*. London, 1936. [Translation of the above].

Torday, E., and T. A. Joyce. Notes ethnographiques sur des populations habitant les bassins du Kasai et du Kwango oriental. *AMCB*, ser. 3, 2(2):1–359. 1922. [Songe, Songomeno, and Tetela].

Van der Kerken, G. L'ethnie Mongo. *MIRCB*, 13:1–1143. 1944.

Van Overbergh, C. Les Basonge. *CME*, 3:1–564. 1908.

Verhulpen, E. *Baluba et Balubaïsés du Katanga*. Anvers, 1936.

Wissmann, H., L. Wolf, C. von François, and H. Mueller. *Im Innern Afrikas*. Leipzig, 1888. [Lulua].

38

Central Bantu

When the ancestors of the Northwestern and Equatorial Bantu and of the Mongo peoples had occupied all their present territory, they reached the far limits of the tropical rainforest. Beyond them, to the east and south, the indigenous hunting population, Pygmies and Bushmen, offered no more of an obstacle to further expansion than they had in the past. The geographical environment, however, was another matter, for this now changed to savanna, dry forest, and upland grasslands (see Map 4). Here the Malaysian food plants provided but an inadequate means of exploiting the new territory. The West African cereals, which would have proved suitable, had been lost in traversing the equatorial forest. It would be 1,000 years before the Portuguese introduced another adaptive complex, the American, and 500 years before the Bantu advance guard, reaching the east coast, could acquire rice and other crops from the Arabs. In the meantime, how could the Bantu who emerged from the rainforest manage to subsist?

The discussion of the Luba and their neighbors has already given a hint of the answer. The Bantu readopted the African cereals. But whence did they obtain them? A clue is provided by the nature of the crops themselves. One was eleusine, an Ethiopian cultigen which never reached the Guinea coast and therefore could not have accompanied the Bantu on their migrations. A second was sorghum. The notable fact about this plant is that, wherever it occurs among the Bantu of eastern or southern Africa, it belongs to varieties developed in East Africa, notably durra and Kafir corn (see Snowden, 1936). Even today these have not spread to the western Sudan, so that again the Bantu could not have brought them with them across the Congo Basin. The source of borrowing, consequently, can only have been a people who cultivated African cereals of Ethiopian origin.

Around the eastern periphery of the rainforest in the early centuries of the Christian era archeological and other evidence reveals only one agricultural people. And they possessed these very plants, for they were the Cushites from the Sidamo country who had emigrated to Uganda and established there a relatively complex civilization (see Chapter 25). Having acquired in Uganda the African cereals in their Ethiopian forms, the Bantu could readily have passed these on from tribe to tribe completely around the edge of the tropical-forest zone until they reached the Atlantic coast near the mouth of the Congo River. With these crops, all groups could then have continued their expansion into the adjacent new geographical environments.

Several auxiliary sources of evidence confirm this interpretation. In the first place, Uganda lies closer to the original homeland of the Bantu than any other section of East Africa, and hence was presumably the first to be reached, especially since the Congo River system leads to the very gates of the lake region (see Map 2). Second, although most of the present Bantu inhabitants of East Africa possess matrilineal forms of social organization, the Interlacustrine group in Uganda and Ruanda-Urundi are patrilineal and thus reasonably to be derived from the adjacent Equatorial Bantu, who likewise have patrilineal social systems. Third, the Bantu who have emerged eastward from the tropical forest have largely abandoned the settlement pattern and house type prevalent there and have adopted dwellings of the cone-cylinder model characteristic of all sedentary Cushites. Finally, as already evidenced by the Luba and their neighbors, nearly the entire circumference of the equatorial forest, from Uganda around to the mouth of the Congo River, is characterized culturally by highly complex states reminiscent of those of the Sidamo peoples. Since, as we have seen, the Bantu inhabitants of the three rainforest provinces nowhere exhibit any consequential degree of political integration, they can scarcely have carried the pattern of large-scale despotic government with them into adjacent territory. It seems reasonable to assume, therefore, that their complex political institutions came from the same source as their cereal agriculture and that both cultural systems subsequently followed approximately the same course of diffusion.

Later historical events of great consequence have markedly changed the culture of the Interlacustrine Bantu, making it necessary to defer considering them until Chapter 45. We shall therefore turn next to the broad belt of Central Bantu which lies immediately south of the rainforest and extends eastward to the shores of the Indian Ocean (see Map 14). Despite the high degree of uniformity in social organization, first noted by Richards (1950), certain local variants in this and other respects make it advisable to divide the peoples of this province into several clusters.

KONGO CLUSTER

A cluster of closely related peoples on the lower reaches of the Congo River and the adjacent coast to the north and south aroused the astonishment of the early Portuguese explorers because of the complexity of their political institutions and their social life.

1. Kongo (Bacongo, Bakongo, Makongo), embracing the Bashikongo (Besikongo, Eshikongo, Exikongo, Mouchicongo), Hungu (Mahungo, Maungo), Mbamba (Bamba, Bambamba), Mbata (Bambata, Batta), Mpangu (Bampangu, Pango), Nzombo (Bazombo, Zombo), and Sorongo (Asolongo, Bashilongo, Basolongo, Misorongo, Mossilongi, Mouchilonge, Musarongo, Mushirongo, Musurongo). Ihle (1929) estimates that they numbered 2,500,000 in 1675.
2. Kunyi (Bakougni, Bakunya), with the Yangela (Bayangela, Nyangela).
3. Sundi (Basoundi, Basundi, Mayanga, Nsundi), with the Bembe (Babembe), Bwende (Babouendi, Babwende), Dondo (Badondo), and Kamba (Bakamba). They formed a province of the old Kongo kingdom.
4. Vili (Bafiote, Bavili, Chiloango, Fiote, Fjort, Loango, Mfioti), with the Kakongo (Cacongo, Kabinda, Kacongo, Makouango).
5. Yombe (Bayombe, Majombe, Mayumbe). They numbered about 170,000 in 1933.

KIMBUNDU CLUSTER

This cluster of tribes, occupying west central Angola, is among the least adequately described in the entire African continent.

6. Holo (Baholo, Hollo).
7. Kimbundu (Ambundu, Mbundu), embracing the Luanda (Loanda), Mbaka (Ambaca, Ambaquista), Mbondo (Bondo), Ndongo (Ndonga, Ngola), Ndembu (Andembu, Atembu, Bandempo, Batembo, Demba, Dembu, Jindembu), and Tamba (Matamba).
8. Kisama (Cisama, Kissama, Quissama). Their population was reduced by smallpox from over 30,000 around 1900 to about 10,000 in 1929.
9. Lupolo (Libolo), with the Esela, Haku (Hako, Oako), Kipala (Cipala, Kibala), and Lemba (Malemba).
10. Mbangala (Bangala, Bangela, Imbangala, Ngala), with the Shinje (Bashinshe, Chinge, Kasinji, Mashinge, Maxingi).
11. Sele (Basele, Esele, Selle), with the Kisanji (Cisanje, Kissandschi, Quissanje), Mbui (Amboim, Ambuin, Mbuiyi, Ombe), and Sumbe (Basumbe).

KWANGO CLUSTER

This cluster embraces a number of well-described tribes in the drainage basin of the Kwango River, a southern affluent of the Congo.

12. Kwese (Bakuese, Bakwese).
13. Luwa (Balua, Baluwa, Lua), with the Nzofo and Sonde (Basonde).
14. Mbala (Ambala, Bambala), with the Huana (Baguana, Bahuana, Bauangana, Wengana) and Humbu (Bahumbu, Bavumbu, Bawumbu).
15. Ngongo (Bangongo), with the Songo (Basongo).
16. Pende (Bapende, Baphendi, Capende, Tupende). They number about 27,000.
17. Suku (Bapindi, Basuku, Pindi, Pindji), with the Samba (Tsaam). They number about 80,000.
18. Yaka (Aiacka, Bayaka, Bayakala, Djakka, Dschagga, Giaca, Jaca, Majacalla, Mayacca, Muyaka, Myaka, Ngiaka, Yacca, Yagga), with the Lula (Balula).

KASAI CLUSTER

The tribes of this cluster lie northeast of the Kwango group on or near the Kasai tributary of the Congo River, and adjacent to the Mongo province.

19. Bunda (Ambundu, Ambuun, Babounda, Babunda, Bambunda, Mbuni).
20. Dzing (Badinga, Badzing, Baringa, Dinga), with the Lori (Alwer, Baloli, Balori), Ngoli (Angul, Bangodi, Bangoli, Bangulu), and Nzari (Bandzadi, Bandzala, Bandjadi, Banzari).
21. Kuba (Bacouba, Bakuba, Tukubba), embracing the Binji (Babindji), Mbala (Bambala), Ngongo (Bangongo), and lesser subtribes. They number about 75,000.
22. Lele (Bachilela, Bashilele, Bouxhilile), with the Wongo (Bagongo, Bakongo, Bawongo, Tukkongo). They number about 12,000.
23. Sakata (Basaka, Basakata), embracing the Baye (Babaye, Bai, Bobai, Tollo), Boma (Baboma, Babuma, Ouabouma, Uabuma, Wabuma), Dia (Badia, Bajia, Jia. Wadia, Wadja), and Lesa (Balesa, Lessa).
24. Yanzi (Bajansi, Baschansi, Bayanchi, Bayanzi, Wachanzi), with the Amput (Bamputu).

LUNDA CLUSTER

The tribes of this cluster live east of the Kimbundu and southeast of the Kwango groups. Most of them were subject to the Lunda empire of Mwata Yamwo (see Chapter 37).

25. Chokwe (Ahioko, Aioko, Atsokwe, Bachoko, Badjok, Bakioko, Batchokwe, Batshoko, Chiboque, Kashioko, Katsokwe, Khioko, Kioko, Kioque, Makioko, Matchioko, Quioco, Shioko, Tschiokwe, Tsiboko, Tsokwe, Tutschokwe, Utshiokwe, Vichioko, Watschokwe), with the Minungu (Tuminungu).
26. Luchazi (Balochasi, Balojash, Kaluchazi, Lutschase, Luxage, Malochazi, Makangala, Mulochazi, Valuchazi).
27. Luimbe (Baluimbi, Loimbe, Lwimbi, Valuimbe), with the Mbande (Kimbande, Quimbande). They number about 40,000.
28. Luvale (Aluena, Balovale, Kaluena, Lobare, Luena, Lovale, Lwena, Malobale, Muluena, Tulwena, Valwena).
29. Mbunda (Ambunda, Mambunda).
30. Mbwela (Amboella, Ambuela).
31. Ndembu (Andembu, Bandempo, Southern Lunda).
32. Songo (Basongo, Masongo).

BEMBA CLUSTER

The tribes of this cluster live east of the Lunda group in Northern Rhodesia and the adjacent Belgian Congo.

33. Aushi (Avausi, Bahushi, Baoussi, Baushi, Umwausi, Ushi, Vouaousi, Wausi, Wauzhi), with the Chisinga (Wenachishinga), Kawendi (Kabende, Wenakawendi), Mukulu, and Ngumbu (Wenangumbu). They number about 100,000.
34. Bemba (Awemba, Ayemba, Babemba, Muemba, Wawemba, Wemba). They number about 150,000.
35. Bisa (Abisa, Aiza, Awisa, Babisa, Bawisa, Invisa, Moize, Moviza, Muviza, Wabisa, Wisa). They number about 50,000.
36. Buye (Babudjue, Babui, Babuye, Bambuyu, Bubui, Luba-Hemba, Wabudjwe, Wabuyu, Waruwa), with the Bwari (Ouabouari, Ubwari, Wabwari), Goma (Wagoma), Hombo (Bango, Bangobango), Kalanga (Bakalanga), Kunda (Bakunda), and Lumbu (Balumbu).
37. Holoholo (Baholoholo, Wahorohoro), also called Guha (Bagua, Baguha, Vuaguha, Waguha) and Tumbwe (Batumbwe, Watombwe).
38. Kaonde (Bakahonde, Bakaonde), with the Sanga (Basanga). They number about 40,000.
39. Lala (Balala, Bukanda), with the Ambo (Kambonsenga) and Luano. They number about 75,000.
40. Lamba (Balamba, Walamba), with the Lima, Sewa, and Swaka. They number about 70,000.
41. Luapula (Bena Kazembe), with the Londa (Alonda, Aronda, Balonda, Lunda, Varunda). They number about 100,000.
42. Lungu (Alungu, Marungu, Walungu, Warungu), with the Mambwe (Amambwe).
43. Senga (Asenga). These people, numbering about 25,000, are an offshoot of the Bisa and are strongly acculturated to the Tumbuka.
44. Shila (Awasira, Bachila, Bashila, Messira, Wasira).
45. Tabwa (Batabwa, Batambwa, Itawa, Watabwa), with the Bwile (Babwile, Bwire).
46. Unga (Bahonga, Bahunga, Baunga, Honja, Waunga). They number about 10,000.

MARAVI CLUSTER

The tribes of this cluster, who are known collectively as the Maravi, live mainly in Nyasaland and on the lower Zambesi River.

47. Chewa (Achewa, Ancheya, Cewa, Masheba, Sheva), with the kindred Chipeta (Achipeta). They number about 650,000.
48. Chuabo (Achwabo, Atxuabo, Chwampo), with the Podzo.
49. Kunda (Achikunda, Chikunda), with the Nyungwe (Wanyongwe). They number about 75,000 in Nyasaland alone.
50. Nsenga (Senga). They number about 50,000.
51. Nyanja (Anyanja, Wanyanja), with the Manganja (Maganja, Waganga). They number in excess of 300,000.
52. Nyasa (Anyassa, Wanyassa).
53. Sena (Asena, Wasena).
54. Tumbuka (Batumbuka, Matumboka, Watumbuka), with the Fulilwa, Fungwe (Wafungwe), Henga (Bahenga, Wahenga), Hewe (Hewa), Kamanga (Wakamanga), Kandawire, Nthali, Phoka (Poka), Sisya (Siska), Tonga (Batonga, Matoka), Wenya, and Yombe. They number about 120,000.
55. Zimba (Azimba, Bazimba, Ouazimba, Vasimba, Wazimba).

YAO CLUSTER

The tribes of this cluster live mainly in northern Mozambique and adjacent coastal Tanganyika, although a few spill over into southern Nyasaland.

56. Lomwe (Acilowe, Alomwe, Anguru, Nguru, Walomwe, Wanguru), with the Mihavani. They number about 400,000 exclusive of those in Portuguese territory.
57. Makonde (Wakonde, Wamakonde), with the Matambwe (Wamatambwe) and Mawia (Mabiha, Mavia, Mawiha, Wamavia, Wawia). Those in British territory, a small fraction of the total, number about 150,000.
58. Makua (Makoa, Makoane, Wakua, Wamakua). They number about 850,000.
59. Mwera (Wamuera), with the Kiturika (Kitusika).
60. Ngindo (Wangindo), with the Chobo (Choo), Hamba, Ikemba, Ndonde (Wandonde), and Ndwewe.
61. Yao (Achawa, Adjao, Adsawa, Adsoa, Ajawa, Ayo, Hiao, Mudsau, Mujano, Mujoa, Myao, Veiao, Wahaiao, Waiyau, Wayao). Those in British territory, a small fraction of the total, number about 360,000.

Among the eastern Central Bantu, particularly those of the Maravi cluster, reside a number of intrusive peoples known collectively as the Ngoni. They represent the descendants of military bands of Nguni who fled Natal in the 1820s to escape Zulu hegemony, ranged northward as far as Lake Victoria raiding for cattle and women, and eventually settled down in the vicinity of Lake Nyasa. Here they married women of the Central Bantu tribes and have become to a considerable extent acculturated to the latter. They will be considered along with their South African kinsmen in Chapter 50.

The economy of the Central Bantu rests primarily upon swidden agriculture. Their original dependence upon the Malaysian food plants survives today only in the Kongo cluster. Elsewhere bananas and yams appear only sporadically, and taro disappears altogether. Eleusine, millet, and sorghum, the African cereals which supplanted them, still retain a prominent position among the tribes of the Bemba, Kasai, Lunda, and Yao clusters; and lesser crops of the Sudanic complex, notably cow peas, earth peas, gourds, and sesame, occur here and there. The plants that dominate the agriculture of the province today, however, are those of American origin, all introduced subsequent to 1500. Manioc constitutes the staple in the Kasai and Kwango clusters, and maize in the Maravi cluster, whereas both share the top position in the Kimbundu and Lunda clusters and are even important in the Bemba, Kongo, and Yao clusters. Among other American plants, peanuts and sweet potatoes are especially widely cultivated. Rice, acquired from the Arabs, also enjoys a modest standing in the eastern part of the province.

The Central Bantu augment their starchy vegetable diet with animal proteins in various ways. They do considerable hunting. They fish to an even greater extent, and the Luimbe, Songo, Unga, and some Shila depend more on fishing than on agriculture. A few tribes in the west even practice cannibalism; the Dzing, Mbangala, Sele, and Yanzi do so extensively, the Bunda, Mbala, Pende, and Suku sporadically. Animal husbandry, however, provides little meat and no milk. Although all groups keep dogs and chickens, most of them a few goats as well, and some of them even pigs and sheep, the overwhelming majority of the tribes of the province have no cattle at all. In the west, the Holo of the Kimbundu cluster keep them in considerable number today, but only the southernmost Chokwe and the westernmost Mbwela, who adjoin the pastoral Southwestern Bantu, had them in precontact times. In the east, an occasional chief among the Holoholo, Luapula, Lungu, and Nyasa maintains a small herd as a matter of prestige, but the striking ignorance of herding and milking techniques demonstrates that cattle are a rarity. Only the Tumbuka in the extreme north of the Maravi cluster seem to have kept them in appreciable numbers prior to the Ngoni invasions of the nineteenth century. Even the intrusive Ngoni, though strongly pastoral when they arrived, have in several instances lost their cattle today. There exists, in short, not a shred of justification for including the eastern Central Bantu in an alleged "East African cattle area."

Intergroup trade plays a prominent role in the economic life of the peoples in the four westernmost clusters. More than half the tribes in this region maintain regular markets and possess conventional media of exchange, such as cowrie shells, salt, raffia cloth, brass rods, and iron bars. The peoples of the four easternmost clusters, on the other hand, conduct relatively little trade and are characterized, indeed, by a striking poverty in material possessions.

The province reveals some variation in settlement patterns. A few tribes in the extreme north, e.g., the Dzing, Holoholo, Kuba, Sakata, Sundi, and Yombe, align their dwellings in two rows along either side of a single street, as do the Bantu of the adjacent rainforest. The members of the Kwango cluster and some of their immediate neighbors live in settlements of dispersed homesteads or small hamlets, and this pattern recurs in the extreme east among the tribes of the Yao cluster. Elsewhere, for the most part, the Central Bantu occupy compact and frequently stockaded villages, often with the dwellings arranged around a central plaza. From the western Kaonde to the Atlantic coast the prevailing house type is a rectangular hut with a thatched gable roof and walls of palm leaves, grass, wood, or wattle and daub. The Bunda, Chokwe, Luimbe, Mbala, Ndembu, and Pende, however, prefer square houses with pyramidal roofs, and beehive dwellings occur among the Kisama. From the eastern Kaonde to the Indian Ocean, all groups have exchanged the rectangular house type of the tropical forest for the old Sudanic hut with a conical thatched roof and cylindrical walls of wattle and daub, and this same structure recurs in the extreme southwest among the Mbangala and Mbwela.

The inhabitants of the province reveal a somewhat surprising complexity in social stratification. Besides the universality of slavery, usually hereditary, and the widespread practice of enslavement for debt and for serious crimes, most groups differentiate a privileged nobility from ordinary freemen, and a number also recognize a special class of royalty. The sources specifically deny such privileged classes only for the Kisama, Ngongo, Sakata, and Yanzi in the west and for the peoples of the Maravi and Yao clusters in the east. Age-grades and secret societies are rare. Most tribes of the five western clusters, with the noteworthy exception of the Kuba, practice circumcision, but the eastern societies do not, and genital mutilations for females are nowhere reported.

Each settlement has a hereditary headman and an advisory council of elders. The Makonde, Mwera, and Ngindo in the extreme northeast recognize no higher political authority, but all other tribes have at least paramount chiefs over districts, although in some instances these are small and the chief's functions are more religious than regulative. Genuinely complex states occur with a frequency probably greater than anywhere else in Africa south of the Sahara-Sudan fringe. In addition to powerful tribal states among the Bemba, Chokwe, Kimbundu, Kuba, Luapula, Vili, Yaka, and formerly also the Buye and Tumbuka, the province had two empires of even greater magnitude at the time of first European contact. We have already described the Lunda empire of Mwata Yamvo, which during the seventeenth century reduced to vassalage the Chokwe, Luchazi, Luvale, Mbangala, Ndembu, and Yaka tribes (Chapter 37). Resisting the temptation to summarize the extremely interesting political systems of the Bemba and Kuba, we shall take the organization of the Kongo empire as our sole example. Since, however, it was destroyed by the Yaka about 1569, a few details missing in the early sources must be filled in from accounts of the adjacent and very similar Vili state of Loango.

The Kongo king maintained an elaborate court at the capital town of San Salvador, where he was surrounded by numerous slaves, pages, and personal attendants; a harem of wives; and such special officials as a chief priest and a royal executioner. The Queen-Mother held a respected position, though one appreciably less prominent than in the Bemba, Chokwe, Kuba, and Vili states. The ruler was an absolute monarch with a ritual relationship to the land, and no one might observe him eating or drinking, on pain of death. The symbols of his high office included a throne with ivory carvings, a white cap, and a zebra's tail. He exercised supreme judicial power and reserved for himself the exclusive right to inflict the death penalty.

A hierarchical administrative organization, with six great provinces divided into districts with a number of villages in each, assured the maintenance of order and a regular flow of tribute in cowrie-shell money, livestock, and agricultural produce. The hereditary headman in each community had the responsibility of making these collections once a year and transmitting them to the capital. Other sources of revenue included tolls from trade, fines paid in slaves for breaches of court etiquette, a royal monopoly on productive cowrie fisheries, and the reservation for the king of all pelts of particular animals and all fish of certain favored species.

The king appointed all provincial governors and district chiefs, usually from among his own relatives. Each maintained a local capital and court in his own administrative territory, and a courier system provided communication between them and San Salvador. Each territorial official also maintained a residence at the national capital. Here the provincial governors formed an advisory council of state and also exercised specialized individual functions. One, for example, served as commander in chief of the army, a second as minister of commerce and markets, a third as supreme ruler during the interregnum following the death of a king.

When the ruler died, the sacred fire which had been maintained throughout his reign was extinguished, as were hearth fires throughout the kingdom, and all work ceased. His corpse was mummified by smoking, wrapped in many cloths, and interred with human sacrifices. Meanwhile the council of state, acting as an electoral college, chose his successor from among the male members of the royal matrilineage. He was then installed with much pomp, including a new-fire ceremony.

The Kisama in the west and the Ngindo and Tumbuka in the east have social systems characterized by patrilineal descent and patrilocal residence. In the last two cases, and very likely in the first as well, these represent recent shifts from the matrilineal types of social organization which prevail everywhere else in the Central Bantu province. Since the latter reveal two somewhat divergent patterns, we shall deal with them separately. The first and most basic one occurs among the Buye, Holoholo, and Shila tribes on the northwestern edge of the Bemba cluster; throughout the Kasai, Kongo, Kwango, and Lunda clusters to the west thereof; and also, so far as the scanty available information can tell us, in the Kimbundu cluster in Angola. When we have described this pattern, we shall note the departures from it which occur in the three easternmost clusters.

The regulations governing marriage among the western Central Bantu usually prescribe both local and lineage exogamy. They prevent unions with a parallel cousin, and most tribes of the Kasai cluster also prohibit cross-cousin marriage. The latter is preferred, however, among the Bunda, the northwestern tribes of the Bemba cluster, and throughout the Kongo, Kwango, and Lunda clusters, although the Pende and Vili permit such unions only with a father's sister's daughter. On the basis of incomplete evidence, all groups prescribe the levirate, and all except the Kimbundu allow the sororate, for the remarriage of widowed persons.

A primary marriage always entails a bride-price. Although usually substantial in amount, this consists only of a small or token payment among the Pende and most tribes of the Lunda cluster. The Kuba allow both alternatives. If the payment is large, the wife's family must replace her if she dies, and she is obligated to reside with her husband and to marry his brother on his death; with only a token payment, however, these obligations do not prevail, and the couple reside alternately with the relatives of each for periods of five or six years.

Polygyny is preferential, general, and, except among the Bunda, exclusively nonsororal. The first wife enjoys a special status, but each co-wife has a separate hut, and the husband spends a prescribed period with each in rotation. The household unit normally assumes the form of an independent polygynous family, an extended family organization being reported only for the Sundi.

The Lele, one of the few tribes of the area possessing organized age-grades, exhibit an interesting form of polyandry. A girl abducted from another group becomes for six months the "wife of the village" and has sex relations with any or all of its male members. Thereafter she is reserved as the exclusive common wife of the unmarried men of the junior age-set. As these obtain wives of their own, they lose their communal rights. When only one man remains, he and the girl become husband and wife in a permanent monogamous union. Similar practices prevail among the adjacent Bunda, Dzing, and Pende.

With remarkable unanimity the western tribes of the province conform to a single basic pattern of social organization, characterized by matrilineal descent, inheritance, and succession; avunculocal residence; noncorporate matrisibs (usually exogamous and often totemic); and exogamous matrilineages, each localized in a village as an avunculocal clan-community. Only for the Kimbundu cluster does some uncertainty exist because of inadequate ethnographic coverage; the available sources clearly attest matrilineal descent, inheritance, and succession but do not specify whether residence follows the avunculocal or patrilocal rule.

Different tribes naturally reveal minor variations. Thus boys leave their paternal homes to join their maternal uncles in another village at the age of five or six in the Lunda cluster, at ten or twelve in the Kongo cluster, but often not until their marriage or the death of their father in the Kasai and Kwango clusters. In a few tribes a minority of men even reside permanently in the villages of their fathers, a tendency which has been increasing in recent years. Perhaps in consequence of this, the clan or localized lineage comprises only a segment of a village in some societies. Different groups also vary in regard to whether a younger brother or the eldest son of the eldest sister takes precedence in inheritance and succession. Some variation likewise occurs in kinship terminology. Cousin terms of the Iroquois type prevail throughout the Lunda cluster and in many tribes of the Kasai, Kwango, and northwest Bemba clusters as well, but the Pende and apparently the Kongo kinship systems reveal features of the Crow pattern.

That so clear an over-all picture of a rather exceptional type of social structure emerges from the descriptive sources must be taken as a tribute to the competence of the Belgian and other ethnographers who have worked in the area. Particularly significant, however, is the fact that this, the largest of all Bantu provinces and in most respects the most conservative, provides full confirmation of the reconstruction made in Chapter 13 of the original form of social organization among the closest linguistic relatives of the Bantu on the Nigerian plateau.

Social organization in the eastern part of the province reveals an interesting shift from that prevailing in the west. Though descent, inheritance, and succession conform to the matrilineal rule, only the Buye, Holoholo, and Shila, as we have seen, still exhibit the presumptive ancestral pattern characterized by a substantial bride-price, avunculocal residence, local exogamy, and avuncuclans. All groups, to be sure, have exogamous matrisibs, typically divided into lineages and often aggregated into phratries on the basis of the complementary or antipathetic characteristics of their totems, but the principles governing the localization of kin groups diverge markedly from those prevailing farther west.

The source of these differences appears to lie in the relative poverty of the people in movable and heritable wealth. The eastern tribes lack the iron money and quantities of trade goods held by their western cousins. Of the Bemba, for example, it is reported that the only important physical object which a man can leave to his heir is his bow. In the absence of movable property of consequence, inheritance tends to assume the form of *positional succession*, according to which a man's nonmaterial acquisitions—such as his name, his social status, and his guardian spirit—tend to descend as a unit, along with his widows and his few material possessions, to his preferred heir, i.e., his younger brother or perhaps his sister's son.

In the absence of livestock, native money, or other movable property in substantial amounts, the bride-price dwindles to a small and purely symbolic gift or disappears entirely, and is replaced as a consideration by bride-service. Throughout the area, consequently, a man must pay for his wife by working for her parents over a period of at least one year and usually several. This renders residence initially matrilocal, instead of being avunculocal from the beginning as among the western Central Bantu.

When he has served his period of bride-service, a man can usually remove with his wife and family to either (1) his father's settlement in patrilocal residence, (2) a new village which he founds himself in neolocal residence, or (3) his mother's original home in avunculocal residence. British ethnographers, through their habitual use of the one ambiguous term "virilocal" for these three very different residence patterns, too often present a confused picture of the resulting structural relationships. It seems reasonably clear, nevertheless, that removal after bride-service entails avunculocal residence far more often than it does either of the alternatives. Removal is by no means inevitable, however, for a man may always choose to remain in permanent matrilocal residence after he has fulfilled his service obligation, and the widespread preference for sororal polygyny provides a motive for such a decision. Among the Yao and neighboring groups, moreover, removal depends upon an opportunity for positional succession to a chiefship or the headship of an extended family. Ultimate residence is thus variable—often matrilocal, often avunculocal, sometimes patrilocal or neolocal.

The early German ethnographers called attention to a structural point which has since been overlooked, namely, the effect of cross-cousin marriage. Preferential marriage between cross-cousins, coupled with Iroquois cousin terminology, prevails throughout the area, and a number of tribes, e.g., the Chewa, Kaonde, Lamba, and Makonde, are specifically reported to favor unions with a matrilateral over a patrilateral cross-cousin, i.e., with a mother's brother's daughter rather than a father's sister's daughter. Whenever a man marries his mother's brother's daughter and resides matrilocally, he lives, of course, with his maternal uncle. The preferential rule of marriage thus equates matrilocal with avunculocal residence, and in all such cases removal naturally becomes unnecessary. Ultimate residence in the area is thus resolvable into combinations of four distinct patterns:

1. Permanent matrilocal residence which is at the same time avunculocal
2. Matrilocal but nonavunculocal residence persisting beyond bride-service
3. Avunculocal and nonmatrilocal residence resulting from removal
4. Patrilocal or neolocal residence after removal

The first three patterns are common; the fourth, exceptional. Regional differences within the area appear to reflect the varying incidence of patterns two and three in different tribal clusters.

Statistically or descriptively, matrilocal residence probably preponderates, at least if one overlooks the avunculocality implicit in preferential cross-cousin marriages. Historically, however, the social systems of the area appear to be derived, not from an original matrilocal form of the matrilineate, but from an avunculocal form in which an initial period of matrilocal residence has been extended to the point where, in the extreme case, avunculocality survives only in cases of positional succession. Such a development, though unusual, is by no means unprecedented. Murphy (1956), for example, has documented a case where a patrilineal and formerly patrilocal society has become matrilocal, except for local headmen, through a progressive extension of the period of bride-service.

The complexity of residence practices has in general prevented the development of localized clans of any of the standard types. Instead, kin ties are utilized in unusual combinations to produce local groups. The Yao, for example, add to a matrilocal extended family, or localized minor matrilineage, the family of the senior male of the lineage, who lives, as it were, in sororilocal residence with his married sisters and their families. Among the Bemba, a local group evolves out of shifting ties to an influential man, beginning usually with his sons and younger brothers and their families, who are later replaced by his sisters and their families (and perhaps an affine or two), and ultimately by his sisters' sons and their families.

The area also provides an actual case of transition from matrilineal to patrilineal descent, documented for three successive stages. The Tumbuka, prior to 1780, resembled most of the neighboring tribes in adhering to matrilineal descent, inheritance, and succession, in requiring matrilocal bride-service rather than a bride-price, and in permitting an ultimate shift to avunculocal residence.

Between 1780 and 1800 some ivory traders from the east conquered the Tumbuka and established the Kamanga kingdom. Under the influence of these patrilineal invaders, bride-service was reduced to a nominal period, the token bridal gift was increased to enable the husband to remove his wife almost immediately to his own village, and rights to inherit and succeed, after younger brothers had had their turn, were transferred from sisters' sons to own sons.

Around 1855 a new invasion, this time by the Ngoni, overthrew the Kamanga dynasty and subjugated the Tumbuka to new rulers with even stronger patrilineal institutions. In consequence of their influence the Tumbuka abandoned even nominal bride-service, adopted the full-fledged South African bride-price, or *lobola*, substituted the eldest son for the younger brother as the preferred heir and successor, and transformed what had originally been matrisibs into indubitable exogamous patrisibs. The process of change here attested for the Tumbuka has doubtless been recapitulated in Tanganyika among peoples for whom we unfortunately lack comparable documentation.

Selected Bibliography

Baeyens, M. Les Lesa. *RC*, 4:129–143, 193–206, 257–270, 321–336. 1913. [Sakata].

Baumann, H. *Lunda*. Berlin, 1935. [Lunda cluster].

Beaucorps, R. de. *Les Bayansi du Bas-Kwilu*. Louvain, 1931.

———. Les Basongo de la Luniungu et de la Gobari. *MIRCB*, 10(3):1–175. 1941. [Ngongo].

Behr, H. F. von. Die Völker zwischen Rufiji und Rovuma. *MDS*, 6:69–87. 1893. [Makonde].

Brau, C. Le droit coutumier Lunda. *BJIDC*, 10:155–267. 1942. [Luwa].

Brelsford, W. V. Fishermen of the Bangweulu Swamps. *RLP*, 12:1–169. 1946. [Unga].

Brohez. Les Balubas. *BSRBG*, 29:460–478. 1905. [Shila].

Bruwer, J. P. van S. The System of Guardianship in Cewa Matrilineal Society. *AS*, 14:113–122. 1955.

———. Matrilineal Kinship among the Kunda. *Africa*, 28:207–224. 1958.

Bruyns, L. De sociaal-economische ontwikkeling van de Bakongo. *MIRCH*, 20(3): 1–343. 1951.

Capello, N., and R. Ivens. *From Benguella to the Territory of Yacca*. 2 vols. London, 1882. [Mbangala].

Chatelain, H. Folk-Tales of Angola. *Memoirs of the American Folklore Society*, 1:1–315. 1894. [Kimbundu].

Colle, P. Les Baluba. *CME*, 10–11:1–918. 1913. [Buye].

Coxhead, J. C. C. The Native Tribes of Northeastern Rhodesia. *RAIOC*, 5:1–64. 1914. [Bemba cluster].

Cross-Upcott, A. R. W. Social Aspects of Ngindo Bee-keeping. *JRAI*, 86(2):81–108. 1956.

Cunnison, I. Kinship and Local Organization in the Luapula. *Communications from the Rhodes-Livingstone Institute*, 5:1–32. Livingstone, 1950.

———. Perpetual Kinship. *RLJ*, 20:28–48. 1956. [Luapula].

Cuvelier, G. La vie sociale des Balamba orientaux. *Congo*, 6(1):1–21; 6(2):161–184. 1932.

Decker, J. M. de. Contribution à l'étude du mariage chez les Bambunda. *BJIDC*, 10:125–246. 1942. [Bunda].

De Cleene, N. La structure de la société Yombe. *BIRCB*, 8:44–51. 1937.

———. La famille dans l'organisation sociale du Mayombe. *Africa*, 10:1–16. 1937.

Deleval, H. Les tribus Kavati du Mayombe. *RC*, 3:32–40, 103–115, 170–186, 253–264. 1912. [Yombe].

Delhaise, C. Chez les Wabemba. *BSRBG*, 32:173–227, 261–283. 1908.

Denis, P. J. L'organisation d'un peuple primitif. *Congo*, 16(1):481–502. 1935. [Sakata].

Dennett, R. E. Laws and Customs of the Fjort. *JAS*, 1:259–287. 1902. [Vili].

———. Bavili Notes. *FL*, 16:371–406. 1905.

D'Hanis. Organisation politique, civile, et penale de la tribu des Mousseronghes. *BSRBG*, 14:135–153. 1890. [Kongo].

Doke, C. M. *The Lambas of Northern Rhodesia*. London, 1931.

Douglas, M. Alternate Generations among the Lele. *Africa*, 22:59–65. 1952.

Even, A. Quelques coutumes des tribus Badondos et Bassoundis. *BSRC*, 13:17–31. 1931. [Sundi].

Gouldsbury, C. Notes on the Customary Law of the Awemba and Kindred Peoples. *JAS*, 14:366–385; 15:36–53, 157–183. 1915–1916. [Bemba].

Gouldsbury, C., and A. Sheane. *The Great Plateau of Northern Rhodesia*. London, 1911. [Bemba].

Hulstaert, G. Carte linguistique du Congo Belge. *MIRCB*, 14(5):1–67. 1950.

Hutereau, A. Notes sur la vie familiale et juridique des Mayumbe. *BSRBG*, 32:299–315, 357–371. 1909. [Yombe].

———. Les Manyanga. *BSRBG*, 34:15–39. 1910. [Sundi].

Ihle, A. Das alte Königreich Kongo. *SV*, 1:1–285. 1929.

Jaspert, F., and W. Jaspert. Die Völkerstämme Mittel-Angolas. *VSVM*, 5:1–155. 1930. [Chokwe and Luvale].

Johnson, W. P. *Nyasa*. London, 1922.

Lamal, F. Essai d'étude démographique d'une population du Kwango. *MIRCB*, 15(4):1–189. 1949. [Suku].

Laman, K. The Kongo. *SEU*, 4:1–155. 1953. [Sundi].

Lambo, L. Étude sur les Balala. *BJIDC*, 14:231–256, 273–300, 313–346. 1946.

Maes, J. *Notes sur les populations des bassins du Kasai, de la Lukenie, et du Lac Leopold II*. Bruxelles, 1924. [Sakata].

Magyar, L. *Reisen in Süd-Afrika*, vol. 1. Pest and Leipzig, 1859. [Kimbundu cluster].

Mair, L. P. Marriage and Family in the Dedza District of Nyasaland. *JRAI*, 81:103–119. 1951. [Chewa].

Marchal, R. La famille chez les Bashila. *BJIDC*, 3:98–112. 1935.

Marwick, M. G. The Kinship Basis of Cewa Social Structure. *SAJS*, 48:258–262. 1952.

———. The Social Context of Cewa Witch Beliefs. *Africa*, 22:120–135. 1952.

Mattenklodt. Die Kisama, ed. H. Baumann. *WBKL*, 6:71–108. 1944.

Maugham, R. C. F. *Zambesia*. London, 1910. [Nyanja and Sena].

McCulloch, M. *The Southern Lunda and Related Peoples*. London, 1951.

Melland, F. H. Bangweulu Swamps and the Wa-Unga. *GJ*, 38:381–395. 1911.

———. *In Witchbound Africa*. London, 1923. [Kaonde].

Mertens, J. Les Ba Dzing de la Kamtsha. *MIRCB*, 4:1–381. 1935.

———. L'esclavage chez les Ba Dzing. *Congo*, 17(1):641–676. 1936.

———. Les chefs couronnés chez les Ba Kongo orientaux. *MIRCB*, 11(1):1–455. 1942.

Mitchell, J. C. The Yao of Southern Nyasaland. *STBCA*, pp. 292–353. 1911.

———. *The Yao Village*. Manchester, 1956.

Mitchell, J. C., and J. A. Barnes. The Lamba Village. *CSAS*, n.s., 24:1–69. 1950.

Monteiro Lopes, M. Usages and Customs of the Natives of Sena. *JAS*, 6:350–366. 1906.

Munday, J. T. Some Traditions of the Nyendwa Clan of Northern Rhodesia. *BS*, 14:435–454. 1940. [Lala].

Murphy, R. F. Matrilocality and Patrilineality in Mundurucú Society. *AA*, 58:414–434. 1956.

Nauwelaert, P. La société Yombe. *Congo*, 19(1):405–415. 1938.

Ntara, S. Y. *Man of Africa*. London, 1934. [Chewa].

Pechuel-Loesche, E. *Volkskunde von Loango*. Stuttgart, 1907. [Vili].

Peters, D. U. Land Use in Serenje District. *RLP*, 19:1–100. 1950. [Lala].

Richards, A. I. Preliminary Notes on the Babemba. *BS*, 9:225–253. 1935.

———. *Land, Labour and Diet in Northern Rhodesia*. London, 1939. [Bemba].

———. The Political System of the Bemba Tribe. *APS*, pp. 83–120. 1940.

———. Bemba Marriage and Present Economic Conditions. *RLP*, 4:1–123. 1940.

———. Some Types of Family Structure amongst the Central Bantu. *ASKM*, pp. 206–251. 1950.

———. The Bemba of North-Eastern Rhodesia. *STBCA*, pp. 164–191. 1951.

Sanderson, M. Relationships among the Wayao. *JRAI*, 50:369–376. 1920.

Sanderson, M. Some Marriage Customs of the Wahenga. *JAS*, 22:131–138. 1923.

———. The Relationship Systems of the Wangonde and Wahenga Tribes. *JRAI*, 53:448–459. 1923. [Tumbuka].

Schebesta, P. Ethnographie der Asena am unteren Sambesi. *Bibliotheca Africana*, 2:201–208. Innsbruck, 1926.

Schmitz, R. Les Baholoholo. *CME*, 9:1–605. 1912.

Slaski, J. *Peoples of the Lower Luapula Valley*. London, 1951.

Snowden, J. D. *The Cultivated Races of Sorghum*. London, 1936.

Sousberghe, L. de. Structures de parenté et d'alliance d'après les formules Pende. *MIRCH*, n.s., 4(1):1–93. 1955.

Stannus, H. S. Notes on Some Tribes in British Central Africa. *JRAI*, 40:285–335. 1910. [Nyanja].

———. The Wayao of Nyasaland. *HAS*, 3:229–272. 1922.

Steytler, J. G. Ethnographic Report on the Achewa Tribe. Unpublished ms.

Tew, M. *Peoples of the Lake Nyasa Region*. London, 1950.

———. A Form of Polyandry among the Lele. *Africa*, 21:1–12. 1951.

———. Alternate Generations among the Lele. *Africa*, 22:59–65. 1952.

Torday, E. The Northern Babunda. *Man*, 19:49–55. 1919.

Torday, E., and T. A. Joyce. Notes on the Ethnography of the Ba-Mbala. *JRAI*, 35:398–426. 1905.

———. Notes on the Ethnography of the Ba-Yaka. *JRAI*, 36:39–58. 1906.

———. Notes on the Ethnography of the Ba-Huana. *JRAI*, 36:272–301. 1906. [Mbala].

———. Notes on the Southern Ba-Mbala. *Man*, 7:81–84. 1907.

———. Notes ethnographiques sur les peuples communément appelés Bakuba. *AMCB*, ser. 3, 2(1):1–271. 1910.

———. Notes ethnographiques sur des populations habitant les bassins du Kasai et du Kwango oriental. *AMCB*, ser. 3, 2(2):1–359. 1922. [Kwango cluster].

Turner, V. W. The Spatial Separation of Generations in Ndembu Village Structure. *Africa*, 25:121–137. 1955.

Van Overbergh, C. Les Mayombe. *CME*, 2:1–470. 1907.

Van Reeth, E. P. De rol van den moederlijken oom in de inlandsche familie. *MIRCB*, 5:3–35. 1935. [Yombe].

Vansina, J. Les tribus Ba-Kuba et les peuplades apparentées. *AMRCB*, 1:1–64. 1954. [Kuba and Lele].

Van Wing, J. Études Bakongo. *BC*, 3:1–318. 1921.

Viaene, E., and F. Bernard. Chez les Lessa. *BSRBG*, 23:464–510; 24:198–229. 1909–1910. [Sakata].

Watson, W. The Kaonde Village. *RLJ*, 20:28–48. 1956.

Weeks, J. H. Notes on Some Customs of the Lower Congo Peoples. *FL*, 19:409–437; 20:32–63, 181–201, 304–311, 457–480. 1908–1909. [Kongo].

———. *Among the Primitive Bakongo*. London, 1914.

Weekx, G. La peuplade des Ambundu. *Congo*, 18(1):353–373; 18(2):13–35. 1937. [Bunda].

Werner, A. *The Natives of British Central Africa*. London, 1906. [Nyanja].

Weule, K. Wissenschaftliche Ergebnisse meiner ethnographischen Forschungsreise in den Südosten Deutsch-Ostafrikas. *MDSE*, 1:1–124. 1908. [Makonde, Makua, and Yao].

White, C. M. N. Factors in the Social Organization of the Luvale. *AS*, 14:97–112. 1955.

Whiteley, W. *Bemba and Related Peoples of Northern Rhodesia*. London, 1951.

———. Modern Local Government among the Makua. *Africa*, 24:349–358. 1954.

Wissmann, H., L. Wolf, C. von François, and H. Mueller. *Im Innern Afrikas.* Leipzig, 1888. [Kuba].

Young, T. C. *Notes on the Customs and Folk-Lore of the Tumbuka-Kamanga Peoples.* Livingstonia, 1931.

———. *Our African Way of Life.* London, 1946. [Chewa].

39

Northeast Coastal Bantu

When the Central Bantu penetrated northern Mozambique, they presumably exterminated the indigenous Bushmen, since no traces of the latter survive today. Fanning out as they neared the coast, one branch turned north into Tanganyika, and another turned south. The southern branch, which has left evidences of its occupation of Southern Rhodesia in the seventh century at Zimbabwe, will receive consideration in Chapter 49. For the present we shall follow only the northern branch.

In Tanganyika the Bantu likewise found Bushmanoid hunters in possession of most of the country. We have already encountered their remnants in the Khoisan-speaking Kindiga and Sandawe (Chapter 10). Conceivably the Bantu might have entered Tanganyika by way of Uganda rather than from the south, but the widespread survival of matrilineal forms of social organization in the area strongly suggests that the first immigrants were Central Bantu rather than the patrilineal Interlacustrine Bantu. In the interior, the subsequent adoption of cattle markedly altered the culture, as will be indicated in Chapter 46. Consequently we shall consider here only the Bantu who followed the coast of the Indian Ocean to the northeast.

When the invaders reached the coastal region opposite Zanzibar, they encountered for the first time a people utterly different from the Bushmanoid hunters whom they had thus far been displacing. These were the descendants of the ancient Azanians (see Chapter 26), to whom we shall return in a moment. From such archeological evidence as we possess, it appears that the Megalithic Cushites, who presumably constituted the principal element of the Azanian population, occupied only the trading ports along the coast and restricted mountainous sections of the interior that had sufficient rainfall to support their intensive irrigated agriculture. We may hazard the conjecture that the Bantu, now habituated to adapting to one new environment after another, were less selective and that they infiltrated and preempted the less desirable land along the river valleys and in the hinterland. Whatever their mode of occupying the country, they certainly established themselves solidly, for they constitute the overwhelmingly preponderant element in the population today.

The newcomers pressed steadily forward into Kenya and thence into Somalia, where the valley of the Shebelle River represents the limit of their intensive penetration. In Kenya and Somalia they found the Azanians confined to a few coastal trading settlements. The hinterland contained only Bushmanoid hunters, even in favored sections such as the valleys of the Tana, Juba, and Shebelle Rivers. The Bantu populated the latter, driving the indigenes back into the arid steppe and savanna country, where agriculture was impossible. Here a few remnants, like the Boni and Sanye tribes, still survive.

Ultimately, as we shall see in Chapters 41 and 42, the pastoral Galla and Somali descended from the Ethiopian plateau with their herds, depriving the indigenous hunters of their remaining land and subjugating the Bantu tillers. Some of the latter escaped southwestward into coastal Kenya, where their descendants today combine pastoral practices learned from the Cushites with their own ancient agricultural economy. Others remained in Somalia as agricultural serfs of the Galla and Somali. A few of these groups, notably the Bosha and Shebelle tribes, succeeded in retaining their Bantu speech until very recent times.

In all probability it was during the period from A.D. 575 to 879, when the Persians held a dominant position in the trade with the East via the Sabaean Lane, that the Bantu arrived on the Azanian coast. Here dwelt an exceedingly mixed population, probably basically Megalithic Cushitic but certainly with strong Persian, Yemenite Arab, and Malay ingredients. To this potpourri the Negroid Bantu now added a new element, which gradually became increasingly prominent, as we know from the fact that the Malagasy who migrated from this region to settle Madagascar carried in their blood a strong Negroid component. This mixed population, when it acquired elements of Islamic culture from the Arabs and absorbed new acculturated and detribalized Bantu groups along the coast and in the offlying islands, evolved into the Swahili people of today.

After the Persians lost control of the trade with the East in 879, the Arabs, by now converted to Islam, rapidly expanded their mercantile interests in East Africa. They founded strong trading posts at Mogadisho and Brava in southern Somalia around 908, gradually adding others in coastal Kenya, Tanganyika, and Mozambique until they had acquired a complete monopoly of all commerce along the East African coast, broken only with the arrival of the Portuguese on Zanzibar in 1503. A number of these settlements developed into strong states and enjoyed marked economic prosperity. Kilwa on the Tanganyika coast, for example, which was founded in 975, holds the distinction of being the only African state south of the Mediterranean coast to strike its own independent coinage during the medieval period. From the maritime ports, Arab and Swahili merchants penetrated into the interior as far as the present Belgian Congo, trading for ivory, gold, and slaves, and introducing rice and other crops as well as novel merchandise.

The foregoing historical discussion provides an explanation of the three distinct clusters into which it seems advisable to divide the Northeast Coastal Bantu.

ZIGULA CLUSTER

This cluster embraces the peoples in the immediate hinterland of the Tanganyika coast who still retain reasonably intact their original tribal identities and who have not been markedly affected by contact with the pastoral Cushites.

1. Bondei (Wabondei, Waschensi). This tribe appears to be an amalgam of Digo, Shambala, and Zigula elements.
2. Kwere (Oukwere, Wakwere), with the Doe (Oudoe, Wadoe).
3. Luguru (Waluguru), with the Kami (Wakami) and Khutu (Kutu, Wakhutu). The Khutu are largely detribalized today. The Luguru proper were reported in 1934 to number about 150,000.
4. Nguru (Ngulu, Nguu, Wangulu, Wanguru).
5. Zigula (Ouazigoua, Wazegura, Zeguha, Zigua), with the Ruvu (Rouvou, Ruwu).

NIKA CLUSTER

This cluster includes the "Hamitized Bantu" tribes in the immediate hinterland of the Kenya coast, together with remnants of the former Bantu occupation of the major river valleys of Somalia. The independent tribes of the cluster are known collectively as the Nika (Wanika, Wanyika).

6. Digo (Adigo, Wadigo). They number about 110,000 and are mainly Moslems.
7. Duruma (Derouma, Waduruma). They number about 35,000.
8. Giryama (Dziryama, Kiriama, Wagiliama), with the Chonyi (Dschogni), Jibana (Dzihana), Kambe (Wakambe), Kaura, Rabai (Warabai), and Ribe (Waribe). They number about 155,000.
9. Gosha (Wagoscia, Wagosha), with the detached Gobawein. Remnants of the Bantu who formerly occupied the valley of the Juba River, they are now completely acculturated to the Sab tribe of Somali. They numbered about 30,000 in 1922.
10. Pokomo (Wapokomo), with the kindred Elwana (Malakote), Korokoro, and Malachini. They occupy the valley of the Tana River, number about 20,000, and are subject to the Bararetta tribe of Galla.
11. Shebelle, with the detached Dube, Eile, Shidle, and Tunni Torre. Remnants of the Bantu who formerly occupied the valley of the Shebelle River, they are now completely acculturated to the dominant Somali.

SWAHILI CLUSTER

The Swahili (Soahili, Suaheli, Wasuaheli) do not actually constitute a separate ethnic group but embrace the strongly Arabized and detribalized people along the coast and in the offlying islands who derive from many tribes and often incorporate significant elements of diverse alien stocks. They are Moslems and have a total population of approximately a million. Their Bantu language serves as the lingua franca over a large area in the interior as well as on the coast.

12. Bajun (Badjouni, Bagiuni, Bajoni, Barjun, Bayoun, Gunya, Patschuni, Wagunya, Watikuu). They inhabit the coast and offlying islands in southern Somalia and adjacent Kenya and number about 2,000.
13. Comorians, embracing the Ngazija and Nzwani. They inhabit the Comoro Islands and were reported in 1936 to number about 130,000.
14. Hadimu (Wahadimu), with the Tumbatu (Watumbatu). They inhabit the island of Zanzibar and the adjacent small island of Tumbatu and were reported in 1924 to number about 100,000.
15. Pemba (Wapemba). They inhabit the island of Pemba and were reported in 1924 to number about 80,000.
16. Segeju (Asegedzu, Mossegale, Wasegeju), with other Arabized and Islamized tribes along the coast of Kenya. They have a total population of about 75,000, of whom 25,000 are specifically Segeju.
17. Zaramo (Dzalamo, Wasaramo), with the Ndengereko, Rufiji, and other Arabized and Islamized tribes along the coast of Tanganyika, in the hinterland of Dar es Salaam, and on the offlying island of Mafia.

All the Northeast Coastal Bantu subsist primarily by agriculture, which they usually conduct by brand-tillage, although the Pokomo and some Giryama practice irrigation. They cultivate the African cereals—eleusine, millet, and especially sorghum—to a considerable extent, as well as small quantities of such Sudanic crops as cow peas, okra, and sesame. The insular Swahili possess the entire roster of Malaysian and Indian plants, but only rice is extensively grown on the mainland. The American complex, however, strongly predominates today, with maize or manioc as the usual staples, followed by peanuts and sweet potatoes as well as smaller quantities of cucurbits, legumes, and fruit trees. Their only close rivals are bananas among the Comorians, rice among the Hadimu, Pemba, and Pokomo, and sorghum among the Bajun, Duruma, Kwere, and Zigula.

Animal husbandry assumes considerable auxiliary importance in the Nika and Swahili clusters. These groups keep cattle, goats, sheep, and often donkeys and bees, as well as dogs, cats, and poultry, and they use milk and make butter. The Bondei, Kwere, Luguru, Zaramo, and Zigula of coastal Tanganyika, on the other hand, keep either extremely few cattle or none at all, affiliating in this respect with the Central Bantu to the south.

Though hunting and gathering are rarely significant, fishing holds a prominent place in the economies of the Nika and insular Swahili peoples. Most of the coastal and island groups engage very extensively in trade and maintain regular markets. In the division of labor by sex, the men generally do the hunting, fishing, herding, milking, and trading, but leave most of the cultivation to the women. On the other hand, women fish among the Zigula, gather shellfish among the Hadimu, and participate in milking among the Bajun and Giryama, whereas men assume an equal or sometimes even preponderant share of the agricultural tasks among the Bajun, Bondei, Hadimu, and Nguru.

Marriage invariably involves a substantial bride-price. All groups allow polygyny in the nonsororal form, but it occurs relatively infrequently among the Bondei, Duruma, Giryama, Luguru, and Pokomo and practically never among the Bajun. Polygynous wives always occupy separate dwellings, and the first married enjoys a superior status. The Bajun permit marriage with any first cousin, the Digo and Luguru with a cross-cousin only, and most other tribes with none. With the possible exception of the Luguru, all the peoples of the province adhere to the patrilocal rule of residence, but the Bajun, Luguru, Nguru, and Zigula require an initial year or so of matrilocal residence. The household unit consists of an independent nuclear or polygynous family among all Swahili groups and the coastal tribes of the Zigula cluster, but patrilocal extended families prevail among the Duruma and Giryama.

Despite the universal patrilocality, descent is only infrequently patrilineal. Exogamous matrilineal sibs still survive, or have only recently disappeared, among all the tribes of the Zigula cluster and even among the adjacent Swahilized Zaramo. Moreover, the southern tribes of the Nika cluster—the Digo, the Duruma, and the Rabai subtribe of the Giryama—along with their exogamous patrisibs still retain functional matrilineages and are thus characterized by double descent. In at least some of the tribes of this cluster patrilineages are localized as clans. Kinship terminology in the province follows a variety of patterns—Crow among the Luguru, Iroquois among the Kwere and apparently also the Digo and Giryama, descriptive among the Bajun, and Hawaiian among the Hadimu, Pokomo, and Zigula. Wherever matrilineal descent survives, even among the Digo and Duruma, inheritance also follows the matrilineal rule.

Most of the tribes of the Nika and Swahili clusters occupy compact villages, formerly often palisaded, but the Zaramo live in neighborhoods of dispersed homesteads, and the prevailing settlement pattern among the Bondei, Kwere, Luguru, and formerly the Zigula consists of a cluster of separated hamlets. The original house type of the province—a rectangular dwelling with a thatched gable roof—has been superseded by the Sudanic cone-cylinder hut among most Kwere, Luguru, Zaramo, and Zigula and

Giryama Girls in Ceremonial Attire. (Courtesy of British Information Services.)

by a hemispherical structure of poles covered with grass among the Pokomo.

Normally each settlement has a headman, a council of elders, or both, and most tribes of the Zigula cluster have achieved no higher form of political integration. The Swahili tribes, except for the Bajun and Segeju, have states of Arabic type with sultans. The Nika peoples and the Segeju, however, borrowed cycling age-grades from the adjacent Galla and also the type of political organization which we have termed the Gada republic (see Chapter 6), and the Digo, Duruma, and Giryama still retain both.

The Giryama, who may serve as an example, have a complex system with age-grades of two distinct types: (1) *rika* grades, each consisting of thirteen annual age-sets of boys initiated by circumcision during a given year, and (2) *kambi* grades, in which promotion depends upon the payment of substantial fees rather than the passage of time. In the *rika* system, advancement to the next higher grade comes automatically, though with appropriate ceremonial, every thirteenth year. All political offices, on the tribal as well as the district and local levels, are filled by men who belong to both the third or ruling *rika* grade and to the ninth *kambi* grade. A triumvirate of three such men administers the affairs of the tribe for thirteen years, after which they become *rika* elders and are succeeded in office by three other men of the same *kambi* grade but of the next *rika* grade.

Selected Bibliography

Baker, E. C. Notes on the History of the Wasegeju. *TNR*, 37:16–41. 1937.

Barrett, W. E. H. Notes on the Customs and Beliefs of the Wa-Giriama. *JRAI*, 41:20–28. 1911.

Baumann, O. *Usambara und seine Nachbargebiete*. Berlin, 1891. [Bondei, Digo, and Segeju].

Cerulli, E. Gruppi etnici negri nella Somalia. *AAE*, 64:177–184. 1934. [Bosha and Shebelle].

Dale, G. An Account of the Principal Customs and Habits of the Natives Inhabiting the Bondei Country. *JRAI*, 25:182–239. 1895.

Fischer, G. A. Das Wapokomo-Land und seine Bewohner. *MGGH*, 2:1–57. 1878–1879.

Fontoynont and Raomandahy. La Grande Comore. *Mémoires de l'Académie Malgache*, 23:1–105. Tananarive, 1937. [Comorians].

Grottanelli, V. L. *Pescatori dell'Oceano Indiano*. Roma, 1955. [Bajun].

Ingrams, W. H. *Zanzibar*. London, 1931. [Hadimu].

Johnstone, H. B. Notes on the Customs of the Tribes occupying Mombasa Sub-District. *JRAI*, 32:263–274. 1902. [Giryama].

Kraft, A. Die Wapokomo. *REVAO*, pp. 283–293. 1903.

Le Roy, A. Au Zanguebar anglais. *MC*, 22:568–573. 1890. [Pokomo].

McVicar, T. The Position of Woman among the Wanguru. *Primitive Man*, 7:17–22. 1934.

Niese, R. Das Personen- und Familienrecht der Suaheli. *ZVR*, 16:203–248. 1903.

Picarda. Notes sur l'Ouzigoua, l'Oukwere et l'Oudoe. *MC*, 18:184–189, 197–201, 208–211, 225–228, 234–236, 246–249, 258–261, 269–274, 281–285, 294–297, 322–324, 342–346. 1886. [Kwere and Zigula].

Prins, A. H. J. *The Coastal Tribes of the North-Eastern Bantu*. London, 1952.

Repiquet, J. *Le sultanat d'Angouan*. Paris, 1901. [Comorians].

Robinson, A. E. The Shirazi Colonizations of East Africa. *TNR*, 3:40–81. 1937.

Rolleston, I. H. C. The Watumbatu of Zanzibar. *TNR*, 8:85–97. 1940. [Hadimu].

Scheerder and Tastevin. Les Wa lu guru. *Anthropos*, 45:241–286. 1950.

St. Paul-Hilaire, von. Ueber die Rechtsgewohnheiten der im Bezirk Tanga ansässigen Färbigen. *MDS*, 8:191–209. 1895. [Digo].

Stuhlmann, F. *Mit Emin Pascha ins Herz von Afrika*. Berlin, 1894. [Kwere].

———. Forschungsreisen in Usaramo. *MDS*, 7:225–232. 1894. [Zaramo].

Vanden Bergh, L. J. *On the Trail of the Pigmies*. New York, 1921. [Duruma].

Velten, C. Sitten und Gebräuche der Suaheli. *MSOS*, 1(3):9–85. 1898.

Wallis, P. Waluguru Sibs. *Primitive Man*, 7:58–63. 1934.

Wedell, H. Das Sachen- und Vertragsrecht und die politische Organisation der Suaheli. *ZVR*, 18:119–183. 1905.

Werner, A. The Bantu Coast Tribes of the East Africa Protectorate. *JRAI*, 45:326–354. 1915. [Digo, Duruma, and Giryama].

Werth, E. *Das Deutsch-Ostafrikanische Küstenland*. 2 vols. Berlin, 1915.

Zache, H. Sitten und Gebräuche der Suaheli. *ZE*, 31:61–86. 1899.

PART NINE
EAST AFRICAN PASTORALISM

─●●─

40

─●●─

Beja

With the exception of a few remnants of ancient hunters and gatherers, and of occasional fishing populations, the peoples considered up to
this point have exhibited economies based primarily upon agriculture.
We have encountered no pastoral nomads. Many of the tillers surveyed,
to be sure, have made considerable use of domesticated animals and their
products, and the Berbers (Chapter 15) have provided an outstanding
example of a balanced economy resting upon agriculture and animal husbandry in approximately equal proportions. From now on we shall meet
a variety of peoples who depend much more strongly on herding and
who in many instances have virtually abandoned cultivation to lead an
independent pastoral existence (see Map 15).

The earliest pastoral nomads in Africa were the Beja, or Bega, a nation located immediately southeast of the ancient Egyptians and east of
the Nubians. They first appear in Egyptian history around 2700 B.C., at
which time they seem already to have been living a life of independent
pastoralism. This they had doubtless acquired from their northeastern
neighbors, the Semites of the Sinai Peninsula and adjacent Arabia. Like
the Egyptians and the Arabs, they spoke languages of the Hamitic stock,
but these belonged to a distinct subfamily thereof, the Cushitic. Their
modern descendants, who continue to occupy the same general area, still
preserve for the most part their ancient speech and mode of life.

Both the Pharaonic and the Ptolemaic Egyptians exploited the Beja
country for gold and occasionally suffered incursions from its nomadic

314

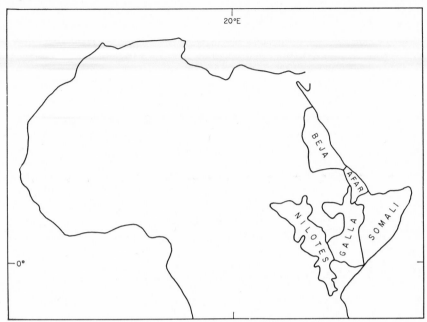

Map 15. East African Pastoralists

inhabitants. Between A.D. 268 and 451 the Beja even exercised political domination over part of Upper Egypt and also exerted considerable influence in Nubia. Although they accepted Christianity shortly after 600, they were converted to Islam between 1150 and 1300 and remain Moslems today. During their Christian period they came strongly under the influence of the Semitic state of Axum, reflected in the adoption by some of the southern Beja of the language and class structure of their Tigrinya neighbors.

The Beja belong to the Caucasoid race and are characterized physically by the following traits: copper-red to deep-brown skin, moderate stature (about 5 feet 5 or 6 inches in adult males), head of medium breadth (cephalic index 75 to 79), narrow nose, thin lips, and clearly Caucasoid features. They possess wavy rather than kinky hair, which is usually black, although red and even blond shades occasionally appear. They speak languages of the Northern branch of the Cushitic subfamily. The tribal classification below, however, includes one Central Cushitic tribe, the Bogo, and one Semitic people, the Tigre, who have adopted the pastoral habits of their Beja neighbors.

1. Ababda, with the Qireijab coastal fishermen. They number about 20,000, are heavily mixed with Arabs, and have largely abandoned their original Cushitic language.

2. Amarar. This group has a population of approximately 45,000.
3. Amer (Beni Amer). These people, numbering about 60,000, have in part adopted the Semitic language of the adjacent Tigre, or are bilingual.
4. Bisharin (Besarin, Bisariab), embracing the Atbai, Atbara, and other lesser tribes. They number about 60,000.
5. Bogo (Belen, Bileni). They number about 25,000, of whom nearly half are Christians. They speak a Central Cushitic language.
6. Hadendowa (Hendawa), with the Halenga. They have a population of about 70,000.
7. Tigre (Tigrai), embracing the Habab, Maria (Marea), Mensa (Mansa), and other subtribes. They number about 200,000 and speak a Semitic language akin to the Amharic and Tigrinya of Ethiopia.

From their entrance into history the Beja have followed an almost exclusively pastoral economy. Even today they do a minimum of hunting and gathering, observe a taboo on fish, except in a few isolated groups on the coast of the Red Sea, and limit their agriculture to a little durra cultivation in an occasional favored spot. They subsist almost entirely on the milk, butter, and meat provided by their large flocks of sheep and goats and their considerable herds of cattle (in the south) and camels (in the north). They have, to be sure, had camels only since the first century. Here and there the Beja also keep horses, donkeys, dogs, cats, and chickens. The Bisharin are reported to drink the fresh blood of their animals. Men alone engage in herding and milking, whereas women till the rare plots of cultivated land. The reader is advised henceforth to note particularly the sex to which milking is assigned, since this has considerable diagnostic significance in the historical analysis of African pastoralism.

The Beja wander in small bands with their flocks and herds, sometimes throughout the year, sometimes only during periods of transhumance. They camp in rectangular tents with a framework of poles and a cover of grass or palm-leaf mats, each occupied by a single nuclear family. The Bogo, Tigre, and some Amer more commonly live in hemispherical shelters roofed with grass or mats, or even in substantial thatched huts. A council of family heads typically handles the affairs of the band. In addition, each subtribe or occasionally a whole tribe has a chief, whose authority is limited and who is chosen by seniority or election from a privileged lineage. Formal age-grades are lacking, but boys are subjected to circumcision and girls to clitoridectomy.

The northern tribes reveal a relatively egalitarian social system; they keep no slaves and recognize no distinct noble class. The Amer, Bogo, and Tigre, however, possess hereditary slaves, originally recruited by capture in war or by purchase from abroad, and the rest of the population is divided into a small class of nobles and a large class of serfs, between which intermarriage does not occur. Each serf owes his master numerous onerous obligations, e.g., among the Tigre an annual present of grain and beer, a weekly contribution of milk, a portion of the meat of all slaughtered animals, and a cow as a funeral offering for each death in his lord's family. He receives a few gifts and services in return, but these by no means constitute complete reciprocity. When a serf woman marries, she becomes subject to her husband's master. Serfs cannot be sold, nor can they obtain freedom in any manner. If mistreated, they can only appeal to a council of the master's lineage to be transferred to another master.

A Hadendowa Beja with His Camel. (Courtesy of United Nations.)

All tribes follow the Moslem practice of preferential marriage with a father's brother's daughter, and all require a substantial bride-price in livestock. Polygyny is permitted, but only in the nonsororal form, and it is rarely practiced except by rich and influential men. Both the levirate and the sororate are customary. Extended forms of the family do not occur, but all tribes possess a social organization of segmentary type, with patrilineal but agamous sibs, subsibs, and lineages. Cousin terminology conforms to the Eskimo pattern among the Hadendowa, to the descriptive pattern among the Tigre.

Residence everywhere follows the patrilocal rule, but the true Beja require a preliminary period of from one to three years of matrilocal residence, commonly with bride-service. Medieval Arabic sources report matrilineal inheritance and succession, and traces of both have survived into modern times. These facts, coupled with intimations of the avunculate, suggest the possibility of former matrilineal descent obliterated through subsequent Ethiopian and Arabic influences. In view, however, of the lack of any evidence of matrilineal descent, or of elements commonly associated therewith, among other peoples of Cushitic speech, it seems preferable to ascribe these Beja customs to prolonged contact with, and borrowing from, the Nubian peoples to the west.

Selected Bibliography

Clark, W. T. Manners, Customs and Beliefs of the Northern Bega. *SNR*, 25:1–30. 1938. [Amarar].

Klunzinger, C. B. *Upper Egypt*. New York, 1878. [Ababda].

Littmann, E. Tales, Customs, Names and Dirges of the Tigrē Tribes. *Publications of the Princeton Expedition to Abyssinia*, vol. 2. Leiden, 1910.

Munzinger, W. *Ueber die Sitten und das Recht der Bogos*. Winterthur, 1859.

——. *Ostafrikanische Studien*. Schaffhausen, 1864. [Amer and Tigre].

Nadel, S. F. Notes on Beni Amer Society. *SNR*, 25:51–94. 1945.

Newbold, D. The Beja Tribes of the Red Sea Hinterland. *The Anglo-Egyptian Sudan from Within*, ed. J. A. de C. Hamilton, pp. 140–164. London, 1935.

Owen, T. R. H. The Hadendowa. *SNR*, 20:183–288. 1937.

Paul, A. Notes on the Beni Amer. *SNR*, 31:223–245. 1950.

——. *A History of the Beja Tribes of the Sudan*. Cambridge, 1954.

Sandars, G. E. R. The Bisharin. *SNR*, 16:119–149. 1933.

41

Afar and Somali

For thousands of years the Beja seem to have remained the only independent pastoralists in Africa, for this mode of life does not appear elsewhere on the continent until near the end of the first millennium. Then, however, it was adopted by three nations which now occupy the arid desert and savanna country of the Eastern Horn. Two of them, the Afar and Somali (see Map 15), will occupy our attention in the present chapter; the third, the Galla nation, in the following one.

From Paleolithic times until almost the middle of the Christian era the Eastern Horn was inhabited almost exclusively by hunting and gathering peoples of Bushmanoid race with cultures of the Stillbay type, of whom no traces survive today except probably the Midgan and other submerged castes of hunters among the Somali. With the development of complex agricultural civilizations in southern Arabia and highland Ethiopia, however, an extensive trade grew up between the two centers across the narrow strait which connects the Red Sea with the Gulf of Aden. The ports of what is now French Somaliland and the adjacent sections of Eritrea and British Somaliland thus came to be frequented, settled, and ultimately developed into mercantile towns by Yemenite Arabs and by

Cushites from the Ethiopian hinterland. These groups, however, did not occupy or utilize the arid back country except for caravan trails and for the intermittent exploitation of some of its natural resources.

The Pharaonic Egyptians knew this region as the land of Punt, and their hieroglyphic writings record a number of exploring and trading expeditions to the country. We know from the *Periplus of the Erythraean Sea* that its principal exports in the first century, in addition to ivory, tortoise shell, and a few slaves, were frankincense, myrrh, and other aromatic gums that had long been in strong demand in the eastern Mediterranean. The coastal towns, moreover, were already participating fully in the trade with India. From other historical sources we know that the Himyaritic Arabs of southern Arabia had exercised political and mercantile control over the region for perhaps ten centuries prior to the date of the *Periplus*.

At some time early in the second half of the first millennium, as we have seen (Chapter 39), the agricultural Bantu, who had recently arrived in East Africa, spread northeastward along the coast of Somalia and occupied the fertile valleys of the Juba and Shebelle Rivers, driving the indigenous hunters into the arid sections of the interior. During the ninth and tenth centuries the Yemenite Arabs extended their commercial activities around the Horn, establishing a series of fortified trading posts in southern Somalia and ultimately as far south as Sofala.

Until about this time the ancestors of the Afar, Galla, and Somali had been confined largely to southeastern Ethiopia in the region separated from the rest of the plateau by the great rift valley. Here they practiced an agricultural economy supplemented by animal husbandry and by commerce, which they conducted with the coastal towns. Now, however, some of them—perhaps influenced by the Beja or the Arabs—elaborated the pastoral aspect of their economy into an independent nomadic mode of life and descended from the highlands into the arid steppe and savanna country.

How this occurred, of course, we do not know. We can, however, make certain inferences from our previous observations concerning the spread of animal husbandry in Africa. Since cattle occur throughout West Africa, whereas milking has diffused only halfway across the Sudan, we have concluded (Chapter 19) that the Nubians did not adopt the milking complex until a considerable time after they had borrowed and transmitted the animals themselves. Since Nubia is likewise the obvious link connecting Egypt with Ethiopia, we have also concluded (Chapter 22) that the Central Ethiopians, too, acquired domestic animals first and the knowledge of how to milk them and make butter only at some later date. Independent pastoralism depends, of course, upon milking and dairy operations, not upon animal husbandry alone. The late development of this mode of economic life among the Afar, Galla, and

Somali may therefore merely reflect the relative recency of the adoption of the milking complex by the Cushites of southeastern Ethiopia.

The first of these people to embark on a career of independent pastoralism were presumably the Afar, who moved north into the Danakil semidesert and adjacent coastal Eritrea. The second were the Galla, who clearly preceded the Somali into the interior of the Eastern Horn. The parallel expansion of the Somali, the third and culturally most advanced of the three, can scarcely have begun much before the tenth century. Once initiated, however, it proceeded apace. Carrying Islam, which they had accepted in the ninth century at the ports of Berbera and Zeila, the Somali expanded eastward to the Horn and southward into Ogaden, displacing or absorbing the last remnants of the ancient hunting population. During the fourteenth and fifteenth centuries they occupied the entire valley of the Shebelle River, reducing the agricultural Bantu inhabitants to the status of serfs. Their further advances to the southwest at the expense of the Galla will be recounted in the next chapter.

The Afar and Somali divisions of the Horn peoples speak related languages of the Eastern branch of the Cushitic subfamily of the Hamitic stock. All except a few Christian Saho adhere to the Sunni sect of Islam. All, moreover, are definitely Caucasoid and have received a substantial infusion of Arab blood. The Afar are characterized by moderately tall stature, wavy hair, narrow noses, thin lips, and a skin color of coffee shade. The Somali are darker than other Eastern Cushitic peoples but otherwise reveal fewer evidences of Negroid admixture; kinky hair, for example, is almost completely absent. Though they have unquestionably incorporated a certain amount of Negro blood through intermarriage with imported slaves and with their Bantu subjects in the valleys of the Shebelle and Juba Rivers, their dark complexion possibly derives mainly from some other source, conceivably in part from Indians who may at some time have been involved in trade with the ports on the Gulf of Aden. The peoples of the Horn may be classified as follows.

1. Afar (Danakil). They number about 110,000.
2. Esa (Eesa, Eissa, Isa), with the kindred Gadabursi (Derbussi, Gadabirsky). They number about 125,000, including 10,000 urbanized inhabitants of Djibouti.
3. Geri (Girri), with the kindred Bartire (Bartera, Bertirri), Bursuk (Barsub, Bersub), and Yabarre. They number about 300,000.
4. Hawiya (Auijja, Hawiyel), with the Abgal, Ajuran, Hawadla, and other associated tribes. They number about 500,000.
5. Ishaak, embracing the Awal (Habr Awal), Gerhajis (Habr Gerhajis), and Toljaala (Habr Toljaala). They number about 420,000.
6. Mijertein (Medscharten, Midshurtin, Mijjertheyn), with the kindred Desishe, Dolbohanta (Dulbahente), and Warsangeli (Wassingali, Wursungeli). They number about 450,000.
7. Ogaden (Ugadin, Wogadin), with the Abaskul, Gelimes, and Marehan. They number about 350,000.

8. Sab, embracing the Bimal, Digil, Rahanwein, Tunni, and other lesser tribes, of whom several spoke Galla until quite recently. They number about 300,000.
9. Saho (Sao, Shiho). This group, who are linguistically akin to the Afar, number about 50,000, of whom the 10,000 members of the Irob subtribe are Christians.
10. West Somali, including the Aulihan, Digodia, Dir, Gerra, Harti, Makabul, Talmoje, and other tribes intrusive into the former territory of the Bararetta Galla. They number about 120,000, plus an unspecified number enumerated under other Somali groups.

Agriculture provides the principal means of subsistence of the Geri, who may well represent the original core of the Somali nation; the Sab, who include substantial numbers of assimilated Bantu; and some Hawiya. The staple crop of these groups is the durra variety of sorghum, supplemented by maize, beans, melons, cotton, and in some instances wheat, eleusine, vetch, sesame, sweet potatoes, and bananas. All other tribes subsist primarily by animal husbandry. Cattle are the chief animals of the agricultural tribes, but camels assume first place among the nomads. Sheep and goats are numerous everywhere. All these animals provide meat, hides, milk, and butter, but only the Sab and West Somali exhibit the Galla practice of drinking fresh blood. Horses, which are few and highly valued, are ridden exclusively by men. Women ride donkeys, which are also, like camels, used for transport. Dogs, cats, and chickens occur only sporadically. The true Somali do not eat fish, game, or fowl and leave hunting and fishing to the Midgan and other despised groups, but the Afar observe none of these taboos. Both peoples do an appreciable amount of gathering, especially of honey, wild fruits, and such gums as frankincense and myrrh. They maintain regular markets and conduct considerable coastwise and caravan trade. The Afar mine salt and export it in the form of bars, which formerly served widely as currency throughout Northeast Africa. In the division of labor by sex the men herd camels, cattle, and horses, whereas the women tend sheep, goats, and donkeys. Each sex usually milks the animals it tends, but the Afar assign this task mainly to women. Both sexes engage in agriculture among the Hawiya and Sab, women alone among the Geri.

The agricultural groups inhabit permanent settlements, but the pastoral tribes wander in nomadic bands, construct temporary camps encircled by fences of thorns, and occupy shelters consisting of a hemispherical framework of dismountable curved poles supported by a central upright post and covered with mats woven from palm leaves or bast fibers. Sedentary villagers normally live in huts with cylindrical walls and conical thatched roofs, but town dwellers often have rectangular houses with whitewashed walls of sun-dried brick or coral and flat or gabled roofs. Socially, the local community is usually a localized patrilineage or clan, but in the towns and among the Sab this gentile form of organization has given way to a territorial one.

To obtain a wife a man must pay her father a negotiated bride-price in livestock, money, or slaves. The Afar practice preferential cross-cousin marriage, and formerly required a young man to kill an enemy in battle before he became eligible to wed. The Somali forbid unions with any first cousin. Though deviating from normal Islamic marriage preferences, all tribes practice nonsororal polygyny up to the Moslem limit of four wives. Each co-wife has her own dwelling, and the husband spends an equal time with each in turn. Both the levirate and the sororate are preferential. Since residence is regularly patrilocal, a camp normally consists of patrilineally related males and their families, but this group is basically a localized lineage rather than an extended family. Kin groups are nontotemic and of segmentary type. Each nation and tribe traces its descent in the male line from a traditional eponymous common ancestor, as do sibs, subsibs, and lineages. Exogamy prevails with respect at least to the subsib, often to the sib.

The Afar and Somali peoples formerly possessed slaves and engaged intensively in the slave trade. Slave status was hereditary, and marriage with freemen was forbidden, though the offspring of a slave woman by her master were free. Outcaste groups exist among the Somali but not among the Afar. They include hunters, smiths, and leatherworkers, but coast dwellers who eat fish are almost as thoroughly despised. These groups intermarry amongst themselves and to some extent with slaves, in which case children take the status of their father. Outcastes are free to move as they like, and they are paid for their services, which include magic and the manufacture of amulets as well as their special crafts. The indigenous Bantu, especially among the Sab, are attached to tribes of superior status as serfs or clients. Marked wealth distinctions prevail among freemen, and chiefly families exist, but the Somali possess no truly differentiated hereditary aristocracy. The Afar, however, recognize some tribes as Red, or noble; others as White, or common. Inheritance is patrilineal, with sons sharing equally. Among the Esa, Mijertein, and some other tribes, daughters receive half shares in accordance with Koranic law.

Local groups, each with a headman and a council of family heads, are successively integrated into subtribes, tribes, and occasionally larger confederations. At each level authority is vested in a chief, sometimes hereditary and sometimes elective, and a council composed of the heads of the next smaller groups. Except for an occasional sultanate, true states do not exist. Warfare, cattle raiding, and blood feuds are endemic. As a consequence, agricultural groups, especially among the Hawiya, often organize themselves under the leadership of a mullah, or holy man, whose sanctity lends them protection. All groups practice circumcision, clitoridectomy, and infibulation. The Afar and Esa possess age-grades of unspecified type, and the Sab and West Somali retain remnants of the cycling system of the former Galla inhabitants of their territory.

Selected Bibliography

Cruttenden, C. J. Notes on the Mijjertheyn Somalees. *Journal of the Asiatic Society of Bengal*, 13:319–335. 1844.

Drake-Brockman, R. E. *British Somaliland*. London, 1912. [Mijertein].

Haggemacher, G. A. Reise im Somali-Lande. *PME*, 10(47):1–45. 1876. [Ishaak].

Hildebrandt, N. M. Vorläüfige Bemerkungen über die Sómal. *ZE*, 7:1–15. 1875. [Esa].

King, J. S. Marriage Customs at Zayla. *Folk-Lore Journal*, 6:119–125. 1888. [Esa].

Lewis, I. M. *Peoples of the Horn of Africa*. London, 1955.

Lucas, M. Renseignements ethnographiques et linguistiques sur les Danakils de Tadjourah. *JSA*, 5:181–202. 1935. [Afar].

Paulitschke, P. *Beiträge zur Ethnographie und Anthropologie der Somâl, Galla und Harari*. 2d edit. Leipzig, 1888. [Esa, Geri, Ishaak, and Ogaden].

———. *Ethnographie Nordost-Afrikas*. 2 vols. Berlin, 1893–1896.

Puccioni, N. *Anthropologia e etnografia delle genti della Somalia*, vol. 3. Bologna, 1936. [Hawiya].

Scaramucci, F., and E. H. Giglioli. Notizie sui Danakil. *AAE*, 14:17–44. 1884. [Afar].

Schoff, W. H., ed. *The Periplus of the Erythraean Sea*. London, 1912.

Swayne, H. G. C. *Seventeen Trips through Somaliland*. London, 1895. [Ishaak and Mijertein].

42

Galla

The Galla, who evolved an independent pastoral economy at about the same time as the Afar and Somali, seem to have lived originally on the southern edge of the Ethiopian plateau and on the slopes which descend thence into Somalia. Here they had as their neighbors two peoples of kindred Eastern Cushitic speech—the ancestral Somali on the east and the Konso cluster of presumptive Megalithic Cushites (see Chapter 25) on the west. The modern Ittu and northern Arusi tribes still inhabit this area.

Like the Somali, but apparently slightly earlier, the plateau Galla who had adopted independent pastoralism descended into the savanna and steppe country to the south, where they displaced or absorbed the indigenous Bushmanoid hunters. We can fix the approximate date of this advance by the fact that they found the Northeast Coastal Bantu already firmly settled in and cultivating the valleys of the Tana, Juba, and Shebelle Rivers and the arable land between them. Medieval Arabic sources, indeed, indicate that the Bantu had entered into symbiotic relationships with the indigenous hunters of the bush country prior to the arrival of the Galla, which can be tentatively dated at about A.D. 1000. Like the Somali, the Galla reduced the Bantu in part to a dependent status. However, they intermarried with them to a greater extent, and many Bantu fled southwestward into Kenya. The Gosha and Shebelle tribes of Somalia, as we have seen (Chapter 39), constitute surviving pockets of comparatively unmixed Negroes, who are still basically agricultural though they have recently exchanged their original Bantu language for Cushitic.

The pastoral Galla did not long enjoy the fruits of their victory, however, for they were soon to encounter pressure from their nomadic cousins to the east, the Somali. By the end of the fourteenth century the Hawiya had occupied the coast of Somalia as far south as the Shebelle River, and during the following century the Somali displaced the Galla even on the upper Shebelle. When they were defeated in their effort to conquer Ethiopia in the first half of the sixteenth century, the Somali again turned against the Galla, extending their occupation from the Shebelle to the vicinity of the Juba River. The displaced Galla, in their turn, invaded highland Ethiopia, occupying extensive tracts of territory west and northwest of their original homeland. They infiltrated parts of the Sidamo country before 1550, wrested western Ethiopia from the Prenilotes, and had occupied substantial sections of former Agau and Semitic country in central Ethiopia by 1600. Back in the highlands, they rapidly reverted to their earlier sedentary mode of life. The Gibe, who became assimilated to Sidamo culture, have already been considered in Chapter 23. The Macha, Tulama, Walaga, and Wallo adapted rather to the Semitic Amhara, but they still retain many of the most distinctive features of traditional Galla culture.

The Somali renewed their pressure in the nineteenth century. Between 1842 and 1848 they drove the Galla across the Juba River, and in the years following 1909 they consolidated their control over all the country as far as the Tana. It thus happens that the first modern ethnographers to study the inhabitants of the country between the Tana and Juba Rivers found Galla peoples in possession, whereas more recent students have encountered only Somali there. The tribal map at the end of the volume attempts a compromise; the region labeled "Bararetta" was Galla territory at the beginning of the present century but is held today by the West Somali.

The pastoral Galla are largely pagan, but many of the tribes in highland

Ethiopia have accepted either Islam or Christianity. The major ethnic groups are identified below.

1. Arusi (Arsi). This group is largely sedentary in the north, pastoral in the south. A few are Moslems, but the great majority are pagan. Though specific population data are lacking, the Arusi, Bararetta, and Boran combined probably number between 200,000 and 300,000.
2. Bararetta (Baole, Kobaba, Tana Galla, Wajole, Wardai). This pagan group is the principal Galla tribe in the region between the Tana and Juba Rivers occupied by the West Somali during the present century.
3. Boran (Borana). These pagan people, in addition to the territory mapped for them, formerly occupied the northern portion of the region recently preempted by the West Somali.
4. Ittu (Itu), with the kindred Ala, Ania (Ennia), Babile (Babulli, Bajabili), Jarso (Djarso), and Nole (Nola, Noli). Largely Moslem, except for the Nole, they number about a million, a figure which may include some of the Arusi.
5. Macha (Metja). A preponderantly Christian group, they also include a fair number of Moslems and pagans. Together with the Wallaga, they probably number about 600,000.
6. Rendile (Randili). The language of this tribe is allegedly an archaic Somali rather than a Galla dialect.
7. Tulama (Shoa Galla). These people, who are considerably mixed with Amhara, are predominantly Christian. With the Wallo, they number about a million.
8. Wallaga (Walega). This group is predominantly pagan.
9. Wallo (Wollo). They are strongly mixed with Amhara, and most are Moslems.

The agriculture of the sedentary Galla differs in no essential respects from that of the Central Ethiopians, described in Chapter 22. Animal husbandry, which is important in all groups, becomes almost the exclusive source of subsistence among the pastoral Galla. Though they do a little gathering, they observe strict taboos against eating fish, game, or fowl and consequently do no hunting or fishing. All Galla tribes possess substantial numbers of cattle, sheep, goats, and donkeys, as well as a few dogs, cats, and chickens. In addition, the Arusi, Bararetta, Boran, and Rendile have many horses and camels. Pigs are reported only for one subtribe of the Macha. Milk and meat, along with butter and fresh blood, constitute the mainstays of the diet among the pastoral Galla and are important supplements in the highlands. Men do most of the herding, and women most of the milking, as well as the bulk of the field work where agriculture is practiced.

The Macha and Wallaga live in neighborhoods of dispersed homesteads, but most highland Galla, as well as some Arusi, occupy compact villages. In all sedentary groups the prevailing house type is a round hut with a conical thatched roof and cylindrical walls of wattle and daub. The pastoral Galla wander in nomadic bands, and their temporary camps consist of a number of huts arranged around a central cattle corral and surrounded by an outer enclosure of thorns. The dwelling is typically hemispherical in shape and transportable, consisting of bent poles set in the ground in a circle, fastened together at the top, and covered with mats or occasionally brush or hides. This obviously represents an adaptation of the house type of the earlier East African hunters. Some Boran build circular walls of stone and cover them with camel mats, and some Arusi construct conical huts without walls.

Marriage regularly involves a substantial bride-price, usually in livestock. General polygyny prevails, with each co-wife occupying a separate dwelling, but extended family households do not occur. The levirate is preferential, and the Arusi practice institutionalized cicisbeism, allowing each married woman to have a recognized lover. The Galla prohibit unions between first cousins and favor local exogamy. All tribes follow the patrilocal rule of residence and the patrilineal rule of descent. In addition to exogamous sibs and lineages, which are universal, the Bararetta and Boran are reported to possess exogamous patrimoieties. Inheritance is likewise patrilineal, with males alone participating and the eldest son receiving the major share. Hereditary slavery prevails, and most groups place smiths, hunters, and leatherworkers in the status of despised and endogamous castes. With certain exceptions in the highlands, the Galla are relatively egalitarian, recognizing distinctions in wealth and seniority in descent but not a hereditary aristocracy.

As among the Konso cluster of Megalithic Cushites, government operates through a system of age-grades of the Gada, or cycling, type. With the possible exception of the Rendile, for whom information is lacking, one basic system prevails throughout both the pastoral and sedentary Galla tribes. This consists of five grades, typically named the Daballe, Folle, Kondala, Luba, and Yuba grades. Age-sets, in which membership endures for life, spend eight years successively in each grade, with a spectacular ceremony marking each transition. In some tribes the fourth, or ruling, grade is divided into two subgrades of four years' duration each, called respectively Dori and Luba. Age-sets likewise bear names, either five or ten in number, which succeed one another in a standard cycling order. Where there are five, a son belongs to a set bearing the same name as his father's, and is initiated into the first grade when his father retires from the fifth, i.e., exactly forty years later. Where there are ten named age-sets, a son enters one which is paired with his father's after the same interval of time, and only grandfathers and grandsons belong to sets with the same name. Circumcision accompanies admission to the first grade among the Bararetta, to the third grade among the Boran, to the second subgrade of the fourth grade among the Macha, to the fifth grade among the Tulama. (Girls are subjected to clitoridectomy and sometimes to infibulation).

Particular functions and stereotyped patterns of behavior are associated with each grade and are essentially similar throughout both lowland and highland tribes. Since, however, they are most fully described for the Tulama, with data suggestive of the possible origin of the system in actual maturational levels, the data for this tribe may be summarized as a sample. During the first grade Tulama males are forbidden to have sex relations, and they wander about begging food, which is always termed "milk," from married women. This is strongly suggestive of the behavior of infants. During the second grade they become initiated into sexual life but without forming stable relationships, and they engage in masked processions and behave generally in an irresponsible manner suggestive of adolescence. In the third grade they serve as warriors and are permitted to marry. Military valor is encouraged in some tribes, though not specifically attested for the Tulama, by requiring the taking of the genitals of a slain enemy as a trophy to qualify for full participation in the activities of the next, or ruling, grade. When an age-set enters the fourth, or Luba, grade, its members take over all important administrative, judicial, and priestly offices in the tribe and run its affairs for eight years. Each position is typically filled from a particular sib, but with this qualification the particular incumbent is democratically chosen on the basis of personal merit. The chief of the age-set, elected when it occupied the second grade, now becomes the high chief (*hayu*) of the tribe. Another man becomes speaker (*boku*) of the general assembly. Others assume various administrative and judicial offices—chief priest, finance minister, and so on. During the last, or Yuba, grade these men relinquish their posts and become "guardians," serving the new officials in a purely advisory capacity.

Selected Bibliography

Arkell-Hardwick, A. *An Ivory Trader in North Kenia*. London, 1903. [Rendile].

Cecchi, A. *Da Zeila alla frontiere del Caffa*. 3 vols. Roma, 1885. [Tulama].

Cerulli, E. *Etiopia occidentale*. 2 vols. Roma, 1932–1933. [Macha and Tulama].

Chambard, R. Sur l'organisation sociale des Oromo du Harar. *RETP*, 7:69–79. 1926. [Ittu].

Huntingford, G. W. B. *The Galla of Ethiopia*. London, 1955.

Maud, P. Exploration in the Southern Borderland of Abyssinia. *GJ*, 23:552–579. 1904. [Boran].

Paulitschke, P. *Beiträge zur Ethnographie und Anthropologie der Somâl, Galla und Harari*. 2d edit. Leipzig, 1888. [Ittu].

———. *Ethnographie Nordost-Afrikas*. 2 vols. Berlin, 1893–1896. [Arusi, Boran, and Ittu].

Prins, A. H. J. *East African Age-Class Systems*. Groningen, 1953.

Salviac, M. de. *Les Galla*. Paris, 1901. [Ittu].

Wakefield, E. S. Marriage Customs of the Southern Gallas. *FL*, 18:319–325. 1907. [Bararetta].

Werner, A. The Galla of the East Africa Protectorate. *JAS*, 13:131–142, 262–287. 1914. [Bararetta and Boran].

43

Nilotes

At approximately the same time as the Eastern Cushitic peoples were evolving an independent pastoral mode of life, a parallel development was taking place to the west of them among the Negroes of the tall, slender subrace known as the Nilotes (see Chapter 2). These people today occupy a large territory extending from the border of Kordofan in the northwest through southern Sudan, northern Uganda, and western Kenya to northern Tanganyika in the southeast, and from the edge of Ethiopia in the northeast to the border of the Belgian Congo in the southwest (see Map 15). They have had an extremely complex history, which will become more readily understandable if we begin with a linguistic and cultural classification of their component tribes.

All the Nilotes speak languages of the Eastern subfamily of the Sudanic stock. A few tribes in the northeast, on and near the Ethiopian border, belong to the Beir branch of the Eastern Sudanic subfamily and are therefore segregated from the rest as the Beir cluster. All other groups belong to the Nilotic branch of the same subfamily. The Nilotic languages proper fall into two subdivisions, of which one, called "Great Lakes" by Greenberg but "Nilo-Hamite" by most other authorities, differs from the other in reflecting an obvious Cushitic influence. Since the present writer dislikes geographical terms for language groupings and considers the term "Nilo-Hamite" a linguistic monstrosity, he finds both names unacceptable. He prefers to call both groups Nilotes and to distinguish the one from the other, where necessary, as the "Cushitized Nilotes," since they are characterized as strongly by cultural as by linguistic borrowings.

The Cushitized groups lie mainly in the east, where three distinct clusters are distinguishable, namely, from north to south, the Karamojong, Nandi, and Masai clusters. A fourth, or Bari, cluster extends westward and separates the tribes that reveal little Cushitic influence into a northern, or Dinka, and a southwestern, or Luo, cluster.

BEIR CLUSTER

This cluster occupies the relatively inhospitable lowlands adjacent to the Sidamo peoples of southwestern Ethiopia. Its tribes exhibit a number of specific borrowings from the latter but seem otherwise to have remained comparatively static. They practice agriculture where geographic conditions permit but elsewhere are predominantly pastoral.

1. Didinga (Birra, Dodinga, Karoko, Toi). This group, whose population is variously estimated at from 10,000 to 25,000, leads a seminomadic existence with seasonal migrations.
2. Murle (Ajiba, Beir, Irenge, Merule, Mourle, Murule), embracing the Epeita (Boma, Epeta, Kapeta), Longarim (Boya), and Pibor. They number about 30,000 and are seminomadic.
3. Nyangiya (Nangiya), with the Arom and Niporen (Napore, Ngitaio, Nyipori). The specific linguistic affiliations of this sedentary group, numbering about 3,000, are as yet unknown.
4. Suri (Churi, Dhuak, Dhuri, Dzuak, Kachipo, Kachuba, Kichepo, Ngachopo, Shuri, Thuri), with the Mekan (Men, Mieken, Tishana), Murzu (Dama, Merdu, Meritu, Mourse, Murdhu, Muritu, Mursi, Mursu, Tama, Tdama), and Surma (Karoma, Korma, Makurma, Mokurma, Mursia, Nikorma, Nyikoroma). The Tid (Chach, Dolot, Tod), Tirma (Chima, Cirma, Dirma, Terema, Terna, Tilma, Turmu), and Zilmamu (Tsilmanu, Zelmamu, Zulimamu) are subtribes of the Surma. This group, numbering about 25,000, subsists primarily by agriculture, with some terraced-field cultivation.

DINKA CLUSTER

In the northeast the peoples of this cluster adjoin the Anuak, Meban, and Shilluk tribes of the Prenilote province, to whom they are both linguistically and culturally akin. They differ, however, in being primarily pastoral rather than agricultural and in lacking the complex political institutions of the Prenilotes.

5. Dinka (Denkawi, Jang). Together with the Padang, they number about 500,000.
6. Jur (Djur, Gour, Luo, Lwo), with the Bor (Baer, Behr, Boor, Mberidi, Mverodi), Dembo (Bodho, Bwodho), Fujiga, Kamum, Manangier (Manangeri), Shatt (Cat, Thuri), and Shilluk-Luo. This group, numbering about 20,000, subsists largely by agriculture today. It was shattered, dispersed, and depopulated by Azande invasions and Arab slave raids during the nineteenth century.
7. Nuer, with the Atwot. They number about 300,000.
8. Padang. They are a detached branch of the Dinka, from whom they separated about two centuries ago.
9. Pari (Beri, Berri, Bori, Fari, Feri, Fori). These people, numbering about 7,000, are a branch of the Anuak, from whom they split off about ten generations ago.

LUO CLUSTER

The tribes of this cluster, who subsist primarily by agriculture, inhabit northern Uganda, but the Alur extend into the Belgian Congo and the Luo into Kenya.

10. Acholi (Atscholi, Gan, Gang, Makdschuru, Shuli). They number nearly 250,000.
11. Alur (Aloro, Alua, Alulu, Lour, Lur, Luri). They number about 200,000.
12. Labwor (Tobur). They number about 5,000 and are closely akin to the Acholi.
13. Lango (Umiro). They number about 275,000 and are about equally agricultural and pastoral.
14. Luo (Jaluo, Luwo, Nilotic Kavirondo, Nyifwa), with the detached Gaya (Girange, Wageia) and Jopadhola (Dama). They number about 800,000.

BARI CLUSTER

These tribes, wedged between the Dinka cluster on the north and the Luo cluster on the south, extend into the Belgian Congo. In addition to being Cushitized, they reveal considerable intermixture with, and acculturation to, their Central Sudanic neighbors on the west.

15. Bari. These people, numbering about 35,000, were primarily pastoral until Arab depredations in the nineteenth century forced them into greater dependence upon agriculture.
16. Fajulu (Fagdelou, Fajelu, Fedgelu, Pojulu), with the Kakwa (Kakuak), Ligi, and Nyangbara (Nyambara). They number about 90,000 and are primarily agricultural.
17. Kuku, with the Nyepu (Nieffu). This tribe, numbering about 30,000, is predominantly agricultural.
18. Lotuko (Latuka), with the Koriuk, Lafit (Lofit, Lopit), Lango, Lokoiya (Leria, Oghoriok), Lomya, and Lowudo (Laudo). In this group, numbering about 70,000, agricultural and pastoral activities are evenly balanced.
19. Mondari (Mandari, Mundar), embracing the Bori, Boronga (Tali), and Sere (Kir, Shir). This group, numbering about 36,000, was predominantly pastoral until the Arab depredations of the nineteenth century.

KARAMOJONG CLUSTER

This Cushitized group resides east of the Bari and Luo clusters in northwestern Kenya and an adjacent strip of Uganda. Most have pastoral economies characterized by transhumance. Among them live a few Teuso remnants of the indigenous hunting population.

20. Jie (Ajie, Egye, Giye, Gye, Jibbeh, Jiwe, Jiye, Kum, Kumi, Negye, Ngie, Nigye, Njie), with the Dodoth (Dodoso). They number about 40,000.
21. Karamojong, with the Tepes (Entepes, Tepeth). They number about 60,000.
22. Teso (Bakedi, Bateso, Iteso, Kedi, Kedo, Kidi, Wakedi), with the kindred Kumam (Akum, Ikokolemu, Lango) and Itesyo (Elgumi, Wamia). They number about 560,000.
23. Topotha (Dabosa, Tabosa, Taposa), with the Donyiro (Buma, Bumie, Dongiro, Idongiro, Ignahatom, Nyangatom, Orogniro), Jiye, and Magoth (Magois, Magos). They number about 45,000.
24. Turkana (Elgume), with the Ngamatak, Nibelai (Billai, Ngebellai), and Nithir (Nyissir). They number about 80,000.

NANDI CLUSTER

This strongly Cushitized group lives in the mountainous section of western Kenya northeast of Lake Victoria and on the slopes of nearby Mount Elgon. Except for an occasional subtribe living in an unfavorable habitat, all its members practice an intensive agriculture, characterized in some places by irrigation on terraced mountain slopes. Most of them reveal evidences of admixture with a Caucasoid racial element.

25. Keyu (Elgeyo), with the Kamasya (Tuken). They number about 110,000.
26. Kipsigi (Lumbwa, Sikisi), with the kindred Buret and Sotek. They number about 160,000.
27. Nandi, with the Terik (Nyangori, Tiriki). They number about 115,000.
28. Sabei (Basabei, Mbai, Sabaot, Sapaut, Sapei), with the Bambe, Kipsorai (Kipsorak, Sore, Sorek), Kony (Elgonyi), Ngomakek (Wangoma), and Pok (Lako, Walako). They number about 50,000.
29. Suk (Bawgott, Pakot, Pokot, Pokwut, Sukku), with the Endo (Chebleng, Ndo), Kadam (Debasien), and Marakwet (Maragwetta). They number about 90,000, of whom the central core are sedentary tillers in the hill country. To the east and west of these live about 40,000 pastoral nomads, the Plains Suk.
30. Tatoga (Datoga, Mangati, Taturu), with the Barabaig. This detached group, shattered in wars with the Masai, live in northern Tanganyika. They number about 20,000 and were primarily pastoral until their dispersion.

MASAI CLUSTER

These Cushitized people reside east of the Karamojong and Nandi clusters and extend southward across Kenya into northern Tanganyika, where they form a wedge deep into Bantu territory. Except for the Arusha and small dispossessed groups elsewhere, they subsist exclusively by animal husbandry. Scattered among them, as well as among the adjacent Nandi, live the Dorobo, a remnant group of hunters and gatherers.

31. Arusha (Warush). Numbering about 62,000, they resemble the Masai except for their dependence upon agriculture.
32. Masai (Massai), with the dispersed Kwafi (Kuavi) and Lumbwa (Bumba, Ilumpua). They number in excess of 100,000.
33. Samburu (Sambur), with the Elburgu, Elmolo (Ngaboto), Laikipiak (Koikop, Leikipia, Leukop, Oikop), Mogogodo (Mokogodo), and Njamus (Eljemasi, Enjemasi, Iltiamus, Njemps). Closely akin to the Masai, this group numbers about 12,000 today but was formerly much more numerous.

The linguistic and cultural distributions summarized above, coupled with the various fragments of other evidence presented in earlier chapters, enable us to reconstruct the culture history of the Nilotic province with a fair degree of assurance. We shall attempt to tell a connected story without belaboring the obvious fact that parts of it are highly tentative.

Prior to the introduction of agriculture, the eastern and southern portions of the province were occupied by Bushmanoid hunters with cultures of the Stillbay type, and the northern and western portions by Negroid peoples who also were still at the hunting and gathering level of economic development. The Negroes almost certainly spoke languages of the Sudanic stock—Eastern Sudanic in at least the northeastern fringe of the area now occupied by the Dinka cluster, and Central Sudanic in at least the present territory of the Bari cluster. Bushmanoids inhabited the country of the present Beir, Karamojong, Masai, and Nandi peoples. The precise boundary between the Negroid and Bushmanoid hunters must await determination through archeological research.

Sometime around 3000 B.C. Sudanic agriculture, diffusing eastward, reached the northern border of the province, where the adjacent and kindred Prenilotes, as we have seen (Chapter 21), transmitted it to highland Ethiopia. It doubtless penetrated the northern part of the Nilotic province to a certain extent, and it almost certainly enabled the Beir linguistic group to expand eastward into former Bushmanoid territory as far as the edge of the Ethiopian plateau. Diffusion to the south, however, may well have proceeded only gradually, partly because of the unfavorable character of much of the terrain and partly because of the unsuitability of the West African crops to low latitudes and high humidity. Indeed, the dominant position held by durra and eleusine in the present roster of food plants suggests that agriculture may actually first have reached many parts of the province from Ethiopia rather than from the northwest.

Archeological and other evidence already adduced (Chapter 25) shows that, by about 1000 B.C., Megalithic Cushites had descended from the Ethiopian highlands into favored sections in the east of the province, especially in the present territory of the Nandi cluster, and that a Sidamo people, at an as yet undetermined date, similarly moved southwest across the province into Uganda. We may reasonably ascribe to them the introduction of the Ethiopian food plants.

A century or two before the advent of the Christian era, the Malaysian crops acquired by the Cushites on the Azanian coast passed westward through Uganda and the Central Sudanic province (see Chapter 28). They exerted only a modest effect on Nilotic culture, however, although the tribes of the Luo and Bari clusters still cultivate them to a limited extent.

Five or six centuries after the time of Christ the Bantu, having wrested the tropical-forest region of the Congo Basin from the Pygmies, arrived in Uganda and encircled Lake Victoria, completely occupying its shores. The account of their conquest and its results will receive our attention in Chapter 45. What is important in the present connection is that the people they found in possession of the country were not Nilotes of the Luo cluster, who hold portions of it today, but Cushitic descendants of the Sidamo immigrants. At this period the Nilotes seem to have been a relatively backward agricultural people occupying only a fraction of their present territory. In the entire eastern section, the present habitat of the Karamojong, Nandi, and Masai groups, there still lived only Bushmanoid hunters and, in well-watered districts, dispersed settlements of Cushitic tillers.

Within two or three centuries, however, the Nilotes had developed a full-fledged pastoral complex, which they could either combine with their traditional agricultural pursuits or detach from the latter and practice independently where the geographic environment did not permit extensive cultivation. Whether they made the discovery by themselves or borrowed it from the Eastern Cushites or from the Beja by way of the Prenilotes we do not know. We assume, however, that it depended upon the late acquisition of the technique of milking their domestic animals.

Once the Nilotes had learned to subsist primarily by pastoral nomadism with only auxiliary dependence upon agriculture, they expanded with explosive force. They marched southward and occupied all the territory now held by the Dinka and Luo clusters, probably wresting much of it from their Central Sudanic cousins, and they even penetrated Bantu country on the northeastern shores of Lake Victoria. The powerful states of the Interlacustrine Bantu, however, blocked their further progress southward and deflected them to the southeast, where they infiltrated the territory of the Megalithic Cushites, who were politically less well organized. With their superior economic adjustment the Nilotes easily wrested the uncultivated savanna country from the Bushmanoid hunters, leaving only the Dorobo and Teuso as vanishing remnants. They encircled and engulfed the scattered agricultural settlements in the mountainous sections, intermarried with the Cushitic tillers there, and in time largely absorbed them. There thus resulted a mixed population speaking a Nilotic language with strong Cushitic increments and exhibiting a culture which combined Nilotic and Cushitic elements. Those of Cushitic derivation predominate today in the hilly and more strongly agricultural regions, notably the area inhabited by the Nandi cluster. Elsewhere, as in the Karamojong and Masai regions, Nilotic physical and cultural traits prevail more strongly, although the language has become unquestionably Cushitized.

The Bantu, who had previously replaced the Megalithic Cushites in southern Kenya, here lacked the military and political strength of their cousins in Uganda and were thus no better prepared than the Cushites to withstand the aggressive Nilotes, whose spearhead, the Masai, had penetrated well into Tanganyika by the time the first Europeans arrived in East Africa. One group of the Cushitized Nilotes reversed their course and moved westward across Uganda into the country previously occupied by the Central Sudanic peoples. Merging with the latter as they had previously done with the Cushites, they produced there the mixed population and culture of the Bari cluster.

In summary, the Negroid Nilotes and Bantu have constituted, respectively, the upper and nether millstones that in the last millennium or so have crushed and obliterated the Caucasoid Cushites of the Megalithic branch who had previously dominated much of northeastern Africa and had played there a culture-historical role of the utmost significance. Recent European settlement in highland Kenya may thus be regarded as a relatively feeble, and perhaps temporary, reversal of a long historical trend.

Nilotic agriculture consists primarily in the cultivation of cereal grains, with sorghum of the durra variety, eleusine, and millet, in this order, ranking as the staples. The more strongly pastoral tribes grow little else, but those that depend substantially on tillage supplement the African cereals with ambary, cotton, cow peas, earth peas, gourds, okra, and sesame from the Sudanic complex; gram beans, hemp, hyacinth beans, Jew's mallow, and pigeon peas from the Indian complex; bananas and yams from the Malaysian complex; and cucurbits, maize, manioc, peanuts, sweet potatoes, and tobacco from the American complex.

Animal husbandry ranks on a parity with, or surpasses, agriculture everywhere except in the Luo cluster and among the Teso. The principal domesticated animals are cattle, goats, and sheep, though dogs are widely used for hunting. Most groups also keep chickens, and cats and bees occur sporadically. The tribes of the Beir, Karamojong, Masai, and Nandi clusters keep donkeys. Camels, introduced about a century ago, are reported for the Karamojong, the Suk, and especially the Turkana. Milk consti-

Masai Drawing Blood from a Cow's Neck with a Miniature Arrow. (Courtesy of British Information Services.)

tutes a dietary staple in nearly all groups. Most of them also make butter, and the Bari and Fajulu prepare a kind of cheese. The peoples of the Masai and Nandi clusters observe dietary regulations, forbidding the consumption of milk and meat on the same day. Since we shall find this custom again among some of the Interlacustrine Bantu, it may well reflect an ancient Cushitic practice. All the eastern peoples—those of the Beir, Karamojong, Masai, and Nandi clusters—drink quantities of fresh blood drawn from the necks of their cattle by means of a miniature arrow. This specifically Cushitic custom also appears, though only sporadically, among the tribes of the Bari and Dinka clusters in the northwest.

Hunting and gathering, though rarely important, often add a modest supplement to the daily fare, as does fishing among the Murle and Suri and many tribes of the Bari, Dinka, and Luo clusters. The Didinga tribe and all members of the Karamojong, Masai, and Nandi groups, however, observe the characteristic Cushitic taboo against eating fish. Only the Suri have developed commerce to any considerable extent, trading lion and leopard pelts, ivory, honey, and slaves to the highland Ethiopians.

The men do the hunting, fishing, and land clearance. They also perform all agricultural work among the Tatoga, but this task is shared by both sexes among most tribes of the Dinka and Luo clusters and is assigned mainly, and sometimes exclusively, to women everywhere else. Sex participation in milking reveals an interesting regional contrast. Women do all or most of the milking in the Dinka, Karamojong, Masai, and Nandi clusters as among most North and East African pastoralists, notably the Arabs, the Berbers, and the Afar, Galla, and Somali. Among the Didinga and all tribes of the Bari and Luo clusters, on the other hand, cattle are strictly taboo to adult women, and only men and children can milk. We have hitherto encountered the assignment of milking to the male sex only among the Beja and the Central Sudanic peoples. Since the latter are immediate neighbors, we can reasonably ascribe to them the origin of the ritual separation of women and cattle. This could have been acquired by the invading Bari peoples, who coalesced with them, and then transmitted to the neighboring Luo cluster and thence to the adjacent Interlacustrine Bantu. In any event, the widespread assumption that this taboo is a "Hamitic" trait lacks any factual support.

Marriage everywhere involves a substantial bride-price in livestock, and in the Bari and Beir clusters usually a period of agricultural bride-service as well. Incest taboos prevent unions with any first cousin and commonly also with remoter relatives. General polygyny prevails, nearly always in the nonsororal form, and each wife is established in a separate dwelling. Though residence is uniformly patrilocal, the Lotuko and Nuer commonly observe an initial matrilocal period. Small extended families occur in the majority of tribes, but independent polygynous families predominate in the Masai and Nandi clusters.

Descent is invariably patrilineal, with segmentary lineage systems among at least the Luo, Mondari, Nuer, and Tatoga. Exogamy extends to all members of the father's patrisib in all tribes except the Kipsigi and Nandi, and in most groups to the mother's sibmates as well. Localized clans tend, in general, to be present in the western clusters but absent in the eastern ones. Cousin terminology conforms basically to the Omaha pattern among the Acholi, Bari, Lango, Masai, Nandi, and Suk; to the Iroquois pattern among the Kipsigi and Lotuko; to the descriptive pattern among the Dinka, Luo, Nuer, and Turkana; and to the Hawaiian pattern among the Teso.

The Masai and Samburu tribes are fully nomadic and wander in bands throughout the year. The Didinga, Mondari, pastoral Suk, Tatoga, and most tribes of the Dinka and Karamojong clusters are seminomadic, living in temporary camps only during the dry season. Although the Acholi, Labwor, Lango, Pari, and the tribes of the Beir cluster inhabit compact and usually stockaded villages, the prevailing settlement pattern, among seminomadic and sedentary peoples alike, is a neighborhood of dispersed homesteads or small hamlets, each surrounded by a fence, a thorn hedge, or a palisade. Dwellings characteristic of adjacent areas have penetrated a few of the marginal tribes, notably the central Tanganyikan *tembe* among the Tatoga and the beehive hut of the Interlacustrine Bantu among the southeastern Alur and formerly among the Teso, but two other house types dominate the area as a whole. Round huts with conical thatched roofs and walls of wattle and daub prevail in the Bari, Beir, Dinka, Luo, and Nandi clusters and in the permanent settlements of some of the Karamojong tribes. In the temporary camps of the Nuer and of all tribes of the Karamojong cluster and in the wet-season settlements of some of the latter, however, the house type approaches that of the pastoral Galla and was probably borrowed from the preexisting hunting population. Hemispherical in shape, it consists of a frame of bent poles fastened together at the top and covered with interlaced branches, grass, reed mats, or skins. The dwellings of the Masai represent a variant of this pattern; they are elongated rather than round, and both top and sides are smeared with a mixture of mud and dung.

Except for wealth distinctions, inevitable among people for whom livestock are so important, the Nilotes are remarkably egalitarian. They completely lack any hereditary aristocracy, and even slavery occurs only among the Dinka, Jur, and Padang of the Dinka cluster and the Alur, Lango, and Teso of the Luo cluster. Most tribes of the Bari group, however, have a class of hereditary serfs, called *dupi*. These are of alien stock and are presumably descended from the subjected Central Sudanic indigenes of the region. Depressed and endogamous castes of smiths occur throughout the Bari, Masai, and Nandi clusters of Cushitized Nilotes, and hunters constitute a comparable group among the Bari, Masai, and Suri.

No Nilotic people has a complex political organization. A handful of tribes, notably the Alur, Labwor, and Suri, acknowledge petty paramount chiefs over small districts, but the rest reveal no secular integration transcending the level of the village or neighborhood. A fair number of these, however, have ritual experts who exert an influence over a group of neighboring settlements, notably rainmakers in the Bari cluster and diviners capable of predicting success in offensive warfare among the tribes of the Masai and Nandi clusters. Particularly interesting in this category are the spear chiefs of Dinka subtribes. These act as rainmakers, sacrificial priests, and peacemakers in feuds. Each possesses special insignia of office, such as a stool, a string of ostrich-eggshell beads, and a sacred war spear. Like the divine kings of the Shilluk, of whom their status is clearly a pale reflection, the spear chiefs are ceremonially killed when too old to perform their ritual functions.

The Cushitic practices of circumcision and clitoridectomy have spread only to the Masai and Nandi clusters. With occasional exceptions, all other tribes adhere to the ancient initiatory rite of the Sudanic-speaking peoples and extract the two lower front incisor teeth in one or both sexes. The Masai peoples, indeed, have not abandoned this custom despite their adoption of genital mutilations. Neither cannibalism nor headhunting occurs among the Nilotes.

Organized age-grades constitute the most distinctive feature of Nilotic social organization and are lacking only in the peripheral Alur, Fajulu, Jur, Kuku, and Luo tribes. Despite differences, all systems have in common the fact that they are entered by initiation, usually during adolescence, and that the boys or young men who are initiated together form a closely knit age-set. In nearly all of them, moreover, initiations occur at specified intervals, normally ranging from four to ten years, and one or more sets, forming an age-grade, constitute the warrior class of the society. The great majority of tribes have grades of the linear type, which succeed one another indefinitely. The tribes of the Nandi cluster, however, resemble the Galla and the Megalithic Cushites in possessing age-grades of the cycling type. In a cycling system there are a limited number of named grades, and when the last grade is preempted, the next one takes again the name of the first in the series.

A relatively simple type of linear system occurs widely in the Bari, Beir, Dinka, and Luo clusters. Here the age-set and the age-grade are commonly identical. A new set is formed most typically every fourth year, though the interval is six years among the Murle and ten among the Acholi, Nuer, and Suri. From one to four of the junior sets form the society's body of warriors. A number of tribes, e.g., the Didinga and Murle, do not allow a man to marry until his age-set either has attained the status of senior warriors or has graduated to the status of elders.

The Masai have a somewhat similar system but with a normal interval of fifteen years. During this time there are two periods, of four to six years each, during which boys may be circumcised; when they subsequently enter the grade of junior warriors, they form a "right-" and a "left-hand" division thereof. Promotion of the preceding age-set to the grade of senior warriors does not occur, however, until several years later, and in the meantime members of two completely different age-sets occupy the same grade. After about fifteen years as senior warriors, an age-set advances to the status of junior elders; after fifteen more, to that of senior elders; and so on at like intervals as long as the set has living members. Between circumcision and their formal initiation as junior warriors, boys wander in bands all over the Masai country. After initiation they sleep in special bachelor huts with the unmarried girls. Only when they become senior warriors are they permitted to marry.

The pastoral Suk and the tribes of the Karamojong cluster reveal a still more complex type of linear system, of which that of the Jie may serve as an example. Here an age-grade is composed exclusively of men of the same genealogical generation. Each grade is divided into about three age-classes, and each class into three or four age-sets. A new age-set is initiated every one to three years, but no man may be initiated until all those senior to him, according to a strict traditional definition of seniority, have already entered an age-set. In the most favorable case he will be eighteen or twenty years of age when he becomes eligible, but he may be as old as forty. When all the men of a generation have finally been initiated, they are formally constituted into an age-grade by the surviving oldsters of their grandfathers' grade, and the sets of the new grade are grouped into classes on the basis of relative age. One man in each grade inherits from his paternal grandfather the title of chief of his generation for the entire Jie tribe.

All the tribes of the Nandi cluster except the pastoral Suk and the Tatoga possess systems of the cycling type, of which that of the Kipsigi may be taken as representative. Seven named age-grades succeed one another in regular rotation every fifteen years, a single full cycle being completed every 105 years. Initiation into an age-set, however, occurs every fifth year, three such sets forming a grade. The junior grade at a given time constitutes the warriors of the society. Every fifteen years the warriors as a body advance to the status of elders, and the first set of the next warrior grade is initiated. Whatever his actual age, however, no man can enter the warrior grade until his father graduates from the status of elder to that of an old man, i.e., thirty years later. As among the Masai, the warriors live apart in special bachelor houses, where they are visited by the uninitiated girls.

The Nilotes unquestionably acquired their age-grade systems through fusion with, or imitation of, the Eastern Cushites. The reason for the spread of these systems must lie in their survival value. They clearly promoted military strength and social integration and thus doubtless served to offset in large measure the disadvantages inherent in a minimal development of political organization.

Selected Bibliography

Barton, J. Notes on the Suk Tribe. *JRAI*, 51:82–100. 1921.
———. Notes on the Turkana Tribe. *JAS*, 20:107–115, 204–211. 1921.
———. Notes on the Kipsikis or Lumbwa Tribe. *JRAI*, 53:42–78. 1923.
Baumann, O. *Durch Massailand zur Nilquelle*. Berlin, 1894. [Masai and Tatoga].
Beaton, A. C. The Bari. *SNR*, 19:109–145. 1936.

Masai Dwelling and Its Equipment. (Courtesy of British Information Services.)

Bedri, I. E. Notes on Dinka Religious Beliefs and Their Hereditary Chiefs and Rain Makers. *SNR*, 22:125–132. 1939. [Padang].

Beech, M. W. H. *The Suk*. Oxford, 1911.

Bernardi, B. The Age-System of the Nilo-Hamitic Peoples. *Africa*, 22:316–332. 1952.

——. The Age-System of the Masai. *AL*, 18:257–318. 1954.

Butt, A. *The Nilotes of the Anglo-Egyptian Sudan*. London, 1952.

Crazzolara, J. P. Zur Gesellschaft und Religion der Nuer. *Studia Instituti Anthropos*, 5:1–221. Wien-Mödling, 1953.

Demuenyck. Au pays de Mahagi. *BSRBG*, 32:36–80, 93–133. 1908. [Alur].

Driberg, J. H. A Preliminary Account of the Didinga. *SNR*, 5:208–222. 1922.

——. *The Lango*. London, 1923.

——. Lafon Hill. *SNR*, 8:47–57. 1925. [Pari].

——. Didinga Customary Law. *SNR*, 8:153–175. 1925.

——. Some Aspects of Lango Kinship. *Sociologus*, 8:44–61. 1932.

Dyson, W. S., and V. E. Fuchs. The Elmolo. *JRAI*, 67:327–338. 1937. [Samburu].

Elmley, E. D. The Turkana of Kolosia District. *JRAI*, 57:157–201. 1927.

Evans-Pritchard, E. E. The Mberidi (Shilluk Group) and Mbegumba (Basiri Group) of the Bahr-el-Ghazal. *SNR*, 14:15–48. 1931. [Jur].

——. The Nuer: Tribe and Clan. *SNR*, 16:1–53. 1933.

——. The Nuer: Age-Sets. *SNR*, 19:233–271. 1936.

——. Some Aspects of Marriage and the Family among the Nuer. *ZVR*, 52:306–392. 1938.

——. *The Nuer*. Oxford, 1940.

——. The Political Structure of the Nandi-speaking Peoples. *Africa*, 13:250–267. 1940.

——. Bridewealth among the Nuer. *AS*, 6:181–188. 1947.

——. Luo Tribes and Clans. *RLJ*, 7:24–40. 1949.

——. Nuer Rules of Exogamy and Incest. *SS*, pp. 85–103. 1949.

——. Kinship and the Local Community among the Nuer. *ASKM*, pp. 360–391. 1950.

——. Marriage Customs of the Kenya Luo. *Africa*, 20:132–142. 1950.

——. The Nuer of the Southern Sudan. *APS*, pp. 272–296. 1950.

——. *Kinship and Marriage among the Nuer*. Oxford, 1951.

Fosbrooke, H. A. An Administrative Survey of the Masai Social System. *TNR*, 26:1–50. 1948.

Ghawi, J. B. Notes on the Law and Custom of the Jur Tribe. *SNR*, 7(2):71–81. 1924.

Grove, E. T. N. Customs of the Acholi. *SNR*, 2:157–182. 1919.

Gulliver, P., and P. H. Gulliver. *The Central Nilo-Hamites*. London, 1953.

Gulliver, P. H. A Preliminary Survey of the Turkana. *CSAS*, n.s., 26:1–281. 1951.

——. The Karamojong Cluster. *Africa*, 22:1–21. 1952.

——. The Age-Set Organization of the Jie Tribe. *JRAI*, 83:147–167. 1953.

——. *The Family Herds*. London, 1955. [Jie and Turkana].

——. Interim Report on Land and Population in the Arusha Chiefdom. Unpublished ms.

Hartmann, H. Some Customs of the Luwo. *Anthropos*, 23:263–275. 1928.

Hayley, T. T. S. *Anatomy of Lango Religion and Groups*. Cambridge, 1947.

Hobley, C. W. Eastern Uganda. *RAIOC*, 1:1–95. 1902. [Luo].

Hollis, A. C. *The Masai*. Oxford, 1905.

——. *The Nandi*. Oxford, 1909.

——. A Note on the Masai System of Relationship. *JRAI*, 40:473–482. 1910.

Howell, P. P. Notes on the Ngork Dinka. *SNR*, 32:240–293. 1951.

Huffman, R. *Nuer Customs and Folk-Lore*. London, 1931.

Huntingford, G. W. B. Miscellaneous Records Relating to the Nandi and Kony Tribes. *JRAI*, 57:417–461. 1927.

———. Nandi Work and Culture. *CRS*, 4:1–126. 1950.

———. *The Northern Nilo-Hamites.* London, 1953.

———. *The Southern Nilo-Hamites.* London, 1953.

Jackson, H. C. The Nuer of the Upper Nile Province. *SNR*, 6:59–107. 1923.

Jacobs, A. H. Masai Age-Groups and Some Functional Tasks. Unpublished ms.

Köhler, O. Die Ausbreitung der Niloten. *BGVT*, pp. 159–194. 1950.

Lawrance, J. C. D. *The Iteso.* London, 1957. [Teso].

Leakey, L. S. B. Some Notes on the Masai. *JRAI*, 60:185–209. 1930.

Logan, M. H. The Beirs. *SNR*, 1:238–248. 1918. [Murle].

Lyth, R. R. The Suri Tribe. *SNR*, 28:106–114. 1947.

Marchetti, M. Notizie sulle popolazioni del Tirma, Tid e Zilmamo. *AAE*, 69:59–76. 1939. [Suri].

Massam, J. A. *The Cliff Dwellers of Kenya.* London, 1927. [Keyu].

Merker, M. *Die Masai.* Berlin, 1904.

Molinaro, L. I Didinga. *Anthropos*, 30:421–431. 1935.

———. Appunti circa gli usi, costumi e idee religiose dei Lotuko. *Anthropos*, 35–36: 166–201. 1940–1941.

Nalder, L. F., ed. *A Tribal Survey of Mongalla Province.* London, 1937. [Bari, Didinga, Fajulu, Kuku, Mondari, and Topotha].

Northcote, C. A. S. The Nilotic Kavirondo. *JRAI*, 37:58–66. 1907. [Luo].

O'Sullivan, H. Dinka Laws and Customs. *JRAI*, 40:171–191. 1910. [Padang].

Pauli, E. Die Splitterstämme nördlich des Rudolfsees. *AL*, 4(4):61–189. 1950. [Suri].

Peristiany, J. G. *La vie et le droit coutumier des Kipsigis.* Paris, 1938.

———. The Age-Set System of the Pastoral Pokot. *Africa*, 21:188–206. 1951. [Suk].

Prins, A. H. J. *East African Age-Class Systems.* Groningen, 1953.

Roscoe, J. *The Bagesu and Other Tribes.* Cambridge, 1924. [Sabei].

Schlippe, P. de, and L. Batwell. Preliminary Study of the Nyangwara System of Agriculture. *Africa*, 25:321–351. 1955. [Fajulu].

Seligman, C. G., and B. Z. Seligman. The Social Organization of the Lotuko. *SNR*, 8:1–45. 1926.

———. The Bari. *JRAI*, 58:409–479. 1928.

———. *Pagan Tribes of the Nilotic Sudan.* London, 1932. [Acholi, Bari, Dinka, Fajulu, Lotuko, Nuer, and Topotha].

Snell, G. S. *Nandi Customary Law.* London, 1954.

Southall, A. W. Lineage Formation among the Luo. *MIAI*, 26:1–43. 1952.

———. *Alur Society.* Cambridge, 1956.

Stirton, S. Moeurs et coutumes des Alour. *BSRBG*, 49:210–215. 1925.

Stubbs, N. M., and C. G. T. Morrison. The Western Dinkas. *SNR*, 21:251–265. 1938.

Stuhlmann, F. *Mit Emin Pascha ins Herz von Afrika.* Berlin, 1894. [Alur].

Titherington, G. W. The Raik Dinka. *SNR*, 10:159–209. 1927.

Tothill, J. D., ed. *Agriculture in the Sudan.* London, 1948.

Vanden Plas, J. Les Kuku. *CME*, 6:1–407. 1910.

Wayland, E. J. Preliminary Studies of the Tribes of Karamoja. *JRAI*, 41:187–230. 1931. [Jie and Labwor].

Wilson, G. McL. The Tatoga of Tanganyika. *TNR*, 23:35–47; 24:35–54. 1952–1953.

PART TEN
SPREAD OF PASTORALISM TO THE BANTU

——————————

44

——————————

Kenya Highland Bantu

When the Northeast Coastal Bantu arrived in Kenya, one branch, instead of following the coast into Somalia, moved north into the eastern section of the highlands, where a substantial number of Bantu reside today. That the latter are descended from the former is attested by an unmistakably close linguistic relationship. The immigrants occupied both the plateau country, where they presumably found only Bushmanoid hunters in possession, and the more elevated slopes of the Pare Mountains and of Mounts Kenya, Kilimanjaro, and Meru. Here they seem to have been preceded by Megalithic Cushites practicing intensive irrigated agriculture on terraced fields, for the mountain Bantu still continue these practices and also exhibit a variety of other customs of indubitable Cushitic origin. They doubtless followed the same process of encirclement, infiltration, intermarriage, and ultimate absorption to which the Nilotes of the Nandi cluster subjected the indigenous Cushites whom they found in the mountainous country northeast of Lake Victoria. The parallel will become strikingly apparent when we survey the ethnographic data.

The Bantu of the Kenya highlands form a progressive and relatively homogeneous cultural province, in which the following seven tribal groups can be distinguished.

1. Chaga (Chagga, Dschagga, Jagga, Wadschagga), with the Kahe and Meru. They occupy the slopes of Mounts Kilimanjaro and Meru and number about 260,000.
2. Kamba (Akamba, Wakamba). They number about 600,000.

342

3. Kikuyu (Akikuyu, Giguyu, Wakikuyu). Recent population estimates range from 665,000 to 1,115,000.
4. Meru (Mweru), with the Chuka (Suka), Embu, Mbere (Emberre), Mwimbe (Amwimbe), and Tharaka (Atharaka). They occupy the slopes of Mount Kenya and number about 150,000.
5. Pare (Asu, Wapare), with the Taveta. They occupy the Pare Mountains and number about 100,000.
6. Shambala (Sambara, Wasambara, Washambala). They were reported in 1935 to number about 80,000.
7. Teita (Taita, Wateita). They number about 60,000.

Agriculture provides the primary basis of subsistence among all the peoples of the province, and the methods of cultivation followed by the mountain tribes reveal a special affinity to those prevailing on the southern slopes of the Ethiopian plateau. Like the Konso, the presumptive kinsmen of the Megalithic Cushites (see Chapter 25), the Chaga, Meru, Pare, Shambala, and Teita make extensive use of irrigation and keep their fields in permanent cultivation through the use of animal manure as fertilizer. The Chaga even resemble the Konso in confining their animals in order to conserve their manure. Instead of grazing them, they bring grass, leaves, and other fodder to them in their stalls.

Cereal grains rank first in the agricultural economy of the province.

Kikuyu Girls Grinding Meal. (Courtesy of the American Museum of Natural History.)

Only the Kamba and Kikuyu, to be sure, cultivate sorghum to any considerable extent, but eleusine constitutes the staple among the Chaga, millet among the Kamba and Meru, and maize among the Kikuyu, Pare, and Shambala; the last two crops, in fact, hold important positions everywhere. Except for cereals, the Sudanic complex provides only small quantities of cow peas and gourds, and the Ethiopian complex only coffee, a major modern cash crop. Besides maize and sweet potatoes, a near staple in many societies, the American complex is represented only by small amounts of haricot and lima beans, manioc, pumpkins, and tobacco.

The cereals are supplemented mainly by importations from India and Southeast Asia. Nearly all groups depend heavily on the Indian legumes—pigeon peas and gram, hyacinth, and sword beans—and cultivate substantial quantities of the Malaysian bananas, sugarcane, taro, and yams. Bananas, indeed, attain the status of the ranking staple among the Shambala and of a co-staple among the Chaga.

The major crops of the Chaga fall into three categories which differ in the amount of ritual associated with their cultivation and in their allocation in the division of labor by sex. The first category, grown only by women and with the heaviest ritual incrustations, includes beans, sweet potatoes, taro, and yams. The second, cultivated only by men and with less prominent attendant rituals, embraces bananas and eleusine. The third, comprising only maize, may be grown indifferently by either sex, and its cultivation involves no ritual activities. We have already alluded to the hypothesis (Gutmann, 1913) that these categories reflect successive levels of historical introduction and to its bearing on the problem of the antiquity of the sweet potato in East Africa (Chapter 28).

Animal husbandry adds variety to the diet and also provides an important supplement. All groups keep considerable numbers of cattle, goats, sheep, and bees, but remarkably few have dogs and chickens. They use milk and in most cases make butter. They likewise exhibit the Cushitic practice of drinking blood drawn from the necks of living animals. The Meru, and doubtless other tribes as well, observe dietary regulations in the consumption of meat and milk. Except for the Teita, the Bantu of this province do very little hunting and little or no fishing, and in general observe the Cushitic taboos against eating fish and game fowl. They engage fairly extensively in trade, and many groups hold regular markets. The men clear land, construct and maintain irrigation ditches, and herd livestock, though Chaga women feed the animals. Except among the Chaga and Pare, women do the bulk of the cultivation. They also do the milking among at least the Chaga, Kamba, and Meru, although the Kikuyu apparently assign this task to men.

Marriage invariably entails the payment of a substantial bride-price in livestock. Most tribes prohibit unions between first cousins, but the Pare allow them in the case of cross-cousins; and the Chaga, who favor marriage with a woman of one's mother's sib, permit marriage with a mother's brother's daughter. General polygyny prevails, but only in the nonsororal form. The first wife enjoys a preferred status, but each married woman has a house of her own. Residence adheres strictly to the patrilocal rule. The Kamba and Teita have extended families, but in all other groups the household unit comprises only a nuclear or polygynous family. Except for minor traces of a possible former matrilineate among the Chaga and Shambala, descent, inheritance, and succession follow the patrilineal principle. All tribes are organized into patrisibs, usually exogamous and occasionally totemic, within which a segmentary lineage system prevails. Kin groups tend to be localized as patriclans, coextensive sometimes with the local community as a whole, sometimes only with segments within it. Kinship terminology conforms to the Omaha pattern among the Chaga, Kikuyu, and Teita, but the Shambala use cousin terms of the Hawaiian type.

All the peoples of the province live in neighborhoods of dispersed family homesteads, though the Shambala formerly occupied palisaded villages, and all groups build houses of the cone-cylinder type with low walls of mud or wattle and daub and with thatched roofs descending nearly to the ground. Despotic forms of government have developed only recently, and in only a few tribes. Thus the Shambala have a tribal state with a Zigula dynasty imposed by conquest, the Teita are ruled by petty district chiefs, and during the nineteenth century strong leaders among the Chaga created about thirty small chiefdoms controlling a few settlements each and exacting tribute from their inhabitants. Except for the development of a class of chiefs' retainers and dependents among the Chaga, social stratification scarcely exists. The Chaga, Kikuyu, and Teita, indeed, have never even kept slaves.

This relatively egalitarian social system reflects the former prevalence of republican political institutions of the Eastern Cushitic, or Gada, type among all the tribes of the province save the Shambala and Teita. With these exceptions, all groups are organized into age-grades of the linear type, and most of them still vest political authority in a council of elders representing a particular age-class during its occupancy of the ruling grade. Boys enter the first grade by initiation with circumcision (girls are subjected to clitoridectomy), and the age-classes, composed of annual age-sets initiated over a period of from twelve to fifteen years, advance at regular intervals through the sequence of grades, holding political office during one such period and retiring at its termination.

The Kikuyu tribe has attained world-wide notoriety in recent years through its participation in the ill-fated Mau Mau movement, led, interestingly enough, by the author of one of the authoritative ethnographic monographs cited in the bibliography below. The Chaga people have achieved a lesser but more solid reputation through the extraordinary financial success of their tribally managed coffee-marketing cooperative. Its profits have gone into the erection of a multistoried and ultramodern block of buildings in the town of Moshi which, in addition to housing a commercial college, provides the community with its finest business offices, an arcade of high-class specialty shops, and an excellent roof restaurant commanding a magnificent view of Mount Kilimanjaro. The reader who wishes to glimpse for himself the future of Africa should visit Moshi.

Selected Bibliography

Baumann, O. *Usambara und seine Nachbargebiete*. Berlin, 1891. [Pare and Shambala].
Bostock, P. G. *The Taita*. London, 1950.
Cagnolo, C. *The Akikuyu*. Nyeri, 1933.
Champion, A. M. The Atharaka. *JRAI*, 42:68–90. 1912. [Meru].
Dobson, E. B. Land Tenure of the Wasambaa. *TNR*, 10:1–27. 1940. [Shambala].
Dundas, C. History of Kitui. *JRAI*, 43:480–549. 1913. [Kamba and Meru].
———. The Organization and Laws of Some Bantu Tribes of East Africa. *JRAI*, 45:234–306. 1915. [Kamba, Kikuyu, and Meru].
———. *Kilima-Njaro and Its Peoples*. London, 1924. [Chaga].
Eichhorn, A. Beiträge zur Kenntnis der Waschambaa. *BA*, 1:155–222; 3:69–131; 7:56–98; 8:1–53. 1911–1924. [Shambala].
Gutmann, B. Die Frau dei den Wadschagga. *Globus*, 92:29–32, 49–51. 1907. [Chaga].
———. Feldbausitten und Wachstumsbräuche der Wadschagga. *ZE*, 45:475–511. 1913.
———. Das Recht der Dschagga. *Arbeiten zur Entwicklungspsychologie*, 7:1–778. 1926.
Hildebrandt, J. M. Ethnographische Notizen über Wakamba und ihre Nachbaren. *ZE*, 10:347–406. 1878.
Holding, E. M. Some Preliminary Notes on Meru Age Grades. *Man*, 42:58–65. 1942.
Hollis, C. Notes on the History and Customs of the People of Taveta. *JAS*, 1:98–125. 1901. [Pare].
Kenyatta, J. *Facing Mount Kenya*. London, 1938. [Kikuyu].
Lambert, H. E. The Systems of Land Tenure in the Kikuyu Land Unit. *CSAS*, n.s., 22:1–85. 1950.
———. *Kikuyu Social and Political Institutions*. London, 1956.
Lang, F. H. Die Waschambala. *REVAO*, pp. 218–267. 1903.
Leakey, L. S. B. *Mau Mau and the Kikuyu*. London, 1952.
Lindblom, G. *The Akamba*. Uppsala, 1916.
Merker, M. Rechtsverhältnisse und Sitten der Wadschagga. *PME*, 30(1):1–40. 1902.
Middleton, J. *The Kikuyu and Kamba of Kenya*. London, 1953.
Orde Brown, G. St. J. *The Vanishing Tribes of Kenya*. London, 1925. [Meru]
Penwill, D. J. *Kamba Customary Law*. London, 1951.
Prins, A. H. J. Notes on the Kinship Terminology of the Wa-Teita. *Man*, 50:145–147. 1950.
———. An Outline of the Descent System of the Teita. *Africa*, 20:26–37. 1950.
———. *The Coastal Tribes of the North-Eastern Bantu*. London, 1952. [Teita].
———. *East African Age-Class Systems*. Groningen, 1953. [Kikuyu].

Routledge, W. S., and K. Routledge. *With a Prehistoric People.* London, 1910. [Kikuyu].

Storch. Sitten, Gebräuche und Rechtspflege bei den Bewohnern Usambaras und Pares. *MDS,* 8:310–331. 1895. [Pare and Shambala].

Tate, H. R. Notes on the Kikuyu and Kamba Tribes. *JRAI,* 34:130–143. 1904.

———. The Native Law of the Southern Giguyu. *JAS,* 9:233–254. 1910.

———. Further Notes on the Southern Giguyu. *JAS,* 10:285–297. 1911.

Warburg, O. Die Kulturpflanzen Usambaras. *MDS,* 7:131–199. 1894. [Shambala].

Widenmann, A. Die Kilimandscharo-Bevölkerung. *PME,* 27(5):1–101. 1899. [Chaga]

Wohlrab, I. von. Das Recht der Schambala. *AFA,* 44:160–181. 1918.

45

Interlacustrine Bantu

A great ring of lakes—Tanganyika, Kivu, Edward, Albert, Kioga, and Victoria—nearly surrounds an important group of peoples known collectively as the Interlacustrine Bantu. They have thrice played a crucial role in the culture history of the Bantu as a whole. In assessing their influence, however, we must divide them into three clusters, since the regions which these occupy, though sharing today one fairly homogeneous culture, have differed substantially from one another at various times in the past.

RUANDA CLUSTER

For the sake of brevity we shall call the first of these regions Ruanda, although it also includes Urundi and portions of adjacent Tanganyika, Uganda, and the Belgian Congo. Its component tribes are listed below.

1. Bashi (Banyabungu, Wanyabungu), with the kindred Fulero (Bafulero, Wafulero) and Havu (Bahavu). This large nation inhabits the Belgian Congo immediately west of Ruanda-Urundi.
2. Chiga (Bachiga, Bakyiga, Batciga, Ciga, Kiga). This tribe, numbering in excess of 100,000, lives north of Ruanda near Lake Edward.
3. Ha (Abaha, Waha), with the Jiji (Wajiji) and Vinza (Vinsa). This group, numbering about 180,000, lives northeast of Lake Tanganyika.
4. Hunde (Bahunde), with the Nyanga (Banianga, Wanyanga). This large group lives north of the Bashi in the Belgian Congo.
5. Konjo (Bakondjo, Banande, Wakondjo, Wanande). This tribe, with a culture transitional toward that of the Equatorial Bantu, lives west of Lake Edward and has a population of about 70,000.

6. Nkole (Banyankole). This tribe, numbering about 260,000, inhabits the extreme southwestern part of Uganda.
7. Ruanda (Banyaruanda, Rwanda), with the Horohoro (Wahorohoro, Wampororo). This nation, inhabiting Ruanda proper, numbers about 2,150,000.
8. Rundi (Barundi, Warundi). These people, the inhabitants of Urundi, number nearly 2 million.

UGANDA CLUSTER

The second region embraces most of the southern half of Uganda and includes the tribes enumerated below.

9. Ganda (Baganda, Waganda). This nation numbers approximately a million.
10. Haya (Basiba, Heia, Kiziba, Wahaya, Wassiba, Ziba). These people, numbering about 300,000, live on Lake Victoria in the extreme northwest of Tanganyika.
11. Kerewe (Bakerewe, Wakerewe). This tribe, numbering about 40,000, occupies the island of Ukerewe in Lake Victoria and an adjacent promontory of the mainland.
12. Nyoro (Bakitara, Banyoro, Kitara). This tribe, with a population of about 110,000, lives to the east of Lake Albert.
13. Soga (Basoga), with the Gwere, Kene (Bakene), and Nyuli. This group, numbering about 500,000, lives in Uganda north of Lake Victoria.
14. Toro (Batoro), with the Tuku. This nation, numbering about 150,000, lives south of Lake Albert adjacent to the Ganda and Nyoro.
15. Zinza (Basindja, Sinja, Wassindja), with the Banyaisanga. This large group lives southwest of Lake Victoria in northwestern Tanganyika.

EAST NYANZA CLUSTER

The third region, known as East Nyanza, lies immediately east and northeast of Lake Victoria in Tanganyika, western Kenya, and a small adjacent section of Uganda. Its component tribes are listed below.

16. Gisu (Bageshu, Bagish, Geshu, Gishu, Masaba, Sokwia). This small tribe occupies the western slopes of Mount Elgon in Uganda.
17. Gusii (Gizii, Kisii, Kosova), with the Kulya (Bakulia, Bulia, Kuria, Tende), Simbiti (Simbeti), and Suba (Soba, Wassuba). This group, numbering about 250,000, lives southeast of the Nilotic Luo in Kenya and Tanganyika.
18. Kara (Wakarra). This tribe, numbering about 20,000, inhabits the island of Ukara in Lake Victoria.
19. Shashi (Washashi), embracing the Ikuzu, Ikoma, Jita (Wajita), Kwaya, Nguruimi (Ngoroine, Wangoroine), Ruri (Waruri), and Zanaki tribes east of Lake Victoria. They number at least 20,000.
20. Sonjo. This tribe, numbering about 4,500, occupies an enclave among the Masai east of the Shashi.
21. Wanga (Bahanga, Hanga, Wawanga), with the kindred Hayo (Khavi, Khayo, Xayo), Logoli (Lokoli, Maragole, Walako), Marach (Mrashi), Nyole, Samia, Tadjoni (Tasoni), Vugusu (Kitosh), and other tribes of the group commonly known collectively as the Bantu Kavirondo. They number well over 300,000.

Pygmoid hunters and gatherers with cultures of the Sangoan complex originally inhabited most of the Interlacustrine province. Modest remnants still survive among some tribes of the Ruanda cluster, but they have disappeared completely in Uganda and East Nyanza. This we can reasonably ascribe to the Cushitic immigrants from southern Ethiopia whose presence in the area in the first millennium B.C. has been revealed by archeological research (see Chapter 25). Different groups of these Caucasoid invaders seem to have occupied East Nyanza and Uganda. The present Kara tribe of the former cluster reflect an earlier Megalithic Cushitic population in their highly intensive agriculture, with permanent cultivation made possible by crop rotation and the use of animal manure conserved through stall feeding. In Uganda, on the other hand, massive prehistoric earthworks attest the former presence of Western Cushites, a conclusion confirmed, as we shall shortly see, by the extraordinarily detailed resemblances between the political institutions of Uganda and those of the Sidamo province of southwestern Ethiopia. The survival of Pygmies in Ruanda would suggest that neither group of immigrant Cushites occupied this region, doubtless because its geography did not suit their agricultural techniques.

Centuries later, but still before the time of Christ, the Cushites of Uganda, as we have seen (Chapter 28), acquired the Malaysian food plants from the coastal Azanians and transmitted them westward to the Central Sudanic peoples. They thus acted as mediators in the major historical process which would shortly eventuate in the explosive expansion of the Bantu into the tropical rainforest. As noted in Chapter 28, it was probably the Equatorial Bantu who first emerged from the forest, entering Uganda from the west or southwest and there meeting the agricultural Cushites. This encounter, too, was fraught with far-reaching consequences, for from the Cushites the Bantu borrowed the East African cereals, especially durra and eleusine, which, when spread around the periphery of the Congo Basin, enabled them successfully to penetrate in all directions the adjacent vegetation zones of savanna and dry forest. Thus indirectly, on two different occasions, the Cushites of Uganda mediated the expansion of the Bantu.

The newcomers could occupy the Ruanda region without serious opposition, entering there into their usual symbiotic relationship with the indigenous Pygmies. In East Nyanza they had no more difficulty in displacing or absorbing the Megalithic Cushites than their cousins, the Northeast Coastal Bantu, encountered nearer the coast. In Uganda, however, the presumably strong Cushitic states must have presented a more serious problem. They ultimately, of course, succeeded in infiltrating these as well, and in absorbing their Caucasoid inhabitants, since the present population speaks only Bantu languages. We already know (see Chapter 38) that complex despotic states occur among all the Bantu peoples around the periphery of the rainforest, and we may reasonably conclude that the conquest of Uganda was achieved, so to speak, by meeting fire with fire, i.e., by adopting the political system of the Cushites and using it to subdue them.

Around the close of the first millennium, as we have seen (Chapter 43), the Nilotes, acquiring the milking complex and thus the capacity for living an independent pastoral mode of life, expanded southward until they encountered the Interlacustrine Bantu. Checked by the political strength of the latter, they turned southeastward into western Kenya and northern Tanganyika. Here they not only dispossessed and absorbed the Megalithic Cushites but also displaced some of the Bantu in East Nyanza, as is evidenced by the occupation of the northeastern shore of Lake Victoria by the Luo and by the survival of the Sonjo deep in the heart of Masai territory.

The Nilotes also infiltrated the Bantu tribes of the Uganda cluster, where rulers and chiefs welcomed them as herders for their new-found wealth in cattle and permitted them to graze their livestock in sections unsuited to agriculture. Their descendants, known as the Hima (Bahima, Huma), constitute a modest fraction of the population today and still live a largely pastoral life, although they have long since exchanged their original Nilotic speech for Bantu. Because of their usefulness to the ruling class they enjoy a respected status, but the assumption that the political systems of Uganda are conquest states founded through the subjugation of agricultural Bantu by invading pastoral nomads lacks any real basis in fact.

On the other hand, something very much like this may well have happened in the Ruanda region. Here most of the societies today reveal a sharp stratification into endogamous castes with a ruling aristocracy of herders called Tussi (Batusi, Watutsi), a subject agricultural peasantry called Hutu (Bahutu, Wakhutu), and often also a depressed caste of Pygmy hunters called Twa (Batwa). Physically the Hutu are clearly Bantu, whereas the Tussi exhibit unmistakably the tall stature, slender bodies, and other characteristic traits of the Nilotic subrace (see Chapter 2).

In consequence of their interpenetration by the Hima and Tussi Nilotes the Interlacustrine Bantu early became thoroughly habituated to the herding and milking of cattle, and they transmitted these skills southward to the Bantu provinces, to be considered in subsequent chapters, whose inhabitants are sometimes known collectively as the Cattle Bantu. Since pastoralism has transformed the lives of many of these peoples, the inhabitants of Uganda have played for the third time a major mediating role in the historical development of the Bantu peoples. To be sure, the Bantu of the Kenya highlands also acquired cattle at about the same time, though from the Galla rather than from the Nilotes. Nevertheless it was not they but the Interlacustrine peoples who served as the crucial intermediaries.

Cattle may well have spread to some of the East African Bantu in advance of the adoption of milking, as has often happened elsewhere in Africa. The fact that the Kara stall-feed their cattle to conserve manure suggests, indeed, that this almost certainly occurred in East Nyanza. In our subsequent discussion, however, we shall assume that cattle and milking diffused together, which seems somewhat more probable for at least the Southern Bantu.

Most authorities in the past have classed the Interlacustrine tribes as "Hamitized Bantu" having derived their cattle complex from the Cushites of Ethiopia and the Horn. They were clearly mistaken. If the reader will compare the pastoral practices of the Bantu described in this and subsequent chapters with those of the Galla (Chapter 42) and the Nilotes (Chapter 43), he can readily confirm for himself the specific affiliation of Bantu pastoralism with that of the Luo cluster of Nilotes and its divergence in important respects from the cattle culture of all Cushites and Cushitized peoples. The Interlacustrine Bantu did, of course, become strongly "Hamitized" at a much earlier date through their contacts with the Sidamo immigrants into Uganda, but the results of this ancient cultural interchange do not include the acquisition of the cattle complex.

Tussi Dancers in Ruanda-Urundi. (Courtesy of United Nations.)

Animal husbandry approaches agriculture in economic importance throughout the province except among the marginal Konjo and Sonjo, and wherever Hima or Tussi are present they subsist almost exclusively on the products of their herds. In addition to cattle, the Interlacustrine Bantu keep goats, sheep, dogs, chickens, and bees. They use milk and make butter, and the drinking of fresh blood is reported for the Chiga, Haya, Nkole, and Rundi. The African cereals—sorghum, millet, and eleusine—play the leading role in the agriculture of most East Nyanza groups and of the Bashi, Chiga, Ha, Nyoro, Ruanda, and Toro tribes in the two western clusters. Bananas, however, rank as the staple crop among the Gisu and the great majority of the Ruanda and Uganda tribes. Among auxiliary food plants the most important are Malaysian yams, the Indian legumes, and maize, manioc, peanuts, and sweet potatoes from the American complex. Only the East Nyanza peoples practice irrigation and other intensive techniques of cultivation, reflecting therein their Megalithic Cushite antecedents, and the Kara rival the Chaga of highland Kenya as the foremost agriculturists of Bantu Africa.

The Interlacustrine peoples depend very little on hunting or gathering, but many of them fish extensively, and commerce is moderately well developed. The prevailing pattern in the division of labor by sex assigns land clearance, hunting, fishing, herding, and milking to the men, buttermaking and the bulk of the field labor to the women. Men, however, assume an equal share in cultivation among the Bashi, Hunde, Kara, Ruanda, and Shashi; and in several East Nyanza tribes women participate in the tending and milking of livestock. This last again reflects the influence of the Megalithic Cushites, whereas everywhere else in the province it is the Central Sudanic pattern of separating women from cattle that prevails.

Marriage universally entails a substantial bride-price in livestock. The Bashi, Kara, and Ruanda permit unions between cross-cousins, the Rundi prefer them, and the Chiga favor them in the case of a mother's brother's daughter only, but most groups forbid marriage with any first cousin. Local exogamy tends to prevail nearly everywhere, even in the absence of clans. The Kara, Rundi, and Wanga practice only limited polygyny, but other groups observe no comparable restraint. No society favors sororal polygyny, though the Chiga, Ganda, Haya, Nyoro, and Ruanda permit it. The first wife regularly enjoys a preferred status, but each co-wife has a hut of her own and the husband visits each in rotation. Residence follows the patrilocal rule, with only occasional individual exceptions. Among the Chiga, married sons live with their father until his death, but extended forms of family organization occur nowhere else.

Descent, inheritance, and succession conform to the patrilineal mode, with no obvious matrilineal survivals. In general, a segmentary lineage organization prevails. Exogamy applies to all members of one's own patrisib, and the Ganda, Gisu, Gusii, Haya, Nyoro, and Wanga extend it to one's mother's patrilineal kinsmen as well. The local community tends to assume the form of a patriclan in Ruanda and East Nyanza, but the Uganda tribes lack clans, though certain indications point to their former existence. Cousin terminology follows the Hawaiian pattern among the Gisu, Kerewe, and Nkole, the Omaha pattern among the Haya, Nyoro, and Soga, and the Iroquois pattern among the Ganda, Wanga, and most tribes of the Ruanda cluster. On the whole, the forms of social organization diverge markedly from those of the Central Bantu and peoples derived from them and show an unmistakable basic resemblance to those prevailing among the Equatorial Bantu (see Chapter 36). This confirms our surmise that the Interlacustrine Bantu derive historically from the latter.

No Interlacustrine tribe, on the other hand, retains any trace of the settlement pattern or house type characteristic of the tropical forest. Only the Hunde and the East Nyanza peoples live, or formerly lived, in compact villages, all other groups having adopted the pattern of dispersed family homesteads. As in other regions of former Megalithic Cushite occupation, the Sudanic cone-cylinder type of dwelling predominates in East Nyanza. The Kara and all tribes of the Ruanda and Uganda clusters,

Kulya Girls, Gusii Group. (Courtesy of British Information Services.)

however, exhibit a distinctive house type peculiar to the province, namely, a dwelling of beehive shape, without walls, thatched from the point of the roof to the ground. Fundamentally, this probably derives from the Sudanic dwelling by an elaboration of the covering cone and the elimination of the supporting cylinder.

The Gusii and possibly some of their neighbors practice clitoridectomy, and, except for the Nyanga subtribe of the Hunde, circumcision is also confined to a few groups in East Nyanza. The Nyoro and Wanga have adopted the old Nilotic pattern of extracting the lower incisor teeth as an initiatory rite. Age-grades, always diagnostic of ancient Megalithic Cushite influence in this part of Africa, occur only among the Gusii, Shashi, Sonjo, and Wanga of East Nyanza. Most of these tribes vest political authority at the local level in a set of age-grade elders. Throughout the rest of the province, however, a hereditary headman typically administers the affairs of the village or neighborhood, often with the assistance of a council of elders.

Political integration does not transcend the level of the local community among the Chiga and Konjo in the extreme west or, with insignificant exceptions, in the East Nyanza cluster. Ruanda and Uganda, however, are characterized by the extraordinary prevalence of despotic states. These embrace the entire society among the Ganda, Kerewe, Nkole, Nyoro, Ruanda, Ruandi, Toro, and Zinza; attain only a slightly lesser magnitude among the Bashi, Haya, and Hunde; and occur on a somewhat smaller scale among the Ha and Soga. A complex social stratification into hereditary classes of royalty, nobility, commoners, and slaves or into endogamous ethnic castes prevails among precisely the same societies, and is lacking elsewhere. The Interlacustrine states conform to a single pattern. They are, to be sure, typical African despotisms, but, beyond this, their forms exhibit such numerous and specific resemblances to the political institutions of the Cushites of the Sidamo province (see Chapter 23) that there is little doubt of their historical connection. A brief description of the traditional political system of the Ganda should make this clear.

At the head of the Ganda state stands an absolute king (*Kabaka*), who is also the high priest and the supreme judge of the land. He enjoys great respect, since the power of the state is believed to be embodied in his person. No one may observe him eat, and he can be approached only with servile prostration. He lives in a magnificent residence on a hilltop in the capital, surrounded by guards, retainers, slaves, personal officials, and a harem of wives. The insignia of his office include drums, a spear-scepter, and a throne. A sacred fire is maintained at the palace; it is generated when the king assumes office, carried along when he travels, and extinguished when he dies.

The realm is divided for administrative purposes into ten provinces, each with a governor, and these are subdivided into districts, each with an appointive chief. These territorial officials organize *corvées* for labor on public works and collect and transmit taxes in livestock, cowries, hoes, and barkcloth. The king reserves half of these revenues for himself and allocates the remainder for the support of his ministers and the administrative bureaucracy. The governors and district chiefs maintain residences not only in their own jurisdictions but also at the capital, where they form a great council which meets frequently with the king. An appointive vizier, or prime minister, the Katikiro, heads the administrative hierarchy, and the king keeps informed of its operations through a corps of secret police.

A second important minister, the Kimbugwe, has charge of the royal fetishes, including the monarch's umbilical cord, or so-called "twin." The territorial officials often exercise specialized functions at court. One governor, the Kago, presides over the council and supervises the royal household. A second, the Mugema, serves as custodian of the royal tombs and is the only minister whose office is hereditary and does not terminate with the death of the king. A third, the Kasuju, has charge of the princes and princesses of royal blood. One district chief, the Gabunga, does double duty as admiral of the canoe fleet.

Among the wives of the ruler, the one chosen for him by his father assumes the position of Queen-Consort. She takes precedence over the rest of the harem and has charge of the king's amulets and other very personal possessions. She is, however, outranked by the Queen-Sister, a half sister of the monarch who shares his royal status, and by the Queen-Mother, his own mother or, after her death, a substitute selected from the royal lineage. The two latter women maintain separate residences, are endowed with independent estates, and are forbidden to marry or bear children.

When the king dies, the fact is kept concealed while the Kasuju summons the royal princes and consults on the succession with the Katikiro and Kimbugwe, who form with him an electoral college. Their choice is confined to the sons of the deceased ruler and is sometimes settled by force of arms. In any event an anarchic interregnum supervenes until the new ruler assumes office. The body of the deceased king is mummified, human sacrifices are offered, and the new Queen-Mother, as soon as she takes office, has most of the rejected princes put to death.

The Ganda state is organized for war, with the Nyoro in particular as its hereditary enemies. Periodic censuses keep account of potential manpower and provide a basis for conscription. A network of roads, connecting each district capital with that of its province and each of the latter with the capital of the state, facilitates rapid mobilization of the armed forces. Finally, a special drum language, with hundreds of distinctive beats or rhythms representing as many specific meanings, makes possible almost instantaneous communication throughout the kingdom.

Selected Bibliography

Autenreith, H. Recht der Kissibaleute. *ZVR*, 21:354–392. 1908. [Haya].

Baumann, O. *Durch Massailand zur Nilquelle*. Berlin, 1894. [Shashi and Zinza].

Beattie, J. H. M. Nyoro Kinship, Marriage and Affinity. *Africa*, 27:317–340; 28:1–22. 1957–1958.

Biebuyck, D. L'organisation politique des Nyanga. *KO*, 22:310–341. 1956. [Hunde].

Césard, E. Le Muhaya. *Anthropos*, 20:75–106, 451–462; 21:489–508, 821–849; 22:15–60. 1935–1937. [Haya].

Colle, P. L'organisation politique des Bashi. *Congo*, 2(2):657–684. 1921.

———. Les clans au pays des Bashi. *Congo*, 3(1):337–352. 1922.

———. Le mariage chez les Bashi. *Congo*, 3(2):535–551. 1922.

Cory, H., and M. M. Hartnoll. *Customary Law of the Haya Tribe*. London, 1945.

Czekanowski, J. *Forschungen im Nil-Kongo-Zwischengebiet*, vols. 1–2. Leipzig, 1917–1924. [Konjo and Ruanda].

Delacauw, A. Droit coutumier des Barundi. *Congo*, 17(1):332–357, 481–522. 1936.

Delhaise, C. Chez les Warundi et les Wahorohoro. *BSRBG*, 32:386–421. 1908.

Dundas, K. R. The Wawanga and Other Tribes of the Elgon District. *JRAI*, 43:19–75. 1913.

Edel, M. M. The Bachiga of East Africa. *CCPP*, pp. 127–152. 1937.

———. *The Chiga of Western Uganda*. New York, 1957.

Fallers, L. A. *Bantu Bureaucracy*. Cambridge, 1956. [Soga].

Felkin, R. W. Notes on the Waganda Tribe. *PRSE*, 13:699–770. 1886.

Grant, C. H. B. Uha in Tanganyika Territory. *GJ*, 66:411–422. 1925. [Ha].

Griffiths, J. E. S. Notes on Land Tenure and Land Rights among the Sonjo. *TNR*, 9:15–19. 1940.

Hurel, E. Religion et vie domestique des Bakerewe. *Anthropos*, 6:62–94, 276–301. 1911.

Irstam, T. The King of Ganda. *PEMS*, n.s., 8:1–203. 1944.

Kagame, A. Les organisations socio-familiales de l'ancien Rwanda. *MIRCB*, 38:1–355. 1954.

Mair, L. P. *An African People in the Twentieth Century*. London, 1934. [Ganda].

Maquet, J. J. Le système des relations sociales dans le Ruanda ancien. *AMCBE*, 1:1–221. 1954.

Mayer, P. The Lineage Principle in Gusii Society. *MIAI*, 24:1–35. 1949.

———. Gusii Bridewealth, Law and Custom. *RLP*, 18:1–67. 1950.

Meyer, H. H. J. *Die Barundi*. Leipzig, 1916.

Oberg, K. The Kingdom of Ankole. *APS*, pp. 121–161. 1940.

———. Kinship Organization of the Banyankole. *Africa*, 11:129–160. 1940.

Pages, G. Un royaume hamite au centre de l'Afrique. *MIRCB*, 1:1–703. 1933. [Ruanda].

Paulssen, E. Rechtsanschauungen der Eingeborenen auf Ukarra. *BA*, 4:39–45. 1914. [Kara].

Rehse, H. *Kiziba*. Stuttgart, 1910. [Haya].

Roscoe, J. Notes on the Bageshu. *JRAI*, 39:181–195. 1909. [Gisu].

———. *The Baganda*. London, 1911.

———. *The Bakitara or Banyoro*. Cambridge, 1923.

———. *The Banyankole*. Cambridge, 1923.

Roscoe, J. *The Bagesu and Other Tribes of the Uganda Protectorate*. Cambridge, 1924. [Chiga, Gisu, Konjo, Ruanda, and Soga].

Roy, R. Notes sur les Banyabungu. *Congo*, 5(2):327–347; 6(1):83–108. 1924–1925. [Bashi].

Schumacher, P. Die Ehe in Ruanda. *Anthropos*, 5:870–906. 1910.

———. Das Eherecht in Ruanda. *Anthropos*, 7:1–32. 1912.

———. Die physische und soziale Umwelt der Kivu-Pygmäen. *MIRCB*, 3:1–509. 1949. [Bashi, Hunde, and Rundi].

Simons, E. Coutumes et institutions des Barundi. *BJIDC*, 12:137–161, 163–179, 181–204, 213–227, 237–265, 269–283. 1944.

Stam, N. The Bahanga. *PCAC*, 1:143–179. 1929. [Wanga].

Thornton, D., and N. V. Rounce. Ukara Island and the Agricultural Practices of the Wakara. *TNR*, 1:25–32. 1936.

Van der Burgt, J. M. M. *Un grand peuple de l'Afrique équatoriale*. Bois-le-Duc, 1903. [Rundi].

Vanhove, J. Essai de droit coutumier du Ruanda. *MIRCB*, 10:1–125. 1941.

Vervloet, G. Aux sources du Nil. *BSRBG*, 34:108–137, 262–273. 1910. [Rundi and Toro].

Viaene, L. La vie domestique des Bahunde. *KO*, 17:111–156. 1951.

———. L'organisation politique des Bahunde. *KO*, 18:8–34, 111–121. 1952.

Wagner, G. The Changing Family among the Bantu Kavirondo. *Africa*, 12(Supplement):1–52. 1939. [Wanga].

———. The Political Organization of the Bantu of Kavirondo. *APS*, pp. 197–236. 1940.

———. *The Bantu of North Kavirondo*. 2 vols. London, 1949–1956.

Weiss, M. *Die Völkerstämme im Norden Deutsch-Ostafrikas*. Berlin, 1910. [Ruanda].

46

———•◦•———

Tanganyika Bantu

On the fringes of the present trust territory of Tanganyika we have already encountered several Bantu peoples—the Central Bantu in the south (Chapter 38), the Northeast Coastal Bantu in the east (Chapter 39), and the Interlacustrine Bantu in the north (Chapter 45). The remaining inhabitants of the country, who constitute the bulk of its present population, must now receive attention. The Tanganyika Bantu, as we shall designate them, arrived as part of the Central Bantu immigration which also peopled the south and east. Since the Cushites had not penetrated this part of East Africa, the immigrants found it occupied only by Bushmanoid hunters and gatherers with cultures of the Stillbay complex, who had held it since Paleolithic times. The Kindiga and Sandawe in the north (see Chapter 10) constitute the only surviving remnants of this earlier population.

It was the African cereals—sorghum, eleusine, and millet—diffusing from Uganda, where the Interlacustrine Bantu had acquired them from the Cushites, that made possible the agricultural occupation of central and western Tanganyika. That the immigrants themselves belonged to the Central rather than the Interlacustrine group of Bantu is indicated both by linguistic evidence and by the widespread survivals of matrilineal institutions among the present inhabitants of the province.

Several centuries later, probably early in the second millennium, the Tanganyika Bantu received a second valuable cultural gift from their neighbors in Uganda—namely, cattle, or, if these perchance had been borrowed somewhat earlier, at least the knowledge of how to milk them and to make butter. This introduced an important new form of movable property and strengthened the economic position of the male sex, thereby initiating a transition from matrilineal to patrilineal forms of social organization, as will shortly be demonstrated.

Surrounded by peoples of differing cultures and of greater economic and political strength, the Tanganyika Bantu accepted in varying degrees the innovations offered to them, with the result that they fall into a number of somewhat disparate clusters.

RIFT CLUSTER

The tribes of this cluster reside in the extreme northeast adjacent to the Masai, with whom they share a number of Cushitic and Nilotic traits not prevalent in the province as a whole. The Gogo, Rangi, and Turu, for example, practice circumcision, clitoridectomy, and also the extraction of the lower median incisor teeth, and most groups drink fresh blood drawn from the necks of their animals.

1. Gogo (Wagogo), with the Ngomwia (Wangomwia). They number about 110,000. The Ngomwia, who occupy an enclave in Gogo territory, appear to be of Southern Cushitic origin.
2. Iramba (Aniramba), with the kindred Izanzu (Issansu) and Irambi (Yambi). They number about 125,000.
3. Mbugwe (Wambugwe). They are an offshoot of the Rangi and number about 8,000.
4. Rangi (Irangi, Langi, Walangi, Warangi). They number about 80,000.
5. Turu (Lima, Nyaturu, Toro, Walimi, Waniaturu). They number about 150,000.

NYAMWEZI CLUSTER

The tribes of this cluster adjoin the Interlacustrine Bantu in the northwest, and the Sumbwa in particular have become strongly acculturated to the latter. The Nyamwezi peoples do not practice genital mutilations, and the central tribes keep few cattle because of the prevalence of the tsetse fly.

6. Bende (Vende, Wabende), with the Tongwe. With them live numerous Holoholo immigrants from across Lake Tanganyika.
7. Kimbu. They form the southeastern branch of the Nyamwezi.
8. Konongo. They form the southwestern branch of the Nyamwezi.
9. Nyamwezi (Banyamwezi, Wanyamwezi), embracing the Gala, Galaganza, Irwana (Bilwana), and Nankwili. With the Kimbu and Konongo, they number at least half a million.
10. Sukuma (Basukuma, Wassukuma), with the Longo (Rongo). They number about a million.
11. Sumbwa, with the Msalala and other subtribes. They adjoin the Ha and Zinza tribes of the Interlacustrine Bantu.

RUKWA CLUSTER

The tribes of this cluster reside in the southwestern part of the province adjacent to the Bemba group of Central Bantu, with whom they reveal an unmistakable linguistic connection.

12. Fipa (Wafipa), with the Nyika (Banyika, Wanjika). The Nyika number about 15,000.
13. Iwa (Awiwa, Wawiwa, Wiwa), with the Nyamwanga (Ainamwanga, Inamwanga, Namwanga, Winamwanga). They were reported in 1910 to number about 20,000.
14. Lambya (Rambia, Warambia), with the Malila (Penya), Ndali, Tambo, and Wandya.
15. Pimbwe (Bapimbwe), with the Rungwa.
16. Safwa (Wassafwa), with the Nyiha (Nyixa). The Safwa proper number about 15,000.

RUFIJI CLUSTER

The tribes of this cluster inhabit the eastern section of the province adjacent to the Zigula group of Northeast Coastal Bantu and to the Yao cluster of the Central Bantu, and their cultures are in some measure transitional toward both. In addition, they were strongly affected by the Ngoni invasions of the nineteenth century. The Matumbi and Mbunga tribes contain substantial Ngoni ingredients, and the Hehe defeated the Ngoni by adopting and turning against them their own military organization and tactics.

17. Bena (Wabena), with the Sowe (Sovi, Wasove) and Vemba. They number at least 20,000
18. Hehe (Wahehe), with the Chungwe (Zungwa). They number about 100,000.
19. Matumbi (Wamatumbi), with the Ndendehule.
20. Mbunga (Bunga, Wambunga).
21. Ndamba (Gangi, Wandamba). They number about 30,000.
22. Pogoro (Wapogoro, Weganga). Their language and that of the Ndamba are mutually intelligible.
23. Sagara (Sagala, Wasagara, Wassungara), with the Kaguru and Vidunda.
24. Sangu (Rori, Sango), with the Poroto.

NYASA CLUSTER

The tribes of this cluster reside in the extreme south around the northern end of Lake Nyasa. Except for the Nyakyusa, who reveal a highly distinctive form of social organization, they are ethnographically almost undescribed and are apparently culturally very divergent.

25. Kinga, with the Mahasi, Mwelya, Pangwa, and Wanji. They inhabit the Livingstone Mountains northeast of Lake Nyasa.
26. Kisi, with the Mpoto and Sandia. They subsist primarily by fishing along the precipitous shores of Lake Nyasa.
27. Matengo (Wamatengo). They were reported in 1933 to number about 40,000.
28. Nyakyusa (Niakiusa, Sochile, Sokile), with the Kukwe, Mwamba, Ngonde (Konde, Nkonde, Wangonde), Selya (Salya, Seria), and Sukwa. They number well over 200,000.

The Tanganyika Bantu subsist primarily by cereal agriculture. Maize has joined millet, sorghum, and eleusine as one of the principal crops, and actually outranks them among the Bende, Hehe, and Pimbwe. The Bena and Ndamba differ from the rest of the province in cultivating rice as their staple; the Nyakyusa and Sumbwa, in depending chiefly upon bananas. Other crops of consequence include cow peas, earth peas, and sesame from the Sudanic complex; gram beans and pigeon peas from the Indian; beans, cucurbits, manioc, peanuts, and sweet potatoes from the American.

All groups keep goats, sheep, dogs, and chickens, and the tribes of the Rift cluster usually have donkeys as well. About one-third of the tribes of the province—the Bende, Fipa, Kisi, Konongo, Matengo, Matumbi, Mbunga, Ndamba, Nyamwezi, Pimbwe, and Pogoro—have few if any cattle, largely on account of the tsetse fly; all other groups, however, possess them in fair numbers, and they assume exceptional importance in the economies of the Nyakyusa, Sangu, Sumbwa, and peoples of the Rift cluster. The Tanganyika Bantu, indeed, served as the intermediaries who transmitted cattle and milking to the Bantu provinces south of the Zambesi River.

As far as geographical propinquity is concerned, the Tanganyika Bantu could have acquired their pastoral skills and knowledge equally well from either the Masai or the Interlacustrine Bantu. The position of milking in the division of labor by sex provides the probable answer, for the Masai, like other Cushitized Nilotes and the Cushites themselves, assign this task to women, whereas the Interlacustrine Bantu, like the Central Sudanic peoples and the Nilotes of the Luo cluster, rigorously segregate women from all contact with cattle. Significantly, the Tanganyika Bantu observe the same taboo in all reported instances—with a single exception. In the Rift cluster, which reveals so many other instances of Cushitic influence,

a number of tribes lack this taboo; men, to be sure, do most of the milking, but no objection is raised to female participation. Men, of course,
universally do the herding. Except among the Iramba, Iwa, Matumbi,
Nyakyusa, and Rangi, where men share equally in field labor, women do
the bulk of the agricultural work.

The Kinga, Matumbi, Sumbwa, northern Hehe, and all tribes of the
Rift cluster except the Gogo inhabit neighborhoods of dispersed family
homesteads, but the predominating settlement pattern for the province as a
whole is a fairly compact and sometimes stockaded village. The Sumbwa
have adopted the beehive houses of the adjacent Interlacustrine Bantu,
while the southern tribes of the Rufiji cluster occupy rectangular dwellings with thatched gable roofs like those of the neighboring coastal
peoples. A house type peculiar to the Tanganyika province prevails
among the northern Rufiji tribes and those of the Rift cluster, and has
recently spread to the Kimbu, Konongo, and some Nyamwezi. This is the
so-called *tembe*, an elongated rectangular structure with mud walls and
a nearly flat roof covered with earth. Often several such dwellings form
a quadrangle around an interior courtyard. The tribes of the Nyasa and
Rukwa clusters and many in the Nyamwezi group live in cone-cylinder
huts of the widespread Sudanic type.

Political integration does not transcend the local level among the
Iramba, Mbugwe, Rangi, and Turu of the Rift cluster. All the other
peoples of the province, however, possess true states. Often these embrace only districts or subtribes, but among the Bena, Fipa, Hehe, Iwa,
Pimbwe, Sangu, and Sukuma political organization extends to the entire
tribe. Whatever its size, the state nearly always assumes the form of a
typical African despotism, with an absolute ruler possessing divine attributes, a capital and court, a territorial administrative hierarchy for the
collection of tribute, a central council of ministers, and frequently a
prestigeful Queen-Mother. Slavery prevails in all except the stateless
tribes, and a hereditary nobility tends to emerge where states are complex. The ruling aristocracy is of Hima or Tussi origin among the
Nyamwezi tribes that adjoin the Interlacustrine Bantu.

The Nyakyusa exhibit a highly distinctive type of social and political
organization. At the age of eleven to thirteen all the boys of a district remove from their paternal homes and establish a new village of their own.
Until they marry they return daily to eat with their mothers and hoe
with their fathers. Ultimately, however, their wives join them in their
village. Local groups among the Nyakyusa consequently consist of age-
mates, not of kinsmen. Each has a headman, or "great commoner," selected by the paramount chief of the district. A district chief is succeeded
by two sons, the firstborn of his two "great wives." Some years before
his death, when these sons are about thirty-five years of age, he formally

retires at a great "coming out" ceremony, dividing his territory between the two sons and assigning definite tracts of land to each recently established age-village. Being a successful and expanding people, the Nyakyusa have been able to perpetuate this system without excessive fractionation.

The Tanganyika Bantu represent various phases of a general transition from matrilineal to patrilineal forms of social organization. The Iramba, Mbugwe, and Rangi in the extreme northeast still preserve their original exogamous matrisibs, as did the Ndamba until very recent times. Since the Mbugwe also possess exogamous patrilineages they are characterized by double descent. Among the Nyakyusa, the development of age-villages has removed the local basis for any form of unilinear kin group, with the result that patrilineal descent has very nearly disappeared. The strictly matrilineal rule of succession followed by the Fipa, Pimbwe, and most tribes of the Nyamwezi cluster and the matrilineal inheritance prevalent among the Mbunga and Sagara bear witness to the former existence of matrilineal descent in these tribes. As a matter of fact, in the entire province only the Sumbwa of the Nyamwezi cluster, the Iwa and Safwa of the Rukwa cluster, the Gogo and Turu of the Rift cluster, the Bena, Hehe, and Sangu of the Rufiji cluster, and doubtless some of the tribes on which information is lacking (the Kinga, Kisi, Lambya, Matengo, Matumbi, and Pogoro) have completed the transition to a thoroughly patrilineal and patrilocal form of social organization.

Matrilocal residence appears, though only during the initial period of marriage, among the Bena, Iramba, Nyamwezi, Safwa, and Sukuma, and avunculocal residence is confined to individual cases. Except among the Nyakyusa, whose age-village organization requires neolocal residence, patrilocality prevails throughout the province. Extended forms of the family occur in some of the northeastern tribes but not elsewhere. The Mbugwe stand alone in practicing monogamy. The Hehe, Nyakyusa, Pimbwe, Safwa, and Turu permit polygyny in the sororal form, but the Nyamwezi tribes and the Bena do not. Cross-cousin marriage occurs, sometimes preferentially, among the Bena, Gogo, Hehe, Iramba, Kimbu, and Sangu, and exclusively with the mother's brother's daughter among the Iwa and Mbunga; but most other groups forbid unions with any first cousin. Kinship terminology conforms to the Crow pattern among the Mbugwe and Sukuma, to the Hawaiian pattern among the Nyakyusa and Turu, and to the Iroquois pattern among the Bena, Bende, Gogo, Hehe, Mbunga, Nyamwezi, Pimbwe, Sangu, and Sumbwa.

Marriage normally entails the payment of a substantial bride-price, and the Bena, Fipa, Iwa, Nyamwezi, Safwa, and Sangu require bride-service in addition. Most tribes of the Nyamwezi cluster, however, recognize an alternative mode of marriage. A man who lacks sufficient livestock for the usual bride-price makes only a token gift and then subsequently a standard payment whenever his wife bears him a child. In such cases, however, the children belong to their mother's sib, not their father's, and they inherit from their maternal kinsmen. This practice suggests how the introduction of cattle into the province initiated a transformation in the social organization. By acquiring the wherewithal to pay bride-prices for their sons, men could affiliate the latter with their own kin group, and when this became sufficiently common it wrought a shift from matrilineal to patrilineal descent.

Selected Bibliography

Avon. Vie sociale des Wabende. *Anthropos*, 10–11:98–113. 1915–1916.

Baumann, O. *Durch Massailand zur Nilquelle*. Berlin, 1894. [Mbugwe].

Baumstark. Die Warangi. *MDS*, 13:45–60. 1900.

Blohm, W. *Die Nyamwezi*. 3 vols. Bamburg, 1931–1933.

Bösch, F. *Les Banyamwezi*. Münster, 1930.

Brown, G. G. Bride-Wealth among the Hehe. *Africa*, 5:145–158. 1932.

Brown, G. G., and A. M. B. Hutt. *Anthropology in Action*. London, 1935. [Hehe].

Chisholm, J. A. Notes on the Manners and Customs of the Winamwanga and Wiwa. *JAS*, 9:360–387. 1910. [Iwa].

Claus, H. Die Wangomwia. *ZE*, 42:489–497. 1910. [Gogo].

———. Die Wagogo. *BA, Beihefte*, 2:1–72. 1911.

Cory, H. *Sukuma Law and Custom*. London, 1953.

Culwick, A. T., and G. M. Culwick. The Functions of Bride-Wealth in Ubena. *Africa*, 7:140–159. 1934. [Bena].

———. *Ubena of the Rivers*. London, 1935.

Dempwolff, O. Beiträge zur Volksbeschreibung der Hehe. *BA*, 4:87–163. 1914.

Desoignies. Die Msalala. *REVAO*, pp. 268–282. 1903. [Sumbwa].

Fabry, H. Aus dem Leben der Wapogoro. *Globus*, 91:197–201, 218–224. 1907.

Fromm, P. Ufipa. *MDS*, 25:79–101. 1912. [Fipa].

Gray, R. F. Notes on Irangi Houses. *TNR*, 35:45–52. 1953.

———. Outline of an Anthropological Study of the Wambugwe. Unpublished ms.

Heese. Sitte und Brauch der Sango. *AFA*, 40:134–146. 1913.

Hodgson, A. G. O. Some Notes on the Wahehe of Mahenge District. *JRAI*, 56:37–58. 1926.

Kannenberg. Reise durch die hamitischen Sprachgebiete um Kondoa. *MDS*, 13:144–172. 1900. [Rangi].

Kohl-Larsen, L. *Auf den Spuren des Vormenschen*. 2 vols. Stuttgart, 1943. [Iramba].

Kootz-Kretschmer, E. *Die Safwa*. 3 vols. Berlin, 1926–1929.

Last, J. T. A Visit to the Wa-itumba Iron-workers and the Mangaheri. *PRGS*, n.s., 5:581–592. 1883. [Sagara].

Mackenzie, D. R. *The Spirit-ridden Konde*. London, 1925. [Nyakyusa].

Majerus. Das Eherecht der Wabende. *Anthropos*, 10–11:781–788. 1915–1916.

Malcolm, D. W. *Sukumaland*. London, 1953.

Maurice, M. Le pays des Bapimbwe. *Géographie*, 64:20–31, 228–237, 309–316; 66:171–289; 67:86–95, 147–165, 209–221; 68:224–236, 289–296; 69:18–33, 264–270; 70:83–102. 1935–1938.

Meinhardt. Provisional Outline of the Ethnographic Provinces of East Africa. Unpublished ms.

Merensky, A. *Deutsche Arbeit am Nyassa*. Berlin, 1894. [Kinga].

Mumford, W. B. The Hehe-Bena-Sangu Peoples. *AA*, 36:203–222. 1934.
Nigmann, E. *Die Wahehe*. Berlin, 1908.
Paulssen, F. Rechtsanschauungen der Wagogo. *BA*, 6:161–175. 1922.
Popplewell, G. D. Notes on the Fipa. *TNR*, 3:99–105. 1937.
Reche, O. *Zur Ethnographie des abflusslosen Gebietes Deutsch-Ostafrikas*. Hamburg, 1914. [Iramba and Turu].
Sanderson, M. The Relationship Systems of the Wangonde and Wahenga Tribes. *JRAI*, 53:448–459. 1923. [Nyakyusa].
Schaegelen, R. T. Le tribu des Wagogo. *Anthropos*, 33:195–217, 515–657. 1938.
Sick, E. von. Die Waniaturu. *BA*, 5:1–62. 1916. [Turu].
Spellig, F. Die Wanjamwezi. *ZE*, 59:201–252. 1927.
Tanner, R. E. S. Maturity and Marriage among the Northern Basukuma. *AS*, 14:123–133, 159–170. 1955.
Weckauf. Die Wamatumbi. *ZE*, 48:373–383. 1916.
Wilson, G. An Introduction to Nyakyusa Society. *BS*, 10:253–292. 1936.
———. Introduction to Nyakyusa Law. *Africa*, 9:16–36. 1936.
———. The Land Rights of Individuals among the Nyakyusa. *RLP*, 1:1–52. 1938.
———. The Constitution of the Ngonde. *RLP*, 3:1–86. 1939. [Nyakyusa].
———. The Nyakyusa. *STBCA*, pp. 252–291. 1951.
Wilson, M. Nyakyusa Kinship. *ASKM*, pp. 111–139. 1950.
———. *Good Company*. London, 1951. [Nyakyusa].
———. *Rituals of Kinship among the Nyakyusa*. London, 1957.

47

Middle Zambesi Bantu

All the Bantu peoples to be considered in this and the following four chapters possess cattle. They can, of course, only have received them from the north. A glance at Map 8, however, will reveal that they are separated from the closest cattle-raising people to the north by a band of Central Bantu who lack cattle. This gap, approximately 300 miles in width, must certainly have been crossed at some time in the past. The Ngoni, who raided north from Natal into Tanganyika during the nineteenth century, proved that it could be crossed. Their Mpezeni branch, who occupy today the Fort Jameson region in the middle of the gap and keep large herds there, likewise demonstrate that cattle can thrive in at least certain sections of the intervening Central Bantu territory despite the wide prevalence of the tsetse fly.

Since the gap was crossed, it seems logical to postulate that this occurred at its narrowest point. This falls unquestionably in Northern Rhodesia between the Iwa and Tumbuka tribes in the northeast and the Ila-Tonga cluster of peoples on the middle Zambesi River. We therefore assume that the ancestors of the latter were the first group of Southern Bantu to acquire cattle and the milking complex and that they acted as the mediators who transmitted pastoral skills to the rest.

The Ila, Tonga, and their neighbors, whom we shall designate collectively as the Middle Zambesi Bantu, fall into the following tribal groups.

1. Ila (Baila, Baschukulompo, Mashukolumbwe), with the Bizhi, Lumbu (Nanzela), Lundwe, Mbala, and Sala (Basala). They number about 40,000.
2. Koba (Bakoba, Bakuba, Bayei, Maiye, Yeii, Yeye). They number about 20,000.
3. Lenje (Balenje, Beni Mukuni, Lengi), with the Soli (Sodi). They number about 50,000.
4. Lozi (Barotse, Barozi, Barutse, Marotse, Rotse, Rozi), embracing the dominant Luyi (Alui, Aluyi, Luyana) and the subject but related Kwandi, Mbowe (Mamboe), Muenyi, and Mwanga. They number about 180,000.
5. Lukolwe (Balukolwe), with the Mbwela (Bambwela, Mambwela, Mbwera).
6. Mashasha (Bamasasa).
7. Mashi (Bamaschi), with the Makoma (Bamakoma), Mishulundu, Ndundulu, Nyengo, Old Mbunda, Shanjo, and Simaa. They are akin to the Lozi but subject to them.
8. Mbukushu (Mambukuschu, Mucusso). They number about 10,000.
9. Nkoya (Mankoya), with the Lushange (Baushanga, Ushanga).
10. Subia (Massubia, Masupia, Subya), with the Leya. They number about 10,000.
11. Tonga (Batonga), with the Gowa, Namainga, Toka, Tonka (Batonka), and We. They number about 130,000.
12. Totela (Batotela, Matotela). They number about 20,000.

In this province the Bantu have by no means exterminated the earlier hunting and gathering population. Scattered groups of Pygmies still live among many of the eastern tribes, and even more substantial remnants of the indigenous Bushmen survive in the west. As elsewhere in southern Africa, this doubtless points to the comparative recency of Bantu occupation. The Koba have incorporated in their speech a number of the Khoisan clicks, or implosive consonants.

The economy of the Middle Zambesi, as compared with that of most other Bantu peoples, rests to an exceptional extent upon gathering, e.g., of water roots among the Koba and Subia; upon hunting, especially of aquatic animals; and upon fishing, in the rivers and in the swamps and flood plains of the Zambesi and Okavango. Among the Nkoya these activities even take precedence over agriculture. Most tribes keep a considerable number of goats, sheep, dogs, and chickens. The Lukolwe, Mashasha, Mbukushu, Nkoya, and Totela have few cattle, in at least some instances primarily because of the tsetse fly, but these animals assume considerable importance in all other groups. On the whole, however, agriculture provides the principal economic support. The Lozi, for example, are estimated to derive about 40 per cent of their food from cultivated plants as compared with 20 per cent from animal husbandry, 25 per cent from hunting, and 15 per cent from fishing.

The staple crops are sorghum, millet, eleusine, and, more recently, maize. Lesser food plants include cow peas, earth peas, okra, and sesame from the Sudanic complex and cucurbits, manioc, peanuts, and sweet potatoes from the American complex, as well as Malaysian yams and beans of unreported species. Men hunt, clear land, and do all the herding and milking, cattle being taboo to women. They also do most of the fishing (although women catch small fry in baskets) and participate to a limited extent in agricultural work. The bulk of the field labor, however, together with gathering, falls within the province of the female sex.

The Middle Zambesi Bantu occupy small, compact villages, commonly surrounded by a fence or palisade and usually arranged with a cattle corral in the center, or occasionally, as among the Nkoya, an open plaza. Lozi communities maintain two villages each—one on an artificial mound in the flood plain of the Zambesi and another on the margin of this plain, to which they remove during the period of annual inundation. The prevailing house type is a round hut with a low cylindrical wall of rush mats or of wattle and daub and with a conical thatched roof. Some Koba, however, live in hemispherical mat lodges resembling those of the Hottentot (see Chapter 9).

Aboriginally the Ila were politically organized into small districts under a chief and a council of local headmen, and the Mashasha and Mbukushu likewise had petty paramount chiefs, but most groups lacked any form of integration more complex than an autonomous local community under a headman with nominal authority. In 1838, however, the Kololo, a Sotho tribe from South Africa, invaded the middle Zambesi region and established a powerful conquest state in what is now called Barotseland. They subjugated the Luyi, or ancestral Lozi, as well as the Mashi, Nkoya, Subia, and Totela, and reduced the Mbukushu and southwestern Tonga to tributary status. In 1864 the Luyi overthrew and expelled the Kololo, but succeeded to their hegemony over the neighboring tribes and came eventually to be known as the Lozi (Barotse). Their state conforms to the pattern prevailing among the Sotho (see Chapter 51), with a divine monarch, a ruling aristocracy, a territorial bureaucracy, a council of ministers residing at the capital, and a prominent and independent Queen-Sister.

Only the Ila, and in very recent times also the Lozi and Tonga, require a bride-price. Other groups demand only bride-service or token gifts. Most tribes, with the exception of the Ila and Tonga, show a preference for local exogamy and also, with the exception of the Lozi, for cross-cousin marriage. Polygyny is general and exclusively nonsororal.

The first wife enjoys a preferred status, but each co-wife has a hut of her own. Ila men permit their wives to have publicly recognized paramours, from whom the husbands receive regular payments. The household unit regularly assumes the form of an independent nuclear or polygynous family rather than an extended family.

If we except the Lozi as a special case, to be considered separately, the province as a whole exhibits a uniform basic pattern of social organization, with certain modifications resulting from the introduction of cattle. All groups, so far as we can determine from the descriptive information available, possess exogamous matrisibs and corporate matrilineages, the latter usually localized as clans. The rule of residence accords basically with the norms prevailing among the Central Bantu immediately to the north (see Chapter 38), i.e., avunculocal in the west and, in the east, matrilocal with the right of removal to avunculocal residence in the case of positional succession. Where cattle are common, their use in marriage payments has resulted in the appearance of patrilocal residence, which now occurs with moderate frequency among the Tonga and has become general, except for chiefs, among the Ila. The latter tribe, as a consequence, has evolved exogamous patrilineages in addition to its older matrilineal kin groups, and is thus characterized by double descent. Cousin terminology, wherever reported, conforms to the Iroquois pattern. In general, the forms of social organization in the province are unmistakably derived from those prevailing among the adjacent Central Bantu, and the modest deviations are readily attributable to the influence exerted by the introduction of cattle.

The Lozi have a social system which differs in every conceivable respect from that outlined above. They possess no unilinear kin groups and are thus characterized by bilateral descent. They have eight noncorporate name groups, and an individual can claim membership in any or all of them provided that he is a direct descendant in any line of a person who was a member. Kinship terminology conforms to the Hawaiian rather than to the Iroquois pattern. Residence follows no single rule. Though patrilocality is preferred, a man, upon marrying, frequently cannot find an available house site on the small mound where his father's dwelling is located and must look elsewhere for a home. In such a case he seeks a site in the settlement of some close bilateral kinsman—a maternal or paternal grandparent, an uncle or aunt, or even in some instances his father-in-law. Lozi residence might thus be called multilocal. A village definitely constitutes a kin group, a "clan" of sorts, though the bonds of affiliation are bilateral and diverse rather than unilinear. Even inheritance reveals a fluid character. A man has one heir, carefully selected either by himself or by his close kinsmen after his death. Though the choice normally falls upon a son, this is by no means invariable, and a grandson or a fraternal or sororal nephew is not infrequently picked in preference to a son.

Gluckman, to whom we are indebted for an admirably complete description of this unique social system, assumes that it has great antiquity because it exhibits so excellent an adaptation to the peculiar local geographical conditions and such thoroughgoing internal consistency. In this assumption he is almost certainly wrong, for cogent historical evidence makes another interpretation very much more probable. From a distributional point of view, the Bantu neighbors of the Lozi in every direction, without exception, have strictly matrilineal forms of social organization, rendering it highly improbable that the ancestral Luyi could have been characterized by a social system of any other type.

We must not forget, moreover, the important historical events which Gluckman himself relates, namely the Kololo conquest of 1838 and the successful Luyi rebellion in 1864. The Kololo must have brought with them the type of social organization exemplified by all their Sotho kinsmen (see Chapter 51), namely, a decadent system of agamous patrisibs largely superseded by a strongly functional territorial ward organization. Twenty-six years of political domination could well have shattered the indigenous matrilineal social structure without providing the model of a functional patrilineal system to take its place. Bilateral descent would thus emerge as a natural consequence.

It is further significant that the Luyi, who replaced the Kololo in the seat of power, had adopted the language of the conquerors and still today, as the Lozi, speak a Sotho dialect rather than one related to the speech of the surrounding tribes. This indicates that they had undergone a very high degree of acculturation before they revolted and assumed control of the kingdom. A people who had changed their language were unlikely to have preserved their kinship organization intact. It would seem clear, therefore, that the social system of the Lozi, far from being ancient, is the natural product of known and relatively recent historical events.

Selected Bibliography

Allan, W., M. Gluckman, D. U. Peters, and C. G. Trapnell. Land Holding and Land Usage among the Plateau Tonga. *RPL*, 14:1–192. 1948.

Bertrand, A. *The Kingdom of the Barotsi*. London, 1899. [Lozi].

Brelsford, V. History and Customs of the Basala. *JRAI*, 65:205–215. 1935. [Ila].

Colson, E. Life among the Cattle-owning Plateau Tonga. *Rhodes-Livingstone Institute Occasional Papers*, 6:1–40. 1949.

———. The Plateau Tonga of Northern Rhodesia. *STBCA*, pp. 94–162. 1951.

———. The Role of Cattle among the Plateau Tonga. *RLJ*, 11:10–46. 1951.

———. Residence and Village Stability among the Plateau Tonga. *RLJ*, 12:41–67. 1951.

Gluckman, B. Economy of the Central Barotse Plain. *RLP*, 7:1–130. 1941. [Lozi].

Gluckman, B. Essays on Lozi Land and Royal Property. *RLP*, 10:1–99. 1943.

———. Kinship and Marriage among the Lozi of Northern Rhodesia and the Zulu of Natal. *ASKM*, pp. 166–206. 1950.

———. The Lozi of Barotseland. *STBCA*, pp. 1–93. 1951.

Holub, E. *Seven Years in South Africa*. London, 1881. [Lozi].

———. *Von der Capstadt ins Land der Maschukulumbe*. Wien, 1890. [Ila].

Jaspan, M. A. *The Ila-Tonga Peoples*. London, 1953.

McCulloch, M. *The Southern Lunda and Related Peoples*. London, 1951. [Lukolwe, Mashasha, and Nkoya].

Passarge, S. Das Okawangosumpfland und seine Bewohner. *ZE*, 37:649–716. 1905. [Koba, Mbukushu, and Subia].

Richards, A. I. Some Types of Family Structure amongst the Central Bantu. *ASKM*, pp. 206–251. 1950. [Ila].

Richter, M. Kultur und Reich der Marotse. *BKUG*, 8:1–196. 1908. [Lozi].

Smith, E. W., and W. M. Dale. *The Ila-speaking Peoples*. 2 vols. London, 1950.

Turner, V. M. *The Lozi Peoples*. London, 1952.

48

——— •◦• ———

Southwestern Bantu

In the southern half of Angola and the northern half of South-West Africa reside a number of tribes whose languages form a distinct subdivision within the Bantu group as a whole and who likewise constitute a fairly homogeneous cultural province. These Southwestern Bantu, as they are commonly called, adjoin the Central Bantu in the north and northeast, the Hottentot and Bushmen in the south and southeast. They are also connected, by a narrow corridor along the Okavango River, with the Middle Zambesi Bantu, from whom they unquestionably acquired cattle and the milking complex. They have no geographical contact whatsoever with the Southeastern Bantu, who will receive our attention in the following three chapters, and they differ markedly from the latter in both language and culture. The common assumption that they constitute merely a branch of the Southeastern Bantu lacks even a shred of factual support.

The aboriginal inhabitants of the province belonged to three distinct groups of hunting and gathering peoples. A very few Pygmy remnants survive in the north. Larger numbers of Bushmen live in enclaves within Bantu territory as well as along its southeastern margin; the Hottentot to the south are, as we have seen (Chapter 9), merely pastoral Bushmen. The third group of indigenous hunters, Negroid in race but Khoisan in language, includes the Koroca on the coast and the Bergdama in the extreme south. The Nyaneka, alone among all Negro peoples, are personally familiar with remnants of all three groups of hunters and sharply differentiate them.

The tribes of the province, though extremely numerous, fall into the following eight distinguishable groups.

1. Ambo (Ovambo), embracing the Eunda, Evale, Kuanyama (Ovakuanyama, Ukuanyama, Vakuanyama), Okafima (Kafima), Ombalantu (Ombarandu), Ombandja (Bandya, Cuamato), Ondonga (Aandonga, Ovandonga), Ongandjera (Ovagandjera), Onguangua, Ukualuthi (Ovanguuruze), and Ukuambi (Ovamguambi). They number about 175,000.

2. Herero (Damara, Ovaherero), with the Mbanderu and Shimba (Himba). Reduced from 100,000 to 25,000 in the Herero War of 1904–1906 against the Germans, they have appreciably recovered since then.

3. Kwangare (Kwengare, Makwangare, Ovakuangari). This completely undescribed tribe is perhaps actually a branch of the Ambo.

4. Mbundu (Banano, Bimbundu, Mambari, Mbali, Munano, Nano, Ovimbali, Ovimbundu, Umbundu, Vakuanano, Vanano), embracing the Bailundu (Mbailundu), Cenga (Chilenge), Cingolo (Quingolo), Cipeyo (Quipeyo), Citata (Quitata), Civula (Quibula), Ciyaka (Quiaca), Eketete (Quiquete), Elende (Lende), Kakonda (Caconda, Cilombo, Quilombo), Kalukembe (Caluquembe), Kasongi (Cassongue), Mbongo (Bongo), Namba, Ndulu (Andulo, Ondura), Ngalanga (Galanga), Ngalangi (Galangue), Sambu (Sambo), Sange, Viye (Bie, Bihe), and Wambu (Huambo). They were reported in 1940 to number about 1,300,000.

5. Ndombe (Andomba, Bandombe, Dombe, Mundombe), with the Hanya (Hanha, Muhanha), Kilenge (Cilenge, Quilenge), and Nganda (Ganda).

6. Ngonyelu (Ngonzelo), with the Nhemba (Nyamba, Nyemba).

7. Ngumbi (Bangumbi, Humbe, Khumbi, Muhumbe, Nkumbe, Ovakumbi, Vahumbi, Vankumbe), with the Hinga (Ehinga, Ovahinga), Kipungu (Cipungu, Pungu, Quipungu, Vatyipungu), and Mulondo (Balondo). These peoples were depopulated by severe famines in 1912 and 1915, when the Ngumbi proper were reduced from 80,000 to 10,000.

8. Nyaneka (Banianeka, Munhaneca, Ovanyaneka, Vanhaneca). They were reduced by the famines of 1912 and 1915 from over 120,000 to about 40,000.

The economy of the Southwestern Bantu rests almost equally upon agriculture and animal husbandry. Agriculture assumes first place in the north, among the Mbundu, Ndombe, and Ngonyelu. The two activities display an even balance among the central tribes, i.e., the Ambo, Ngumbi, and Nyaneka. In the south, however, the Herero have abandoned agriculture and pursue a life of independent pastoral nomadism —the only Bantu tribe in Africa to do so. Moreover, they transmitted this mode of life to their southern neighbors, the Hottentot. Hunting, fishing, and gathering augment the food supply of the Southwestern Bantu to only a modest extent, and the Mbundu alone engage extensively in trade.

The agricultural tribes practice hoe cultivation with brand-tillage. The original staples were sorghum and millet, which still hold first place among the Ambo and Ngumbi and are extensively grown everywhere else. In general, however, the American complex has superseded the Sudanic. Maize ranks as the staple among the Mbundu and Nyaneka, manioc among the Ndombe, and both are widely cultivated elsewhere. Among lesser crops, American beans, cucurbits, peanuts, and sweet potatoes assume the greatest importance, rivaled only by the Indian legumes.

All tribes possess cattle, sheep, goats, and dogs, and most of them also keep chickens, bees, and pigs, a recent introduction from Europe. Cattle enjoy exceptional importance, not only for the milk and butter they yield but also for marriage payments, as a source of wealth and prestige, and for religious reasons. The three northern tribes, indeed, rarely milk their animals, although dairy products constitute a dietary staple everywhere else. A widespread trait, distinctive of the province, is the keeping of "sacred cows." Among the Nyaneka, for example, every respected adult male has at least two of these, one given him by his father, the other by his mother's brother. They are dedicated, respectively, to a deceased paternal and maternal relative, whose spirits allegedly reside in them and communicate through them to the living. The Nyaneka consequently observe their behavior with great care for possible revelations. They feed them exceptionally well, dedicating the milk and sacrificing the first calf of each to the ancestral spirit. It is taboo, incidentally, to consume their milk with meat—a reflection of the dietary regulations which we have already encountered among the Nilotes (Chapter 43) and which also occur among the Interlacustrine Bantu, e.g., the Nyoro.

A Nyaneka man's chief wife tends his sacred cows, performs the cult activities associated with them, and for this reason must remain absolutely faithful. This suggests that the taboo segregating women from cattle did not spread to the Southwestern Bantu. Other evidence supports this inference. Among the Ambo, though men do most of the milking, their wives often assist. The Herero, moreover, assign milking primarily to females. In other respects the division of labor by sex reveals complete uniformity. The men hunt, herd, and clear new land. Both sexes fish, although women catch only small fry. Women gather and do most, but not all, of the field labor.

Except for the Herero, who wander in nomadic bands, all tribes live in compact and semipermanent hamlets or villages. Sizable towns occur only among the Mbundu, usually associated with a royal residence. Formerly each settlement was defended by an encircling wooden palisade, in the case of the Herero a thorn fence. Dwellings are grouped in family compounds around a central open space—a cattle corral among the

Herero and Nyaneka, elsewhere usually a plaza or courtyard with a building used as a council house and the headman's residence. Here the headman or his wife maintains a sacred fire, the invariable symbolic center of the community. Most Southwestern Bantu live in round huts with conical thatched roofs and cylindrical walls of poles or of wattle and daub. The Herero, however, occupy hemispherical dwellings resembling those of the Hottentot. These are constructed of flexible saplings inserted in the ground in a circle, bound together at the top, often with support from a central post, covered with twigs or bark, or sometimes with hides, and frequently surfaced with clay or dung.

Government at the local level rests in the hands of a hereditary headman with priestly functions, assisted by a council of elders. The Herero, among whom the community is a patriclan composed of a number of family bands, lack any more elaborate form of political organization. The other tribes, however, all have genuine states. Though relatively small in size, these exhibit the usual characteristics of African despotisms. Each has a divine king, who rules from a capital town with the aid of a council of ministers and collects tribute through appointive territorial officials. Among the Ngumbi he has a special stool as his throne. Among the Ambo, a Queen-Mother enjoys great prestige and maintains an independent court, and the chief wife, or Queen-Consort, tends the sacred fire, which is kindled at the ruler's installation and extinguished at his death. All groups keep slaves, and all except the Herero have hereditary aristocracies.

In contrast to the Middle Zambesi Bantu, who require no bride-price, all tribes of the Southwestern province make substantial marriage payments, nearly always in cattle. Most of them reveal a preference for local exogamy. They differ, however, in regard to cross-cousin marriage. The Ambo, with certain local exceptions, forbid unions with any first cousin. The Herero and Mbundu prefer marriage with a cross-cousin, the former particularly favoring a father's sister's daughter and the latter a mother's brother's daughter. The Nyaneka permit unions of either type, but only if a cow is sacrificed in a kin-severing rite. General polygyny prevails universally, but the Herero alone allow a man to marry two sisters. The first wife enjoys seniority of status, but each has her own hut and the husband visits each in regular rotation. Extended forms of the family appear only among the Herero and Nyaneka.

Patrilocal residence prevails in almost direct proportion to the importance of cattle, with avunculocal rather than matrilocal residence as the alternative. The pastoral Herero permit a man to reside with his maternal uncle rather than with his father, but as a rule only poor men exercise this privilege. Avunculocal residence occurs with greater frequency among the Ambo and becomes the rule in chiefly lineages. Further north, a married man regularly lives with or near his father until the latter's death, when a Nyaneka usually, and a Mbundu occasionally, shifts to avunculocal residence. Since all the tribes of the province observe matrilineal descent, the Southwestern Bantu reveal an unmistakable affinity to the adjacent Central Bantu in the fundamental structure of their social systems. This fact, coupled with comparable resemblances in language, in political organization, and in mode of marriage, argues strongly for their original derivation from the north.

It was from the east, however, that they received cattle, and therewith the stimulus toward the intensification of bride-price payments and the emergence of patrilocality. By aggregating patrilineally related males in a single locale, patrilocal residence favors the development of patrilineal descent. In two geographically remote sections of the province, i.e., among the Herero in the south and the Mbundu in the north, patrilocality has actually given rise to patrilineal lineages and sibs. Since this has occurred without disturbing the older matrilineal kin groups, these two tribes are characterized by double descent.

Gibson (1956), in discussing the Herero, argues that "double descent must have occurred in both lines simultaneously, possibly over a long period of time, for the disjunctive and conjunctive forces associated with them are complementary." That the distributional evidence, both for the Southwestern province and for Bantu Africa as a whole, proves his conclusion to be incorrect is less important than the serious fallacy in his reasoning. The modern social anthropologist who takes account both of the processes of culture change and of the evidence of history should certainly recognize that social systems rarely lose their internal consistency as they readjust to changing conditions. On the contrary, they ordinarily exhibit a dynamic or shifting equilibrium in which their parts maintain their integration though altering their interrelationships. Although historical inferences may often be made from minor or temporary internal inconsistencies, it is never legitimate to infer historical depth from the fact of integration, as Gibson has done in this instance and Gluckman, though less explicitly, in the Lozi case considered in the previous chapter.

Selected Bibliography

Childs, G. M. *Umbundu Kinship and Character*. London, 1949.
Estermann, C. Ethnographische Beobachtungen über die Ovambo. *ZE*, 63:40–46. 1931.
Gibson, G. D. Double Descent and Its Correlates among the Herero of Ngamiland. *AA*, 58:109–139. 1956.
———. The Social Organization of the Southwestern Bantu. Unpublished ms.
Hahn, C. H. L. The Ovambo. *NTSWA*, pp. 1–36. 1928.
Hambly, W. D. The Ovimbundu of Angola. *FMAS*, 21:89–362. 1934.
Irle, J. *Die Herero*. Gütersloh, 1906.

Jaspert, F., and W. Jaspert. Die Völkerstämme Mittel-Angolas. *VSVM,* 5:1–155. 1930. [Mbundu].

Kraft, M. Die Rechtsverhältnisse der Ovakuanyama und der Ovandonga. *MDS,* 27:17–35. 1914. [Ambo].

Lang, A., and C. Tastevin. La tribu des Va-Nyaneka. *Mission Rohan-Chabot,* 5:1–213. Corbeil, 1937.

Lebzelter, V. *Eingeborenenkulturen in Südwest- und Südafrika.* Leipzig, 1934. [Ambo].

Lehmann, F. R. Das Häuptlingstum der Herero. *Sociologus,* n.s., 5:28–43. 1955.

Loeb, E. M. Transition Rites of the Kuanyama Ambo. *AS,* 7:1–27. 1948.

Luttig, H. C. *The Religious System and Social Organization of the Herero.* Utrecht, 1933.

Magyar, L. *Reisen in Süd-Afrika,* vol. 1. Pest and Leipzig, 1859. [Mbundu and Ndombe].

McCulloch, M. *The Ovimbundu of Angola.* London, 1952.

Rautanen, M. Die Ondonga. *REVAO,* pp. 326–345. 1903. [Ambo].

Schachtzabel, A. *Im Hochland von Angola.* Dresden, 1923. [Ngonyelu].

Schlosser, K. Die Herero in Britisch Betschuanaland-Protektorat. *ZE,* 80:200–258. 1955.

Tastevin, C. Le famille "Nyaneka." *Semaine International d'Ethnologie Religieuse,* 5:269–287. 1931.

Tönjes, H. *Ovamboland.* Berlin, 1911.

Vedder, H. The Herero. *NTSWA,* pp. 153–211. 1928.

Viehe, G. Die Ovaherero. *REVAO,* pp. 294–312. 1903.

Wunenberger, C. La mission et la royaume de Cunène. *MC,* 20:224–225, 234–236, 250–252, 261–264, 269–272. 1888. [Ngumbi].

Zastrow, B. von. Die Herero. *ER,* 2:213–268. 1930.

49

Shona and Thonga

Two great Bantu nations, the Shona and Thonga, occupy Southern Rhodesia and the southern half of Mozambique. On the north they have the Central Bantu as their neighbors, and in the northwest they abut on the Middle Zambesi Bantu, from whom they apparently acquired cattle and the milking complex. Linguistically, the Shona reveal a particularly close relationship with the adjacent Maravi peoples of the Central Bantu province, and the Thonga occupy an intermediate position between them and the Nguni and Sotho to the south.

The earlier hunting and gathering population, presumably Bushmen, have left no surviving remnants in the Shona or Thonga country. Conceivably they may have suffered extinction at the hands of the seekers after gold who left behind the spectacular ruins of Zimbabwe and numerous other traces of their occupation. Since we have already considered the problem of Zimbabwe (Chapter 26), we shall not discuss it further except to note that most authorities ascribed the ruins and gold workings to the modern Shona peoples until recent radiocarbon research fixed the occupation at the unexpectedly early date of around A.D. 600. Negroid skeletal remains, however, demonstrate that the expanding Bantu had already reached the province at that time. The discovery of remains of sorghum, cow peas, and watermelons at Mapungubwe, but apparently not of cattle, suggests that the original immigrants were exclusively agricultural.

The numerous Shona and Thonga tribes can be classified into ten groups, forming two distinct clusters.

SHONA CLUSTER

The Shona (Mashona) constitute a culturally homogeneous nation numbering more than a million people. They inhabit Southern Rhodesia and adjacent Mozambique. In 1838, an army of Nguni raiders, the Ndebele, occupied the country of the Kalanga and Rozwi tribes in the west and established there a powerful conquest state.

1. Karanga (Makaranga, Vakaranga, Wakaranga), with the Duma, Govera, Gwena (Abagwena), Kalanga (Bakaa, Makalaka, Wakalanga), Limima (Humbe), Mari, Matopo, Nanzwa (Abananzwa), Nyai (Abanyai, Banyai, Wanyai), Nyubi (Banyubi), and Shabi (Abashabi, Bashabi).
2. Korekore (Korikori, Makorekore, Wakorikori), with the Shangwe (Abashankwe, Bashankwe, Washangwe).
3. Manyika (Bamanyeka, Manika, Wamanyika, Wanyika).
4. Ndau (Ndzawu, Njao, Vandau, Vandzau), embracing the Danda (Madanda, Vadanda, Wadondo, Watande), Gova (Magova, Vagova, Wagowa), Shanga (Mashanga, Wasanga), Teve (Vateve, Wateve), and Tomboji (Matomboji, Vatombotse).
5. Tawara (Matawara, Mtarawa, Tavara, Wataware), with the Barwe (Bargwe, Barue, Barwa, Wabarwe), Bujga (Wambudjga), Fungwe (Bafungwi, Basungwe, Baungwe, Phungwe, Wafungwe, Wahungwe, Waungwe), and Tonga (Abatonga, Atonga, Batoka, Batonga, Watonga).
6. Zezuru (Bazezuru, Bazuzura, Mazizuru, Vazezuru, Wazezuru), with the Hera (Abahela, Bahera), Gova, Mbire, Njanja (Bajanja, Sinjanja), Nohwe (Noe, Wanoe), Rozwi (Amalozwi, Balozwe, Baroswi, Warozwi), and Shawasha.

THONGA CLUSTER

The Thonga (Bathonga, Shangana-Tonga) constitute a culturally homogeneous nation numbering well in excess of a million. They live southeast of the Shona in southern Mozambique and have received substantial Nguni increments, who are known as the Shaangan (Shangana).

7. Chopi (Batchopi, Tshopi, Vachopi), with the Lenge (Valenge) and Tonga (Vatoka, Vatonga).
8. Hlengwe, with the Nwanati and Tswa (Batswa).
9. Ronga (Baronga).
10. Thonga (Bathonga, Tonga).

The Shona and Thonga subsist primarily by agriculture. Kafir corn, the former staple, has yielded first place to maize in the majority of tribes. Subsidiary crops include other varieties of sorghum as well as millet, eleusine, rice, beans, earth peas, manioc, peanuts, pumpkins, and sweet potatoes. As an example of overemphasis in anthropology the author should perhaps record his experience in attempting to ascertain the nature of the Shona economy. After reading the fourteen sources on this nation which appeared most promising from available bibliographies, he found that he had obtained nine independent lists of kinship terms but not a single mention of the crops grown by this basically agricultural people.

Animal husbandry, though important in the Thonga cluster, plays a definitely subsidiary role in the economy of the Shona. All groups keep goats and chickens, and most of them possess cattle, but sheep are rare and pigs recent. The Tawara have no cattle, and the Chopi and Zezuru keep very few. Although they provide milk, cattle are chiefly important for bride-price payments. Hunting and gathering add little to the food supply. Fishing makes a more substantial contribution, especially among the Ndau and Tawara. The men hunt, fish (except for small fry), and do the herding and milking, since cattle are taboo to women. Among the Shona they also share equally in the agricultural work, but this is not true in the Thonga cluster.

The Shona and Thonga peoples live in dispersed hamlets, or kraals, each a cluster of thatched cone-cylinder huts with walls of wattle and daub arranged in a circle around a cattle corral or sometimes, as among the Lenge tribe of the Chopi group, around a central plaza with a sacred tree. Socially, the hamlet has the structure of a patriclan, its members constituting either a large extended family or a small localized patrilineage. Authority within the hamlet is vested in a hereditary headman, who arbitrates disputes, officiates at sacrifices to the ancestors, and is assisted by an informal council of family heads.

Descent, inheritance, and succession, with certain exceptions to be noted below, follow the patrilineal principle. Kin groups reveal a segmentary character. Though sibs are agamous, their localized segments are invariably exogamous, and the Shona, but not the Thonga, extend exogamy to the mother's as well as the father's patrilineage. Thonga sibs bear ancestral names, but among the Shona they have totemic names and taboos and are aggregated into phratries on the basis of totemic resemblances, precisely as among the adjacent Central Bantu (see Chapter 38). In sharp contrast to practically all Bantu tribes of the surrounding Central, Middle Zambesi, Southwestern, Nguni, and Sotho provinces, who exhibit kinship systems of the Iroquois type, the Shona and Thonga tribes employ cousin terms exclusively of the Omaha type, a widespread feature of societies with strongly patrilineal social systems. Abundant evidence nevertheless exists that they followed only the matrilineal rule of descent in the not very distant past. We shall first examine the case for the Shona, which is very clear, and then turn to the more controversial situation among the Thonga.

Matrilineal descent, inheritance, and succession still prevail in a few Shona groups in the extreme north, notably the Dombe subtribe of the Tonga tribe of Tawara. Marriage practices provide even more convincing evidence of former matrilineal descent. All the Shona recognize two distinct modes of marriage: a preferred mode involving a substantial bride-price in cattle and an alternative mode entailing only a token gift of a few hoes coupled with prolonged matrilocal premarital and postmarital bride-service. Even when a bride-price is paid, matrilocal residence is normally required during the first year of married life. Thereafter the husband removes with his wife, normally to patrilocal residence but sometimes to avunculocal residence, which everywhere exists as a patterned alternative. Where no bride-price has been paid, removal becomes possible only when the oldest daughter has grown up and married and her bride-price has been turned over to the wife's father or brother in lieu of that not paid for her mother. Other Shona marriage usages accord with those of the Thonga, e.g., local exogamy, the prohibition of unions with any first cousin, and preferential sororal polygyny.

In those Shona tribes that possess few cattle, notably the Tawara and some groups of Zezuru, marriages of the second type naturally preponderate, and prolonged matrilocal residence is usual. This situation, incidentally, doubtless explains the preference for sororal polygyny. Such practices reveal a striking resemblance to those prevailing among the Central Bantu immediately to the north (see Chapter 38), especially when one takes into consideration the alternative of removal to avunculocal residence. The conclusion seems inescapable that the Shona once shared the social system of their northern neighbors and linguistic kinsmen and that the shift to bride-price payments, patrilocal residence, and patrilineal descent occurred as a direct consequence of the introduction of cattle.

Junod (1927) reaches an identical conclusion for the Thonga through a careful analysis of ethnographic data. Some of the features of Thonga culture which support this historical reconstruction are cited below, together with brief parenthetical comments.

1. Avunculocal residence is customary in childhood. Boys and girls, as soon as they are weaned, go to live in the village of their maternal uncle and remain there for several years, in the case of girls sometimes until they are fully grown. (This is normal in matrilineal societies with avunculocal residence, e.g., the central and western tribes of the Central Bantu.)
2. When a man has no patrilineal heirs to carry on his line, he may require one of his sisters to remain in his settlement. Her children reside in his house, and the males continue his lineage and clan. (This recapitulates the household pattern of the matrilineal eastern Central Bantu.)
3. If a man has no immediate patrilineal heirs, his sisters' sons inherit his property in preference to remoter patrilineal kinsmen. Even when he has patrilineal heirs, his sisters' sons can claim certain items from his estate, e.g., his spears. (Inheritance by sisters' sons is normal in matrilineal societies.)
4. A maternal uncle has a right to a definite share in the bride-price received for a sister's daughter. (He can ordinarily claim most of it in a matrilineal society.)
5. The officiant at all sacrifices in a man's life-crisis ceremonies is his mother's brother. (In a matrilineal society this duty naturally falls to a man's maternal uncle as the head of his lineage.)

In a paper that has been widely acclaimed by those who have not examined the evidence, Radcliffe-Brown (1924) offers an alternative interpretation of Shona and Thonga usages relating to the mother's brother. Refraining from citing any of the specific ethnographic data, and arguing exclusively from general assumptions, he ascribes the Southeastern Bantu forms of the avunculate to an alleged law that "the special pattern of behaviour between a sister's son and the mother's brother is derived from the pattern of behaviour between the child and the mother." The aim of his paper, as stated by Radcliffe-Brown (1952, p. 14) himself, was "to contrast with the explanation by pseudo-history the interpretation of the institution to which it refers as having a function in a kinship system with a certain type of structure." The indicated contrast is clear. In the eyes of the present writer, however, it takes the form of an opposition between sound historical scholarship and untrammeled sociological speculation.

Both the Shona and Thonga are politically organized in states of relatively modest size. At the head of each stands a paramount chief with the characteristics of a divine king. He is hedged in by taboos and in some cases is killed if he develops any physical defect, even the loss of a tooth. He resides in a capital town, where he maintains a court and is advised by a council of ministers with specialized functions. A hierarchy of territorial officials assures him a regular flow of tribute. A new fire is kindled at his accession and maintained throughout his life.

Most authorities have assumed that these political institutions represent a heritage from the builders of Zimbabwe. We already possess evidence which casts doubt on this interpretation, for complex political systems occur nowhere in the territory once occupied by the Megalithic Cushites, who presumably founded Zimbabwe. It seems much more likely that the Shona and Thonga acquired their political forms from the Central Bantu peoples to the northwest, amongst whom we have previously encountered institutions of a very similar character (Chapter 38).

Selected Bibliography

Barnes, B. H. Relationships in Mashonaland. *Man,* 31:213–216. 1931. [Manyika and Zezuru].

Bernardi, B. The Social Structure of the Kraal among the Zezuru. *CSAS,* n.s., 23:1–60. 1950.

Boas, F. Das Verwandtschaftssystem der Vandau. *ZE,* 54:41–54. 1922.

Bullock, C. *The Mashona.* Cape Town and Johannesburg, 1928.

Clerc, A. The Marriage Laws of the Ronga Tribe. *BS,* 12:75–104. 1938.

Dos Santos, J. Eastern Ethiopia. *Records of South-Eastern Africa,* ed. G. M. Theal, 7:183–383. London, 1901. [Ndau and Ronga].

Earthy, E. D. Sundry Notes on the Vandau. *BS,* 4:95–107. 1930.

———. *Valenge Women.* London, 1933. [Chopi].

Fouché, L. *Mapungubwe.* Cambridge, 1937.

Fuller, C. E. Native Tradition and History. Unpublished ms. [Chopi].

Goldman, I. The Bathonga. *CCPP,* pp. 354–381. 1937.

Herskovits, M. J. Some Property Concepts and Marriage Customs of the Vandau. *AA,* 25:376–386. 1923.

Holleman, J. F. The Pattern of Hera Kinship. *RLP,* 17:1–58. 1949. [Zezuru].

———. Some "Shona" Tribes of Southern Rhodesia. *STBCA,* pp. 354–396. 1951. [Zezuru].

———. *Shona Customary Law.* London, 1952. [Zezuru].

Jacques, A. A. Terms of Kinship and Corresponding Patterns of Behaviour among the Thonga. *BS,* 3:327–349. 1929.

Junod, H. A. *The Life of a South African Tribe.* 2 vols. London, 1927. [Thonga].

Junod, H. P. A Contribution to the Study of Ndau Demography, Totemism and History. *BS,* 8:17–37. 1934.

———. The VaThonga. *BTSA,* 4(1):7–28. 1935.

Kuper, H. *The Shona.* London, 1955.

Posselt, F. W. T. *Fact and Fiction.* Salisbury, 1935. [Tawara and Zezuru].

Radcliffe-Brown, A. R. The Mother's Brother in South Africa. *SAJS,* 21:542–555. 1924.

———. *Structure and Function in Primitive Society.* Glencoe, 1952.

Schapera, I. Matrilocal Marriage in Southern Rhodesia. *Man,* 29:113–117. 1929. [Tawara and Zezuru].

Seed, J. H. The Kinship System of a Bantu Tribe. *NADA,* 10:65–73; 11:35–56. 1932–1933. [Karanga and Zezuru].

Stead, W. H. The Clan Organization and Kinship System of Some Shona Tribes. *AS,* 5:1–20. 1946. [Zezuru].

Taberer, W. S. Mashonaland Natives. *JAS*, 4:311–336. 1905. [Zezuru].
Taylor, G. A. The Genealogical Method of Anthropological Enquiry. *NADA*, 15:71–
86. 1938. [Manyika].
Wieschhoff, H. A. Marriage among the Babudja in Southern Rhodesia. *Publications
of the Philadelphia Anthropological Society*, 1:221–235. 1937. [Tawara].
———. The Zimbabwe-Monomotapa Culture. *GSA*, 8:1–115. 1941. [Zezuru].

50

Nguni

The nation known as the Nguni represents the southernmost extension
of the Bantu. At the time of the discovery of South Africa these people
occupied what is now Natal and had penetrated deeply into the Cape of
Good Hope. They were still gradually expanding at the expense of the
indigenous Bushmen, but it is not true, as certain historians claim, that
they were recent arrivals, for they had already held for a century or more
all except the frontiers of the country they inhabited when Vasco da
Gama arrived. The original invaders almost certainly intermarried extensively with Bushman women, for it would otherwise be difficult to
account for the fact that all Nguni languages today have adopted some
of the clicks, or implosive consonants, so characteristic of the Khoisan
languages.

Since their discovery the Nguni have expanded northward at the expense of other Bantu peoples, a fact which makes it advisable to separate
the contemporary tribes into three clusters.

NGUNI CLUSTER

This cluster embraces the tribes that still occupy approximately their
original habitat. The Pondo, Tembu, and Xosa are commonly distinguished from the Swazi and Zulu as the South Nguni and North Nguni,
respectively.

1. Pondo (Amapondo, Mpondo). They number nearly 300,000.
2. Swazi (Amaswazi). They occupy Swaziland and adjacent portions of the Transvaal, where Zulu conquerors welded indigenous Nguni and Sotho elements into
   a state in the late eighteenth century. They number about 400,000.
3. Tembu (Tembo, Thembu), with the Bomvana, Mpondomise, Ngabe, and Qwathi.
4. Xosa (Amakosa, Amaxosa, Kaffir, Xhosa) Together with the Tembu, they number
   appreciably more than 2 million.

5. Zulu (Amazulu), with the Bhaca, Bhele, Fingo, Hlubi, and Zizi. They represent an amalgamation of many original tribes in Natal and number over 2 million.

NDEBELE CLUSTER

This cluster includes three tribes descended from North Nguni emigrants to other parts of South Africa within the historical period. These are the Rhodesian Ndebele, or Ndebele proper, who established a conquest state in Shona territory in 1838, and the Transvaal Ndebele, embracing the Laka and Manala, who settled among the Sotho in the Transvaal about two centuries earlier.

6. Laka (Black Ndebele, Langa), with the Maune (Letwaba), Motetlane (Sebitiela), and Seleka. Together with the Manala, they number nearly 150,000.
7. Manala, with the Hwaduba and Ndzundza (Mapoch).
8. Ndebele (Amandebele, Landeen, Matabele, Tebele). They number about 300,000 and are much mixed with Shona, Sotho, and other alien elements.

NGONI CLUSTER

This cluster includes the mixed descendants of Zulu bands that fled from Natal around 1820 to escape the rule of King Shaka and raged northward on a career of cattle raiding and pillage, picking up on the way large elements of Sotho, Swazi, Thonga, and other ethnic elements. They passed west of Lake Nyasa and east of Lake Tanganyika and advanced to the vicinity of Lake Victoria, where they turned south and eventually conquered and settled their present territories in southern Tanganyika, Nyasaland, and Northern Rhodesia. Here they intermarried extensively with the indigenous Central Bantu. Their heterogeneous descendants are known collectively as the Ngoni (Angoni, Mangoni, Wangoni). The extent to which the several Ngoni tribes have accepted the cultures of their new neighbors, while retaining elements of their own traditional ways, presents a fascinating problem in acculturation, but one which lies outside the scope of the present work. Although we cannot deal with this subject here, the various tribes are listed below, and the interested reader may pursue their study with the aid of the appended bibliography.

9. Gomani, with the Chiwere. They inhabit a section of southern Nyasaland and speak the Nyanja language today. They number about 50,000.
10. Magwangara (Machonde, Mafiti, Mazitu, Watutu). They inhabit a section of southern Tanganyika, and most of them speak either Pangwa or Yao today.
11. Mombera. They conquered the Tumbuka of northern Nyasaland and welded them into a conquest state. They number about 45,000 and speak the Tumbuka language.
12. Mpezeni. They settled in the vicinity of Fort Jameson in Northern Rhodesia, where, unlike other Ngoni, they still live a primarily pastoral life. They number about 85,000 and speak the Nsenga language.

Agriculture and animal husbandry play approximately equal roles in the Nguni economy. Maize has everywhere superseded sorghum, the indigenous staple. Subsidiary crops include bananas, beans, earth peas, eleusine, gourds, millet, peanuts, pumpkins, sweet potatoes, and water-melons. In addition to cattle, important for prestige and bride-price payments as well as for their milk, the Nguni keep goats, sheep, and dogs, as well as horses, donkeys, pigs, and chickens, which have been introduced since the first European contact. They do little hunting or gathering, and most groups display an almost Cushitic aversion to fish. Since cattle are taboo to women, men do the herding and milking. They also clear land but leave most other agricultural operations to the women.

Despite the importance of pastoral activities, the Nguni are sedentary rather than nomadic. The ruling class among the Ndebele formerly oc-cupied large palisaded towns, but the prevailing pattern of settlement throughout the province consists of neighborhoods of dispersed family homesteads, or kraals. In the Ngoni and Ndebele clusters, cone-cylinder dwellings have replaced the original house type, which still predominates in the Nguni cluster. This is a hut of beehive shape consisting of a circle of bent saplings fastened together at the top, interlaced with horizontal

Ndebele Couple at Home. (Courtesy of Union of South Africa State Information Office.)

elements, and supported by a central post; the exterior is thatched with grass, or occasionally with mats, and the interior walls are often plastered with a mixture of earth and dung. A number of such huts, arranged in a circle around a cattle corral, form a kraal. The group inhabiting a kraal tends to be a polygynous family among the Ndebele and Xosa, an extended family among the Pondo, Swazi, and Zulu.

Marriage invariably entails the payment of a substantial bride-price (*lobola*) in cattle. Incest taboos prevent unions with any first cousin, and exogamous rules prohibit marriage with any member of the sib of either parent. Polygyny is general and, except among the Xosa, preferably sororal. Each wife has her own hut within the kraal. A polygynous family is divided into "houses," among which the husband distributes land and livestock. In South Nguni tribes, the first wife heads a "great house" and the second a "right-hand house," other wives being assigned alternately to each as "rafters." The Ndebele and Zulu add a third major division, the "left-hand house" of the third wife. The eldest son of each house inherits the property allocated to it, with the son of the great house as the principal heir. Although not previously mentioned, this form of family organization has a sporadic distribution as far north as the Nilotes of the Luo cluster, from whom it perhaps ultimately derives. The so-called "seed-raising" levirate, another Nguni practice, has a somewhat similar distribution. According to this custom a widow lives with, but does not marry, her spouse's younger brother, and the children she bears by him are ascribed to the deceased husband.

Residence invariably follows the patrilocal rule, and descent, inheritance, and succession conform strictly to the patrilineal principle. Sibs, as well as their segmentary lineage divisions, are exogamous and bear ancestral names. Nguni social structure reveals no apparent survivals of former matrilineal institutions, which can be inferred only from distributional evidence and from the general picture we have presented of the social history of the Bantu as a whole.

Kinship terminology conforms to the Iroquois pattern. Since the Bantu who exhibit this pattern frequently reveal different roots in their terms for cross-cousins, a listing of those that are clearly cognate with the Nguni term and have an identical application may conceivably offer a clue to linguistic affiliations and hence to past migration routes.

mubiala	Rega of the eastern Equatorial Bantu province
muzara	Hunde of the Interlacustrine Bantu province
muzala	Bashi and Chiga of the Interlacustrine Bantu province
mubyara	Ruanda of the Interlacustrine Bantu province
umuvyara	Rundi of the Interlacustrine Bantu province
muvyala	Kimbu, Nyamwezi, and Sumbwa of the Tanganyika Bantu province

muyalaye	Bende of the Tanganyika Bantu province
mvyala	Pimbwe of the Tanganyika Bantu province
mvyara	Tumbuka of the Central Bantu province
mufyala	Bemba, Luapula, and Shila of the Central Bantu province
mvyala	Nsenga of the Central Bantu province
vavyala	Kunda of the Central Bantu province
umufyala	Lamba of the Central Bantu province
mufiala	Lala of the Central Bantu province
muzwala	Lovedu and Venda of the Sotho province
motswala	Kgatla, Pedi, Sotho, and Tlokwa of the Sotho province
ntsala	Kwena, Ngwaketse, Ngwato, Rolong, and Tawara of the Sotho province
umzala	Manala, Pondo, Swazi, and Zulu of the Nguni province
umza	Xosa of the Nguni province

All the peoples of the province are organized into states of considerable complexity. The political systems of the South Nguni still preserve strong traces of their original kinship basis, with the ruler as the senior representative of the senior sib and the higher administrative offices filled by patrilineal kinsmen appointed by him. In Natal, however, an energetic paramount chief named Shaka succeeded, about 1818, in organizing a powerful conquest state in which territorial ties largely replaced the bonds of kinship and practically obliterated tribal divisions. Shaka established himself as the personal owner of the land and its inhabitants. In addition to exercising supreme executive and judicial authority, he arrogated to himself the responsibility for performing all religious and magical rites on behalf of the nation, even expelling all private rainmakers from his kingdom. He maintained his absolute power by instituting a standing army consisting of all unmarried men, who were organized into regiments on the basis of age. Warriors were not permitted to marry until the king gave collective permission to the members of a regiment to mate girls of their own age. He stationed these regiments in barracks in various parts of the country, but especially in the vicinity of the capital, where they underwent military training and also tended his herds and tilled his fields. Since he received additional support from gifts, judicial fines, tribute in game, and especially the bulk of all cattle and women captured in war, he was in a position to dispense generous largesse.

The elements of the Zulu political system—conquest, territorial organization, and age-regiments—spread to other North Nguni peoples, notably the Ndebele and Swazi. Associated with it was a social stratification into classes of royalty, hereditary nobility, and commoners. To this the Ndebele added slavery, which the other tribes did not practice, and a class of dependent aliens.

Selected Bibliography

Barnes, J. A. Some Aspects of Political Development among the Fort Jameson Ngoni. *AS*, 7:98–109. 1948. [Mpezeni].

——. The Fort Jameson Ngoni. *STBCA*, pp. 194–252. 1951.

——. Marriage in a Changing Society. *RLP*, 20:1–136. 1951. [Mpezeni].

Cook, P. A. W. *Social Organisation and Ceremonial Institutions of the Bomvana.* Cape Town and Johannesburg, 1931. [Tembu].

Elmslie, W. A. *Among the Wild Ngoni.* Edinburgh, 1899. [Mombera].

Frazer, M. *Winning a Primitive People.* London, 1914. [Mombera].

Gluckman, M. The Kingdom of the Zulu. *APS*, pp. 25–55. 1940.

——. Kinship and Marriage among the Lozi of Northern Rhodesia and the Zulu of Natal. *ASKM*, pp. 166–206. 1950.

Hodgson, A. G. O. Notes on the Achewa and Angoni. *JRAI*, 63:123–164. 1933. [Gomani].

Holleman, J. F. Die Zulu Isigodi. *BS*, 15:91–118. 1941.

Hughes, A. J. B. Kin, Caste and Nation among the Rhodesian Ndebele. *RLP*, 25:1–86. 1956.

Hughes, A. J. B., and J. van Velsen. *The Ndebele.* London, 1955.

Hunter, M. *Reaction to Conquest.* London, 1936. [Pondo].

Jackson, H. M. G. Notes on Matabele Customary Law. *NADA*, 4:30–34; 5:7–14. 1926–1927. [Ndebele].

Kohler, M., and N. J. van Warmelo. Marriage Customs in Southern Natal. *DNAEP*, 4:1–103. 1933. [Zulu].

Krige, E. J. *The Social System of the Zulus.* London, 1936.

Kropf, A. *Das Volk der Xosa-Kaffern.* Berlin, 1889.

Kuper, H. *An African Aristocracy.* London, 1947. [Swazi].

——. Kinship among the Swazi. *ASKM*, pp. 86–110. 1950.

——. *The Swazi.* London, 1952.

Marwick, B. A. *The Swazi.* Cambridge, 1940.

Myburgh, A. C. The Tribes of the Barberton District. *DNAEP*, 25:1–146. 1949. [Swazi].

Read, M. *The Ngoni of Nyasaland.* London, 1956. [Gomani and Mombera].

Reader, D. H. Marriage among the Makhanya. *IAE*, 47:69–107. 1954. [Zulu].

Schapera, I., ed. *The Bantu-speaking Tribes of South Africa.* London, 1937.

Soga, J. H. *The Ama-Xosa.* London, 1932.

Tew, M. *Peoples of the Lake Nyasa Region.* London, 1950. [Ngoni cluster].

Thomas, T. M. *Eleven Years in Central South Africa.* London, 1872. [Ndebele].

Warmelo, N. J. van. Transvaal Ndebele Texts. *DNAEP*, 1:1–108. 1930. [Manala].

——. Kinship Terminology of the South African Bantu. *DNAEP*, 2:1–119. 1931.

51

---•◦•---

Sotho

The last wave of Bantu expansion, occurring within the historical period, carried the Tswana branch of the Sotho peoples westward into the country now known as Bechuanaland, where they engulfed the indigenous Bushmen. This began around 1720 and continued until after the beginning of European contact in 1801.

The tribes that constitute the Sotho province occupy Basutoland and a considerable area in the interior of the Union of South Africa, in addition to Bechuanaland. Aboriginally they adjoined the Shona and Thonga in the northeast, the Nguni in the southwest, and Bushmen in other directions. Whatever the reason, political or otherwise, none of the many ethnographers who have described the Sotho peoples has mapped the territories they occupied prior to the Great Trek and to subsequent encroachments by Europeans. The tribal locations indicated on Map 17 are based on fragmentary scraps of information in the literature, and thus doubtless err in serious respects.

The Sotho fall into four major divisions: the Southern branch, or Sotho proper; the Western, or Tswana, branch; the Eastern, or Pedi, branch; and the Northeastern, or Venda, branch. The Kgalagadi, though here placed in the Western branch, actually constitute a distinct division from a linguistic point of view. The Lovedu, though linguistically closer to the Eastern branch, belong culturally with the Venda. The following classification of tribes omits population data on those of the large Tswana (Bechuana, Becwana, Betschuana) cluster, who number in all about 800,000.

1. Hurutshe (Bahuruthse, Khurutshe).
2. Kgalagadi (Bakalahari, Bakxalaxadi, Batlaopa, Dighoya, Kalahari, Makalahari, Vaalpens). They are strongly mixed with and acculturated to the Bushmen.
3. Kgatla (Bakgatla, Bakxatla).
4. Kwena (Bakwena).
5. Lovedu (Balovedu, Lobedu), with the Khaha, Makxiba, Mamidja, Narene, Phalaborwa (Borwa), Sai (Shai, Tsubye), and Thabina (Moxoboya). They number about 80,000.
6. Ngwaketse (Bangwaketse).
7. Ngwato (Bamangwato).
8. Pedi (Bapedi), with other tribes of the Eastern branch. They number about 770,000.
9. Rolong (Barolong).

10. Sotho (Basotho, Bassouto, Basuto). Their language, alone among Sotho dialects, contains clicks. They number about 1,400,000.
11. Tawana (Batawana, Batwana).
12. Tlhaping (Bachapin, Batlaping).
13. Tlharu (Batlaro, Batlharu).
14. Tlokwa (Batlokwa, Dokwa, Tokwa), with the Birwa (Babirwa, Virwa), Kolobe, Koni, Malete (Moletse), Mamavolo, Matala (Madala), Molepu, Tlhako, and Xananwa.
15. Venda (Bavenda, Bavesha, Bawenda, Vhavenda), with the Lemba (Abalempa, Bahere, Balemba, Bamwenya, Baremba, Malepa, Muwenji, Nalemba, Namgeni, Vhalemba, Wahere, Waremba). They number about 135,000.

A number of authorities have bracketed the Venda with the Shona as the Bantu tribes associated with the culture of Zimbabwe. As evidence they cite the presence among them of the Lemba, an itinerant tribe of metalworkers, potters, and merchants, who allegedly possess markedly Semitic features and who exhibit a number of cultural traits that distinguish them sharply from their neighbors, e.g., circumcision, absence of totemism, tribal endogamy (unless the alien spouse is ceremonially adopted), a predilection for fish, burial in an extended rather than a crouched position, a distinctive new-moon ceremony, and a taboo on eating the flesh of animals unless their throats have been cut before death. The fact that they reveal no trace of either Judaic or Islamic religion, however, argues against the hypothesis of their descent from Jewish or Moslem traders of the Arabic period. Could they be a remnant of the Cushitic founders of Zimbabwe? Their fondness for fish, to be sure, is un-Cushitic, but the *Periplus of the Erythraean Sea* records a similar exception for the ancient Azanians (see Chapter 26).

The Lovedu and Venda tribes in the northeast closely resemble the neighboring Shona in most aspects of culture. From this we may reasonably assume that they reflect the ancestral culture of the Sotho as a whole in the many respects in which these people differ from other Southern Bantu. The basic economy provides one example. The Lovedu and Venda raise the very same crops as the Shona and display the same emphasis upon agriculture as opposed to animal husbandry. In all Sotho tribes except these two, together with the Pedi and Tlokwa, animal husbandry ranks with agriculture in importance. Goats, dogs, chickens, and a few sheep are kept, but cattle hold the center of interest. The roster of food plants duplicates that of the Nguni, and maize here too has replaced sorghum as the staple. The Sotho peoples do a moderate amount of hunting but no fishing, even among the Lovedu and Venda. Men hunt, herd and milk the livestock, and clear new land, but leave most agricultural operations to the women. In contrast to all other Sotho, the Lovedu and Venda do not observe the usual ritual separation of women and cattle, although women usually milk only in emergencies.

Cone-cylinder dwellings with thatched roofs and walls of wattle and daub prevail throughout the province. They are grouped in small hamlets, or kraals, among the Lovedu and Pedi, in larger villages with a central plaza among the Venda. Other tribes exhibit a totally different settlement pattern, consisting of a large town with a number of satellite villages or hamlets. Tswana towns often have populations of 5,000 or more and are divided into wards.

In general, a territorial organization into wards has replaced a structure based on kinship. Though wards and subwards bear some resemblance to clans in their composition, this is merely incidental, resulting from the prevalence of patrilocal residence. Patrilineal sibs with animal names exist, but they do not regulate marriage or fulfill any other significant function. Most Sotho, indeed, permit marriage with any first cousin, even a father's brother's child.

The Lovedu and Venda resemble other Sotho tribes in requiring a substantial bride-price in cattle, in practicing general and preferentially sororal polygyny, in establishing each co-wife in a separate hut, in observing patrilocal residence, and in possessing kinship terminology of the Iroquois type, but they differ radically in most other aspects of social organization. Both have exogamous, corporate, and localized patrilineages, though sibs are agamous. The Venda are even characterized by double descent, since they also possess matrilineages which function prominently in the ancestor cult. The Lovedu, like the Shona, group their sibs into phratries on the basis of totemic resemblances.

Both the Venda and the Lovedu favor marriages with a mother's brother's daughter, which in the latter tribe actually constitute 60 per cent of all marital unions. The Lovedu even group lineages into rings to expedite and stabilize their rule of matrilateral cross-cousin marriage. Within such a ring, women pass from lineage to lineage in one direction, and the cattle received for them in marriage payments circulate in the opposite direction. This exemplifies perfectly the system of "generalized exchange" described by Lévi-Strauss (1949).

The Lovedu, incidentally, demonstrate how unsafe it is to infer the functioning of a social system from its structure. With polygyny, patrilocal residence, patrilineal descent, local exogamy, and patriclans, the Lovedu structure brings together in a settlement a group of closely related men who have known one another since childhood and a disparate collection of adult women assembled from other localities and often initially strangers to each other. It might seem reasonable to infer from this a low and depressed status for the female sex. The exact reverse is true. By capitalizing upon certain possibilities inherent in the system, women have gained for themselves an enviable position.

First of all, they have turned polygyny to their own advantage. Most

African societies require a polygynous husband to treat his wives impartially. The Lovedu women insist on this with unusual strictness, so that if a man exhibits the slightest act of favoritism toward one wife, all of them "gang up on him" and render his life miserable until he makes amends. Since a single wife lacks such a punitive weapon and can perhaps even be dominated with relative impunity, the first objective of a woman, when she marries, is to plan and scheme to obtain a second wife for her husband. Small wonder that the Lovedu women, when they observed the deterioration in status of the wives of the first monogamous converts to Christianity, presented a solid front against further missionary enterprise.

Second, the women have assumed the principal role in the arrangement of marriages. The preference for matrilateral cross-cousin marriage gives the mother an obvious advantage over the father in negotiating with her brother to obtain a daughter of the latter as a wife for her son. In this way women have gained large control over bride-price payments. If one wife has more daughters than sons, bringing in more cattle than are going out, the husband cannot claim the surplus to pay the bride-prices for his sons by other wives. Instead, the fortunate mother "invests" the excess cattle with her lineage mates in prepayment of the bride-prices of her daughters' sons. Alternatively, a woman with a plethora of daughters may assume a male role, paying bride-prices for women as her own "wives."

Women have even achieved political power. Like the Venda and many Shona tribes, the Lovedu have long been organized in a moderately complex state with a territorial administrative organization and a divine monarch. The latter must be physically fit and may not continue to live if any serious blemish develops. Around 1800 a woman succeeded to the throne, presumably in default of male heirs, and the Lovedu have not had a male ruler since. Indeed, over approximately the next century and a half they had only three monarchs, all women, suggesting that female common sense overrode all such nonsense as killing the divine king. Actually the case is not quite so simple, for the female kings continued to respect the principle, and the second of them, in 1894, committed suicide by poison when she judged herself no longer fit to rule.

We have spoken advisedly of the Lovedu monarchs as "female kings" rather than as queens because they very consciously play a male role. They take no husbands but do marry a large number of wives. It is apparently from among the children of these latter women, not those borne by the ruler in her own promiscuous sex life, that the successor is chosen. If such is actually the case, the Lovedu present the only instance on record where a woman's own children are, by cultural definition, necessarily illegitimate.

The Southern and Western Sotho reveal a totally different type of political organization. Their states are based on conquest and resemble closely in many respects those of the Zulu and other Nguni tribes, which doubtless served as their model. However, they incorporate a number of features specifically adapted to the absorption and integration of alien peoples, including both voluntary immigrants and conquered groups. Individual tribes differ in modest respects, but the organization of the Tawana will serve as a reasonably representative example.

The Tawana themselves reside mainly in the capital town of Maun, where they are organized into wards under hereditary leaders. When the ruler dies, new wards are split off for his younger sons, being strengthened by the affiliation of dependent alien elements. Such accretions, coupled with the occasional affiliation of the families of resident sons-in-law and sisters' sons, prevent the ward from becoming a genuine patriclan. The principal conquered tribes, the Koba and Mbukushu, are organized into districts, each with its hereditary native chief, and these in turn into wards. Tribute flows through this territorial hierarchy into the capital, where the district chiefs are required to live and where the ruler has his counselors and personal servants and retainers.

Like all Sotho tribes except the Lovedu, the Tawana keep no slaves. They do, however, exhibit a complex stratification into four social classes: (1) a hereditary aristocracy comprising the ruling Tawana tribe; (2) commoners, consisting largely of the fully absorbed Koba and Mbukushu people; (3) aliens, comprising recent and as yet unabsorbed refugees from other Bantu tribes; and (4) hereditary serfs, mainly Bushmen and Kgalagadi, who are attached to chiefs and other prominent men for whom they herd, till the soil, and perform menial household labor.

A special form of conditional servitude also prevails among the Tawana upper classes. Chiefs and other wealthy men give cattle and other livestock to friends, who are free to use them in any way, even to kill them, and to transmit them to their heirs. The donor, however, may repossess them at any time, together with, not only their increase, but all the recipient's possessions. This, however, occurs extremely rarely, usually only for disloyalty or refusal to render assistance when called upon. The ruler makes much use of this technique to bind his friends and leading counselors to him in such a way as to assure their enduring loyalty.

Selected Bibliography

Ashton, E. H. Notes on the Political and Judicial Organization of the Tawana. *BS*, 11:67–83. 1937.

———. Political Organization of the Southern Sotho. *BS*, 12:287–320. 1938.

Ashton, E. H. A Sociological Sketch of Sotho Diet. *Transactions of the Royal Society of South Africa*, 27:147–214. 1939.

――. The Social Structure of the Southern Sotho Ward. *CSAS*, n.s., 15:1–33. 1946.

――. *The Basuto*. London, 1952.

Brown, J. T. *Among the Bantu Nomads*. London, 1926. [Tswana].

Burchell, W. J. *Travels in the Interior of Southern Africa*, vol. 2. London, 1824. [Tlhaping].

Campbell, J. *Travels in South Africa*. 2 vols. London, 1922. [Tlhaping].

Casalis, E. A. *Les Bassoutos*. Paris, 1859.

――. *The Basutos*. London, 1861. [Translation of the above].

Coertze, P. J. Huweliksgewoontes en erfreg by de Batlokwa. *BS*, 7:257–273. 1933.

Dornan, S. S. *Pygmies and Bushmen of the Kalahari*. London, 1925. [Kgalagadi and Kwena].

Du Plessis, H. Die territoriale organisasie van die Venda. *AS*, 4:122–127. 1945.

Dutton, E. A. T. *The Basuto of Basutoland*. London, 1923.

Harries, C. L. *The Laws and Customs of the Bapedi*. Johannesburg, 1929.

Hoffman, C. Verlöbnis und Heirat bei den Bassutho in Holzbuschgebirge Transvaals. *Zeitschrift für Kolonialsprachen*, 3:124–139. Berlin, 1912. [Pedi].

Junod, H. A. The Belemba of the Zoutpansberg. *FL*, 19:276–287. 1908. [Venda].

Krige, E. J. Notes on the Phalaborwa. *BS*, 11:357–366. 1937. [Lovedu].

――. The Place of the North-Eastern Sotho in the South Bantu Complex. *Africa*, 11:265–293. 1938. [Lovedu and Tlokwa].

Krige, E. J., and J. D. Krige. *The Realm of a Rain-Queen*. London, 1943. [Lovedu].

Laydevant, J. Étude sur la famille en Basutoland. *JSA*, 1:207–257. 1931.

Lebzelter, V. Das Betschuanendorf Epukiro. *ZE*, 65:44–74. 1933. [Tlharu].

Lestrade, G. P. Some Notes on the *Bogadi* System of the Bahurutshe. *SAJS*, 23:937–942. 1926.

――. Some Notes on the Political Organization of the Bechwana. *SAJS*, 25:427–432. 1932. [Hurutshe].

Lévi-Strauss, C. *Les structures élémentaires de la parenté*. Paris, 1949.

Matthews, Z. K. Marriage Customs among the Barolong. *Africa*, 13:1–24. 1940.

Passarge, S. Das Okawangosumpfland und seine Bewohner. *ZE*, 37:649–716. 1905. [Tawana].

Schapera, I. *A Handbook of Tswana Law and Custom*. London, 1938. [Kgatla].

――. The Political Organization of the Ngwato. *APS*, pp. 56–82. 1940.

――. *Married Life in an African Tribe*. New York, 1941. [Kgatla].

――. Some Features of the Social Organization of the Tlokwa. *SWJA*, 2:16–47. 1946.

――. The Political Annals of a Tswana Tribe. *CSAS*, n.s., 18:1–131. 1947. [Ngwaketse].

――. Kinship and Marriage among the Tswana. *ASKM*, pp. 140–165. 1950.

――. The Ethnic Composition of Tswana Tribes. *MSA*, 11:1–136. 1952.

――. *The Tswana*. London, 1953.

――. *Government and Politics in Tribal Societies*. London, 1956.

Schapera, I., and D. F. van der Merwe. Notes on the Tribal Groupings, History and Customs of the Bakgalagadi. *CSAS*, n.s., 13:1–195. 1945.

Schultze, L. *Aus Namaland und Kalahari*. Jena, 1907. [Ngwaketse].

Sheddick, V. G. J. *The Southern Sotho*. London, 1953.

Stayt, H. A. *The Bavenda*. Oxford, 1931.

――. Notes on the Balemba. *JRAI*, 61:231–239. 1931. [Venda].

Warmelo, N. J. van. Venda Law. *DNAEP*, 23:1–1047. 1948.

Wessmann, R. *The Bawenda of the Spelonken*. London, 1908. [Venda].

PART ELEVEN

NORTH AND WEST AFRICAN PASTORALISM

52

Bedouin Arabs

Within less than a decade after the death of Mohammed, the disciplined forces of the Abbassid caliphate at Baghdad embarked on a career of conquest in North Africa. Egypt fell before them in 639, Cyrenaica and Fezzan in 642, Tripolitania in 647, and then successively Tunisia, Algeria, and Morocco. By the end of the century the Arabs had achieved political hegemony over all the former Greco-Roman territory and over nearly all the Berber homeland. Islamization and Arabization proceeded apace. Within a generation Christianity had disappeared completely except for the Copts of Egypt, who survive as a small sect to the present day, and for a few Berber Christians who held out briefly through flight into the desert. Only the Jews withstood this onslaught. Though subjected to severe restrictions, they have persisted in this area until the present century in such surprisingly large numbers as to arouse suspicion that they may have been joined by numerous Christians and perhaps, even earlier, by Carthaginians who preferred the faith of their Semitic cousins to the alien religion of Rome.

This Arab conquest introduced Islam, the Arabic language, and many features of Arab culture, but it was primarily political in character and did not involve any large-scale immigration from Arabia. Before long the Arabized Berbers revolted and established independent dynasties of their own—in Morocco in 788, in Algeria in 761, and in Tunisia in 800. Only Libya and Egypt continued, at least nominally, to acknowledge the suzerainty of the caliphs of Baghdad. The Moroccan Berbers, however, carried on the momentum of Islamic expansion. They moved northward into Spain, where they laid the foundations of Moorish civilization, and southward into Mauritania and the fringe of the western Sudan, where they established themselves as early as the ninth century. Around 910 the Berber dynasties in Algeria and Tunisia were supplanted by the Arab Fatimids, who assumed the title of caliph, wrested Egypt from the Abbassids in 969, and in 973 removed their capital to Cairo.

Throughout this early Islamic period the rulers of North Africa, whether Arab or Berber, strove with some success to maintain the economic order and the essentials of the urbane civilization which they had inherited from their Greco-Roman predecessors and which the Moors perpetuated and even elaborated in Spain. In the eleventh century, however, their efforts came to nought, and North Africa was plunged suddenly into an era even darker than that which had engulfed Europe. The cause was a mass invasion of Bedouin nomads from central Arabia, beginning about 1045 and continuing at a decreasing rate for several centuries. These "Hilalian" invaders—who numbered, according to various estimates, anywhere from several hundred thousand to several million—poured into Egypt and spread like a swarm of locusts throughout the former Berber regions of North Africa. Illiterate nomads, intolerant alike of agricultural and urban civilization, they preempted all land suitable for grazing, upsetting everywhere the fine balance which the Berbers had achieved between cultivation and animal husbandry. They converted fertile fields to pasture by destroying or neglecting the waterworks constructed by the labor of centuries. Their flocks devoured the natural cover of vegetation, ultimately ruining the forests that had once supplied the timber for the Carthaginian and Roman fleets, and by overgrazing induced erosion which converted even pasture lands to barren semidesert. Population, of course, withered. The vast Roman amphitheater of Thysdrus in central Tunisia, which seated 60,000 spectators, overlooks today a scene of utter desolation, and, on the coast, hamlets of a few score fishermen now occupy the sites of once flourishing cities of 100,000.

Socially, the consequences were similar. Fighting indiscriminately with one another and with the settled Berbers, they infiltrated everywhere, depriving the vanquished of their independent livelihood and reducing them to the status of tributary serfs. The Berbers were faced with the alternative of adopting the new predatory mode of life in self-defense or of fleeing to the oases of the Sahara and there similarly exploiting the indigenous Negroes. Commerce stagnated, and the port towns turned from trade to piracy. Only a few cities, notably Fez, Tangier, Tlemcen, and Tunis, were able to keep alive a few feeble flickers of the arts and urbane living, preserved mainly by cultivated Moors returning thence after their expulsion from Spain. Conquest by the Turks, achieved in Egypt in 1517, in Tripolitania in 1553, and in Algeria in 1557, brought no improvement. The occupation of North Africa by the European colonial powers, begun in Algeria in 1830 and completed in Libya a century later, at least reestablished peace and commerce, even though it did not bring the democratic self-government which the Berbers covet so dearly but have, over the past millennium, so rarely enjoyed.

The classification and mapping of the North African Arabs and Arabized Berbers present exceptional difficulties. Ethnographic accounts are few and, with some notable exceptions, of inferior quality. Scholars have concerned themselves principally with unraveling complex tribal histories and genealogies, with the result that for some regions we possess hundreds of names of "tribes" and "fractions" arranged according to their genealogical relationships, whereas for others even the names of the principal tribes are lacking. In accordance with the practice followed elsewhere in this volume, we have attempted to group tribes into units on the basis of cultural similarities and geographical contiguity. The resulting classification, as a highly tentative pioneer effort, will satisfy few. Nor will the names which we have chosen for these clusters —sometimes that of a region, sometimes that of a single particularly well-known tribe, and in one case, the Sanusi, the name of an indigenous religious movement. The groups which we have distinguished are listed below and may be located on Map 17 in the pocket at the back of the book.

1. Algerians, embracing the Arabized Berber inhabitants of the coastal zone of Algeria with the Angad and related tribes of adjacent Morocco. They are sedentary and in 1936 numbered approximately 4 million.
2. Arad, including the sedentary inhabitants of Gabes (population about 20,000) and the outlying tribes of southern Tunisia, e.g., the Attia, Gumrage (Ghoumrage), Hamerna, Hazzem, Yakub (Uled Yacoub), and Zid (Beni Zid).
3. Bahariya (Beharia), embracing the sedentary inhabitants of the oases of Bahariya and Frafra in western Egypt. They number about 7,000.
4. Berabish. This nomadic tribe, inhabiting the Sahara northwest of Timbuktu, numbers about 35,000 together with the adjacent Kunta.
5. Chaamba (Shaanba), with other Bedouin tribes of the Algerian Sahara between the Atlas Mountains and the Tuareg country. They number about 25,000.
6. Cyrenaicans, embracing the sedentary population of the coastal fringe of Cyrenaica in Libya. They number about 50,000.
7. Dakhla (Dachel), embracing the sedentary inhabitants of the oasis of Dakhla in western Egypt. They number about 10,000.
8. Delim (Oulad Delim), embracing the Amar (Ulad ba Amar), Seba (Bou Sba, Oulad Bu-Seba), Sheukh (Oulad Chouekh, Ulad Chouick), and other subtribes in Mauritania. They number about 70,000.
9. Dui-Menia (Doui Menia), with the Atauna (Uled Atauna), Jerir (Uled Djerir), and Nacem (Uled Nacem) tribes and the sedentary oasis dwellers along the

Kanatsa, Saura, and lower Zusfana Rivers in southeastern Morocco and adjacent Algeria.

10. Egyptians, embracing the sedentary inhabitants of the Nile Valley in Egypt. They number about 20 million.

11. Fezzan, including the Murahidya tribe and other inhabitants of the oases of Fezzan in Libya. They number about 40,000, of whom 10,000 inhabit the town of Murzuk.

12. Gafsa, embracing the sedentary inhabitants of the oases of El Ksar, Gafsa, and Lala in central Tunisia. They number about 15,000.

13. Gil (Beni Guil), with the Lhadj (Uled Lhaddj) and other Bedouin tribes of the steppe region of eastern Morocco.

14. Hamama, with the kindred Aun (Uled Aoun, Uled Sidi ben Aoun), Fraichich (Frechich), Majeur (Majer), Mehadba, Methellith (Metellit), Neffet, Swassi (Souassi), and Zlass (Djelass, Jlass) tribes of the interior steppe region of Tunisia. They number about 150,000.

15. Hamyan (Hamian), embracing the Hamyan proper and numerous other Bedouin tribes of the steppe zone of Algeria. They number nearly a million.

16. Imragen (Imeragen), with the Aita (Ulad bu Aita), Foikat, and Lammiar. These people lead a precarious existence by fishing along the Atlantic coast.

17. Jebala (Djebala), embracing the Anjera (Endjra), Arus (Beni Arous), Gorfet (Beni Gorfet), Mesgilda (Beni Mesguilda), Mestara (Beni Mestara), Rhuna (Rehouna, Rhona), Serif (Ahal Srif, Ehl Serif), Setta, Sless (Slass), Tzul (Dsoul, Tsoul), Zerwal (Beni Zeroual), and other Arabized Berber tribes of the mountainous Rif region of northern Morocco, together with the towns of Ceuta and Tetuan. They number about 600,000.

18. Jerid (Djerid), embracing the sedentary inhabitants of the oases of El Guettar, El Hamma, El Udian (El Oudian), Kriz, Nefta, and Tozeur in southern Tunisia, as well as the Nefzawa tribe to the east. They number about 40,000.

19. Kharga, embracing the inhabitants of the Egyptian oases of Kharga and Selima. They number about 10,000.

20. Kufra (Cufra), embracing the inhabitants of the Libyan oases of Kufra and Wanyanga. They number about 6,000. Prior to 1813 these oases were occupied by Saharan Negroes of the Teda group.

21. Kunta (Kounta). This Bedouin tribe inhabits the Sahara north of Timbuktu.

22. Laguat (Aruat, Laghouat), embracing the inhabitants of the Algerian oases of Ain Madhi and Laguat. They number about 10,000.

23. Maaza, with the Haweitat and a few other Bedouin tribes who extend from the Sinai Peninsula into Egypt along the Gulf of Suez.

24. Moroccans, embracing the Ahsen, Cherarda, Chiadma, Dukkala (Doukkala), Fahsya, Gharbya (Rharbya), Khlot, Rehamna, Shawia (Chaouia), Sragna, Tadla, Tliq, and other sedentary tribes of the plains region of western Morocco, together with the inhabitants of the cities of Casablanca, Fez, Marrakech, Mazagan, Meknes, Rabat, Sali, Sofi, and Tangier. They numbered over 3 million in 1936.

25. Nail (Uled Nail). The nomadic inhabitants of the central Atlas region of Algeria between Biskra and Laguat.

26. Regeibat (Ergeibat, Rgibat), embracing the Ajur (Ahel Ajur), Daud (Uled Daued), Elguasem (Guassem), Mussa (Oulad Moussa), Othman (Ahel Othman, Oulad Iahia ben Othman, Yaya-ben-Othman), Rehalat, Reilane (Oulad Reilane), Shej (Oulad Cheikh, Ulad Sej), Suaad, and Taleb (Oulad Talet) tribes of interior Mauritania. They are nomads and number about 35,000.

27. Riyah (Riah), with the Busaif (Uled Busaif), Hasauna, Hutman (Hotma),

Maqarha (Megarha), Mozda, Urfil'a (Ourfellah), Zintan, and other Bedouin tribes and small oasis populations in the desert region of western Libya.

28. Ruarha, embracing the sedentary inhabitants of the oases of Chema (Dschema), Megharin, Mraier, Sidi Khelil, Tamerna, Temassin, Tinedla, Tuggurt (Touggourt), and Urhlana on the Oued Rir in the northeastern Algerian Sahara. They number about 60,000 and include a few Berber-speaking remnants.

29. Saadi, with the tributary Murabitin and lesser Bedouin tribes of western Egypt.

30. Sanusi, including the sedentary Arafa and Darsa, the seminomadic Abaidat, Awaqir, and Hasa, the nomadic Abid, Baraasa, Fayid, and Magharba, and various smaller client tribes in interior Cyrenaica. They number about 150,000 and were united by the Sanusiya movement in the nineteenth century.

31. Sahel, embracing the now sedentary Riyah (Riah), Said (Uled Said), and Urazla (Ourazla) tribes and the inhabitants of the towns of Kairouan, Sfax, and Sousse and of some fifty smaller villages in the Sahel or eastern coastal zone of Tunisia, together with the people of the Kerkena Islands. They number over a million.

32. Sidi (Uled Sidi Sheikh), with the Aissa (Uled Aissa), Jagub (Uled Jagub), Mahiyan, and Trafi tribes of Bedouins in the region south of Geryville in Algeria, together with the sedentary inhabitants of Brezina, El Abiod, and neighboring oases.

33. Sirticans, including the Jamaat, Qadharhfa, Soliman (Uled Soliman), and other Bedouin tribes of the arid coast of Sirtica in Libya.

34. Soliman (Uled Sliman). This branch of the Sirtican tribe of the same name, numbering about 5,000, migrated to Kanem in the early nineteenth century.

35. Suafa, embracing the sedentary inhabitants of El Oued and other oases on the Oued Souf in the northeastern Algerian Sahara, together with the neighboring pastoral Acheche, Ftaiet, and Messaaba. They number about 40,000.

36. Tajakant (Djakana, Tazzerkant, Tenaker), with the Arib, Aruisin (Arosien, Arouissiin, Arusin), Blal (Daublal, Dui Belal, Ida u Blal), and Meribda (Ait u Mribet). These nomads inhabit northern Mauritania and number about 30,000.

37. Trarza, with the kindred Brakna of southwestern Mauritania. They were reported in 1912 to number about 75,000.

38. Tripolitanians, embracing the inhabitants of coastal Tripolitania in Libya. They numbered about 525,000 in 1931.

39. Tunisians, including the inhabitants of northern Tunisia and a small strip of adjacent Algeria. They number over a million.

40. Yahi (Beni Bou Yahi), with the Settut (Uled Stut). They inhabit the valley of the lower Moulouya River in eastern Morocco and number about 40,000.

41. Zenaga, embracing the Allush (Allouch), Girganke (Massin), Mbarek (Oulad Mbarek), Meshduf, Nasser (Oulad Nasser), Sirifou (Chorfa), and Tichit (Ahl Tichit). These Arabized Berbers occupy the Hodh region of the French Sudan and number more than 100,000.

42. Ziban, embracing the inhabitants of the oases of the Ziban and Zab Chergui districts of the Algerian Sahara. The town of Biskra alone had a population of 22,000 in 1936.

Among the groups listed above should be segregated a number of Arabic-speaking peoples who are descended from the coastal populations that participated fully in the earlier Greco-Roman civilization. These Littoral peoples, as we shall term them, include the Algerians, Cyrenaicans, Egyptians, Jebala, Moroccans, Sahel, Tripolitanians, and Tunisians. All are sedentary and partially urbanized, and all were Islamized and Arabized in the first period of Arab political conquest. All have received some infusion of Arab blood, but in every instance the bulk of the population is descended from the earlier inhabitants with increments of alien origin —European officials, businessmen, and colonists; the so-called Kulugli, the descendants of crosses between Turks and native women; many Spanish and Levantine as well as local Jews; and a very large number of people descended from the Moors expelled from Spain, many of whom still speak Spanish. These Littoral groups have remained to a considerable extent aloof from the Hilalian Bedouins, and the comments which follow will apply to them only when specifically so indicated.

The economy of the Littoral peoples still resembles that of Greco-Roman times, though far less flourishing. It is based primarily on cereal agriculture, with barley and wheat as the staples, but with important auxiliary aboriculture, animal husbandry, urban handicraft manufactures, and trade. The following is a list of the crops specifically reported in the sources for at least half of the societies of this group:

Cereal grains: barley, maize, millet, oats, rice, sorghum, wheat
Legumes and forage crops: alfalfa, broad beans, chick peas, lentils, peas, vetch
Tubers and root crops: carrots, onions, radishes, turnips
Leaf and stalk vegetables: cabbage, celery, okra, rape
Vine and ground fruits: cucumbers, eggplant, grapes, melons, pumpkins, to-
    matoes, watermelons
Tree fruits and nuts: almonds, apples, apricots, carob, citrons, dates, figs, jujubes,
    mulberries, olives, oranges, peaches, pears, plums, pomegranates, quinces
Condiments and indulgents: coriander, cumin, fennel, garlic, peppers, tobacco
Textile plants: cotton, flax, hemp
Dye plants: henna, indigo

In contrast to the Littoral peoples, the Bedouin Arabs of North Africa have retained, wherever possible, the nomadic pastoral economy which they brought with them from Arabia. They subsist primarily on the meat, milk, and dairy products provided by their herds, though many tribes also practice a little subsidiary agriculture. They often possess a certain number of cattle, donkeys, and horses, but their principal animals are sheep, goats, and camels, with sheep in general predominating near the coast and camels toward the interior. Only those tribes who have penetrated the farthest into the Sudan depend primarily upon cattle. These include the Kunta and Zenaga, as well as the Baggara of the eastern Sudan, who will be separately treated in Chapter 54.

The Bedouin Arabs leave agriculture, industry, and commerce to the indigenous peoples, both Caucasoid and Negroid. When forced to adopt such pursuits they do so reluctantly, depending, where they can, on the labor of slaves and serfs. So strong is their aversion to settled life that they have refused even to adopt the balanced, seminomadic economy characteristic of the earlier Berbers. The only groups that have become sedentary are the Imragen fishermen and those Arab groups that have replaced or absorbed the Egyptians, Teda, or Berbers previously in possession of certain Saharan oases, namely, the Bahariya, Dakhla, Dui-Menia, Fezzan, Gafsa, Jerid, Kharga, Kufra, Laguat, Ruarha, Suafa, and Ziban. Even among these people, the politically dominant tribes commonly lead a nomadic existence in the neighborhood of the oases, leaving the actual cultivation to dependent subject peoples.

Aside from animal husbandry, the economy of Arab North Africa rests primarily on exploitation, on predatory rather than productive pursuits. The history of the region since the eleventh century is a sordid record of the application of force in every conceivable manner to wrest from others the fruits of their labor. Through warfare one tribe, Arab or Arabized Berber, reduces another, Berber or Arab, to dependent status, extorting from it regular tribute in the products of despised agriculture. Through conquest, a sedentary people is dispossessed of its lands and reduced to peonage; among the Algerians one source reports that the sharecropping tenant works the land for one-fifth of the produce, the remaining four-fifths being appropriated by the landlord. Captured coastal cities have repeatedly been converted from ports of sea-borne commerce to centers of piracy and of kidnapping on the high seas for ransom—activities which offer quicker and more spectacular immediate profits. The Negro tribes of the Sudan have been systematically raided for slaves. The occupation or domination of an oasis offers a double exploitative reward. The hapless inhabitants can easily be mulcted of their agricultural surplus, and the caravan traders can be blackmailed for "protection." Along every route in the Sahara the nomadic tribes extort a substantial fee from each caravan crossing their territory, in return for which they not only refrain from raiding it themselves but undertake to fend off raiders from other tribes. They commonly attempt to extract, of course, only what the traffic will bear, for excessive greed would force the merchants to take an alternative route.

The essentially exploitative and predatory character of the Bedouin invaders, coupled with their intolerance of settled life, explains why they have established no urban civilization in North Africa and why they have blighted those which they found already in existence. Civilization has flourished and the arts of life have been advanced in other Arab regions, such as Moorish Spain and Baghdad under the caliphs, but among African Arabs we encounter little more than the exaltation of naked force. Even the Berbers, who, though warlike, followed a basically productive rather than parasitic mode of livelihood, have widely succumbed to the racketeering standards of their conquerors.

Social organization is remarkably uniform throughout Arabic-speaking North Africa and shows strong affinities with Bedouin Arabia. In the division of labor by sex, for example, the men normally do the herding and the bulk of the agricultural labor not performed by slaves or serfs, whereas the women do the milking (except of camels) and perform all dairy operations. Only in groups where Berber influence is still strong, e.g., the Jebala and Tunisians, do women participate in agriculture. Occasionally, as among the Saadi, they herd sheep and goats, but never the larger animals.

Marriage regularly involves a bride-price, paid usually in money but occasionally in livestock. Virginity is demanded and is tested on the wedding night. Monogamy prevails only in a few Arabized Berber tribes, notably the Jebala, Kunta, Trarza, and Zenaga. Elsewhere polygyny is permitted, exclusively in the nonsororal form, up to the Koranic limit of four wives. In general, however, it is practiced extensively only by the more undiluted Bedouin tribes. Among the Egyptians its frequency is reported to be about 5 per cent, and this seems to be fairly typical as well for the Littoral peoples, the oasis Arabs, and the Bedouin tribes with a substantial Berber infusion. Residence is universally patrilocal, and the prevailing form of domestic organization is a small patrilocal extended family under a patriarchal head. In the sedentary tribes this normally constitutes a household unit; in nomadic tribes, a camp group or segment thereof, with each component nuclear family occupying a separate tent.

Descent is patrilineal, with a highly segmentary lineage organization. We may distinguish a series of levels of increasing size and depth: (1) the minimal patrilineage, forming the core of an extended family; (2) the minor lineage, commonly localized as a camp group in nomadic tribes; (3) the major lineage, often constituting a band; (4) the sib, "fraction," or subtribe; and (5) the tribe (*qabila*). Urban groups, particularly those of Berber origin, rarely carry kinship reckoning this far, but nomadic groups even keep careful count of the genealogical relationships between tribes. The bonds of union, primarily those of kinship in the smaller segments, become increasingly political in larger segments. Collective responsibility for wrongs committed by its members and the obligation for blood vengeance normally appear in association with the minor lineage. The universal preference for marriage with a father's brother's daughter renders exogamy impossible at any level of the lineage structure. Kinship terminology, wherever reported, conforms to the typical Arabic descriptive pattern.

Settlement patterns differ with the mode of life. The nomadic tribes are organized in bands and live in tents, which they transport from one camp site to the next. These are usually pitched in a circle, but in some tribes they are arranged in a single line, as among the Chaamba, or in two parallel rows. The sedentary peoples live in permanent houses, which are grouped in compact towns or villages with narrow streets and commonly also an encircling fortified wall. In social composition, both nomadic bands and all but the largest villages are patriclans, i.e., localized patrilineages.

The typical nomad tent consists of a framework of upright posts and a central horizontal ridgepole, supporting a cover which is pegged to the ground with ropes at the sides and ends. The Bedouins usually make their tent covers of strips of cloth woven from goat's or camel's hair and vegetable fibers, sewn together, and dyed black, but some cattle tribes, like the Kunta, substitute hides. The prevailing type of permanent dwelling is a rectangular house, often several stories in height, with external walls of stone or sun-dried brick (frequently whitewashed), an interior courtyard, and flat terraced roofs of horizontal beams and beaten earth. This structure occurs in Egypt, in the Saharan oases, and in many parts of the Maghreb (the coastal zone of original Berber occupation); but in other parts of the last region, especially among rural Algerians, Jebala, Moroccans, and Tunisians, it has not replaced an earlier type, also rec-

Group of Bedouin Arabs in Egypt. (Courtesy of the Peabody Museum of Archaeology and Ethnology, Harvard University.)

tangular but with a thatched gable or hip roof and no interior courtyard. The Sudanese cylindrical hut with conical roof appears occasionally on the fringes of the Sudan and also, curiously enough, among the distant Moroccans of the Dukkala and Rehamna tribes, where it must have been introduced by Negro slaves.

The political system of the Bedouin Arabs is simplicity itself. Above the extended family with its patriarchal head, each segment from minor lineage to tribe has a sheikh. This office descends typically from father to eldest son in the senior patrilineal line, but the political authority of its occupant depends largely upon his wealth and personal influence. Judicial authority is exercised by a hereditary judge (*qadi*); there is usually one in each sib or fraction. The judge decides questions of fact; on questions of law he commonly seeks guidance from learned men who are versed in the Koran but who do not necessarily have any official standing.

Where genuine states have developed, sheikhs and judges are replaced by appointive officials. The head of the state, e.g., the Moroccan Sultan or the Tunisian Bey, typically appoints a governor (*caid*) over each tribe or province subject to him, a sheikh over each sib or district, and commonly judges and local officials as well. Turkish rule followed a similar system, with provincial governors appointed from Constantinople, appointive district chiefs (*qaimaqam*), and subdistrict heads (*mudir*). In societies with a strong Berber substratum, e.g., the Algerians, Dui-Menia, Hamyan, Jebala, Moroccans, Regeibat, and Zenaga, councils of Berber type have survived with considerable success on the local level, despite Arab and Turkish influence.

A special type of ecclesiastical government, centered on Marabouts, or holy men, deserves special note. Marabouts first appeared in southern Morocco, as a product of a medieval Islamic reformation, and have since spread throughout much of North Africa. They are devout men who renounce military and other mundane pursuits and devote themselves to the study of the Koran and Islamic lore. They conduct schools, are called upon to arbitrate disputes, and often acquire such reputations for saintliness, learning, and the ability to bring rain and cure illness that people flock to their support and cults grow up around their tombs after their death. They and their hereditary successors receive landed endowments and a flow of gifts from their pious admirers and are exempted from secular political rule. Out of the Marabout movement there arose among the Sanusi, in 1843, the Sanusiya, or Mahdist, movement, a religious order with a conservative and antiforeign ideology, which spread like wildfire throughout Libya, Egypt, the Sahara, and the eastern Sudan. It was the Mahdists who defeated the British under Gordon at Khartoum in 1885.

Their power was shattered in the Sudan by Kitchener in 1898 and in their homeland by the Italian military conquest of Libya in 1923–1932.

The nomadic peoples recognize the collective right of each tribe, sib, and lineage to particular tracts of grazing land and natural water resources. Tilled land, however, is universally subject to private property, including full rights to lease or sell. In a few societies, e.g., the Sahel, small peasant holdings predominate, but usually the land is unequally divided, mainly into large estates worked by tenant farmers. Inheritance is strictly patrilineal and usually follows Islamic law, which reserves one-eighth of a man's estate to his widow and divides the balance equally among his children, except that daughters receive half rather than full shares. The Hamama, Nail, and Soliman, however, follow the Berber practice and exclude daughters from inheritance, at least of land.

In marked contrast to the egalitarian Berbers, the Bedouin Arabs reveal an elaborate stratification into strongly differentiated and usually endogamous castes. Six separate strata must be distinguished: nobles, freemen, vassals, serfs, slaves, and outcastes. In no society, even of relatively simple nomads, do the sources reveal fewer than four of these divisions, and frequently, especially in the west, all six are clearly indicated.

The nobles, at the top of the hierarchy, fall into three distinct subgroups: (1) *shorfa*, or genealogical nobles, allegedly the direct descendants of Mohammed, who are exempted from taxation and all labor and are supported by endowments and voluntary gifts; (2) Marabouts, or religious nobles, who have already been described; and (3) military and political nobles. The last group, where states exist, is further subdivided into royalty and a ruling aristocracy.

Freemen consist of the ordinary members of politically dominant or at least independent tribes. They are internally differentiated on the basis of wealth, e.g., into herders who are relatively rich or poor in livestock and, in sedentary groups, into large landowners, small peasants, and tenant farmers.

Vassals are the members of subjugated tribes who pay a regular tribute to their dominant neighbors. They may be Arabs, Berbers, or Negroes, but in the last case they are more often reduced to the still lower status of serfs. Even when they are Arabs, as in the case of the tributary Murabitin among the dominant Saadi, they are despised by their masters, who do not intermarry with them.

Serfs, usually of Negro or mixed origin, appear only in those regions where Bedouin tribes have conquered an indigenous sedentary population and have reduced them to a dependent and tributary status. They differ from vassals chiefly in being even more thoroughly despised and more ruthlessly exploited. They are especially prevalent in the western

Sahara among such peoples as the Chaamba, Delim, Kunta, Regeibat, Trarza, and Zenaga. Here, as noted in Chapter 16, they are known as Haratin and represent remnants of the autochthonous Negro inhabitants of the region.

Slavery prevailed in every Arab tribe until its relatively recent abolition, usually by European colonial governments. Slaves in former times were occasionally Caucasian, e.g., the European galley slaves of the Barbary pirates, but more recently they have been exclusively Negroes from the Sudan, obtained either through Arab raiders or through purchase in the trans-Saharan trade. The descendants of slaves today, as in the Southern United States, form an endogamous caste.

At the bottom of the social hierarchy, despised by all, are certain outcaste groups following occupations that are considered unclean. In cities like Fez, for example, they include street cleaners and donkey drivers; in Mauritania, bards, or *griots*. The commonest categories, however, are smiths, leatherworkers, and artisans of related specialties. Almost without exception they are Caucasoid in race. Among them must be included the Jews, who, in North Africa, are mainly artisans rather than merchants and who are everywhere confined to ghettos and subjected to repressive restrictions.

Rural residents, whether nomadic or sedentary, have as little in common with the urban inhabitants of the larger towns as do the segregated castes with one another. The urban population, largely of alien origin as previously noted, is divided into castes along ethnic lines and also into social classes based on economic criteria, both tending strongly toward endogamy. The class hierarchy comprises four principal divisions: (1) wealthy families engaged mainly in foreign commerce; (2) middle-class retail merchants, who are organized in guilds; (3) master artisans, who are organized separately in craft guilds; and (4) unskilled laborers and poor journeymen. Literacy prevails only in the two highest classes.

Coon (1951) has depicted vividly the "mosaic" composition of Middle Eastern society, including that of Arab North Africa. He has perhaps not sufficiently stressed, however, that this structure, striking as it certainly is, rests on a caste stratification so extreme that it can be paralleled elsewhere in the world only in India and the Union of South Africa. It is at least possible that the caste, as opposed to class, distinctions found today in societies of European origin, once perhaps as egalitarian as those of the Berbers, may be ultimately derived historically from Arab North Africa, mediated first by the Spaniards and then by the Dutch and English. If so, the principal contributions of the North African Arabs to Western civilization may well be the Jewish ghetto and the inferior and segregated status of the Negro race.

Selected Bibliography

Adeler. Coutume maure. *PCEHS*, ser. A, 9:373–400. 1939. [Zenaga].

Ammar, H. *Growing Up in an Egyptian Village*. London, 1954.

Ascherson, P. Die Bewohner der Kleinen Oase in der libyschen Wüste. *ZE*, 8:343–358. 1876. [Bahariya].

Bardin, P. Les populations arabes du contrôle civil de Gafsa et leurs genres de vie. *Publications de l'Institut des Belles Lettres Arabes*, 6:1–64. Tunis, 1944.

Bel, A. La population musulmane de Tlemcen. *REES*, 1:201–225, 417–447. 1908. [Algerians].

Bernard, A. *L'Algérie*. Paris, 1929. [Algerians, Hamyan].

———. *Afrique septentrionale et occidentale*. 2 vols. Paris, 1937–1939.

Bessis, A., P. Marthelot, H. de Montety, and D. Pauphilet. *Le territoire des Oulad Sidi ben Aoun*. Paris, 1956. [Hamama].

Blackman, W. S. *The Fellahin of Upper Egypt*. London, 1929.

Bonniard. F. *Le tell septentrional en Tunisie*. Paris, 1934.

Bouillié, R. *Les coutumes familiales au Kanem*. Paris, 1937. [Soliman].

Caro Baroja, J. *Estudios saharianos*. Madrid, 1955. [Delim, Regeibat, and Tajakant].

Chavanne, J. *Die Sahara*. Wien, 1879.

Coon, C. S. *Caravan*. New York, 1951.

Despois, J. *La Tunisie*. Paris, 1930. [Sahel and Tunisians].

———. *La Tunisie orientale*. Paris, 1940. [Hamama and Sahel].

———. *Le Hodna*. Paris, 1953. [Algerians].

Dubie, P. La vie matérielle des Maures. *MIFAN*, 23:111–252. 1953. [Trarza].

Evans-Pritchard, E. E. *The Sanusi of Cyrenaica*. Oxford, 1949.

Herkommer, J. *Libyen*. Freiburg, 1941.

Hrdlicka, A. The Natives of Kharga Oasis. *Smithsonian Miscellaneous Collections*, 59(1):1–118. 1912.

Julien, C. A. *Histoire d'Afrique du Nord*. Paris, 1931.

Kennett, A. *Bedouin Justice*. Cambridge, 1925. [Saadi].

King, W. J. H. *Mysteries of the Libyan Desert*. London, 1923. [Dakhla].

Le Tourneau, R. *Fès avant le protectorat*. Casablanca, 1949. [Moroccans].

Lotte. Coutume maure. *PCEHS*, ser. A, 10:1–91. 1939. [Delim].

Marty, P. Les tribus de la haute Mauritanie. *RCD*, 25:73–82, 118–126, 136–145. 1915. [Regeibat].

———. *L'émirat des Trarzas*. Paris, 1919.

Mercier, E. *Histoire de l'Afrique septentrionale*. 3 vols. Paris, 1888–1891.

Michaux-Bellaire, E. Quelques tribus de montagnes de la région du Habt. *AM*, 17:1–542. 1911. [Jebala].

———. Casablanca et les Châouia. *VTM*, 1:1–306; 2:1–338. 1915. [Moroccans].

———. Le Gharb. *VTM*, 6:1–316. 1918. [Moroccans].

———. Rabat et sa région. *VTM*, 5:1–372. 1920. [Moroccans].

———. Région des Doukkala. *VTM*, 10:1–178; 11:1–219. 1932. [Moroccans].

Michaux-Bellaire, E., and G. Salmon. Les tribus arabes de la vallée du Lemkoûs. *AM*, 4:1–151; 5:1–133; 6:219–297. 1905–1906. [Moroccans].

Miner, H. *The Primitive City of Timbuctoo*. Princeton, 1953. [Berabish].

Modat. Aperçu sur la société maure de l'Adrar. *BCEHS*, 5:264–278. 1922. [Regeibat].

Mouliéras, A. *Le maroc inconnu*, vol. 2. Paris, 1899. [Jebala].

Murray, G. W. *Sons of Ishmael*. London, 1935. [Maaza and Saadi].

Nachtigal, G. *Sahara und Sudan*. 2 vols. Berlin, 1879–1881.

Regnier, Y. *Les Chaamba sous le régime français.* Paris, 1938.
Rohlfs, G. *Quer durch Afrika,* vol. 1. Liepzig, 1874. [Fezzan].
———. *Drei Monate in der libyschen Wüste.* Cassel, 1875. [Bahariya and Dakhla].
Salmon, G. Les Fahçya. *AM,* 1:149–261. 1904. [Moroccans].
Scotti, P. *L'etnologia del Fezzan.* Genova, 1949.
Tauxier, L. *Le noir du Soudan.* Paris, 1912. [Kunta and Zenaga].
Tharaud, Jérome, and Jean Tharaud. *Fez.* Paris, 1930. [Moroccans].
Ubach, E., and E. Rackow. *Sitte und Recht in Nordafrika.* Stuttgart, 1923. [Hamama, Nail, and Sahel].
Villot, C. *Moeurs, coutumes et institutions des indigènes de l'Algérie.* 2d edit. Constantine, 1875. [Algerians and Hamyan].
Westermarck, E. *Marriage Ceremonies in Morocco.* London, 1914.
Winkler, H. A. *Bauern zwischen Wasser und Wüste.* Stuttgart, 1934. [Egyptians].

53

Tuareg

The Hilalian immigration of Bedouin Arabs in the eleventh century resulted in the displacement of many Berber groups, some of whom sought refuge in the oases of the Sahara and adopted there a nomadic and predatory mode of life modeled on that of the invaders. The principal body of these refugees, stemming for the most part from Tripolitania, gave rise to the modern Tuareg nation. Though long since completely Islamized, the Tuareg still bear witness to their Christian past in the retention of the cross as their favorite decorative motif. They fall into the following seven major divisions.

1. Ahaggaren (Ihaggaren, Kel Ahaggar). They inhabit the Hoggar region in the northwestern portion of the Tuareg country and number about 5,000.
2. Antessar (Kel Antessar), with the Tengeredief. They occupy the hinterland of Timbuktu in the extreme southwestern section of the Tuareg country and number about 40,000.
3. Asben (Kel Air), embracing the Itesan (Kel Geres), Owey (Kel Oui), Tadele (Kel Tadele), and other tribes of the Air region in the southeastern part of the Tuareg country. They number about 30,000.
4. Aulliminden (Awelliminden, Iullemmeden, Oulliminden). They are located in the south central section of the Tuareg country and number about 100,000.
5. Azjer (Adjeur, Ajjer, Ashar, Kel Azdjer), with the Ihajenen of the oasis of Gat. They occupy the northeastern portion of the Tuareg country and number about 6,000.

6. Ifora. They inhabit the Iforas region in the western part of the Tuareg country and number about 5,000.
7. Udalan (Oudalen, Wadalen), with the Gossi (Kel Gossi), Igwadaren, Imedreden, Irreganaten, Logomaten, Tingeregdech, and other lesser tribes. They reside south of the Niger River and number about 100,000.

Since we have already become acquainted with the original culture of the Berbers in Chapter 15 and with that of the indigenous Saharan Negroes in Chapter 16, we shall view the Tuareg primarily from the point of view of the processes of culture change which they exemplify. They retain the language and many of the most distinctive customs of their Berber ancestors. In other respects, however, they have completely abandoned their ancestral way of life and have adopted that of the invading Arabs. In still other respects their culture is neither Berber nor Arab, nor a blend of both, but represents a genuine creative synthesis. The resulting combination, moreover, is a relatively stable one, revealing only relatively slight regional variation.

The economic life conforms closely to the pattern introduced into North Africa by the Bedouin Arabs. The Tuareg are camel nomads. They despise agriculture and leave it exclusively in the hands of the subjugated indigenous Negroes. Except for herding, they have abandoned productive enterprise and live off the tribute extorted from their subjects and the "protection" exacted from caravans. They are organized in migratory bands rather than settled villages, and they live in tents. The latter, however, differ markedly from those of the Arabs. They are covered with tanned sheep or goat hides rather than with cloth, and these are dyed red rather than black.

Political organization represents a fusion of Berber and Arab elements. In general, each band and subtribe has an assembly or council, as among the Berbers, and also a chief, comparable to the sheikhs of the Arabs. Chiefs are sometimes elected by the council in Berber fashion, but are sometimes hereditary. The Aulliminden follow the Arab rule of patrilineal succession, but this is exceptional. Most Tuareg tribes with hereditary chiefship adhere to the matrilineal principle of succession, thus deviating sharply from both Berber and Arab practice.

The system of property and inheritance is likewise unique. The form in which it appears among the Azjer may be briefly summarized, both because it is the most adequately described and because it seems to be typical for at least the northern Tuareg. The Azjer divide property into two categories—"personal" and "illegitimate." Personal property includes everything which an individual acquires through his own economic effort, e.g., money, livestock, and purchased weapons and slaves. Whether owned by men or women, it is always inherited by their children, who receive equal shares regardless of sex. So-called "illegitimate" property includes whatever has been acquired by force, e.g., rights to land and water sources, customary fees exacted from caravans and travelers, "protection" paid by other groups to avoid being raided, personal and property privileges with respect to vassals and serfs, and the authority to command and exact obedience from political subordinates. Such rights are held collectively by lineages rather than by individuals, are administered by the head of the lineage, and are transmitted on his death, without partition, to his eldest sister's eldest son, who succeeds him.

In sharp contrast to other Berber peoples, most of whom are strongly democratic and egalitarian, the Tuareg have adopted the caste system of the Arabs in its fullest range. In addition to Marabouts, or religious nobles, five separate castes are clearly differentiated: (1) the Imochar, or ruling Tuareg, who lead a strictly parasitic life of warfare and political domination; (2) the Imrad, or vassal Tuareg, who engage in herding, bear arms in support of the Imochar groups to which they are attached, and render regular tribute to the latter; (3) the Bella or Haratin, Negro serfs who cultivate the land and are attached and pay tribute to particular groups of Imochar or Imrad; (4) the Iklan, privately owned Negro slaves who are obtained from the Sudan through purchase or capture and who are employed in domestic service and other menial labor; (5) the Inaden, outcaste groups of Negro artisans, especially smiths and leather-workers. A woman is permitted to marry a man only of her own or a higher caste, whereas a man may marry a woman only of his own or a lower caste. Since social status is transmitted through women, this rule of caste hypergamy has protected the dominant Imochar, and with insignificant exceptions also the vassal Imrad, from any infusion of Negro blood. The sources suggest, indeed, that it was instituted for this purpose.

Like both Arabs and Berbers, the Tuareg require a bride-price and permit marriage between first cousins, but their Berber affiliations are revealed in their insistence on strict monogamy and in the high status which they accord to women. The men spend most of their time in herding, in raiding, and in protecting client caravans, whereas the women are relieved of all economic and most household responsibilities by Negro serfs and slaves. With their time thus freed, the women devote themselves to the fine arts. Music and poetry are exclusively feminine accomplishments. Whereas only a few men are literate—approximately one-third in the Azjer tribe—all women can read and write in the peculiar Tuareg script, which is derived from a Libyan alphabet of the fourth century B.C. Moreover, at least among the northern Tuareg tribes, the bulk of all livestock and other movable property is owned by the women. Finally, it is perhaps symbolic that among the Tuareg—alone among all Moslem peoples—it is the men rather than the women who wear veils.

Residence is sometimes matrilocal for an initial period, as among the

Ahaggaren and Ifora, but it is typically patrilocal for the lifetime of the husband's father. When the latter dies, however—and also if he divorces his wife—his sons normally remove to the band of their mother and maternal uncle, in whose "illegitimate" property they can expect to share.

In descent, as in residence, the Tuareg peoples differ markedly both from the Arabs and from other Berber tribes. That they are matrilineal is asserted by nearly all the ethnographers. What the latter seem usually to have in mind, however, is social-class rather than kin-group affiliation. In a hypergamous marriage, involving a man and woman of different castes, it is clear that children regularly take the status of their mother. But what happens when the parents belong to the same caste? In such a case, kin-group affiliation could theoretically be either matrilineal, patrilineal, or bilateral. Unfortunately, the ethnographic sources, though excellent in many respects, do not meet the demanding standards of modern kinship investigation and do not supply the wealth of detail required for complete understanding. That descent is unilinear seems certain, as does the existence of a segmentary lineage system in all castes except possibly the Iklan, or slaves. The mode of affiliation, however, seems to differ from tribe to tribe. The sources strongly suggest that lineages are patrilineal among the Aulliminden and Ifora but matrilineal among the Asben, the Udalan, and probably also the Ahaggaren, Antessar, and Azjer.

The matrilineal institutions of the Tuareg raise an interesting problem of historical reconstruction, to which there are at least three possible solutions. One possibility is that the Tuareg have preserved the matrilineate from a very early period of Berber culture, perhaps also reflected among the extinct Guanche of the Canary Islands. This is rendered improbable, however, by the fact that none of the numerous other Berber tribes of the African mainland provides any corroborative evidence and by the additional fact that the present relative isolation of the Tuareg is historically recent, dating only from the Hilalian Arab invasion. A second possibility is that the indigenous Bella were characterized by avunculocal residence and matrilineal descent and that they transmitted these rules to the conquering Tuareg. This, too, seems improbable. The Bella, as noted in Chapter 16, were presumably akin to the Hausa on the southern border of the Tuareg country, and these Hausa peoples are strictly patrilineal.

The third and most probable hypothesis is that the ancestral Tuareg, while still resident in Tripolitania, were patrilineal, like all other mainland Berbers, and that the matrilineate was developed as an adjustment to special local conditions after their displacement into the Sahara. Adopting the very un-Berber caste stratification of the Arabs, they may well have instituted matrilineal affiliation for intercaste marriages in order to preserve their purity of race. This accords with the view of most Tuareg ethnographers and may well have been facilitated by the unusually high status of women. Lineage affiliation could have remained patrilineal for a time, as indeed is still the case among the Aulliminden and Ifora. The two contradictory rules, however, must inevitably have come into conflict whenever an intercaste marriage occurred. To have accepted the patrilineal rule in such instances would have resulted in the unwelcome transmission of "illegitimate" property rights in land, vassals, and serfs to people of mixed blood. Matrilineal descent would thus have gained ascendancy in cases of conflict. Then, wherever intercaste unions became common, it could readily have come to replace patrilineal descent even in regard to kin-group affiliation. If this reconstruction, which seems to the author much the most probable, is actually correct, we have in the Tuareg the first authenticated case in the world of a people that has moved directly from patrilineal to matrilineal descent without passing through a transitional period of bilateral descent.

Selected Bibliography

Aymard, A. *Les Touareg*. Paris, 1911. [Antessar].

Bissuel, H. *Les Touareg de l'ouest*. Alger, 1888. [Ahaggaren].

Cortier, M. *D'une rive à l'autre du Sahara*. Paris, 1908. [Ifora].

Coutouly, F. de. Les populations du cercle de Dori. *BCEHS*, 6:269–301, 471–496, 636–671. 1923. [Udalan].

Demoulin, F. La vie des Touareg du Hoggar. *Annales de Géographie*, 37:137–162. 1928. [Ahaggaren].

Duveyrier, H. *Les Touareg du nord*. Paris, 1864. [Ahaggaren and Azjer].

Foley, H. *Moeurs et mèdecine des Touareg de l'Ahaggar*. Alger, 1930. [Ahaggaren].

Gaalon, R. de. Coutume Touareg. *PCEHS*, ser. A, 10:217–237. 1939. [Udalan].

Hourst, L. *The Exploration of the Niger*. New York, 1899. [Aulliminden].

Jean, C. *Les Touareg du sud-est*. Paris, 1919. [Asben].

Joubert. Les coutumes et le droit chez les Kel Tadélé. *BIFAN*, 1:245–281. 1939. [Asben].

Lhote, H. *Les Touaregs du Hoggar*. Paris, 1944. [Ahaggaren].

Miner, H. *The Primitive City of Timbuctoo*. Princeton, 1953. [Antessar].

Nicolas, F. Les industries de protection chez les Twareg de l'Azawagh. *Hesperis*, 25:43–84. 1938. [Aulliminden].

Rodd, F. R. *People of the Veil*. London, 1926. [Asben].

Zeltner, F. de. Les Touareg du sud. *JRAI*, 44:351–375. 1914. [Antessar].

Zöhrer, L. G. A. Die Tuareg der Sahara. *AV*, 11:152–201. 1956.

54

Baggara

The Bedouin Arabs of the Hilalian invasion, who poured across the Sinai Peninsula into Egypt after A.D. 1045, encountered a block in northern Nubia, where the Christian kingdom of Dongola was strong enough to prevent their passage up the Nile, thus diverting the flood westward into North Africa. Even when Dongola fell in the fourteenth century, a second Christian kingdom, that of Alwa to the south, manned the dike for another two centuries. After the fall of Alwa in 1504, however, the Arabs surged unchecked up the Nile and thence westward into the central Sudan, where their advance guard penetrated as far as Lake Chad. In these regions the people they displaced were not Caucasoid Berbers, as in North Africa, but Negroes, the major victims being the Nubians, the Prenilotes, and the Central Sudanic tribes. The invaders often intermarried extensively with the indigenous populations, as well as with slaves obtained farther south, with the result that many tribes have received a heavy infusion of Negroid blood. In addition, they exhibit somewhat less noticeable evidences of cultural borrowing.

The Arabs of Nubia and the eastern Sudan may be designated collectively as the Baggara, although this name is often reserved for those groups whose animal husbandry revolves primarily around cattle. They have a total population of around 5 million and can be classified into the following major tribal groupings.

1. Batahin, with the Fadnia. They are camel nomads who occupy the "Island of Meroe" between the White Nile and Atbara Rivers and reveal only slight Negroid admixture.
2. Bederia (Bedayria), with the Dubab, Ghodiat, Hamayd (Aulad Hamayd), Hawazma, Terayfia, Tomam, Tumbab, and other seminomadic tribes in Kordofan north of the Nuba, with whom some of the Bederia are strongly mixed.
3. Dekakire. A detached tribe in Bagirmi, much mixed with the indigenous Negroes.
4. Fertit, including the Mandala (Bandala) and other Arabic-speaking tribes of escaped Negro slaves in the Dar Fertit region. They are sedentary tillers.
5. Fezara, with the Bazaa, Gerar (Beni Gerar), Hamid, Kawahla, Maakla, Maalia, Shenabla, and Zayadia tribes of northern Kordofan. They are largely cattle and sheep nomads.
6. Gaaliin (Jaalyyin), with the Gamuia, Gemaab, Gimiab, Manasir, Mesallania, Mirafab, Rubatab, and other tribes along the Nile River in Nubia. They are largely sedentary and reveal a strong Nubian component.
7. Gimma. A seminomadic tribe along the White Nile.
8. Habbania, with the kindred Helba (Beni Helba), Rizeigat (Rizaykat), Taaisha,

and Taelba of southern Darfur. They are primarily pastoral and exhibit considerable Negroid admixture.

9. Hamar. A seminomadic tribe of Dar Hamar in Kordofan.
10. Hasania (Hassanyah), with the Husseinat (Husaynat). A seminomadic tribe on
    the White Nile above Khartoum.
11. Hemat (Heimad), with the Kirdi, Salamat, and other tribes in southern Wadai.
    They are seminomadic and reveal substantial Negroid admixture.
12. Kababish (Kubbabish), with the Hawawir and Kerriat. They are camel nomads
    with a comparatively slight Negroid admixture.
13. Kerarish. An Arabized Nubian tribe of camel nomads in the Dongola region.
14. Mahamid, with the Atayfat, Eraykat, Mahria, Nawaiba (Nuwaiba), and other
    tribes in northern Wadai. They are camel nomads with a moderate degree of
    Negroid admixture.
15. Messiria, with the kindred Humr (Homr) of the Dar el Homr region of Kordo-
    fan. They are cattle nomads with considerable Negroid admixture.
16. Rufaa (Abu Rof), with the Abdullab, Ahamda, Amarna, Awamra, Gubayna,
    Hamran, Kawasma, Kenana, Khawalda, Lahawiin, and other tribes of the Blue
    Nile region. They are seminomadic herders of sheep and goats.
17. Selim (Beni Selim). They are cattle nomads along the White Nile, with a strong
    Negroid admixture.
18. Shaikia (Cheykye, Shegya). They are camel nomads ruling over Nubian serfs
    along the Nile.
19. Shukria, with the Dubania (Dubaina) and Dubasiin tribes on the Atbara tribu-
    tary of the Nile. They are camel nomads.
20. Shuwa (Choua, Shiwa, Shoa), with the Assale (Lesiye), Dagana (Degena), Khoz-
    zam (Chozzam, Khuzam), and other tribes of Bornu and western Bagirmi. They
    are nomadic or seminomadic cattle herders and number about 100,000.
21. Tungur (Toundjour, Tunzer), inhabiting Darfur, Kanem, and Wadai. They
    are sedentary remnants, with a strong Negroid admixture, of the earliest Arabized
    immigrants into the central Sudan, probably refugees from Dongola.

Among the Baggara tribes, only the Batahin, Fezara, Hamar, Kababish,
Kerarish, Mahamid, Shaikia, and Shukria have been able to cling substantially to the traditional camel nomadism preferred by the Bedouin.
The majority have shifted to cattle as their chief animals and have come
to depend to a considerable extent upon agriculture, adopting the cultivation of sorghum, millet, and other Sudanic crops from the indigenous
Negroes. The Fertit, Gaaliin, and Tungur, indeed, are almost completely
sedentary. In contrast to the Arabs of North Africa and the Sahara, men
rather than women do most of the milking.

Social organization deviates in only minor respects from the norms
prevailing among other African Arabs. Polygyny, however, shows a very
much higher incidence. Nubian influence, moreover, is often revealed in
an initial period of matrilocal residence, notably among the Gaaliin,
Hasania, Kababish, and Shaikia. The Mandala tribe of Fertit, who are
Arab only in language, have a curious and aberrant social system. These
people, the descendants of escaped Negro slaves formerly held by the
Habbania, base their organization on the fiction that they are still slaves.

Children are assumed to be the property of the mother's Arab owner and are thus affiliated with their matrilineal kinsmen, and a son can inherit from his father only if the latter has the same traditional master as the mother.

Although many Baggara tribes cling to the Bedouin tent, the usual cloth cover is occasionally replaced by hides, as among the Messiria, or by mats, as among the Gimma, Mahamid, and Shukria. Its form also varies, being cylindrical among the Gimma and Selim, hemispherical among the Habbania, and beehive-shaped among some Shuwa. The Sudanese cylindrical hut with conical thatched roof crops up among some Bederia and Shuwa.

The Baggara keep slaves, but in general they reveal a much less complex caste stratification than most African Arabs. They likewise depend for their livelihood more on economic productivity than on predatory exploitation. The latter, to be sure, is by no means absent, especially among the more nomadic tribes of the Nile Valley. An outstanding exception must be noted in the mass slave raiding conducted in the southern Sudan during the nineteenth century. Here the presence of politically unorganized Negro tribes, especially of the Central Sudanic linguistic subfamily, provided an opportunity, and their pagan beliefs an excuse, for slave raids on a scale, and with a degree of ferocity, unparalleled elsewhere in the unhappy history of the continent. Of the Bongo tribe, for example, whose population was estimated at 100,000 by Schweinfurth when he visited their country in the 1870s, only 5,000 survived the Arab depredations. Other tribes, less fortunate, left no survivors.

Selected Bibliography

Bouillié, R. Les coutumes familiales au Kanem. Paris, 1937. [Shuwa].
Burckhardt, J. L. Travels in Nubia. 2d edit. London, 1922. [Shaikia].
Carbou, H. La région du Tchad et du Ouadaï, vol. 2. Paris, 1912. [Mahamid].
Cunnison, I. The Humr and Their Land. SNR, 35(2):50–68. 1954. [Messiria].
Herbert, G. K. C. The Bandala of the Bahr el Ghazal. SNR, 8:187–194. 1925. [Fertit].
Lagrange. La circonscription du Bartha. Géographie, 28:157–171. 1913. [Hemat].
Lampen, G. D. The Baggara Tribes of Darfur. SNR, 16:97–118. 1933. [Habbania].
MacMichael, H. A. The Tribes of Northern and Central Kordofan. Cambridge, 1912.
———. A History of the Arabs in the Sudan, vol. 1. Cambridge, 1922.
Martine. Essai sur l'histoire du pays Salamat et les moeurs et coutumes de ses habitants. BSRC, 5:19–83. 1924. [Hemat].
Parkyns, M. The Kubbabish Arabs. JRGS, 20:254–275. 1851.
Reid, J. A. Some Notes on the Tribes of the White Nile Province. SNR, 8:149–209. 1930. [Gimma, Hasania, and Selim].
———. The Nomad Arab Camel Breeding Tribes of the Sudan. The Anglo-Egyptian Sudan from Within, ed. J. A. de C. Hamilton, pp. 113–129. London, 1935.
Seligman, C. G., and B. Z. Seligman. The Kabâbîsh. HAS, 2:105–185. 1918.
Zenkovsky, S. Marriage Customs in Omdurman. SNR, 26(2):241–255. 1945. [Gaaliin].

55

Fulani

Scattered throughout the western Sudan from Senegal in the west to Cameroon and French Equatorial Africa in the east live a curious people known as the Fulani, but also variously called Fellani, Fellata, Filani, Foulah, Ful, Fulbe, Peul, and Pullo. For the most part they reside in the midst of other peoples. Particularly large groups live as ethnic minorities among such populous nations as the Bambara, Gurma, Hausa, Malinke, Mossi, Soninke, and Zerma, and others are dispersed among many smaller Voltaic and Plateau Nigerian tribes. Only in a few discontinuous districts do they constitute the dominant element in the population. These are shown in Map 16 and include, from west to east, the Senegal Valley, Fouta Toro, Fouta Djalon, Kita, Masina, Liptako, Sokoto, Bauchi, and Adamawa. Because of their dispersion and their interpenetration of other peoples they cannot be said to constitute an independent culture province despite their unquestioned distinctiveness.

The latest detailed estimate of their population, by Lavergne de Tressan (1953), assigns the Fulani a total of more than 5 million people, distributed by political divisions as follows:

Cameroon	275,000	Haute Volta	240,000
Dahomey and Togo	115,000	Mauritania	70,000
French Equatorial Africa	50,000	Northern Nigeria	2,025,000
French Guinea	880,000	Portuguese Guinea	110,000
French Niger	275,000	Senegal	510,000
French Sudan	460,000	Sierra Leone and Gambia	20,000

Few regional groups of Fulani bear distinctive names. For this reason, we shall classify them by their principal areas of concentration, omitting minority groups, however large, that reside amongst other peoples.

1. Adamawa. In this region the Fulani have usurped large tracts of grazing land from the indigenous Plateau Nigerian and Eastern Nigritic peoples, over many of whom they also exercise political sovereignty.
2. Bauchi. In this region the Fulani have penetrated deep into the heart of the plateau Nigerian province.
3. Fouta Djalon. This region, whose present inhabitants are known as the Foutaja-lonke, was wrested by the Fulani from the Dialonke tribe of Nuclear Mande.
4. Fouta Toro. This region, in Senegal, was occupied very early by the Fulani.
5. Kita. This region, whose present inhabitants are known as Fuladugu (Fouladou-gou), was taken by the Fulani from the Bambara and Malinke groups of Nuclear Mande.
6. Liptako. This region was seized from the Voltaic Gurma tribe.

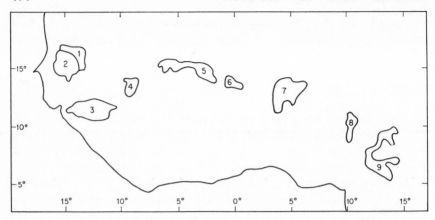

Map 16. **Major Concentrations of Fulani** (1—Senegal Valley, 2—Fouta Toro, 3—Fouta Djalon, 4—Kita, 5—Masina, 6—Liptako, 7—Sokoto, 8—Bauchi, 9—Adamawa)

7. Masina. This region was largely taken from the Bambara tribe of Nuclear Mande.
8. Senegal Valley. This region, where the inhabitants are known as the Tukulor (Takruri, Tekarir, Torodo, Toucouleur, Tukri), has long been occupied by the Fulani.
9. Sokoto. This region, whose nomadic inhabitants are known as the Bororo, was wrested by the Fulani from the Hausa.

Accounts of the Fulani in regions remote from their place of origin, such as Northern Nigeria, describe and sometimes confuse two seemingly quite different peoples. We shall call them tentatively the A Fulani and the B Fulani. Table 4 summarizes some of their most notably contrasting characteristics.

Table 4: Characteristics of Contrasting Fulani Groups

A Fulani	*B Fulani*
Non-Negroid in physique: "straight-nosed, straight-haired, relatively thin-lipped, wiry, copper-or-bronze complexioned"	Strongly Negroid, though often displaying some admixture of other ethnic elements
Pastoral nomads	Sedentary village dwellers
Indifferent Moslems and not infrequently even pagans	Fanatic Moslems committed to proselytizing their faith
Peaceful herders, readily accommodating to their neighbors	Aggressive addicts of "holy wars" against pagan peoples
Lacking any indigenous political organization above the level of the autonomous band and its headman	Noted state builders through wars of conquest and aggrandizement

Attempts to account for these contradictory facts have usually started with the assumption that the A Fulani constitute the original nucleus of the people and that the B Fulani have been derived from them by long miscegenation with Negro slaves and subjects. The origin of the A Fulani, who everywhere contrast sharply with all their immediate neighbors in both physique and culture, has then been sought in a variety of fantastic hypotheses of their derivation by migration from some remote region, usually one inhabited by Caucasians of Hamitic speech. Those which have enjoyed the widest popularity include the theory of Delafosse that they are sprung from Syrians of Semitic (Aramaic) speech, who allegedly penetrated Negro Africa from Cyrenaica about A.D. 200, and that advanced by Meinhof deriving them from the Cushites of the Eastern Horn.

Actually, the Fulani present no insoluble mystery. We start with the fact that the A and B groups, however greatly they may differ in physical and cultural characteristics, share the same language, and we then look for its closest cognates. Greenberg (1949), rejecting the curious use of the herding and milking of cattle as diagnostic criteria of linguistic relationships, has demonstrated conclusively that the Fulani, far from being Hamitic in speech, possess a Nigritic language belonging specifically to the Atlantic subfamily of that stock and related especially closely to the Sin dialect of Serer and nearly as closely to Wolof. Except for the Fulani, most speakers of this group of languages reside in the Senegambian culture province (see Chapter 34) along the Atlantic coast and in its immediate hinterland. The ancestral Fulani can hardly have come from anywhere else. As a matter of fact, abundant historical evidence traces them back definitely to the former inhabitants of the middle region of the Senegal Valley and the savanna region of Fouta Toro immediately south thereof. Here they actually had as their immediate neighbors the linguistically kindred Serer and Wolof.

Our earliest historical information relates to the Tukulor, who still occupy the middle Senegal and whose name, significantly enough, is said to be a corruption of English "two colors." The Tukulor enter history about the seventh century after Christ, when they ruled a powerful state independent of the empire of Ghana. In the eleventh century they relinquished their territory in Mauritania to the Berbers, then expanding southward from Morocco under Arab pressure from the rear, but they held fast against the intruders in the valley of the Senegal.

History tells us something of the interaction of the Tukulor and the Berbers, and the rest can be reconstructed with little difficulty. We know that the Tukulor, led by their ruling dynasty, accepted Islam with enthusiasm in the eleventh century and that, as the first Negro converts in the western Sudan, they were largely instrumental in spreading the new faith among the Soninke to the east and the Wolof to the west. At this time doubtless began the transition, now complete, from the original matrilineal and avunculocal social structure of the Senegambians to the present patrilineal and patrilocal system. That the Tukulor were reacting to Berber influence in this respect is reflected in their retention today of certain traits that are specifically Berber rather than Negro, e.g., the transfer of the bride-price by the girl's parents to their daughter as a dowry.

Stopped in their political expansion by the strength of the Tukulor state, the Berbers presumably resorted to economic penetration, infiltrating with their herds into sections relatively unsuited to agriculture. On the fertile and well-watered land along the Senegal River, where there was little room for grazing, the Tukulor merely added the use of milk and butter to their dual economy and replaced their older humpless cattle with the new humped, or zebu, breed from the north. South of the river, however, the savanna country of Fouta Toro offered excellent pasturage, and was probably only sparsely occupied by tillers because of the difficulty of cultivation and the scarcity of water. Hence it was doubtless here that most of the Berber herdsmen established themselves. And here favorable conditions caused them to flourish. Politically subject to the Tukulor state and geographically isolated from their independent Berber kinsmen north of the Senegal, they gradually became acculturated to the dominant Negro population, accepted their language as a replacement for their own, and intermarried with them to at least some extent. In the resulting mixture, however, economic and demographic factors produced a preponderantly Caucasoid cross in the pastoral population of Fouta Toro but a predominantly Negroid cross among the sedentary tillers and townspeople along the Senegal. There thus arose two divisions among the "two-colored" Tukulor, ancestral respectively to our A and B Fulani.

The Tukulor state dominated Senegal until 1350, though under a Soninke dynasty after 1250. It was conquered by the Wolof around 1350, but regained its independence in 1520 and retained it until defeated by the French in 1893. The pastoral Fulani meanwhile prospered and spread. Their success is best accounted for in ecological terms, for they filled a previously unoccupied niche in the economic life of the region. Their expansion into the territory of their neighbors caused no alarm since they took over at first only lands ill suited to agriculture. Indeed they were usually welcomed by the indigenous tillers, who gladly exchanged their agricultural products for milk and butter, employed skilled Fulani herdsmen to tend their own livestock, and were happy to have the newcomers pasture their cattle on tilled fields after the crop was harvested, for the manure served as fertilizer. There developed a close symbiotic relationship which is repeatedly attested in essentially the same form across the entire breadth of the western Sudan, for the Fulani infiltrated ever farther to the east as their healthy life and diet brought rapid population increase and consequently a continuous pressure for new grazing land.

The expansion of the pastoral Fulani can be traced historically with fair accuracy. During the twelfth and thirteenth centuries they spread from Fouta Toro southward into Ferlo and eastward into Kaarta, mingling with the Malinke and ultimately forming populations of mixed blood that survive in many parts of the area today. One such group, in which the Fulani element predominates, is the Fuladugu of Kita. During the fourteenth century the Fulani penetrated eastward through Soninke and Bambara country and reached Masina, where a heavy concentration still survives. In the sixteenth century a Fulani vanguard infiltrated southward from Senegal into Fouta Djalon, where small remnants persist as the Fulakunda (Foulacounda) and Hubu (Houbbou). In the meantime the main movement continued eastward, forming an enclave in Liptako and penetrating the Hausa country, where they are first mentioned historically in the fifteenth century. Here their principal concentrations occur in Sokoto and Bauchi. Their vanguard reached Adamawa, another center of concentration, by at least the early eighteenth century, and smaller groups expanded eastward as far as Wadai and penetrated southeast into parts of Cameroon during the nineteenth century.

The pastoral Fulani did not migrate alone. Always they were accompanied by at least some of their sedentary and more Negroid kinsmen— better educated, more sophisticated in political matters, and far less tolerant of the infidel. When the nomads encountered local opposition to their encroachments, as was inevitable, they could call upon their Tukulor or B Fulani cousins to provide the military and political means for resistance and aggrandizement. In extreme situations the latter were prone to launch a jihad, or holy war, against the pagan "oppressors." Several of these deserve special mention.

Around 1750 a fanatic Fulani Marabout, who had established a theocratic state in Fouta Toro, launched a holy war against the pagan Dialonke and Senegambians who then inhabited Fouta Djalon; in a series of savage campaigns he drove many of them out of the country and converted and subjugated the rest. From a mixture of the conquerors and their subjects has sprung the present dominant population of Fouta Djalon, the Fulani-speaking but largely sedentary Futajalonke. Between 1848 and 1862 an equally fanatic Tukulor named El Hadj Omar carried Islam by fire and sword as far east as Djenne and initiated a period of ruthless devastation which ended only with the arrival of the French in 1893.

Still more famous is the career of the religious zealot and conqueror Osman dan Fodio, a sedentary Fulani reared in the Hausa state of Gobir. In 1804, his fervor having brought him into conflict with the native ruler, he fled the country, assumed the title of Ruler of the Faithful, and embarked on a holy war of conquest. Between 1804 and 1809 he successively reduced the Hausa states of Gobir, Zamfara, Zaria, Katsena, Kebbi, and Kano, establishing in each conquered territory a Fulani emir, subject and tributary to him. On his death he split his dominions, leaving his son Mohammed Bello as sultan in Sokoto and his brother Abdullai as ruler in Gwandu. This dual empire ruled most of Northern Nigeria until the arrival of the British in 1903.

Disciples of Osman carried his conquests far beyond the Hausa states. One established a tributary emirate in Bauchi in 1812; a second, one over the Nupe nation around 1820. A third, Modibo Adama by name, in 1809 launched a holy war against the pagan Negroes of the country now known, after him, as Adamawa and established himself as a tributary emir, with his capital first at Gurin but later, after 1841, in Yola. Thence his followers extended his conquests into Cameroon, where Fulani dominance and exploitation terminated only with the arrival of the Germans in 1899.

The techniques of government instituted by the conquering Fulani are well illustrated by those of Masina. Being based on warlike predation, the state depended on a complex military organization. Five great military commanders were made responsible for border defense and aggressive warfare against as many groups of bordering peoples, namely, (1) the Bobo and Minianka, (2) the Bambara, (3) the Soninke and Zenaga, (4) the Tuareg, and (5) the Mossi and Dogon. Each village was required to maintain a fixed military contingent, of which a third was called up each year for police work, raids, or wars of conquest. They were supported by requisitions levied on the villages where they were billeted, and their families received recompense while they were on active duty.

Lands seized from conquered peoples became state property. Enemies who submitted voluntarily and accepted Islam escaped enslavement. Others were reduced to serfdom and required to labor on the lands owned by the state. Livestock captured in raids or ordinary warfare were placed in the charge of district chiefs under the over-all supervision of two national officials. Those taken in a holy war were pooled and then distributed. The ruler took a fifth, giving half his share to the military commanders of the successful operation and using the other half to ransom war captives and succor the destitute. The warriors divided the remaining four-fifths, with cavalrymen receiving double shares.

The state derived its normal revenues from indemnities, confiscations, disinheritances, and a variety of regular imposts. These included (1) an annual tax of one-tenth of all agricultural produce, of which the tax collector kept 10 per cent, the ruler 20 per cent, and the district chief 70 per cent for his own support and that of his troops; (2) an annual livestock tax to the ruler, consisting of one steer in thirty, one cow in forty, one sheep in forty, and one goat in a hundred; (3) a capital levy of 2½ per cent per annum on all gold, cowrie currency, and salt owned by individuals; (4) a sales tax on all merchandise sold by tradesmen; and (5) a head tax of a measure of threshed millet for each adult, of which the ruler kept a fifth and used the rest for the support of mosque officials and the poor.

The riverain Tukulor and the mixed Fulani of Bauchi, Fouta Djalon, and Kita engage in agriculture to a substantial extent, cultivating crops similar to those of their neighbors. Elsewhere, however, the Fulani subsist almost exclusively by animal husbandry, leaving tillage to serfs or resorting to it only under pressure of circumstances. They do very little hunting, fishing, or gathering but depend heavily upon trade. They leave this largely, however, to other peoples, notably the Marka and Hausa; only in Liptako do mercantile Fulani constitute an important group. Transhumance is especially highly developed in Masina and Sokoto. Cattle, by far the most important domestic animals, are usually of the humped zebu breed, but the Futajalonke have adopted the humpless cattle of the indigenous Dialonke, and a similar Bambara strain rivals the zebu one in Masina. Meat is little used, but milk and butter are dietary staples everywhere. Nearly all Fulani keep sheep, goats, dogs, and chickens as well as cattle, and many of them have horses and donkeys as well. Men ordinarily herd cattle, though women often tend goats and sheep. Milking and dairy operations are normally performed by women, though men sometimes participate, especially in Adamawa.

The sedentary Fulani and Tukulor inhabit permanent villages or towns and occupy either thatched mud dwellings of the cone-cylinder type or occasionally rectangular houses with walls of sun-dried brick, flat terrace roofs, and an interior courtyard. The pastoral Fulani wander in nomadic bands and occupy only temporary camps consisting of a cluster of huts of dismountable and portable construction commonly surrounded by a thorn hedge. The dwellings are round in ground plan and of either hemispherical or beehive shape, with a framework of poles covered with mats, leaves, or grass. All Fulani practice circumcision, but clitoridectomy is reported only for the inhabitants of Fouta Djalon, Kita, and Liptako and is specifically denied for the Tukulor and the Fulani of Adamawa and Sokoto. Neither headhunting nor cannibalism prevails.

Marriage always involves a bride-price in cattle, but the amount tends to be small among the pastoral Fulani. The latter also reflect their Senegambian affiliations, and contrast with most Moslems, in their lack of insistence upon premarital chastity in girls. Polygyny prevails universally in the nonsororal form, and the household unit is a polygynous rather than an extended family. The co-wives have separate huts, and the husband rotates among them. Strongly Islamized sedentary Fulani favor unions with a father's brother's daughter, but all others proscribe marriage with a parallel cousin, regarding a cross-cousin as the ideal spouse. This preference is correlated with cousin terminology of the Iroquois type, at least in Adamawa and Fouta Djalon. The levirate rule prevails for secondary marriages, but only for the widow of an elder brother.

Residence is patrilocal, but among the pastoral Fulani a wife usually returns to her parental home for the birth of her first child and remains there until it is weaned. Descent is patrilineal, with a segmentary lineage system. Exogamy characterizes at least the lineages of relatively shallow depth, except where parallel-cousin marriage has been adopted. A nomadic band normally assumes the form of an exogamous patriclan. The pastoral Fulani are egalitarian except for wealth distinctions and slavery. Sedentary groups, however, are commonly stratified into nobles, commoners, serfs, slaves, and endogamous castes of *griots* and artisans.

Selected Bibliography

Coutouly, F. de. La famille, les fiançailles et le mariage chez les Peuls du Liptako. *RETP*, 4:259–270. 1923.

———. Les populations du cercle de Dori. *BCEHS*, 6:269–301, 471–496, 637–671. 1923. [Liptako].

Delafosse, M. *Haut-Sénégal-Niger*. 3 vols. Paris, 1912.

Durand, O. Moeurs et institutions d'une famille peule du cercle de Pita. *BCEHS*, 12:1–85. 1929. [Fouta Djalon].

Forde, D., and R. Scott. *The Native Economies of Nigeria*. London, 1946.

Froelich, J. C. Le commandement et l'organisation sociale chez les Foulbé de l'Adamaoua. *EC*, 45–46:1–91. 1954.

Gaalon, R. de. Coutume peul. *PCEHS*, ser. A, 8:239–260. 1939. [Liptako].

Greenberg, J. H. Studies in African Linguistic Classification. *SWJA*, 5:190–198. 1949.

Hopen, C. E. *The Pastoral Fulbe Family in Gwandu*. London, 1958. [Sokoto].

Kane, A. S. Coutume civile et pénale toucouleur. *PCEHS*, ser. A, 8:55–115. 1939.

Lafont. Coutume toucouleur. *PCEHS*, ser. A, 9:247–301. 1939.

Lavergne de Tressan, M. de. Inventaire linguistique de l'Afrique Occidentale Française et du Togo. *MIFAN*, 30:1–241. 1953.

Meek, C. K. *The Northern Tribes of Nigeria*. 2 vols. London, 1925.

Monteil, C. *Djénné*. Paris, 1932. [Masina].

Pfeffer, G. Die Djafun-Bororo. *ZE*, 68:150–196. 1936. [Adamawa].

Rohlfs, G. *Quer durch Afrika*, vol. 2. Liepzig, 1875. [Bauchi].

Sarrazin, H. *Races humaines du Soudan Français*. Chambéry, 1901.

Sidibé, M. La famille chez les Foula du Birgo, du Fouladougou Arbala et du Fouladougou Saboula. *BCEHS*, 18:462–539. 1935. [Kita].

St. Croix, F. E. de. *The Fulani of Northern Nigeria*. Lagos, 1945. [Sokoto].

Stenning, D. J. Household Viability among the Pastoral Fulani. *Cambridge Papers in Social Anthropology*, 1:92–119. 1958. [Bauchi].

Tauxier, L. *Le noir du Soudan*. Paris, 1912. [Fulani of the Mossi country].

———. *Moeurs et histoire des Peuls*. Paris, 1937. [Fouta Djalon and Masina].

Urvoy, T. *Petit atlas ethno-démographique du Soudan*. Paris, 1942.

Vieillard, G. Notes sur les coutumes des Peuls au Fouta Djallon. *PCEHS*, ser. A, 11:1–127. 1939.

———. Notes sur les Peuls du Fouta-Djallon. *BIFAN*, 2:95–210. 1940.

Westermann, D. *Geschichte Afrikas.* Köln, 1952.

Wilson-Haffenden, R. J. Ethnological Notes on the Shuwalbe Group of Bororo Fulani. *JRAI*, 57:275–293. 1925. [Sokoto].

———. *The Red Men of Nigeria.* London, 1930. [Sokoto].

Wolff, K. Die Entstehung der frühen Ful-Staaten in Senegambien. *BGVT*, pp. 435–445. 1950.

KEY TO BIBLIOGRAPHICAL ABBREVIATIONS

In the bibliographies at the end of the several chapters, important or recurrent periodicals, series, and symposia are indicated by abbreviations in order to conserve space. The complete references are listed below according to the alphabetical order of the symbols employed.

AA   *American Anthropologist*, new series. New York, Lancaster, and Menasha.
AAE   *Archivio per l'Antropologia e la Etnologia*. Firenze.
AB   *Archives Berbères*. Paris.
AFA   *Archiv für Anthropologie*. Braunschweig.
AHKI   *Abhandlungen des Hamburgischen Kolonialinstituts*. Hamburg.
AL   *Annales Lateranensi*. Città del Vaticano.
AM   *Archives Marocaines*. Paris.
AMCB   *Annales du Musée du Congo Belge, Ethnographie et Anthropologie*. Bruxelles.
AMCBE   *Annales du Musée du Congo Belge, Sciences de l'Homme, Ethnologie*. Tervuren.
AMRCB   *Annales du Musée Royal du Congo Belge, Sciences de l'Homme, Monographies Ethnographiques*. Tervuren.
APS   *African Political Systems*, ed. M. Fortes and E. E. Evans-Pritchard. London, 1950.
AQ   *Anthropological Quarterly*, new series. Washington.
AS   *African Studies*. Johannesburg.
ASKM   *African Systems of Kinship and Marriage*, ed. A. R. Radcliffe-Brown and D. Forde. London, 1950.
AV   *Archiv für Völkerkunde*. Wien.
BA   *Baessler-Archiv*. Berlin and Leipzig.
BAM   *Bulletin de l'Académie Malgache*. Tananarive.
BC   *Bibliothèque Congo*. Bruxelles.
BCEHS   *Bulletin du Comité d'Études Historiques et Scientifiques de l'Afrique Occidentale Française*. Paris.
BCGP   *Boletim Cultural da Guiné Portuguesa*. Bissau.
BGVT   *Beiträge zur Gesellungs- und Völkerwissenschaft Professor Dr. Richard Thurnwald zu seinem achtzigsten Geburtstag gewidmet*. Berlin, 1950.
BIEC   *Bulletin de l'Institut d'Études Centrafricaines*. Brazzaville.
BIFAN   *Bulletin de l'Institut Français d'Afrique Noire*. Paris and Dakar.
BIFSH   *Bulletin de l'Institut Français d'Afrique Noire, Série B, Sciences Humaines*. Dakar.
BJIDC   *Bulletin des Juridictions Indigènes et du Droit Coutumier Congolais*. Elisabethville.
BKUG   *Beiträge zur Kultur- und Universalgeschichte*. Leipzig.
BS   *Bantu Studies*. Johannesburg.

BSAP	*Bulletin de la Société d'Anthropologie de Paris.* Paris.
BSG	*Bulletin de la Société de Géographie.* Paris.
BSRBG	*Bulletin de la Société Royale Belge de Géographie.* Bruxelles.
BSRC	*Bulletin de la Société des Recherches Congolaises.* Brazzaville.
BTSA	*The Bantu Tribes of South Africa,* ed. A. M. Duggan-Cronin. Kimberley.
CCPP	*Cooperation and Competition among Primitive Peoples,* ed. M. Mead. New York, 1937.
CME	*Collection de Monographies Ethnographiques.* Bruxelles.
CRS	*Colonial Office, Colonial Research Studies.* London.
CSAS	*Communications from the School of African Studies, University of Capetown.* Cape Town.
DNAEP	*Union of South Africa, Department of Native Affairs Ethnological Publications.* Pretoria.
EC	*Études Camerounaises.* Douala.
EN	*Ethnologisches Notizblatt.* Berlin.
ER	*Das Eingeborenenrecht,* ed. E. Schultz-Ewerth and L. Adam. Stuttgart.
ESEJ	*Études de Sociologie et d'Ethnologie Juridiques.* Paris.
FL	*Folk-Lore.* London.
FMAS	*Field Museum of Natural History Anthropological Series.* Chicago.
GJ	*Geographical Journal.* London.
GSA	*General Series in Anthropology.* Menasha.
HAS	*Harvard African Studies.* Cambridge.
JAS	*Journal of the [Royal] African Society.* London.
JMV	*Jahrbuch des [Städtischen] Museums für Völkerkunde.* Leipzig.
JRAI	*Journal of the [Royal] Anthropological Institute.* London.
JRGS	*Journal of the Royal Geographical Society.* London.
JSA	*Journal de la Société des Africanistes.* Paris.
KO	*Kongo-Overzee.* Antwerpen.
MAGW	*Mitteilungen der Anthropologischen Gesellschaft in Wien.* Wien.
MC	*Les Missions Catholiques.* Lyon.
MDS	*Mitteilungen aus den Deutschen Schutzgebieten.* Berlin.
MDSE	*Mitteilungen aus den Deutschen Schutzgebieten, Ergänzungshefte.* Berlin.
MGGH	*Mitteilungen der Geographischen Gesellschaft zu Hamburg.* Hamburg.
MGGJ	*Mitteilungen der Geographischen Gesellschaft zu Jena.* Jena.
MGGW	*Mitteilungen der Geographischen Gesellschaft zu Wien.* Wien.
MIAI	*Memoranda of the International African Institute.* London.
MIEC	*Mémoires de l'Institut d'Études Centrafricaines.* Brazzaville.
MIFAN	*Mémoires de l'Institut Français d'Afrique Noire.* Paris and Dakar.
MIFCC	*Mémoires de l'Institut Français d'Afrique Noire, Centre du Cameroun, Série Populations.* Douala.
MIRCB	*Mémoires de l'Institut Royal Colonial Belge, Section des Sciences Morales et Politiques.* Bruxelles.
MIRCQ	*Mémoires de l'Institut Royal Colonial Belge, Section des Sciences Morales et Politiques,* quarto series. Bruxelles.
MSA	*Monographs on Social Anthropology, London School of Economics and Political Science.* London.
MSAP	*Mémoires de la Société d'Anthropologie de Paris.* Paris.
MSOS	*Mitteilungen des Seminars für Orientalische Sprachen.* Berlin.
NADA	*Southern Rhodesia Native Affairs Department Annual.* Salisbury.
NTSWA	*Native Tribes of South-West Africa.* Cape Town, 1928.

PCAC	*Publications of the Catholic Anthropological Conference.* Washington.
PCEHS	*Publications du Comité d'Études Historiques et Scientifiques de l'Afrique Occidentale Française.* Paris.
PEMS	*Publications of the Ethnographic Museum of Sweden.* Lund.
PM	*Petermanns Mitteilungen.* Gotha.
PME	*Petermanns Mitteilungen, Ergänzungshefte.* Gotha.
PPM	*Papers of the Peabody Museum of American Archaeology and Ethnology, Harvard University.* Cambridge.
PRGS	*Proceedings of the Royal Geographical Society.* London.
PRSE	*Proceedings of the Royal Society of Edinburgh.* Edinburgh.
RAIOC	*Royal Anthropological Institute Occasional Papers.* London.
RC	*Revue Congolaise.* Bruxelles.
RCD	*Renseignements Coloniaux et Documents publiés par le Comité de l'Afrique Française et le Comité du Maroc.* Paris. (Published as supplements in *Bulletin du Comité de l'Afrique Française* and its continuation, *L'Afrique Française,* to which the volume numbers refer).
RE	*Revue d'Ethnographie.* Paris.
REES	*Revue des Études Ethnographiques et Sociologiques.* Paris.
RES	*Revue d'Ethnographie et de Sociologie.* Paris.
RETP	*Revue d'Ethnographie et des Traditions Populaires.* Paris.
REVAO	*Rechtsverhältnisse von eingeborenen Völkern in Afrika und Ozeanien,* ed. S. R. Steinmetz. Berlin, 1903.
RIS	*Revue de l'Institut de Sociologie, Instituts Solvay.* Bruxelles.
RLJ	*Rhodes-Livingstone Journal.* Lusaka.
RLP	*Rhodes-Livingstone Papers.* Livingstone and Cape Town.
RSE	*Rassegna di Studi Etiopici.* Roma.
SAJS	*South African Journal of Science.* Cape Town.
SEU	*Studia Ethnographica Upsaliensia.* Uppsala.
SGM	*Scottish Geographical Magazine.* Edinburgh.
SLS	*Sierra Leone Studies.* Freetown.
SNR	*Sudan Notes and Records.* Khartoum.
SS	*Social Structure,* ed. M. Fortes. Oxford, 1949.
STBCA	*Seven Tribes of British Central Africa,* ed. E. Colson and M. Gluckman. London, 1951.
SV	*Studien zur Völkerkunde.* Leipzig.
SWJA	*Southwestern Journal of Anthropology.* Albuquerque.
TMIE	*Travaux et Mémoires de l'Institut d'Ethnologie.* Paris.
TNR	*Tanganyika Notes and Records.* Dar es Salaam.
UJ	*Uganda Journal.* Kampala.
VSVM	*Veröffentlichungen der Städtischen Völker-Museum.* Frankfurt am Main.
VTM	*Villes et Tribus du Maroc.* Paris.
WBKL	*Wiener Beiträge zur Kulturgeschichte und Linguistik.* Wien.
ZE	*Zeitschrift für Ethnologie.* Berlin.
ZGE	*Zeitschrift der Gesellschaft für Erdkunde.* Berlin.
ZVR	*Zeitschrift für Vergleichende Rechtswissenschaft.* Stuttgart.

INDEX OF TRIBAL NAMES

All tribes and peoples mentioned in the text, including synonymous names, are listed below in alphabetical order. For ready reference, each name is followed by numbers, usually in pairs. The number preceding the colon refers to the chapter in which the tribe is mentioned, and the second figure gives the numerical position which it occupies in the classified list of tribes contained in the chapter.

Aandonga, 48:1
Ababda, 40:1
Ababua, 36:2
Abagwena, 49:1
Abaha, 45:3
Abahela, 45:6
Abaidat, 52:30
Abaiyonga, 31:8
Abaka, 28:12
Abalempa, 51:15
Abananzwa, 49:1
Abangba, 28:15
Abango, 36:3
Abani, 31:8
Abanyai, 49:1
Abarambo, 29:13
Abashabi, 49:1
Abashankwe, 49:2
Abaskul, 41:7
Abatonga, 45:5
Abaw, 35:4
Abayong, 31:8
Abbe, 32:24
Abdullab, 54:16
Abe, 32:24
Abewa, 31:18
Abgal, 41:4
Abi, 32:24
Abid, 52:30
Abidji, 32:27
Abine, 31:8
Abire, 29:30
Abisa, 38:35
Abisinga, 28:22

Abo, 13:23, 35:4
Abol, 20:2
Abong, 13:23
Abrignon, 33:1
Abrinyo, 33:1
Abriwi, 33:1
Abron, 32:21
Abuan, 31:4
Abu Derreg, 17:6
Abuguru, 29:15
Abure, 32:28
Abu Rof, 54:16
Abu Semen, 17:18
Aby, 32:4
Achawa, 38:61
Achbar, 15:9
Ache, 13:61
Acheche, 52:35
Acheron, 20:4
Achewa, 38:47
Achifawa, 13:16
Achikouya, 35:14
Achikunda, 38:49
Achipeta, 38:47
Achlo, 32:12
Acholi, 43:10
Achwabo, 38:48
Acilowe, 38:56
Aculo, 12:19
Ada, 13:15, 31:20, 32:1
Adamawa, 55:1
Adampa, 32:1
Adangme, 32:1

Adara, 13:15
Adarawa, 17:37
Adaymat, 34:6
Adda, 31:26
Adea, 25:2
Adele, 32:7
Adeli, 32:7
Aderaoua, 17:37
Adidji, 32:27
Adigo, 39:6
Adija, 35:1
Adio, 29:25
Adioukrou, 32:25
Adja, 32:3
Adjao, 38:61
Adjer, 11:10
Adjeur, 15:23, 53:5
Adjolo, 12:19
Adjumba, 35:12
Adong, 13:18
Adsawa, 38:61
Adsoa, 38:61
Aduma, 35:10
Adun, 31:5
Afao, 31:9
Afar, 41:1
Afatime, 32:10
Afawa, 13:50
Afema, 32:28
Afitti, 19:6
Afo, 31:9
Afu, 31:9
Afusare, 13:1
Afutu, 32:4

Agala, 31:13
Agaro, 21:3
Agatu, 31:13
Agau, 9:8, 22
Agaumeder, 22:2
Agbegnyau, 32:20
Agbisherea, 31:4
Age, 30:13
Aghbar, 15:19
Aghem, 30:14
Agi, 28:13
Aglu, 15:22
Agnagan, 32:9
Agnamkpase, 32:14
Agni, 32:17
Agoi, 31:8
Agolik, 13:18
Agonglin, 32:3
Agwa, 32:20
Agwaaguna, 31:8
Agyukru, 32:25
Ahaggaren, 15:23, 53:1
Ahaju, 31:3
Ahal Srif, 52:17
Ahamda, 54:16
Ahanta, 32:18
Ahel Aglou, 15:22
Ahel Ajur, 52:26
Ahel Othman, 52:26
Ahel Sahel, 15:22
Ahenklo, 32:14
Ahioko, 38:25

Ahl Feqqous, 15:26
Ahlo, 32:12
Ahl Tichit, 52:41
Ahsen, 52:24
Aiacka, 38:18
Aid Djemel, 15:22
Aike, 13:21
Ainamwanga,
  46:13
Ain Madhi, 52:22
Aioko, 38:25
Aissa, 52:32
Aita, 52:16
Ait Atta, 15:1
Ait Ba Amran,
  15:22
Ait Bella, 15:22
Ait Brahim, 15:22
Ait Chokhman,
  15:2
Ait Dades, 15:2
Ait Djagut, 15:22
Ait Djerrar, 15:19
Ait Iafelman, 15:2
Ait Jussa, 15:22
Ait Khebbache,
  15:24
Ait Lahsen, 15:22
Ait Massat, 15:9
Ait Medjat, 15:22
Ait Moussa ou Ali,
  15:22
Ait Ndhir, 15:2
Ait Oureggou,
  15:26
Ait Oussa, 15:22
Ait Sahel, 15:22
Ait Seddrat, 15:3
Ait Seghrouchen,
  15:2
Ait Seri, 15:2
Ait Ssimig, 15:9
Ait Tinerst, 15:26
Ait u Mribet,
  52:36
Ait Warain, 15:27
Ait Yahia, 15:1
Ait Yemel, 15:22
Ait Youssi, 15:2
Ait Zerri, 15:3
Aiza, 38:35

Aizangbe, 32:3
Aizi, 32:25
Aizo, 32:3
Aja, 28:3
Ajawa, 13:50,
  38:61
Ajiba, 43:2
Ajie, 43:20
Ajjer, 15:23, 53:5
Ajukru, 32:25
Ajur, 52:26
Ajuran, 41:4
Ajure, 13:5
Aka, 8:4
Akabu, 32:13
Akaju, 31:3
Akalai, 36:13
Akale, 29:27
Akamba, 44:2
Akanda, 31:18,
  31:26
Akapless, 32:28
Akari, 29:27
Akasele, 12:30
Akaza, 16:4
Akebu, 32:13
Akelle, 36:13
Akhsas, 15:22
Akikuyu, 44:3
Akka, 8:4
Akkele-Guzai, 22:7
Akoa, 8:1
Akoko, 31:24,
  31:28
Akonto, 13:3
Akounga, 28:4
Akpafu, 32:12
Akpenu, 32:11
Akposo, 32:8
Akpoto, 31:13
Akripon, 32:4
Akum, 43:31
Akunakuna, 31:8
Akunga, 28:4
Akurumba, 12:30
Akwahu, 32:16
Akwamu, 32:16
Akwapim, 32:16
Akweya, 31:11
Akye, 32:19
Akyem, 32:16

Ala, 42:4
Alaba, 25:2
Alada, 25:3
Aladia, 32:26
Alago, 31:10
Alagya, 32:26
Alawa, 24:1
Alendu, 28:8
Alga, 23:7
Algerians, 52:1
Ali, 17:8
Allaba, 25:2
Alladians, 32:26
Alleira, 20:2
Allouch, 52:41
Allush, 52:41
Alomwe, 38:55
Alonda, 38:41
Aloro, 43:11
Alua, 43:11
Aluena, 38:28
Alui, 47:4
Alulu, 43:11
Alunda, 37:14
Alungu, 38:42
Alur, 43:11
Aluyi, 47:4
Alwer, 38:20
Amadi, 29:13
Amago, 29:13
Amakosa, 50:4
Amalozwi, 49:6
Amam, 31:9
Amambwe, 38:42
Amanaya, 32:28
Amandabele, 50:8
Amap, 13:12
Amapondo, 50:1
Amar, 23:1, 52:8
Amara, 23:7
Amarar, 40:2
Amarcocche, 23:1
Amarna, 54:16
Amarro, 23:7
Amaswazi, 50:2
Amaxosa, 50:4
Amazulu, 50:5
Amba, 36:1
Ambaca, 38:7
Ambala, 38:14
Ambamba, 36:14

Ambaquista, 38:7
Ambete, 35:10
Ambo, 38:39, 48:1
Amboella, 38:30
Amboim, 38:11
Ambuela, 38:30
Ambuin, 38:11
Ambunda, 38:29
Ambundu, 38:7,
  38:19
Ambuun, 38:19
Amer, 40:3
Amhara, 22:1
Amiangba, 28:15
Amkwe, 8:11
Ammur, 23:1
Amo, 13:12
Amput, 38:24
Amubenge, 36:4
Amwimbe, 44:4
Ana, 31:25
Anag, 19:1
Anago, 31:27
Anaguta, 13:1
Anakaza, 16:4
Anang, 31:4
Ancheya, 38:47
Andembu, 38:7,
  38:31
Andombe, 48:5
Andoni, 31:4
Andorobo, 10:2
Andri, 28:13
Andulo, 48:4
Andumbo, 35:10
Anecho, 32:6
Anenga, 35:12
Anfillo, 21:9
Angad, 52:1
Angas, 13:33
Angassawa, 13:33
Angbandi, 29:31
Anglo, 32:2
Angoni, 50
Angul, 38:20
Anguru, 38:56
Ania, 42:4
Aniramba, 46:2
Anjang, 31:1
Anjera, 52:17
Ankutshu, 37:10

Ankwe, 13:33
Anna, 16:2, 17:37
Anno, 12:44
Ano, 32:17
Antaimoro, 27:1
Antaimorona, 27:1
Antaisaka, 27:1
Antaiva, 27:10
Antambahoaka, 27:1
Antambongo, 27:8
Antanala, 27:10
Antandroy, 27:2
Antankarana, 27:8
Antankay, 27:10
Antanosy, 27:2
Antessar, 15:23, 53:2
Antiboina, 27:8
Antifasina, 27:1
Antifasy, 27:1
Antifiherena, 27:8
Antimailaka, 27:8
Antimanambondro, 27:1
Antimaraka, 27:8
Antimena, 27:8
Antimerina, 27:7
Antimilanja, 27:8
Antisihanaka, 27:8
Anuak, 21:1
Anufo, 12:41
Anyana, 32:9
Anyang, 31:1
Anyanja, 38:51
Anyassa, 38:52
Anyi, 32:17
Aogo, 29:13
Aouaka, 28:4
Aowin, 32:17
Apambia, 29:13
Apfourou, 36:3
Apingi, 35:13
Apinyi, 35:13
Apollonians, 32:28
Apono, 35:13
Arabs, 42, 54
Arad, 52:2
Arafa, 52:30
Arago, 31:10
Aragya, 32:26

Arbore, 25:4
Are, 23:1
Aregwa, 13:7
Aretou, 28:4
Ari, 23:1, 32:27
Arib, 52:36
Arichin, 32:17
Arindrano, 27:4
Arna, 17:37
Arom, 43:3
Aronda, 38:41
Arosien, 52:36
Arouissiin, 52:36
Arringeu, 13:17
Arro, 23:1
Arsi, 42:1
Aruat, 52:22
Aruisin, 52:36
Arun, 31:5
Arunda, 37:14
Aruro, 23:7
Arus, 52:17
Arusha, 43:31
Arusi, 42:1
Arusin, 52:36
Asa, 10:2
Asandeh, 29:14
Asango, 35:11
Asante, 32:18
Asaye, 32:17
Asben, 15:23, 53:3
Asegedzu, 39:16
Asena, 38:53
Asenga, 38:43
Asen-Twifo, 32:18
Aser, 11:10
Asergiin, 15:22
Ashaku, 13:27
Ashango, 35:11
Ashanti, 32:18
Ashar, 53:5
Ashogo, 35:13
Asiga, 31:8
Asikaso, 32:17
Asimba, 35:13
Asna, 17:37
Asoko, 32:28
Asolio, 13:18
Asolongo, 38:1
Assale, 54:20
Assini, 32:28

Assongo, 35:11
Asu, 44:5
Asuamara, 32:17
Atagara, 31:14
Ataka, 13:18
Atakpame, 31:25
Atam, 31:3
Atauna, 52:9
Atayfat, 54:14
Atbai, 40:4
Atbara, 40:4
Ategue, 36:14
Atembu, 38:7
Aten, 13:4
Atharaka, 44:4
Atjuti, 32:9
Atonga, 45:5
Atsam, 13:7
Atscholi, 43:10
Atshefa, 13:16
Atsokwe, 38:25
Atsuku, 13:27
Atta, 15:1
Attaqua, 9:2
Attia, 52:2
Attie, 32:19
Atwot, 43:7
Atxuabo, 38:48
Atyo, 35:14
Atyode, 32:9
Atyulo, 12:19
Atyuti, 32:9
Auen, 9:8
Auijja, 41:4
Aulad Hamayd, 54:2
Aulihan, 41:10
Aulliminden, 15:23, 53:4
Aulopo, 33:1
Aun, 62:14
Auni, 9:12
Aushi, 38:33
Auyokawa, 17:22
Avare, 28:10
Avatime, 32:10
Avausi, 38:33
Avekwom, 32:29
Avikam, 32:29
Avukaya, 28:9
Awaka, 28:4

Awal, 41:5
Awamba, 36:1
Awamra, 54:16
Awaqir, 53:30
Awasira, 38:44
Awawa, 46:13
Awawar, 22:2
Awe, 16:2
Awellimiden, 15:23, 53:4
Awemba, 38:24
Awerri, 31:23
Awisa, 38:35
Awiya, 22:2
Awori, 31:27
Aworo, 31:26
Awuna, 12:9
Awunlen, 34:11
Awutu, 32:4
Axumites, 22
Ayahu, 32:20
Ayamat, 34:6
Ayembe, 38:34
Ayesegn, 32:14
Ayo, 38:61
Ayob, 13:21
Ayu, 13:21
Azande, 29:14
Azanians, 26
Azena, 17:37
Azimba, 38:55
Azjer, 15:23, 53:5
Azna, 17:37
Azouafit, 15:22
Azuafidi, 15:22

Baamba, 31:1
Baati, 36:4
Baba, 13:23, 30:8
Babadjou, 30:1
Babagani, 37:15
Babale, 36:22
Babalia, 17:16
Babamba, 36:14, 38:1
Babangi, 36:3, 36:8
Babango, 36:22
Babanki, 30:4
Babati, 36:4
Babelu, 28:19
Babemba, 38:34

Babembe, 38:3
Babenga, 8:1
Babeo, 36:2
Babessi, 30:8
Babeyru, 28:19,
   36:6
Babila, 36:6
Babile, 42:4
Babili, 36:6
Babimbi, 35:3
Babindi, 37:15
Babindji, 38:21
Babinga, 8:1
Babinja, 36:5
Babinza, 36:5
Babira, 36:6
Babirwa, 51:14
Babisa, 38:35
Baboa, 36:2
Baboma, 38:23
Babong, 35:4
Babonga, 8:1
Babouendi, 38:3
Babouissi, 35:11
Babounda, 38:19
Babudja, 49:5
Babudjue, 38:36
Babudschu, 30:1
Babudu, 36:9
Babui, 38:36
Babukur, 29:15
Babulli, 42:4
Babuma, 38:23
Babumbu, 36:15
Babunda, 38:19
Babungo, 30:8
Babur, 13:36
Baburu, 36:6
Babute, 29:33
Babvanuma, 36:25
Babwa, 36:2
Babwendi, 38:3
Babwile, 38:45
Babwissi, 35:11
Babwizi, 36:1
Bacha, 10:4
Bachada, 23:1
Bachama, 13:34
Bachapin, 51:12
Baciada, 23:1
Bachiga, 45:2

Bachila, 38:44
Bachilangue, 37:13
Bachilela, 38:22
Bachoko, 38:25
Bacongo, 38:1
Bacouba, 38:21
Bacuisso, 9:7
Bacusu, 37:11
Badagri, 31:27
Badawa, 13:11
Badditu, 23:7
Bade, 17:27
Badia, 38:23
Badian, 34:11
Badiaranke, 34:11
Badiele, 8:1
Badinga, 38:20
Baditu, 23:7
Badjo, 28:14
Badjok, 38:25
Badjouni, 39:12
Badjue, 36:10
Badondo, 38:3
Baduma, 35:10
Badyaranke, 34:11
Badzing, 38:20
Baele, 16:2
Baenya, 36:31
Baer, 43:6
Bafang, 30:1
Bafaw, 35:4
Bafia, 30:2
Bafiote, 38:4
Bafo, 35:4
Bafourou, 36:3
Bafoussam, 30:1
Bafreng, 30:4
Bafulero, 45:1
Bafumbum, 30:3
Bafungwi, 49:5
Bafut, 30:4
Bafute, 29:33
Baga, 34:1
Bagam, 30:1
Baganda, 45:9
Bagane, 11:4
Bagata, 23:1
Bagbira, 36:6
Bagengele, 36:31
Bageshu, 45:16

Baggara, 54
Bagirmi, 17:12
Bagish, 45:16
Bagiuni, 39:12
Bagnoun, 34:3
Bago, 34:1
Bagoko, 35:3
Bagongo, 38:22
Bagua, 38:37
Baguana, 38:14
Baguielli, 8:1
Bagunda, 28:24,
   36:26
Baham, 30:1
Bahamba, 36:1,
   37:11
Bahanga, 45:21
Bahariya, 52.3
Bahavu, 45:1
Bahenga, 38:54
Bahera, 49:6
Bahere, 51:15
Bahima, 45
Baholo, 38:6
Baholoholo, 38:37
Bahom, 30:5
Bahoumbou, 36:14
Bahuana, 38:14
Bahuku, 28:16
Bahumbu, 38:14
Bahunde, 45:4
Bahuruthse, 51:1
Bahushi, 38:33
Bahutu, 45
Bai, 13:58, 28:6,
   29:30, 38:23
Baila, 47:1
Bailundu, 48:4
Bainuk, 34:3
Baja, 29:20
Bajabili, 42:4
Bajanja, 49:6
Bajanzi, 38:24
Baji, 35:6
Bajia, 38:23
Bajoni, 39:12
Baju, 13:18
Bajun, 39:12
Baka, 28:12
Bakaa, 49:1
Bakahonde, 38:38

Bakaka, 35:4
Bakalahari, 51:2
Bakalai, 36:13
Bakalanga, 38:36
Bakale, 36:13
Bakamba, 38:3
Bakango, 36:2
Bakanike, 35:10
Bakaonde, 38:38
Bakare, 29:27
Bakedi, 43:22
Bakela, 37:3
Bakelle, 36:13
Bakem, 35:4
Bakene, 45:13
Bakerewe, 45:11
Baketa, 37:15
Bakgatla, 51:3
Bakioko, 38:25
Bakitaro, 45:12
Bakka, 17:6
Bako, 23:1
Bakoa, 8:1
Bakogo, 35:6
Bakoko, 35:3
Bakola, 8:1
Bakolle, 35:5
Bakondjo, 45:5
Bakone, 33:1
Bakongo, 38:1,
   38:22
Bakoroka, 9:7
Bakosi, 35:4
Bakota, 36:14
Bakougni, 38:2
Bakoumou, 36:15
Bakoussou, 37:11
Bakoutou, 37:8
Bakouya, 8:1
Bakpele, 32:12
Bakuba, 38:21
Bakuele, 36:10
Bakuese, 38:12
Bakulia, 45:17
Bakum, 36:12
Bakumbu, 36:15
Bakumu, 36:15
Bakunda, 38:36
Bakundu, 35:6
Bakunya, 38:2
Bakutsu, 37:4

Bakutu, 37:8
Bakwange, 36:31
Bakwe, 33:1
Bakwedi, 35:5
Bakwele, 35:5
Bakwena, 51:4
Bakwese, 38:12
Bakwili, 36:10
Bakwiri, 35:5
Bakxalaxadi, 51:2
Bakxatla, 51:3
Bakyiga, 45:2
Balala, 38:39
Balali, 35:14
Balamba, 38:40
Balanga, 37:3
Balante, 34:2
Balda, 13:39
Bale, 28:8, 36:8
Balega, 28:8
Balegga, 36:28
Baleka, 36:21
Balemba, 51:15
Balembe, 36:28
Balemi, 32:12
Balendu, 28:8
Balenge, 35:9
Balengora, 36:16
Balenje, 47:3
Balesa, 28:16, 38:23
Balesse, 28:16
Bali, 30:6, 36:22
Balika, 36:17
Balinga, 37:8
Balissi, 28:16
Ballante, 34:2
Ballohi, 36:3
Ballue, 35:6
Balochasi, 38:26
Baloi, 36:3
Balojash, 38:26
Baloki, 36:24
Baloli, 38:20
Balolo, 37:6
Balom, 30:2
Balombo, 35:11
Balon, 35:4
Balonda, 37:14, 38:41
Balondo, 35:4, 48:7
Balong, 35:4

Balongo, 35:6
Balori, 38:20
Balouba, 37:12
Baloumbo, 35:11
Baloundou, 37:14
Balovale, 38:28
Balovedu, 51:5
Balozwe, 49:6
Balu, 30:6
Balua, 38:13
Balue, 35:6
Balui, 36:3
Baluimbi, 38:27
Balukolwe, 47:5
Balula, 38:18
Balulu, 36:21
Balumbu, 35:11, 38:36
Balundu, 35:6
Balung, 35:4
Balunga, 37:12
Baluva, 37:12
Baluwa, 38:13
Bamakoma, 47:7
Bamanga, 28:21
Bamangala, 36:24
Bamangwato, 51:7
Bamanyeka, 49:3
Bamasasa, 47:6
Bamaschi, 47:7
Bamba, 36:1, 38:1
Bambala, 38:14, 38:21
Bambamba, 36:14
Bambanga, 28:21
Bambao, 36:14
Bambare, 11:1
Bambaro, 13:11
Bambata, 38:1
Bambe, 43:28
Bamberawa, 13:11
Bambete, 35:10
Bamboko, 35:5
Bambole, 37:7
Bambuba, 28:16
Bambugu, 11:8
Bambuku, 35:5
Bambuli, 37:3
Bambunda, 38:19
Bambuti, 8:4
Bambuyu, 38:36

Bambwela, 47:5
Bamekom, 30:5
Bamenda, 30:4
Bamendjou, 30:1
Bamendzo, 30:1
Bamessi, 30:8
Bamessing, 30:8
Bamfono, 35:14
Bamfumungu, 35:14
Bamileke, 30:1
Bamlunda, 37:14
Bamongo, 37:6
Bamouba, 28:16
Bamoum, 30:7
Bampangu, 38:1
Bamputu, 38:24
Bamrane, 15:22
Bamum, 30:7
Bamungo, 30:8
Bamwenya, 51:15
Bana, 13:40, 23:1, 29:8
Banabuddu, 36:9
Banadoula, 17:6
Banaha, 35:8
Banana, 29:8
Banande, 45:5
Banano, 48:4
Banda, 29:16
Bandaka, 36:22
Bandala, 54:4
Bandassa, 36:14
Bandawa, 13:51
Bandempo, 38:7, 38:31
Bandeng, 30:4
Bandja, 32:23
Bandjabi, 35:10
Bandjali, 36:25
Bandjambi, 36:14
Bandjo, 29:22
Bandjoun, 30:1
Bandombe, 48:5
Bandomo, 36:14
Bandschu, 30:1
Bandula, 17:6
Bandumbo, 35:10
Bandya, 29:14, 48:1
Bandzadi, 38:20
Bandzala, 38:20

Bane, 36:11
Baneka, 35:4
Banen, 30:9
Banend, 30:9
Banfumu, 35:14
Banfunuka, 35:14
Banga, 13:59
Bangala, 36:24, 38:10
Bangandu, 29:17, 37:7
Bangangoulou, 35:14
Bangangte, 30:1
Bangangtu, 29:17
Bangawa, 13:8
Bangba, 28:15, 36:2
Bangbele, 28:23
Bange, 36:4
Bangela, 38:10
Bangelima, 36:2
Banghie, 36:14
Bangi, 36:3
Bangili, 36:3, 36:29
Bangiri, 36:3
Bango, 36:8, 38:36
Bangobango, 38:36
Bangodi, 38:20
Bangoli, 38:20
Bangombe, 37:8
Bangomo, 36:13
Bangone, 36:13
Bangongo, 38:21, 38:15
Bangu, 30:1
Banguie, 36:14
Bangulu, 38:20
Bangumbi, 48:7
Bangwa, 30:1
Bangwaketse, 51:6
Bangwe, 36:13
Banhun, 34:3
Bani, 30:6
Banianeka, 48:8
Banianga, 45:4
Banjadi, 38:20
Banjangi, 31:1
Bankalawa, 13:11
Bankon, 35:4
Bankundu, 37:9
Bankusu, 37:10

Bankutshu, 37:4
Bankutsu, 37:10
Bankutu, 37:10
Banna, 23:1
Banoh, 35:8
Banoko, 35:8
Bansaw, 30:10
Banso, 30:10
Bantu, 30, 35–39,
    44–51
Banua, 33:3
Banun, 30:7
Banunu, 35:14
Banyabungu, 45:1
Banyai, 49:1
Banyaisanga, 45:15
Banyamwezi, 46:9
Banyang, 31:1
Banyankole, 45:6
Banyari, 36:25
Banyaruanda, 45:7
Banyika, 46:12
Banyin, 30:9
Banyaro, 45:12
Banyubi, 49:1
Banyun, 34:3
Banza, 29:18
Banzari, 38:20
Banziri, 29:19
Bao, 35:6
Baole, 42:2
Baoule, 32:20
Baoussi, 38:33
Bape, 30:2
Bapedi, 51:8
Bapei, 30:1
Bapende, 38:16
Bapere, 36:6
Baphendi, 38:16
Bapi, 30:1
Bapili, 36:6
Bapimbwe, 46:15
Bapindi, 38:17
Bapindji, 30:13,
    35:13
Bapo, 33:1
Bapopoie, 28:24
Bapoto, 36:27
Bapou, 36:14
Bapoubi, 35:13
Bapouno, 35:13

Bapu, 36:14
Bapuku, 35:8
Bapuno, 35:13
Bara, 27:3
Baraasa, 52:30
Barabaig, 43:30
Barabra, 19:2
Barain, 17:20
Baram, 13:33
Barama, 35:11
Barambo, 29:13
Bararetta, 42:2
Barawa, 13:11
Barba, 12:36
Barburr, 13:36
Bare, 13:24, 29:30
Barea, 21:2
Barega, 36:28
Barein, 17:20
Bareko, 35:4
Baremba, 51:15
Bareshe, 13:26
Bargu, 12:36
Bargwe, 49:5
Bari, 13:24, 29:30,
    43:15
Baria, 21:2
Bariba, 12:36
Baribu, 17:27
Barimba, 8:1
Baringa, 37:8,
    38:20
Barjun, 39:12
Barma, 28:6
Barobe, 27:3
Barolong, 51:9
Barombi, 35:6
Baron, 13:33
Barondo, 35:6
Baronga, 49:9
Baroswi, 49:6
Barotse, 47:4
Barozi, 47:4
Barsub, 41:3
Barta, 21:3
Bartera, 41:3
Bartire, 41:3
Barue, 35:6, 49:5
Barumbi, 28:25
Barundi, 45:8
Barwe, 49:5

Barya, 21:2
Basa, 13:2, 32:14,
    33:2
Basabei, 43:28
Basaka, 38:23
Basakata, 38:23
Basakomo, 13:2
Basala, 47:1
Basanga, 38:38
Basange, 31:17
Basari, 12:30, 34:11
Baschansi, 38:24
Bascho, 31:1
Baschukulompo,
    47:1
Baseda, 32:11
Baseka, 37:2
Baseke, 35:9
Basele, 38:11
Basengele, 37:2
Bashabi, 49:1
Bashada, 23:1
Bashama, 13:34
Bashankwe, 49:2
Bashar, 13:14
Basheke, 35:9
Basherawa, 13:5
Bashi, 45:1
Bashikongo, 38:1
Bashila, 38:44
Bashilele, 38:22
Bashilenge, 37:13
Bashilongo, 38:1
Bashinshe, 38:10
Basiba, 45:10
Basiki, 35:9
Basila, 32:11
Basindja, 45:15
Basiri, 29:30
Basissiou, 36:13
Baskatta, 23:7
Basketo, 23:7
Basoga, 45:13
Basoko, 36:30
Basolongo, 38:1
Basonde, 38:13
Basonge, 37:16
Basonge-Meno,
    37:10
Basongo, 38:15,
    38:32

Basongola, 36:31
Basosi, 35:4
Basotho, 51:10
Basoundi, 38:3
Bassa, 13:2, 33:2,
    35:3
Bassa-Kaduna, 13:2
Bassa-Komo, 13:2
Bassanga, 36:29
Bassange, 31:7
Bassari, 12:30,
    34:11
Bassen, 32:9
Basso, 33:2
Bassongo, 37:16
Bassongo-Meno,
    37:10
Bassonje, 37:16
Bassouto, 51:10
Basuku, 38:17
Basukuma, 46:10
Basumbe, 38:11
Basundi, 38:3
Basungwe, 49:5
Basuto, 51:10
Bata, 13:34, 13:35
Batabwa, 38:45
Batache, 31:18
Batahin, 54:1
Batambwa, 38:45
Batanga, 35:8
Batatela, 37:11
Batawana, 51:11
Batchangui, 35:10
Batchenge, 36:11
Batchokwe, 38:25
Batchopi, 49:7
Batciga, 45:2
Bategue, 35:14
Bateke, 35:14
Batembo, 38:7
Bateso, 43:22
Bathonga, 49:10
Bati, 36:4
Batitu, 37:2
Batlaopa, 51:2
Batlaping, 51:12
Batlaro, 51:13
Batlharu, 51:13
Batlokwa, 51:14
Batoka, 49:5

Batonga, 38:54,
47:11, 49:5
Batongtu, 30:1
Batonka, 47:11
Batoro, 45:14
Batotela, 47:12
Batshoko, 38:25
Batswa, 49:8
Batta, 13:34,
13:35, 38:1
Batu, 13:3
Batumbuka, 38:54
Batumbwe, 38:37
Batwa, 8
Batwana, 51:11
Bauangana, 38:14
Bauchi, 55:2
Baule, 32:20
Baungwe, 49:5
Baushanga, 47:9
Baushi, 13:17,
38:33
Bavarama, 35:11
Bavenda, 51:15
Bavesha, 51:15
Bavili, 38:4
Bavira, 36:6
Bavo, 35:6
Bavoumbo, 36:14
Bavoungo, 35:11
Bavumbu, 38:14
Bavungo, 35:11
Bawenda, 51:15
Bawgott, 43:29
Bawisa, 38:35
Bawongo, 38:22
Bawumbu, 36:14,
38:14
Baya, 29:20
Bayaga, 8:1
Bayaka, 8:1, 35:11,
38:18
Bayakala, 38:18
Bayanchi, 38:24
Bayangela, 38:2
Bayanzi, 36:3,
38:24
Baye, 38:23
Bayeke, 37:17
Bayele, 8:1
Baygo, 17:1

Bayi, 35:6
Bayombe, 38:5
Bayot, 34:6
Bayoun, 39:12
Bayugu, 28:20,
35:12
Baza, 13:42
Bazaa, 54:5
Bazanche, 32:11
Bazen, 21:8
Bazezuru, 49:6
Bazigaba, 8:3
Bazimba, 37:16,
38:55
Bazoko, 36:30
Bazombo, 38:1
Bazuzura, 49:6
Bechuana, 51
Becwana, 51
Bedanga, 17:20
Bedayria, 54:2
Bedde, 17:23
Bede, 17:23
Bedere, 32:7
Bederia, 54:2
Bedeyat, 16:2
Bedjelib, 12:30
Bedouin Arabs, 52
Befang, 30:13
Bega, 40
Bego, 17:1
Beharia, 52:3
Behli, 28:12
Beigo, 17:1
Beir, 43:2
Beja, 40
Bekaburum, 12:34
Bekhti, 15:29
Bekom, 30:5
Bekpokpak, 12:32
Beku, 8:1
Bekwom, 12:32
Belen, 40:5
Beli, 28:12
Bella, 15:22, 16
Belle, 33:18
Bemba, 38:34
Bembance, 36:13
Bembe, 36:28, 38:3
Ben, 12:44
Bena, 46:17

Bena Kalundwe,
37:12
Bena Kanioka,
37:12
Bena Kazembe,
38:41
Bena Lulua, 37:13
Bende, 46:6
Bene, 36:11
Benesho, 23:3
Benga, 35:8
Benge, 35:8, 36:4
Beni, 31:18
Beni Amer, 40:3
Beni Arous, 52:17
Beni Bou Yahi,
52:40
Beni Bou Zeggou,
15:29
Beni Chebel, 15:29
Beni Gerar, 54:5
Beni Gorfet, 52:17
Beni Guil, 52:13
Beni Helba, 54:8
Beni Iznacen, 15:17
Beni Kanz, 19:2
Beni Menasser,
15:14
Beni Mesguilda,
52:17
Beni Mestara, 52:17
Beni Mtir, 15:2
Beni Mukuni, 47:3
Beni Mzab, 15:15
Benischo, 23:3
Beni Selim, 54:17
Beni Shangul, 21:3
Beni Snous, 15:29
Beni Yaala, 15:29
Beni Zeroual, 52:17
Beni Zid, 52:2
Bennecho, 23:3
Benu, 31:18
Beraber, 15:2
Berabish, 52:4
Berba, 12:38
Berberi, 19:2
Berbers, 15
Bere, 33:18
Bergdama, 9:1
Beri, 43:9

Beriberi, 17:24,
17:28
Berom, 13:4
Berrian, 15:15
Bersub, 41:3
Berta, 21:ɔ
Berti, 16:1
Bertirri, 41:3
Besarin, 40:4
Besikongo, 38:1
Besimbo, 36:12
Besom, 36:29
Besorube, 12:38
Betammadibe,
12:38
Betammaribe, 12:38
Betanimena, 27:5
Bete, 31:2, 33:3
Betiabe, 12:38
Betjek, 35:3
Betschuana, 51
Betsileo, 27:4
Betsimisaraka,
27:5
Betsinga, 36:11
Betta, 13:59
Bettie, 32:17
Betye, 32:17
Beundo, 35:8
Bezanozano, 27:10
Bhaca, 50:5
Bhele, 50:5
Biafada, 34:4
Biafar, 34:4
Biakumbo, 36:12
Bideyat, 16:2
Bidjuk, 36:29
Bidyago, 34:5
Bie, 48:4
Bienescio, 23:3
Bifra, 34:4
Bihe, 48:4
Bijago, 34:5
Bijogo, 34:5
Bijuga, 34:5
Bikay, 36:19
Bikele, 36:19
Bikom, 30:5
Bikwombe, 12:32
Bileni, 40:6
Billai, 43:24

Billiri, 13:47
Bilwana, 46:9
Bimal, 41:8
Bimbi, 35:3
Bimbia, 35:5
Bimbundu, 48:4
Bimenso, 23:3
Binari, 34:1
Binawa, 13:20
Bindi, 37:15
Binga, 8:1, 28:2
Bini, 31:18, 31:19,
    32:17
Binji, 38:21
Binjombo, 36:29
Binna, 13:59
Binye, 32:17
Binza, 36:5
Bio, 23:1
Bira, 36:6
Birguid, 19:3
Biri, 29:30
Birifon, 12:23
Birifor, 12:23
Birked, 19:3
Birom, 13:4
Birra, 43:1
Birri, 29:30
Birwa, 51:14
Bisa, 12:40, 38:35
Bisano, 12:40
Bisapele, 12:40
Bisariab, 40:4
Bisharin, 40:4
Biskra, 52:42
Bissago, 34:5
Bitare, 13:31
Bite, 28:12
Biti, 28:12
Bitu, 28:12
Biya, 23:1
Biyan, 34:11
Biye, 23:1
Bizhi, 47:1
Bjakum, 36:12
Black Bobo, 12:8
Black Jews, 22:6
Black Ndebele,
    50:6
Blal, 52:36
Blapo, 33:1

Bmoba, 12:33
Bo, 35:4
Bobai, 38:23
Bobangi, 36:3
Bobango, 36:8
Bobate, 36:4
Bobe, 35:5
Bobea, 35:5
Bobo, 12:8
Bobofign, 12:47
Bobwa, 33:3, 36:2
Boda, 23:1
Bodde, 32:19
Bodho, 43:6
Bodi, 23:7
Bodiman, 35:2
Bodjili, 8:1
Bodo, 33:1
Bodongo, 36:7
Bodu, 23:7
Boem, 32:12
Boeni, 34:11
Boffi, 29:21
Bofi, 29:21
Boghorom, 13:5
Bogo, 40:5
Bogon, 32:12
Bogoro, 28:15
Bogoto, 29:20
Boi, 13:58
Boka, 36:7
Bokaka, 36:7
Bokala, 37:4
Boki, 31:2
Bokiba, 36:14
Boko, 12:39, 13:3,
    29:12, 35:5
Bokongo, 37:2
Bokote, 37:9
Bokre, 33:1
Bokwe, 33:1
Bola, 34:9
Bole, 17:25, 37:5
Bolemba, 37:9
Bolendu, 37:4
Bolewa, 17:25
Bolia, 37:2
Bolki, 13:35
Bolo, 35:6, 37:7
Boloki, 36:24
Bolom, 33:10

Bolongo, 37:4
Bolto, 16:3
Boluki, 36:24
Boma, 38:23, 43:2
Bomali, 36:29
Bomam, 36:29
Bomba, 28:15
Bomesa, 36:20
Bombo, 36:29
Bomitaba, 36:7
Bomofwe, 32:20
Bomome, 36:29
Bomongo, 37:6
Bon, 10:1
Bonai, 32:17
Bonda, 32:17
Bondei, 39:1
Bondjo, 29:22
Bondo, 38:7
Bonga, 8:1, 36:7
Bongandu, 37:7
Bongio, 29:22
Bongkeng, 35:3
Bongo, 28:7, 48:4
Bongombe, 37:8
Bongondjo, 36:29
Bonguili, 36:3
Boni, 10:1
Bonjo, 29:22
Bonkesse, 37:4
Bonna, 32:17
Boo, 33:24
Boobe, 35:1
Booli, 37:4
Boor, 43:6
Bor, 43:6
Borali, 23:1
Boran, 42:3
Borana, 42:3
Borgawa, 12:36
Bori, 29:4, 43:9,
    43:19
Borlawa, 17:25
Boro, 32:12
Borodda, 23:7
Boronga, 43:19
Bororo, 55:9
Borrom, 13:5
Borwa, 51:5
Bosaka, 37:1
Bosanga, 36:29

Bosha, 23:2
Bota, 35:5
Bote, 28:15
Boua, 12:8
Bouaka, 29:23
Bouanda, 32:17
Bouchamai, 36:14
Boudja, 36:8
Boudouma, 17:26
Boulala, 17:18
Boulba, 12:38
Boulea, 12:38
Boulgheda, 16:3
Boulou, 36:11
Boumaoali, 36:29
Bounguili, 36:29
Boura, 12:16
Bourake, 29:19
Bousanou, 12:40
Bou Sba, 52:8
Boussa, 12:39
Bouxhilile, 38:22
Bouzantchi, 12:40
Boya, 43:2
Boyaeli, 8:1
Boyela, 37:3
Boyeu, 36:2
Bozo, 11:2
Brahim, 15:22
Brakna, 52:37
Bram, 34:9
Brass, 31:21
Brignan, 32:29
Brinya, 32:29
Brisa, 32:17
Brofi, 32:17
Brong, 32:21
Brossa, 32:17
Brussa, 32:17
Bua, 12:8, 17:13
Bubangi, 36:3
Bubi, 35:1
Bubui, 38:36
Budja, 36:8, 49:5
Budu, 36:9
Budugum, 29:8
Budukwa, 33:1
Buduma, 17:26
Buem, 32:12
Bugakwe, 9:14
Buguru, 29:15

Builsa, 12:16
Bujawa, 13:12
Bujeba, 35:7
Bujga, 49:5
Buji, 13:12
Bukanda, 38:39
Buku, 35:8
Bula, 13:24, 21:10
Bulaba, 37:12
Bulabai, 13:45
Bulai, 13:35
Bulala, 17:18
Bulba, 12:38
Buldiit, 21:7
Bulea, 12:16
Bulega, 36:28
Bulem, 33:10
Bulgeda, 16:3
Buli, 35:2
Bulia, 45:17
Bulibuli, 36:1
Bulla, 13:24
Bullom, 33:10
Bulo, 12:16
Bulom, 33:10
Bultoa, 16:3
Bulu, 35:6, 36:11
Buluk, 12:16
Bum, 29:10, 30:3
Buma, 43:23
Bumali, 36:29
Bumba, 43:32
Bumbe, 29:17
Bumbon, 36:29
Bumie, 43:23
Buna, 21:10
Bunda, 38:19
Bunga, 46:20
Bungbon, 36:29
Bungwili, 36:29
Bunno, 23:1
Bunu, 31:26
Bura, 12:16, 13:36
Buraka, 29:19
Buram, 20:4
Burama, 34:9
Burburi, 32:25
Buresya, 32:17
Buret, 43:26
Burgu, 12:36

Burji, 25:3
Burle, 23:1
Burmawa, 13:5
Burra, 13:36
Burrum, 13:5
Bursuk, 41:3
Burum, 13:4
Burun, 21:11
Burungi, 24:1
Busa, 12:39
Busanga, 12:40
Busaif, 52:27
Busansi, 12:40
Busasi, 21:9
Busawa, 12:39
Bush Grebo, 33:6
Bush Kru, 33:6
Bushmen, 9
Bussansi, 12:40
Busso, 17:12, 25:3
Busy, 33:25
Butawa, 13:6
Bute, 29:33
Buye, 38:36
Buzi, 33:25
Bviri, 29:30
Bwa, 12:8
Bwaka, 29:23
Bwamba, 36:1
Bwari, 38:36
Bwende, 38:3
Bwenum, 32:12
Bwezi, 36:1
Bwile, 38:45
Bwire, 38:45
Bwissi, 35:11
Bwol, 13:33
Bworo, 21:5
Byafada, 34:4
Byerre, 29:5
Byetri, 32:31

Caba, 23:3
Cabrai, 12:34
Caconda, 48:4
Cacongo, 38:4
Cakpang, 31:18
Caluquembe, 48:4
Camant, 22:6
Camba, 13:52
Cambate, 25:2

Camma, 35:12
Cangborong, 32:14
Cape Bushmen, 9:15
Cape Hottentot, 9:2
Capende, 38:16
Carthaginians, 18
Cassongue, 48:4
Cat, 43:6
Cenga, 48:4
Cewa, 38:47
Chaamba, 52:5
Chach, 43:4
Chaga, 44:1
Chagga, 44:1
Chainoqua, 9:2
Chako, 23:3
Chakosi, 12:41
Chakpang, 31:18
Chale, 17:8
Cham, 13:47
Chamai, 36:14
Chamba, 12:30, 13:52
Chambuli, 32:9
Chamir, 22:5
Chang, 30:1
Changi, 35:10
Chaouia, 15:18, 52:24
Chara, 13:12, 23:7
Chariguriqua, 9:2
Chaucho, 12:35
Chawai, 13:7
Chebel, 15:29
Chebleng, 43:29
Cheke, 13:40
Chema, 52:28
Chemant, 22:6
Cherarda, 52:24
Chere, 17:15, 29:30
Cherre, 23:1
Chewa, 38:47
Cheykye, 54:18
Chiadma, 52:24
Chibak, 13:44
Chibbuk, 13:44
Chiboque, 38:25
Chiga, 45:2
Chikide, 13:49
Chikunda, 38:49

Chilenge, 48:4
Chiloango, 38:4
Chima, 43:4
Chimboro, 32:14
Chinge, 38:10
Chip, 13:33
Chipeta, 38:47
Chiri, 17:15
Chiroa, 17:27
Chisinga, 38:33
Chiwere, 50:9
Chleuch, 15:19
Chobo, 38:60
Chokobo, 13:12
Chokosi, 12:41
Chokwe, 38:25
Chongee, 13:47
Chongwom, 13:47
Chonyi, 39:8
Choo, 38:60
Chorfa, 52:41
Choua, 54:20
Chozzam, 54:20
Chtouka, 15:19
Chuabo, 38:48
Chuka, 44:4
Chungwe, 46:18
Churi, 43:4
Chwampo, 38:48
Ciara, 23:7
Cibak, 13:44
Ciga, 45:2
Cimba, 35:13
Cilenge, 48:5
Cilombo, 48:4
Cingolo, 48:4
Cipala, 38:9
Cipeyo, 48:4
Cipungu, 48:7
Cirma, 43:4
Cirra, 25:3
Cisama, 38:8
Cisanje, 38:11
Citata, 48:4
Civula, 48:4
Ciyaka, 48:4
Coira, 23:7
Comende, 33:23
Commi, 35:12
Como, 21:7
Comorians, 39:13

Coniagui, 34:11
Conso, 25:3
Conta, 23:7
Coroca, 9:7
Crau, 33:7
Cuamato, 48:1
Cuccia, 23:7
Cufra, 52:20
Cuiscia, 23:7
Cule, 23:1
Culle, 23:7
Cunama, 21:7
Cushites, 22, 23, 24,
    25, 26, 42, 43, 44
Cyrenaicans, 52:6

Da, 33:16
Daba, 13:40
Dabosa, 43:23
Dach, 21:5
Dachel, 52:7
Dadio, 17:1
Dadye, 32:17
Dafi, 12:42
Dafing, 12:42
Daga, 13:23
Dagaba, 12:17
Dagamba, 12:24
Dagana, 54:20
Dagari, 12:17
Dagati, 12:17
Dagba, 28:5
Dagboma, 12:24
Dago, 17:1
Dagom, 12:10
Dagomba, 12:24
Dagra, 17:24
Dagu, 17:1, 17:4
Dahomeans, 32:3
Daju, 17:1
Daka, 13:53
Dakakari, 13:8
Dakarawa, 13:8
Dakha, 13:53
Dakhla, 52:7
Dakoka, 20:4
Dakpa, 28:5
Dakpwa, 29:16
Dakuya, 33:3
Dalatoa, 17:27
Dalea, 16:3

Dalia, 16:3
Dalinga, 17:2
Dama, 29:1, 43:4,
    43:14
Damaqua, 9:2
Damara, 9:1, 48:2
Damot, 22:2
Dan, 33:16
Danagla, 19:2
Danakil, 41:1
Danawa, 17:27
Danda, 49:4
Danoa, 17:27
Darasa, 25:1
Darassa, 25:1
Dari, 29:2
Darsa, 52:30
Darsonich, 25:5
Dasa, 16:4
Dashi, 21:3
Dassa, 31:27
Dathanaic, 25:5
Dathanik, 25:5
Datoga, 43:29
Daublal, 52:36
Daud, 52:26
Daurawa, 17:38
Dauro, 23:7
Dawaro, 23:7
Day, 28:5
Daya, 28:5
Daza, 16:4
Dazagarda, 16:4
De, 33:2
Debe, 12:19
Debue, 33:1
Deforo, 12:9
Degena, 54:20
Degha, 12:18
Dek, 29:7
Dekakire, 54:3
Dekka, 13:53
Delami, 20:2
Delim, 52:8
Delo, 32:7
Demba, 38:7
Dembo, 43:6
Dembu, 38:7
Demik, 20:5
Demsa, 13:34
Denawa, 13:38

Dendi, 17:43, 29:34
Dendje, 28:6
Dengese, 37:4
Denkawi, 43:5
Dennassena, 9:5
Dera, 13:37
Derbussi, 41:2
Deressia, 17:21
Derouma, 39:7
Desishe, 41:6
Dewoi, 33:2
Dga, 12:18
Dhuak, 43:4
Dhuri, 43:4
Dia, 38:23
Diabe, 32:17
Diabouala, 33:16
Diabu, 17:27
Diafoba, 33:16
Diagada, 16:3
Diakhambe, 11:8
Dialonke, 11:3
Diamande, 11:6
Diammou, 12:18
Dian, 12:11
Diawara, 11:10
Dibo, 31:18
Dibum, 35:3
Dida, 33:4
Didinga, 43:1
Die, 12:38
Diele, 13:45
Diezem, 36:10
Difale, 12:34
Digbue, 33:1
Dighoya, 51:2
Digil, 41:8
Digo, 39:6
Digodia, 41:10
Dilling, 19:4
Dima, 23:1
Dime, 23:1
Dimuk, 13:33
Dindje, 28:6
Dinga, 38:20
Dinka, 43:5
Diola, 34:6
Diongor, 17:16
Dioro, 33:1
Dioula, 12:43
Dir, 41:10

Dirma, 43:4
Dirrim, 13:53
Diryawa, 13:50
Dissu, 23:3
Diula, 12:43
Diwala, 35:2
Dizu, 23:3
Djakana, 52:36
Djakka, 38:18
Djanti, 30:2
Djarso, 42:4
Dje, 31:27
Djebala, 52:17
Djebel, 17:5
Djedj, 32:3
Djeggut, 15:22
Djelass, 52:14
Djem, 36:10
Djennenke, 11:9
Djerba, 15:10
Djerid, 52:18
Djerma, 17:45
Djimi, 13:40
Djinge, 28:6
Djioko, 28:6
Djiwat, 34:6
Djofra, 15:11
Djoloff, 34:12
Djompra, 13:32
Djumperi, 13:32
Djur, 43:6
Do, 28:9, 33:2
Doado, 29:12
Doco, 23:7
Dodinga, 43:1
Dodoso, 43:20
Dodoth, 43:20
Doe, 39:2
Dogara, 17:24
Dogon, 12:10
Dogorda, 16:4
Dokhosie, 12:12
Dokko, 23:7
Doko, 23:7
Dokwa, 51:14
Dolbohanta, 41:6
Dollo, 23:7
Dollong, 13:29
Dolot, 43:4
Dombe, 48:5
Dompago, 12:24

Domwa, 32:4
Dondo, 38:3
Donga, 13:52
Dongiro, 43:23
Dongo, 28:9
Dongosa, 16:4
Donyiro, 43:23
Doo, 33:24
Dor, 28:7
Dorhosye, 12:12
Dormo, 17:15
Dorobo, 10:2
Dorosie, 12:12
Dorze, 23:7
Douala, 35:2
Doui Menia, 52:9
Doukkala, 52:24
Douma, 35:10
Doza, 16:4
Dozza, 16:4
Drawa, 15:3
Drugu, 28:8
Dschagga, 38:18, 44:1
Dschamba, 13:52
Dscherma, 36:29
Dschogni, 39:8
Dschubu, 13:13
Dsimu, 36:10
Dsoul, 52:17
Duaish, 15:4
Duala, 35:2
Dubab, 54:2
Dubaina, 54:19
Dubania, 54:19
Dubasin, 54:19
Dube, 39:11
Duga, 29:13
Dui, 29:3
Dui Belal, 52:36
Dui-Menia, 52:9
Dukawa, 13:16
Dukkala, 52:24
Dukwe, 9:13
Dulbahente, 41:6
Duma, 23:1, 35:10, 49:1
Dumbo, 13:27
Dume, 23:1, 31:23
Dungi, 13:10
Durru, 29:3

Duru, 29:3
Duruma, 39:7
Dwela, 35:2
Dwingi, 13:10
Dya, 12:11
Dyabo, 33:5
Dyakosi, 12:41
Dyalonka, 11:3
Dyamu, 12:18
Dye, 12:38, 33:4
Dyerma, 17:45
Dyida, 33:4
Dyoura, 12:43
Dzalamo, 39:17
Dzalia, 37:7
Dzem, 36:10
Dzihana, 39:8
Dzimou, 36:10
Dzing, 38:20
Dziryama, 39:8
Dzuak, 43:4
Dzungle, 30:11

Ebagi, 31:18
Ebe, 31:18
Ebrie, 32:20
Echira, 35:11
Edda, 31:20
Edea, 35:3
Ediye, 35:1
Edo, 31:19
Eesa, 41:2
Efe, 8:4
Effium, 31:7
Efik, 31:4
Efu, 35:6
Ega, 33:4
Egabo, 31:27
Egba, 31:27
Egbiri, 31:16
Egede, 31:11
Eggon, 13:21
Egon, 13:21
Egu, 31:16
Egun, 32:5
Egwa, 33:4
Egye, 43:20
Egyptians, 14, 52:10
Ehinga, 48:7
Ehl Serif, 52:17
Eibe, 32:2

Eile, 39:11
Eisa, 41:2
Ejagham, 31:3
Ekbebe, 32:12
Ekele, 37:3
Eket, 31:4
Eketete, 48:4
Ekiti, 31:28
Ekoi, 31:3
Ekombe, 35:6
Ekonda, 37:2
Ekopo, 33:4
Ekota, 37:1
Ekumuru, 31:8
Ekuri, 31:8
El Achsass, 15:22
Elanga, 37:9
Elburgu, 43:33
Elende, 48:4
Elgeyo, 43:25
Elgonyi, 43:28
Elguasem, 52:26
El Guettar, 52:18
Elgume, 43:24
Elgumi, 43:22
El Hamma, 52:18
Elinga, 37:1, 37:8
Eljemasi, 43:33
El Ksar, 52:12
El Menaba, 15:19
Elmolo, 43:33
Elong, 35:4
Elonga, 37:9
El Oudian, 52:18
El Oued, 52:35
El Udian, 52:18
Elwana, 39:10
Emberre, 44:4
Embu, 44:4
Empoongwe, 35:12
Enarya, 23:2
Endjra, 52:17
Endo, 43:29
Enenga, 35:12
Engassana, 21:6
Enjemasi, 43:33
Enna, 31:8
Ennia, 42:4
Entepes, 43:21
Entifa, 15:19
Enya, 36:31

Enyong, 31:4
Ephe, 32:2
Epeita, 43:2
Epeta, 43:2
Erakwa, 31:22
Eraykat, 54:14
Erenga, 17:5
Ergeibat, 52:26
Ermbeli, 17:3
Erokh, 24:3
Erorup, 31:6
Esa, 31:19, 41:2
Esel, 36:29
Esela, 38:9
Esele, 38:11
Eshikongo, 38:1
Eshira, 35:11
Eshupum, 31:5
Esimbi, 31:13
Eso, 36:32
Essel, 36:29
Essiga, 31:8
Essouma, 32:28
Esuma, 32:28
Ethiopians, 22
Eton, 36:11
Etsako, 31:24
Etulo, 31:11
Etun, 36:11
Eunda, 48:1
Evale, 38:1
Evalue, 32:28
Eve, 8:4
Ewe, 32:2
Ewodi, 35:2
Ewoutire, 32:31
Ewuni, 35:6
Ewutile, 32:31
Exikongo, 38:1
Eyap, 30:1
Eyarra, 35:2

Faawa, 13:50
Fachara, 13:12
Fadnia, 54:1
Fagdelou, 43:16
Fagnia, 17:14
Fahsya, 52:24
Fajelu, 43:16
Fajulu, 43:16
Fakawa, 13:8

Fala, 17:6
Falafala, 12:3
Fali, 13:40, 13:44
Famalla, 16:4
Fan, 36:11
Fang, 36:11
Fanian, 17:14
Fanwe, 36:11
Fanyan, 17:14
Fari, 43:9
Fayid, 52:30
Fedgelu, 43:16
Fellani, 55
Fellata, 55
Fem, 13:4
Feqqus, 15:26
Feram, 12:19
Feri, 43:9
Ferkla, 15:6
Fero, 13:47
Fertit, 54:4
Fezara, 54:5
Fezwata, 15:3
Fezzan, 52:11
Figig, 15:5
Figuig, 15:5
Fika, 17:25
Filala, 15:6
Filani, 55
Fingo, 50:5
Fiote, 38:4
Fipa, 46:12
Fizere, 13:1
Fjort, 38:4
Foikat, 52:16
For, 17:2
Forawa, 17:2
Forenga, 17:2
Forgha, 15:11
Fori, 43:9
Foto, 36:27
Foulacounda, 55
Fouladougou, 55:5
Foulah, 55
Foulse, 12:20
Fouta Djalon, 55:3
Foutajalonke, 55:3
Fouta Toro, 55:4
Fra, 12:19
Frafra, 12:19, 52:3
Fraichich, 52:14

Frechich, 52:14
Frouga, 15:19
Fruga, 15:19
Ftaiet, 52:35
Fuga, 10:4
Fujiga, 43:6
Ful, 55
Fuladugu, 55:5
Fulakunda, 55
Fulani, 55
Fulbe, 55
Fulero, 45:1
Fulilwa, 38:54
Fulse, 12:20
Fungwe, 38:54, 49:5
Fur, 17:2
Furu, 36:3

Ga, 32:4
Gaaliin, 54:6
Gaberi, 17:15
Gabes, 52:2
Gabin, 13:42
Gabri, 17:15, 20:2
Gadabirsky, 41:2
Gadabursi, 41:2
Gadames, 15:7
Gade, 13:41
Gaeda, 16:2
Gafsa, 52:12
Gagembe, 23:7
Gagou, 33:7
Gagu, 33:7
Gaida, 16:2
Gala, 46:9
Galabu, 17:27
Galaganza, 46:9
Galebagba, 12:19
Galembawa, 13:38
Galikwe, 9:5
Galim, 13:9
Galla, 42
Gallab, 25:4
Gallina, 33:26
Galloa, 35:12
Galoa, 35:12
Galoi, 35:12
Galua, 35:12
Galuba, 25:4
Gamawa, 17:29
Gamba, 29:30

Gamergu, 17:32
Gamila, 21:3
Gamo, 23:7
Gamole, 25:3
Gamuia, 54:6
Gan, 12:12, 12:44,
  32:4, 43:10
Ganagana, 31:18
Ganawuri, 13:4
Ganda, 45:9, 48:5
Gandole, 13:53
Gang, 43:10
Gangaran, 11:8
Gangi, 46:21
Ganin, 9:10
Ganne, 12:44
Ganra, 12:44
Ganyanga, 17:6
Ganza, 21:7
Gardula, 25:3
Garikwe, 9:14
Garo, 23:2
Gat Tuareg, 15:23
Gatzamba, 23:7
Gauar, 13:39
Gauwada, 25:3
Gaya, 43:14
Gayi, 23:1
Gbamende, 33:23
Gban, 33:7
Gbanda, 32:29
Gbande, 33:18
Gbandi, 29:21
Gbandja, 32:23
Gbanziri, 29:19
Gbari, 13:60
Gbasa, 33:2
Gbassi, 33:18
Gbaya, 28:3, 29:20
Gbe, 33:2, 33:24
Gbedye, 31:18
Gben, 12:44
Gberi, 28:12
Gbese, 33:21
Gbundi, 33:18
Gbuwhe, 13:49
Gbwaka, 29:23
Ge, 32:6, 33:24
Gedmiwa, 15:19
Gehri, 28:12
Geinin, 9:10

Gelab, 25:4
Gele, 28:1
Geleba, 25:4
Gelebda, 13:49
Gelimes, 41:7
Gelubba, 25:4
Gemaab, 54:6
Gemirra, 23:3
Gen, 32:6
Gengele, 36:31
Gengle, 13:57
Gentafa, 15:19
Gerar, 54:5
Gerawa, 13:38
Gerba, 15:10
Gerhajis, 41:5
Geri, 41:3
Gerkawa, 13:33
Gerra, 41:10
Gerse, 33:21
Gerumawa, 13:38
Gesera, 8:3
Geshu, 45:16
Geso, 36:31
Gezawa, 13:38
Ghadames, 15:7
Gharbya, 52:24
Ghat, 15:23
Gheleba, 25:4
Gheria, 15:6
Ghidole, 25:3
Ghimirra, 23:3
Ghizi, 33:12
Ghodiat, 54:2
Ghomara, 15:17
Ghomera, 15:17
Ghoumrage, 52:2
Giaca, 38:18
Gialo, 15:9
Gibe, 23:2
Gibya, 32:23
Gidar, 13:40
Gidder, 13:40
Gidole, 25:3
Gien, 33:6
Gigeagi, 33:1
Giguyu, 44:3
Gil, 52:13
Gili, 31:12
Gimiab, 54:6
Gimira, 23:3

Gimma, 54:7
Gimz, 21:5
Ginkwe, 9:11
Gio, 33:16
Giofra, 15:11
Girange, 43:14
Girganke, 52:41
Girri, 41:3
Giryama, 39:8
Gisei, 29:8
Gishu, 45:16
Gisiga, 13:39
Gisohiga, 13:39
Gisu, 45:16
Giti, 33:1
Givi, 33:2
Giye, 43:20
Gizii, 45:17
Glaoua, 15:19
Glawa, 15:19
Goa, 36:31
Goale, 13:60
Gobawein, 39:9
Gobir, 17:38
Gobo, 23:7
Gobu, 29:24
Godye, 33:4
Gofa, 23:7
Goffa, 23:5
Gogo, 46:1
Gokwe, 9:11
Gola, 13:57, 33:11
Goliba, 25:4
Golo, 29:30
Goma, 38:36
Gomani, 50:9
Gombe, 36:20, 36:24, 37:8
Gomla, 13:57
Gomma, 23:2
Gomwa, 32:4
Gonaqua, 9:2
Gondaffa, 15:19
Gonga, 23:5
Gontafa, 15:19
Gonya, 32:23
Gorachouqua, 9:2
Goram, 13:33
Gorane, 16:4
Gorensi, 12:25
Gorfet, 52:17

Gori, 13:57
Goringhaiqua, 9:2
Gorise, 12:19
Goroa, 24:2
Gosha, 39:9
Gossi, 53:7
Goua, 32:30
Gouin, 12:1
Goula, 28:1
Goulay, 28:5
Gouma, 36:10
Goun, 32:5
Goundi, 36:26
Goundafa, 15:19
Gour, 43:6
Gouraghe, 22:3
Gourmantche, 12:31
Gouro, 33:19
Gourounsi, 12:19
Gova, 49:4, 49:6
Govera, 49:1
Gowa, 47:11
Gowaze, 25:3
Gragui, 33:1
Grebo, 33:5
Grigriqua, 9:2
Grio, 33:16, 33:24
Grippuo, 33:1
Gruinse, 12:19
Grunshi, 12:19
Grusi, 12:16–22
Grussi, 12:19
Guala, 12:7
Guanche, 15:8
Guang, 32:23
Guarara, 15:24
Guardaia, 15:15
Guassem, 52:26
Gubayna, 54:16
Gubba, 21:5
Gubei, 17:37
Gude, 13:40
Gudela, 25:2
Gudilla, 25:2
Gudji, 25:1
Gudjiru, 17:27
Gudo, 13:35
Guemra, 17:3
Guerara, 15:15
Guere, 33:24

Guerze, 33:24
Guha, 38:37
Guider, 13:40
Guimr, 17:3
Guin, 12:1
Guissiga, 13:39
Gula, 28:1
Gulai, 28:5
Gule, 21:4
Gulfan, 19:4
Gulla, 28:1
Gullop, 25:4
Guma, 32:2, 36:10
Gumba, 29:30
Gumrage, 52:2
Gumus, 21:5
Gumuz, 21:5
Gumzawi, 21:5
Gun, 32:5
Gundi, 36:26
Gundo, 37:9
Gungawa, 13:26
Guniz, 21:5
Gunya, 39:12
Gunza, 21:5
Gupa, 31:18
Gura, 21:11
Gurage, 22:3
Gure, 13:10
Gurensi, 12:25
Guri, 13:10
Gurka, 13:33
Gurma, 12:31
Guro, 33:19
Guroji, 13:23
Gurumo, 24:2
Gurunsi, 12:19
Gusii, 45:17
Gussum, 13:12
Gusuwa, 13:12
Gwa, 32:30
Gwabyo, 32:30
Gwagba, 31:18
Gwali, 13:60
Gwama, 21:7
Gwan, 32:4, 32:23
Gwandara, 13:41
Gwanya, 32:23
Gwari, 13:60
Gweabo, 33:5
Gwena, 49:1

Gwere, 45:13
Gwin, 12:1
Gwio, 33:19
Gworam, 13:33
Gye, 43:20
Gyo, 33:16
Gyomande, 11:6
Gyula, 12:43
Gyuman, 32:30

Ha, 45:3
Habab, 40:6
Habbania, 54:8
Habe, 12:10
Habr Awal, 41:5
Habr Gerhajis, 41:5
Habr Toljaala, 41:5
Haddad, 17:27
Hadea, 25:2
Hadendowa, 40:6
Hadimu, 39:14
Hadiya, 25:2
Hadj, 15:21
Hadya, 25:2
Hadzapi, 10:3
Haha, 15:19
Hako, 38:9
Haku, 38:9
Halenga, 40:6
Ham, 13:18
Hamama, 52:14
Hamar, 54:9
Hamarkoke, 23:1
Hamarro, 23:7
Hamasien, 22:7
Hamayd, 54:2
Hamba, 37:11, 38:60
Hambbe, 12:10
Hamedj, 17:27
Hameg, 21:4
Hamej, 21:4
Hamerna, 52:2
Hamian, 52:15
Hamid, 54:5
Hamir, 22:5
Hamran, 54:16
Hamta, 22:5
Hamyan, 52:15
Hancumqua, 9:2
Handa, 13:59

Hanga, 45:21
Hanha, 48:5
Hanya, 48:5
Haouara, 15:19
Haoussa, 17:38
Harari, 22:4
Haratin, 16
Harbora, 25:4
Harti, 41:10
Haruro, 23:7
Hasa, 52:30
Hasania, 54:10
Hasauna, 52:27
Hassan, 15:21
Hassanyah, 54:10
Hatsa, 10:3
Haualla, 16:4
Haukoin, 9:1
Haulo, 33:1
Hausa, 17:38, 17:40
Havu, 45:1
Hawadla, 41:4
Hawara, 15:19
Hawawir, 54:12
Hawazma, 54:2
Haweitat, 52:23
Hawiya, 41:4
Hawiyel, 41:4
Haya, 45:10
Hayo, 45:21
Hazzem, 52:2
Hehe, 46:18
Heia, 45:10
Heiban, 20:2
Heikum, 9:3
Heimad, 54:11
Helba, 54:8
Hemat, 54:11
Hena, 33:1
Hendawa, 40:6
Henga, 38:54
Her, 34:6
Hera, 49:6
Herero, 48:2
Hessequa, 9:2
Hewa, 38:54
Hewe, 38:54
Hiao, 38:61
Hide, 13:45
Hidkala, 13:49
Hiechware, 9:4

Higi, 13:43
Hiji, 13:43
Hill Jarawa, 13:1
Hill Mada, 13:21
Hill Margi, 13:43
Hima, 31:16, 45
Himba, 48:2
Hina, 13:40, 17:36
Hinga, 48:7
Hinna, 17:36
Hisala, 12:19
Hlengwe, 49:8
Hlubi, 50:5
Hoggar, 15:23
Holli, 31:27
Hollo, 38:6
Holo, 38:6
Holoholo, 38:37
Holma, 13:40
Hombo, 38:36
Homr, 28:2, 54:15
Hona, 13:42
Honja, 38:46
Horohoro, 45:7
Hotma, 52:27
Hottentot, 9
Houbbou, 55
Houne, 33:1
Hova, 27:7
Huambo, 48:4
Huana, 38:14
Hubu, 55
Huela, 12:45
Hukwe, 9:5
Hula, 32:6
Huluf, 34:6
Huma, 29:15, 45
Humbe, 48:7, 49:1
Humbu, 38:14
Hummurcocche,
   23:1
Humr, 54:15
Hunde, 45:4
Hungu, 38:1
Hungwe, 36:14
Huntu, 13:61
Hura, 9:13
Hurutshe, 51:1
Husaynat, 54:10
Husseinat, 54:10
Hutman, 52:27

Hutu, 45
Hwaduba, 50:7
Hwanne, 33:1
Hwelanu, 32:3
Hwine, 33:1
Hyapa, 31:18

Iaggut, 15:22
Ibadan, 31:31
Ibaji, 31:14
Ibau, 13:12
Ibbedde, 31:26
Ibea, 35:7
Ibeno, 31:4
Ibibio, 31:4
Ibo, 31:20
Idab-el-Hassan,
   15:21
Idaouich, 15:4
Ida ou Mamoud,
   15:19
Ida ou Semlal,
   15:19
Ida ou Tanan, 15:19
Ida u Blal, 52:36
Ida-u-el-Hadj,
   15:21
Ida u Sal, 15:19
Ida u Siki, 15:19
Idenic, 10:4
Idio, 29:25
Idoma, 31:13
Idongiro, 43:23
Idrassen, 15:2
Ife, 31:25, 31:29
Ifora, 15:23, 53:6
Igala, 31:14
Igara, 31:14
Igbamina, 31:3
Igbira, 31:16
Igbo, 31:5
Igbolo, 31:31
Igbono, 31:31
Iggout, 15:22
Ignahatom, 43:23
Igu, 31:16
Igula, 31:14
Igulua, 35:12
Igumale, 31:13
Igwadaren, 15:25,
   53:7

Ihaggaren, 15:23,
   53:1
Ihajenen, 15:23,
   53:5
Ijaw, 31:21
Ijebu, 31:30
Ijesha, 31:29
Ijo, 31:21
Ijumu, 31:26
Ika, 31:20
Ikasa, 29:26
Ikele, 37:3
Ikemba, 38:60
Ikenga, 29:26
Ikokolemu, 43:22
Ikolu, 13:18
Ikoma, 45:19
Ikongo, 27:10
Ikota, 36:14
Ikulu, 13:18
Ikumunu, 31:8
Ikuzu, 45:19
Ila, 47:1
Ilalangina, 27:4
Ilesha, 31:29
Illa, 31:29
Ilorin, 31:31
Iltiamus, 43:33
Ilumpua, 43:32
Imamono, 27:3
Imbangala, 38:10
Imbara, 29:11
Imedreden, 53:7
Imentagen, 15:19
Imeragen, 52:16
Imerina, 27:7
Imoma, 37:5
Imragen, 52:16
Imssegin, 15:19
Imtuggen, 15:19
Inamwanga, 46:13
Indiki, 30:9
Ineme, 31:24
Inemu, 33:1
Ingassana, 21:6
Ingessana, 21:6
Ingkum, 31:15
Ingouesse, 36:13
Ininga, 35:12
Inkundo, 37:9
Inqua, 9:2

Invisa, 38:35
Ipanga, 37:2
Iraku, 24:3
Iramba, 46:2
Irangi, 46:4
Irapwe, 33:1
Iraqw, 24:3
Irecapo, 33:1
Irenge, 43:2
Iria, 16:3
Iribue, 33:1
Irie, 16:3
Irigwe, 13:7
Iringa, 17:5
Irreganaten, 15:25,
  53:7
Irrigwe, 13:7
Irwana, 46:9
Isa, 31:19, 41:2
Isaian, 15:2
Isala, 12:19
Isalen, 12:19
Isandra, 27:4
Iseksawan, 15:19
Ishaak, 41:5
Ishan, 31:19
Ishogo, 35:13
Isoko, 31:22
Issangili, 35:6
Issansu, 46:2
Issinese, 32:28
Issogo, 35:13
Issynois, 32:28
Isuwu, 35:5
Itawa, 38:45
Itesan, 53:3
Iteso, 43:22
Itesyo, 43:22
Itsekiri, 31:23
Itsha, 31:27
Ittu, 42:4
Itu, 42:4
Iullemmeden, 53:4
Ivbiosakon, 31:24
Iwa, 41:13
Iya, 13:61
Iyace, 31:11
Iyala, 31:15
Iyambi, 46:2
Iyembe, 37:2
Iyon, 13:28

Izanzu, 46:2
Izargien, 15:22
Izerguiin, 15:22

Jaalyyin, 54:6
Jaba, 13:18
Jabo, 33:5
Jaca, 38:18
Jackjack, 32:26
Jagada, 16:3
Jagga, 44:1
Jagub, 52:32
Jagut, 15:22
Jakri, 31:23
Jal, 13:4
Jallonke, 11:3
Jalo, 15:9
Jaloff, 34:12
Jaluo, 43:14
Jamaat, 52:33
Jambo, 21:2
Jamjam, 25:1
Jang, 43:5
Jangere, 29:35
Janjero, 23:4
Janji, 13:12
Jar, 13:11
Jara, 17:36
Jarawa, 13:1, 13:11
Jarso, 42:4
Jassing, 29:11
Jasua, 36:29
Jaunde, 36:11
Jebala, 52:17
Jebelawin, 21:3
Jedina, 17:26
Jekri, 31:23
Jelli, 8:1
Jemel, 15:22
Jen, 13:54
Jenge, 13:35
Jenji, 13:12
Jera, 17:36
Jerawa, 13:12
Jerba, 15:10
Jerid, 52:18
Jerir, 52:9
Jerra, 17:36
Jerrar, 15:19
Jesko, 13:30
Jia, 38:23

Jibana, 39:8
Jibbeh, 43:20
Jibu, 13:13
Jie, 43:20
Jiji, 45:3
Jimo, 13:35
Jindembu, 38:7
Jita, 45:19
Jiwat, 34:6
Jiwe, 43:20
Jiye, 43:20, 43:23
Jlass, 52:14
Jofra, 15:11
Joko, 28:6
Jolof, 34:12
Jopadhola, 43:14
Jorto, 13:33
Jubu, 13:13
Jukon, 13:14
Jukun, 13:14
Jumba, 35:12
Jumjum, 21:11
Jur, 43:6

Kaba, 23:3, 28:6
Kababish, 54:12
Kabakwe, 9:13
Kabalai, 17:21
Kabba, 28:6, 31:26
Kabende, 38:33
Kabil, 34:6
Kabinda, 38:4
Kabo, 23:3
Kabre, 12:34
Kabu, 32:13
Kabure, 12:34
Kaburi, 17:27
Kabyle, 15:12
Kachama, 23:7
Kache, 13:18
Kacherda, 16:6
Kachicheri, 13:18
Kachipo, 43:4
Kachmere, 17:6
Kachuba, 43:4
Kacongo, 38:4
Kadallu, 21:4
Kadalo, 21:4
Kadam, 43:29
Kadara, 13:15
Kadaru, 19:4

Kadero, 19:4
Kadjidi, 17:27
Kado, 12:10
Kadodo, 20:5
Kadugli, 20:5
Kaduna, 13:2
Kafa, 23:5
Kafficho, 23:5
Kaffir, 50:4
Kafima, 48:1
Kagoma, 13:18
Kagoro, 11:4,
  13:18
Kaguru, 46:23
Kahe, 44:1
Kahugu, 13:10
Kai, 17:31
Kaibi, 13:20
Kajaja, 20:2
Kaje, 13:18
Kajjara, 19:3
Kajji, 13:18
Kajuru, 13:15
Kaka, 13:27, 36:12
Kaka-Banjo, 13:27
Kakande, 31:18
Kakonda, 48:4
Kakongo, 38:4
Kakuak, 43:16
Kakwa, 43:16
Kalabari, 31:21
Kalahari, 51:2
Kalai, 36:13
Kalanga, 38:36,
  49:1
Kaleri, 13:22
Kali, 29:1
Kaliko, 28:9
Kalkadda, 20:1
Kaluchazi, 38:26
Kaluena, 38:28
Kalukembe, 48:4
Kalum, 34:1
Kalunda, 37:14
Kam, 13:55
Kama, 35:12
Kamanga, 38:54
Kamant, 22:6
Kamantan, 13:18
Kamasya, 43:25
Kamba, 38:3, 44:2

Kambali, 13:16
Kambari, 13:16
Kambata, 25:2
Kambe, 39:8
Kamberi, 13:16
Kambonsenga,
    38:39
Kamdang, 20:5
Kami, 39:3
Kamir, 22:5
Kamkam, 13:23
Kamminga, 17:2
Kamo, 13:47
Kamu, 13:47
Kamudu, 13:17
Kamum, 43:6
Kanakuru, 13:27
Kanawa, 17:38
Kanda, 35:13
Kandawire, 38:54
Kanderma, 20:1
Kanembu, 17:27
Kanga, 20:5
Kangeju, 10:3
Kangu, 29:4
Kanike, 35:10
Kanikon, 13:18
Kanjaga, 12:16
Kanka, 17:27
Kankena, 17:27
Kanoury, 17:28
Kaonde, 38:38
Kapala, 28:3
Kapeta, 43:2
Kapo, 33:1
Kapsiki, 13:43
Kara, 28:2, 45:18
Karaboro, 12:2
Karakarit, 17:2
Karamojong, 43:21
Karan, 33:6
Karanga, 17:6,
    49:1
Karbo, 17:10
Kare, 29:9, 29:27
Karekara, 17:29
Karo, 23:1
Karoko, 43:1
Karoma, 43:4
Karon, 34:6
Karondi, 20:5

Karra, 16:6
Kaschilange, 37:13
Kaschua, 35:7
Kaselem, 12:30
Kasena, 12:19
Kashioko, 38:25
Kashmere, 17:6
Kasinji, 38:10
Kasom, 12:19
Kasongi, 48:4
Kasonke, 11:5
Kassanga, 34:3
Kasson, 11:5
Kassonbura, 12:19
Kassonfra, 12:19
Kassuna, 12:19
Katab, 13:18
Katla, 20:1
Katsamma, 23:7
Katsenawa, 17:38
Katsokwe, 38:12
Kattei, 20:1
Kaura, 39:8
Kaure, 12:34
Kavirondo, 43:14,
    45:21
Kawahla, 54:5
Kawalib, 20:1
Kawar, 16:5
Kawasma, 54:16
Kawendi, 38:33
Kaya, 29:9
Kayla, 22:6
Keaka, 31:3
Kebbawa, 17:38
Kebeirka, 21:7
Kebu, 32:13
Kede, 31:18
Kedemane, 32:10
Kederu, 28:13
Kedi, 43:22
Kediru, 28:13
Kedo, 43:22
Kegueme, 34:10
Keiga, 20:5
Keiga-Girru, 20:6
Kela, 37:3
Kel Ahaggar, 15:23,
    53:1
Kel Air, 15:23,
    53:3

Kel Antessar,
    15:23, 53:2
Kelawa, 13:8
Kel Azdjer, 15:23,
    53:5
Kele, 36:13
Kel Geres, 53:3
Kel Gossi, 53:7
Keliko, 28:9
Kelingane, 17:6
Kelinguen, 17:6
Kel Oui, 53:3
Kel Tadele, 53:3
Kemaltu, 17:36
Kemant, 22:6
Kenana, 54:16
Kene, 45:13
Kenga, 17:16
Kengawa, 12:48
Kenous, 19:2
Kenozi, 19:2
Kentu, 13:19
Kenuzi, 19:2
Kenya, 17:16
Kepere, 29:5
Kerarish, 54:13
Kere, 23:1
Kerekere, 17:29
Kerewe, 45:11
Kerkena, 52:31
Kerre, 23:1
Kerriat, 54:12
Kerzaz, 15:24
Kete, 37:15
Ketu, 31:27
Keyu, 43:25
Kgalagadi, 51:2
Kgatla, 51:3
Khaha, 51:5
Khamir, 22:5
Khamta, 22:5
Kharga, 52:19
Khasonke, 11:5
Khavi, 45:21
Khawalda, 54:16
Khayo, 45:21
Khebbache, 15:24
Khenga, 17:16
Khioko, 38:25
Khlot, 52:24
Khoke, 17:13

Khoma, 21:7
Khozzam, 54:20
Khumbi, 48:7
Khurutshe, 51:1
Khutu, 39:3
Khuzam, 54:20
Kiam, 12:8
Kiba, 36:14
Kibala, 38:9
Kiballo, 13:20
Kibbo, 13:4
Kibyen, 13:4
Kichepo, 43:4
Kidi, 43:22
Kien, 33:6
Kienga, 12:48
Kiga, 45:2
Kigelle, 21:7
Kikuyu, 44:3
Kilba, 13:44
Kilenge, 48:5
Kilinga, 12:37
Kilir, 12:37
Kim, 29:8
Kimbande, 38:27
Kimbu, 46:7
Kimbundu, 38:7
Kimbuzi, 33:18
Kimr, 17:3
Kinderma, 20:1
Kindiga, 10:3
Kinga, 46:25
Kinuku, 13:20
Kioko, 38:25
Kioque, 38:25
Kipala, 38:9
Kipsigi, 43:26
Kipsorai, 43:28
Kipsorak, 43:28
Kipungu, 48:7
Kir, 43:19
Kirdi, 54:11
Kiriama, 39:8
Kirifawa, 13:38
Kisama, 38:8
Kisanji, 38:11
Kisi, 33:12, 46:26
Kisii, 45:17
Kissama, 38:8
Kissandschi, 38:11
Kissi, 33:12

Kita, 55:5
Kitara, 45:12
Kitimi, 13:20
Kitosh, 45:21
Kiturika, 38:59
Kitusika, 38:59
Kiziba, 45:10
Kiziere, 29:11
Klepo, 33:2
Ko, 33:23
Koa, 8:1
Koalib, 20:1
Koba, 34:1, 47:2
Kobaba, 42:2
Kobochi, 13:35
Kobiana, 34:3
Kobo, 23:7
Kobore, 12:34
Kochoqua, 9:2
Kodo, 28:12
Kodvi, 17:6
Kofo, 13:35
Kogo, 35:6
Koigi, 10:4
Koikop, 43:33
Koira, 23:7
Koisha, 23:7
Kojam, 17:31
Koko, 17:13, 35:3
Kokorda, 16:4
Kola, 8:1, 13:40
Kolano, 12:13
Kolbila, 29:12
Kole, 35:5
Kolo, 33:20
Kolobe, 51:14
Kololo, 47
Kolomende, 33:23
Kom, 30:5
Koma, 9:10, 13:58, 21:7
Komba, 12:32
Kombe, 35:6, 35:8
Komo, 21:7, 36:15
Komono, 12:3
Kona, 13:40
Konambembe, 36:29
Konde, 46:28
Kongo, 38:1
Konguan, 31:1

Koni, 51:14
Koniagi, 34:11
Konianke, 11:6
Konjo, 45:5
Konka, 12:32
Konkomba, 12:32
Konku, 17:27
Konnoh, 33:20
Kono, 13:20, 33:20
Konongo, 46:8
Konso, 25:3
Konta, 23:7
Kontomba, 25:2
Kony, 43:28
Konyanke, 11:6
Kopo, 33:1
Kora, 9:2
Korana, 9:6
Koranko, 11:7
Korara, 21:7
Korawp, 31:6
Korbo, 17:10
Korekore, 49:2
Korikori, 49:2
Koriuk, 43:18
Korma, 43:4
Koro, 13:61, 31:12
Koroa, 16:3
Koro Ache, 13:61
Koroca, 9:7
Koro Funtu, 13:61
Korokoro, 39:10
Korongo, 20:5
Koron Huntu, 13:6
Koron Iya, 13:61
Koron Zani, 13:61
Korop, 31:6
Kororofawa, 13:14
Korro, 13:61
Kosho, 21:3
Kosi, 35:4
Kosova, 45:17
Kossi, 35:4
Kossob, 29:8
Kota, 36:14
Kotofo, 29:6
Kotoko, 17:30
Kotokoli, 12:35
Kotokori, 31:16
Kotopo, 29:6
Kouayegou, 10:4

Koubou, 17:8
Koudia, 28:1
Kouka, 17:18
Koulango, 12:13
Koule, 23:1
Koulfa, 28:1
Kounta, 52:21
Kourbo, 17:10
Koure, 23:1
Kourfey, 17:39
Kouri, 17:26
Kouroumba, 12:20
Kousansi, 12:25
Koutinn, 29:5
Kouya, 33:3
Koyam, 17:31
Kpa, 33:23
Kpankpam, 12:32
Kpe, 35:5
Kpedji, 31:25
Kpeli, 35:5
Kpelle, 33:21
Kper, 29:5
Kpese, 33:21
Kpin, 12:1
Kpone, 32:1
Kposo, 32:8
Kra, 33:6
Krachi, 32:14
Kran, 33:6
Krao, 33:7
Kratyi, 32:14
Krawi, 33:7
Kre, 33:5
Krebo, 33:5
Krech, 28:3
Kreda, 16:6
Kreish, 28:3
Krejy, 28:3
Kreki, 28:3
Krepe, 32:2
Krim, 33:14
Kriz, 52:18
Krobo, 32:1
Krobu, 32:19
Krongo, 20:5
Kru, 33:7
Ksima, 15:19
Ktawa, 15:3
Kuang, 17:17
Kuanyama, 48:1

Kuavi, 43:32
Kuba, 38:21
Kubbabish, 54:12
Kubu, 17:8
Kucha, 23:7
Kudawa, 13:6
Kudia, 28:1
Kudu, 17:6
Kuera, 23:7
Kufra, 52:20
Kugama, 13:57
Kuka, 17:18
Kuku, 43:16
Kukuruku, 31:24
Kukwe, 46:28
Kulambo, 12:13
Kulango, 12:13
Kule, 23:1
Kulfa, 28:1
Kulfe, 28:1
Kullo, 23:7
Kulu, 13:51
Kulya, 45:17
Kum, 43:20
Kumam, 43:22
Kumba, 13:57
Kumbe, 35:6, 35:8
Kumi, 43:20
Kumra, 28:6
Kumu, 36:15
Kumwe, 32:17
Kun, 17:17
Kunabembe, 36:29
Kunama, 21:8
Kunante, 34:2
Kunda, 38:36, 38:39
Kundu, 35:6, 37:9
Kung, 9:8, 17:17
Kungara, 17:2
Kungau, 9:8
Kunta, 52:21
Kunuzi, 19:2
Kunya, 32:14
Kunyi, 38:2
Kuontab, 23:7
Kupa, 31:18
Kurama, 13:20
Kuranko, 11:7
Kure, 23:1
Kurfei, 17:39

Kuri, 17:26
Kuria, 45:17
Kuroba, 32:19
Kurumba, 12:20
Kusae, 12:25
Kusale, 12:25
Kusan, 12:25
Kusasi, 12:25
Kusopa, 31:18
Kussi, 12:25
Kusu, 37:11
Kuta, 36:14
Kutev, 13:32
Kutin, 29:5
Kutshu, 37:4
Kutu, 37:8, 39:3
Kuturmi, 13:15
Kuvoko, 13:49
Kuya, 8:1, 33:3
Kwa, 33:3
Kwadre, 33:3
Kwadya, 33:3
Kwafi, 43:32
Kwahu, 32:16
Kwakwa, 32:29
Kwandi, 47:4
Kwangare, 48:3
Kwange, 36:31
Kwara, 22:6
Kwaya, 33:4, 45:19
Kwayegu, 10:4
Kwele, 36:10
Kweli, 35:5
Kwena, 51:4
Kwendre, 33:19
Kwengare, 48:3
Kwengo, 9:5
Kweni, 33:19
Kwere, 23:7, 39:2
Kwese, 38:12
Kwia, 33:2
Kwiri, 35:5
Kwise, 9:7
Kwolla, 13:33
Kwotba, 13:59
Kwotto, 31:16
Kyama, 32:30
Kyan, 12:8
Kyato, 13:19
Kyedye, 31:18
Kyenga, 12:48

Kyeto, 13:19
Kyilina, 12:37

Labwor, 43:11
Laccara, 28:10
Laego, 13:52
Lafana, 32:12
Lafit, 43:18
Laghouat, 52:22
Lagos, 31:30
Laguat, 52:22
Lahawiin, 54:16
Laikipiak, 43:33
Laka, 29:7, 50:6
Lakamaki, 28:13
Lakka, 29:7
Lako, 43:28
Lala, 13:59, 38:39,
    52:12
Lali, 35:14
Lamba, 12:34,
    38:40
Lambya, 46:14
Lame, 29:2
Lamja, 13:53
Lammiar, 52:16
Landeen, 50:8
Landoma, 34:7
Landouman, 34:7
Landro, 32:22
Landuma, 34:7
Langa, 50:6
Langbwasse, 29:16
Lange, 37:13
Langi, 46:4
Lango, 43:13,
    43:18, 43:22
Lareschiat, 25:4
Laro, 20:2
Latuka, 43:18
Laudo, 43:18
Lebu, 20:2, 34:12
Leco, 13:52
Lefana, 32:12
Lega, 28:8, 36:28
Leikipia, 43:33
Lekon, 13:52
Lekpokpam, 12:32
Lele, 11:7, 17:15,
    38:22
Lemande, 30:2

Lemba, 35:2, 38:9,
    51:15
Lende, 48:4
Lendu, 28:8
Lenge, 49:7
Lengi, 35:9, 47:3
Lengola, 36:16
Lenje, 47:3
Leria, 43:18
Lesa, 38:23
Lese, 28:16
Lesiye, 54:20
Lessa, 38:23
Leto, 28:4
Letwaba, 50:6
Leukip, 43:33
Leya, 47:10
Lhadj, 52:13
Lhassen, 15:22
Li, 30:6
Libo, 13:59
Libolo, 38:9
Lifumba, 37:9
Ligbi, 12:45
Ligi, 43:16
Ligoue, 12:45
Lika, 36:17
Likile, 36:18
Likpe, 32:12
Lilima, 49:1
Liliwa, 13:8
Lilse, 12:20
Lima, 13:58, 38:40,
    46:5
Limba, 33:13, 35:2
Limmu, 23:2
Linga, 37:8
Lino, 36:29
Lipkawa, 13:50
Liptako, 55:6
Lisi, 17:18
Lissel, 36:29
Litime, 32:8
Lo, 33:19
Loanda, 38:7
Loango, 38:4
Lobala, 36:24
Lobare, 38:28
Lobedu, 51:5
Lober, 12:23
Lobi, 12:14

Lofa, 13:47
Lofit, 43:18
Lofofa, 20:4
Logba, 12:34, 32:10
Logbwari, 28:10
Logo, 28:9
Logoli, 45:21
Logomaten, 15:25,
    53:7
Logone, 17:30
Loi, 36:3
Loimbe, 38:27
Lokele, 36:18
Lokko, 33:22
Loko, 32:22
Lokoiya, 43:18
Lokoli, 45:21
Lolia, 37:7
Lolo, 32:7, 37:6
Lolobi, 32:12
Loma, 33:25
Lombi, 28:25
Lomwe, 38:56
Lomya, 43:18
Londa, 38:41
Longarim, 43:2
Longo, 46:10
Longuda, 13:56
Lopit, 43:18
Lorho, 12:13
Lori, 28:12, 38:20
Loro, 12:13
Loron, 12:12
Loron-Lobi, 12:14
Loso, 12:28
Losso, 12:28
Lotuko, 43:18
Louagouare, 28:10
Louba, 37:12
Lounda, 37:14
Lour, 43:11
Lovale, 38:28
Lovedu, 51:5
Lowudo, 43:18
Lozi, 47:4
Lua, 38:13
Luanda, 38:7
Luano, 38:39
Luapula, 38:41
Luba, 37:12
Luba-Hemba, 38:36

Lubala, 36:24
Lubare, 28:10
Luchazi, 38:26
Luena, 38:28
Lugbara, 28:10
Lugori, 28:10
Luguru, 39:3
Lugwaret, 28:10
Luheka, 9:7
Luimbe, 38:27
Lukelle, 36:18
Lukerou, 36:18
Lukha, 20:2
Lukolwe, 47:5
Lula, 38:18
Lulua, 37:13
Luluba, 28:11
Luluwa, 37:13
Luman, 20:4
Lumba, 35:11
Lumbo, 35:11
Lumbu, 38:36, 47:1
Lumbwa, 43:26,
    43:32
Lumun, 20:4
Lunda, 37:14,
    38:31, 38:41
Lundu, 35:6
Lundwe, 47:1
Lungu, 13:18,
    13:21, 38:42
Luo, 43:6, 43:14
Lupolo, 38:9
Lur, 43:11
Luri, 43:11
Lushange, 47:9
Luto, 28:4
Lutschase, 38:26
Luvale, 38:28
Luwa, 38:13
Luwo, 43:14
Luxage, 38:26
Luyana, 47:4
Luyi, 47:4
Lwena, 38:28
Lwo, 43:6
Lwimbi, 38:27
Lyela, 12:20

Maakla, 54:5
Maalia, 54:5

Maaza, 52:23
Maba, 17:6
Mabale, 36:8
Maban, 21:11
Mabass, 13:45
Mabea, 35:7
Mabendi, 28:8
Mabenga, 35:8
Mabiha, 38:57
Mabinja, 36:5
Mabisanga, 28:22
Mabodo, 36:9
Mabudu, 36:9
Macha, 42:5
Machango, 35:11
Machonde, 50:10
Maciu, 23:6
Mada, 13:21, 13:46
Madaba, 17:6
Madala, 17:6, 51:14
Madanda, 49:4
Madennassena, 9:5
Madi, 28:11, 29:13
Madjinngay, 28:5
Madjo, 28:14
Madsche, 23:6
Maduma, 35:10
Madyo, 29:13
Mafiti, 50:10
Mafoto, 36:27
Maga, 17:18
Maganja, 38:51
Magbea, 35:7
Magengo, 21:10
Magharba, 52:30
Magi, 23:6
Magianghir, 21:10
Magiano, 21:10
Maginza, 36:8
Magois, 43:23
Magomi, 17:28
Magos, 43:23
Magoth, 43:23
Magova, 49:4
Magu, 13:23
Maguemi, 17:27
Magumi, 17:28
Magwangara, 50:10
Mah, 33:24
Mahafaly, 27:4
Mahamid, 54:14

Mahas, 19:2
Mahasi, 46:25
Mahi, 32:3
Mahiyan, 52:32
Mahoungoue, 36:14
Mahria, 54:14
Mahu, 11:6
Mahungo, 38:1
Maigo, 28:20
Maiye, 47:2
Majacalla, 38:18
Majer, 52:14
Majeur, 52:14
Maji, 23:6
Majolo, 25:3
Majombe, 38:5
Maka, 36:19
Makabul, 41:7
Makalahari, 51:2
Makalaka, 49:1
Makangala, 38:26
Makaraka, 29:25
Makaranga, 49:1
Makari, 17:30
Makbe, 12:10
Makdschuru, 43:10
Makere, 28:17
Makioko, 38:25
Makoa, 38:58
Makoane, 38:58
Makoma, 47:7
Makonde, 38:57
Makongo, 38:1
Makorekore, 49:2
Makouango, 38:4
Makua, 38:58
Makurma, 43:4
Makwangare, 48:3
Makwengo, 9:5
Makxiba, 51:5
Malabu, 13:35
Malachini, 39:10
Malakote, 39:10
Malanga, 17:6
Malegga, 28:8
Malele, 28:17
Malemba, 38:9
Malepa, 51:15
Malete, 51:14
Malhundo, 37:14
Mali, 28:1

Malika, 36:17
Malimba, 35:2
Malinke, 11:8
Malo, 23:7
Malobale, 38:28
Malochazi, 38:26
Mama, 13:22
Mamavolo, 51:14
Mambanga, 28:21
Mambari, 48:4
Mambecto, 28:19
Mambere, 28:23
Mambila, 13:23
Mamboe, 47:4
Mambukuschu, 47:8
Mambunda, 38:29
Mambwela, 47:5
Mamidja, 51:5
Mampelle, 12:26
Mamprusi, 12:26
Mampua, 33:14
Mampulugu, 12:26
Mamud, 15:19
Mamun, 28:2
Mamyu, 28:18
Mana, 33:24
Manadriana, 27:4
Manala, 50:7
Manangeri, 43:6
Manangier, 43:6
Manasir, 54:6
Mancagne, 34:9
Mandala, 54:5
Mandara, 17:32
Mandari, 43:19
Mande, 11
Mandenyi, 34:1
Manding, 11:8
Mandingo, 11:8
Mandja, 29:28
Manduri, 34:1
Mandyako, 34:9
Manehas, 35:4
Manga, 17:33,
    28:21
Mangala, 36:24
Manganapo, 12:34
Manganja, 38:51
Mangati, 43:30
Mangawa, 17:33
Mangba, 28:15

Mangbei, 29:11
Mangbele, 28:23
Mangbetu, 28:19
Mangbutu, 28:18
Mangia, 29:28
Mangoni, 50
Mangoro, 12:44
Mangutu, 28:18
Manigri, 31:27
Manika, 49:3
Manjo, 10:4
Mankanya, 34:9
Mankoya, 47:9
Mano, 33:24
Mansa, 40:7
Manta, 31:3
Manyang, 31:1
Manyika, 49:3
Mao, 21:9
Maouri, 17:41
Mapoch, 50:7
Mapungubwe, 26
Maqarha, 52:27
Marach, 45:21
Maragwetta, 43:29
Marakwet, 43:29
Mararet, 17:8
Maravi, 38
Marba, 29:8
Marea, 40:7
Marehan, 41:7
Marfa, 17:6
Marghi, 13:44
Margi, 13:43, 13:44
Margole, 45:21
Mari, 49:1
Maria, 40:7
Marille, 25:4
Marka, 12:42
Marki, 13:58
Marle, 25:4
Marmale, 25:4
Marotse, 47:4
Marungu, 38:42
Masa, 29:8
Masaba, 45:16
Masai, 43:32
Masalit, 17:7
Masanga, 36:29
Masango, 21:10,
    35:11

Masarwa, 9:12
Mashanga, 49:4
Mashasha, 47:6
Masheba, 38:47
Mashi, 47:7
Mashinge, 38:10
Mashona, 49
Mashongo, 21:10
Mashukolumbwe,
    47:1
Masi, 23:6
Masina, 55:7
Masmadje, 17:16
Masongo, 38:32
Massa, 29:8
Massai, 43:32
Massalat, 17:7
Massange, 35:11
Massat, 15:19
Massubia, 47:10
Masupia, 47:10
Matabele, 50:8
Matakam, 13:45
Matala, 51:14
Matamba, 38:7
Matambae, 38:57
Matawara, 49:5
Matchioko, 38:25
Matengo, 46:27
Matlambe, 17:6
Matmata, 15:13
Matoka, 38:54
Matomboji, 49:4
Matopo, 49:1
Matotela, 47:12
Matuka, 32:12
Matumba, 37:2
Matumbi, 46:19
Matumboka, 38:54
Mau, 11:6, 21:9
Maune, 50:6
Maungo, 38:1
Mauri, 17:41
Mavia, 38:57
Mawia, 38:57
Mawiha, 38:57
Maxi, 32:3
Maya, 17:32
Mayacca, 38:18
Mayanga, 28:15
Mayo, 21:9, 34:11

Mayogo, 28:20
Mayugu, 28:20
Mayumbe, 38:5
Mazi, 23:6
Mazitu, 50:10
Mazizuru, 49:6
Mazugawa, 17:40
Mbae, 28:21
Mbagani, 37:15
Mbai, 28:6, 43:28
Mbailundu, 48:4
Mbaka, 29:23, 38:7
Mbala, 38:14, 38:21,
    47:1
Mbale, 36:20
Mbali, 36:8, 48:4
Mbam, 30:12
Mbamba, 26:14,
    38:1
Mbande, 38:27
Mbanderu, 48:2
Mbang, 35:3
Mbanga, 28:21
Mbangala, 38:10
Mbanza, 29:18
Mbao, 36:14
Mbaon, 36:14
Mbarawa, 13:11
Mbarek, 52:41
Mbarike, 12:32
Mbat, 30:11
Mbata, 38:1
Mbato, 32:20
Mbaw, 30:11
Mbegumba, 29:30
Mbem, 30:11
Mbembe, 13:27,
    31:5
Mbenga, 35:8
Mbere, 29:9, 44:4
Mberidi, 43:6
Mberre, 29:9
Mbessa, 36:20
Mbete, 35:10
Mbia, 35:5
Mbimu, 36:29
Mbire, 49:6
Mbo, 35:4
Mboe, 37:5
Mboi, 13:59
Mboko, 35:5

Mbole, 37:5
Mbondjo, 29:22
Mbondo, 38:7
Mbonge, 35:6
Mbongo, 37:6,
    48:4
Mbotuwa, 13:6
Mboue, 36:13
Mbouin, 12:1
Mbowe, 47:4
Mboye, 13:59
Mbuba, 28:16
Mbudja, 36:8
Mbugu, 24:4
Mbugwe, 46:3
Mbui, 38:11
Mbuiyi, 38:11
Mbukushu, 47:8
Mbula, 13:24
Mbulu, 24:3
Mbulunge, 24:1
Mbulunich, 34:1
Mbum, 29:10
Mbunda, 38:29,
    47:7
Mbundu, 38:7, 48:4
Mbunga, 46:20
Mbuni, 38:19
Mburekem, 30:8
Mbutawa, 13:6
Mbuti, 8:4
Mbwela, 38:30,
    47:5
Mbwera, 47:5
Meban, 21:11
Medela, 16:4
Medje, 28:22
Medjimi, 36:10
Medogo, 17:18
Medscharten, 41:6
Megarha, 52:27
Megharin, 52:28
Mehadba, 52:14
Mehele, 30:2
Meidob, 19:5
Mejja, 15:22
Mekan, 43:4
Mekyibo, 32:31
Men, 43:4
Menaba, 15:19
Menabe, 27:10

Menasser, 15:14
Mende, 33:23
Mendsime, 36:10
Menemo, 30:13
Menka, 30:13
Menkiera, 12:21
Mensa, 40:7
Mentaga, 15:19
Merarit, 17:8
Merdu, 43:4
Mere, 28:3
Merelle, 25:4
Meribda, 52:36
Merina, 27:7
Meritu, 43:4
Merniang, 13:33
Meru, 44:1, 44:4
Merule, 43:2
Mesakin, 20:4
Mesallania, 54:6
Mesgilda, 52:17
Mesgina, 15:19
Mesgita, 15:3
Meshduf, 52:41
Mesme, 17:21
Messaba, 52:35
Messira, 38:44
Messiria, 54:15
Mestara, 52:17
Meta, 30:13
Metabi, 21:6
Metalsa, 15:17
Metcho, 13:27
Metellit, 52:14
Methellith, 52:14
Metja, 42:5
Mezguita, 15:3
Mfang, 36:11
Mfioti, 38:4
Mfumte, 13:27
Mfumungu, 35:14
Mfute, 29:33
Mgoumba, 35:7
Mhammid, 15:3
Miamilo, 35:4
Midgan, 10:5
Midobi, 19:5
Midogo, 17:18
Midshurtin, 41:6
Mieken, 43:4
Migili, 31:12

Mijertein, 41:6
Mijjertheyn, 41:6
Mikifore, 11:8
Miltu, 17:21
Mima, 17:9
Mimi, 17:9
Mimidza, 21:6
Mina, 32:6
Mindassa, 36:14
Mindoumbo, 35:10
Mineo, 13:45
Minew, 13:45
Minianka, 12:4
Minjombo, 36:29
Minungu, 38:25
Mirafab, 54:6
Miriam, 13:33
Miru, 20:5
Misaje, 13:27
Misanga, 36:29
Mishulundu, 47:7
Misorongo, 38:1
Mitshi, 13:28
Mittu, 28:12
Mituku, 36:21
Miyawa, 13:50
Miza, 28:13
Mnebba, 15:19
Mo, 12:18
Moab, 12:33
Moare, 12:3
Moba, 12:33
Mobali, 36:8
Mobanghi, 36:4
Mobango, 36:8
Mobati, 36:4
Mobber, 17:34
Mober, 17:34
Mocha, 23:3
Mochebo, 36:13
Modgel, 17:21
Modshafra, 15:9
Mofu, 13:39
Mogamaw, 30:13
Mogogodo, 43:33
Mogum, 28:2
Mogwandi, 29:31
Moize, 38:35
Mojat, 15:22
Mokogodo, 43:33
Mokurma, 43:4

Moldwa, 13:46
Mole, 12:27
Molepu, 51:14
Moletse, 51:14
Molingi, 35:9
Molosa, 10:4
Moquisse, 9:7
Mom, 30:7
Mombati, 36:4
Mombattou, 28:19
Mombera, 50:10
Mombesa, 36:20
Momboutou, 28:18
Momfou, 28:18
Momvu, 28:18
Monbuttu, 28:19
Mondari, 43:19
Mondonga, 36:27
Mondu, 29:29
Mongalla, 36:24
Mongandu, 37:7
Mongbutu, 28:19
Mongbwandi, 29:31
Mongelima, 36:2
Mongo, 35:2, 37:6
Mono, 29:1, 33:19
Monsengere, 37:2
Montoil, 13:33
Montol, 13:33
Mopoi, 28:24
Mora, 13:46
Moreb, 20:3
Morib, 20:3
Morille, 25:4
Moro, 20:2, 32:17
Moroa, 13:18
Moroccans, 52:24
Moru, 28:13
Moru-Agi, 28:13
Moru-Endri, 28:13
Moru-Kediru, 28:13
Moru-Kodo, 28:12
Moru-Misi, 28:13
Moruno, 32:17
Moru-Wadi, 28:12
Morwa, 13:18
Moshi, 12:27
Mossegale, 39:16
Mossi, 12:27
Mossilongi, 38:1

Motelane, 50:6
Moubi, 17:10
Mouchicongo, 38:1
Mouchilonge, 38:1
Moufa, 28:1
Moundan, 29:11
Mountain Damara,
   9:1
Mountou, 29:29
Mourdia, 16:2
Mourle, 43:2
Mourse, 43:4
Mousgou, 17:19
Moutou, 13:39
Moutoutou, 17:9
Moviza, 38:35
Moxoboya, 51:5
Moyo, 17:6
Mozabites, 15:15
Mozda, 52:27
Mpama, 37:2
Mpangu, 38:1
Mpangwe, 36:11
Mpezeni, 50:11
Mpomama, 36:29
Mpondo, 50:1
Mpondomise, 50:3
Mpongwe, 35:12
Mpoto, 46:26
Mraier, 52:28
Mrashi, 45:21
Msalala, 46:11
Mtalsa, 15:17
Mtarawa, 49:5
Mtioua, 15:19
Mtougga, 15:19
Mtuga, 15:19
Mubali, 36:22
Mubenge, 36:4
Mubi, 17:10
Mucoroca, 9:7
Mucusso, 47:8
Mudogo, 17:18
Mudsau, 38:61
Muemba, 38:34
Muenyi, 47:4
Mufa, 28:1
Muffo, 13:39
Muhanha, 48:5
Muhumbe, 48:7
Mujano, 38:61

Mujoa, 38:61
Muktale, 13:46
Mukulehe, 13:46
Mukulu, 38:33
Muleng, 13:35
Mulochazi, 38:26
Mulondo, 48:7
Muluena, 38:28
Mum, 30:7
Mumbake, 13:52
Mummu, 20:2
Mumuye, 13:57
Mumvu, 28:18
Munano, 48:4
Mundang, 29:11
Mundar, 43:19
Mundombe, 48:5
Mundu, 29:29
Munga, 13:53
Mungo, 35:2
Munhaneca, 48:8
Munshi, 13:28
Murabitin, 52:29
Murahidya, 52:11
Murdhu, 43:4
Murdia, 16:2
Muritu, 43:4
Murle, 43:2
Mursi, 43:4
Mursia, 43:4
Mursu, 43:4
Murta, 20:5
Murule, 43:2
Murundu, 35:6
Murzu, 43:4
Musarongo, 38:1
Musawali, 15:22
Musei, 29:8
Museki, 35:9
Musgoi, 13:39
Musgu, 17:19
Musgum, 17:19
Mushirongo, 38:1
Musmenam, 35:4
Mussa, 52:26
Mussoi, 29:8
Musugeu, 13:39
Musuk, 17:19
Musur. :go, 38:1
Mutsaya, 35:14
Muturua, 13:39

Muviza, 38:35
Muwenji, 51:15
Muyaka, 38:18
Mvae, 36:11
Mvegumba, 29:30
Mvele, 36:11
Mverodi, 43:6
Mvumba, 35:7
Mwa, 33:19
Mwai, 36:11
Mwamba, 46:28
Mwan, 12:23
Mwanga, 47:4
Mwei, 36:11
Mwele, 35:3
Mwelle, 36:11
Mwelya, 46:25
Mwera, 38:59
Mweru, 44:4
Myaka, 38:18
Myao, 38:61
Mydob, 19:5
Mzab, 15:15

Naa, 23:3
Nabdam, 12:25
Nabe, 12:13
Nabte, 12:25
Nacem, 52:9
Nafame, 12:5
Nafana, 12:5
Nafarha, 12:5
Nafusa, 15:16
Naga, 21:5
Nagaya, 21:5
Nago, 31:27
Nagot, 31:27
Naguta, 13:1
Nagwa, 12:19
Naho, 23:3
Nail, 52:25
Naji, 23:3
Naka, 28:3
Nakatsa, 16:4
Nalemba, 51:15
Nalou, 34:8
Nalu, 34:8
Nama, 9:9, 13:27
Namainga, 47:11
Naman, 9:9
Namaqua, 9:9

Namba, 12:34, 48:4
Namchi, 29:12
Namgeni, 51:15
Namib, 9:10
Namnam, 12:25
Namshi, 28:12
Namwanga, 46:13
Nana, 33:7
Nancere, 17:15
Nandi, 43:27
Nanerge, 12:4
Nangire, 17:15
Nangiya, 43:3
Nankana, 12:25
Nankanse, 12:25
Nankwili, 46:9
Nano, 48:4
Nanumba, 12:21
Nanune, 12:24
Nanzela, 47:1
Nanzwa, 49:1
Nao, 23:3
Naoudemba, 12:28
Napore, 43:3
Narabuna, 13:12
Narene, 51:5
Naron, 9:11
Nasser, 52:41
Natemba, 12:38
Natioro, 12:7
Natimba, 12:38
Natyab, 12:38
Naudeba, 12:28
Nautuba, 12:38
Nawaiba, 54:14
Nawuli, 32:14
Nawura, 32:14
Nawure, 32:14
Nayo, 23:3
Nazaza, 16:4
Nchumbulung,
   32:14
Nchumuru, 32:14
Ndaka, 36:22
Ndali, 46:14
Ndam, 17:21
Ndamba, 46:21
Ndamefwe, 32:20
Ndara, 17:32, 28:6
Ndare, 13:45
Ndasa, 36:14

Ndau, 49:4
Nde, 31:3
Ndebele, 50:8
Ndei, 31:3
Ndembu, 38:7,
   38:31
Ndemi, 28:6
Ndendehule, 46:19
Ndengereko, 39:17
Ndengese, 37:4
Ndenye, 32:17
Ndhir, 15:2
Ndiki, 30:9
Ndjavi, 35:10
Ndo, 28:9, 43:29
Ndob, 30:8
Ndogo, 29:30
Ndogpenda, 35:3
Ndoko, 36:23
Ndombe, 48:5
Ndomme, 30:12
Ndomo, 36:14
Ndonde, 38:60
Ndonga, 38:7
Ndongo, 38:7
Ndop, 30:8
Ndoren, 13:9
Ndorno, 20:2
Ndoro, 13:25
Ndouggo, 29:30
Ndouka, 28:4
Ndsime, 36:10
Ndsimu, 36:10
Ndu, 30:11
Nduka, 28:4
Ndulu, 48:4
Ndum, 30:11
Ndumbo, 35:10
Ndumu, 35:10,
   36:14
Ndundulu, 47:7
Ndzawu, 49:4
Ndzem, 36:10
Ndzundza, 50:7
Ndzungli, 30:11
Nedde, 32:19
Nedio, 33:1
Neffet, 52:14
Nefousa, 15:16
Nefta, 52:18
Nefusa, 15:16

Nefzawa, 52:18
Negrillos, 8
Negye, 43:20
Nembai, 12:13
Nen, 30:9
Nene, 33:1
Newole, 33:4
Neyaux, 33:3
Neyo, 33:3
Nfaka, 13:43
Ngabe, 50:3
Ngaboto, 43:33
Ngabre, 17:15
Ngachopo, 43:4
Ngadhado, 20:2
Ngaga, 12:32
Ngala, 17:30,
  36:24, 38:10
Ngalanga, 48:4
Ngalangi, 48:4
Ngaloi, 35:12
Ngama, 28:5
Ngamatak, 43:24
Ngamo, 17:29
Ngan, 12:44
Nganda, 48:5
Ngandu, 37:7
Ngangulu, 35:14
Ngannufwe, 32:20
Ngazija, 39:13
Ngbandi, 29:31
Ngbanye, 32:23
Ngbele, 28:23
Ngbwaka, 29:23
Nge, 31:17
Ngebellai, 43:24
Ngejim, 17:27
Ngell, 13:4
Ngemba, 30:13
Ngere, 29:35, 33:24
Ngezzim, 17:35
Ngiaka, 38:18
Ngie, 30:13, 36:14,
  43:20
Ngindo, 38:60
Ngiri, 36:3
Ngishem, 17:27
Ngitaio, 43:3
Ngizim, 17:35
Ngke, 9:12
Ngola, 36:24, 38:7

Ngoli, 38:20
Ngolo, 35:6
Ngomakek, 43:28
Ngombe, 36:20,
  36:24, 37:8
Ngomwia, 46:1
Ngonde, 46:28
Ngongo, 38:15,
  38:21
Ngoni, 50
Ngonyelu, 48:6
Ngonzelo, 48:6
Ngoroine, 45:19
Ngoulango, 12:13
Nguerze, 33:24
Ngulu, 39:4
Ngumba, 35:7
Ngumbi, 35:8, 48:7
Ngumbu, 38:33
Ngundi, 36:26
Nguni, 50
Ngunu, 30:13
Nguru, 38:56, 39:4
Nguruimi, 45:19
Nguu, 39:4
Ngwaketse, 51:6
Ngwato, 51:7
Ngwili, 36:29
Ngwo, 30:13
Ngwoi, 13:17
Nhemba, 48:6
Niabua, 33:3
Niadrubu, 33:24
Niam-Niam, 29:14
Niao, 33:24
Niapu, 28:17
Nibelai, 43:24
Nibulu, 12:21
Nidu, 13:19
Nieffu, 43:17
Nielim, 17:13
Niende, 12:38
Nienige, 12:8
Nifa, 15:19
Nigabani, 33:1
Nigbi, 12:45, 33:1
Nigwe, 12:45
Nigye, 43:20
Nika, 39
Nikorma, 43:4
Nile Nubians, 19:2

Nimbia, 13:41
Ningawa, 13:6
Ningo, 32:1
Niniha, 12:8
Ninong, 35:4
Ninzam, 13:21
Nioniosse, 12:20
Niporen, 43:3
Nithir, 43:24
Niyo, 33:3
Njabeta, 30:2
Njabi, 35:10
Njamus, 43:33
Njanja, 49:6
Njanti, 30:2
Njao, 49:4
Njawi, 35:10
Njei, 13:35
Njemps, 43:33
Njie, 43:20
Njiem, 36:10
Njillem, 17:13
Njungene, 30:11
Nkatshina, 32:14
Nki, 31:2
Nkim, 31:15
Nkogna, 32:14
Nkole, 45:6
Nkom, 30:5
Nkomi, 35:12
Nkonde, 46:28
Nkossi, 35:3
Nkove, 35:11
Nkoya, 47:9
Nkum, 31:15
Nkumbe, 48:7
Nkundo, 37:9
Nkunya, 32:14
Nkutu, 37:10
Noe, 49:6
Nogau, 9:8
Noho, 35:8
Nohwe, 49:6
Noko, 35:8
Nola, 42:4
Nole, 42:4
Noli, 42:4
Non, 34:10
Nono, 11:9, 34:10
Noo, 35:8
Noumou, 12:45

Nourouma, 12:21
Nozo, 33:1
Nsakkara, 29:32
Nsaw, 30:10
Nsei, 30:8
Nsenga, 38:50
Nso, 30:10
Nsundi, 38:3
Nsungli, 30:11
Ntchan, 12:30
Ntere, 35:14
Nthali, 38:54
Ntomba, 37:2,
  37:8
Ntribu, 32:15
Ntum, 36:11
Ntumba, 37:2
Ntumu, 36:11
Nuba, 17:14, 19:1,
  20
Nubi, 19:2
Nubians, 19
Nuclear Mande, 11
Nuer, 43:7
Nukr, 20:2
Numana, 13:21
Numu, 12:45
Numuna, 13:21
Nungu, 13:21
Nunguda, 13:56
Nunu, 35:14
Nunuma, 12:21
Nupe, 31:18
Nusan, 9:12
Nuwaiba, 54:14
Nyabwa, 33:3
Nyai, 49:1
Nyakyusa, 46:28
Nyamang, 19:6
Nyamba, 48:6
Nyambara, 43:16
Nyamusa, 28:12
Nyamwanga, 46:13
Nyamwezi, 46:9
Nwan, 33:19
Nwanati, 49:8
Nyaneka, 48:8
Nyanga, 45:4
Nyangatom, 43:23
Nyangbara, 43:16
Nyangbo, 32:10

Nyangela, 38:2
Nyangiya, 43:3
Nyangori, 43:27
Nyanja, 38:51
Nyankpo, 32:10
Nyari, 36:25
Nyaro, 20:2
Nyasa, 38:52
Nyaturu, 46:5
Nyei, 13:35
Nyelem, 17:13
Nyem, 36:10
Nyemba, 48:6
Nyende, 12:38
Nyengo, 47:7
Nyepu, 43:17
Nyidu, 13:19
Nyifwa, 43:14
Nyiha, 46:16
Nyika, 46:12
Nyikoroma, 43:4
Nyilam, 21:10
Nyima, 19:6
Nyipori, 43:3
Nyissir, 43:24
Nyivu, 13:19
Nyixa, 46:16
Nyokon, 30:9
Nyole, 45:21
Nyong, 35:8
Nyonyose, 12:20
Nyoro, 45:12
Nyubi, 49:1
Nyukur, 20:2
Nyuli, 45:13
Nyungwe, 38:49
Nzakara, 29:32
Nzangi, 13:35
Nzari, 38:20
Nzima, 32:28
Nzimu, 36:10
Nzofo, 38:13
Nzombo, 38:1
Nzwani, 30:13

Oako, 38:9
Obamba, 36:14
Obanen, 9:10
Obang, 31:3
Obli, 33:1
Ododop, 31:6

Oere, 31:23
Ofutu, 32:4
Ogaden, 41:7
Oghoriok, 43:18
Ogi, 28:13
Ogo, 32:12
Ogowe, 9:8
Ogykru, 32:25
Ohekwe, 9:13
Oida, 23:1
Oikop, 43:33
Ojang, 21:10
Ojiga, 28:13
Okafima, 48:1
Okale, 37:11
Okanda, 35:13
Okande, 35:13
Okefu, 28:10
Okene, 31:16
Okeni, 31:16
Okiek, 10:2
Okoiyang, 31:6
Okota, 36:14
Okpoto, 31:13
Okpoto-Mteze,
    31:7
Okung, 9:8
Okwaga, 31:13
Olam, 21:10
Old Diula, 11:6
Old Mbunda, 47:7
Olemba, 37:11
Oli, 35:2
Olulumaw, 31:3
Omand, 30:2
Omati, 23:7
Ombalantu, 48:1
Ombamba, 36:14
Ombandja, 48:1
Ombarandu, 48:1
Ombe, 38:11
Omelokue, 33:1
Ometi, 23:7
Ometo, 23:7
Ondo, 31:28
Ondonga, 48:1
Ondri, 28:13
Ondura, 48:4
Ongandjera, 48:1
Ongomo, 36:13
Onguangua, 48:1

Ongwe, 36:14
Onitsha, 31:20
Orepue, 33:1
Oro, 17:8
Orogniro, 43:23
Orri, 31:7
Orungu, 35:12
Oshopong, 31:5
Osuduku, 32:1
Otadi, 32:8
Otoro, 20:2
Oturkpo, 31:13
Ouaba, 12:38
Ouabouari, 38:36
Ouabouma, 38:23
Ouaga, 33:3
Ouala, 12:29
Ouara, 12:7
Ouargla, 15:28
Ouassoulou, 11:9
Ouazigoua, 39:5
Ouazimba, 38:55
Oudalen, 15:25,
    53:7
Oudio, 28:4
Oudoe, 39:2
Ouendallah, 16:4
Ouenya, 36:31
Ouere, 31:23
Oukwere, 39:2
Oulad-Bu-Seba,
    52:8
Oulad Cheikh,
    52:26
Oulad Chouekh,
    52:8
Oulad Delim, 52:8
Oulad Iahia ben
    Othman, 52:26
Oulad Mbarek,
    52:41
Oulad Moussa,
    52:26
Oulad Nasser,
    52:41
Oulad Reilane,
    52:26
Oulad Talet, 52:26
Oulliminden,
    15:23, 53:4
Oumbee, 35:10

Ounein, 15:19
Ouobe, 33:9
Ouolof, 34:12
Ourazla, 52:31
Ouregga, 36:28
Ourfellah, 52:27
Ouroungou, 35:12
Ousgita, 15:19
Outeniqua, 9:2
Ovagandjera, 48:1
Ovah, 27:7
Ovaherero, 48:2
Ovahinga, 48:7
Ovakuangari, 48:3
Ovakuanyama, 48:1
Ovakumbi, 48:7
Ovambo, 48:1
Ovamguambi, 48:1
Ovandonga, 48:1
Ovanguuruze, 48:1
Ovanyaneka, 48:8
Ovimbali, 48:4
Ovimbundu, 48:4
Owe, 31:26
Owerri, 31:23
Owey, 53:3
Owo-Ifon, 31:28
Oyo, 31:31

Paawa, 13:50
Pabir, 13:36
Padang, 43:8
Padebu, 33:6
Padorho, 12:12
Pahn, 33:8
Pahouin, 36:11
Pai, 13:33
Paiema, 13:4
Pain, 12:1
Pakara, 13:12
Pakot, 43:29
Pala, 12:3
Pambia, 29:13
Panda, 31:16
Pande, 36:26
Pango, 36:1
Pangpana, 12:32
Pangwa, 46:25
Pangwe, 36:11
Pantera, 12:5
Pape, 29:12

Papel, 34:9
Pare, 44:5
Pari, 43:9
Parkhalla, 12:13
Pasala, 12:19
Patschuni, 39:12
Peda, 32:6
Pedi, 51:8
Pella, 13:59
Pem, 13:4
Pemba, 39:15
Pende, 38:16
Penin, 30:9
Penyin, 30:9
Pepel, 34:9
Pere, 29:5, 36:6
Peri, 36:6
Pero, 13:47
Peske, 29:4
Pessy, 33:21
Peul, 55
Phalaborwa, 51:5
Phoka, 38:54
Phungwe, 49:5
Pia, 13:51, 33:1
Pibor, 43:2
Pie, 33:1
Pilapila, 12:37
Pimbwe, 46:15
Pin, 12:1
Pindi, 38:17
Pindji, 37:17
Pirra, 13:59
Piti, 13:12
Pitti, 13:12
Piyawa, 13:51
Pla, 32:6
Plapo, 33:1
Plateau Nigerians,
    13
Plawi, 33:1
Pobi, 35:13
Podo, 32:11
Podogo, 13:46
Podokwo, 13:46
Podzo, 38:48
Pogoro, 46:22
Pojulu, 43:16
Pok, 43:28
Poka, 38:54
Pokomo, 39:10

Pokot, 43:29
Pokwut, 43:29
Pol, 36:12
Pomo, 36:29
Pomporo, 12:4
Pondo, 50:1
Pongo, 13:17, 35:2,
    35:12
Pongoue, 35:12
Popo, 32:5, 32:6
Poroto, 46:24
Poto, 36:27
Poubi, 35:13
Povi, 35:13
Powi, 35:13
Prampram, 32:1
Prenilotes, 21
Prufa, 33:1
Pu, 36:14
Pubi, 35:13
Puguli, 12:11
Puko, 35:8
Puku, 35:8
Pullo, 55
Pungu, 48:7
Puno, 35:13
Pya, 33:1
Pyem, 13:4

Qadharhfa, 52:33
Qemant, 22:6
Qireijab, 40:1
Quara, 22:6
Queah, 33:2
Quiaca, 48:4
Quibula, 48:4
Quilenge, 48:5
Quilombo, 48:4
Quimbande, 38:27
Quingolo, 48:4
Quioco, 38:25
Quipeyo, 48:4
Quipungu, 48:7
Quiquete, 48:4
Quissama, 38:8
Quissanje, 38:11
Quitata, 48:4
Qwathi, 50:3

Rabai, 39:8
Rachiat, 25:4

Rahawein, 41:8
Rama, 35:11
Rambia, 46:14
Randili, 42:6
Rangi, 46:4
Rashad, 20:3
Rebinawa, 13:12
Red Bobo, 12:8
Rega, 36:28
Regeibat, 52:26
Rehalat, 52:26
Rehamna, 52:24
Rehouna, 52:17
Reilane, 52:26
Rendile, 42:6
Reshe, 13:26
Reshiat, 25:4
Rgibat, 52:26
Rhadames, 15:7
Rharbya, 52:24
Rhat, 15:23
Rhona, 52:17
Rhuna, 52:17
Riah, 52:27, 52:31
Ribam, 13:12
Ribe, 39:8
Ribi, 10:5
Rif, 15:17
Riffians, 15:17
Rigwe, 13:7
Rikabiyyah, 21:3
Rimba, 8:1
Ripere, 29:5
Rishuwa, 13:20
Rissiat, 25:4
Riyah, 52:27, 52:31
Rizaykat, 54:8
Rizeigat, 54:8
Roba, 13:59
Rolong, 51:9
Romans, 18
Ron, 13:33
Ronga, 49:9
Rongo, 46:10
Rori, 46:24
Roro, 21:7
Rotse, 47:4
Rounga, 17:11
Routou, 28:4
Rouvou, 39:5
Rozi, 47:4

Rozwi, 49:6
Ruanda, 45:7
Ruarha, 52:28
Rubatab, 54:6
Rufaa, 54:16
Rufiji, 39:17
Rukuba, 13:12
Rumaiya, 13:20
Rumbi, 28:25
Rundi, 45:8
Runga, 17:11
Rungu, 35:12
Rungwa, 46:15
Ruri, 45:19
Ruruma, 13:20
Russia, 25:4
Ruton, 28:4
Ruvu, 39:5
Ruwu, 39:5
Rwanda, 45:7

Saadi, 52:29
Sab, 41:8
Saba, 17:16
Sabaot, 43:28
Sabei, 43:28
Sablo, 13:58
Saco, 23:3
Sadqi, 32:17
Safwa, 46:16
Sagada, 16:3
Sagala, 46:23
Sagara, 46:23
Sahafatra, 27:1
Sahel, 15:22, 52:31
Saho, 41:9
Sahue, 32:28
Sai, 51:5
Said, 52:31
Saka, 37:1
Sakalava, 27:8
Sakara, 29:32
Sakata, 38:23
Sala, 23:7, 47:1
Salamat, 54:11
Salya, 46:28
Samai, 23:1
Samba, 38:17
Sambara, 44:6
Sambaro, 25:2
Sambo, 48:4

Sambu, 48:4
Sambur, 43:33
Samburu, 43:33
Same, 12:15
Samia, 45:21
Samino, 12:7
Samo, 12:46
Samogho, 12:46
Samoro, 12:46
Samvign, 32:17
San, 12:46, 21:7
Sandawe, 10:6
Sande, 29:14
Sandia, 46:26
Sanga, 13:21, 36:29, 38:38
Sangada, 16:3
Sangawa, 13:12
Sange, 48:4
Sango, 29:34, 46:24
Sangu, 46:24
Sanhadja, 15:17
Sania, 10:11
Sankan, 12:4
Sankaran, 11:8
Sankura, 12:8
Sanmu, 12:7
Santrokofi, 32:12
Sanusi, 52:30
Sanwi, 32:17
Sanye, 10:11
Sao, 41:9
Sapahn, 33:8
Sapaut, 43:28
Sapei, 43:28
Sapo, 33:8
Sarakole, 11:10
Sarer, 34:10
Sari, 29:12
Sarua, 17:21
Sarwa, 9:12, 17:21
Sautsauta, 27:3
Sawa, 13:46
Sayawa, 13:33
Sayirr, 13:29
Schewe, 23:3
Sciacco, 23:3
Scioghile, 21:3
Seawa, 13:33
Seba, 52:8
Sebitiela, 50:6

Seddrat, 15:3
Sefwi, 32:12
Segami, 35:9
Segeju, 39:16
Seiyawa, 13:33
Seke, 35:9
Sekiani, 35:9
Seksawa, 15:19
Seksioua, 15:19
Sele, 38:11
Seleka, 50:6
Selim, 54:17
Selima, 52:19
Selle, 38:11
Selya, 46:28
Semen, 17:18
Semlal, 15:19
Semmeg, 15:19
Semu, 12:15
Sena, 38:53
Sendere, 12:4
Sene, 12:6
Senga, 38:43, 38:50
Sengele, 37:2
Senhaja, 15:17
Senufo, 12:6
Seraculeh, 11:10
Serae, 22:7
Sere, 29:30, 43:19
Serer, 34:10
Seri, 15:2
Seria, 46:28
Serif, 52:17
Serre, 29:30
Serruchen, 15:2
Setta, 52:17
Settut, 52:40
Sewa, 33:23, 38:40
Sewe, 29:12
Sewo, 23:3
Seysse, 23:7
Shaanba, 52:5
Shabi, 49:1
Shai, 51:5
Shaikia, 54:18
Shaire, 29:30
Shake, 35:9
Shako, 23:3
Shambala, 44:6

Shanga, 12:48, 49:4
Shangalla, 21:3
Shangama, 23:1
Shangana, 49:10
Shangi, 47:7
Shango, 35:11
Shangwe, 49:2
Shashi, 45:19
Shatt, 17:4, 43:6
Shawasha, 49:6
Shawia, 15:18, 52:24
She, 23:3
Shebelle, 39:11
Sheekan, 35:9
Shegya, 54:18
Sheir, 29:30
Shej, 52:26
Sheke, 35:9
Shekiani, 35:9
Shekke, 23:3
Shenabla, 54:5
Sherbro, 33:14
Shere, 17:15
Sheukh, 52:8
Sheva, 38:47
Shewo, 23:3
Shidle, 39:11
Shiho, 41:9
Shikuya, 35:14
Shila, 38:44
Shilluk, 21:12
Shilluk-Luo, 43:6
Shimba, 48:2
Shinasha, 21:5
Shinje, 38:10
Shioko, 38:25
Shir, 43:19
Shira, 35:11
Shirawa, 17:22
Shiwa, 54:20
Shluh, 15:19
Shoa, 54:20
Shoa Galla, 42:7
Shogo, 35:13
Shona, 49
Shtuka, 15:19
Shukria, 54:19
Shuli, 43:10
Shuri, 43:4

Shuwa, 54:20
Shwai, 20:2
Sia, 12:47
Sidamo, 23, 25:1
Sidi, 23:7, 52:32
Sidi Khelil, 52:28
Sido, 23:1, 23:7
Sidra, 19:6
Sidyanka, 11:8
Siena, 12:6
Sihanaka, 27:9
Sika, 32:12
Sikisi, 43:26
Sikolo, 12:3
Sikon, 33:2
Sila, 17:4
Sillok, 21:3
Simaa, 47:7
Simba, 35:13
Simbeti, 45:17
Simbiti, 45:17
Sin, 34:10
Sinja, 45:15
Sinjanja, 49:6
Sinsin, 34:10
Sirawa, 13:50
Siri, 29:30
Sirifou, 52:41
Sirticans, 52:33
Siska, 38:54
Sissala, 12:19
Sisya, 38:54
Site, 12:22
Sitemu, 34:1
Siwa, 15:20
Siwu, 32:12
Siya, 32:10
Slass, 52:17
Sless, 52:17
Snus, 15:29
So, 36:19
Soahili, 39
Soba, 45:17
Sobane, 34:1
Sochile, 46:28
Sodi, 47:3
Sodo, 32:8
Sofi, 28:12
Soga, 45:13
Soghaua, 16:8
Sokhman, 1f·2

Sokile, 46:28
Sokna, 15:11
Soko, 36:30
Sokoro, 17:20
Sokoto, 55:9
Sokwele, 33:3
Sokwia, 45:15
Sokya, 33:3
Soli, 47:3
Soliman, 52:33,
   52:34
Somali, 41
Somba, 12:38
Sombaru, 12:38
Some, 12:38
Somno, 12:46
Somono, 11:1
Somrai, 17:21
Sonde, 38:13
Songe, 37:16
Songhai, 17:44
Songhoi, 17:44
Songo, 38:15,
   38:32
Songola, 36:31
Songomeno, 37:10
Sonhray, 17:44
Soninke, 11:10
Sonjo, 45:19
Sore, 43:28
Sorek, 43:28
Sorongo, 38:1
Soruba, 12:38
Sosi, 35:4
Soso, 11:11
Sossi, 35:4
Sotek, 43:26
Sotho, 51:10
Souassi, 52:14
Soudie, 17:39
Soungor, 17:5
Soussou, 11:11
Sovi, 46:17
Sowe, 46:17
Suaad, 52:26
Suafa, 52:34
Suaheli, 39
Suaya, 15:9
Suba, 45:17
Subia, 47:10
Subktu, 13:59

Subu, 35:5
Subya, 47:10
Suga, 13:9
Sugu, 12:37
Sugur, 13:44
Sugurti, 17:27
Suk, 43:29
Suka, 44:4
Sukkot, 19:2
Sukku, 43:29
Suku, 38:17
Sukuma, 46:10
Sukur, 13:44
Sukwa, 46:28
Sula, 17:4
Sragna, 52:24
Srubu, 13:20
Sumbe, 38:11
Sumbwa, 46:11
Sundi, 38:3
Sungor, 17:5
Sungu, 37:11
Suri, 43:4
Surma, 43:4
Susu, 11:11
Swahili, 39
Swaka, 38:40
Swassi, 52:14
Swazi, 50:2
Sya, 12:47
Syenere, 12:4

Taaisha, 54:8
Tabanya, 20:5
Tabetuo, 33:1
Tabi, 21:6
Tabosa, 43:23
Tacho, 20:4
Tadele, 53:3
Tadjoni, 45:21
Tadla, 52:24
Taelba, 54:8
Tafi, 32:10
Tafilalet, 15:6
Tagali, 20:3
Tagba, 12:4
Tagbo, 29:30
Tageli, 20:3
Tagoi, 20:3
Tagu, 17:1
Tahu, 33:1

Taifasy, 27:1
Taimoro, 27:1
Taisaka, 27:1
Taita, 44:7
Tajakant, 52:36
Takruri, 55:8
Tal, 13:33
Tala, 13:46
Taleb, 52:26
Talene, 12:25
Tali, 29:9, 43:19
Tallensi, 12:25
Talmoje, 41:10
Talni, 12:25
Talodi, 20:4
Talok, 13:29
Tama, 17:5, 21:10,
   43:4
Tamba, 12:37, 38:7
Tambahuaca, 27:1
Tambaro, 25:2
Tamberma, 12:34
Tambo, 13:58,
   46:14
Tamboboba, 12:19
Tamerna, 52:28
Tampolense, 12:22
Tamprussi, 12:22
Tanala, 27:10
Tanan, 15:19
Tandruy, 27:2
Taneka, 12:37
Tang, 30:11
Tanga, 35:8
Tangale, 13:47
Tankay, 27:10
Tanna Galla, 42:2
Tannekwe, 9:14
Tanosy, 27:2
Tanusi, 27:2
Tanwa, 38:45
Taposa, 43:23
Tara, 12:8
Taram, 13:53
Tarok, 13:29
Tasoni, 20:4,
   45:21
Tasserkant, 52:36
Tasumsa, 15:21
Tata, 20:4
Tatoga, 43:30

Taturu, 43:30
Taurawa, 13:12
Tavara, 49:5
Taveta, 44:5
Tawana, 51:11
Tawara, 49:5
Tazarawa, 17:42
Tchangbore, 32:14
Tchimboro, 32:14
Tchirra, 25:3
Tchumbuli, 32:9
Tdama, 43:4
Tdamoo, 23:1
Tebele, 50:8
Tebu, 16:7
Teda, 16:7
Tefasi, 27:1
Tegamawa, 17:42
Tegessie, 12:14
Tegue, 12:13, 35:14
Teis, 20:5
Teis-um-Danab,
   20:6
Teita, 44:7
Tekarir, 55:8
Teke, 35:14
Tekele, 20:3
Tekena, 15:22
Tekna, 15:22
Tele, 28:6
Tem, 12:35
Temain, 20:6
Temassin, 52:28
Temba, 12:35
Tembaro, 25:2
Tembo, 50:3
Tembu, 50:3
Teme, 13:57
Temein, 20:6
Temne, 33:15
Temurka, 17:2
Tenaker, 52:36
Tenda, 34:11
Tende, 35:14, 45:17
Tendik, 20:2
Tengeredief, 53:2
Tenuro, 27:1
Tepes, 43:21
Tepeth, 43:21
Tepo, 33:5
Tera, 17:36

Terawa, 17:36
Terawia, 16:2
Terayfia, 54:2
Terema, 43:4
Teria, 13:12
Terik, 43:27
Terna, 43:4
Ternata, 15:3
Tesake, 27:1
Tese, 12:13
Teshenawa, 17:22
Teso, 43:22
Tete, 9:13
Tetela, 37:11
Teuso, 10:8
Teve, 49:4
Tewi, 33:5
Thabina, 51:5
Tharaka, 44:4
Thembu, 50:3
Thonga, 49:10
Thuri, 43:4, 43:6
Tian, 12:8
Tiapi, 34:7
Tibbu, 16:7
Tichit, 52:41
Tid, 43:4
Tidikelt, 15:24
Tie, 28:6, 33:5
Tienga, 12:48
Tigon, 13:27
Tigrai, 40:7
Tigre, 40:7
Tigrinya, 22:7
Tigum, 13:27
Tikar, 30:12
Tilma, 43:4
Tima, 20:1
Timne, 33:15
Timonjy, 27:3
Timu, 12:35
Tindega, 10:3
Tinedla, 52:28
Tinerst, 15:26
Tingelin, 29:4
Tingeregdech,
    53:7
Tinguelin, 29:4
Tinzulin, 15:3
Tira, 20:2
Tiriki, 43:27

Tirma, 43:4
Tishana, 43:4
Tiv, 13:28
Tlhako, 51:14
Tlhaping, 51:12
Tlharu, 51:13
Tliq, 52:24
Tlokwa, 51:14
Toagi, 33:1
Tobote, 12:30
Tobur, 43:12
Tod, 43:4
Todga, 15:6
Tofinu, 32:5
Tofoke, 36:32
Togbo, 29:24
Togi, 13:58
Toi, 43:1
Toka, 47:11
Tokwa, 51:14
Tolakka, 29:7
Toljaala, 41:5
Tollo, 38:23
Toma, 33:25
Tomam, 54:2
Tombo, 12:10
Tonga, 38:54, 47:11,
    49:5, 49:7, 49:10
Tongwe, 46:6
Toni, 36:11
Tonka, 47:11
Topoke, 36:32
Topotha, 43:23
Torbi, 13:23
Toro, 12:10, 45:14,
    46:5
Torodo, 55:8
Torona, 20:4
Toronka, 11:8
Torumbu, 36:18
Totela, 47:12
Touareg, 15:23
Touat, 15:24
Toubou, 16:7
Toubouri, 13:48
Toucouleur, 55:8
Touggourt, 52:28
Touloumey, 17:37
Toummak, 17:21
Touna, 12:14
Toundjour, 54:21

Tounia, 17:13
Toura, 33:16
Tourouka, 12:1
Toyo, 33:1
Toyoke, 36:32
Tozeur, 52:18
Trafi, 52:32
Trarza, 52:37
Trebo, 33:5
Tribu, 32:15
Tripolitanians,
    52:38
Trugbo, 32:10
Tsaam, 38:17
Tsamai, 23:1
Tsamako, 23:1
Tsamba, 13:52
Tsara, 23:7
Tsaukwe, 9:11
Tsautsho, 12:35
Tsaya, 35:14
Tschamba, 12:30
Tschebe, 31:27
Tschikowe, 38:25
Tschiroa, 17:27
Tschokossi, 12:41
Tserekwe, 9:13
Tshabe, 31:27
Tshanga, 12:48
Tshire, 17:15
Tshopi, 49:7
Tsiboko, 38:25
Tsilmanu, 43:4
Tsimihety, 27:11
Tsinga, 36:11
Tsokwe, 38:25
Tsonokwe, 9:11
Tsoul, 52:17
Tsubye, 51:5
Tsugu, 13:53
Tsurgurti, 17:27
Tswana, 53
Tsylina, 12:37
Tuareg, 15:23, 53
Tuat, 15:24
Tubakay, 11:8
Tubindi, 37:15
Tubori, 13:48
Tubu, 16:7
Tuburi, 13:48
Tuggurt, 52:28

Tugong, 13:27
Tugun, 13:27
Tuken, 43:25
Tukete, 37:15
Tuki, 13:58
Tukkongo, 38:22
Tukri, 55:8
Tuku, 54:14
Tukubba, 38:21
Tukulor, 55:8
Tukum, 13:27
Tula, 13:47
Tulama, 42:7
Tuleshi, 20:5
Tullishi, 20:5
Tulumi, 17:37
Tulwena, 38:28
Tum, 13:18
Tumak, 17:21, 20:3
Tumbab, 54:2
Tumbatu, 39:14
Tumbuka, 38:54
Tumbwe, 38:37
Tumeli, 20:3
Tuminungu, 38:25
Tummok, 17:21
Tumtum, 20:5
Tumuk, 20:3
Tuna, 12:14
Tungur, 54:21
Tunia, 17:13
Tunisians, 52:39
Tunni, 41:8
Tunni Torre, 39:11
Tunzer, 54:21
Tuopo, 33:1
Tupende, 38:16
Tupuri, 13:48
Tur, 13:49
Tura, 33:16
Ture, 13:47
Turjak, 20:3
Turka, 12:1
Turkana, 43:23
Turmu, 43:4
Turruba, 37:12
Turu, 46:5
Turug, 20:5
Turuka, 12:1
Turumbu, 36:18
Tusia, 12:47

Tusilani, 37:13
Tusselange, 37:13
Tusyan, 12:15
Tutschokwe, 38:25
Tuy, 33:1
Twa, 8
Twea, 49:8
Twide, 8
Tyaman, 32:30
Tyapi, 34:7
Tyefo, 12:2
Tyenga, 12:28
Tyoko, 12:41
Tzadembe, 23:7
Tzambaro, 25:2
Tzul, 52:17

Uabuma, 38:23
Uadschili, 15:9
Ualamo, 23:7
Uaratta, 23:7
Uassi, 24:1
Uba, 23:7
Ubamer, 23:1
Ubba, 23:7
Ubi, 33:1
Ubwari, 38:36
Udalan, 15:25, 53:7
Udio, 28:4
Udjila, 13:46
Uduk, 21:7
Udyade, 34:11
Ugadin, 41:7
Ugbe, 13:28
Uge, 31:2
Uggi, 28:12
Ukelle, 31:7
Ukualuthi, 48:1
Ukuambi, 48:1
Ukuanyama, 48:1
Ulad ba Amar,
    52:8
Ulad bu Aita,
    52:16
Ulad Chouick, 52:8
Ulad Sej, 52:26
Uled Aissa, 52:32
Uled Aoun, 52:14
Uled Atauna, 52:9
Uled Busaif, 52:27
Uled Daued, 52:26

Uled Djerir, 52:9
Uled Jagub, 52:32
Uled Jerri, 15:3
Uled Lhaddj, 52:13
Uled Nacem, 52:9
Uled Nail, 52:25
Uled Said, 52:31
Uled Sidi ben
    Aoun, 52:14
Uled Sidi Sheikh,
    52:32
Uled Sliman, 52:34
Uled Soliman, 52:33
Uled Stut, 52:40
Uled Yacoub, 52:2
Ulu, 21:11
Umanga, 28:21
Umbete, 35:10
Umbundu, 48:4
Umdasa, 36:14
Umiro, 43:13
Umwausi, 38:33
Unein, 15:19
Unga, 38:46
Unia, 16:2
Uollamo, 23:7
Upoto, 36:14
Uregu, 15:26
Urepo, 33:1
Urfilla, 52:27
Urhlana, 52:28
Urhobo, 31:22
Urku, 13:51
Uroko, 33:1
Uru, 13:17
Urzal, 13:46
Urzla, 52:31
Usa, 15:22
Ushanga, 47:9
Ushi, 38:33
Usongora, 36:31
Usuwu, 35:5
Utange, 13:28
Utschiokwe, 38:25
Uyanga, 31:8
Uzgita, 15:19

Vaalpens, 51:2
Vabembe, 36:28
Vachopi, 49:7
Vadanda, 49:4

Vagala, 12:22
Vagele, 12:22
Vagova, 49:4
Vahumbi, 48:7
Vai, 33:26
Vakaranga, 49:1
Vakuanano, 48:4
Vakuanyama, 48:1
Vakuise, 9:7
Vale, 28:5
Valega, 36:28
Valenge, 49:7
Valuchazi, 38:26
Valuheke, 9:7
Valuimbe, 38:27
Valunda, 37:14
Valwena, 38:28
Vanano, 48:4
Vanda, 51:15
Vandals, 18
Vandau, 49:4
Vandzau, 49:4
Vanhaneca, 48:8
Vankumbe, 48:7
Varama, 35:11
Varunda, 38:41
Vasimba, 38:55
Vasorontu, 9:7
Vateve, 49:4
Vatoka, 49:7
Vatombotse, 49:4
Vatonga, 49:7
Vatyipungu, 48:7
Vazezru, 49:6
Vei, 33:26
Veiao, 38:61
Vemba, 46:17
Vemgo, 13:49
Venda, 51:15
Vende, 46:6
Vere, 13:58
Veso, 27:8
Vezu, 27:8
Vhalemba, 51:15
Vhavenda, 51:15
Vichioko, 38:25
Vidunda, 46:23
Vigye, 12:15
Vili, 38:4
Vinda, 27:3
Vinsa, 45:3

Vinza, 36:5, 45:3
Viri, 29:30
Virwa, 51:14
Vitre, 32:31
Viye, 48:4
Vizik, 13:49
Voko, 29:12
Voltaic peoples, 12
Vomni, 13:58
Vonoma, 36:1
Vouaghenia, 36:31
Vouaousi, 38:33
Vuaguha, 38:37
Vuakuku, 36:15
Vuakussu, 37:11
Vuaregga, 36:28
Vuela, 12:45
Vugusu, 45:21
Vumbo, 36:14
Vungo, 35:11
Vusei, 13:45
Vyetre, 32:31

Wa, 30:11
Waba, 12:38
Wabali, 36:22
Wabarwe, 49:5
Wabembe, 36:28
Wabena, 46:17
Wabende, 46:6
Wabira, 36:6
Wabisa, 38:35
Wabondei, 39:1
Wabuddu, 36:9
Wabudjwe, 38:36
Wabuma, 38:23
Wabuyu, 38:36
Wabwari, 38:36
Wachanzi, 38:24
Wachi, 32:3
Wadaians, 17:6
Wadalen, 15:25,
    53:7
Wadan, 15:11
Wadelka, 20:3
Wadi, 28:12
Wadia, 38:23
Wadigo, 39:6
Wadja, 28:23
Wadoe, 39:2
Wadondo, 49:4

Wadschagga, 44:1
Wadshili, 15:9
Waduruma, 39:7
Waenya, 36:31
Wafipa, 46:12
Wafulero, 45:1
Wafungwe, 38:54, 49:5
Waganda, 45:9
Waganga, 38:51, 45:21
Wageia, 43:14
Wagenia, 36:31
Wagiliama, 39:8
Wagogo, 46:1
Wagoma, 38:36
Wagoscia, 39:9
Wagosha, 39:9
Wagowa, 49:4
Waguha, 38:37
Wagunya, 39:12
Waha, 45:3
Wahadimu, 39:14
Wahaiao, 38:61
Wahaya, 45:10
Wahehe, 46:18
Wahenga, 38:54
Wahera, 49:6
Wahere, 51:15
Wahorohoro, 38:37, 45:7
Wahungwe, 49:5
Waiyau, 38:61
Waja, 13:47
Wajiji, 45:3
Wajita, 45:19
Wajole, 42:2
Waka, 13:57
Wakalanga, 49:1
Wakamanga, 38:54
Wakamba, 44:2
Wakambe, 39:8
Wakami, 39:3
Wakaranga, 49:1
Wakarra, 45:18
Wakedi, 43:22
Wakerewe, 45:11
Wakhutu, 39:3
Wakikuyu, 44:3
Wakindiga, 10:3
Wakkutu, 45

Wakonde, 38:57
Wakondjo, 45:5
Wakorikori, 49:2
Wakua, 38:58
Wakuko, 28:16
Wakumu, 36:15
Wakura, 13:49
Wakusu, 37:11
Wakweli, 35:5
Wakwere, 39:2
Wala, 12:29
Walaitsa, 23:7
Walako, 43:28, 45:21
Walamba, 38:40
Walamo, 23:7
Walangi, 46:4
Walangulo, 10:1
Walega, 36:28, 42:8
Walegga, 28:8
Walendu, 28:8
Walengola, 36:16
Walese, 28:16
Walika, 36:17
Walimi, 46:5
Wallaga, 42:8
Wallamo, 23:7
Wallo, 42:9
Walo, 13:51
Walomwe, 38:56
Waluba, 37:12
Waluguru, 39:3
Walumbi, 28:25
Walungu, 38:42
Wamakonde, 38:57
Wamakua, 38:58
Wamanga, 28:21
Wamanyika, 49:3
Wamatambwe, 38:57
Wamatengo, 46:27
Wamatumbi, 46:19
Wamavia, 38:57
Wamboni, 10:1
Wambu, 48:4
Wambuba, 28:16
Wambudjga, 49:5
Wambugu, 24:4
Wambugwe, 46:3
Wambunga, 46:20

Wambuti, 8:4
Wamfumu, 35:14
Wamia, 43:22
Wammate, 23:7
Wampororo, 45:7
Wamuera, 38:59
Wanande, 45:5
Wandaka, 36:22
Wandala, 16:4, 17:32
Wandamba, 46:21
Wandonde, 38:60
Wandorobbo, 10:2
Wandya, 46:14
Wanga, 45:21
Wangala, 36:24
Wangandi, 29:31
Wangara, 11:8
Wangata, 37:9
Wangindo, 38:60
Wangoma, 43:28
Wangomwia, 46:1
Wangonde, 46:28
Wangoni, 50
Wangoroine, 45:19
Wangulu, 39:4
Wanguru, 38:56, 39:4
Waniaturu, 46:5
Wanie, 49:6
Wanika, 39
Wanji, 46:25
Wanjika, 46:12
Wankutshu, 37:10
Wanyabungu, 45:1
Wanyai, 49:1
Wanyamwezi, 46:9
Wanyanga, 45:4, 52:20
Wanyanja, 38:51
Wanyassa, 38:52
Wanyika, 39, 49:3
Wanyongwe, 38:49
Wapare, 44:5
Wapemba, 39:15
Wapogoro, 46:22
Wapokomo, 39:10
War, 30:11
Wara, 12:7

Warabai, 39:8
Warain, 15:27
Warambia, 46:14
Warangi, 46:4
Waratta, 23:7
Wardai, 42:2
Warege, 36:28
Waremba, 51:15
Wargla, 15:28
Waribe, 39:8
Waribi, 10:5
Waringa, 37:8
Warjawa, 13:50
Warji, 13:50
Warozwi, 49:6
Warri, 31:23
Warsangeli, 41:6
Warumbi, 28:25
Warundi, 45:8
Warungu, 38:42
Waruri, 45:19
Waruwa, 38:36
Warwar, 13:23
Wasa, 32:18
Wasagara, 46:23
Wasambara, 44:6
Wasanga, 49:4
Wasanye, 10:7
Wasaramo, 39:17
Waschensi, 39:1
Wasegeju, 39:16
Wasena, 38:53
Washambala, 44:6
Washangwe, 49:2
Washashi, 45:19
Wasi, 24:1
Wasira, 38:44
Wasonga, 37:16
Wasove, 46:17
Wassafwa, 46:16
Wassalu, 11:8
Wassandaui, 10:6
Wassania, 10:7
Wassiba, 45:10
Wassindja, 45:15
Wassingali, 41:6
Wassuba, 45:17
Wassukuma, 46:10
Wassungara, 46:23
Wasuaheli, 39
Wasulunka, 11:8

Watabwe, 38:45
Watande, 49:4
Watatit, 21:3
Wataware, 49:5
Watchongoa, 36:31
Wateita, 44:7
Wateve, 49:4
Watikuu, 39:12
Watindega, 10:3
Watitu, 50:10
Watombwe, 38:37
Watonga, 49:5
Watschokwe, 38:25
Watta, 10:4
Watumbatu, 39:14
Watumbuka, 38:54
Watyi, 32:3
Waunga, 38:46
Waungwe, 49:5
Wausi, 38:33
Wauzhi, 38:33
Wavinza, 36:5
Wavira, 36:6
Wawa, 13:23,
   46:13
Wawamba, 36:1
Wawemba, 38:34
Wawia, 38:57
Wawiwa, 46:13
Wayao, 38:61
Wayto, 10:4
Wazegura, 39:5
Wazezuru, 49:6
Wazimba, 38:55
We, 47:11
Weima, 33:18
Wemba, 38:34
Wemenu, 32:5
Wen, 33:16
Wenachishinga,
   38:33
Wenakawendi,
   38:33
Wenangumbu,
   38:33
Wengana, 38:14
Wenja, 36:31
Wenya, 38:54
Werre, 13:58
Wewanga, 46:22
White Bobo, 12:8

Whydah, 32:3
Widekum, 30:13
Wile, 12:29
Wimbu, 30:11
Winamwanga,
   46:13
Windjinwindjin,
   32:11
Wira, 28:12
Wisa, 38:35
Wiya, 30:11
Woaba, 12:38
Wobe, 33:9
Woga, 13:49
Wogadin, 41:7
Woko, 29:12
Wollamo, 23:7
Wollo, 42:9
Wom, 13:52
Womboko, 35:5
Wongo, 38:22
Woro, 28:3
Wot, 30:11
Wouri, 35:2
Wovea, 35:5
Wula, 13:45
Wule, 12:29
Wum, 30:14
Wure, 32:20
Wuri, 35:2
Wurkum, 13:51
Wursungeli, 41:6
Wuruku, 13:51
Wushishi, 31:16
Wute, 29:33
Wutella, 25:2
Wuumbu, 36:14

Xam, 9:15
Xananwa, 51:14
Xayo, 45:21
Xhosa, 50:4
Xosa, 50:4

Yabarre, 41:3
Yabouba, 33:16
Yacca, 38:18
Yachi, 31:11
Yadunde, 36:11
Yaelima, 37:4
Yafelman, 15:2

Yaga, 8:1
Yagba, 31:26
Yagga, 38:18
Yahi, 52:40
Yahia, 15:1
Yaka, 35:11, 38:18
Yakka, 35:11
Yako, 31:8
Yakoma, 29:34
Yakori, 31:2
Yakoro, 31:2
Yakout, 15:22
Yakuba, 33:16
Yala, 15:29,
   31:15
Yallof, 34:12
Yalna, 17:20
Yalunka, 11:12
Yambi, 46:2
Yambo, 21:1
Yambuya, 36:22
Yamma, 23:4
Yandan, 13:57
Yang, 13:59
Yangaro, 23:4
Yangela, 38:2
Yangeli, 29:35
Yangere, 29:35
Yankpa, 13:30
Yanzi, 38:24
Yao, 38:61
Yaounde, 36:11
Yarse, 12:27
Yasa, 35:8
Yasayama, 37:7
Yasgua, 13:30
Yasing, 29:11
Yaunde, 36:11
Yaya-ben-Othman,
   52:26
Yedina, 17:26
Yeii, 47:2
Yeke, 37:17
Yela, 37:3
Yem, 23:4
Yendang, 13:57
Yergam, 13:29
Yergum, 13:29
Yesko, 13:30
Yeskwa, 13:30
Yeye, 47:2

Yjang, 21:10
Yoabu, 12:38
Yofo, 13:57
Yola, 34:6
Yom, 12:37
Yomamgba, 28:3
Yombe, 38:5,
   38:54
Yoruba, 31:31
Youlou, 28:2
Youwa, 12:37
Yukutare, 13:31
Yulu, 12:9, 28:2
Yungur, 13:59
Yunguru, 13:59
Yussi, 15:2

Zab Chergui,
   52:42
Zaberma, 17:45
Zaer, 15:2
Zaghawa, 16:8
Zagitse, 23:7
Zague, 33:24
Zahon, 33:24
Zaisse, 23:7
Zal, 15:19
Zala, 23:7
Zalla, 23:7
Zam, 31:18
Zanaki, 45:19
Zande, 29:14
Zanga, 12:17
Zango, 13:58
Zani, 13:35, 13:61
Zara, 12:8, 23:7
Zaramo, 39:17
Zayadia, 54:5
Zayan, 15:2
Zaysse, 23:7
Zazing, 29:11
Zegaoua, 16:8
Zegbe, 33:4
Zeggu, 15:29
Zeguha, 39:5
Zekara, 15:29
Zella, 15:11
Zelmamu, 43:4
Zema, 32:28
Zemmur, 15:2
Zenaga, 52:41

Zerma, 17:45
Zerri, 15:3
Zerwal, 52:17
Zezuru, 49:6
Ziba, 45:10
Ziban, 52:42
Zid, 52:2
Zigaba, 8:3
Zigula, 39:5

Ziki, 15:19
Zilmamu, 43:4
Zimba, 37:16,
    38:55
Zimbabwe, 26
Zimu, 36:10
Zin, 13:57
Zinna, 13:57
Zintan, 52:27

Zinza, 45:15
Zitako, 31:18
Zizi, 50:5
Zkara, 15:29
Zlass, 52:14
Znassen, 15:17
Zombo, 38:1
Zomper, 13:32
Zorhaua, 16:8

Zorotua, 9:7
Zuande, 13:31
Zuba, 13:61
Zulimamu, 43:4
Zulu, 50:5
Zumper, 13:32
Zumu, 13:35
Zungle, 30:11
Zungwa, 46:18